International Law Stories

Second Edition

Edited by

John E. Noyes
Roger J. Traynor Professor of Law Emeritus
California Western School of Law

Laura A. Dickinson
Lyle T. Alverson Professor of Law
The George Washington University Law School

Mark Weston Janis
William F. Starr Professor of Law
University of Connecticut School of Law
Formerly Reader in Law & Fellow of Exeter College
University of Oxford

Carlos M. Vázquez
Scott K. Ginsburg Professor of Law
Georgetown University Law Center

LAW STORIES SERIES®

FOUNDATION PRESS

860 Blue Gentian Road, Suite 350
Eagan, MN 55121
1-877-888-1330

Published in the United States of America

ISBN: 978-1-64708-636-7

Table of Contents

International Law Stories

Second Edition

Introduction

John E. Noyes, Laura A. Dickinson, Mark Weston Janis, and Carlos M. Vázquez

International Law Stories explores the personal, social, political, and historical foundations of seventeen classic international law cases. The authors of our essays—with varied backgrounds in academia, the judiciary, private practice, and government service—bring these stories to life, telling tales helpful, we hope, for those well-acquainted with the cases, as well as for those new to the field. One book cannot address all the important cases in the vast arena of international law, but these essays provide a rich and lucid understanding of modern international law. Almost all of the chapters from the first edition of this book have been updated to reflect recent developments, and this second edition adds six entirely new stories.

International Law Stories has four parts. Part I, "Nuremberg and Its Progeny," begins with the story about the judgment of the International Military Tribunal at Nuremberg, by Judge Theodor Meron of the International Tribunal for the former Yugoslavia and Professor Jean Galbraith of the University of Pennsylvania Law School. Following are four chapters involving cases from other courts and institutions, each building on *Nuremberg*: *Filártiga* from a U.S. federal court, by Professor Harold Koh of Yale Law School; *Pinochet* from Britain's highest court, by Philippa Webb, a barrister and a professor at the University of Oxford, and Yasmin Liberman, a junior fellow at the Centre for International Governance and Dispute Resolution, King's College London; disputes over the treatment of prisoners at Abu Ghraib, by Professor Laura Dickinson of George Washington University Law School; and *Mellet* from the United Nations Human Rights Committee, by Professor Yuval Shany of the Hebrew University of Jerusalem. These five chapters, all of which concern the human rights or humanitarian law obligations of states, feature the individual as a central actor in international law.

Part II, "Regional International Law," introduces three different regional systems of international law. The first two chapters showcase other progeny of Nuremberg: *Velásquez Rodríguez* from the Inter–American Court of Human Rights, by Professor Claudio Grossman of American University's Washington College of Law and Professor Nienke Grossman of the University of Baltimore School of Law; and *Hassan* from the European Court of Human Rights, by Natasha Holcroft-Emmess, a lecturer and tutor at Jesus College, University of Oxford. The third story in this part, by Professor James Gathii of Loyola University Chicago

School of Law, concerns an international environmental law case in the East African Court of Justice.

Part III, "International Law: The Domestic Impact," has five chapters, each of them looking at how the U.S. Supreme Court has treated the complex interplay among international law, constitutional law, and domestic politics and culture. Professor Roger Alford of Notre Dame Law School presents *The Charming Betsy*; Professor Carlos Vázquez of the Georgetown University Law Center explores *Foster*, *Percheman*, and *Medellín*; Professor William Dodge of George Washington University Law School considers *The Paquete Habana*; Professor Mark Janis of the University of Connecticut School of Law writes about *Missouri v. Holland*; and Professor Oona Hathaway of Yale Law School examines *Hamdan*.

Finally, Part IV, "International Law: Interstate Conflicts," contains four chapters showing how international law and process have addressed controversies over the use of force, the overlapping jurisdiction of countries, and the development of international institutions. The chapters in Part IV include *Caroline*, by Professor John Noyes of California Western School of Law; *Lotus*, by Professor Eric Jensen of Brigham Young University Law School; *Reparation for Injuries*, by the late Emory University School of Law Professor David Bederman; and *Nicaragua*, by Professor Mary Ellen O'Connell of Notre Dame Law School.

This Introduction continues with four short essays by the editors of *International Law Stories*, providing perspective on the contents of this volume. The first, by Mark Janis, discusses what makes an international law case a "classic." John Noyes, in the second introductory essay, highlights the wide variety of fora that interpret and apply international law. Third, Carlos Vázquez examines how international law is interpreted and applied in U.S. courts, where rules of international law intersect with constitutional law principles. And fourth, Laura Dickinson reflects on the efficacy of international law in our cases.

"CLASSIC" CASES OF INTERNATIONAL LAW

Mark Weston Janis

What makes an international law case a "classic"? How have we decided what to include as "classic" international law cases for *International Law Stories*? We can think of at least three tests to determine "classic" status. The first is reliance: Is the case one on which international lawyers rely? Do international lawyers make steady reference to the case in subsequent practice? The second test is transformation: Has the case changed international law? Have international lawyers come to think about and to do their discipline differently because of the case? And third is expectation: Is the case one that international lawyers are expected to know? Could one be counted a real international lawyer if one was not familiar with the case?

Since all tests of "classic" status involve opinion, we acknowledge that it will be much harder to agree upon "classic" cases in international law than upon cases in a subject matter drawn from a single legal system, like that of the United States. Plainly, there will always be a greater degree of intellectual, social, and professional coherence among lawyers from a single country about a domestic legal field like U.S. constitutional law, property law, or tort law, than there will be among lawyers from almost two hundred different countries about international law, a fundamentally "shared" legal field. So, to be honest, we must admit that deciding what cases to include in *International Law Stories* is colored by the fact that we four editors are all American, all educated at U.S. law schools (though one was first educated at an English law school), all members of a bar of a state of the United States, and all professors at U.S. law schools. Moreover, we perceive our principal audience to be students, though not necessarily American, taking courses in U.S. law schools or undergraduate and graduate schools, or U.S. lawyers, judges, and academics. Hence, our choice of "classic" international law cases has, and is meant to have, a distinctly American flavor. As international lawyers, of course, we are by trade and emotion keenly sympathetic with foreign audiences; we hope that our choice of cases will also reach out to foreign students, lawyers, judges, and academics.

In choosing our international law cases, we have thought both about the tests marking a "classic" case and about our American focus. Our choice of *Nuremberg* is the most compelling among all seventeen chapters. *Nuremberg* is relied upon as the foundational case in international human rights law; it transformed, indeed perhaps created, the field of international human rights law, itself the most important transformation in international law in general in the twentieth century. No one, in our opinion, should be counted as an international lawyer unless he or she knows about the case. Moreover, Nuremberg is a case of universal import; it is foundational for every country, not just our own. The other stories in Part I—*Filártiga, Pinochet,* the Abu Ghraib controversy, and *Mellet*—all show how *Nuremberg* has played out in almost eighty years of practice. The cases in Part II—*Velásquez-Rodríguez, Hassan,* and *Serengeti*—illustrate *Nuremberg*'s impact on the development of regional systems of international law, another fundamental change in our discipline and in international relations.

Part III has an acknowledged U.S. focus. Each national legal system accounts or does not account for international law in its own way. The rules about using international law in U.S. courts are now more than two centuries old and are deeply imbedded in U.S. constitutional law, a discipline famous for its complexity and ambiguity. All five cases in Part III deal with those complexities and ambiguities. Perhaps the most "classic" of these is *Foster*, which has set the tone for U.S. judicial incorporation, or not, of the rules of treaties in U.S. law. Certainly, the other cases, classics too—*Charming Betsy, Paquete Habana, Missouri,* and *Hamdan*—are equally beset by complexity and ambiguity. All are crucial for anyone who wants to understand the part international law plays in U.S. domestic litigation.

Finally, Part IV deals with cases as they play a part directly in international relations, another crucial role for international law and lawyers. Here perhaps the most "classic" case is *Lotus*, where the Permanent Court of International Justice grappled with the fundamental question, How and when are sovereign states bound by international legal rules? Though probably not as well-known, the other Part IV cases—*Caroline*, *Reparation for Injuries*, and *Nicaragua*—all address the same age-old problem: Are states subject to the rule of law?

DIVERSE DECISION MAKERS

John E. Noyes

Understanding any area of law requires understanding the institutions that interpret and apply it. Most of the time, no court or tribunal decides how rules of international law should be applied. Institutions within nation states often internalize those rules. For example, the story of Abu Ghraib (Chapter 4) notes the U.S. military's traditional role in trying to give effect to rules of international humanitarian law. And when countries disagree about the content of international law rules or their application, they often resolve such disputes solely by negotiation. We see an illustration in the *Caroline* incident (Chapter 14), where the United States and Britain settled a tense dispute over a transborder use of force without the involvement of any third-party decision maker.

Yet prominent international law controversies do at times end up being litigated, and most of our stories focus on decisions rendered by courts or tribunals. The judicial process sharpens thinking about the legal dimensions of disputes and typically results in detailed, reasoned opinions. What third-party decision makers hear and rule on international law disputes?

The diversity of courts and tribunals that hear international law cases is striking. National courts in fact decide such many such cases, applying international law in conjunction with domestic constitutional law. Several of our essays—*Filártiga* (Chapter 2), *The Charming Betsy* (Chapter 9), *Foster*, *Percheman*, and *Medellín* (Chapter 10), *The Paquete Habana* (Chapter 11), *Missouri v. Holland* (Chapter 12), and *Hamdan* (Chapter 13)—feature U.S. judicial decisions. British courts were involved in the disputes in *Pinochet* (Chapter 3) and *Hassan* (Chapter 7). Especially in common law countries such as the United States and the United Kingdom, courts play a central role in deciding disputes and developing the law.

There are also about three dozen international and hybrid courts that hear international law cases. Most of these courts were created by treaty, although the United Nations Security Council has established a few. States and private parties also participate in international arbitrations, with arbitral tribunals making thousands of awards each year. A wide range of domestic and international courts and tribunals thus interpret and apply international law rules.

These various fora are not linked through any overarching hierarchical structure, as is the case in national legal systems. There is no international supreme court. The International Court of Justice (ICJ)—sometimes called the "World Court"—does not hear appeals from other international courts or from national courts. Indeed, the ICJ, the principal judicial organ of the United Nations, serves both as a trial court in contentious cases between countries and as the final judicial word in many of the disputes that come before it. The ICJ is thus but one of many courts providing interpretations of international law. The World Court's prestige has, however, lent considerable weight to its opinions. This is true even though, as a formal matter, an ICJ decision in a contentious case is binding only on the parties to the dispute, and the Court's Statute deems pronouncements of jurists merely "subsidiary means for the determination of rules of law." Two essays in this book—*Lotus* (Chapter 15) and *Nicaragua* (Chapter 17)—involve contentious cases before the World Court.

Some regional and specialized international courts and tribunals—including the Inter–American Court of Human Rights (see *Velásquez Rodríguez* in Chapter 6), the European Court of Human Rights (*Hassan* in Chapter 7), and the East African Court of Justice (*Serengeti* in Chapter 8)—do serve as central components of international regimes and may provide for appellate review. Yet, unlike national supreme courts that typically sit at the apex of a system of courts of general jurisdiction, regional international courts, limited by the treaties creating them, only consider one or a few subjects, *e.g.*, human rights or trade. Some global tribunals, such as the World Trade Organization's Dispute Settlement Body and the International Tribunal for the Law of the Sea, also hear only limited categories of cases.

International law treats individuals as among its subjects, and international legal process has correspondingly recognized them as parties in some venues. Indeed, in only three stories in this book—*Caroline*, *Lotus*, and *Nicaragua*—is the primary focus on disputes between nation states. Individuals may be parties to international law cases in national courts. Some regional and specialized tribunals also allow individuals or even non-governmental organizations to institute cases, a jurisdictional feature that promotes frequent use of those tribunals. In addition, international criminal courts, highlighted in the story about the International Military Tribunal at Nuremberg (Chapter 1), have prosecuted individuals for war crimes and other serious international law offenses.

How jurisdiction is obtained over parties varies from court to court. Defendants in national court cases are subject to compulsory process. That is, a plaintiff or a prosecutor may institute a case within the scope of the national court's jurisdiction against a defendant, however reluctant that defendant may be to participate. Nation states are, however, immune from lawsuits in national courts in many situations, as specified in national laws on sovereign immunity. And a country is not subject to the jurisdiction of an international court unless the country has consented; such consent may take different forms and may be given well before a particular lawsuit begins.

Countries may be affected by formally non-binding advisory opinions, which some courts are authorized to render. We see an example in the International Court of Justice's influential *Reparation for Injuries* case (Chapter 16). To complicate matters further, not all contentious disputes heard by third-party treaty bodies lead to legally binding judgments. The United Nations Human Rights Committee's *Mellet* case (Chapter 5) illustrates that even non-binding decisions about international law may significantly affect the conduct of nation states.

In short, one reason why international law is complex is because of the great variety of fora in which its rules are interpreted and applied. Third-party fora differ in terms of how and where they were created, their scope of application (geographical and subject matter), the functions they serve, the parties that may appear before them, whether their decisions are legally binding, and the mechanisms available to promote compliance with their decisions.

The diversity of third-party international dispute settlement mechanisms leads us to consider how uniform a body of law is "international law" and what roles courts play in developing legal norms. Do different courts take the same view of international legal issues? With such a variety of fora, problems of "conflict of laws" may arise. If one court's interpretation of a rule conflicts with another court's interpretation, or with the other court's determination that a different rule should govern, how should such conflicts be resolved? What if the conflict arises with respect to the same factual dispute? As *Lotus* (Chapter 14) illustrates, different courts may sometimes exercise concurrent jurisdiction over the same matter.

Several essays, *e.g.*, *Filártiga* (Chapter 2), explore how international legal norms develop by filtering among international and national institutions. Some cases, *e.g.*, *Velásquez Rodríguez* (Chapter 6) and *Serengeti* (Chapter 8), show international courts applying international law when national authorities have failed to implement important norms. Conversely, the *Hassan* essay (Chapter 7) posits that national attitudes may at times restrain the rulings of international courts. The stories in this book thus not only introduce a diverse group of international dispute settlement bodies but also illustrate the challenges and opportunities for norm diffusion among tribunals and other institutions.

Despite the diversity of third-party decision makers, the possibility that they may strengthen core universal values remains alluring.

Principles established at Nuremberg (see Chapter 1), for example, are strong candidates for fundamental norms. As several essays in this book demonstrate, the Nuremberg Tribunal not only influenced the creation of later international tribunals but articulated basic international human rights and humanitarian law norms.

INTERNATIONAL LAW IN U.S. COURTS

Carlos M. Vázquez

The status and applicability of international law in domestic courts is, for domestic courts, a matter of domestic, not international, law. The topic falls within the emerging scholarly field of Foreign Relations Law. (For international tribunals, the opposite is true. Domestic law cannot excuse a state's violation of international law.) Though not technically a question of international law, the place of international law in domestic legal systems is usually studied in law school International Law courses. Indeed, non-U.S. scholars have commented that this topic seems to dominate the International Law syllabus in U.S. law schools.

Foreign Relations Law is perhaps most developed as a scholarly field in the United States. Part III of this book tells the stories of some canonical U.S. Foreign Relations cases, and one noncanonical decision that may signal the Supreme Court's future direction. Stories in other chapters, however, also touch upon this topic, notably *Filartíga* (Chapter 2), and some—notably *Pinochet* (Chapter 3)—address the status and applicability of international law in the domestic legal systems of other states. The recent growth of Foreign Relations Law as a scholarly field outside the United States has, in turn, led to the emergence of Comparative Foreign Relations Law as an exciting subfield of Comparative Constitutional Law.

Roughly speaking, states may be classified as either monist or dualist in their treatment of international law. In monist states, international law has the status of domestic law, whereas in dualist states the domestic and international legal systems are largely distinct, with international law having the status of domestic law only to the extent the legislature has incorporated it into the domestic legal system. Few states are entirely monist, however. Even in the most monist of states, for example, the domestic constitution prevails over international law in the event of a conflict. It is more accurate to say that states fall within a spectrum between monism and dualism. Moreover, states might be (relatively) monist with respect to some categories of international law (say, treaty law), while being (relatively) dualist with respect to other categories (say, customary international law).

In the United States, the text of the Constitution appears to establish a monist system with respect to treaties. Article VI declares "all Treaties" of the United States to be the "supreme Law of the Land" and instructs the courts to give effect to them, "any Thing in the Constitution or Laws of any State to the Contrary nothwithstanding." Chapter 10 tells the story of *Foster v. Neilson, Percheman v. United States,* and *Medellín v. Texas,* which established the doctrine that some treaties are "non-self-executing" and thus unenforceable in the courts unless and until they are implemented by legislation. This very limited exception to the Supremacy Clause's monism was recognized in *Foster* and *Percheman* but was expanded in *Medellín*, leading some commentators to claim that there is currently a presumption that treaties in the United States are not directly enforceable in the courts, a view that is difficult to square with the constitutional text. As Chapter 10 explains, in expanding the "non-self-execution" exception to the Supremacy Clause, the *Medellín* opinion misunderstood the holding of *Foster* and *Percheman,* yet *Medellín* does not go as far as to reverse the presumption established in that clause.

The Court's recognition that some treaties require legislative implementation raises important questions about the scope of Congress's power to implement treaties. Chapter 12 tells the story of *Missouri v. Holland,* in which Justice Holmes eloquently reaffirmed what the text of the Constitution appears to say: Congress's power to implement treaties is an independent legislative power and accordingly authorizes legislation that does not fall within the scope of its other enumerated powers. This remains the prevailing view, although some scholars and dissenting Justices have challenged it.

Although the Constitution does not directly address the domestic status of customary international law in the United States, the "modern position" is that this category of international law has the status of federal law in the United States. Chapter 11 tells the story of *The Paquete Habana,* in which the Supreme Court relied on customary international law in holding that the capture of Cuban fishing vessels as prizes of war was not lawful. The Court's famous statement that "international law is part of our law" and enforceable even against executive officials remains a pillar of the modern position. Here, too, however, the traditional understanding has been challenged of late. Chapter 11 explains how revisionist scholars and officials have misunderstood language from *The Paquete Habana* that they have read as licensing executive branch violations of customary international law.

Even when particular treaty provisions or customary norms are not directly enforceable in the courts, they remain relevant to the interpretation of federal statutes. Chapter 9 recounts the story of *The Charming Betsy*, the case whose name is now synonymous with the doctrine that a statute is to be interpreted consistently with international law if at all possible. The *Charming Betsy* doctrine has been applied in innumerable cases in the U.S. courts, and has been adopted in other nations, where it goes by the name of the doctrine of consistent interpretation or the presumption of conformity.

Finally, Chapter 13 tells the story of *Hamdan v. Rumsfeld*, perhaps the most notable recent success story in the pantheon of U.S. cases on the domestic enforcement of international law. The decision has been regarded as a resounding victory for the rule of law even in responding to an armed attack and protecting the nation from terrorism. Yet, though the story of this case does show, as Professor Hathaway writes in Chapter 13, that "domestic enforcement of international law—the enforcement of the law by domestic institutions including against their own government—represents a critical tool for enforcing international law around the globe," the decision, and its aftermath, also reflect the "fragility" of such enforcement as a tool for giving efficacy to international law. As the chapter explains, the Court relied on statutory provisions incorporating international law as a limit on executive action, and Congress soon thereafter enacted amendments to those statutes purporting to restrict the courts' power to enforce international law against the executive.

The domestic enforcement of international law stands on firmer ground when based on *constitutional* incorporation of international law. The U.S. Constitution appears to contemplate a strong judicial role in the enforcement of international law. The Constitution was adopted when the United States was a weak nation whose existence and flourishing depended on respect for international law by stronger nations. Yet, as the chapters in Part III show, as the nation has become more powerful, the Court has interpreted those provisions less robustly, in what might be considered an example of a "living constitutionalist" approach to constitutional interpretation by purportedly originalist judges. Thus, we see expansions of the "non-self-executing" exception to the Supremacy Clause in cases like *Medellín*, and attempts to restrict the canonical holdings of *The Paquete Habana* and *Missouri v. Holland*, albeit so far only in minority opinions. In the end, even if international law is formally binding as a matter of domestic constitutional law, the effectiveness of domestic enforcement as a tool for giving efficacy to international law depends on societal (and judicial) commitment to the rule of law in both domestic and international affairs.

THE EFFICACY OF INTERNATIONAL LAW

Laura A. Dickinson

Although compliance with international legal norms has long been the problem most troubling international lawyers, there has been, until relatively recently, remarkably little real study of why states do and do not obey international law. Thus, liberal internationalists have traditionally assumed that liberal democratic states comply with international law because their norms and values resonate with those contained in international agreements. Others have suggested that if international rules are deemed procedurally and substantively "fair," they compel compliance. And those promoting "transnational legal process" have argued that states obey international law because they come to internalize international norms and values over time. Yet, for years there were only fitful efforts to test these hypotheses with comprehensive data on international law compliance.

For their part, international relations skeptics of international law have long used rational choice and game theoretic models to argue that international law does *not* have any independent valence and that a nation-state obeys international law only when doing so is in that state's own self-interest. But these arguments too have tended not to be empirically grounded, relying far more on logical models and hidden (or not so hidden) assumptions concerning state behavior. And while constructivist scholars have challenged such skeptical assumptions and argued that international law *itself* shapes what comes to be thought of as the state's interest, this proposition—like the others—has not been sufficiently tested. The field, therefore, long cried out for further empirical analysis, and over the past two decades, international law scholars have begun to respond.

Against this backdrop, *International Law Stories*, in addition to its many other virtues, makes a useful contribution to the emerging literature on international law compliance. To be sure, this book is not intended as a work of empiricism, and it in no way obviates the need for more empirical studies, both qualitative and quantitative. Yet, the essays assembled here do—both individually and collectively—shed some light on the vexing question of international law's efficacy by emphasizing both the complexity inherent in how we conceptualize what *counts* as efficacy and compliance in this context, as well as the many difficulties scholars are likely to encounter in trying to measure such compliance.

To begin, we might attempt to measure international law's impact by considering simply the extent to which court judgments finding violations of international law are actually enforced. Clearly they are, at least some of the time. Indeed, even when the ruling under consideration is issued by an international tribunal—where the obstacles to enforcement are likely to be greatest—the volume provides powerful examples of the law's efficacy in this sense. In *Velásquez Rodríguez*, for example, the Honduran government obeyed a judgment of the Inter–American Court of Human Rights imposing a fine for allowing the disappearance of one of its citizens. And of course at Nuremberg, an international tribunal tried twenty-two defendants and convicted nineteen (though certainly the court's effective power was intimately bound up in the Allies' military power over Germany at that time).

Elsewhere, however, the results are more ambiguous. In *Nicaragua*, although the International Court of Justice (ICJ) decided in favor of Nicaragua, the United States refused to appear during the Court's consideration of the merits and threatened to withhold aid from Nicaragua until it withdrew its claim for reparations. In the *Reparation* case, the ICJ ruled that the United Nations had the international personality enabling it to bring an international legal claim against Israel for the death of a U.N. agent, and Israel indemnified the United Nations for this death. But Israel never punished those who committed the assassination that gave rise to the case, although the identities of the individuals involved did ultimately come to light. The *Hassan* case, decided by the European Court of Human Rights, illustrates the general strength of the European system, where states typically follow judgments of the court. Yet, in that particular example, the court—perhaps trying to avoid fueling backlash against the court itself—adopted a somewhat restrictive conception of the right to liberty, upholding the United Kingdom's detention of Hassan during armed conflict even though the United Kingdom did not derogate from the European Convention. A similar concern about avoiding backlash may also explain the decision by the Appellate Division of the East African Court of Justice, in a case involving the Serengeti National Park, a UNESCO World Heritage site. Here, although the trial court had issued an injunction barring Tanzania from building a road across the Park, the appellate panel ruled that the case was ultimately not actionable, even as it seemed to uphold the lower court's judgment.

Turning to examples of U.S. court enforcement of international law, the results are also mixed, as Professor Vázquez recounts in his introductory essay on "International Law in U.S. Courts," above. In *Paquete*, the Court asserted the authority of customary international law, but dictum on the role of the executive has opened the door to recent claims that the President may actually contravene such law. Turning to treaties, *Missouri v. Holland* supports the assertion of federal authority to impose treaty law on the states, but the reach of that authority remains the subject of scholarly debate. In both *Foster* and *Percheman*, the U.S. Supreme Court also asserted the supremacy of treaties, ruling that treaties are presumptively enforceable regardless of legislative implementation. Yet, language in *Foster* has been read to suggest that treaties that are not self-executing might not fall within the U.S. Constitution's Supremacy Clause (although many leading experts dispute that notion). *Medellín*, too, is a bit of a mixed bag. Although the majority did appear to expand the idea that non-self-executing treaties may not be subject to the Supremacy Clause, the Court did not fully reverse the presumption that treaties are generally enforceable in U.S. courts, as Professor Vázquez makes clear. Similarly in *Filártiga*, the U.S. Court of Appeals for the Second Circuit issued a strong judgment that awarded damages to a non-citizen victim of torture, but the victim was never able to collect payment from the defendant, also a non-citizen, and the U.S. Supreme Court subsequently narrowed the reach of the Alien Tort Claims Act, the statute that gave rise to the international law claims in *Filártiga*. Finally, in *Hamdan* the U.S. Supreme Court relied in part on international law to resist claims of the Executive Branch concerning the legal status of military detention centers in Guantánamo Bay, Cuba. But the ultimate outcome of that exchange—particularly in light of Congress's subsequent limitations on the scope of judicial enforcement—remains fragile.

Thus, the core questions of how, when, and under what circumstances international law is or is not effective form at least a subtext underlying all the stories discussed in this book. Indeed, this is part of the benefit of a book on international law *stories*, rather than simply international law *cases*. By looking at the multifaceted stories behind the formal lawsuits, readers may be in a better position to answer these core questions of international law's efficacy.

I. NUREMBERG AND ITS PROGENY

1

Theodor Meron and Jean Galbraith*

Nuremberg and Its Legacy

As the trial of twenty-two Germans opened at Nuremberg in November of 1945, it had all the makings of an historical moment. The identities of those involved alone confirmed this. The top surviving Nazi leaders sat in the dock, including Hermann Goering, Hitler's second-in-command for much of the war. The prosecutors and the judges were as prestigious lawyers as the United States, Great Britain, France, and Russia had to offer. The United States in particular had sent its best: Robert Jackson, on leave from the Supreme Court, served as its prosecutor; and Francis Biddle, a former Attorney General, was its lead judge.

Perhaps even more significant than the identities of the participants, however, was the purpose and nature of the International Military Tribunal (IMT) itself. Established by the London Charter, an agreement made that August among the four major Allies, the IMT's mandate was to carry out the "just and prompt trial and punishment of the major war criminals of the European Axis."[1] In Jackson's words, it was a venture both "novel and experimental"—the first international court in history to hear criminal charges against national leaders.[2] It was also a venture done very much on the fly. The London Charter was strong on mandate but short on details, and the participants were left to flesh out many important issues of substance and procedure over the course of the trial.

---

* The first and third parts of this piece first appeared in an expanded form in an article published by the first author in the *American Journal of International Law*. Theodor Meron, *Reflections on the Prosecution of War Crimes by International Tribunals,* 100 AM. J. INT'L L. 551 (2006). The *Journal* has graciously allowed us to reproduce them here. The second author is primarily responsible for the second part. Predictably, we write in our personal capacities rather than our official ones.

This chapter is reprinted from the first edition of this book. Theodor Meron & Jean Galbraith, *Nuremberg and Its Legacy, in* INTERNATIONAL LAW STORIES 13 (John E. Noyes, Laura A. Dickinson & Mark Weston Janis eds., 2007).

1 Charter annexed to the Agreement for the Prosecution and Punishment of Major War Criminals of the European Axis art. 1, Aug. 8, 1945, 59 Stat. 1544, 1546, 82 U.N.T.S. 279, 284 [hereinafter London Charter]. Nineteen other nations subsequently stated their adherence to the London Charter. *See* 1 TRIAL OF THE MAJOR WAR CRIMINALS BEFORE THE INTERNATIONAL MILITARY TRIBUNAL, NUREMBERG, 14 NOVEMBER 1945–1 OCTOBER 1946, at 171 (1947) [hereinafter IMT TRIAL].

2 1 IMT TRIAL, *supra* note 1, at 99.

In the end, the IMT succeeded in conducting a trial that was both effective and fair, though not without its shortcomings. Nineteen defendants were convicted, with sentences ranging from ten years to death, and the other three acquitted. Along the way, the Allies had successfully assembled a court from scratch, clarified difficult issues of law, and placed the alleged criminal behavior of the defendants in a clear and public light. From an international law perspective, it was unquestionably the trial of the century.

In this essay, we flesh out the trial's significance. We begin by looking at the state of international criminal law prior to the IMT and show how the IMT was a radical—though logical—departure from the approach taken in the aftermath of World War I. We then discuss the trial itself and highlight some of its most crucial substantive and procedural aspects. Twenty years ago, we might have stopped here. But since the Cold War ended, the international community has seen a resurgence in international criminal tribunals, including the International Criminal Tribunal for the former Yugoslavia (ICTY), the International Criminal Tribunal for Rwanda (ICTR), and the International Criminal Court (ICC). The story of the IMT would be incomplete without considering the extent to which these tribunals are its heirs and how they have used or modified the substantive and procedural law that it developed.

I. WAR CRIMES LAW BEFORE NUREMBERG

The Landscape Before World War I. Until the mid-nineteenth century, the laws of war existed solely as custom, evidenced in national laws, military manuals, and religious teachings.[3] During the second half of the century, however, various attempts at codification took place.[4] These culminated in the 1899 and 1907 Hague Peace Conferences and the resulting Hague Conventions.

While the law of war developed significantly over the course of the two Hague Conferences, mechanisms to enforce that law did not keep pace with it. Even though the acts proscribed by the Hague Conventions on land warfare had "long been treated as criminal acts for which members of the armed forces or civilians" could be "held individually

---

[3] Adam Roberts, *Land Warfare: From Hague to Nuremberg*, *in* THE LAWS OF WAR: CONSTRAINTS ON WARFARE IN THE WESTERN WORLD 116, 119 (Michael Howard, George J. Andreopoulos & Mark R. Shulman eds., 1994). *See, e.g.*, U.S. War Dep't, Instructions for the Government of Armies of the United States in the Field, General Orders No. 100, Apr. 24, 1863 (commonly known as the Lieber Code).

[4] *See* UNITED NATIONS WAR CRIMES COMM'N, HISTORY OF THE UNITED NATIONS WAR CRIMES COMMISSION 24 (1948) [hereinafter WAR CRIMES COMM'N HISTORY]; *see also* Roberts, *supra* note 3, at 119. For some of these early instruments, see Geneva Convention for the Amelioration of the Condition of the Sick and Wounded of Armies in the Field, Aug. 22, 1864, *reprinted in* 1 AM. J. INT'L L. SUPP. 90 (1907); Declaration Renouncing the Use, in Time of War, of Explosive Projectiles Under 400 Grammes Weight, St. Petersburg, Nov. 29 (Dec. 11), 1868, *reprinted in id.* at 95; and International Declaration Concerning the Laws and Customs of War, Brussels, Aug. 27, 1875, *reprinted in id.* at 96.

responsible,"[5] the 1899 Convention contained no provisions on the punishment of violations, and the Fourth Hague Convention of 1907 made no allowance for the imposition of individual criminal responsibility upon persons responsible for violations of either its provisions or those of its annexed regulations.[6] Instead, the Convention specified as the chief form of punishment the payment of compensation by states.[7] Moreover, it required states to negotiate the amount of compensation owed as a result of a violation, and these negotiations proved long and complex.[8] Not surprisingly, the Fourth Hague Convention's provision on compensation was criticized as having little deterrent effect.[9]

Other means of enforcing the laws and customs of war at the turn of the century also lacked teeth. States could try their own nationals for war crimes, but they rarely did so.[10] And although an aggrieved state could take military action against the offending state, such reprisals were criticized for simply escalating the hostilities.[11] Even if a belligerent state wished to prosecute foreign war criminals, its entitlement to jurisdiction over captured enemy combatants was uncertain, and in any event the act-of-state defense traditionally immunized heads of state from prosecution in foreign courts. As a result, combatants accused of war crimes were ordinarily relieved of prosecution rather than subjected to an indictment.[12]

World War I and Its Aftermath. War crimes law sprang to the fore at the end of World War I. Even as the war raged, commentators began calling for justice to be done in the wake of the atrocities. At an international law conference in London in 1916, one observer pledged that "the public opinion of the civilised world will not rest satisfied unless, upon the termination of the conflict, not only the instigators but also the actual perpetrators of the more heinous offences against the usages of war are brought to trial before some impartial tribunal."[13]

The process of establishing a legal framework to address the atrocities began shortly after the war. At its first plenary meeting in January 1919, the Paris Peace Conference appointed a multinational

---

[5] WAR CRIMES COMM'N HISTORY, *supra* note 4, at 30.

[6] Convention Respecting the Law and Customs of War on Land [hereinafter Fourth Hague Convention] and annexed Regulations Respecting the Laws and Customs of War on Land, Oct. 18, 1907, 36 Stat. 2277, 1 Bevans 631.

[7] Fourth Hague Convention, *supra* note 6, art. 3.

[8] Roberts, *supra* note 3, at 122.

[9] *See* Hugh H.L. Bellot, *War Crimes: Their Prevention and Punishment*, 2 GROTIUS SOC'Y TRANSACTIONS 31, 37–38 (1916).

[10] Roberts, *supra* note 3, at 126.

[11] *See* Bellot, *supra* note 9, at 34–35; WAR CRIMES COMM'N HISTORY, *supra* note 4, at 29.

[12] *See* Matthew Lippman, *Nuremberg: Forty Five Years Later*, 7 CONN. J. INT'L L. 1, 3 (1991).

[13] Bellot, *supra* note 9, at 54.

commission to inquire into the war's causes and consequences.[14] The establishment of such a commission had been advocated chiefly by the British Prime Minister Lloyd George, who sought to set new international precedent on aggressive warfare.[15] U.S. President Woodrow Wilson opposed the creation of a commission, but Lloyd George's view, which was supported by the Belgians and the French, prevailed, and the Commission on the Responsibility of the Authors of the War and on Enforcement of Penalties—the first modern international investigative body of its kind—was formed.[16]

After two months of secret meetings, the Commission issued its final report,[17] which determined that Germany and Austria-Hungary bore primary responsibility for the war. It criticized Bulgaria and Turkey for supporting the German and Austrian aggression[18] and found that all of these states had practiced "barbarous or illegitimate methods" of warfare.[19] Seeking a precise classification of the criminal acts committed by officials from these states, the Commission prepared a catalog of thirty-two offences that it denoted as falling within the meaning of war crimes. These included, among others, murders and massacres, torture of civilians, rape, and internment of civilians under inhuman conditions.[20] However, an annex that listed instances in which the Central Powers and their allies had committed such offences described the acts in question as violations of "the Laws and Customs of War and the Laws of Humanity."[21] Among the listed atrocities were some committed by Turkish and German forces against Turkish subjects (Armenians), and some by Austrian forces against Austrian subjects.[22] These acts were probably the ones that, in the Commission's view, had violated the "laws of humanity" and not the "laws of war."[23]

Having concluded that officials and soldiers from Germany, Austria-Hungary, Bulgaria, and Turkey had committed illegal acts, the Commission recommended the creation of an international tribunal to try

---

14 JAMES F. WILLIS, PROLOGUE TO NUREMBERG: THE POLITICS AND DIPLOMACY OF PUNISHING WAR CRIMINALS OF THE FIRST WORLD WAR 68 (1982); M. Cherif Bassiouni, *World War I: "The War to End All Wars" and the Birth of a Handicapped International Criminal Justice System*, 30 DENV. J. INT'L L. & POL'Y 244, 253 (2002).

15 WILLIS, *supra* note 14, at 68; Bassiouni, *supra* note 14, at 251–52.

16 WILLIS, *supra* note 14, at 68; Bassiouni, *supra* note 14, at 251–52.

17 WILLIS, *supra* note 14, at 68.

18 Comm'n on the Responsibility of the Authors of the War and on Enforcement of Penalties: Report Presented to the Preliminary Peace Conference (Mar. 29, 1919), *reprinted in* 14 AM. J. INT'L L. 95, 98 (1920) [hereinafter WWI Commission].

19 *Id.* at 115.

20 *Id.* at 114–15. See *id.* for a complete listing.

21 Violation of the Laws and Customs of War: Reports of the Majority and Dissenting Reports of American and Japanese Members of the Commission on Responsibilities, Conference of Paris, Annex I, at 28 (1919).

22 *Id.* at 30, 34–35, 40.

23 WAR CRIMES COMM'N HISTORY, *supra* note 4, at 35. Britain, France, and Russia had previously referred to massacres of Armenians by Turkish forces as "crimes against humanity and civilization." *Id.*

officials responsible for some of the worst offences.[24] The Commission also concluded that criminal liability should extend to all persons responsible for war crimes, including heads of state; in its words, a prohibition on the prosecution of heads of state who were guilty of war crimes "would shock the conscience of the world."[25]

In a memorandum, the United States objected to many of the most significant aspects of the Commission's report. According to the Americans, the Commission should not have concerned itself with violations of the "laws of humanity" because these laws were vague and "var[ied] with the individual."[26] Therefore, trying anyone for violations of such laws would contravene the principle of legality, or *nullum crimen sine lege*.[27] Supported by the Japanese, the American members of the Commission also challenged the notion that a head of state could be placed on trial,[28] while the British suggested that the Americans were simply afraid that the U.S. President would be incriminated some day.[29] Additionally, the United States objected to the concept we now refer to as "command responsibility."[30] The American representatives did agree with the recommendation that criminal charges not be brought for acts that had provoked the war, including breaches of neutrality.[31] Finally, the United States objected to one of the Commission's most significant practical recommendations: that an international tribunal try the offenders. Expressing concerns that would echo eighty years later, the Americans protested the creation of an international criminal court "for which there is no precedent, precept, practice, or procedure."[32] Instead, the Americans argued, military commissions or tribunals should try the offenders.[33]

On June 28, 1919, several months after the Commission filed its report, the Treaty of Versailles was signed. The Treaty contained several critical provisions relating to wartime conduct. The first concerned the responsibility of the Kaiser. Despite the American and Japanese objections, Great Britain remained convinced that a head of state should be liable for crimes of war—and that Kaiser Wilhelm, in particular, should be prosecuted to deter future aggression.[34] Britain's insistence

---

[24] WWI Commission, *supra* note 18, at 121–22.

[25] *Id.* at 116.

[26] Memorandum of Reservations Presented by the Representatives of the United States to the Report of the Commission on Responsibilities (Apr. 4, 1919), *reprinted in* 14 AM. J. INT'L L. 127, 134 (1920) [hereinafter U.S. Reservations].

[27] *Id.*

[28] *Id.* at 135; Reservations by the Japanese Delegation to the Report of the Commission on Responsibilities (Apr. 4, 1919), *reprinted in* 14 AM. J. INT'L L. 151, 152 (1920).

[29] WILLIS, *supra* note 14, at 77.

[30] U.S. Reservations, *supra* note 26, at 128.

[31] *Id.*

[32] *Id.* at 142.

[33] *Id.*

[34] WILLIS, *supra* note 14, at 98; Lippman, *supra* note 12, at 8.

carried the day—sort of. Article 227 of the Treaty provided that "[t]he Allied and Associated Powers publicly arraign William II of Hohenzollern, formerly German Emperor, for a supreme offence against international morality and the sanctity of treaties," and it specified that "[a] special tribunal will be constituted to try the accused."[35]

For the first time, a treaty thus addressed the individual responsibility of a head of state for initiating and conducting what we now call a crime of aggression or crime against peace—even if it did so in language that, as one commentator put it, "simply expressed a 'political' transgression and not an international crime."[36] As a practical matter, however, Article 227 was a dead letter. Queen Wilhelmina of the Netherlands, where the Kaiser had gone after abdicating the throne, would not permit his extradition.[37] A group of American soldiers was thwarted in its effort to seize him forcibly.[38]

The failure to prosecute the Kaiser is not the only respect in which the implementation of the Treaty fell short of the Commission's recommendations. The Treaty contained two other provisions related to the prosecution of individuals for war crimes. Article 228 stated in part: "The German Government recognises the right of the Allied and Associated Powers to bring before military tribunals persons accused of having committed acts in violation of the laws and customs of war."[39] And Article 229 added that "[p]ersons guilty of criminal acts against the nationals of one of the Allied and Associated Powers will be brought before the military tribunals of that Power," while "[p]ersons guilty of criminal acts against the nationals of more than one of the Allied and Associated Powers will be brought before military tribunals composed of members of the military tribunals of the Powers concerned."[40]

These clauses reflected the position expressed in the American memorandum of reservations to the Commission's report of 1919. Thus, they did not call for an international criminal court; instead, they merely contemplated the use of military tribunals. Moreover, through Article 228, the German government recognized only the victorious powers' right to prosecute "violation[s] of the laws and customs of war," eliminating any chance of prosecuting violations of the "laws of humanity"—the type of prosecutions to which the Americans objected.

After the Treaty of Versailles had been signed, German opposition to Allied-conducted trials proved considerable, prompting the Allies to worry that such trials would weaken the German government and enable

---

35 Treaty of Peace with Germany art. 227, June 28, 1919, 2 Bevans 43, 11 Martens Nouveau Recueil (ser. 3) 323 [hereinafter Versailles Treaty].

36 Bassiouni, *supra* note 14, at 271.

37 WILLIS, *supra* note 14, at 66, 98, 104.

38 *Id.* at 100–01.

39 Versailles Treaty, *supra* note 35, art. 228.

40 *Id.* art. 229.

militarists or Bolsheviks to take over.[41] Taking advantage of this fear, the German ambassador, Baron von Lersner, proposed that Germany conduct the trials of alleged war criminals itself, in its national courts.[42] To make his proposal credible, the German legislature enacted a law granting the German Supreme Court at Leipzig jurisdiction to try the accused.[43] The Allies eventually agreed.[44] They also pared down a list of 20,000 alleged war criminals that had been compiled by the Commission to 895 or so names and then, following German protest and warnings of political instability, to 45.[45] But even that was too many for the Germans, and, since the procurator general of the German Supreme Court retained prosecutorial discretion as to which cases would be pursued, ultimately only twelve military officers were brought to trial.[46]

Two-and-a-half years after the signing of the armistice, the trials finally commenced before the Penal Senate of the Reichsgericht in Leipzig.[47] Of the twelve defendants, six were convicted.[48] But even in those cases the German court imposed lenient punishments. The Commission of Allied Jurists determined that the Reichsgericht "had failed in carrying out its mandate and that 'some of the accused who were acquitted should have been condemned and . . . in the case of those condemned the sentences were not adequate.' "[49]

Other attempts to achieve justice for atrocities committed during the war period similarly fell short. The Treaty of Sèvres, an initial peace agreement between the Allies and Turkey, contained provisions consistent with the recommendations of the Commission on Responsibility in 1919. These provisions were never implemented, however, because the treaty was never ratified. The Treaty of Lausanne, which was eventually signed by the Allies and Turkey in 1923, when Turkey was in a much stronger position, contained no war crimes clauses; instead, it was accompanied by a "Declaration of Amnesty" that covered all offences committed during the wartime period.[50] Rather than insist on war crimes clauses, the Allies agreed that Turkey itself would prosecute offenders, just as the Allies had permitted Germany to try offenders in

---

41 WILLIS, *supra* note 14, at 116–24.

42 *Id.* at 118.

43 *Id.*

44 *Id.* at 124; *see also* Theodor Meron, *The Case for War Crimes Trials in Yugoslavia*, FOREIGN AFF., Summer 1993, at 124.

45 Bassiouni, *supra* note 14, at 281–82.

46 WILLIS, *supra* note 14, at 124.

47 Judgment in Case of Commander Karl von Neumann: Hospital Ship "Dover Castle" (Reichsgericht Penal Senate No. 2, June 4, 1921), *reprinted in* 16 AM. J. INT'L L. 704 (1922).

48 Bassiouni, *supra* note 14, at 282.

49 *Id.* at 285 (quoting Comm'n of Allied Jurists, *in* WAR CRIMES COMM'N HISTORY, *supra* note 4, at 48).

50 Treaty of Peace with Turkey, July 24, 1923, Gt. Brit. T.S. No. 16 (1923), *reprinted in* 18 AM. J. INT'L L. SUPP. 4 (1924); Declaration of Amnesty, July 24, 1923, *reprinted in id.* at 92.

Leipzig. The so-called Istanbul trials were no more successful than the Leipzig trials: many defendants were absent, the sentences were light, and the proceedings never gained any popular support.[51] For their part, the Turks denied that crimes against humanity were committed against the Armenians between 1915 and 1917.[52]

In sum, while international humanitarian law saw considerable doctrinal development in the half century preceding the Nuremberg trials—as nations codified many laws of war in treaties, many powers embraced the concepts of crimes against humanity and command responsibility, and many nations rejected the notion of head-of-state immunity—enforcement lagged far behind the doctrinal development. Nobody faced an international tribunal after World War I, few faced domestic prosecution in Germany and Turkey, and in those cases that were actually brought, the few-and-far-between convictions resulted in light penalties. Indeed, as one commentator observed, "[A]part from helping to lay the legal foundations for international criminal justice in the future, the Allies' experiment in retributive justice following the First World War was a dismal failure."[53] Thus, while the contours of war crimes law had been increasingly well established by World War II, persons violating that law faced only a hypothetical possibility of criminal sanction. In a sense, war crimes law had not yet truly become a form of criminal law.

II. THE TRIAL OF THE MAJOR WAR CRIMINALS AT NUREMBERG

The Creation of the IMT. As World War II wore on and victory looked increasingly likely, the Allies began to discuss how they would deal with the Nazi leaders after the war.[54] There was virtually no consideration of leaving it to Germany to try its own leaders. As Jackson later observed, "[a]fter the first World War, we learned the futility of [that] course."[55] The Allied leaders did express some interest in summary executions. At the Tehran Conference, Stalin suggested the summary execution of at least 50,000 Germans, and Roosevelt countered, presumably jokingly, with a figure of 49,000 instead.[56] At Yalta, Churchill "thought a list of the major war criminals . . . should be drawn up here

---

[51] Bassiouni, *supra* note 14, at 288.

[52] *Id.*

[53] *Id.* at 290.

[54] This essay only addresses the Allies' treatment of the Nazi leaders. The decisions made regarding the Japanese leadership, and the Tokyo trials that ultimately resulted from these decisions, are beyond the scope of this piece.

[55] 2 IMT TRIAL, *supra* note 1, at 101.

[56] THE NUREMBERG INTERVIEWS CONDUCTED BY LEON GOLDENSOHN ix (Robert Gellately ed., 2004) [hereinafter NUREMBERG INTERVIEWS].

. . . [and] they should be shot once their identity is established."[57] But early agreements among the Allies also suggested the possibility of trials.[58] In the United States, this position was forcefully advocated by Secretary of War Henry Stimson among others. Indeed, his department prepared memoranda on how the trials could be conducted well before the Allied leadership agreed to trials at all.[59]

When Truman became President in April 1945, he immediately supported trials and offered Jackson the role of U.S. prosecutor.[60] With the United States thus firmly in favor of trials—and with Jackson moving rapidly ahead with organization—the other Allies concurred. At Potsdam, the Allies formalized the position that "[w]ar criminals and those who have participated in planning or carrying out Nazi enterprises involving or resulting in atrocities or war crimes shall be arrested and brought to judgment,"[61] and Jackson met with representatives from Britain, Russia, and France in August to draw up the London Charter.

The Charter set out three types of substantive crimes: first, crimes against peace, which it defined mainly as starting or waging a war of aggression; second, war crimes; and third, crimes against humanity.[62] Although the Americans had opposed the charges both of waging a war of aggression and of "crimes against humanity" in the aftermath of World War I, they now supported their inclusion.[63] Similarly, the Charter rejected head-of-state immunity.[64] The Charter also contained two novel aspects, both stemming from a memorandum prepared earlier by Stimson's department.[65] First, the Charter included conspiracy as a crime—a decision reached over some objections from the French, whose civil law system (like that of the Russians) did not separately criminalize conspiracy.[66] Second, the Charter authorized the IMT to try organizations and stated that if such organizations were convicted, individuals

---

57 FOREIGN RELATIONS OF THE UNITED STATES: DIPLOMATIC PAPERS: THE CONFERENCES AT MALTA AND YALTA 1945, at 849 (1955) (minutes of the Yalta Conference); *see also* ROBERT E. CONOT, JUSTICE AT NUREMBERG 13–14 (1983).

58 *See* M. Cherif Bassiouni, *The International Criminal Court in Historic Context*, 1999 ST. LOUIS-WARSAW TRANSATLANTIC L.J. 55, 60 (discussing the St. James Declaration of 1942 and the Moscow Declaration of 1943).

59 CONOT, *supra* note 57, at 13; TELFORD TAYLOR, FINAL REPORT TO THE SECRETARY OF THE ARMY ON THE NUERNBERG WAR CRIMES TRIALS UNDER CONTROL COUNCIL LAW NO. 10, at 1–3 (1949).

60 CONOT, *supra* note 57, at 14.

61 Potsdam Conference, Protocol of the Proceedings II(A)(5) (Aug. 1, 1945).

62 London Charter, *supra* note 1, art. 6.

63 Indeed, the other three Allies were opposed to including the launch of an aggressive war as a crime, and only energetic efforts by Jackson persuaded them otherwise. *See* CONOT, *supra* note 57, at 21–23.

64 London Charter, *supra* note 1, art. 7.

65 *See* Norman Silber & Geoffrey Miller, *Towards 'Neutral Principles' in the Law: Selections from the Oral History of Herbert Wechsler*, 93 COLUM. L. REV. 854, 893–95, 898–99 (1993).

66 London Charter, *supra* note 1, art. 6; *see also* Henry T. King, Jr., *Robert Jackson's Vision for Justice and Other Reflections of a Nuremberg Prosecutor*, 88 GEO. L.J. 2421, 2425 (2000).

belonging to those organizations could be tried "for membership therein" without having the right to reopen the question of the criminality of the organization.[67]

One article of the Charter was devoted to the rights of the defendants and ensured them (1) copies of the indictments against them; (2) translations of the indictments, incorporated documents, and trial proceedings into their language; (3) the right to conduct their own defense or have the assistance of counsel; and (4) the right to present evidence and cross-examine the prosecution witnesses.[68] Notably lacking were the right to remain silent, the right to be present,[69] and the right of appeal.[70] Nor was there any specification of the burden of proof.

The London Charter also set out the bare-bones structure for how the IMT would proceed. Each of the four signatory nations would provide a judge, an alternate judge, and a chief prosecutor.[71] The judges would elect a president from among their number. Decisions would be made based on majority vote, with the president's vote proving decisive in the event of a tie—except in votes as to convictions or sentences, where a tie would go to the defendant.[72] Finally, the IMT would "not be bound by technical rules of evidence" and it would primarily follow the adversarial system used in common law rather than the inquisitorial system used in civil law—thus the prosecution and the defense were primarily responsible for interrogation and cross-examination of witnesses.[73]

Although brief, the London Charter thus covered important ground. It clearly resolved issues that had proved controversial in the aftermath of World War I, including the nature of the substantive crimes and the question of head-of-state immunity. It also indicated that the IMT would proceed more along common law lines than civil law lines—an approach that showed the comparative sway of the Americans and the British in the negotiations.

The Place and the People. Even before the London Charter was drawn up, preparations for the trial had begun at Nuremberg. Its selection as the site for the first trial came about largely at the Americans' urging. They favored it for several reasons. For one thing, the choice had symbolic resonance: Nuremberg had been a center of Nazi rallies and racist laws.[74] For another, while much of the city had been reduced to rubble, the Palace of Justice remained physically intact and could, with

---

67 London Charter, *supra* note 1, arts. 9–11.

68 *Id.* art. 16.

69 Indeed, the Charter specified that a defendant could be tried *in absentia*. *Id.* art. 12.

70 The Charter did give the Control Council the power to reduce the sentences entered by the IMT. *See id.* art. 29.

71 *Id.* arts. 2, 14.

72 *Id.* art. 4.

73 *See id.* arts. 19, 24.

74 NUREMBERG INTERVIEWS, *supra* note 56, at xviii.

modifications, accommodate the trials. Probably most significantly, though, from the American perspective, was the fact that Nuremberg was within their zone of occupation. With Jackson applying considerable pressure, the other Allies assented over the summer to the proposed site.[75]

An American architect was put in charge of making the necessary modifications to the Palace of Justice. Using former SS personnel from a nearby prison camp for labor,[76] he swiftly transformed the courtroom into one that could accommodate the proceedings. This included enlarging the room, refurnishing it, and adding the translators' booths and related equipment so that participants could listen simultaneously to the proceedings over earphones in English, German, French, or Russian.[77] Preparations began in July, and by November it was ready for the trials.[78]

As the courtroom was being prepared, the cast of participants was also coming together. This took time, as the Allied countries needed to appoint their judges and prosecutors; the prosecutors needed to agree on who the first defendants would be; and these defendants needed counsel.

In its selections, the United States played what Herbert Wechsler, who served as a law clerk to Biddle at the IMT, described as a game of "musical chairs":[79] picking a Justice for its prosecutor and a prosecutor for its judge. Although far from intuitive, this swap ended up working well. Jackson brought unbounded energy and eloquence to the role of prosecutor—and a sense of speed, as he was taking a leave of absence from the Supreme Court. As for Biddle, he had been Attorney General until Roosevelt's death, and his appointment to Nuremberg was essentially a consolation prize for Truman's decision not to keep him on in that role.[80] His cosmopolitan upbringing (including his impeccable French) served him well on the IMT,[81] as did his strong sense of fairness. As an alternate judge, Truman sent John Parker, a well-respected judge on the Fourth Circuit.[82] These high-powered choices demonstrated the U.S. commitment to the project, one made despite pockets of significant skepticism.[83]

---

[75] *See* CONOT, *supra* note 57, at 19–21.

[76] *See* WITNESS TO NUREMBERG: AN ORAL HISTORY OF AMERICAN PARTICIPANTS AT THE WAR CRIMES TRIALS 19–21 (Bruce M. Stave & Michelle Palmer eds., 1998).

[77] *See id.* at 26.

[78] *Id.* at 21.

[79] Silber & Miller, *supra* note 65, at 904.

[80] CONOT, *supra* note 57, at 62.

[81] Silber & Miller, *supra* note 65, at 910.

[82] Indeed, Parker had once been a Supreme Court nominee. His nomination in 1930 failed following strong lobbying efforts by the NAACP, which had turned up a newspaper report of a racist speech given by Parker in 1920. *See* RICHARD KLUGER, SIMPLE JUSTICE 141–43 (1975). Parker subsequently gained a reputation as a fair, able, and "universally admired" jurist. *Id.* at 303, 658.

[83] To give an example, Chief Justice Harlan Fiske Stone viewed the IMT as "Jackson's high-grade lynching party" and refused to swear in Biddle and Parker. CONOT, *supra* note 57, at 63.

The English, the Russians, and the French similarly made their selections. The lead English judge, Lord Geoffrey Lawrence, was a former Lord Chief Justice of England, and the judges selected him as their president. In Wechsler's view, he was an "average workaday" kind of judge, but one whose "imperturbability" suited the role of president.[84]

The prosecutors then sought to draw up a list of defendants for the first trial. They were broadly in agreement that the most senior German leaders should be tried in this first trial—but how to define those leaders and where to draw the line? In the end, they selected leaders drawn broadly from various sectors, including top Nazi leader and air force commander Hermann Goering, Hitler's former deputy Rudolf Hess, navy admiral and Hitler's named successor Karl Doenitz, Wilhelm Keitel from the armed forces, foreign affairs minister Joachim von Ribbentrop, and interior minister Wilhelm Frick. Other considerations affected this list as well. Most of the top Nazi leaders were in American or British custody. Not wishing to be entirely outdone, the French urged the addition of a German diplomat in their custody, Constantin von Neurath, and the Russians insisted on the inclusion of two of their prisoners, including second-rank propagandist Hans Fritzsche.[85] There was thus significant variety in the final list of twenty-two defendants. Indeed, Goering observed that he never heard of some of the "little fellows" on the list until trial.[86]

Finally, the defendants needed counsel. Arranging this proved more of a hurdle than the Allies had anticipated, even though the IMT decided to pay for counsel and provide them with food, lodging, and transportation.[87] Many of the defendants asked for suggestions from another defendant, Hans Frank, who had been the lead lawyer for the Nazi party before becoming governor-general of Poland. One of the defendants actually wanted Frank to serve as his lawyer,[88] but unsurprisingly this did not occur. Doenitz ended up with one of the best lawyers due to a stray memory—he requested a young naval judge, Otto Kranzbuehler, whom he had once seen handle a case skillfully.[89]

In the end, German lawyers were found for all the defendants. The lawyers came from various backgrounds. Some were academics, others were practitioners, and eighteen of the forty-eight were former Nazis.[90] All these lawyers, however, faced one disadvantage in common: as

---

84 Silber & Miller, *supra* note 65, at 910.

85 CONOT, *supra* note 57, at 27–28.

86 NUREMBERG INTERVIEWS, *supra* note 56, at 101.

87 CONOT, *supra* note 57, at 83.

88 *Id.* at 83–84.

89 NUREMBERG INTERVIEWS, *supra* note 56, at 6; *see also* Silber & Miller, *supra* note 65, at 906.

90 CONOT, *supra* note 57, at 83; *see also* Silber & Miller, *supra* note 65, at 905.

members of a civil law system, they were not familiar with the practice of cross-examination and often blundered in conducting it.[91]

The IMT in Session. The IMT held its opening session in Berlin on October 18, 1945. This session was essentially a formality. The judges gave declarations of their impartiality, the Russian prosecutor announced the lodging of the Indictment, and reference was made to the upcoming trial at Nuremberg.[92] Over the next month, the judges dealt with various preliminary issues, such as the publication of their Rules of Procedure (which had a scant eleven rules).[93]

The trial itself opened in Nuremberg on November 20. The next day, the defendants all pled not guilty, and Jackson delivered his famous opening statement. "The wrongs which we seek to condemn and punish," he told the judges, "have been so calculated, so malignant, and so devastating, that civilization cannot tolerate their being ignored, because it cannot survive their being repeated. That four great nations, flush with victory and stung with injury stay the hand of vengeance and voluntarily submit their captive enemies to the judgment of the law is one of the most significant tributes that Power has ever paid to Reason."[94]

With that, the prosecution's case against the individual defendants began. The host of topics covered is mind-boggling: it included evidence related to the planning and waging of aggressive war against Czechoslovakia, Poland, the United Kingdom, France, Denmark, Norway, Belgium, the Netherlands, Luxembourg, Greece, Yugoslavia, the Soviet Union, and the United States; to the deportation, forced labor, persecution, and annihilation of the Jewish people; to the atrocities committed against civilians and soldiers of the occupied countries; to the plunder of these occupied countries and crimes against culture; and to the inhumane treatment of prisoners of war.[95] Yet the trial lasted less than four months,[96] and the number of witnesses was hardly large. Only thirty-three witnesses testified orally for the prosecution.[97]

The prosecution's slim use of witnesses was made possible by the availability of documentary evidence. In Jackson's words, "the defendants had their share of the Teutonic passion for thoroughness in putting things on paper."[98] In the course of their investigations, the prosecution sifted through huge quantities of captured evidence, including 100,000

---

[91] Silber & Miller, *supra* note 65, at 905–06.

[92] 1 IMT TRIAL, *supra* note 1, at 24–26.

[93] *Id.* at 19–23. By contrast, the ICTY currently has 127 Rules of Procedure. *See* International Criminal Tribunal for the Former Yugoslavia, Rules of Procedure and Evidence, IT/32/Rev.38 (June 13, 2006), *available at* https://www.icty.org/x/file/Legal%20 Library/Rules_procedure_evidence/IT032_rev38_en.pdf.

[94] 2 IMT TRIAL, *supra* note 1, at 98–99.

[95] *See generally* 2–8 *id.*

[96] *See* 8 *id.* at 495.

[97] 1 *id.* at 172.

[98] 1 *id.* at 102.

documents, millions of feet of moving film, and 25,000 photographs (many taken by Hitler's personal photographer), of which the prosecution ultimately introduced around 4000 documents, certain sections of the film, and 1800 photographs into evidence.[99] Finds included a complete set of notes taken by Hitler's interpreter at meetings with foreign officials and official reports on the killings of Jews.[100] There were also many documents produced or signed by the defendants themselves, including the thirty-six-volume official diary of Frank's time in Poland.[101] As the Judgment ultimately stated, "[t]he case . . . against the defendants rests in a large measure on documents of their own making, the authenticity of which has not been challenged except in one or two cases."[102] Frank's diary, for example, observed that "[o]f course I could neither eliminate all lice nor all Jews in only 1 year's time. But in the course of time . . . this end will be obtained."[103] Upon receiving a memorandum from Admiral Canaris, the head of German military intelligence, that objected to the inhumane treatment of Soviet POWs,[104] Keitel wrote the following (and signed his name): "These objections arise from the military conception of chivalrous warfare. We are dealing here with the destruction of an ideology and, therefore, I approve such measures and I sanction them."[105]

The case for the individual defendants ran into July. Nineteen of the defendants took the stand, as did sixty-one other witnesses.[106] An additional 143 witnesses provided written answers to interrogatories.[107] The general approach was to acknowledge the atrocities that had occurred but to deny responsibility for them.[108] Relatedly, while the defendants rarely contested the authenticity of documents issued under their name or of minutes of meetings where they were present, they frequently tried to justify their behavior by urging that it was appropriate in context or that they had not meant it. Frank, for example, suggested that while he himself was "shocked at many of the words which I had used" in the diary, nonetheless "[o]ne has to take the diary as a whole."[109]

---

[99] Report to the President by Mr. Justice Jackson, Oct. 7, 1946, *in* INTERNATIONAL CONFERENCE ON MILITARY TRIALS 433 (1949).

[100] CONOT, *supra* note 57, at 37.

[101] *Id.*

[102] 1 IMT TRIAL, *supra* note 1, at 173.

[103] 3 *id.* at 528.

[104] In this 1941 memorandum, Canaris stated that while the " 'Geneva Convention for the treatment of prisoners of war is not binding in the relationship between Germany and the U.S.S.R.,' " nonetheless " 'the principles of general international law on the treatment of prisoners of war apply.' " 1 *id.* at 232. These principles are " 'developed in accordance with the view held by all armies that it is contrary to military tradition to kill or injure helpless people,' " whereas the " 'decrees for the treatment of Soviet prisoners of war enclosed are based on a fundamentally different viewpoint.' " *Id.* (quoting Report of Admiral Canaris, 15 September 1941, Nuremberg Doc. No. EC–338).

[105] 10 *id.* at 623.

[106] 1 *id.* at 172.

[107] *Id.*

[108] *See, e.g.*, 19 *id.* at 453.

[109] 12 *id.* at 20.

Asked on the stand about his position on the treatment of Soviet POWs, Keitel claimed that he had actually agreed with the concerns raised in Canaris's memorandum and suggested that he had written what he did due to compulsion from Hitler.[110]

Other aspects of the defense case were more persuasive. Accused of violating international law through certain submarine warfare practices (namely, attacking merchant ships without warning and doing so without being prepared to rescue the survivors), Doenitz did not deny the practices but claimed that they did not violate international law. His lawyer, Kranzbuehler, sought to introduce an affidavit of U.S. Admiral Nimitz stating that the United States carried out similar practices. The prosecution objected on the grounds that the claim that the other side did it too, also known as the *tu quoque* argument, is no defense.[111] The subject of *tu quoque* was a touchy one in the IMT, for the Allies did not want their own practices to come under judicial scrutiny.[112] In this instance, however, Kranzbuehler cleverly argued that he did not seek to show that the Americans had also violated international law, but instead wished to show that custom and practice demonstrated that there was no violation of international law at all.[113] The IMT allowed the evidence to come in and ultimately found Kranzbuehler's point persuasive.[114]

Moments like these undoubtedly helped the IMT appear relatively fair.[115] Even though the IMT was created by the victorious nations rather than by neutral parties—a fact treated by Jackson in his opening argument as unfortunate but inevitable[116]—it was relatively well-regarded by the Germans within the American occupation zone. Public opinion surveys taken there during the course of the trial showed that seventy-nine percent thought the trial was "conducted fairly."[117]

The trial wrapped up at the end of July with regard to the individual defendants. In his closing remarks, Jackson rather grandiosely gave each defendant an epithet: Goering was "half militarist and half gangster"; Doenitz was "Hitler's legatee of defeat"; Ribbentrop "the salesman of deception"; Keitel "the weak and willing tool."[118] After another month spent hearing evidence related to organizational defendants like the SS, the IMT adjourned, returning to deliver the Judgment on September 30.

---

110 10 *id.* at 622–23.

111 8 *id.* at 547.

112 *See* ANN TUSA & JOHN TUSA, THE NUREMBERG TRIAL 259–60 (1995).

113 8 IMT TRIAL, *supra* note 1, at 549.

114 1 *id.* at 311–13.

115 Of course, there were moments to the contrary. The social ties between the judges and prosecutors, for example, led to some awkward incidents, as when Biddle and Parker attended a party, hosted by Jackson, where a Russian dignitary raised a toast "[t]o the speedy conviction and execution of all the defendants." CONOT, *supra* note 57, at 92.

116 *See* 2 IMT TRIAL, *supra* note 1, at 101.

117 NUREMBERG INTERVIEWS, *supra* note 56, at 457.

118 19 IMT TRIAL, *supra* note 1, at 415–16.

The Judgment and the Aftermath. Herbert Wechsler has remarked that the possibility of acquittals at Nuremberg was inconceivable at the beginning of the process.[119] Certainly the London Charter supports this impression, focusing on "trial and punishment" as though the outcome was not in doubt.[120] The Judgment that came down, however, drew clear distinctions between the different individual defendants and also took a restrictive view of certain substantive crimes.

The 170-page document began with a general overview of the IMT, of the applicable law, and of the major offenses committed by Germany over the course of the war—including the planning and waging of aggressive warfare, the murder and ill-treatment of POWs and civilian populations, and the persecution of the Jews.[121] Two aspects of this discussion are particularly noteworthy. First, as we discuss more later, the IMT discussed and rejected the defendants' claim that the offenses charged were not criminalized under international law at the time of their occurrence.[122] Second, the IMT read the charge of conspiracy narrowly, interpreting the London Charter to permit this charge only with regard to crimes against peace and not with regard to war crimes or crimes against humanity.[123]

The Judgment then turned to the specific defendants—first the organizational defendants and then the individual ones. As to the organizational defendants, it upheld the charges against some of the organizations, including the SS. But while the London Charter had suggested that individual members of these organizations could later be convicted based simply on their membership in the organizations, the IMT ruled that "membership alone is not enough."[124] Instead, in future trials, the prosecution would have to show that these individuals shared in the criminal aims or acts of the organizations.[125]

The Judgment then analyzed the evidence against each defendant. Nineteen were found guilty of various crimes. Of these, twelve were sentenced to hang and the rest received prison terms of various lengths.[126] Convicted of conspiracy to wage aggressive war, the waging of aggressive war, war crimes, and crimes against humanity, Goering was one of those given a death sentence, as were Ribbentrop, Keitel, Frank, and Frick.[127] The IMT was unimpressed by Frank's claims of ignorance and lack of control over the situation in Poland, finding that he was a "willing and knowing participant" in the terrors there, including the

---

[119] Silber & Miller, *supra* note 65, at 906–07.

[120] London Charter, *supra* note 1, art. 1.

[121] 1 IMT TRIAL, *supra* note 1, at 171–254.

[122] *Id.* at 219–23; *see also infra* notes 190–196 and accompanying text.

[123] 1 IMT TRIAL, *supra* note 1, at 226.

[124] *Id.* at 256.

[125] *See id.*

[126] *Id.* at 365–66.

[127] *Id.* at 282, 365–66.

programs of slave labor and of extermination of the Jews.[128] Keitel's disavowals of his actions were similarly found unpersuasive.[129] Those sentenced to prison terms included Doenitz (whose ten-year sentence was the lightest given) and Hess (with a life sentence).[130]

Over the dissent of the Soviet judge, the remaining three defendants were acquitted, including Hans Fritzsche. The IMT deemed him too uninfluential to have conspired to wage aggressive war and held that his propaganda did not rise to the level of incitement.[131] His acquittal must have surprised him. During the course of the trial, Fritzsche had told an American psychiatrist that it was a "completely false trial" and suggested that an outcome of guilt was foreordained.[132]

With the issuances of the sentences, the IMT adjourned. The acquitted men were released, though all chose to remain in U.S. custody for at least several days due to concerns about their personal safety.[133] The convicted men were given four days[134] to seek clemency from the Control Council, which swiftly declined to intervene.[135] On October 16, those who had received death sentences were executed by hanging—with the exception of Goering, who committed suicide the night before.[136] Those who had received prison terms were sent to Spandau prison in Berlin. Six of the seven were released after serving their full terms or for reasons of ill health.[137] The seventh, Hess, remained in prison until his suicide in 1987.[138]

Although the London Charter did not limit the IMT to one trial, no others took place before the Tribunal. The growing rift between the Soviet Union and the Western Allies may have been part of the reason;[139] Jackson's concerns about the expense and hassle of the IMT may have been another.[140] But Allied Control Council Law No. 10, issued in December of 1945, did give each Allied Power the power to prosecute suspected war criminals within its zone of occupation.[141] The United States made use of this law, conducting twelve trials of various

[128] *Id.* at 298.

[129] *Id.* at 288–90.

[130] *Id.* at 365–66.

[131] *Id.* at 336–38.

[132] NUREMBERG INTERVIEWS, *supra* note 56, at 50.

[133] CONOT, *supra* note 57, at 499. They were also justifiably concerned about being seized and tried by a German court. *See id.*; *see also infra* text accompanying note 183.

[134] 22 IMT TRIAL, *supra* note 1, at 587.

[135] 2 DREXEL A. SPRECHER, INSIDE THE NUREMBERG TRIAL: A PROSECUTOR'S COMPREHENSIVE ACCOUNT 1427–29 (1999).

[136] *Id.* at 1432–34.

[137] *Id.* at 1437.

[138] *Id.*

[139] *See* CONOT, *supra* note 57, at 516.

[140] TAYLOR, *supra* note 59, at 25–27.

[141] Control Council Law No. 10, Punishment of Persons Guilty of War Crimes, Crimes Against Peace and Against Humanity art. 3, *available at* https://avalon.law.yale.edu/imt/imt10.asp.

industrialists, SS leaders, lawyers, doctors, and high military officials over the next several years.[142] In all, 177 defendants were tried, leading to 142 convictions.[143] Though not conducted by an international court, these trials have proved important precedents for the ICTY.[144]

III. FROM NUREMBERG TO THE HAGUE

Despite international recognition of the importance of many legal principles set forth by the IMT, no subsequent international criminal tribunal emerged until after the end of the Cold War. Since 1993, however, we have seen the development of the ICTY, the ICTR, and the ICC, as well as hybrid bodies like the Special Court for Sierra Leone. These tribunals are the heirs of the IMT: like it, they are internationally constituted bodies seeking to bring the perpetrators of international crimes to justice. This part outlines some key features of their development, with a particular focus on how they have departed from or expanded upon the approach taken by the IMT.[145]

Offenses Recognized. Prior to the establishment of the IMT, although customary international law existed, it had never been applied in an international criminal court. The challenge for the IMT, then, was to find a way to bring the existing law to bear in a multinational court.

As noted earlier, the London Charter set forth three types of crimes: crimes against the peace, war crimes, and crimes against humanity; it also permitted charges of conspiracy and stated that defenses of state immunity and superior orders would not be relevant to guilt.[146] Each of these legal grounds was controversial. Never before had aggression been treated as a legal, rather than a merely political, wrong, and never had senior officials been held criminally liable as individuals. The concept of conspiracy liability not only was novel in international law, but was especially foreign to lawyers from civil traditions. And although the notion of "crimes against humanity," which defined criminal liability as including citizen-to-citizen acts, seems like second nature to us now, it had never formed the basis for international criminal liability before World War II. Even the charge of war crimes was ambiguous, since the

---

[142] TAYLOR, *supra* note 59, at 91, 115.

[143] *Id.* at 91.

[144] *See, e.g.*, Prosecutor v. Tadić, Judgment, No. IT–94–1–A, ¶¶ 263–264 (July 15, 1999).

[145] This is a necessarily selective endeavor. Due to space constraints, this essay omits many differences that are obvious, such as the point that while the IMT was a court established by four victorious nations, the ICTY and ICTR were established by the U.N. Security Council and thus have a more truly international grounding. Similarly, this essay does not address significant practical differences, such as the fact that the prosecutors of the modern Tribunals have harder times gathering evidence than did those at Nuremberg, due to a lack of comparable written records and the need to rely on the cooperation of supportive governments and individuals.

[146] London Charter, *supra* note 1, arts. 6–9.

laws of war had not previously delimited the boundaries of lawful military conduct with much precision.[147]

Despite the initial controversy, the IMT's legal legacy was rapidly and broadly established.[148] The United Nations quickly ratified the legal principles articulated in the London Charter, and American military law incorporated them as well.[149] The Genocide Convention soon followed (1948), as did the Geneva Conventions for the Protection of Victims of War (1949), and pressure built to establish a permanent international criminal court.[150]

These developments stimulated doctrinal developments. Writings by Hersch Lauterpacht[151] and Richard Baxter[152] were critically important, as were the later writings of Cherif Bassiouni.[153] Then came the Vietnam War. The acts of war by both the United States and North Vietnam sparked a new debate over the applicability of international legal norms and, broadly, over the adequacy of compliance with the law.[154] The growing antiwar movement and the human rights community began to press for the application of international law to human rights violations in Vietnam and elsewhere, not just to war crimes. Significantly, the disagreement was *not* over the definition of the offenses, but, rather, over the capacity of the law to deal with the conduct of hostilities, protection of medical evacuation aircraft, and treatment of prisoners of war. These difficulties were heightened by questions about the applicability of international humanitarian conventions to internal and mixed internal-international conflicts. Although the principles of Nuremberg had settled into place and the debate had moved on,[155] the conflict in Vietnam, combined with national liberation wars, guerrilla wars, and civil wars, created the pressure necessary for renewal of the law through the elaboration of the two Additional Protocols to the Geneva Conventions, which were adopted in 1977.

That is how matters stood until the establishment of the modern tribunals at The Hague and Arusha. Using the London Charter as a

---

147 *See* YORAM DINSTEIN, THE CONDUCT OF HOSTILITIES UNDER THE LAW OF INTERNATIONAL ARMED CONFLICT 57–105 (2004).

148 *See* Jonathan A. Bush, *Nuremberg: The Modern Law of War and Its Limitations*, 93 COLUM. L. REV. 2022, 2063 (1993) (reviewing TELFORD TAYLOR, THE ANATOMY OF THE NUREMBERG TRIALS: A PERSONAL MEMOIR (1992)).

149 Henry T. King, *The Legacy of Nuremberg*, 34 CASE W. RES. J. INT'L L. 335, 347 (2002).

150 *Id.*

151 *See, e.g.*, HERSCH LAUTERPACHT, INTERNATIONAL LAW AND HUMAN RIGHTS (1950).

152 *See, e.g.*, Richard R. Baxter, *Constitutional Forms and Some Legal Problems of International Military Command*, 1952 BRIT. Y.B. INT'L L. 325; Richard R. Baxter, *The Municipal and International Law Basis of Jurisdiction over War Crimes*, 1951 BRIT. Y.B. INT'L L. 382.

153 *See, e.g.*, A TREATISE ON INTERNATIONAL CRIMINAL LAW (M. Cherif Bassiouni & Ved Nanda eds., 1973).

154 *See* Bush, *supra* note 148, at 2065.

155 *See id.* at 2065–69.

model, the U.N. Security Council, exercising its authority under Chapter VII of the U.N. Charter, enacted the statutes that created the ICTY and the ICTR.[156] Those statutes set forth in detail the crimes over which the ad hoc tribunals would exercise jurisdiction. As at Nuremberg, those crimes include war crimes and crimes against humanity, and the crime of genocide was added. Unlike the London Charter, however, the ICTY and ICTR Statutes do not include crimes against peace.[157] They are also marked by more detailed definitions and a broader scope, encompassing war crimes in internal conflicts. Thus, these statutes manifest the growing humanization of humanitarian law under the influence of human rights.[158] And the Statute of the ICC contains even more detailed definitions.[159]

Like the ad hoc tribunals, the ICC did not follow the Nuremberg model of criminalizing crimes against peace, despite intense debate. Many states consider the concept too political, and lacking in the required customary law underpinnings.[160] Nevertheless, attempts to include the crime of aggression in a revised version of the ICC Statute continue unabated.

At the ICTY, although the definitions are more detailed, they still require extensive judicial interpretation. In adding that judicial gloss, the ICTY judges, like the court at Nuremberg, refer to the customary underpinnings of the crimes.[161] The ICTY's resort to customary law, however, is more methodical than Nuremberg, partly because of the criticisms levelled against the Nuremberg convictions. Critics of the Nuremberg trials charged that the law that was applied there originated in the London Charter and that it was unlawfully applied *ex post facto* to the German defendants.[162] To forestall similar criticisms, the ad hoc tribunals take pains to explain the customary and conventional underpinnings of their decisions. Consequently, judgments of the ICTY are helping to revitalize customary law and to anchor international law

---

156 *See* Statute of the International Criminal Tribunal for the Former Yugoslavia, U.N. Doc. S/25704, annex (1993), 32 I.L.M. 1192 (1993) [hereinafter ICTY Statute]; Statute of the International Criminal Tribunal for Rwanda, S.C. Res. 955, annex (1994), 33 I.L.M. 1602 (1994) [hereinafter ICTR Statute].

157 *Compare* London Charter, *supra* note 1, *with* ICTY Statute, *supra* note 156, *and* ICTR Statute, *supra* note 156.

158 Theodor Meron, *The Humanization of Humanitarian Law*, 94 AM. J. INT'L L. 239 (2000). For a detailed discussion of the substantive law applied at the ICTY and ICTR, see GUÉNAËL METTRAUX, INTERNATIONAL CRIMES AND THE AD HOC TRIBUNALS (2005).

159 Rome Statute of the International Criminal Court arts. 6–9, July 17, 1998, 2187 U.N.T.S. 3 [hereinafter ICC Statute].

160 Theodor Meron, *Defining Aggression for the International Criminal Court*, 25 SUFFOLK TRANSNAT'L L. REV. 1 (2001).

161 *See, e.g.*, Prosecutor v. Hadžihasanović, Decision on Jurisdiction in Relation to Command Responsibility, No. IT–01–47–AR72 (July 16, 2003).

162 *See* Kevin R. Chaney, *Pitfalls and Imperatives: Applying the Lessons of Nuremberg to the Yugoslav War Crime Trials,* 14 DICK. J. INT'L L. 57, 71–72 (1995).

firmly in both codified law and judicial decisions.[163] The ICC is different in this respect. Its statute resembles more of a civil law code and is to be applied as such, though, broadly speaking, the crimes it enumerates are declaratory of customary law.

Gender Crimes. Rape and violence against women have long been accepted as natural consequences of war.[164] The London Charter made no specific reference to sex crimes, and the IMT virtually ignored such crimes in its judgment.[165] By contrast, the ICTY and the ICTR have been groundbreaking in this area.[166] Both statutes explicitly include rape as a crime against humanity,[167] and the tribunals have successfully prosecuted various forms of sexual violence as instruments of genocide, crimes against humanity, and crimes of war, thus developing a crucial area of international humanitarian law.[168] The tribunals made a major contribution in grounding the prohibition of rape in customary international law.[169] And the ICC Statute specifically defines sexual crimes such as rape and sexual slavery.[170]

Jurisdiction. The respective jurisdictions of the IMT and the modern tribunals differ in another way. The London Charter limited its definition of crimes against humanity to offenses that had occurred "in execution of or in connection with any crimes within the jurisdiction of the Tribunal."[171] In other words, although the Charter extended international criminal responsibility to atrocities committed within a single country, even between its own citizens ("against any civilian population, before or during the war"),[172] the scope of that liability was limited, because the offenses were required to be *wartime* atrocities within the IMT's jurisdiction. As a result, the IMT did not have jurisdiction over atrocities committed within and by Germany in the years leading up to World War II. Nevertheless, there is no question that crimes against humanity constituted the most revolutionary contribution of the Nuremberg trials to international criminal law, exceeding even

---

163 Theodor Meron, *The Revival of Customary Humanitarian Law*, 99 AM. J. INT'L L. 817 (2005).

164 Theodor Meron, *Rape as a Crime Under International Humanitarian Law*, 87 AM. J. INT'L L. 424, 424–27 (1993); David S. Mitchell, *The Prohibition of Rape in International Humanitarian Law as a Norm of* Jus Cogens*: Clarifying the Doctrine*, 15 DUKE J. COMP. & INT'L L. 219, 224 (2005).

165 *See generally* London Charter, *supra* note 1; 1 IMT TRIAL, *supra* note 1, at 171–341.

166 Mitchell, *supra* note 164, at 237–38.

167 ICTY Statute, *supra* note 156, art. 5(g); ICTR Statute, *supra* note 156, art. 3(g).

168 *See, e.g.*, Prosecutor v. Furundžija, No. IT–95–17/1–T, ¶ 186 (Dec. 10, 1998).

169 *See* Prosecutor v. Kunarac, Nos. IT–96–23 & 96–23/1–A, ¶¶ 127–133 (June 12, 2002); Prosecutor v. Gacumbitsi, No. ICTR–2001–64–A, ¶¶ 147–157 (July 7, 2006).

170 ICC Statute, *supra* note 159, art. 7(1)(g); *see also* Mitchell, *supra* note 164, at 242–44.

171 London Charter, *supra* note 1, art. 6(c); TAYLOR, *supra* note 59, at 239.

172 London Charter, *supra* note 1, art. 6(c).

crimes against peace, which owed at least a semblance of a foundation to the Treaty of Versailles.

Over time, however, the definition of crimes against humanity lost the required nexus with armed conflict. For instance, the U.N. Convention on the Non-Applicability of Statutory Limitations to War Crimes and Crimes against Humanity of 1968 applies to "crimes against humanity whether committed in time of war or in time of peace."[173] The ICTY Statute, in Article 5, defines crimes against humanity subject to the jurisdiction of the Tribunal as certain crimes "committed in armed conflict, whether international or internal in character."[174] Although this provision appears to require a nexus with armed conflict, the appeals chamber has interpreted the requirement of an armed conflict as related only to the Tribunal's subject matter jurisdiction.[175] Under the case law of both ad hoc tribunals, then, a war nexus is not required under customary law.

The ICC Statute confirms that no nexus with armed conflict is required. Under Article 7, crimes against humanity can be committed in all situations—international wars, internal wars of whatever intensity, and peacetime.[176]

These changes relate to another significant legal development: the international criminalization of internal atrocities. The Security Council's statutes for the ad hoc tribunals have contributed significantly to the extension of international humanitarian law to non-international armed conflicts. The ICTY Statute and jurisprudence treat the conflict in the former Yugoslavia as both international and non-international in scope.[177] The ICTR Statute, however, is predicated on the assumption that the conflict in Rwanda was internal.[178] And the ICC Statute sets forth violations not only of the laws and customs of war applicable in international armed conflicts, but also of the laws and customs applicable in armed conflicts not of an international character—within the established framework of international law.[179] These developments are a natural extension of the Nuremberg principles.

Due Process. One of the principal criticisms of Nuremberg was, and is, that it was a victors' court trying the vanquished. That criticism resonates most strongly in the context of due process protections.

---

173 Convention on the Non-Applicability of Statutory Limitations to War Crimes and Crimes Against Humanity art. 1(b), Nov. 26, 1968, 754 U.N.T.S. 73 (entered into force Nov. 11, 1970).

174 ICTY Statute, *supra* note 156, art. 5.

175 Prosecutor v. Tadić, Appeal on Jurisdiction, No. IT–94–1–AR72, ¶¶ 78–79 (Oct. 2, 1995).

176 ICC Statute, *supra* note 159, art. 7.

177 *See Prosecutor v. Tadić*, Appeal on Jurisdiction, ¶¶ 71–93.

178 ICTR Statute, *supra* note 156, art. 1.

179 ICC Statute, *supra* note 159, arts. 8(2)(c)–(f).

Two examples illustrate this point. First, the London Charter expressly provided that trials could be conducted *in absentia* "if [an accused] has not been found or if the Tribunal, for any reason, finds it necessary, in the interests of justice, to conduct the hearing in [the accused's] absence."[180] As it happened, the Allies were unable to locate and arrest Martin Bormann, head of the Nazi Party Chancellery, but the IMT tried, convicted, and sentenced him to death anyway.[181] The second example is that the Charter contained no protection against double jeopardy. On the contrary, Article 11 stated that persons convicted by the IMT could be separately charged and punished by a national, military, or occupation court;[182] and some were. Indeed, the three defendants acquitted by the IMT were later prosecuted in German courts.[183]

All the same, the IMT track record on due process protections was not all bad. The Allies agreed to the Nuremberg enterprise largely because they assumed that the trials would be quick, the outcome never in doubt. Frankly, the London Charter was short on due process protections because they were not among the Allies' chief concerns. But fairness norms inevitably crept into the proceedings, in spite of the conciseness of the IMT's Charter. The Charter, for instance, made no reference to burdens of proof.[184] In fact, the Soviets took the view that the burden should rest on the defense rather than the prosecution.[185] Nonetheless, the IMT imposed a rigorous Anglo-American burden on the prosecution—one so rigorous that some of the accused were acquitted.

Due process protections also triumphed over the American plan to focus on trials of Nazi organizations such as the Gestapo.[186] The intention was to convict these organizations at trial and then use the convictions in follow-on proceedings to bring thousands of individual members to justice.[187] The only question in the later trials would be whether the individual defendants knowingly participated in the criminal conspiracy. But the IMT thwarted this plan by interpreting conspiracy narrowly and reading additional elements of specific intent into the conspiracy and aggressive war charges.[188] As a result, many of the individuals who were charged with conspiracy were acquitted of that charge, as were some of the organizational defendants. And as noted earlier, the IMT held that individual members of organizations that were convicted were liable only

---

180 London Charter, *supra* note 1, art. 12.

181 Jonathan A. Bush, *Lex Americana: Constitutional Due Process and the Nuremberg Defendants*, 45 ST. LOUIS U. L.J. 515, 536 (2001).

182 London Charter, *supra* note 1, art. 11.

183 *See* Chaney, *supra* note 162, at 69–70.

184 Bush, *supra* note 181, at 531–32.

185 *Id.*

186 *Id.* at 533.

187 *Id.*

188 *Id.* at 534.

if their participation or membership was both knowing and willing, and active.[189]

One of the enduring lessons of Nuremberg, then, is that due process protections are not an impediment to the administration of international justice; rather, they are indispensable to it. The ad hoc tribunals at The Hague and Arusha and the permanent ICC are supported by detailed statutes and extensive rules of procedure and evidence—a far cry from the brief London Charter. The ICTY and ICTR Statutes entitle the accused to be present at his trial and accord primacy to the tribunals over national courts, preventing concurrent or consecutive convictions by multiple jurisdictions for the same charges. The U.N. statutes expressly created an appeals chamber to which defendants may appeal not only their convictions, but also certain interlocutory issues. Moreover, in general, the modern tribunals adhere to the catalogue of human rights protections embodied in the International Covenant on Civil and Political Rights, and, increasingly, those in the European Convention on Human Rights. Therefore, while the IMT was hardly a failure from the perspective of due process rights, its shortcomings inspired its heirs to do better, and the result is a rigorous commitment to due process across the international criminal courts.

Sources of Law. The principle of *nullum crimen sine lege*, also known as the legality principle, has been much discussed with respect to the Nuremberg tribunals. Customary law was essential to the ability of the IMT and the later American tribunals to convict Nazi war criminals: the Geneva POW Convention of 1929 was not applicable on the eastern front, and the Fourth Hague Convention was challenged on the ground that the situation of the belligerents did not conform with its *si omnes* clause, as not all the belligerents were party to it.[190] Moreover, the applicable provisions of the Geneva and Hague Conventions that define the relevant substantive proscriptions and are considered declaratory of customary law did not expressly criminalize their violation.[191] The Nuremberg tribunals therefore faced the question as to whether, for the purposes of the legality principle, offenders had been sufficiently on notice that their conduct entailed criminal liability. The IMT described the Nuremberg Charter as both the exercise of the sovereign power of the victorious countries and as "the expression of international law existing at the time of its creation."[192] In dismissing the challenge based on the principle of legality, the IMT noted that the law of war was to be found in

---

[189] *Id.*

[190] *See* THEODOR MERON, HUMAN RIGHTS AND HUMANITARIAN LAW AS CUSTOMARY LAW 41–62 (1989).

[191] *See* Theodor Meron, *International Criminalization of Internal Atrocities*, 89 AM. J. INT'L L. 554, 564 (1995).

[192] 1 IMT TRIAL, *supra* note 1, at 218.

treaties, as well as in the customs and practices of states and the general principles of justice.[193]

Addressing this question, the Military Tribunal under Control Council Law No. 10 similarly explained:

> It is not essential that a crime be specifically defined and charged in accordance with a particular ordinance, statute, or treaty if it is made a crime by international convention, recognized customs and usages of war, or the general principles of criminal justice common to civilized nations generally. If the acts charged were in fact crimes under international law when committed, they cannot be said to be *ex post facto* acts or retroactive pronouncements.[194]

Some criticized the Nuremberg tribunals for this relatively loose approach to the legality principle.[195] To be sure, the IMT did not provide a very satisfactory explanation as to how aspects of the 1929 Geneva POW Convention and the Fourth Hague Convention had so quickly metamorphosed into customary norms.[196] Nonetheless, the crimes with which the Nuremberg defendants were charged—including murder, torture, and enslavement, carried out on an enormous scale—were so clearly criminal under every domestic legal system in the world that it could hardly be said that the prospect of criminal liability for them was unpredictable. Ultimately, the *nullum crimen* principle turns on fairness to the defendant.

The ICTY has likewise declined to engage in an overly formalistic assessment of custom in instances where the criminality of conduct is obvious (or, to use the Nuremberg terminology, where it is clearly established under the relevant "general principles" of law). In its seminal interlocutory decision on jurisdiction in the *Tadić* case, the ICTY Appeals Chamber stated that to be subject to prosecution by the Tribunal as a violation of laws and customs of war, an offense must violate either customary law or a treaty that was unquestionably binding on the parties at the time of the alleged offense.[197] The Nuremberg trials, of course, serve as a precedent for the principle of legality to be satisfied by reference to treaties that were in force at the time of the offense. However, in the case of the ICTY, such reliance on treaties must be reconciled with the statement in the U.N. Secretary-General's 1993 report that the Tribunal should apply rules of international humanitarian law that

---

193 *Id.* at 221.

194 United States v. List, *in* 11 TRIALS OF WAR CRIMINALS BEFORE THE NUERNBERG MILITARY TRIBUNALS UNDER CONTROL COUNCIL LAW NO. 10, at 759, 1239 (1950).

195 Hans-Heinrich Jescheck, *The General Principles of International Criminal Law Set out in Nuremberg, as Mirrored in the ICC Statute,* 2 J. INT'L CRIM. JUST. 38, 40–42 (2004).

196 MERON, *supra* note 190, at 37–41.

197 Prosecutor v. Tadić, Appeal on Jurisdiction, No. IT–94–1–AR72, ¶¶ 94, 143 (Oct. 2, 1995).

beyond any doubt form part of customary law. The *Tadić* panel found that the purpose of this statement was merely to avoid a conflict with the *nullum crimen* principle when a party to the conflict was not a party to a treaty; the statement therefore does not exclude reliance on treaties in the absence of a potential conflict.[198] If the principle of legality can thus be satisfied by grounding a prosecution in a treaty binding the parties, why has the ICTY not made treaty law the principal foundation of its approach to *ratione materiae* jurisdiction, preferring instead to rely on customary principles (especially since treaties have the added advantage of satisfying the principle of specificity[199])? One obvious reason was to follow as closely as possible the language of the Secretary-General's report. Another may have been to avoid doubts as to succession to treaties, their continuing binding character and reservations, and the scope and validity of ad hoc agreements between the belligerents. Reliance on customary law provides additional comfort because of its generality. In addition, where the ICTY has showed some readiness to apply treaties, they were, wholly or largely, declaratory of customary law—for example, the Geneva Conventions and Additional Protocol I.[200] This factor only underscores the point that the ICTY has found customary law to be a more solid basis for its jurisdiction.

The legality principle likewise governs the other international criminal tribunals operating today, including the ICTR, the Special Court for Sierra Leone, and the ICC.[201] Since the conflict in Rwanda was non-international in character, and since (as the Secretary-General noted when the ICTR Statute was adopted) Rwanda had been party to the relevant international humanitarian law treaties, which constituted part of its domestic law, the ICTR generally need not consider whether a violation of its Statute was also a violation of customary law at the time of the offense; it suffices that the treaties were violated.[202]

As much as possible, the Rome Conference sought to formulate the content of customary international law in the language of the Statute. Subjects on which it exceeded customary law may pose particular difficulties when nationals of nonstate parties to the ICC Statute are prosecuted.

---

198 *Id.* ¶ 143; *see* Report of the Secretary-General pursuant to Paragraph 2 of Security Council Resolution 808 (1993), U.N. Doc. S/25704, ¶ 34 (1993).

199 Jescheck, *supra* note 195, at 41.

200 *Cf.* Prosecutor v. Galić, Judgment, No. IT–98–29–A, ¶ 85 (Nov. 30, 2006) (explaining that "while binding conventional law that prohibits conduct and provides for individual criminal responsibility could provide the basis for the International Tribunal's jurisdiction, in practice the International Tribunal always ascertains that the treaty provision in question is also declaratory of custom").

201 *See* Meron, *supra* note 163, at 829–32.

202 Report of the Secretary-General Pursuant to Paragraph 5 of Security Council Resolution 955, U.N. Doc. S/1995/134, ¶¶ 11–12 (1994).

IV. CONCLUDING THOUGHTS

In his opening statement, Jackson remarked that "the record on which we judge these defendants today is the record on which history will judge us tomorrow."[203] By most measures, the IMT has passed the test of history. The trial of the major war criminals may not have been perfect, but it was essentially fair. The defendants had their cases fully considered, and the convictions generally rested upon compelling evidence of guilt.

In considering the impact of the IMT, we have focused on its effect on international law today: on how it provided a model for successful international criminal trials, on the substantive definitions of crimes that it set forth, and on ways in which modern criminal tribunals have implemented or altered its approach. As we close, however, it seems worthwhile to consider the place of the IMT—and international criminal trials generally—in the broader landscape of world affairs. Why should we have these tribunals, and what can we expect from them?

The most obvious justification for international criminal tribunals is simply that they provide a forum for dealing with high-level international war criminals. Without international criminal courts, what would we do with alleged war criminals captured at the end of a period of war or turmoil? Leaving them to go free is untenable, as is summary execution or perpetual detainment without trial. That leaves some form of legal process. But while trials in the accuseds' former countries—or in the countries in which they allegedly committed the crimes—may in some instances prove successful, this will not always be the case. Sometimes, as in the post-World War I trials in Leipzig, the former country will prove unjustly lenient. At other times, the new government of the former country may harbor too much vengeance towards its former leaders, even towards the worst of the worst.[204] With regard to the former Yugoslavia, only recently has the ICTY begun to let courts in Bosnia, Croatia, and Serbia try alleged war criminals indicted by the ICTY prosecutor. To have done so earlier might have risked the application of principles other than justice.

International criminal courts may also play some role in deterring international crimes. As Jackson observed in his opening remarks before the IMT, "I am too well aware of the weaknesses of juridical action alone to contend that in itself your decision under this Charter can prevent future wars. . . . But the ultimate step in avoiding periodic wars, which are inevitable in a system of international lawlessness, is to make

---

[203] 2 IMT TRIAL, *supra* note 1, at 101.

[204] This may have proved the case with regard to Saddam Hussein, where questions have been raised as to both the manner in which his execution was carried out and the decision to execute him before the conclusion of his trial for abuses of the Kurds (though after his conviction for the murder of 148 Shiites). *See, e.g.*, Hendrik Hertzberg, *Desolation Rows*, NEW YORKER, Jan. 15, 2007, at 21, 21–23.

statesmen responsible to law."[205] If there is a deterrent effect, though, it is hard to measure, and there has sadly been no shortage of international crimes in the years since Nuremberg. This, however, may change if more atrocities are adjudicated in international tribunals, and if the ICC proves to be a vibrant, robust, and effective institution.

Finally, international criminal courts may play some role in assisting the post-war recovery of the nations at issue. For Wechsler, the greatest perceived benefit of IMT and the subsequent Control Council trials was that their emphasis on justice provided time for passions to cool and headed off a possible bloodbath against the former Nazi oppressors by the liberated governments and masses.[206] By institutionalizing the process of judgment and punishment, international criminal courts may offer some hope of closure to the crimes they adjudicate.

In light of such benefits, it is no surprise that the idea of international criminal tribunals did not end with Nuremberg. In recent years, they have come to form a small but important piece of the mechanisms of international accountability—and a piece that, with the establishment of the ICC, seems likely to last. Although these international criminal tribunals have moved away from many of the specifics of the IMT's approach, they still share its core purpose of judging alleged perpetrators of grave international crimes with fairness and impartiality. As with the IMT, "many mistakes have been made and many inadequacies must be confessed,"[207] but international criminal law continues to develop and to fulfill the promise of Nuremberg, and its universe is light years away from where it was a century ago.

[205] 2 IMT TRIAL, *supra* note 1, at 153–54.

[206] Silber & Miller, *supra* note 65, at 914.

[207] Report to the President by Mr. Justice Jackson, *supra* note 99, at 440.

2

Harold Hongju Koh*

Filártiga v. Peña-Irala: Judicial Internalization of the Customary International Law Norm Against Torture

Some cases, Justice Frankfurter said, do not simply revise old precedents; they spawn new ways of looking at the law.[1] One such historic decision was the landmark 1980 ruling of the U.S. Court of Appeals for the Second Circuit in *Filártiga v. Peña-Irala*,[2] which inaugurated the era of human rights litigation in which we now live. Supported by an important government amicus brief pressing the Carter administration's human rights policy, *Filártiga* held that a then-obscure federal law, the Alien Tort Claims Act (ATCA),[3] conferred district court jurisdiction over a suit by two Paraguayan nationals against a Paraguayan official who had tortured their son and brother to death in Paraguay, while acting under color of governmental authority. A district court later awarded the plaintiffs a judgment of more than $10 million in damages for their loss.

The case triggered a sea change in international human rights litigation and a series of court battles that continue today. Twenty-four years later, in *Sosa v. Alvarez-Machain*,[4] six Justices of the U.S. Supreme Court confirmed *Filártiga*'s core holding: that when there is a norm of international character accepted by the civilized world and defined with a specificity comparable to recognized paradigms, an alien can sue in a federal court under the ATCA even for extraterritorial violations of that norm.[5] Although the Roberts Court has since sharply limited the applicability of the Alien Tort Claims Act, it has not overruled *Filártiga*,

---

* This law story grows out of the author's Foreword to WILLIAM J. ACEVES, THE ANATOMY OF TORTURE: A DOCUMENTARY HISTORY OF *FILÁRTIGA V. PEÑA-IRALA* (2007).

1 Guaranty Trust Co. v. York, 326 U.S. 99, 101 (1945) (discussing Erie R.R. Co. v. Tompkins, 304 U.S. 64 (1938)).

2 630 F.2d 876 (2d Cir. 1980).

3 28 U.S.C. § 1350 (2007) (Federal courts "shall have original jurisdiction of any civil action by an alien for a tort only, committed in violation of the law of nations or a treaty of the United States.").

4 542 U.S. 692 (2004).

5 *Id.* at 732 (Souter, J., joined by Stevens, O'Connor, Kennedy, Ginsburg, & Breyer, JJ.).

which continues to spawn important progeny in the United States and abroad.

How did *Filártiga* come to be, and what is its legacy?[6]

I. JOELITO'S DEATH AND THE SEARCH FOR A JUDICIAL REMEDY

After seizing power in 1954, for thirty-five years General Alfredo Stroessner Matiauda ruled Paraguay with a brutal fist.[7] "Terror archives" later unearthed in 1992 by human rights activists at a police station in the Lambaré suburb of Asunción, Paraguay's capital, suggested that some 50,000 people had been murdered, 30,000 disappeared, and 400,000 people had been imprisoned in "Operation Condor," a Latin American operation during the 1970s and 80s involving the exchange of intelligence and prisoners among the military governments of Argentina, Bolivia, Brazil, Chile, Paraguay, and Uruguay.[8] One of Stroessner's vocal critics was Dr. Joel Filártiga, who ran a medical clinic about fifty miles from Asunción. On at least three occasions, Filártiga was detained and tortured.[9]

During the night of March 29, 1976, Dr. Filártiga's seventeen-year-old son, Joelito, was kidnapped from his bed while his two sisters lay sleeping elsewhere in the Filártigas' Asunción home. He was taken two doors away to the house of the then-Inspector General of Asunción, Americo Norberto Peña-Irala. There he was whipped, beaten, slashed, and subjected to severe electro-shock. After about forty-five minutes, he died.

At four o'clock in the morning, Joelito's sister Dolly was awakened by a knock on her front door. A policeman told her that "there was a small problem with [her] brother at Peña's house." She walked two doors down and found her brother's body lying on a mattress amid a pool of blood. Later, she saw and confronted Peña, who told her, "[H]ere you have what you have been looking for for so long and what you deserve. Now shut

---

6 *Filártiga*'s story has been told in several places: a 1991 movie entitled ONE MAN'S WAR (Home Box Office 1991), directed by Sergio Toledo and starring Anthony Hopkins; a 2004 book by RICHARD ALAN WHITE, BREAKING SILENCE: THE CASE THAT CHANGED THE FACE OF HUMAN RIGHTS (2004); and in documentary form in WILLIAM J. ACEVES, THE ANATOMY OF TORTURE: A DOCUMENTARY HISTORY OF *FILÁRTIGA V. PEÑA-IRALA* (2007). For two book-length treatments of the doctrines spawned by *Filártiga*, see BETH STEPHENS & MICHAEL RATNER, INTERNATIONAL HUMAN RIGHTS LITIGATION IN U.S. COURTS (1996) (written with the support of Yale Law students); and THE ALIEN TORT CLAIMS ACT: AN ANALYTICAL ANTHOLOGY (Ralph G. Steinhardt & Anthony D'Amato eds., 1999).

7 *See generally* CARLOS R. MIRANDA, THE STROESSNER ERA: AUTHORITARIAN RULE IN PARAGUAY (1990).

8 *See generally* Katie Zoglin, *Paraguay's Archive of Terror: International Cooperation and Operation Condor*, 32 U. MIAMI INTER-AM. L. REV. 57, 59–60 (2001).

9 ACEVES, *supra* note 6, at 18 n.6 (citing Transcript of Hearing Before the Honorable John L. Caden at 31–32, Filártiga v. Peña-Irala, 577 F. Supp. 860 (E.D.N.Y. 1984) (No. 79 C 917)).

up." Peña then threatened Dolly with a similar fate.[10] Dr. Filártiga was summoned back to Asunción; he asked doctor friends to conduct an autopsy that confirmed that torture had been the cause of his son's death.[11] He became convinced that Joelito had been tortured by Paraguayan officials seeking information on his own political activities.

In the months that followed, the Filártiga family tried unsuccessfully to institute Paraguayan legal proceedings against Joelito's murderers. One lawyer who helped them was subsequently disbarred; two others withdrew from the case after being threatened. In 1977, an unsuccessful petition concerning the case was filed against Paraguay with the Inter-American Commission of Human Rights.[12] Meanwhile, the family continued to suffer harassment, threats, and abuse.[13]

In July 1978, Peña-Irala entered the United States on a tourist visa with his common-law wife, son, and niece, ostensibly to visit Disney World. From Florida, they made their way to Brooklyn, New York, where they remained after their visas had expired. Peña's niece wrote a letter back to her father in Asunción, who lived in the same neighborhood as the Filártigas. Incredibly, the letter, which included Peña's return address in New York, was misdelivered to the Filártiga home in Asunción, where Dolly opened it.[14] In October 1978, Dr. Joel Filártiga and Dolly came to the United States as part of an Amnesty International-sponsored tour, but with the real goal of locating Peña-Irala. Finding no initial success, Dr. Filártiga returned to Paraguay, but Dolly stayed on to continue the search.

In March 1979, Dolly finally learned, through a Paraguayan exile, of Peña-Irala's address in Brooklyn. Through lawyer friends, she notified the Immigration and Naturalization Service (INS) of Peña-Irala's whereabouts, which led in April 1979 to his arrest while leaving his Brooklyn apartment. As Peña sat in detention pending deportation at the Brooklyn Naval Yard, Dolly began consulting American lawyers about the possibility of initiating a civil suit against him. Through the Executive Director of Amnesty International USA, she was put in touch with Peter Weiss, a Vice-President and cooperating attorney at New York's Center for Constitutional Rights (CCR). As Weiss later recalled:

> [O]ne day the phone rings and it's Gerhard Elston from Amnesty International who says, "They just arrested a Paraguayan torturer. He's being held at the INS detention

---

[10] The facts in this section draw heavily upon ACEVES, *supra* note 6, at 18–31. Dolly Filártiga recounted the story of her brother's death in Dolly Filártiga, *American Courts, Global Justice*, N.Y. TIMES, Mar. 30, 2004, at A21.

[11] ACEVES, *supra* note 6, at 20 n.11 (citing Affidavit of Dr. Joel Filártiga at 1–2, Filártiga v. Peña-Irala, 577 F. Supp. 860 (E.D.N.Y. 1984) (No. 79 C 917)).

[12] *See* WHITE, *supra* note 6, at 139–40.

[13] ACEVES, *supra* note 6, at 23.

[14] *Id.* at 28 n.36 (citing Affidavit of Dolly Filártiga at 2, Filártiga v. Peña-Irala, 630 F.2d 876 (2d Cir. 1980) (No. 79 C 917).

center in Brooklyn and he is going to be deported in 48 hours. What can we do to keep him here?" . . . That's how *Filártiga* started. Nobody had time to think about what the implications were, where it was going to lead or even what the theory was going to be. All we knew was that something had to be done within 48 hours.[15]

One idea that came to Weiss's mind was suing Peña on behalf of the Filártigas in a federal court under 28 U.S.C. § 1350, sometimes called the Alien Tort Claims Act (ATCA). The ATCA was an obscure statute originally enacted as part of the First Judiciary Act of 1789, which declared that federal courts "shall have original jurisdiction of any civil action by an alien for a tort only, committed in violation of the law of nations or a treaty of the United States."[16] Since its enactment, the ATCA had been cited as a basis for federal court jurisdiction in only two known cases: a 1795 maritime seizure dispute[17] and a 1961 child custody dispute in Maryland.[18] CCR had unsuccessfully invoked the ATCA in a Ninth Circuit case previously brought against Secretary of State Henry Kissinger on behalf of Vietnamese children being massively transferred from Vietnam toward the end of the Vietnam War.[19] In the leading Second Circuit ATCA precedent, *IIT v. Vencap, Ltd.*, the fabled Judge Henry Friendly had stated: "[t]his old but little used section is a kind of legal Lohengrin; although it has been with us since the First Judiciary Act, no one seems to know whence it came."[20] Judge Friendly therefore dismissed the claim before him, reasoning that the only claims for violations of the law of nations cognizable under the statute were those that relate to "international law," literally understood: that is, relations between states or between individuals and foreign states.[21]

---

15 *Proceedings: Conference on International Human Rights Law in State and Federal Courts*, 17 U.S.F. L. REV. 1, 57 (1982) (remarks of Peter Weiss).

16 28 U.S.C. § 1350 (2000). The statute originally provided, in language subsequently omitted from later amendments, that federal district courts "shall also have cognizance, *concurrent with the courts of the several States, or the circuit courts, as the case may be*, of all causes where an alien sues for a tort only in violation of the law of nations or a treaty of the United States." Act of Sept. 24, 1789, ch. 20, § 9(b) (emphasis added). *See generally* William R. Casto, *The Federal Courts' Protective Jurisdiction Over Torts Committed in Violation of the Law of Nations*, 18 CONN. L. REV. 467 (1986), *reprinted in* THE ALIEN TORT CLAIMS ACT, *supra* note 6, at 137–54.

17 Bolchos v. Darrel, 3 F. Cas. 810 (D.S.C. 1795).

18 Adra v. Clift, 195 F. Supp. 857 (D. Md. 1961), *overruled in light of Sosa v. Alvarez-Machain by* Taveras v. Taveraz, 477 F.3d 767 (6th Cir. 2007).

19 Nguyen Da Yen v. Kissinger, 528 F.2d 1194, 1202 n.13 (9th Cir. 1975) (noting in footnote that the ATCA "may be available . . . . [But w]e are reluctant to decide the applicability of § 1350 to this case without adequate briefing. Moreover, we are reluctant to rest on it in any event" because of difficulties in joining other tortfeasors relevant to such action).

20 IIT v. Vencap, Ltd., 519 F.2d 1001, 1015 (2d Cir. 1975). In German literature and opera, Lohengrin arrives in a boat pulled by a swan and offers to defend a beautiful maiden, but he warns her never to ask his name. When she nevertheless asks the forbidden question, he answers, but steps back onto his swan boat, vanishing as mysteriously as he came. *See* ROBERT JAFFRAY, THE TWO KNIGHTS OF THE SWAN: LOHENGRIN AND HELYAS 11 (1910).

21 *See Vencap*, 519 F.2d at 1015 (internal quotation marks omitted).

This adverse Second Circuit precedent notwithstanding, Weiss and several other attorneys at CCR quickly drafted a six-page complaint seeking compensatory and punitive damages of $10 million and charging Peña with wrongful death and "torts in violation of U.S. treaties and the law of nations." On April 6, 1979, they filed their complaint before Judge Eugene Nickerson of the federal district court for the Eastern District of New York. A few days later, they sought a district court order seeking a stay of Peña-Irala's deportation, which the judge swiftly granted. In turn, Peña-Irala's counsel moved to dismiss the lawsuit, arguing that the district court lacked subject matter jurisdiction because the acts alleged did not rise to the level of the jurisdictionally required "tort in violation of the law of nations." The Filártigas responded with affidavits from four prominent international law scholars—Professors Richard Falk of Princeton, Thomas Franck of New York University, Richard Lillich of Virginia, and Myres McDougal of Yale—each asserting that torture is unambiguously proscribed by international law.

Following a May 1979 hearing, Judge Nickerson dismissed the suit in a brief four-page ruling. While plainly sympathetic to the Filártigas' plight, he felt bound by Judge Friendly's prior decision, which had "held that conduct, though tortious, is not in violation of 'the Law of Nations,' as those words are used in 28 U.S.C. § 1350, unless the conduct is in violation of those standards, rules or customs affecting the relationship between states and between an individual and a foreign state, and used by those states for their common good and/or in dealings inter se."[22]

The Filártigas immediately appealed to the Second Circuit. In October 1979, Weiss argued the appeal before a three-judge panel comprised of Chief Judge Irving Kaufman and Judges Wilfred Feinberg and John Smith (who passed away and was replaced by a newly appointed judge, Amalya Kearse). In a memorandum to the author, Judge Kaufman's then-law clerk, Bruce R. Kraus, a 1979 Yale Law School graduate who is now a New York lawyer, recounts what happened next.[23]

> I never took a course in international law. My note was about bankruptcy law and the prisoner's dilemma, but when I arrived for my first day of work as a clerk on the Second Circuit, there were different prisoners and dilemmas to deal with. . . . [My co-clerk and I] learned that all bench memos to the Judge about cases large and small had to be summarized in a page of rough, 4x6-inch foolscap, double spaced, containing everything

---

[22] Filártiga v. Peña-Irala, No. 79 C 917, slip op. at 2 (E.D.N.Y. May 15, 1979), *reprinted in* ACEVES, *supra* note 6, at 349.

[23] What follows is an extract from a memorandum entitled "Filártiga Memoir," sent to the author by Bruce R. Kraus, Willkie Farr & Gallagher LLP. For two more formal accounts by the late Judge Kaufman, see Irving R. Kaufman, *A Legal Remedy for International Torture?*, N.Y. TIMES MAG., Nov. 9, 1980, at 44; Irving R. Kaufman, *The Anatomy of Decisionmaking*, 53 FORDHAM L. REV. 1 (1984). For a recent biographical discussion of the role of the *Filártiga* case in Judge Kaufman's jurisprudence, see Rodger D. Citron, *The Long Shadow of* United States v. Rosenberg*: A Biographical Perspective on the Hon. Irving Robert Kaufman*, 75 RUTGERS L. REV. 55, 119–25 (2022).

important about the case. . . . Briefs for pending cases were kept in upright, green, open-topped boxes cut on the bias to reveal the case names. There was a color coding system for appellants and respondents, replies and sur-replies that has long fled from memory (I'm a deal lawyer now) . . . . In any event, through a random assignment calendar drawn up by [my co-clerk or his predecessor], the *Filártiga* case was to be decided by a panel consisting of the Judge, Judge Feinberg, and Judge Kearse.

I had never read a real brief before I delved into that first stack of them. For all I knew, every Second Circuit docket had a case or two with amicus briefs and affidavits from leading legal scholars. But even I must have been astute enough to realize that most opinions do not come up to the Court of Appeals with a note attached from the District Judge that basically said, "Reverse Me!" Judge Nickerson had felt bound by a recent (1975), powerfully-written Friendly opinion that sneered at Section 1350 ("a legal Lohengrin—no one knows from whence it came") and had all but wiped the provision out of the Judiciary Act of 1789. Whether moved by the cruel facts of this case, or the legal issues at stake, Judge Nickerson's opinion left no doubt that he was hoping for a panel that would reverse *IIT v. Vencap*, notwithstanding Judge Friendly's enormous prestige.

The Second Circuit was a decisive court in those days, a rocket docket, and the Judge (known by his initials IRK) justly claimed credit for the Court's fast turnaround time. As a colleague noted to smiles at the Judicial Conference that year, "he irks us and irks us" to decide our cases and get our opinions out quickly, and preserve our standing as the fastest circuit in the land.

But this case was different. The Friendly opinion was only part of the problem. The Iran hostage crisis began in the middle of all this, and the nation felt itself under siege more than it would again for another 22 years. Everyone knew that if the panel didn't take the easy way out and follow Judge Friendly, we'd be sailing into uncharted waters. This was not just a question of jurisdiction, because a finding of jurisdiction would imply the existence of a new body of substantive law, a law of torts committed in violation of international law. No one seemed to doubt that a finding of jurisdiction comported with our national ideals; the honest question we all had was whether it comported with our national interests as well. So the Judge from the bench did something utterly un-Judge like. He asked (not directing the question to anyone in particular) why we hadn't heard from the State Department about this.

The lawyers were a bit taken aback, but no one raised a separation-of-powers objection to the court's request that the executive branch weigh in. I think the plaintiff's lawyer, Peter Weiss, may have expressed some confidence that the Carter State Department was with him in spirit, but the Judge wouldn't take his word for it, and the decision was postponed until State's views were made known. I don't recall the judge writing to them himself; I think the lawyers for one side or the other must have done that.

So there the case sat, for the rest of the year, while we waited for a response . . . . Briefs from other cases filled our docket boxes: a trademark case, a copyright case, the case of the administrative law judge seeking administrative law judicial independence. The Judge's legendary temper flared on occasion, but the work of the Chambers got done. I recorded our travails as sitcom episode summaries, in the style of TV Guide, and wrote a bench memo in rhymed dactylic hexameter dismissing the appeal of a suit by a high school student who swore under his breath at a teacher who had shut the classroom door in his face. Concurrences were usually evidenced by a signed adhesive tab, the precursor of the Post-It note, but Judge [Charles] Brieant concurred with this one in verse of his own.

When the State Department finally responded, my clerkship was about to end. Someone told me later that our request had caused great consternation within the legal counsel's office. Not only were they distracted by the hostage crisis, it wasn't obvious to them, either, which side of this question this country should be on as a policy matter. But in the end, they came down firmly on the side of the plaintiffs, and this view was, in the end, given dispositive weight by the panel.

But who was going to draft the opinion? The new clerks, who hadn't heard the arguments and hadn't even begun to be broken in? Someone else's clerks? Despite the stresses and conflicts of the year, I wanted to do it and so did the Judge, to the point where he managed to wangle an extra two weeks of salary for me. The new clerks arrived the following Monday, and I moved across the hall to the empty chambers normally occupied by (Senior) Judge Timbers. So with a whole law library at my disposal, I read and read, and drafted and drafted, undisturbed and uninterrupted.

I knew how the case was supposed to come out, but how to get there? The Friendly opinion could be distinguished. Its hostility to the statute was so sweeping that by definition it was 98% dictum. So there's a section at the end, with dense footnotes, that cites dictum with approval, turns it into its opposite, and then moves on.

When it came to the question of whether international law forms part of our law automatically, I really wished I had taken [former Dean and Undersecretary of State] Gene Rostow's course at Yale. At least then I would have had some idea of the received wisdom on this fundamentally important topic. It seemed fairly clear that Chief Justice Marshall had confidently answered this question in the affirmative at the birth of the Republic—back when Americans were grateful and maybe a bit surprised to have been admitted to the comity of sovereign nations at all. Had anyone looked at this question again since the time the newborn nation grew up to be a superpower?

The briefs were all scholarly and excellent, but it was obvious that the plaintiffs and amici were citing scholarship when they'd have cited caselaw, had there been any. So the draft did its best to be balanced, defending its conclusion while bending over backwards not to open any floodgates. (In that, it seems to have succeeded not at all, and some of my partners spend a lot of time litigating Alien Tort Claims suits brought against American multi-national corporations for alleged complicity with oppressive regimes.)

The "color of state law" idea from domestic civil rights law seemed like a tool ready-made to prevent the torturer from escaping the jurisdictional predicate by claiming, in effect, "I was not following orders." The opinion tried not to be creating a private right of action under every provision of the Universal Declaration of Human Rights, and, rhetoric notwithstanding, to decide as little as possible.

The draft passed judicial muster: Judges Feinberg and Kearse sent up their tabs right away.

There's not much more to tell. I later met Peter Weiss (self-described trademark lawyer by day, human rights lawyer by night). I was aware of the explosion of legal scholarship that followed. I was introduced to a prominent NYU professor as the drafter of the famous opinion, but she assumed I had written a student note *about* the opinion and couldn't hear otherwise, so I didn't press the point. Only a few of my friends know of my connection with the case . . . .

II. THE CARTER ADMINISTRATION BRIEF

As Judge Kaufman's clerk recalled, "[t]he Carter Administration's view, which came down firmly on the side of the plaintiffs, . . . was, in the end, given dispositive weight by the [Second Circuit] panel."[24] But how, exactly, did the Carter administration come to support the plaintiffs' position in *Filártiga* in the first place? That story turned on both the

[24] Kraus, *supra* note 23.

administration's human rights policy and the particular personalities involved.

Early in his presidency, Jimmy Carter had decided that "the demonstration of American idealism was a practical and realistic approach to foreign affairs, and [that] moral principles were the best foundation for the exertion of American power and influence."[25] Moreover, Congress had responded to the nation's post-Watergate, post-Vietnam disgust over the perceived amorality of the Nixon-Kissinger foreign policy by enacting an extensive body of legislation conditioning foreign assistance to certain countries on their forbearance from consistent patterns of gross human rights violations.[26] Leading Carter administration officials, including Secretary of State Cyrus Vance and United Nations Ambassador Andrew Young, took prominent public positions advocating for the promotion of human rights.

At the Justice Department, Drew S. Days III, First Assistant Counsel at the NAACP Legal Defense and Educational Fund in New York, had been named Assistant Attorney General for the Civil Rights Division. Although that position had previously been viewed as having an entirely domestic focus, Days had formerly been a Peace Corps volunteer in Honduras and spoke fluent Spanish. Later Solicitor General in the Clinton administration, a professor at Yale Law School, and founding director of that law school's Orville H. Schell, Jr. Center for International Human Rights, Days recalled:

> I went to a reception in Washington and had a casual conversation with someone from the State Department. That person said, "People write us all the time now, and say that President Carter talks about human rights abroad, but what about human rights at home? There are stacks of letters being sent to us that no one is paying attention to, about cases against the United States at the Inter-American Human Rights Commission and other such places. I can understand why the Soviet Union ignores human rights complaints, but why does the United States?"
>
> I thought he had a point, so following that discussion, I made an arrangement with the State Department whereby we had a Memorandum of Understanding under which human

---

[25] JIMMY CARTER, KEEPING FAITH: MEMOIRS OF A PRESIDENT 143 (1982).

[26] That effort was pioneered by Congressman Don Fraser of Minnesota, who in the 1970s held numerous hearings before the House Foreign Affairs Committee's Subcommittee on International Organizations and Movements that led to the enactment of a series of laws designed to elevate the status of human rights in U.S. foreign policy. *See generally* FRANK NEWMAN & DAVID WEISSBRODT, INTERNATIONAL HUMAN RIGHTS 502–44 (1990) (discussing these laws). For examples of such statutes, see Foreign Assistance Act of 1974, Pub. L. No. 93–559, 88 Stat. 1795 (1974) (codified as amended in scattered sections of 22 U.S.C.); Trade Act of 1974, Pub. L. No. 93–618, 88 Stat. 1978 (1975) (codified as amended in scattered sections of 19 U.S.C.); and International Bank for Reconstruction and Development Act of 1977, Pub. L. No. 95–118, 91 Stat. 1067 (1977) (codified as amended in scattered sections of 22 U.S.C.).

> rights complaints brought against the United States would be transferred to the Civil Rights Division at Justice for evaluation and response. We broke with the Soviet practice of declining to address international human rights arguments on the merits. When such complaints would come in, we would review them on the merits and where appropriate, file responses: I remember that we filed one in Geneva about capital punishment in the United States and another about police brutality in Tennessee. I designated my political deputy John Huerta as our point person on cases that intersected civil rights and international human rights. I think the *Filártiga* case came over to us through that interagency channel that we had created between State and Justice.[27]

Accordingly, when the Second Circuit sent in its request for the State Department's views on *Filártiga*, the matter was referred to the State Department Legal Adviser's office. Legal Adviser Roberts Owen (formerly a partner at the Washington firm of Covington & Burling) assigned the matter to Deputy Legal Adviser William Lake (formerly a partner at the Washington firm of Wilmer Cutler & Pickering) and in turn to an international law professor, Stefan Riesenfeld, who was taking a leave from his teaching duties at Berkeley to serve as the Department's Counselor of Public International Law. Born in Breslau, Germany, Riesenfeld had fled Nazi Germany in the 1930s and come to Berkeley, where he began teaching international law and became a U.S. citizen. As civilian legal advisor with the U.S. Office of the High Commissioner in the mid 1940s, Riesenfeld had helped to prepare the West German constitution.[28]

Because the matter called for the filing of a federal appellate brief, the matter was sent over to the Justice Department and routed to the Civil Rights division, where it landed on the desk of Drew Days's political deputy, John E. Huerta.[29] Like Days, Huerta had enjoyed an unusual path to government service. He too had been trained as a civil rights lawyer and had also lived in Latin America for several years working on issues of Latin American law and development. As Huerta later recalled,

---

[27] Telephone Interview with Drew S. Days III, former Assistant Att'y Gen., Civil Rights Div., U.S. Dep't of Justice (May 5, 2007).

[28] Unfortunately, Professor Riesenfeld passed away in 1999 and could not be interviewed for this essay. *See Farewell, Professor Stefan Riesenfeld*, THE BERKELEYAN (Feb. 24, 1999), https://perma.cc/8CUQ-2UUA.

[29] After attending law school at Berkeley, Huerta had studied and taught Latin American law and development at the Catholic University Law School in Lima, Peru. After returning from Peru, he joined California Rural Legal Assistance, then spent four years as a member of the law faculty at the University of California, Davis, and was selected to take a one-year fellowship at the Harvard Law School in 1976 before being appointed Deputy Assistant United States Attorney General for Civil Rights in the Carter administration. Following his Justice Department service, Huerta became, inter alia, executive director of the Southern California office of the Mexican-American Legal Defense and Education Fund, general counsel of a coalition dedicated to the 1981 California reapportionment, and General Counsel of the Smithsonian Institution.

"I testified, for example, about U.S. compliance with the Helsinki Accords. I worked a lot with the State Department on allegations of U.S. violation of international human rights, investigating those allegations. We were bringing prosecutions to show that the United States was following the law."[30]

Huerta later recalled how *Filártiga* came to his attention:

> I joined the Civil Rights Division as a political deputy in September 1978. When the request from the State Department in *Filártiga* came over, I coordinated the Justice Department's response with Brian Landsberg and Irv Gornstein of the Appellate Section of the Civil Rights Division. We had a heads-up from CCR that the request would be coming over, so we had met with them previously to discuss the case.[31] We had developed contingency plans in case we decided to come out pro or con, but we ended up developing a civil rights position supportive of the plaintiffs' position. In developing those positions, I talked to Stefan Reisenfeld, who was working on this at State; I knew him from my law school days at Berkeley, even though I had never had him as a professor for any class. We sat and talked about it, and he gave me the crucial international law background. We also had some discussions with Solicitor General Wade McCree's office and explored the possible ramifications for the U.S. in case we were ourselves ever accused of torture and sued civilly. Barbara Babcock, the head of the civil division [and later a professor at Stanford Law School] was also supportive. Ambassador Robert White, our envoy to Paraguay, also favored the plaintiffs' position. I remember no White House involvement. [Attorney General and former] Judge Griffin Bell had set up a pretty rigorous screening process to prevent the White House from contacting the Justice Department, except through established channels. Our view eventually prevailed in the Solicitor General's office. When we filed our Second Circuit brief, I never expected that the case would have such an impact. Since then, I have been involved in many civil rights and human rights cases, but of all the cases I have ever handled, this case, in which I played a relatively small

---

30 *Oral History Interview with John E. Huerta*, ONLINE ARCHIVE OF CAL. 53 (Mar. 7, 21, Apr. 9, and May 11, 1990), https://perma.cc/5ZED-BLLZ.

31 *See* ACEVES, *supra* note 6, at 47 ("Throughout the drafting process, the Center for Constitutional Rights was in regular contact with the State Department and Justice Department. As early as July 1979, the Center had contacted the Office of the Legal Adviser in the State Department to seek its intervention in the case. Subsequent communications also occurred with the Civil Rights Division of the Justice Department. On several occasions, lawyers at the Center even reviewed drafts of the U.S. amicus brief and offered comments on its development and argumentation. They also emphasized to U.S. government lawyers the benefits that a U.S. submission would provide their case.").

role, has probably gotten more subsequent publicity than any other matter in which I have ever been involved.[32]

The Justice Department therefore recommended that the United States seek leave to file an amicus brief with the Second Circuit.[33] In a letter from then-Deputy Legal Adviser of the State Department (later U.S. Judge on the International Court of Justice) Stephen Schwebel, the State Department concurred and elaborated upon the legal arguments that should be made in such an amicus brief.[34] Incorporating those arguments, the Government's amicus curiae brief asked two questions, both of which it then answered in the affirmative:

> 1. Whether the torture of a foreign citizen by an official of the same country is a violation of the law of nations within the meaning of 28 U.S.C. 1350?
>
> 2. If so, whether such a violation gives rise to a judicially enforceable remedy and is therefore a tort within the meaning of that provision?

With respect to the first issue, the administration argued that "Section 1350 encompasses the law of nations as that body of law may evolve," not as the law of nations may have existed in 1789, when the statute was first enacted. International law, the administration recognized, "now embraces the obligation of a state to respect the fundamental human rights of its citizens . . . . [T]his does not mean that all such rights may be judicially enforced. Indeed, it is likely that only a few rights have the degree of specificity and universality to permit private enforcement and that the protection of other asserted rights must be left to the political branches of government." Freedom from torture, the administration recognized, now ranks among the fundamental human rights protected by international law and is therefore cognizable as a tort "in violation of the law of nations" for the purposes of conferring subject matter jurisdiction under the ATCA. The Government stated the core of its position this way:

> This does not mean that Section 1350 appoints the United States courts as Commissions to evaluate the human rights performance of foreign nations. . . . The courts are properly confined to determining whether an individual has suffered a denial of rights guaranteed him as an individual by customary international law. Accordingly, before entertaining a suit

[32] Telephone Interview with John E. Huerta, former Deputy Assistant Att'y Gen., Civil Rights Div., U.S. Dep't of Justice (May 5, 2007).

[33] Memorandum from Drew S. Days, III, Assistant Att'y Gen., Civil Rights Div., Justice Dep't, to the Solicitor Gen. 1–2 (Aug. 29, 1979), *reprinted in* ACEVES, *supra* note 6, at 485.

[34] Letter from Stephen Schwebel, Deputy Legal Adviser, U.S. Dep't of State, to Richard Allen, Office of the Solicitor Gen., Dep't of Justice (Sept. 14, 1979), *reprinted in* ACEVES, *supra* note 6, at 511. The back and forth between the Justice and State Departments regarding the arguments in the amicus brief is recounted in ACEVES, *supra* note 6, at 41–47.

> alleging a violation of human rights, a court must first conclude that there is a consensus in the international community, that the right is protected and that there is a widely shared understanding of the scope of this protection. . . . When these conditions have been satisfied, there is little danger that judicial enforcement will impair our foreign policy efforts. To the contrary, a refusal to recognize a private cause of action in these circumstances might seriously damage the credibility of our nation's commitment to the protection of human rights. As we have shown . . ., official torture is both clearly defined and universally condemned. Therefore, private enforcement is entirely appropriate.[35]

Significantly, in a footnote, the U.S. government raised and rejected the possibility that "Section 1350 is unconstitutional in conferring jurisdiction on federal courts to entertain tort actions under the law of nations." Citing the Supreme Court's decisions in *Banco Nacional de Cuba v. Sabbatino*[36] and *The Paquete Habana*,[37] the administration argued instead that "[c]*ustomary international law is federal law,* to be enunciated authoritatively by the federal courts. An action for tort under international law is therefore a case 'arising under . . . the laws of the United States' within Article III of the Constitution."[38]

III. THE SECOND CIRCUIT'S OPINION IN *FILÁRTIGA*

Chief Judge Kaufman's opinion for the Second Circuit, issued on June 30, 1980, held that torture constitutes an actionable violation of the law of nations, sufficient to confer subject matter jurisdiction on the federal court under the ATCA.[39] The opinion relied on an array of international agreements, declarations, and state policy and practice as evidence that the law of nations prohibits torture.[40] The court further held that federal jurisdiction over such offenses is consistent with Article III of the Constitution because international law has long been recognized as "part of our law."[41] Accordingly, the court deemed it unnecessary to determine whether the ATCA itself provided the cause of action for the Filártigas' claims and whether the ATCA should be treated as an exercise of Congress's power to define and punish offenses against the law of nations.[42] The ATCA, the court explained, should be understood not to

[35] Brief for the United States as Amicus Curiae Supporting Appellants at 1, Filártiga v. Peña-Irala, 630 F.2d 876 (2d Cir. 1980) (No. 79–6090) (emphasis added), *reprinted in* 19 I.L.M. 585, 606 n.49 (1980) [hereinafter U.S. *Filártiga* Brief].

[36] 376 U.S. 398 (1964).

[37] 175 U.S. 677 (1900).

[38] U.S. *Filártiga* Brief, *supra* note 35, at n.49 (emphasis added).

[39] Filártiga v. Peña-Irala, 630 F.2d 876 (2d Cir. 1980).

[40] *Id.* at 880–85.

[41] *Id.* at 887 (quoting The Paquete Habana, 175 U.S. 677, 700 (1900)).

[42] U.S. CONST. art. I, § 8, cl. 10.

grant new rights to aliens, but to allow individuals to come to federal court to enforce "the rights already recognized by international law."[43] "[F]or purposes of civil liability," Chief Judge Kaufman declared, "the torturer has become—like the pirate and slave trader before him—*hostis humani generis,* an enemy of all mankind."[44] Recognizing civil liability for acts of torture "is a small but important step in the fulfillment of the ageless dream to free all people from brutal violence."[45]

By so saying, the Second Circuit reaffirmed the Nuremberg ideal: that like genocide, torture can never serve as a legitimate instrument of state power. Under the court's reasoning, official torturers may neither invoke comity nor cloak themselves in state sovereignty to avoid individual responsibility to their victims before a court of law. Nor, the *Filártiga* court held, must such cases invariably be dismissed under the doctrine of separation of powers. Even if the executive branch had not supported adjudication, the court found, the core issue in the case was quintessentially legal: whether the victims had a right to be free from torture that was actionable in federal court. Resolution of that question required only standard judicial interpretation of a statute (the ATCA) and human rights treaties. The court concluded that because the customary international law norm against torture was definable, obligatory, and universal, it constituted an actionable "tort in violation of the law of nations" for purposes of the statute.

On remand, U.S. District Judge Eugene Nickerson awarded the Filártigas a judgment of nearly $10.4 million, comprising compensatory damages based on Paraguayan law and punitive damages based on U.S. cases and international law.[46] By so holding, *Filártiga*'s ruling on remand created a federal common law remedy against torture, which fell squarely within the Supreme Court's prior recognition that issues "in ordering our relationships with other members of the international community must be treated exclusively as an aspect of federal law," made by the federal courts, binding on the states, but subject to legislative revision.[47] By the time that ruling issued, however, Peña-Irala had already been deported, and to this day, the Filártigas have yet to recover any part of their judgment.[48]

---

43 *Filártiga*, 630 F.2d at 887.

44 *Id.* at 890.

45 *Id.*

46 Filártiga v. Peña-Irala, 577 F. Supp. 860, 864–67 (E.D.N.Y. 1984).

47 Banco Nacional de Cuba v. Sabbatino, 376 U.S. 398, 425 (1964). For elaboration, see Harold Hongju Koh, *Is International Law Really State Law?*, 111 HARV. L. REV. 1824 (1998).

48 Even while deciding the civil liability of Peña-Irala, the Second Circuit declined to extend the stay of his deportation order, and the Supreme Court denied certiorari on that ruling, leading to Peña-Irala's eventual deportation back to Paraguay. Filártiga v. Peña-Irala, 442 U.S. 901 (1979). Apparently, the default judgment has never been collected. *See* R.H. Hodges, *Letter to the Editor*, N.Y. TIMES, Mar. 26, 1986, at A34.

IV. *FILÁRTIGA*'S LEGACY

In *Filártiga*, human rights litigants and scholars finally found their *Brown v. Board of Education*.[49] The *Filártiga* decision triggered a tidal wave of academic scholarship and more than a quarter-century of human rights litigation in U.S. courts.[50] In subsequent cases, the lower federal courts elaborated on *Filártiga*'s holding that when an act represents a violation of a definable, specific, universal, and obligatory norm of international law, an alien can sue under the ATCA and be awarded civil damages for the tort. *Filártiga* came to provide the governing framework for ATCA litigation not only in the Second Circuit, but also in the First,[51] Fifth,[52] Ninth,[53] and Eleventh[54] Circuits. These lower federal decisions held that not only torture, but also extrajudicial killing,[55] disappearance,[56] arbitrary detention,[57] genocide,[58] and cruel, inhuman, or degrading treatment and other kinds of gross violations[59] also fit within the category of offenses against specific, definable, universal, and obligatory norms.

Sosa v. Alvarez-Machain. These cases culminated on the last day of the U.S. Supreme Court's 2003 Term in the decision in *Sosa v. Alvarez-Machain*.[60] While the Supreme Court's decision did not embrace *Filártiga* unquestioningly, six Justices—Justices Souter, Stevens, O'Connor, Kennedy, Ginsburg, and Breyer—did reaffirm *Filártiga*'s core insight: that when there is a norm of international character accepted by the civilized world and defined with a specificity comparable to recognized paradigms, an alien can sue for violations of that norm in a federal court under the ATCA.[61]

---

[49] 347 U.S. 483 (1954).

[50] A computer-assisted search indicates that as of January 5, 2025, *Filártiga* had been cited in 2436 law review articles and 252 published decisions in the United States.

[51] *See, e.g.*, Xuncax v. Gramajo, 886 F. Supp. 162 (D. Mass. 1995).

[52] Beanal v. Freeport-McMoRan, Inc., 969 F. Supp. 362 (E.D. La. 1997), *aff'd*, 197 F.3d 161 (5th Cir. 1999).

[53] *See In re* Estate of Marcos Human Rights Litig., 25 F.3d 1467, 1475 (9th Cir. 1994) ("We thus join the Second Circuit in concluding that the Alien Tort Act, 28 U.S.C. § 1350, creates a cause of action for violations of specific, universal and obligatory international human rights standards which confer fundamental rights upon all people vis-a-vis their own governments.") (internal quotation marks omitted).

[54] *See, e.g.*, Abebe-Jira v. Negewo, 72 F.3d 844 (11th Cir. 1996) (adopting *Filártiga* approach to claims of torture and cruel, inhuman, or degrading treatment).

[55] *See, e.g.*, *Xuncax*, 886 F. Supp. at 184–85.

[56] *See, e.g.*, Forti v. Suarez-Mason, 694 F. Supp. 707, 711 (N.D. Cal. 1988).

[57] *Xuncax*, 886 F. Supp. at 184.

[58] *See, e.g.*, Kadic v. Karadžić, 70 F.3d 232, 241–42 (2d Cir. 1995).

[59] For a partial list of unsuccessful claims, see Derek P. Jinks, *The Federal Common Law of Universal, Obligatory, and Definable Human Rights Norms*, 4 ILSA J. INT'L & COMP. L. 465, 471–72 (1998) (collecting cases in text and footnotes).

[60] 542 U.S. 692 (2004).

[61] *Id.* at 728–31.

Justice Souter, writing for the Court, adopted a "modified-*Filártiga*" approach to the ATCA. He explained that although the ATCA was a jurisdictional statute, and not an invitation "to mold substantive law,"[62] neither does it require an explicit statutory or treaty-based cause of action. Rather, the history and intent behind the ATCA indicated that the First Congress expected the statute to have practical effect the moment it was enacted, and to enable actions arising directly from customary international law.[63] *Sosa* thus held that courts could infer a private cause of action for certain torts in violation of the laws of nations "as an element of common law,"[64] consistent with its reading of the history and intent behind the ATCA.

Sosa directed courts considering claims under the ATCA to ask three questions. First, a court must assess whether the asserted claim constitutes a violation of the "present-day law of nations," not the law of nations as it existed in 1789. To do so, the Court affirmed the approach laid out by Chief Justice Marshall over a century ago:

> [W]here there is no treaty, and no controlling executive or legislative act or judicial decision, resort must be had to the customs and usages of civilized nations; and, as evidence of these, to the works of jurists and commentators, who by years of labor, research and experience, have made themselves peculiarly well acquainted with the subjects of which they treat.[65]

Second, a court must determine whether the asserted violation of the law of nations is "accepted by the civilized world and defined with specificity comparable to the features of the eighteenth-century paradigms we have recognized" as existing at the time of enactment of the ATCA.[66] Those historical paradigms were the three offenses identified by Blackstone: piracy, violations of safe conduct, and offenses against ambassadors.[67] More generally, these offenses fell within the category of "rules binding individuals for the benefit of other individuals [that] overlapped with the norms of state relationships."[68] When enacting the ATCA, the Founders were thinking of these violations of the law of nations, "admitting of a judicial remedy and at the same time threatening serious consequences in international affairs."[69]

---

62 *Id.* at 713.

63 *Id.* at 719.

64 *Id.* at 725.

65 *Id.* at 734 (quoting The Paquete Habana, 175 U.S. 677, 700 (1900)).

66 *Id.* at 725; *see also id.* at 732 ("Whatever the ultimate criteria for accepting a cause of action subject to jurisdiction under § 1350, we are persuaded that federal courts should not recognize private claims under federal common law for violations of any international law norm with less definite content and acceptance among civilized nations than the historical paradigms familiar when § 1350 was enacted.").

67 *Id.* at 715.

68 *Id.*

69 *Id.*

Third and finally, *Sosa* warned that any inquiry into whether an ATCA claim is judicially enforceable must account for the "collateral consequences" of recognizing such an action,[70] particularly the foreign policy implications of permitting a judicial remedy for such a claim.[71] Applying this test to the facts before it, the *Sosa* Court rejected Alvarez-Machain's claim that the law of nations prevented his arbitrary arrest and detention, "defined as officially sanctioned action exceeding positive authorization to detain" under any domestic law.[72] The Court noted that although a survey of national constitutions revealed that many countries prohibit arbitrary detention, the consensus about this prohibition was "at a high level of generality."[73] In effect, the Court concluded that Alvarez-Machain's claim of temporary arbitrary arrest did not rise to the well-settled violation of prolonged arbitrary detention—and thus lacked the required level of specificity or acceptance of the human rights prohibition under the Court's test.

Sosa thus affirmed *Filártiga*'s core insight. A clear Court majority finally held that U.S. courts could recognize actionable "torts in violation of the law of nations" under the ATCA. Such actionable torts included gross violations of such core norms of modern international human rights law—such as the norm against torture—that were as widely accepted and specifically defined as the three traditional violations of the law of nations that Congress recognized in 1789. Significantly, in so holding, the *Sosa* Court effectively rejected three narrower theories of the ATCA that had been asserted throughout the post-*Filártiga* ATCA litigation in the lower courts. The first such theory posited that courts should not hear these cases because, by their nature, they raise nonjusticiable political questions, a theory first offered by Judge Roger Robb of the D.C. Circuit in 1984.[74] But if courts are simply construing an enacted statute, the Alien Tort Claims Act, and the words being interpreted are the words "torts in violation of law of nations," it is hard to see why construing those words should not be a quintessentially judicial task.

The *Sosa* Court also rejected a second, originalist position, first taken by Judge Bork in his concurring opinion in the *Tel-Oren* case in

---

70 *Id.* at 727. Specifically, the Court identified five reasons that counsel "caution" in recognizing a private right of action to adjudicate new violations of the law of nations: They included: (1) that the prevailing conception of the common law has changed since 1789; (2) post-*Erie* reluctance to involve courts in generating federal common law rules of decision; (3) the general preference for leaving the creation of a private right of action to the legislature; (4) potential disruption of U.S. foreign policy; and (5) the lack of legislative encouragement of "judicial creativity" in this field. *Id.* at 725–29.

71 *Id.* at 727–28 ("[M]any attempts by federal courts to craft remedies for the violation of new norms of international law would raise risks of adverse foreign policy consequences . . . .").

72 *Id.* at 736.

73 *Id.* at 736 n.27.

74 Tel-Oren v. Libyan Arab Republic, 726 F.2d 774, 823 (D.C. Cir. 1984) (Robb, J., concurring).

1984.[75] Judge Bork asserted that courts were wrong to infer a private cause of action for violations of the law of nations directly from the ATCA, federal common law, or international law itself.[76] He acknowledged that certain kinds of claims could be heard in these ATCA cases, but argued that this could only happen if the claims had actually existed in the eighteenth century, when the statute was first enacted. Contrary to modern views of dynamic statutory interpretation,[77] Judge Bork essentially asserted that the list of "law of nations" claims cognizable in ATCA cases should be frozen in time and limited to piracy, attacks on diplomats, and violations of safe conduct. Thus, under Judge Bork's originalist view, a traveler denied safe conduct could recover under the ATCA, but a victim of modern genocide could not, even though customary international law had long since evolved to recognize both an individual human right to be free from genocide and the universal jurisdiction and obligation of all nations to punish it.[78]

Third and finally, *Sosa* refused to adopt a view of the ATCA urged by two law professors, Curtis Bradley and Jack Goldsmith, and also pressed by some of the briefs in the *Sosa* case: namely, that the courts should recognize no cause of action unless the political branches had expressly consented to it by enacting such claims into positive law.[79] Under this theory, if the national political branches have not internalized an international law rule into U.S. law, that international law rule either has no status in U.S. law, or must be construed as some species of state law.

As I have argued elsewhere, it makes no sense to argue that customary international law is really state law.[80] Professors Bradley and Goldsmith asserted that the canonical case of *Erie R.R. Co. v. Tompkins*[81] supported their conclusion, but as every first-year law student knows, the Supreme Court's landmark decision in *Erie* rested on the constitutional argument that in exercising general federal common lawmaking power, the federal courts had "invaded rights which are reserved by the Constitution to the several States."[82] But no such constitutional problem arises when federal courts determine rules of customary international law, because "[f]ederal judicial determination of most questions of

75 *Id.* at 798 (Bork, J., concurring). For a discussion of the relationship between the ATCA and the common law, see William S. Dodge, *The Historical Origins of the Alien Tort Statute: A Response to the "Originalists,"* 19 HASTINGS INT'L & COMP. L. REV. 221, 231–37 (1996).

76 *See Tel-Oren*, 726 F.2d at 798–823 (Bork, J., concurring).

77 *See generally* WILLIAM N. ESKRIDGE, JR., DYNAMIC STATUTORY INTERPRETATION (1994).

78 *See* RESTATEMENT (THIRD) OF FOREIGN RELATIONS LAW OF THE UNITED STATES § 702 cmt. d & reporters' note 3, § 404 cmt. D, and § 907 cmt. a (1986).

79 Curtis A. Bradley & Jack L. Goldsmith, *Customary International Law as Federal Common Law: A Critique of the Modern Position*, 110 HARV. L. REV. 815 (1997).

80 Koh, *supra* note 47.

81 304 U.S. 64, 79 (1938).

82 *Id.* at 90.

customary international law transpires not in a zone of core state concerns, such as state tort law, but in a foreign affairs area in which the Tenth Amendment has reserved little or no power to the states."[83]

Significantly, only three members of the *Sosa* Court would have held—as the revisionists urged—that the *Erie* doctrine somehow precluded the federal courts from making federal common law to enforce international human rights law.[84] Justice Souter's majority opinion rejected that claim, declaring: "*Erie* did not in terms bar any judicial recognition of new substantive rules, no matter what the circumstances, and post-*Erie* understanding has identified limited enclaves in which federal courts may derive some substantive law in a common law way," including foreign relations law.[85] The *Sosa* majority further noted that " 'international disputes implicating . . . our relations with foreign nations' are one of the 'narrow areas' *in which 'federal common law' continues to exist*."[86] And, Justice Souter added, "it would be unreasonable to assume that the First Congress would have expected federal courts to lose all capacity to recognize enforceable international norms simply because the common law might lose some metaphysical cachet on the road to modern realism" in *Erie*.[87] Accordingly, the Court found "consistent with the division of responsibilities between federal and state courts after *Erie*" its recognition that the ATCA "was enacted on the congressional understanding that courts would exercise jurisdiction by entertaining some common law claims derived from the law of nations."[88]

Writing soon after *Sosa*, one distinguished federal courts expert, Judge William Fletcher of the Ninth Circuit, concluded:

> [From] *Sosa*, [w]e now know two things that perhaps we did not know before.
>
> First, we know—because the Supreme Court has told us—that there is a federal common law of international human rights based on customary international law.
>
> Second, we also know—though *not* because the Court has told us—that the federal common law of customary international law is federal law in both the jurisdiction-conferring and the supremacy-clause senses. . . . [T]he Court's decision necessarily implies that the federal common law of customary international law is jurisdiction-conferring. [T]he only basis for the federal court to hear an alien versus alien suit

83 Koh, *supra* note 47, at 1831–32.

84 Sosa v. Alvarez-Machain, 542 U.S. 692, 739–50 (Scalia, J., concurring in part and concurring in the judgment, joined by Rehnquist, C.J., and Thomas, J.).

85 *Id.* at 729–30.

86 *Id.* at 730 (quoting Texas Industries, Inc. v. Radcliff Materials, Inc., 451 U.S. 630, 641 (1981) (alteration in original) (emphasis added)).

87 *Id.* at 730.

88 *Id.* at 731 n.19.

under the [Alien Tort Claims Act] is the federal nature of the substantive claim.[89]

Despite *Sosa*'s clear rejection of the claim that customary international law lacks status as federal common law in U.S. law, academic critics of *Filártiga* sought to reassert that claim, but were again soon rebuffed.[90] Subsequent Court decisions confirmed that, despite changes in the Court's membership, claims under customary international law arise under federal law for purposes of Article III. In *Jesner v. Arab Bank*, only two concurring Justices, Gorsuch and Thomas, argued that customary international law claims do not arise under federal law for purposes of Article III.[91] As a circuit judge, Justice Kavanaugh also adopted some of the revisionists' critiques.[92] Nevertheless, in both *Jesner* and *Kiobel v. Royal Dutch Shell Petroleum Corp.*,[93] the Supreme Court decided ATCA suits between aliens *on the merits*, which it could not have done had federal courts genuinely lacked Article III federal question jurisdiction over the international law question at issue.[94]

Perhaps as significant, as I learned during four stints in the U.S. government spanning five decades, executive branch and congressional lawyers have never seriously questioned the status of international law as federal law. This is an issue they consider long-settled. Particularly when matters such as official immunities arise, the executive branch has expressly stated that it looks to customary international law to articulate federal principles of foreign official immunity.[95] The U.S. government has

---

[89] William A. Fletcher, Essay, *International Human Rights in American Courts*, 93 VA. L. REV. IN BRIEF 1, 7–8 (2007).

[90] *Compare* Curtis A. Bradley, Jack L. Goldsmith & David H. Moore, Sosa, *Customary International Law, and the Continuing Relevance of* Erie, 120 HARV. L. REV. 869 (2007) (reasserting Bradley and Goldsmith position after *Sosa*), *with* William S. Dodge, *Customary International Law and the Question of Legitimacy,* 120 HARV. L. REV. F. 19 (2007) (rebutting that position).

[91] 584 U.S. 241, 274 (2018) (Thomas, J., concurring); *id.* at 287–88 (Gorsuch, J., concurring in part and concurring in the judgment).

[92] *See* Al-Bihani v. Obama, 619 F.3d 1, 17–36 (D.C. Cir. 2010) (Kavanaugh, J., concurring).

[93] 569 U.S. 108 (2013).

[94] In a footnote, *Sosa* denied that Section 1331's *statutory* grant of federal question jurisdiction invariably applies to claims under customary international law recognized under the ATCA, but conspicuously did not address the *constitutional* question of whether issues of customary international law fall within the broader scope of the federal judicial power created by Article III. *See* 542 U.S. at 731 n.19.

[95] *See, e.g.*, Suggestion of Immunity by the United States at 2, Cengiz v. Salman, No. 1:20-cv-3009-JDB (D.D.C. Nov. 17, 2022) (recognizing head-of-state immunity "[u]nder common law principles of immunity articulated by the Executive Branch in the exercise of its Constitutional authority over foreign affairs and informed by customary international law"); Suggestion of Immunity by the United States at 7, Dogan v. Barak, No. 2:15-CV-08130-ODW (C.D. Cal. June 10, 2016) (similar). *See generally* JENS DAVID OHLIN, THE ASSAULT ON INTERNATIONAL LAW 15–48 (2015); William S. Dodge, *Revisiting Bradley and Goldsmith's "Critique of the Modern Position,"* TRANSNAT'L LITIG. BLOG (Mar. 31, 2022), https://perma.cc/KT4M-MMRG; William S. Dodge & Chimène I. Keitner, *A Roadmap for Foreign Official Immunity Cases in U.S. Courts*, 90 FORDHAM L. REV. 677, 693 n.106 (2021)

so argued following the Supreme Court's ruling in *Samantar v. Yousuf* that the executive branch must determine official immunities.[96] *After Sosa*, lower federal courts have largely continued their tradition of following the executive's lead and incorporating customary international law into federal common law binding on the states, whether or not any particular statute or treaty authorizes them to do so.[97] Thus, contrary to the revisionists' claims, human rights plaintiffs may still invoke federal common law causes of action to enforce certain claims under the customary international law of human rights.[98] So *Filártiga*'s core insight still stands: under certain conditions, the ATCA provides today's federal judges with the power to fashion "a cause of action" for a "modest number" of claims based on the present-day law of nations."[99]

Filártiga *and Transnational Public Law Litigation.* Nor has there been any indication that *Sosa*'s adoption of the modified *Filártiga* test has opened the floodgates of ATCA litigation. To be sure, the *Sosa* majority articulated reasons for "judicial caution" in recognizing such implied causes of action. As described further below, the Court has subsequently imposed territorial limits on the places and the kinds of defendants against whom an ATCA case may be brought. Nevertheless, *Filártiga* has remained seminal, not just for what it held, but also for what it triggered.

Filártiga sparked what I have elsewhere called an era of "transnational public law litigation," a novel and expanding effort by state and individual plaintiffs to fuse international legal rights with domestic judicial remedies.[100] As I have argued elsewhere,

> [t]ransnational public law litigation is characterized by: (1) a *transnational party structure*, in which states and nonstate entities equally participate; (2) a *transnational claim structure*, in which violations of domestic and international, private and public law are all alleged in a single action; (3) a *prospective focus*, directed as much upon obtaining judicial declaration of transnational norms as upon resolving past disputes; (4) the litigants' strategic awareness of the *transportability of those norms* to other domestic and international fora for use in judicial interpretation or political bargaining; and (5) a

("[L]ower courts have considered the common law of foreign official immunity to be 'federal common law.' ").

[96] 560 U.S. 305 (2010).

[97] *See* MICHAEL J. GLENNON & ROBERT D. SLOANE, FOREIGN AFFAIRS FEDERALISM: THE MYTH OF NATIONAL EXCLUSIVITY ch. 7 (2016) (reviewing cases that demonstrate the survival of customary international law as part of federal common law); Bart M.J. Szewczyk, *Customary International Law and Statutory Interpretation: An Empirical Analysis of Federal Court Decisions*, 82 GEO. WASH. L. REV. 1118, 1134–46 (2014).

[98] *See generally* Gary Born, *Customary International Law in United States Courts*, 92 WASH. L. REV. 1641, 1642 (2017).

[99] *Sosa*, 542 U.S. at 724–25.

[100] *See* Harold Hongju Koh, *Transnational Public Law Litigation*, 100 YALE L. J. 2347, 2347 (1991).

> subsequent process of *institutional dialogue* among various domestic and international, judicial and political fora to achieve ultimate settlement.[101]

The paradigm of transnational public law litigation couples a substantive notion—individual and state responsibility—with the process of adjudication in pursuit of a normative goal—promotion of universal norms of international conduct.

In bringing their human rights cases in domestic courts, transnational public law litigants such as the Filártigas pursue several goals: not only norm-enunciation of clearly established international human rights norms, but also compensation, deterrence, and denial of safe haven to the human rights violator defendant. In *Filártiga*, the Second Circuit acknowledged that the phenomenon of "transnational litigation"—which had originated in the context of private commercial suits in U.S. courts against foreign governments—had properly migrated into the realm of public human rights suits against the United States and foreign governments and officials of the kind discussed in the Supreme Court's 2004 ruling in *Sosa*.

Filártiga created a judicial channel for human rights activism in U.S. courts during an era in which other avenues of human rights change often appeared blocked. In the same way that *Brown v. Board of Education*[102] enabled a generation of public interest lawyers to devote themselves to the judicial pursuit of civil rights, *Filártiga* empowered U.S. human rights activists and legal scholars of the late twentieth century to employ domestic litigation to promote normative commitments to uphold human rights.[103] *Filártiga* opened the door not just for expanded scholarly work in international human rights and transnational law, but also for the activist work of human rights clinics and law professors engaged in transnational public law litigation.[104]

---

101 *Id.* at 2371 (emphasis in original).

102 347 U.S. 483 (1954).

103 For discussions of judicial internalization of human rights in other domestic legal systems, see, *e.g.*, Eyal Benvenisti, *The Influence of International Human Rights Law on the Israeli Legal System: Present and Future*, 28 ISR. L. REV. 136 (1994); Eyal Benvenisti, *Judges and Foreign Affairs: A Comment on the Institut de Droit International's Resolution on "The Activities of National Courts and the International Relations of their State,"* 5 EUR. J. INT'L L. 423 (1994); Gennady M. Danilenko, *The New Russian Constitution and International Law*, 88 AM. J. INT'L L. 451 (1994); Henry G. Schermers, *The Role of Domestic Courts in Effectuating International Law*, 3 LEIDEN J. INT'L L. 77 (1990); and Eric Stein, *International Law in Internal Law: Toward Internationalization of Central-Eastern European Constitutions?*, 88 AM. J. INT'L L. 427 (1994).

104 *See, e.g.*, Neal Kumar Katyal, Hamdan v. Rumsfeld*: The Legal Academy Goes to Practice*, 120 HARV. L. REV. 65 (2006). *Filártiga* helped spawn clinical impact litigation in human rights and trained numerous human rights clinicians and public interest lawyers, many of whom have become actively involved in litigation surrounding civil liberties after September 11. *See generally* BRANDT GOLDSTEIN, STORMING THE COURT: HOW A BAND OF YALE LAW STUDENTS SUED THE PRESIDENT—AND WON (2005); Deena R. Hurwitz, *Lawyering for Justice and the Inevitability of International Human Rights Clinics*, 28 YALE J. INT'L L. 505 (2003).

Filártiga *and Transnational Legal Process.* Upon examination, the transnational public law litigation pioneered by *Filártiga* represents only the judicial face of a broader procedural phenomenon that I have called "Transnational Legal Process": the transubstantive process whereby states and other transnational private actors use the blend of domestic and international legal process to internalize international legal norms into domestic law.[105] As I have argued, key agents in promoting this process of internalization include transnational norm entrepreneurs, governmental norm sponsors, transnational issue networks, and interpretive communities.[106] In this story, one of these agents triggers an interaction at the international level, works together with other agents of internalization to force an interpretation of the international legal norm in an interpretive forum, and then continues to work with those agents to persuade a resisting nation-state to internalize that interpretation into domestic law. Through repeated cycles of "interaction-interpretation-internalization," interpretations of applicable global norms are eventually internalized into states' domestic legal systems.

A transnational legal process approach helps to explain how transnational law functions in a *dynamic* way to constrain state behavior. In a second, *normative* sense, it illustrates how law and legal process help to create norms and construct interests. Transnational Legal Process scholars see international norms as filtering through legal process mechanisms to play a critical role in reformulating national interests and reconstituting national identities. Third, as one scholar put it, the goal of transnational legal process is *constitutive*: "not simply to change behavior, but to change minds."[107]

These ideas connect the Transnational Legal Process school to the "constructivist" school of international relations. Unlike interest theorists, who tend to treat state interests as given, "constructivists" have long argued that states and their interests are socially constructed by "commonly held philosophic principles, identities, norms of behavior, or

---

[105] *See generally* Harold Hongju Koh, *The 1994 Roscoe Pound Lecture: Transnational Legal Process*, 75 NEB. L. REV. 181 (1996); Harold Hongju Koh, *Why Do Nations Obey International Law?*, 106 YALE L.J. 2599 (1997); OONA HATHAWAY & HAROLD HONGJU KOH, FOUNDATIONS OF INTERNATIONAL LAW AND POLITICS 173–204 (2006). Those legal scholars who apply a transnational legal process approach have been called the Yale School of International Law. *See generally* Harold Hongju Koh, *The Yale School of International Law*, YALE J. INT'L L. ONLINE (Sept. 22, 2024), https://yjil.yale.edu/posts/2024-09-22-the-yale-school-of-international-law. *See infra* text accompanying note 174.

[106] Transnational legal process highlights the interactions among both private citizens, whom I call "transnational norm entrepreneurs," and governmental officials, whom I call "governmental norm sponsors." The interaction among transnational norm entrepreneurs and governmental norm sponsors creates transnational networks and law-declaring fora, which create new rules of international law that are construed by interpretive communities. Through the work of these "agents of internalization," these international law rules trickle down from the international level and become domesticated into national law. *See generally* Harold Hongju Koh, *The 1998 Frankel Lecture: Bringing International Law Home*, 35 HOUS. L. REV. 623, 646–48 (1998).

[107] Melissa A. Waters, *Normativity in the "New" Schools: Assessing the Legitimacy of International Legal Norms Created by Domestic Courts*, 32 YALE J. INT'L L. 455, 463 (2007).

shared terms of discourse."[108] Rather than arguing that state actors and interests create rules and norms, constructivists argue that "rules and norms constitute the international game by determining who the actors are, [and] what rules they must follow if they wish to ensure that particular consequences follow from specific acts."[109]

Filártiga and its progeny illustrate the "vertical" dimension of transnational legal process, by which international norms infiltrate domestic law through "trickle-down lawmaking."[110] But the doctrine's evolution also reveals two other facets of transnational legal process: the "horizontal" and "bottom-up" channels whereby such norms are transplanted horizontally from one country to another or "uploaded" from national into international legal institutions.[111] Through these channels, domestic courts interpreting international law help to shape the development of international legal norms and the ability of transnational actors to invoke those norms in other national and international fora.[112]

In submissions to the United Nations, the U.S. executive branch called *Filártiga* a "pivotal decision" demonstrating the nation's commitment to protecting human rights and cited the line of ATCA cases as a model for redressing human rights violations.[113] In turn, an array of

---

[108] MARTHA FINNEMORE, NATIONAL INTERESTS IN INTERNATIONAL SOCIETY 15 (1996). *See also* HATHAWAY & KOH, *supra* note 105, at 112–32 (describing constructivist school). Leading constructivists have included Friedrich Kratochwil, John Ruggie, Nicholas Onuf, Hayward Alker, Richard Ashley, Ernst B. Haas, and Alexander Wendt. For samples of this work, see, for example, ALEXANDER WENDT, SOCIAL THEORY OF INTERNATIONAL POLITICS (1999); Alexander Wendt, *Collective Identity Formation and the International State*, 88 AM. POL. SCI. REV. 384 (1994); and Alexander Wendt, *Constructing International Politics*, 20 INT'L SECURITY 71 (1995). For a systematic treatment of norms from a constructivist perspective, *see* THE CULTURE OF NATIONAL SECURITY: NORMS AND IDENTITY IN WORLD POLITICS (Peter J. Katzenstein ed., 1996).

[109] Ngaire Woods, *The Uses of Theory in the Study of International Relations*, *in* EXPLAINING INTERNATIONAL RELATIONS SINCE 1945, at 9, 26 (Ngaire Woods ed., 1996).

[110] *See, e.g.*, Sarah H. Cleveland, *Norm Internalization and U.S. Economic Sanctions*, 26 YALE J. INT'L L. (2001); Koh, *Bringing International Law Home*, *supra* note 106, at 627.

[111] Janet Koven Levit, *A Bottom-Up Approach to International Lawmaking: The Tale of Three Trade Finance Instruments*, 30 YALE J. INT'L L. 125 (2005); Janet Koven Levit, *Bottom-Up International Lawmaking: Reflections on the New Haven School of International Law*, 32 YALE J. INT'L L. 393 (2007).

[112] The discussion that follows in the text derives from the Brief of International Jurists as Amici Curiae Supporting Respondent, Sosa v. Alvarez-Machain, 542 U.S. 692 (2004) (No. 03-339), for which the author served as counsel of record.

[113] In 1995, the United States government reported to the U.N. Commission on Human Rights that the ATCA "represents an early effort by the United States Government to provide a remedy to individuals whose rights have been violated under international law." *See* U.N. Secretary-General, Addendum, *Question of the Human Rights of All Persons Subjected to Any Form of Detention or Imprisonment*, ¶¶ 13, 15, U.N. Doc. E/CN.4/1996/29/Add.2 (Jan. 18, 1996); *see also* Comm. Against Torture, *Consideration of Reports Submitted by States Parties Under Article 19 of the Convention: Initial Report of the United States of America*, ¶¶ 4–8, U.N. Doc. CAT/C/SR.424 (Feb. 9, 2001). Several years later, in a report to the U.N. Committee Against Torture, the U.S. government again emphasized the importance of the ATCA, repeating key language from its 1996 report:

> U.S. law provides statutory rights of action for civil damages for acts of torture occurring outside the United States. One statutory basis for such suits, the Alien Tort Claims Act of 1789, codified at 28 U.S.C. § 1350, represents an early effort

United Nations bodies—including the U.N. Secretariat,[114] the U.N. Commission and Sub-Commission on Human Rights,[115] and various human rights Special Rapporteurs[116]—have all incorporated the principles expressed in *Filártiga* into different areas of human rights law. Regional[117] and treaty bodies[118] have also cited *Filártiga* and its progeny in the process of developing international legal norms prohibiting torture, genocide, and other serious violations of international law. And both the International Court of Justice[119] and the International Criminal Tribunal

---

to provide a judicial remedy to individuals whose rights had been violated under international law.

Comm. Against Torture, Addendum, *Consideration of Reports Submitted by States Parties Under Article 19 of the Convention: Report of the United States of America*, ¶ 277, U.N. Doc. CAT/C/28/Add.5 (Feb. 9, 2000). The U.S. government also described the subsequent extension of this "pivotal" decision to other human rights claims. *Id.* ¶ 280 (citing *In re Estate of Ferdinand E. Marcos*, 25 F.3d 1467 (9th Cir. 1994) and *Kadic v. Karadžić*, 70 F.3d 232 (2d Cir. 1995)).

114 The Division for Social Policy and Development of the United Nations Secretariat relied on *Filártiga* to conclude that "[t]he domestic enforceability of customary international law is manifest in the case of *Filártiga v. Peña-Irala* . . . . [D]omestic court[s] may discover international legal principles by consulting executive, legislative and judicial precedents, international agreements, the recorded expertise of jurists and commentators, and other similar sources." Division for Social Policy and Development of the United Nations Secretariat, *Compilation of International Norms and Standards Relating to Disability*, §§ 1.2 & 1.4 (draft July 2002).

115 In 1993, the U.N. Sub-Commission on Human Rights relied on *Filártiga* in developing appropriate standards for determining whether conditions of imprisonment fall below fundamental human rights guarantees. *See* Hum. Rts. Comm., *The Administration of Justice and the Human Rights of Detainees*, ¶ 69, U.N. Doc. E/CN.4/Sub.2/1993/21 (June 25, 1993).

116 The Special Rapporteur appointed by the Commission on Human Rights to elaborate "the right to restitution, compensation and rehabilitation for victims of gross violations of human rights and fundamental freedoms" relied upon the ATCA as a leading example for states to "provide remedies for violations occurring outside their territory." High Comm'r for Human Rights, Note, *The Right to a Remedy and Reparation for Victims of Violations of International Human Rights and Humanitarian Law*, ¶ 114, U.N. Doc. E/CN.4/2003/63 (Dec. 27, 2003). Similarly, the Special Rapporteur on Contemporary Forms of Slavery lauded the ATCA as "a potential forum for redress" in cases in which foreign fora have proven inadequate. Gay J. McDougall, Special Rapporteur on Contemporary Forms of Slavery, *Contemporary Forms of Slavery: Systematic Rape, Sexual Slavery, and Slavery-Like Practice During Armed Conflict*, ¶ 52, U.N. Doc. 4/Sub.2/1998/13 (June 22, 1998). Another Special Rapporteur cited the ATCA as an example of "effective remedies" for gross violations of international law, recognizing that ATCA is limited in its "appli[cation] to customary international law norms, such as the prohibition of slavery, genocide, torture, crimes against humanity and war crimes." Secretary-General, Note, *The Right to Food*, ¶ 40 & n.32, U.N. Doc. A/58/330 (Aug. 28, 2003) (reporting the findings of the Special Rapporteur on the Right to Food on the potential of the ATCA as a method of redress for violations of human rights by transnational corporations and citing U.S. cases following *Filártiga*).

117 The Inter-American Commission on Human Rights has held that the ATCA, as interpreted in *Filártiga*, constitutes an adequate and effective domestic remedy for international human rights violations. Walker v. United States, Case P12.049, Inter-Am. Comm'n H.R., Report No. 62/03, OEA/Ser.L/V/II.118 doc. 70 rev. 2 at 550 n.18 (2003).

118 The Human Rights Committee of the International Covenant on Civil and Political Rights has followed *Filártiga* in urging that under Article 2.3 of that treaty, civil remedies must be available for all individuals, including non-citizens, within the territory of a state party. *See, e.g.*, Human Rights Comm., Bakhtiyari v. Austl., Communication No. 1069/2002, at 550 & ¶ 12, U.N. Doc. CCPR/C/79/D/1069/2002 (Nov. 6, 2003).

119 In *Arrest Warrant of 11 April 2000* (Dem. Rep. Congo v. Belg.), 2002 I.C.J. 1 (Feb. 14), the U.S., British, and Dutch judges filed a joint concurring opinion that addressed the

for the former Yugoslavia (ICTY)[120] have drawn guidance from the *Filártiga* jurisprudence.

Similarly, foreign domestic courts have also followed the *Filártiga* approach in selectively incorporating fundamental norms of international law into domestic law. In the *Pinochet* case, for example, the British House of Lords cited *Filártiga* for the proposition that only a select group of customary international norms are justiciable in national courts—including torture.[121] The English Court of Appeal echoed these sentiments, discussing approvingly *Filártiga*'s characterization of torturers as "hostis humani generis."[122]

Following *Filártiga*'s example, other democratic countries have engaged in remedial efforts parallel to the ATCA, recognizing that their international responsibilities require them to exercise jurisdiction over serious violations committed outside their territory, by their nationals as well as foreign nationals. The National Commission on Human Rights in India, for example, highlighted *Filártiga*'s importance in the development of national judicial remedies for violations of fundamental human rights.[123] In recognition of these responsibilities, many states now indirectly provide civil remedies for serious violations of international law, even when they are committed abroad, by allowing victims to append civil claims to criminal prosecutions.[124] Fittingly, throughout Latin

appropriate scope of universal criminal jurisdiction, inter alia, by highlighting ATCA jurisprudence, and describing it as conforming to global trends of extending civil jurisdiction over extraterritorial conduct in appropriate cases. *Id.* ¶¶ 47–48 (Higgins, Kooijmans & Buergenthal, JJ., joint separate opinion).

[120] In the first case prosecuted at the ICTY, the international judges relied on the Second Circuit's post-*Filártiga* decision in *Kadic v. Karadžić*, 70 F.3d 232 (2d Cir. 1995), to determine that crimes against humanity do not require an element of state action. Prosecutor v. Tadić, Case No. IT–94–1–T, Judgment, ¶ 655 (Int'l Crim. Tribunal for the former Yugoslavia May 7, 1997) (citing *Kadic*, 70 F.3d at 232). In another significant case before the ICTY, the judges relied on *Filártiga* in determining the status of the prohibition against torture during wartime. Prosecutor v. Furundžija, ICTY Trial Chamber Opinion, No. IT–95–17/1–T, Judgment, ¶ 147 (Dec. 10, 1998) ("There exists today universal revulsion against torture: as a USA Court put it in *Filártiga v. Peña-Irala*, 'the torturer has become, like the pirate and the slave trader before him, *hostis humani generis*, an enemy of all mankind.' ") (quoting *Filártiga*, 630 F.2d at 876). In the *Kunarac* case, the ICTY Trial Chamber cited both *Filártiga* and *Kadic* to conclude that an international criminal tribunal could convict a defendant of war crimes for committing torture during an armed conflict, even if that defendant is not a government official or acting in concert with a government official. Prosecutor v. Kunarac, Case No., IT–96–23–T, Judgment, ¶ 470 (Feb. 22, 2001).

[121] *See* Regina v. Bow St. Metro. Stipendiary Magistrate, *Ex parte* Pinochet Ugarte (No. 3) [2000] 1 A.C. 147, 159 (H.L.).

[122] Al-Adsani v. Gov't of Kuwait, 100 I.L.R. 465 (Eng. C.A. 1994), 107 I.L.R. 536 (CH. L. 1996).

[123] *See* Nat'l Comm'n on Human Rights, Sardar Patel Bhawan, Case No. 1/97/NHRC, ¶ 23 (Aug. 4, 1997). In particular, the Commission noted the effect of these developments on Indian law: "In India great strides have since been made in the field of evolving legal standards for remedial, reparatory, punitive and exemplary damages for violation of human rights." *Id.* ¶ 24.

[124] *See, e.g.*, CODE DE PROCEDURE PÉNAL [C. PR. PÉN.] [CRIMINAL PROCEDURE CODE] arts. 689, 689–2 to –10 (Fr.) (extraterritorial jurisdiction for crimes of torture, terrorism, and others); *id.* arts. 2–3 (authorizing victims to join criminal prosecution as *parties civile*); International Crimes Act of 2003 §§ 2–8, 10, 21 (Neth.) (extraterritorial jurisdiction for

America, the *Filártiga* case and its progeny fortified a movement of human rights activists who sought to bring the leaders of Operation Condor to justice in their home countries.[125]

To bring matters full circle, the United States Congress built on the *Filártiga* line of cases by enacting several statutes providing causes of action or lifting foreign sovereign immunity to make civil remedies available for particular kinds of gross human rights violations: the Torture Victim Protection Act of 1991 (TVPA) to address torture and summary execution,[126] the Trafficking Victims Protection Act of 2000 (TRVPA) to address human trafficking,[127] and, to address terrorist acts, the Anti-Terrorism Act (ATA) of 1990[128] and the Justice Against Sponsors of Terrorism Act of 2016 (JASTA).[129] As the House Report to the TVPA

genocide, war crimes, torture, and crimes against humanity); Art. 51(f), ¶¶ 1–2, SR (Neth.) (authorizing victims and, if deceased, their relatives to join criminal prosecution); POINIKOS KODIKAS [P.K.] [PENAL CODE] 1:8 (Greece) (extraterritorial jurisdiction for many serious international offenses); KODIKAS POINIKES DIKONOMIAS [KPOI.D.] [CODE OF CRIMINAL PROCEDURE] 4.2:70, 4.3:82–88, 4.4:108, 6.1:137(d), 1:468, 2.1:480, 3.1:488 (Greece) (authorizing victims to append civil claims to criminal cases); VÖLKERSTRAFGESETZBUCH [VstGB] [CODE OF CRIMES AGAINST INTERNATIONAL LAW] § 1 (Ger.) (criminalizing war crimes and crimes against humanity; "[t]his Act shall apply to all criminal offences against international law designated under this Act, to serious criminal offences designated therein even when the offence was committed abroad and bears no relation to Germany"); STAFPROZESSORDNUNG [STPO] [CODE OF CRIMINAL PROCEDURE] §§ 403–406(c) (Ger.) (authorizing victims to append civil claims to criminal cases); Codice penale [C.p.] [Penal Code] art. 10 (It.) (extraterritorial criminal jurisdiction for serious violations of international law, including torture, crimes against humanity, war crimes, genocide, and international terrorism); Legge 3 novembre 1988, n.498, G.U. Nov. 18, 1988, n.271 (It.) (same); Codice di procedura penale [C.p.p] [Code of Criminal Procedure] arts. 74, 90, 101, 394, 396 (It.) (enabling victims to bring civil claims for compensation and restitution within criminal proceedings); LEY ORGANICA DEL PODER JUDICIAL [L.O.P.J.] [LAW ON THE JUDICIARY] art. 23.4 (Spain) (extraterritorial criminal jurisdiction for serious violations of international law, including torture, crimes against humanity, war crimes, genocide, and international terrorism); LEY DE ENJUICIAMIENTO CRIMINAL [L.E. CRIM.] [CODE OF CRIMINAL PROCEDURE] art. 112 (Spain) (providing that any criminal complaint filed by a victim is also a civil claim unless the claimant expressly states otherwise).

125 *See generally* Zoglin, *supra* note 8.

126 Torture Victim Protection Act, Pub. L. No. 102–256, 106 Stat. 73 (1992) [hereinafter TVPA] (codified at 28 U.S.C. § 1350 (2000)) (codifying and extending to citizen plaintiffs statutory causes of action for torture and summary execution suffered under the actual or apparent authority, or under color of law, of any foreign nation).

127 Trafficking Victims Protection Act, Pub. L. No. 106–386, 114 Stat. 1466 (2000). *See generally* Luis C. deBaca & Griffin Black, *The Development of US Anti-Slavery Law: A Historical Review, in* THE HISTORICAL ROOTS OF HUMAN TRAFFICKING: INFORMING PRIMARY PREVENTION OF COMMERCIALIZED VIOLENCE 127, 157–63 (Makini Chisolm-Straker & Katherine Chon eds., 2021).

128 Pub. L. No. 102–572, § 1003(a)(4), 106 Stat. 4522 (1992) (codified at 18 U.S.C. § 2333(a)). Congress exercised criminal jurisdiction over terrorist acts in 1986, and the ATA was designed to provide a complementary civil remedy for the victims of such acts. The ATA also added 18 U.S.C. § 2333(a), which provides: "Any national of the United States injured in his or her person, property, or business by reason of an act of international terrorism, or his or her estate, survivors, or heirs, may sue therefor in any appropriate district court of the United States and shall recover threefold the damages he or she sustains and the cost of the suit, including attorney's fees." *Id.*

129 Congress enacted the JASTA in response to lower-court rulings that had narrowly interpreted the ATA—"to provide civil litigants with the broadest possible basis, consistent with the Constitution of the United States, to seek relief against [any person or entity that] provided material support, directly or indirectly, to foreign organizations or persons that

made explicit, Congress designed these statutes to supplement and complement, not replace, the *Sosa/Filártiga* interpretation of the ATCA. Significantly, the TVPA's legislative history expressly declared Congress's understanding that "international human rights cases predictably raise legal issues—such as interpretations of international law—*that are matters of Federal common law* and within the particular expertise of Federal courts."[130] Thus, even if a future Supreme Court ruling should further narrow, or even overrule, *Filártiga*, by spurring this legislative movement, the case has left an indelible legacy on the landscape of United States and international human rights law.

The Torture Debate. *Filártiga* also affirmed that U.S. courts must be critical players not just in the general pursuit of human rights, but particularly in the elimination of the practice of torture and cruel, inhuman, or degrading treatment. *Filártiga* inspired a movement within the U.S. human rights community to promote domestic judicial incorporation of the norm against torture that eventually helped push President George H.W. Bush to ratify the U.N. Convention Against Torture and Congress to enact the Torture Victim Protection Act of 1991.[131] Unexpectedly, nearly a quarter century after *Filártiga,* the stability of the domestic incorporation of that norm was called into question by the revelation that torture and other forbidden methods were being used by the United States against detainees both in an Iraqi prison at Abu Ghraib, and as part of "extreme interrogation methods" being deployed in the "War Against Terror" after September 11, 2001.

An August 1, 2002 memorandum opinion came to light, which had been sent by then-Assistant Attorney General Jay S. Bybee of the Office of Legal Counsel (OLC) at the U.S. Department of Justice to then-Counsel to the President Alberto R. Gonzales regarding coercive interrogation tactics ("Torture Opinion").[132] The Torture Opinion, which Mr. Gonzales as White House Counsel apparently requested in early summer 2002, explored the question whether U.S. officials could use tactics tantamount to torture against suspected terrorists, without being held liable under a federal statute that criminalizes torture. Following the release of the opinion, a firestorm ensued, and the Justice Department officially withdrew the opinion. In late 2005, a governmental norm sponsor, Senator John McCain, introduced the McCain Amendment to the Defense

---

engage in terrorist activities against the United States." Justice Against State Sponsors of Terrorism Act, Pub. L. No. 114–222, § 2(b), 130 Stat. 852, 853 (2016); *see, e.g.*, Kaplan v. Lebanese Can. Bank, SAL, 999 F.3d 842, 855 (2d Cir. 2021) (discussing this language).

[130] S. REP. NO. 102–249, at 6 n.6 (1991) (emphasis added).

[131] Convention Against Torture and Other Cruel, Inhuman or Degrading Treatment or Punishment, Dec. 10, 1984, S. TREATY DOC. NO. 100–20, 1465 U.N.T.S. 85 (1988) (ratified by United States Oct. 21, 1994); TVPA, *supra* note 126.

[132] Memorandum from Jay S. Bybee, Assistant Att'y Gen., Office of Legal Counsel, to Alberto R. Gonzales, Counsel to the President, Regarding Standards of Conduct for Interrogation under 18 U.S.C. §§ 2340–2340A (Aug. 1, 2002), https://perma.cc/WPF8-DXYX. For a substantive critique of this opinion, see Harold Hongju Koh, *Can the President Be Torturer in Chief?*, 81 IND. L.J. 1145 (2005), from which the discussion in the text derives.

Authorization Act, prohibiting the use of cruel, inhuman, or degrading treatment against any individual in the custody or physical control of the United States.[133] The Amendment sought to ban cruel, inhuman, or degrading treatment or punishment of people in U.S. custody or under the effective control of the U.S. Department of Defense. In addition, the McCain Amendment required all U.S. troops to follow *Army Field Manual* procedures when they detain and interrogate military prisoners.

The McCain Amendment soon became another example of a transnational effort to enforce the international human rights norm against torture. Against the vigorous objections and lobbying efforts of the George W. Bush administration, a transnational network arose, consisting of private citizens and some twenty-eight retired generals, led by former Secretary of State Colin Powell, who came forward to speak in favor of the Amendment. At the same time, numerous human rights NGOs, such as Human Rights First[134] and Human Rights Watch,[135] vigorously pressed the case for the Amendment. The federal courts again became a player in the public debate, as Judge Alvin Hellerstein of the Southern District of New York ordered the release of dozens more pictures of prisoners being abused at Abu Ghraib.[136] Despite vigorous White House lobbying, the Republican-controlled Senate and House overwhelmingly voted to strengthen the guidelines governing the treatment of prisoners in U.S. military custody.[137] On the day after the House approved the McCain Amendment, the White House reversed itself, and President Bush accepted a compromise that Senator McCain had been offering for weeks.[138] On December 30, 2005, President Bush finally signed the 2006 Defense Appropriations Act, which included the McCain Amendment. On its face, the McCain Amendment applies to all U.S. personnel everywhere, without regard to whom they are interrogating.

Thus, a transnational network against torture provoked an interaction, which led to an interpretation of law that apparently promoted the internalization of a norm against torture and cruel, inhuman, or degrading treatment into U.S. law. Yet, even after the

---

[133] Detainee Treatment Act of 2005, Pub. L. No. 109–148, § 1003, 119 Stat. 2680, 2739–40 (2005) (prohibiting "Cruel, Inhuman, or Degrading Treatment or Punishment of Persons Under Custody or Control of the United States Government").

[134] *See Congress Puts Bush Administration on Notice: Stop Using Abusive Interrogation Methods*, HUMAN RIGHTS FIRST (Dec. 22, 2005), https://perma.cc/DTE5-SXTM.

[135] *See U.S. Landmark Torture Ban Undercut*, HUMAN RIGHTS FIRST (Dec. 16, 2005), https://perma.cc/TKW4-33A8.

[136] *See* A.C.L.U. v. Dep't of Def., 389 F. Supp. 2d 547 (S.D.N.Y. 2005).

[137] Eric Schmitt, *House Defies Bush and Backs McCain on Detainee Torture*, N.Y. TIMES, Dec. 15, 2005, at A14 (reporting that the House voted 308 to 122 and that the Senate voted 90 to 9 to support the McCain Amendment).

[138] Eric Schmitt, *Bush Will Support McCain on Torture: Bipartisan Support Leads to Reversal*, S.F. CHRON., Dec. 16, 2005, at A7 (reporting that it was a "stinging defeat" for Bush that both chambers had defied his threatened veto to resoundingly support McCain's measure, especially considering that his party controlled both houses of Congress).

President accepted the law, his presidential signing statement accompanying the Act made only a qualified commitment to follow the new law "in a manner consistent with the President's constitutional authority to supervise the unitary executive branch."[139] But under intense public pressure, President Bush backed off such extreme claims, finally telling an interviewer: "I don't think a president can order torture, for example. . . . Yes, there are clear red lines."[140] In short, the norm against torture has apparently once again been internalized into U.S. law, as a matter of judicial decision, legislation, and executive policy.

During the Obama administration, the President himself stressed that the U.S. government had genuinely foresworn the use of torture as an interrogation device in the war on terror.[141] As a presidential candidate, Donald Trump welcomed the renewed use of torture, although the actual practice of torture did not appear to have returned under his administration.[142] Yet through it all, the 1980 judicial decision in *Filártiga* remained the leading statement by a U.S. governmental institution unambiguously condemning the use of torture. And so, nearly twenty years after the abuses at Abu Ghraib, a *Filártiga*-style torture lawsuit by ATCA plaintiffs went to trial in 2024 against CACI, a U.S. army contractor that operated at that prison. In the end, a federal jury awarded the plaintiffs $42 million.[143]

Corporate Responsibility for Human Rights Violations. The Abu Ghraib case exemplified a shift in transnational public law litigation in the early twenty-first century. Private litigants began to invoke the basic principles of *Filártiga* to try to hold global corporations responsible for human rights violations committed outside the United States. In response, failed Supreme Court nominee Robert Bork argued that "[t]he modern expansion of the Alien Tort Claims Act is judicial activism—indeed, moral presumption—at its highest pitch."[144] Other skeptics of *Filártiga* called the ATCA an "awakening monster," under whose auspices "millions of impoverished people" may be "denied an opportunity

---

139 Statement on Signing the National Defense Authorization Act for Fiscal Year 2006, 42 WEEKLY COMP. PRES. DOC. 23 (Jan. 6, 2006).

140 Interview by Bob Schieffer with President George W. Bush, in Washington, D.C., CBS NEWS (Jan. 27, 2006), https://www.presidency.ucsb.edu/documents/interview-with-bob-schieffer-cbs-news.

141 *See generally* Harold Hongju Koh, *The Emerging Law of 21st Century War*, 66 EMORY L.J. 487, 496–500 (2017).

142 *See, e.g.*, Tom McCarthy, *Donald Trump: I'd Bring Back 'A Hell of a Lot Worse than Waterboarding,'* GUARDIAN (Feb. 7, 2016), https://perma.cc/JM5Y-7QVH.

143 *See* Al Shimari v. CACI Premier Tech., 684 F. Supp. 3d 481 (E.D. Va. 2023); Matthew Barakat, *Judge rejects military contractor's bid to end Abu Ghraib torture suit,* FED. TIMES, Aug. 2, 2023, https://perma.cc/T7K2-QFR8 ("In a previous hearing, [Judge Leonie] Brinkema said there is evidence implicating CACI in the torture regime at Abu Ghraib, including an email from a CACI employee assigned to Abu Ghraib that she described as a potential 'smoking gun.' ").

144 ROBERT BORK, COERCING VIRTUE: THE WORLDWIDE RULE OF JUDGES 27 (2003).

to participate in global markets."[145] The George W. Bush administration weighed in heavily against ATCA plaintiffs, arguing that litigation against corporate defendants under the statute would threaten U.S. foreign policy, endanger corporations, discourage trade and foreign investment in dozens of developing countries, and undermine the war against terrorism.[146]

In the string of cases that followed, the Roberts Court dramatically narrowed, but did not entirely eliminate, the ATCA as a tool for challenging extraterritorial human rights abuse. In *Kiobel* v. *Royal Dutch Petroleum,* by a vote of 5–4, the Court applied the presumption against extraterritoriality to the ATCA cause of action, holding that a claim under the statute arising from "violations of the law of nations occurring outside the United States is barred" for lack of subject matter jurisdiction unless it "touches and concerns" the United States.[147] In *Jesner v. Arab Bank,* the Court extended that reasoning to hold that "foreign corporations may not be defendants in suits brought under the ATS."[148] Finally, in *Nestlé v. Doe,* the Court refused to allow extraterritorial application of the ATCA to slave labor claims by Malian cocoa workers in Cote d'Ivoire against U.S. companies that buy cocoa from that country with reason to know that the cocoa was being harvested by slave labor. The Court held that claims against U.S. corporations required more conduct occurring in the United States than general corporate decisionmaking.[149]

Taken together, these decisions have sharply limited U.S. suits by alien survivors against foreign corporations and individuals based on human rights violations committed abroad. Significantly, in *Kiobel,* the Second Circuit had ruled that corporate liability for human rights violations was not well-enough established to meet the *Sosa* standard. The Supreme Court granted certiorari to decide the corporate liability question, but instead disposed of the case by limiting the ATCA cause of action to claims that "touch and concern" the territory of the United States. In 2018, the Court again granted certiorari to decide the corporate liability question in *Jesner,* but again avoided the question by holding that the ATCA cause of action did not apply to foreign corporations. In 2021, in *Nestle v. Doe,* the Court for a third time took up the corporate liability issue, but again failed to resolve the question, holding instead that application of the ATCA cause of action to a U.S. corporation engaged in general corporate decisionmaking would be impermissibly extraterritorial. Thus, the Supreme Court has *not* held, as the respondents in each of those cases invited them to do, that domestic courts cannot hold private corporations civilly liable for torts in violations

---

145 GARY CLYDE HUFBAUER & NICHOLAS K. MITROKOSTAS, AWAKENING MONSTER: THE ALIEN TORT STATUTE OF 1789, at 2 (2003).

146 Brief for the United States of America as Amicus Curiae, Doe v. Unocal Corp., 403 F.3d 708 (9th Cir. 2005) (en banc) (Nos. 00-566-3, 00-56628).

147 569 U.S. 108, 124 (2013).

148 585 U.S. 241, 272 (2018).

149 593 U.S. 628, 634 (2021).

of international law. If and when the Court finally takes on this question, it will find a great deal of law pointing in the other direction.

Many treaties and international instruments do impose substantive duties upon corporations. The International Labor Organization (ILO) Tripartite Declaration, for example, obliges corporations not to interfere with employees' rights to form unions and not to use child or slave labor.[150] Nuclear treaties, such as the Paris Convention[151] and oil spill treaties, hold shipowners and operators of nuclear facilities liable for damage or loss of life to persons and property from private nuclear accidents or oil spills.[152] Hazardous waste conventions, such as those concluded at Basel, impose strict liability on corporate generators of hazardous waste.[153] The OECD Anti-Bribery Convention effectively holds corporations liable for bribery.[154] It would make little sense if corporations can be held responsible under international law for their complicity in oil spills, or under European law for anticompetitive behavior, but then not held liable for profiting from slavery or complicity in genocide.

The commonsense fact remains that if states and individuals can be held liable under international law, then so too should corporations, for the simple reason that both states and individuals *act through* corporations. Given that reality, why let states and individuals immunize themselves from liability for gross violations through the mere artifice of corporate formation? Had that been allowed at the time of *Filártiga,* Peña absurdly could have escaped liability simply by incorporating as "Peña-Irala, Inc."

---

[150] *See* International Labour Office [ILO], *Tripartite Declaration of Principles Concerning Multinational Enterprises and Social Policy*, at 10, 16, 37, 41 (Nov. 1977), https://perma.cc/FL2J-2WAS.

[151] Paris Convention on Third Party Liability in the Field of Nuclear Energy, July 29, 1960, 956 U.N.T.S. 251.

[152] *See, e.g.*, International Convention on Civil Liability for Oil Pollution Damage, Nov. 29, 1969, 973 U.N.T.S. 3 [hereinafter Civil Liability Convention]; Brussels Convention Relating to Civil Liability in the Field of Maritime Carriage of Nuclear Material, Dec. 17, 1971, 974 U.N.T.S. 255; Convention on Civil Liability for Oil Pollution Damage Resulting from Exploration for and Exploitation of Seabed Mineral Resources, Dec. 17, 1976, 16 I.L.M. 1450 (1977). The 1969 Civil Liability Convention states: "The owner of a ship at the time of an incident, or where the incident consists of a series of occurrences at the time of the first such occurrence, *shall be liable* for any pollution damage caused by oil which has escaped or been discharged from the ship as a result of the incident." Civil Liability Convention, *supra*, art. III(1), 973 U.N.T.S. at 5 (emphasis added).

[153] Basel Convention on the Control of Transboundary Movements of Hazardous Wastes and Their Disposal arts. 4(3), 9(5), Mar. 22, 1989, 1673 U.N.T.S. 57; *see also id.* art. 2(14) (" 'Person' means any natural or legal person.").

[154] *See* Convention on Combating Bribery of Foreign Public Officials in International Business Transactions art. 3, Dec. 17, 1997, https://www.oecd.org/daf/anti-bribery/oecdantibriberyconvention.htm ("The bribery of a foreign public official shall be punishable by effective, proportionate and dissuasive criminal penalties. The range of penalties shall be comparable to that applicable to the bribery of the Party's own public officials and shall, in the case of natural persons, include deprivation of liberty sufficient to enable effective mutual legal assistance and extradition.").

As history and precedent make clear, corporations can be held liable in two ways, particularly when they are involved in *jus cogens* violations.[155] First, corporations can be held liable as agents of the state committing what Andrew Clapham calls "complicity offenses," namely, acting under color of state law or in concert with state actors.[156] Second, private actors, including corporations, can be held directly liable under international law if they commit certain "transnational offenses"—namely, heinous offenses that can be committed by either a public or a private entity.[157] Indeed, it was on this basis that the Nuremberg Tribunal held private German industrialists—Flick, I.G. Farben, and Krupp—criminally liable for their support of, and participation in, the Holocaust, finding that the Nuremberg Charter permitted prosecution of a private group or organization and stating that the actions of the company and its representatives "under these circumstances cannot be differentiated from acts of plunder or pillage committed by officers . . . or . . . officials of the Third Reich."[158] Moreover, under Article 4 of the Genocide Convention, a private corporation can commit or aid and abet in genocide, for example, by producing lethal toxic gas for use in a concentration camp.[159] The same goes for Common Article 3 of the Geneva Conventions, which binds all parties to an armed conflict, including those who may be nonstate actors.[160]

It makes no sense to argue that international law may impose criminal liability on corporations, but not civil liability. Congress passed several statutes described above—e.g., the ATCA and the Torture Victim

[155] *See generally* Steven R. Ratner, *Corporations and Human Rights: A Theory of Legal Responsibility*, 111 YALE L.J. 443 (2001).

[156] Andrew Clapham, *On Complicity*, *in* LE DROIT PÉNAL À L'ÉPREUVE DE L'INTERNATIONALISATION 241 (Marc Henzelin & Robert Roth eds., 2002).

[157] Even Judge Bork acknowledged that if a corporation committed piracy or slave trade or fostered an attack on an ambassador, it would be considered *hostis humani generis* (enemies of all mankind) even if it acted in a purely private capacity. *See* Tel-Oren v. Libyan Arab Republic, 726 F.2d 774, 798, 813–14 (D.C. Cir. 1984) (Bork, J., concurring). *See also id.* at 794–95 (Edwards, J., concurring) (there are a "handful of crimes," including slave trading, "to which the law of nations attributes individual liability," such that state action is not required for ATCA liability).

[158] United States v. Krauch (I.G. Farben Case), 8 Trials of War Criminals before the Nuernberg Mil. Tribunals 1081, 1140 (1952). In three cases decided by American courts sitting in occupied Germany under Control Council Law No. 10—*United States v. Flick*, *United States v. Krauch* (*I.G. Farben Case*), and *United States v. Krupp*—leading German industrialists were prosecuted for crimes against peace (i.e., initiating World War II), war crimes, and crimes against humanity. *See* 6–9 Trials of War Criminals Before the Nuernberg Mil. Tribunals xvi (1950–1953). These trials led to convictions of the industrialists not only for slave labor, but also, in the case of Flick, for financial contributions to the SS.

[159] Convention on the Prevention and Punishment of the Crime of Genocide art. IV, *adopted* Dec. 9, 1948, 78 U.N.T.S. 277 ("Persons committing genocide or any of the other acts enumerated in article III shall be punished, whether they are constitutionally responsible rulers, public officials *or private individuals*.") (emphasis added). *Cf.* The Zyklon B Case: Trial of Bruno Tesch and Two Others, 1 Law Reports of Trials of War Criminals 93 (1997) (Brit. Mil. Ct. 1946) (holding individuals liable for producing and supplying lethal gas to concentration camp).

[160] *See, e.g.*, Geneva Convention Relative to the Treatment of Prisoners of War art. 3, Aug. 12, 1949, 6 U.S.T. 3316, 75 U.N.T.S. 135.

Protection Act (TVPA)—precisely to provide civil remedies for international law violations.[161] These statutes constitute a form of domestic legislative internalization of an international norm.

Even if for some reason international law did not impose civil liability directly, there is nothing to prevent domestic law (e.g., the ATCA) from supplementing international criminal law remedies with civil remedies arising out of domestic law.[162] Indeed, in *Kadic v. Karadžić* and its progeny, the Second Circuit and other circuits have held that the ATCA provides domestic civil remedies against nonstate actors who violate international law.[163] Like any aider and abettor, corporations can be held liable for the small class of cases that arise out of a claim of violation of obligatory, definable, and universal norms of international law (direct offenses) as well as for their complicity in a public actor's violation of international law. Indeed, it was precisely the theory of the historic Holocaust Assets Deal that private companies, banks, and officials were part of a common plan or conspiracy to commit war crimes or crimes against humanity.[164]

The International Law Commission's rules of state responsibility suggest that complicity constitutes provision of "aid or assistance to another . . . facilitating the commission of the wrongful act by the latter."[165] Similarly, Article 7(1) of the ICTY statute[166] and Article 25 of the International Criminal Court treaty hold private citizens criminally liable for committing crimes jointly with or through another person.[167] So, there seems to be little reason why private corporations could not

---

161 28 U.S.C. § 1350, 1350a.

162 *See, e.g.*, RESTATEMENT (THIRD) OF FOREIGN RELATIONS LAW OF THE UNITED STATES § 404 cmt. B (1987) ("International law does not preclude the application of non-criminal law on [the] basis [of universal interests], for example, by providing a remedy in tort or restitution for victims of piracy.").

163 70 F. 3d 232, 239 (2d Cir. 1995) ("certain acts violate the law of nations whether undertaken by those acting under the auspices of a state or only as private individuals"). *See also* Doe v. Unocal Corp., 395 F.3d 932, 946 (9th Cir. 2002) ("Thus, under *Kadic*, even crimes like rape, torture, and summary execution, which by themselves require state action for ATCA liability to attach, do *not* require state action when committed in furtherance of other crimes like slave trading, genocide or war crimes, which by themselves do not require state action for ATCA liability to attach. We agree with this view and apply it below to Plaintiffs' various ATCA claims.") (emphasis in original).

164 *See generally* STUART E. EIZENSTAT, IMPERFECT JUSTICE: LOOTED ASSETS, SLAVE LABOR, AND THE UNFINISHED BUSINESS OF WORLD WAR II (2003) (describing evolution of Holocaust Assets Deal).

165 James Crawford (Special Rapporteur), *Second Report on State Responsibility*, ¶ 159, U.N. Doc. A/CN.4/498/Add.1 (Apr. 1, 1999).

166 Statute of the Int'l Trib. for the Prosecution of Pers. Responsible for Serious Violations of Int'l Humanitarian Law Committed in the Territory of the Former Yugoslavia Since 1991, art. 7(1), U.N. Doc. S/RES/827, as amended, https://www.icty.org/x/file/Legal%20Library/Statute/statute_sept09_en.pdf ("A person who planned, instigated, ordered, committed, or otherwise aided and abetted in the planning, preparation or execution of a crime [under this Statute] shall be individually responsible for the crime.")

167 Rome Statute of the International Criminal Court art. 25(3), *adopted* July 17, 1998, 2187 U.N.T.S. 3 ("[A] person shall be criminally responsible . . . if that person . . . aids, abets, or otherwise assists in its commission or attempted commission.").

equally be held liable for either their direct human rights violations or their acts in complicity with state human rights violations.

The Roberts Court's rulings limiting the ATCA and *Filártiga* have created a noticeable divergence in the law as compared with like-minded democratic countries. In March 2020, the Supreme Court of Canada, in a landmark opinion by Justice Rosalie Silberman Abella, held in *Nevsun Resources Ltd. v. Araya* that Canadian corporations may be sued in tort for gross violations of international human rights law that occur abroad.[168] The *Nevsun* plaintiffs sued a Canadian company that owned a mine in Eritrea, claiming that by conscripting them into forced labor, the Eritrean military had subjected them to compensable breaches of customary international law prohibitions against forced labor, slavery, cruel, inhuman, or degrading treatment, and crimes against humanity.

The *Nevsun* decision let those claims proceed, resolving under Canadian law the question that the U.S. Supreme Court has repeatedly failed to answer under U.S. law: that as a matter of domestic law, international human rights norms impose corporate tort liability for gross human abuses. The ruling recognized that there should be a domestic law remedy for this international law right, and held that domestic courts could develop "a civil remedy in domestic law for corporate violations of the customary international law norms adopted in Canadian law" "to adequately address the heinous nature of the harm caused by this conduct."[169] At the same time, Justice Abella acknowledged that every nation must decide whether and how its own legal system should provide redress for corporate violations of those norms, leaving to the trial court on remand to decide whether to recognize new domestic common law torts against slavery based on customary international law or to apply customary international law directly to the defendant's conduct, because of the gravity of the offenses.[170]

The *Nevsun* ruling added Canada to a growing list of nations recognizing the possibility of corporate liability for human rights violations abroad. In 2019, the U.K. Supreme Court, in *Vedanta Resources PLC v. Lungowe*, allowed claims to go forward against a U.K. corporation and its Zambian subsidiary seeking damages for toxic

---

[168] Nevsun Resources Ltd. v. Araya, [2020] S.C.R. 166 (Can.), https://perma.cc/9E6W-7E5Z.

[169] *Id.* ¶¶ 120, 122, 125. Justice Abella ruled that norms of customary international law are fully integrated into, and absent conflicting law, form a self-executing part of, Canadian domestic common law, subject to legislative revision. *Id.* ¶ 94. The norms alleged to have been breached in this case prohibiting crimes against humanity, slavery, forced labor, and cruel, inhuman, and degrading treatment were all found to be well established as *jus cogens* in customary international law, *id.* ¶¶ 99–103, in some cases "regardless of whether the perpetrator is a state," *id.* ¶ 105, and therefore potentially applicable to corporations. *Id.* ¶ 111. The majority concluded: "it is not 'plain and obvious' that corporations today enjoy a blanket exclusion under customary international law from direct liability for violation of 'obligatory, definable, and universal norms of international law,' or indirect liability for their involvement in . . . 'complicity offenses.' " *Id.* ¶ 113.

[170] *Id.* ¶¶ 127–129.

emissions from a mine in Zambia.[171] A Dutch district court in The Hague held, in *Kiobel v. Royal Dutch Shell*—contrary to the U.S. Supreme Court ruling of the same name—that it had jurisdiction over claims by widows of activists executed in Nigeria alleging that Dutch and U.K. parent companies and their Nigerian subsidiary were accessories to the unlawful arrests, detentions, and executions.[172] So, even while the U.S. Supreme Court has repeatedly limited the availability of suits against corporate defendants, other democratic nations have moved the other way, influenced by *Filártiga* to recognize the availability of corporate liability for human rights violations against parent companies domiciled in those countries.

It remains unclear at this writing whether U.S. courts will follow this emerging trend. For now, the Supreme Court's rulings have left open a narrow window for ATCA suits against U.S. corporations when their activities abroad aid and abet gross human rights abuse, and the U.S.-located activity constitutes more than general corporate decision-making. In a prominent 2023 Ninth Circuit decision, a divided panel allowed a case by Chinese practitioners of Falun Gong to go forward against a U.S. corporation that they alleged had designed and built a surveillance system that had been used against them by Chinese officials. The panel held that the facts had alleged substantial conduct by the corporate defendant in the United States with knowledge that it was facilitating human rights abuses abroad, and that under the *Sosa* test, aiding and abetting liability is a norm of customary international law with sufficient definition and universality to establish corporate liability under the Alien Tort Claims Act.[173] The obvious question arises: if a U.S. corporation operating in Paraguay had actively aided and abetted Joelito's torture, would that American corporation today escape liability in an American court for its involvement in such a gross human rights violation?

---

[171] Vedanta Resources PLC v. Lungowe [2019] UKSC 20 (Eng.), https://perma.cc/K25K-CDGB (observing that the parent company may have intervened sufficiently in the management of the mine to have assumed a duty of care under Zambian common law or fault-based liability under Zambian legislation).

[172] Rb. Den Haag 1 juli 2019, ECLI:NL:RBDHA:2019:6670 (Kiobel/Shell) (Neth.) https://perma.cc/EG3Q-2358. The Dutch suit involved the same plaintiffs as the U.S. *Kiobel* case, but alleged violations of fundamental rights under Nigerian law, rather than customary international law. In March 2022, the Hague court dismissed Esther Kiobel's civil case due to insufficient evidence to link Shell to the bribing of witnesses to give false testimony at the trial of the "Ogoni Nine." Kiobel announced her intent to appeal the decision, but ultimately did not do so. *Nigeria: Dutch court rejects suit of 'Ogoni Nine' widows against Shell*, ALJAZEERA (Mar. 23, 2022), https://perma.cc/69VJ-42AC.

[173] Doe I v. Cisco Sys., Inc., 73 F.4th 700 (9th Cir. 2023). *See* William S. Dodge, *Ninth Circuit Allows Human Rights Claims Against Cisco to Proceed*, TRANSNATIONAL LITIGATION BLOG (July 19, 2023), https://perma.cc/Q35M-UHP7. The Ninth Circuit also denied petitions by Cisco for panel rehearing and rehearing en banc. Doe I v. Cisco Systems, Inc., 113 F.4th 1230, 1231 (9th Cir. Sept. 3, 2024). The same aiding-and-abetting issue obviously also arises in the Abu Ghraib case against the U.S. corporation, CACI, discussed at note 143 *supra*.

V. CONCLUSION

Despite the judicial counterrevolution it sparked, *Filártiga* showed conclusively that domestic courts need not be bystanders in modern human rights controversies. The *Filártiga* doctrine promoted a growing partnership among the work of U.S. courts, international tribunals, and human rights organs. This transnational legal process has illustrated a key claim of the Yale School of International Law by highlighting the role of legal pluralism—multiple communities for law development, interpretation, and enforcement—in creating transnational law absent a single global "Leviathan."[174] *Filártiga*'s key legacy thus rests in the norm that emerged from the dialogue it fostered: that all nations must provide all individuals, whether citizens or not, with an effective judicial remedy for acts of torture, genocide, and other serious violations of international law, wherever those acts are committed.

On the day that *Sosa* was argued at the U.S. Supreme Court, Dolly Filártiga wrote in an op-ed article in the *New York Times*:

> I came to this country in 1978 hoping simply to look a killer in the eye. With the help of American law, I got so much more. Eventually I received political asylum, then became a citizen. I am proud to live in a country where human rights are respected, where there is a way to bring to justice people who have committed horrible atrocities.[175]

More than two years later, an obituary in the same newspaper reported that the author of Paraguay's reign of torture, Alfredo Stroessner Matiaude, had finally died in exile in Brazil. Buried in that story was mention that while in exile, Stroessner had written to an American diplomat, asking whether he could come to the United States for gallbladder surgery. The diplomat had "advised the general to stay away, warning that he could become the target for a lawsuit [in the United States] by Paraguayans." The general ended up having his surgery in Brazil.[176]

Too often, we hear that violence must be met with more violence. But *Filártiga* showed instead how violence can be met with law. The case and its progeny revealed how international human rights law, invoked in a domestic judicial forum, can illumine life, redress pain, and declare norms to guide future governmental action. In that way, international

---

[174] Paul Schiff Berman, *A Pluralist Approach to International Law*, 32 YALE J. INT'L L. 301, 307, 311 (2007). Yale School theorists see "dialectical legal interactions" among these law-declaring forums as helping to refine the scope of international legal obligations, particularly through transnational judicial dialogue. *Id.* at 315–16. *See also* Robert B. Ahdieh, *Between Dialogue and Decree: International Review of National Courts*, 79 N.Y.U. L. REV. 2029 (2004); Waters, *supra* note 107. *See generally* Koh, *The Yale School of International Law*, *supra* note 105.

[175] Filártiga, *American Courts, Global Justice*, *supra* note 10, at A21.

[176] Diana Jean Schemo, *Alfredo Stroessner, Paraguayan Ex-Dictator, Dies*, N.Y. TIMES, Aug. 17, 2006, at B7.

law—and the human beings it touches—can rise above violence to tell the truth, heal, and teach.

3

Philippa Webb and Yasmin Liberman

The *Pinochet* Case: General, President, Defendant

The *Pinochet* case continues to stir debate amongst the international community as to whether a former head of state is (and whether they should be) legally immune from prosecution of alleged international crimes committed whilst in office. In particular, the House of Lords' judgment in *Pinochet (No. 3)*[1] is the leading case on immunity *ratione materiae* and is cited extensively by domestic and international courts.[2] The case is a prominent and historic example of international efforts to hold a former head of state, in this case Augusto Pinochet, the former dictator of Chile, to account for crimes committed by their regime. Furthermore, whilst it is debatable whether the *Pinochet* case fomented a trend towards accountability in the international legal community, the case was followed by an apparent uptick in efforts to hold other dictators to account, including Slobodan Milošević and Hissène Habré.

This chapter explores the law, politics, and controversies surrounding the *Pinochet* case beginning with a discussion of Pinochet's capture of power in 1973 and subsequent seventeen-year-long dictatorship in Chile. It details the alleged human rights abuses committed by Pinochet's forces throughout this period, including the widespread practice of enforced disappearance, which remains synonymous with the Pinochet regime and was carried out by various military governments during the Latin American "dirty wars" between 1960 and 1980.[3] The chapter next details the investigations carried out in Spain looking into the abuses committed by the Pinochet regime, which culminated in the arrest of Pinochet in London on the basis of two international arrest warrants in October 1998. The chapter then turns to

---

[1] R v. Bow St. Metro. Stipendiary Magistrate, *ex parte* Pinochet Ugarte (No. 3) (2000) 1 AC 147 (HL).

[2] Immunity *ratione materiae* in this context can be understood as an immunity granted to individuals who perform certain state functions and thus extends "to acts that are official acts or performed in an official capacity." *See* Roger O'Keefe, *Immunity Ratione Materiae from Foreign Criminal Jurisdiction and the Concept of "Acts Performed in an Official Capacity"* (Council of Europe Seminar on the Immunity Ratione Materiae of State Officials from Foreign Criminal Jurisdiction, 2014), https://rm.coe.int/1680097836.

[3] Off. High Comm'r for Hum. Rts., *Enforced Disappearances: Progress and Challenges in South America* (Aug. 31, 2012), https://www.ohchr.org/en/stories/2012/08/enforced-disappearances-progress-and-challenges-south-america.

discuss the *Pinochet* case itself, detailing the legal back-and-forth within the English courts over several years whilst Pinochet lived under house arrest in Surrey. Critically, in *Pinochet (No. 3)*, the House of Lords held by majority that Pinochet was not immune as a former head of state for acts of torture or conspiracy to torture committed following the United Kingdom's ratification of the 1984 U.N. Convention against Torture.[4] Subsequently, whilst it appeared as if Pinochet's extradition to stand trial in Spain was imminent, the British Home Secretary Jack Straw called off the extradition on medical grounds, and Pinochet was allowed to return to Chile.

As is discussed towards the end of the chapter, Pinochet's return to Chile ignited efforts within Chile's domestic legal system to hold Pinochet and other regime collaborators accountable for this dark chapter in the country's history. In addition to domestic effects within Chile itself, the chapter also looks at the broader legacy of the *Pinochet* case and evaluates whether it set a precedent for an international crimes exception to immunity *ratione materiae* moving forward.

I. BACKGROUND

The Coup. As with many dictators, General Augusto Pinochet entered the world stage through a coup d'état. On September 11, 1973, the democratically elected government of President Salvador Allende was violently overthrown by the Chilean military. The coup was led by General Pinochet as Commander-in-Chief. The world watched these events unfold on television, as British-made Hawker Hunter jets bombed the presidential palace, *La Moneda,* with President Allende still inside.

Following the fall of *La Moneda,* the armed forces, under the direction of a military junta with Pinochet at the helm, assumed total control of Chile. Initially, it was believed that President Allende had been murdered by military forces. However, a forensic investigation by Chilean experts in 2011 revealed that in fact Allende had committed suicide with an AK-47 rifle, which had been a gift from Fidel Castro.[5]

Notably, the coup that ousted democracy from Chile was instigated under the pretext of a fight against Communism. As Chile's first socialist president, Allende had ambitious plans to take Chile on the "road to socialism."[6] After taking office, he moved quickly by nationalizing copper

---

[4] Convention Against Torture and Other Cruel, Inhuman or Degrading Treatment or Punishment, Dec. 10, 1984, 1465 U.N.T.S. 85 [hereinafter Torture Convention].

[5] Alexei Barrionuevo & Pascale Bonnefoy, *Allende's Death was a Suicide, an Autopsy Concludes,* N.Y. TIMES (July 19, 2011), https://www.nytimes.com/2011/07/20/world/americas/20allende.html; Michael Guerrin, *The Story of the 'Last Photo' of Salvador Allende, the Chilean President who Killed Himself in the 1973 Coup,* LE MONDE (Sept. 11, 2023), https://www.lemonde.fr/en/history/article/2023/09/11/the-story-of-the-last-photo-of-salvador-allende-the-chilean-president-who-killed-himself-in-the-1973-coup_6132828_157.html.

[6] Jon Lee Anderson, *The Dictator,* NEW YORKER (Oct. 11, 1998), https://www.newyorker.com/magazine/1998/10/19/the-dictator-2.

mines and other industries, conducting land reform, and increasing government expenditure on social welfare programs.[7] These policies were divisive and ultimately alienated a significant portion of the population, the military, and the private sector.[8]

Many of Pinochet's most ardent supporters—those who called themselves "*Pinochetistas*"—argued that the military coup was necessary. According to Pinochet's eldest daughter Lucía Pinochet, the coup was needed to prevent Chile from turning into "another Cuba."[9] She believed that if the armed forces had not stepped in, a bloody civil war would have been inevitable.

Concerns about Allende were also felt beyond Chile, as his socialist experiment stirred up angst in Washington, D.C. Notoriously, from the moment that Allende was elected President of Chile in 1970, the Central Intelligence Agency (CIA) under U.S. President Richard Nixon waged a secret campaign of destabilization against his government. According to declassified U.S. government documents, Nixon's plan was to make Chile ungovernable under Allende, to provoke social chaos, and ultimately to bring about a military coup.[10] One method of doing so was via economic sabotage, as conveyed by Richard Helms, Director of the CIA at the time: "make the economy scream."[11] The Nixon administration also funneled money and arms to right-wing paramilitary groups and facilitated press disinformation in Chile throughout this period.

According to journalist John Dinges, the Nixon Administration wanted Allende to fail because "they were very afraid that the socialist experiment would be successful [in Chile]" and that this would have a ripple effect throughout Latin America.[12] While the United States did not directly participate in the coup, Washington ultimately did not oppose a military takeover.

Abuses Under the Pinochet Regime. The overthrow of Allende's government paved the way for a systematic campaign of repression and terror against various groups in Chile, a campaign that continued throughout Pinochet's seventeen-year-long dictatorship. On the day of the coup, the military rounded up thousands of people and herded them at gunpoint into the National Stadium in Santiago. Out of sight, these ordinary Chileans, who were suspected by the regime of being subversives, were detained, tortured, and murdered.[13]

---

7 *Id.*

8 *Id.*

9 *Id.*

10 *Id.*

11 Peter Kornbluh, *Extreme Option: Overthrow Allende*, NAT'L SEC. ARCHIVE (Sept. 15, 2020), https://nsarchive.gwu.edu/briefing-book/chile/2020-09-15/extreme-option-overthrow-allende.

12 Sarah Gilbert, *The Other 9/11*, SBS (Sept. 11, 2013), https://www.sbs.com.au/theother911/.

13 Anderson, *supra* note 6.

This reign of terror was mostly carried out by agents of the National Directorate of Intelligence (DINA), which struck out against anyone suspected of being an enemy of the new Chile. All evidence of abuse was concealed as bodies were dumped in mine shafts and unmarked graves, and even dropped from helicopters into the Pacific Ocean.[14] According to various official commissions, the total number of victims of the dictatorship was 40,175 people, with over 1000 still missing today.[15] The Valech Commission, which heard testimony from over 30,000 people, established that firing squads, systematic torture, deprivation of liberty, and human rights violations had been a "state policy" during the Pinochet years.[16]

Enforced Disappearance. The Pinochet government was particularly known for the practice of enforced disappearance. As suggested by journalist Jon Lee Anderson, Pinochet can probably be credited with adding los desaparecidos—"the disappeared"—to the modern lexicon.[17] Enforced disappearance involves the kidnapping of individuals by undercover agents from their homes or the street and then their killing, often after prolonged incommunicado detention and torture.[18] Victims' bodies are then disposed of in clandestine locations, and family members are never notified of death or the whereabouts of the victim. When practiced in a systematic manner or on a massive scale, forced disappearance is a crime against humanity.[19]

genocide?

Unfortunately, the Chilean courts obstructed attempts to investigate these disappearances at the time. According to Roberto Garretón, a lawyer who led judicial investigations by the Vicaría de la Solidaridad during the Pinochet dictatorship, when presented with indisputable evidence of a disappearance, the courts would ultimately deny the existence of the person: "that man was never born."[20] Garretón lamented that the courts denied everything and therefore, "we were never able to separate them [the courts] from the official lie they were endorsing, that they had made their own."[21]

Operation Condor. In addition, the Pinochet government spearheaded a cross-border conspiracy known as "Operation Condor."

---

14 *Id.*

15 Ivan Alvarado & Natalia A. Ramos Miranda, *Chile Political Prisoners Reclaim Torture Sites to Preserve Coup Memory*, REUTERS (Sept. 9, 2023), https://www.reuters.com/world/americas/chile-political-prisoners-reclaim-torture-sites-preserve-coup-memory-2023-09-09/.

16 *Id.*

17 Anderson, *supra* note 6.

18 U.N. Working Grp. on Enforced or Involuntary Disappearances, *About Enforced Disappearance*, OFF. HIGH COMM'R FOR HUM. RTS., https://www.ohchr.org/en/special-procedures/wg-disappearances/about-enforced-disappearance (last visited Oct. 4, 2024).

19 International Convention for the Protection of All Persons from Enforced Disappearance art. 26, Dec. 20, 2006, 2716 U.N.T.S. 3 (entered into force Dec. 23, 2010).

20 See the testimony of Roberto Garretón in Patricio Guzmán's documentary *The Pinochet Case* (2002) at 11.34 minutes. THE PINOCHET CASE (Icarus Films 2002).

21 *Id.*

This was a collaborative agreement between the governments of Argentina, Bolivia, Brazil, Chile, Paraguay, and Uruguay that provided for the sharing of information, trading of prisoners, and orchestration of assassinations.[22] This covert reign of terror targeted suspected communists, leftist intellectuals, and supposed subversive individuals.[23] For example, one high-profile assassination was that of Allende's former Foreign Secretary Orlando Letelier and his American secretary Ronnie Moffitt, who were blown up by a car bomb in Washington, D.C., in 1976.[24] The former director of DINA, General Manuel Contreras Sepúlveda, was eventually put on trial in Chile and sentenced to seven years in prison for the Washington assassination. He declared before the Supreme Court of Chile that he was carrying out the orders of Pinochet and "informed him daily" about DINA's activities.[25]

Measures for Self-Protection. While Chile did eventually transition from dictatorship to democracy beginning in 1990, this process did not provide for justice for victims of the Pinochet regime. In part, this was because Pinochet had implemented measures of self-protection before conceding power, including a 1978 Amnesty Law and his designation as a "senator for life" in the Chilean Senate,[26] which provided Pinochet and several other military officials with immunity from domestic prosecution. Thus, the road towards accountability looked long and had to begin outside of Chile.

Investigations in Spain. The legal background of the *Pinochet* case began in Spain, where significant investigations were conducted by various groups into abuses committed during the Pinochet era. In 1996, an association of Spanish prosecutors, acting in their private capacities, filed criminal charges of genocide and terrorism against former military leaders in both Argentina and Chile.[27]

---

[22] INT'L COMM'N OF JURISTS, CRIMES AGAINST HUMANITY—PINOCHET FACES JUSTICE 17 (1999), https://www.icj.org/wp-content/uploads/1999/07/Chile-Pinochet-fact-finding-mission-report-1999-eng.pdf.

[23] Karen DeYoung et al., *This was Not an Accident. This was a Bomb.*, WASH. POST (Sept. 20, 2016), https://www.washingtonpost.com/sf/national/2016/09/20/this-was-not-an-accident-this-was-a-bomb/.

[24] This led to, among other things, a famous U.S. case on the territorial tort exception to state immunity: *Letelier v. Chile,* 488 F. Supp. 665 (D.D.C. 1980).

[25] INT'L COMM'N OF JURISTS, *supra* note 22, at 17.

[26] Ministerio Del Interior, *Decreto Ley 2191*, Biblioteca del Congreso Nacional de Chile (Apr. 19, 1978), https://www.bcn.cl/leychile/navegar?idNorma=6849.

[27] Richard J. Wilson, *Prosecuting Pinochet: International Crimes in Spanish Domestic Law,* 21 HUM. RTS. Q. 927, 933–34 (1999).

Pinochet Meeting with Henry Kissinger, U.S. Secretary of State, in 1976

Subsequently, two Spanish magistrates, Baltasar Garzón and Manuel García-Castellón, took up the Argentine and Chilean cases, respectively, and conducted meticulous investigations over the course of two years.[28] Both magistrates heard volumes of witness testimony and documentary evidence presented in separate courtrooms of the *Audiencia Nacional*, a special court sitting in Madrid with jurisdiction over international crimes.

At the time of investigation, Spanish law recognized universal jurisdiction[29] for criminal offences and codified international crimes—including genocide, torture, and terrorism—in its domestic statutes.[30] As originally filed, the complaints for both Argentina and Chile named only Spanish citizens as victims. They therefore seem to have been grounded in the criminal jurisdictional principle of passive personality, which is based on the nationality of the victim.[31] Accordingly, Spanish jurisdiction

[28] *Id.* at 932.

[29] Universal jurisdiction in this context means "the competence of a State to prosecute alleged offenders and to punish them if convicted, irrespective of the place of commission of the crime and regardless of any link of active or passive nationality, or other grounds of jurisdiction recognized by international law." Institut de Droit International, Resolution on Universal Criminal Jurisdiction with Regard to the Crime of Genocide, Crimes Against Humanity and War Crimes (2005), https://www.idi-iil.org/en/publications/iii-la-competence-universelle-en-matiere-penale-a-legard-du-crime-de-genocide-des-crimes-contre-lhumanite-et-des-crimes-de-guerre/.

[30] Judicial Power Organization Act, 1985 (No. 6/1985, art. 23.4) (Spain).

[31] Wilson, *supra* note 27, at 951.

Passive personality

was founded on the idea that states have a duty to protect their citizens wherever they may be.

International Warrants and Arrest. In what turned out to be an accurate premonition, General Pinochet told *The New Yorker* in early October 1998 that "history teaches you that dictators never end up well."[32] Only a few weeks later, on October 16, 1998, the eighty-two-year-old former dictator was arrested at London Bridge hospital while recovering from back surgery.[33]

The arrest was carried out on the basis of two international arrest warrants issued by Judge Garzón, who sought Pinochet's extradition to Spain to face charges of genocide, terrorism, and torture. It was of considerable assistance to Garzón that both Spain and the United Kingdom had ratified the 1957 European Convention on Extradition. The Convention provides for judicial cooperation with respect to the transfer of accused persons between European countries.[34]

Following the arrest, those who supported Pinochet immediately claimed that he was immune from arrest and prosecution. As reported in the *Sunday Mirror*, Chile's Ambassador to London at the time, Mario Artaza, said that he would be seeking Pinochet's release: "[W]hat we must do is make clear that Mr. Pinochet is a senator, who travels with a diplomatic passport."[35] Yet in the months following the arrest, three more states—Switzerland, Belgium, and France—filed requests for Pinochet's extradition.[36] At the very least, these further extradition requests confirmed that a strong case existed against Pinochet and that a movement for accountability was growing.

Pinochet was placed under provisional house arrest at a luxury estate in Wentworth, Surrey, where a neighbor complained, "it's a bit like having Adolf Hitler move in next door."[37] And so began a seventeen-month legal battle to hold the former dictator accountable for the crimes of his regime.

---

32 Anderson, *supra* note 6.

33 David Connett, John Hooper & Peter Beaumont, *Pinochet Arrested in London*, GUARDIAN (Oct. 17, 1998), https://www.theguardian.com/world/1998/oct/18/pinochet.chile.

34 European Convention on Extradition art. 1, Dec. 13, 1957, 359 U.N.T.S. 273.

35 Tim Luckett, *Death Charges Dictator Held in London Clinic*, SUNDAY MIRROR, Oct. 18, 1998, at 2.

36 These requests were generally made in connection with the disappearance of these countries' nationals by Chilean forces. For example, the Swiss request was made pursuant to the kidnapping and presumed death of Alexei Jaccard, a Swiss-Chilean citizen in 1977. Michael Byers, *The Law and Politics of the Pinochet Case*, 10 DUKE J. COMPAR. & INT'L L. 415, 423 (2000).

37 *Pinochet Retreats to Luxury Estate*, BBC NEWS (Dec. 2, 1998, 02:30 GMT), https://news.bbc.co.uk/2/hi/225567.stm.

Pinochet in Uniform, 1986

Politics of the Arrest. In addition to questions around immunity, Pinochet's arrest was also a subject of considerable political sensitivity. The arrest raised an important political question about the appropriateness of interfering in the domestic affairs of states undergoing delicate transitions from authoritarianism to democracy. This was a primary concern of Chilean Ambassador Mario Artaza, who publicly proclaimed, "we are not here to protect the dictator of yesterday, we are here to protect and defend our transition to democracy."[38]

Pinochet's arrest was also complex as it forced Chile as a nation to re-examine a convulsive past that its leaders may have preferred to put to rest. Transitions from authoritarianism to democracy are challenging for most nations, but it was particularly challenging in Chile where "historical memory is contentious, tarnished, and unstable in its resolution."[39]

The arrest also put Britain in a difficult diplomatic position. On the one hand, Chile had been a long-time friend, an active trading partner, and a valued ally of Britain during the 1982 Falklands War. On the other hand, any attempt by Britain to rid itself of the Pinochet proceedings would have run counter to the commitment of Prime Minister Tony Blair's government to an "ethical" foreign policy.[40] This diplomatic sensitivity may explain why the British Home Secretary Jack Straw was

---

[38] Warren Hoge, *Pinochet's Case Moves to Realm of Blair's Aides*, N.Y. TIMES (Nov. 27, 1998), https://www.nytimes.com/1998/11/27/world/pinochet-s-case-moves-to-realm-of-blair-s-aides.html.

[39] Anderson, *supra* note 6.

[40] Hoge, *supra* note 38.

careful to insist that the Pinochet matter was ultimately one for the courts, and not for politicians.[41]

II. U.K. PROCEEDINGS

In response to his arrest, Pinochet hired some of London's leading criminal defense lawyers. They immediately filed a petition for a writ of habeas corpus before the High Court and sought leave for judicial review, alleging that Home Secretary Jack Straw had acted wrongfully by not ordering Pinochet's release.[42] The crux of their argument was that, as the Chilean head of state during the period in which most of the alleged crimes were committed, Pinochet was immune from the jurisdiction of the British courts under the 1978 State Immunity Act.[43]

High Court of England and Wales. On October 28, 1998, the *Pinochet* case was heard for the first time by a panel of three judges headed by Lord Chief Justice Bingham in the High Court. Lord Bingham held that the first arrest warrant was defective, as the crimes for which extradition had been requested by Spain—the murder of Spanish citizens in Chile—did not qualify as extradition crimes under the 1989 U.K. Extradition Act.[44]

By contrast, the second arrest warrant focused on alleged crimes of torture. This was important, as torture was an extraterritorial offence under English law following the adoption of section 134 of the 1988 Criminal Justice Act. Nevertheless, the High Court held that Pinochet was immune from the United Kingdom's jurisdiction, as the alleged crimes were official acts performed in the exercise of Pinochet's functions as head of state.[45] The legal basis of this immunity was section 20 of the 1978 State Immunity Act, which grants to heads of state the same privileges and immunities, subject to "any necessary modification," as those conferred on the heads of diplomatic missions under the 1961 Vienna Convention on Diplomatic Relations.[46]

Throughout the litigation, the Crown Prosecution Services submitted two notable arguments on behalf of Spain that the High Court straightforwardly rejected. The first was that the alleged crimes were of such a serious nature that they could not amount to "official acts" performed by Pinochet in the exercise of his functions as a head of state.[47] This argument was dismissed by Justice Collins, who noted that "history

---

[41] Rory Carroll, Ian Black & John Hopper, *Pinochet Decision for Straw*, GUARDIAN (Oct. 19, 1998, 1:10 PM EDT), https://www.theguardian.com/politics/1998/oct/19/immigrationpolicy.

[42] Byers, *supra* note 36, at 423.

[43] State Immunity Act 1978, ch. 33, *reprinted in* 17 I.L.M. 1123 (1978).

[44] Extradition Act 1989, ch. 33 (U.K.); *In re* Pinochet Ugarte (High Ct. of Justice, Q.B. Div., 1998), 38 I.L.M. 68, ¶ 34 (1999).

[45] *In re Pinochet*, 38 I.L.M. ¶ 34.

[46] Vienna Convention on Diplomatic Relations, Apr. 18, 1961, 500 U.N.T.S. 95.

[47] *In re Pinochet*, 38 I.L.M. ¶ 80.

shows us that it has indeed on occasions been state policy to exterminate or to oppress particular groups," and that he could accordingly see "no justification for reading any limitation based on the nature of the crimes committed into the immunity which exists."[48]

Second, the Court rejected the argument submitted by Alun Jones KC that there can be no immunity for a former head of state who is accused of committing crimes against humanity. Jones argued that these crimes, which include genocide, torture, the taking of hostages, and "other crimes of a similarly offensive character," are "deeply repugnant to any notion of morality."[49] In assessing this argument, the Court took into account that the Nuremburg Charter (1945) and the Statutes of the International Tribunals for the former Yugoslavia (1993) and Rwanda (1994) all explicitly exclude claims of immunity by a former head of state as a method of averting criminal responsibility.[50] But the Court distinguished these instruments from the case at hand on the ground that they addressed prosecutions before international tribunals established by international agreement.[51]

Ultimately, while Pinochet was found to be immune, the High Court did not immediately quash the second arrest warrant as the Court granted leave to appeal to the House of Lords on the point of immunity.

***House of Lords:* Pinochet (No. 1).** As expected, the *Pinochet* case was appealed to the House of Lords, the court of final appeal in the United Kingdom at the time. The Law Lords rendered their judgment—known as *Pinochet (No. 1)*—on November 25, 1998, which also happened to be Pinochet's eighty-third birthday. Reversing the lower court's ruling, the Lords held by a three to two majority that Pinochet was not immune, as the alleged acts of torture and hostage-taking were not "official" acts performed in the exercise of his functions as head of state within the meaning of the statute.

Of the majority, Lord Nicholls (with whom Lord Hoffmann concurred) reasoned that Pinochet's alleged acts could not be regarded by international law as a function of a head of state. This was on the ground that international law has "made plain that certain types of conduct, including torture and hostage-taking, are not acceptable conduct on the part of anyone" and that "the contrary conclusion would make a mockery of international law."[52]

---

48 *Id.*

49 *Id.* ¶ 63.

50 Charter of the International Military Tribunal art. 7, Aug. 8, 1945, 82 U.N.T.S. 279; Updated Statute of the International Criminal Tribunal for the former Yugoslavia art. 7, Sept. 2009, https://www.icty.org/x/file/Legal%20Library/Statute/statute_sept09_en.pdf; S.C. Res. 827, ¶ 7, U.N. Doc. S/RES/827 (May 25, 1993); Statute of the International Criminal Tribunal for Rwanda art. 6, Nov. 8, 1994, 33 I.L.M. 1598, 1602 (1994).

51 *In re Pinochet*, 38 I.L.M. ¶ 68.

52 R v. Bow St. Metro. Stipendiary Magistrate, *ex parte* Pinochet Ugarte (No. 1) (2000) 1 AC 61, 109 (HL).

Lord Steyn took a slightly different approach, drawing attention to the evolution of international law. He said, "the development of international law since the Second World War justifies the conclusion that by the time of the 1973 coup d'état, and certainly ever since, international law condemned genocide, torture, hostage taking and crimes against humanity . . . as international crimes deserving of punishment."[53] Given this evolution, it was impossible for Lord Steyn to "maintain that the commission of such high crimes may amount to acts performed in the exercise of the functions of a Head of State."[54]

In dissent, Lord Lloyd held that Pinochet was immune as a former head of state both under customary international law and under the 1978 State Immunity Act. He pointed out that under customary international law, immunity is not accorded for the benefit of the former head of state himself, but rather for the state of which he was once head.[55] Therefore, any international law obligations are owed to that state and not to the individual. Lord Lloyd pointed out that, rather than carrying out the alleged acts "with his own hands," Pinochet was accused of organizing the "commission of such crimes, including the elimination of his political opponents, as head of the Chilean government."[56] In essence, he gave the orders. This supported Lord Lloyd's conclusion that Pinochet's alleged crimes were sovereign acts and thus covered by immunity.

In response to the argument that some crimes are so horrific that an exception must be made to immunity under customary international law, Lord Lloyd suggested that it is difficult to know "where to draw the line."[57] In his mind, it would be "unjustifiable in theory, and unworkable in practice, to impose any restriction on head of state immunity by reference to the number or gravity of the alleged crimes."[58] Furthermore, the special international tribunals set up to adjudicate crimes committed in the former Yugoslavia and Rwanda supported his conclusion that when crimes against humanity are committed by heads of state or other responsible government officials, they "cannot be tried in the ordinary courts of other states."[59]

Also in dissent, Lord Slynn held that Pinochet benefited from immunity both under the 1978 State Immunity Act and customary international law. Notably, Lord Slynn conceded the possibility that immunity *ratione materiae* retained by a former head of state after ceasing service could be affected by the emerging notion of individual crimes under international law. However, he found that there was no evidence of "any state practice or general consensus let alone a widely

53 *Id.* at 115.

54 *Id.*

55 *Id.* at 90.

56 *Id.* at 95.

57 *Id.*

58 *Id.* at 96.

59 *Id.* at 98.

supported convention that all crimes against international law should be justiciable in national courts on the basis of the universality of jurisdiction."[60] Therefore, he concluded that there is "no universal rule that all crimes are outside immunity *ratione materiae*."[61]

Finally, Lord Slynn also considered whether the United Kingdom and Chile had agreed to override immunity enjoyed by a former head of state with regard to the crime of torture via ratification of the 1984 U.N. Torture Convention.[62] This would depend on whether a former head of state was covered by the words "a public official or other person acting in an official capacity" under Article 1. Ultimately, he found that the reference to public officials in the Convention did not cover former heads of state. Therefore, according to Lord Slynn, if states did wish to exclude immunity of former heads of state in respect of specific crimes, they must do so in "clear terms."[63]

Following the Law Lords' judgment in *Pinochet (No. 1)*, the case then passed to Home Secretary Jack Straw who had the option to either quash or grant authority to proceed with the extradition process as stipulated by sections 7 and 12 of the 1989 Extradition Act. On December 9, 1999—one day before the fiftieth anniversary of the Universal Declaration of Human Rights[64]—Straw granted authority to proceed with the extradition.

Pinochet (No. 2). The Pinochet saga then took an unexpected turn as Pinochet's counsel made a significant discovery. They found that Lord Hoffmann, who sat on the *Pinochet (No. 1)* case, also served as Director of Amnesty International Charity Limited, a branch of Amnesty International. Crucially, Amnesty International, along with a number of other human rights organizations, had been granted leave to intervene in the *Pinochet (No. 1)* appeal. At this point, they argued, Lord Hoffmann should have disclosed his connections with Amnesty International. His failure to do so, they argued, undermined confidence in the House of Lords' decision.[65]

Pinochet's legal team petitioned for the House of Lords to set aside its previous decision, on the ground that the link between Lord Hoffmann and Amnesty International gave the appearance of bias. In an unprecedented ruling on January 15, 1999, the House of Lords set aside its previous decision in *Pinochet (No. 1)* and ordered a rehearing.[66] This was done on the ground that, by virtue of his relationship with Amnesty

---

60 *Id.* at 79.

61 *Id.* at 80.

62 Torture Convention, *supra* note 4.

63 R v. Bow St. Metro. Stipendiary Magistrate, *ex parte* Pinochet Ugarte (No. 1) (2000) 1 AC 61, 84 (HL).

64 G.A. Res. 217 (III) A, U.N. Doc. A/RES/217(III) (Dec. 10, 1948).

65 R v. Bow St. Metro. Stipendiary Magistrate, *ex parte* Pinochet Ugarte (No. 2) (2000) 1 AC 119 (HL).

66 *Id.*

International, Lord Hoffmann was automatically disqualified from sitting on the hearing of the appeal. As stated by Lord Browne-Wilkinson, "if the absolute impartiality of the judiciary is to be maintained, there must be a rule which automatically disqualifies a judge who is involved, whether personally or as a director of a company, in promoting the same causes in the same organization as is a party to the suit."[67] While there had been no suggestion that Lord Hoffmann had actually been biased, this was beside the point, as "it is of fundamental importance that justice should not only be done, but should manifestly and undoubtedly be seen to be done."[68]

Friendship and Margaret Thatcher. During these tumultuous months for Pinochet, he had one particularly vocal supporter: former U.K. Prime Minister Margaret Thatcher. While they never met while in power, Thatcher was impressed by the success of Chile's neoliberal economic program under Pinochet and his approach to dealing with communism in Latin America.[69] Furthermore, it seems that Thatcher felt somewhat indebted as Chile had provided significant assistance to Thatcher's government during the 1982 Falklands War.[70]

According to *The New Yorker*, the relationship between the pair became "downright cozy,"[71] so much so that Pinochet would send Thatcher flowers and chocolate and the pair would meet for tea on his annual trips to London.[72] Following Pinochet's arrest, Thatcher was outspoken in her support of the former dictator, writing in a letter to *The Times* that "it is not for Spain, Britain or any other country to interfere in what is an internal matter for Chile."[73] While Pinochet was under house arrest in Surrey, Thatcher sent him a bottle of single malt whisky with an accompanying note that read, "scotch is one British institution that will never let you down."[74]

Pinochet (No. 3). A seven-judge panel was constituted to rehear the *Pinochet* case, so as to lend greater authority to the new decision in this highly unusual situation. The Law Lords handed down their new judgment—*Pinochet (No. 3)*—on March 24, 1999, the same day NATO

---

67 *Id.* at 135.

68 *Id.*

69 Mat Youkee, *Thatcher Sent Pinochet Finest Scotch during Former Dictator's UK House Arrest*, GUARDIAN (Oct. 4, 2019, 15:16 EST), https://www.theguardian.com/world/2019/oct/04/margaret-thatcher-pinochet-chile-scotch-malt-whisky.

70 Jon Lee Anderson, *Neruda, Pinochet, and the Iron Lady*, NEW YORKER (Apr. 9, 2013), https://www.newyorker.com/news/daily-comment/neruda-pinochet-and-the-iron-lady; Associated Press Archive, *Various: Reaction to Pinochet Decision*, YOUTUBE (Mar. 2, 2000), https://youtu.be/gIL2sfOkAe0?si=IPITA0_GWy7Wyn0v.

71 Anderson, *supra* note 70.

72 Anderson, *supra* note 6.

73 *Thatcher Pleads 'Free Pinochet,'* ABERDEEN PRESS & J., Oct. 22, 1998, at 1.

74 Youkee, *supra* note 69.

aircraft began dropping bombs on the Federal Republic of Yugoslavia "to halt the humanitarian catastrophe that was then unfolding in Kosovo."[75]

The world awaited the decision with anticipation, especially in Chile. As reported in the *Irish Independent*, the city of Santiago came to a standstill to hear the Law Lords' ruling. Football matches were canceled and companies gave their workers an extended lunch break to watch the decision announced on television.[76]

By a majority of six to one, it was held that a former head of state was not immune for acts of torture or conspiracy to torture committed after December 8, 1988, the date when the United Kingdom ratified the 1984 U.N. Convention against Torture. This judgment was quite different from *Pinochet (No. 1)* in its treatment of two critical issues: the qualification of extradition crimes, and the role attributed to the Torture Convention for the purpose of denying immunity.

As noted above, the power to extradite Pinochet to Spain for an "extradition crime" was contained in the 1989 Extradition Act. An important requirement under the Act was that the conduct complained of must have constituted a crime under both Spanish and U.K. law at the time—the double criminality rule. As a result, two dates played an important role in the judgment—September 28 and December 8, 1988—being the dates when the Convention against Torture was incorporated into English law and was ratified. As a result, criminal charges for offenses committed before these critical dates were excluded, thereby radically reducing the number of charges upon which Pinochet's extradition could be sought.

On the central issue of immunity, instead of basing their decision on customary international law, the majority relied primarily on the Torture Convention and the Criminal Justice Act.[77] Of the majority, Lord Browne-Wilkinson's approach was that the idea of continued immunity for a former head of state was inherently inconsistent with the provisions of the Torture Convention. In his view, the Torture Convention provided worldwide jurisdiction for the crime of torture and further required all state parties to ban and outlaw torture under Article 2. Accordingly, he posited, "how can it be for international law purposes an official function to do something which international law itself prohibits and criminalises?"[78]

As immunity for ex-heads of state is not explicitly excluded in the Convention, his reasoning seemed to depend on an implied waiver in the Convention. His opinion appealed to pragmatism, suggesting that the

---

75 *Kosovo Air Campaign (March–June 1999)*, NATO (updated Oct. 21, 2024, 15:44), https://www.nato.int/cps/en/natohq/topics_49602.htm.

76 *Pinochet Ruling Casts Doubt on Extradition*, IRISH INDEP., Mar. 25, 1999, at 28.

77 Criminal Justice Act, 1988, ch. 33, § 134, 22 Halsbury's Statutes 357 (4th ed. 2003 reissue) (U.K.).

78 R v. Bow St. Metro. Stipendiary Magistrate, *ex parte* Pinochet Ugarte (No. 3) (2000) 1 AC 147, 205 (HL).

implementation of a universal torture regime through the Torture Convention that also upheld immunity *ratione materiae* would produce "bizarre results" and "render abortive" the notion of universal jurisdiction over torture committed by state officials.[79]

Three of the Law Lords—Lord Hope, Lord Millett, and Lord Phillips—focused their analysis on the fact that state torture had been recognized as an international crime that could not viably coexist with immunity *ratione materiae*. This conflict was summarized by Lord Millett, who stated, "international law cannot be supposed to have established a crime having the character of a *jus cogens*[80] and at the same time to have provided an immunity which is coextensive with the obligation it seeks to impose."[81] In other words, the official or governmental nature of the act of torture is an essential ingredient of the offense under the Convention. This official or governmental quality cannot also form the basis of a claim of immunity *ratione materiae*, otherwise the offense would be self-defeating. Therefore, the ratification of the Torture Convention by Chile, Spain, and the United Kingdom was viewed as an affirmation that state torture is an international crime of universal jurisdiction that should be prevented and punished accordingly.

In a solo dissent, Lord Goff discussed both the issue of international crimes and implied waiver of immunity. In the first place, he suggested that former heads of state can be held internationally accountable for certain crimes, including torture, referring to the Nuremburg and Tokyo Charters, the Statute of the International Tribunal for the former Yugoslavia, and the 1996 International Law Commission Draft Code of Crimes.[82] However, he pointed out that these instruments are "all concerned with international responsibility before international tribunals, and not with the exclusion of state immunity in criminal proceedings before national courts."[83] He then agreed with the conclusion of Lord Slynn in *Pinochet (No. 1)*, that "except in regard to crimes in particular situations before international tribunals these measures did not in general deal with the question whether otherwise existing immunities were taken away."[84] Following from this conclusion, he

---

[79] *Id.*

[80] These are peremptory norms of general international law that "reflect and protect fundamental values of the international community. They are universally applicable and are hierarchically superior to other rules of international law." Int'l Law Comm'n, Draft Conclusions on Identification and Legal Consequences of Peremptory Norms of General International Law (*Jus Cogens*), Conclusion 2, *in* Rep. of the Int'l Law Comm'n, 73d Sess., Apr. 18–June 3, July 4–Aug 5, 2022, U.N. Doc. A/77/10 (2022), ¶ 43, at 11; GAOR, 77th Sess., Supp. No. 10 (2022).

[81] *Pinochet (No. 3)*, at 278.

[82] Int'l Law Comm'n, Draft Code of Crimes against the Peace and Security of Mankind, July 5, 2006, *in* 2 YEARBOOK OF THE INTERNATIONAL LAW COMMISSION 1996, Part 2, U.N. Doc. A/CN.4/SER.A/1996/Add.1 (Part 2), ¶ 50 (2008).

[83] *Pinochet (No. 3)*, at 211.

[84] *Id.* at 211–12.

suggested that if former head of state immunity in respect of torture was to be excluded at all, this could only have occurred via the Torture Convention.

Lord Goff argued that a state's waiver of its immunity by treaty must always be express.[85] In support, he pointed to the 116 state parties to the Convention as reinforcing the "strong impression" that no state would have silently agreed to the exclusion of state immunity *ratione materiae* via ratification.[86] He then cautioned, "how extraordinary it would be, and indeed what a trap would be created for the unwary, if state immunity could be waived in a treaty sub silentio."[87] He reasoned that "common sense" supported the conclusion that this could not be done.[88]

Ultimately, despite the strong dissent, the majority of the Law Lords held that Pinochet was not immune for the alleged acts of torture or conspiracy to torture committed after December 8, 1988.

Reactions to the Judgment. The global reaction to the outcome of *Pinochet (No. 3)* was mixed. Some heralded the decision as a milestone in international law. Following the verdict, thousands of human rights activists and families of victims who disappeared during the Pinochet era marched through the Chilean capital with banners hailing the verdict as a "landmark victory in defense of humanity."[89] The reaction was similarly positive in Geneva, where the U.N. High Commissioner for Human Rights Mary Robinson welcomed the ruling as a "vigorous endorsement of the view that torture is an international crime subject to universal jurisdiction. National courts can try torturers even when the crime has been committed elsewhere."[90] The International Commission of Jurists went even further, suggesting that "the decision will have a dissuasive effect on the perpetrators of horrendous crimes such as genocide, crimes against humanity and war crimes."[91]

On the other hand, several leading academics in international law were not as optimistic. In the United Kingdom, Hazel Fox suggested that a close reading of the *Pinochet (No. 3)* judgment tended to elicit a "sense of disquiet for an international lawyer."[92] In particular, they pointed out fundamental issues with the majority's attempt to occupy a moral high ground; deploy matters of international law that were not accepted or

---

85 *Id.* at 223.

86 *Id.* at 222.

87 *Id.* at 223.

88 *Id.*

89 *Pinochet Ruling Casts Doubt on Extradition*, *supra* note 76.

90 Off. U.N. High Comm'r for Hum. Rts., Press Release HR/99/24, Law Lords' Decision in Pinochet is Another Significant Step in Struggle against Impunity (Mar. 24, 1999).

91 INT'L COMM'N OF JURISTS, *supra* note 22, at 48.

92 Hazel Fox, *The Pinochet Case No. 3*, *in Current Developments: Public International Law* (Colin Warbrick & Dominic McGoldrick eds.), 48 INT'L & COMP. L.Q. 687, 687 (1999).

recognized by the majority of states; and intervene in a dispute that was inherently political in nature.[93]

Final Magistrate Decision. Following the Law Lords' decision in *Pinochet (No. 3)* and subsequent grant of authority to proceed with extradition by Home Secretary Jack Straw, the final legal hurdle to extradition was a hearing that took place in Bow Street Magistrates' Court. The judge considered charges from *Pinochet (No. 3),* as well as a number of new charges subsequently filed by Judge Garzón. Garzón's allegations included accounts of brutal beatings, burnings, partial asphyxiation, and fatal electronic shock treatment.[94] According to Alun Jones KC, who represented the Spanish authorities, these were "some of the most serious allegations of crime ever to come before English criminal courts."[95]

On October 8, 1999, the magistrate ruled that Pinochet could be extradited to Spain and committed him on thirty-four charges of torture and one charge of conspiracy to commit torture.[96] Pinochet's extradition to Spain to stand trial appeared to be imminent.

However, in response to the magistrates' decision, the Chilean government requested that Jack Straw consider releasing Pinochet on medical grounds.[97] Straw acceded to this request and arranged a medical examination of Pinochet by four prominent British doctors, which ultimately established that he was unfit to stand trial.[98] While the examination was not released publicly for reasons of confidentiality, it was eventually leaked to the media.[99] It revealed that Pinochet was in fact quite ill. He was suffering extensive brain damage, and his memory had been severely affected; therefore, the doctors concluded, he would be incapable of following the process of a trial so as to instruct his lawyers.[100]

On the basis of the medical examination results, Straw called off Pinochet's extradition to Spain and allowed the former dictator to return to Chile on March 2, 2000.[101] While Pinochet was taken out of the United Kingdom in a wheelchair, upon arriving in Santiago he stood from his

---

[93] *See id.* at 687–702.

[94] Jamie Wilson, *Pinochet Accused of 35 Torture Charges at Hearing*, GUARDIAN (Sept. 27, 1999), https://www.theguardian.com/world/1999/sep/28/pinochet.chile.

[95] *Id.*

[96] *The Extradition of General Pinochet*, HUM. RTS. WATCH (Oct. 14, 1999), https://www.hrw.org/news/1999/10/14/extradition-general-augusto-pinochet.

[97] Jonathan Franklin, *Chile Makes Pinochet Plea to Straw*, GUARDIAN (Oct. 15, 1999), https://www.theguardian.com/world/1999/oct/16/pinochet.chile.

[98] Byers, *supra* note 36, at 437.

[99] *Id.* at 438.

[100] *Id.*

[101] Nicholas Watts, *Pinochet to be Set Free*, GUARDIAN (Jan. 12, 2000), https://www.theguardian.com/world/2000/jan/12/pinochet.chile3; Associated Press Archive, *supra* note 70.

chair and triumphantly walked, slowly but steadily, across the tarmac to the music of a military brass band.[102]

III. RETURN TO CHILE

Upon Pinochet's return to Chile, significant efforts began to prosecute the former dictator under the domestic legal system, driven by Chilean lawyers.[103] Dozens of cases were lodged against him in Chilean courts, with dozens more following in the weeks after his return.[104] Previously, Chile's court system had been paralyzed by a Pinochet-era amnesty law that prevented the prosecution of those responsible for abuses committed from 1973 to 1978.[105] It was not until Pinochet's arrest in London and eventual return to Chile that the judiciary stopped using this amnesty law to dismiss cases, and special judges were appointed to investigate these crimes.[106] Two days after Pinochet's return, the Chilean Judge Juan Guzmán requested the Court of Appeals of Santiago to lift Pinochet's immunity as a senator for life in order to indict him.[107] This request was granted and later upheld by the Supreme Court of Chile, which stripped Pinochet of his parliamentary immunity in August 2000.[108]

Following the removal of immunity, on December 1, 2000, Judge Guzmán ordered Pinochet to be held under house arrest after charging him as the mastermind of acts in the so-called "Caravan of Death," a Chilean Army death squad that carried out the kidnapping and forced disappearance of at least seventy political prisoners shortly after Pinochet came to power.[109] At this point in time, Pinochet faced 177 criminal complaints, all stemming from alleged human rights violations committed during his time in power.[110] However, shortly after this order,

---

[102] Alex Bellos & Jonathan Franklin, *Pinochet Receives a Hero's Welcome on his Return*, GUARDIAN (Mar. 3, 2000), https://www.theguardian.com/world/2000/mar/04/pinochet.chile1.

[103] Anthony Faiola, *Chile Reacts Emotionally to Pinochet Ruling*, WASH. POST (Jan. 12, 2000), https://www.washingtonpost.com/archive/politics/2000/01/12/chile-reacts-emotionally-to-pinochet-ruling/eb317bcf-8d47-402f-8bc1-a08b793a2ad4; Associated Press Archive, *supra* note 70.

[104] Rebecca Evans, *Pinochet in London: Pinochet in Chile: International and Domestic Politics in Human Rights Policy*, 28 HUM. RTS. Q. 235 (2006).

[105] Pascale Bonnefoy, *Decades after Dictatorship, Chile Mounts Search for Hundreds Who Vanished*, N.Y. TIMES (Aug. 30, 2023), https://www.nytimes.com/2023/08/30/world/americas/chile-military-coup-disappeared-search.html.

[106] Stacie Jonas, *The Ripple Effect of the Pinochet Case*, 11 HUM. RTS. BRIEF 36, 37 (2004).

[107] Clifford Krauss, *Freed by Britain, Pinochet is Facing a Battle at Home*, N.Y. TIMES (Mar. 3, 2000), https://www.nytimes.com/2000/03/03/world/freed-by-britain-pinochet-is-facing-a-battle-at-home.html.

[108] *Chile Supreme Court Rejects Pinochet Immunity*, HUM. RTS. WATCH (Aug. 8, 2000), https://www.hrw.org/news/2000/08/08/chile-supreme-court-rejects-pinochet-immunity.

[109] *Pinochet Charged with Kidnapping*, BBC NEWS (Dec. 1, 2000), http://news.bbc.co.uk/2/hi/americas/1050374.stm.

[110] *Id.*

on December 11, 2000, Judge Guzmán's ruling was suspended by the Court of Appeals of Santiago on due process grounds.[111]

While the attempts to hold Pinochet legally accountable only gained momentum, this back-and-forth continued in the Chilean courts right up until Pinochet's death on December 10, 2006. Ultimately, Pinochet died without having been convicted of any of the crimes of which he was accused, with 300 criminal charges still pending against him in Chile.[112]

IV. LEGACY: A *PINOCHET* PRECEDENT?

Accountability Within Chile. In addition to the political and social impacts of the *Pinochet* case, questions remain as to its legacy for the evolution of international law as a whole. In the first place, the former dictator's arrest and extradition forced Chilean society into a reckoning with the darkest chapters of the country's history. As suggested by Chilean law professor José Zalaquett, while the *Pinochet* case initially polarized Chile by re-igniting old passions between supporters and opponents of the former dictator, it ultimately helped to usher in a new era of openness about the past.[113] Zalaquett suggested that this openness was facilitated by a new generation of judges, who were appointed following the return of democracy to Chile in 1990, and who actively pursued investigations into human rights abuses under the regime.[114] This national reckoning with the past is still underway within Chile and elsewhere, as demonstrated by Spain's recent decision to strip Pinochet of a Spanish military honor bestowed on him more than forty years ago.[115]

In terms of legal accountability, most Chileans believed that Pinochet should be held accountable. In 1999, opinion polls in Chile showed that over sixty percent of respondents believed that Pinochet should be tried for his alleged crimes.[116] Yet Pinochet never had his day in court, either in Spain or in Chile. Following Pinochet's death in 2006, Chilean courts have continued to prosecute and convict former military personnel accused of committing grave crimes under the military dictatorship from 1973 to 1990. For example, in March 2021, a Chilean court convicted thirty-one former agents for their role in the 1974 disappearances of moviemakers Carmen Bueno Cifuentes and Jorge

---

[111] Anthony Faiola, *Chilean Court Voids Pinochet Indictment, House Arrest*, WASH. POST (Dec. 12, 2000), https://www.washingtonpost.com/archive/politics/2000/12/12/chilean-court-voids-pinochet-indictment-house-arrest/03e7922b-ad17-41dc-992e-8ce9bb428460/.

[112] Charis McGowan, *Chile Marks 50 Years Since Pinochet's Brutal Coup*, AL JAZEERA (Sept. 11, 2023), https://www.aljazeera.com/news/2023/9/11/chile-marks-50-years-since-pinochets-brutal-coup.

[113] Cynthia Arnson, *Pinochet Case Brings Catharsis to Chile*, WILSON CENTER (Jan. 14, 2000), https://www.wilsoncenter.org/article/pinochet-case-brings-catharsis-to-chile.

[114] *Id.*

[115] *Spain Strips Deceased Former Chilean President Pinochet of a Spanish Military Honor*, ASSOCIATED PRESS (Sept. 12, 2023), https://apnews.com/article/spain-chile-pinochet-medal-withdrawn-ebd4c700ca7b3c6739129ef982bdeb52.

[116] Richard Lagos & Heraldo Muñoz, *The Pinochet Dilemma*, 114 FOREIGN POL'Y 26, 37 (1999).

Muller Silva through *Operación Colombo*, during which state security forces forcibly disappeared 119 political prisoners.[117] As of January 2023, the Supreme Court of Chile had issued some 640 rulings, sending hundreds to prison, and had seventeen judges exclusively dedicated to nearly 1500 cases relating to crimes under the dictatorship.[118]

While these prosecutions are a positive development, legal hurdles remain. For example, as part of Chile's transition to democracy, the National Commission on Political Prisoners and Torture was formed to collect the testimony of torture victims from September 2003 to June 2005.[119] Following this process, a fifty-year secrecy order was placed on all information collected by the Commission, prohibiting access to the archives by any person, authority, or magistrate, except for the right of the holders of the statements and documents to make them public.[120] This secrecy order is still in force today.

Impact on International Law. For many years, there has been lively debate as to whether the *Pinochet* case has set a precedent for an international crimes exception to immunity *ratione materiae*.

Accountability for Abuses. Many argued that the *Pinochet* case was transformational, including Human Rights Watch, which viewed Pinochet's London arrest as having strengthened a new international movement—spurred by the killings committed in Bosnia and Rwanda and facilitated by the end of the Cold War—to end impunity for the worst abuses.[121] Arguably, this position did ring true in the immediate aftermath of the case and likely contributed to the increasing momentum towards the establishment of the International Criminal Court in 2002. As suggested by Lord Lloyd of Berwick during a House of Lords debate on the International Criminal Court Bill on January 15, 2001, the "Pinochet case proves the need for a court such as the International Criminal Court."[122]

---

[117] *Chile: Events of 2020*, HUM. RTS. WATCH (2020), https://www.hrw.org/world-report/2021/country-chapters/chile.

[118] Pascale Bonnefoy, *Decades after Dictatorship, Chile Mounts Search for Hundreds Who Vanished*, N.Y. TIMES (Aug. 30, 2023), https://www.nytimes.com/2023/08/30/world/americas/chile-military-coup-disappeared-search.html.

[119] National Comm'n on Political Imprisonment and Torture, *Commission of Inquiry: Chile 03*, U.S. INST. PEACE (Dec. 10, 2009), https://www.usip.org/publications/2003/09/commission-inquiry-chile-03.

[120] Felipe Téllez Guzmán, *The Secrecy of the Archives of Chile's National Commission on Political Prisoners and Torture and its Problematic Relationship with the Right to Justice*, NUREMBERG HUM. RTS. CENTER (2023), https://www.menschenrechte.org/en/wp-content/uploads/sites/2/2023/02/Secrecy-of-the-archives-of-the-Valech-comission-1.pdf.

[121] *Pinochet: Justice and the General*, HUM. RTS. WATCH (Dec. 11, 2006), https://www.hrw.org/news/2006/12/11/pinochet-justice-and-general.

[122] 620 PARL. DEB., H.L. (5th ser.) (2001) col. 956 (U.K.).

A Tribute to the Disappeared Persons (*Los Desaparecidos*) Under the Dictatorship, on Display at the Museum of Memory and Human Rights in Santiago, Chile[123]

In addition, the judgment of the House of Lords in *Pinochet (No. 3)* was soon followed by international indictments for other former heads of state, including former President of the Federal Republic of Yugoslavia Slobodan Milošević and former Chadian dictator Hissène Habré, often referred to as "Africa's Pinochet."[124] As regards the alleged crimes of Habré, a commission set up in 1992 uncovered that Chadian security forces had committed an estimated 40,000 political murders and 200,000 acts of torture during his eight years in power before he was deposed in 1990.[125] Following years of legal back-and-forth and pressure from Belgium, in August 2012 the International Court of Justice ordered Senegal (where Habré was residing in exile) to either prosecute or extradite him so that he could stand trial without further delay.[126] In response, Senegal and the African Union established the Extraordinary

[123] The empty frames represent over 1000 individuals who are still unaccounted for.

[124] David Sugarman, *The Arrest of Augusto Pinochet: Ten Years On*, GLOBAL POL'Y F. (Oct. 29, 2008), https://archive.globalpolicy.org/intljustice/wanted/2008/1029tenyears on.htm; Krishnadev Calamur, *The Legacy of the Pinochet Trial*, ATLANTIC (Oct. 17, 2015), https://www.theatlantic.com/international/archive/2015/10/chad-habre-trial-pinochet/411 004/.

[125] *'Africa's Pinochet' Faces Extradition and Trial for Crimes against Humanity*, HUM. RTS. WATCH (Sept. 29, 2005), https://www.hrw.org/news/2005/09/29/africas-pinochet-faces-extradition-and-trial-crimes-against-humanity.

[126] Questions Relating to the Obligation to Prosecute or Extradite (Belg. v. Sen.), 2012 I.C.J. 144, 422 (July 20).

African Chambers (EAC) within the courts of the Republic of Senegal to prosecute Habré for crimes committed by his regime in Chad.[127]

Following a long trial, Habré was convicted by the EAC in May 2016 of war crimes, crimes against humanity, and acts of torture, and he was later sentenced to life in prison.[128] The historic trial was the first time that an African defendant was convicted of war crimes committed on African soil, and the first time that a deposed head of state faced justice for atrocities committed by his security forces in the courts of another country.[129] Overall, in addition to highlighting the need for an International Criminal Court, the *Pinochet* case also sent a strong message that the prosecution of former heads of state for grave crimes is not only laudable but also legally possible.

Immunity of State Officials. The prevailing narrative surrounding the legacy of the *Pinochet* case has increasingly focused on the legal issue at the heart of the case: immunity. At the time, many commentators suggested that the judgment in *Pinochet (No. 3)* represented an "immunity watershed" insofar as the immunity of former heads of state could now be waived[130] on the basis of state treaty obligations.[131] This view was in some ways reinforced by Article 27 of the Rome Statute of the International Criminal Court, which expressly provides that immunity, whether under national or international law, does not bar the Court from exercising its jurisdiction.[132] But we still do not have a consensus that such a broad removal of immunity exists vis-à-vis domestic courts. As conveyed by the International Law Commission, there are currently "insufficient grounds for concluding that the existence of such treaty obligations can automatically and generally be understood to waive the immunity of State officials."[133]

The absence of an automatic waiver of immunity is also seen in practice around the world. In recent decisions, both national and

---

[127] Habré v. Senegal, ECW/CCJ/JUD/06/10, Judgment after Rejection of Preliminary Objections Raised by Defendant (Ct. of Just. of the Econ. Cmty. of States of W. Afr. (ECOWAS), Nigeria, Nov. 18, 2010); *Statute of the Extraordinary African Chambers*, HUM. RTS. WATCH (Sept. 2, 2013), https://www.hrw.org/news/2013/09/02/statute-extraordinary-african-chambers.

[128] *Chad: Hissène Habré Appeal Ruling Closes Dark Chapter for Victims*, AMNESTY INT'L (Apr. 27, 2017), https://www.amnesty.org/en/latest/news/2017/04/chad-hissene-habre-appeal-ruling-closes-dark-chapter-for-victims.

[129] The EAC was established within the courts of the Republic of Senegal. *See Statute of the Extraordinary African Chambers*, *supra* note 127, art. 2; Charlotte Mohr, *The President on Trial: Prosecuting Hissène Habré*, INT'L REV. RED CROSS No. 918 (May 2022), https://international-review.icrc.org/articles/the-president-on-trial-prosecuting-hissene-habre-918.

[130] Whilst academics and the International Law Commission have described immunity in this context as having been "waived," a preferable expression would be that immunity has been "removed."

[131] Ingrid Wuerth, *Pinochet's Legacy Reassessed*, 106 AM. J. INT'L L. 731, 765 (2012).

[132] Rome Statute of the International Criminal Court art. 27, July 17, 1998, 2187 U.N.T.S. 90 (entered into force July 1, 2002).

[133] Rep. of the Int'l Law Comm'n, 73d Sess., Apr. 18–June 3 and July 4–Aug 5, 2022, U.N. Doc. A/77/10 (2022), ch. VI, at 259; GAOR, 77th Sess., Supp. No. 10 (2022).

international courts have now ruled in favor of state and status-based immunity, even in cases alleging grave human rights violations.[134] Some courts have distinguished the holding in *Pinochet (No. 3)* on a variety of bases, such as the fact that it concerned issues of criminal jurisdiction or that the outcome depended upon the ratification of the Torture Convention. For example, in *Al-Adsani v. United Kingdom*, while the European Court of Human Rights accepted that the prohibition of torture had achieved the status of a peremptory norm in international law, it distinguished the majority view in *Pinochet (No. 3)*, holding that the case did not provide a firm basis to conclude that the immunity *ratione personae* of foreign sovereign states is no longer enjoyed in respect of civil liability for claims of acts of torture.[135]

The distinction between criminal and civil jurisdiction was reaffirmed by Lord Bingham in *Jones v. Ministry of Interior for the Kingdom of Saudi Arabia*, where he stated that "the distinction between criminal proceedings (which were the subject of universal jurisdiction under the Torture Convention) and civil proceedings (which were not) was fundamental to [the decision in *Pinochet (No. 3)*]. This is not a distinction which can be wished away."[136]

Therefore, while the *Pinochet* case can be seen as the high-water mark of attempts to hold senior officials accountable for human rights violations, it has not yet created a broader legal precedent.

The Debate Continues: ILC Draft Articles. Finally, whilst the *Pinochet* case was certainly a milestone in the development of international law, the debate over the immunity of state officials accused of international crimes continues, as highlighted by recent work of the International Law Commission (ILC). In August 2022, the Commission adopted, on first reading, eighteen draft articles (with commentaries) on *Immunity of State Officials from Foreign Criminal Jurisdiction*.[137]

Chapter VI, Part Three of the Draft Articles specifically addresses the issue of immunity *ratione materiae* from foreign criminal jurisdiction.[138] The current position taken by the Draft Articles is that there should be exceptions to immunity *ratione materiae* from criminal jurisdiction, as set out in Draft Article 7. This Draft Article contains a list of "crimes under international law" that, if allegedly committed, would

---

134 *See, e.g.*, Al-Adsani v. United Kingdom, App. No. 35763/97 (Nov. 21, 2001), https://hudoc.echr.coe.int/fre?i=001-59885; Jurisdictional Immunities of the State (Ger. v. It.; Greece intervening), 2012 I.C.J. 99 (Feb. 3); Jones v. United Kingdom, App. Nos. 34356/06 & 40528/06 (Jan. 12, 2014), https://hudoc.echr.coe.int/fre?i=001-140005. Note also, for example, the refusal of the U.K. Metropolitan Police to arrest Lt. General Mahmoud Hegazy on the basis of special mission immunity. *See* TRIAL INT'L, MAKE WAY FOR JUSTICE #4—MOMENTUM TOWARDS ACCOUNTABILITY 95 (2018), https://trialinternational.org/wp-content/uploads/2018/03/UJAR-Make-way-for-Justice-2018.pdf.

135 *Al-Adsani*, App. No. 35763/97, ¶ 63.

136 Jones v. Saudi Arabia [2006] UKHL 26 (appeal from [2004] EWCA Civ 1394).

137 Rep. of the Int'l Law Comm'n, *supra* note 133, ch. VI, at 188–287.

138 *Id.* at 225.

prevent the application of immunity *ratione materiae* from criminal jurisdiction to a foreign official, even if the official committed those crimes while acting in an official capacity during his or her term of office. Such crimes include genocide, crimes against humanity, war crimes, the crime of apartheid, torture, and enforced disappearance.[139]

The Commission's decision to include this article was based in part on its recognition of "a discernible trend [amongst national courts] towards limiting the applicability of immunity from jurisdiction *ratione materiae* in respect of certain types of behavior that constitute crimes under international law."[140] The first case referenced by the Commission "in support of such a trend" is *Pinochet (No. 3)*.[141] Furthermore, the Commission appeared to justify the inclusion of Draft Article 7 in light of a need to "pursue its mandate of promoting the progressive development and codification of international law."[142] While it is not clear whether states agree with the suggestion that there has been a "trend" towards limiting immunity *ratione materiae*, some may see the *Pinochet* case as the tinderbox behind this legal evolution.[143]

The response of states to the Draft Articles has been mixed. According to Sir Michael Wood KC, the immunity of state officials is "one of the most controversial topics taken up by the Commission," which is only reinforced by the fact that "there is no general agreement on what the existing law is or on what the law should be."[144] As a result, controversy over Draft Article 7 had the effect of overshadowing the adoption of the first reading text.[145] Those ILC members who were critical of Draft Article 7 took the view that the Commission was conducting a "normative policy" exercise that bore no relation to either the codification or progressive development of international law.[146] For such members, the Draft Article was seen as a proposal for "new law" that could not be considered as *lex lata* nor a desirable progressive development of international law.[147]

V. CONCLUSION

In sum, the story of Pinochet and his transition from head of state to defendant is a microcosm of the international community's efforts over

---

139 *Id.* at 236.

140 *Id.* at 232.

141 *Id.*

142 *Id.* at 234.

143 For further context, see Michael Wood's suggestion that even after adoption on first reading of the Draft Articles in 2022, Draft Article 7 "remains highly contested within the Commission." Michael Wood, *The ILC's First Reading Draft Articles on 'Immunity of State Officials from Foreign Criminal Jurisdiction,'* 26 MAX PLANCK Y.B. UNITED NATIONS L. ONLINE 717, 733 (2023).

144 *Id.* at 719.

145 *Id.* at 731.

146 Rep. of the Int'l Law Comm'n, *supra* note 133, at 235.

147 *Id.* at 236.

the decades to secure accountability for the crimes that most shock humanity's conscience. The pendulum swings between efforts to stamp out impunity, facilitated by universal jurisdiction and progressive development of the law, and a formalist, state-centric approach that limits such prosecutions to international courts with circumscribed jurisdiction that are reliant on state cooperation.

At this moment in time, a renewed push for accountability triggered by the war in Ukraine could potentially revive the precedential value of the *Pinochet* case. In March 2023, owing to an investigation by the Prosecutor of the International Criminal Court (ICC) into allegations of war crimes, crimes against humanity, and genocide being committed in Ukraine, the ICC issued arrest warrants against Russian President Vladimir Putin and Russian Presidential Commissioner for Children's Rights Maria Lvova-Belova on the basis of unlawful deportations of children from Ukraine to Russia.[148] In addition to the ICC warrants, in July 2023 the International Centre for the Prosecution of the Crime of Aggression against Ukraine (ICPA) began operations in the Hague, hosted by the European Union Agency for Criminal Justice Cooperation (Eurojust).[149] The creation of the ICPA is the first step towards the possible introduction of a Special Tribunal for the crime of aggression against Ukraine.[150]

In May 2024, the Prosecutor of the ICC also applied for a warrant against current Israeli Prime Minister Benjamin Netanyahu, in addition to several other individuals, on the basis of alleged war crimes and crimes against humanity committed during the ongoing Israel-Hamas war in Gaza.[151]

Finally, progress towards accountability has also been made in the context of the protracted and bloody Syrian Civil War. Following a civil party complaint and judicial investigations, in November 2023 a French court issued an international arrest warrant for Syria's President Bashar al-Assad over the use of banned chemical weapons against civilians in

---

[148] *Situation in Ukraine: ICC Judges Issue Arrest Warrants against Vladimir Vladimirovich Putin and Maria Alekseyevna Lvova-Belova*, INT'L CRIM. CT. (Mar. 17, 2023), https://www.icc-cpi.int/news/situation-ukraine-icc-judges-issue-arrest-warrants-against-vladimir-vladimirovich-putin-and.

[149] The ICPA was created via joint efforts by the European Commission and the European External Action Service to ensure full accountability for crimes committed in the Russian war against Ukraine. Directorate-General for Neighbourhood & Enlargement Negots., *Ukraine: International Centre for the Prosecution of Russia's Crime of Aggression against Ukraine Starts Operations*, EUR. NEIGHBOURHOOD POL'Y & ENLARGEMENT NEGOTS. (July 3, 2023), https://neighbourhood-enlargement.ec.europa.eu/news/ukraine-international-centre-prosecution-russias-crime-aggression-against-ukraine-starts-operations-2023-07-03_en.

[150] *The International Centre for Prosecution for the Crime of Aggression against Ukraine*, INST. FOR WAR & PEACE REPORTING (Aug. 8, 2023), https://iwpr.net/global-voices/international-centre-prosecution-crime-aggression-against-ukraine.

[151] *Statement of ICC Prosecutor Karim A.A. Khan KC: Applications for Arrest Warrants in the Situation in the State of Palestine*, INT'L CRIM. CT. (May 20, 2024), https://www.icc-cpi.int/news/statement-icc-prosecutor-karim-aa-khan-kc-applications-arrest-warrants-situation-state.

Syria.[152] Judges from the crimes against humanity unit at the Paris tribunal have issued a total of eleven arrest warrants for crimes committed by Syrian officials.[153] Ultimately, while it is not clear how this story will conclude, the fact that current international efforts are geared towards fighting impunity reignites hope that the *Pinochet* precedent will prevail.

---

[152] *France Issues Arrest Warrant for Syria's President Assad—Source*, REUTERS (Nov. 15, 2023), https://www.reuters.com/world/france-issues-arrest-warrants-against-syrias-president-assad-source-2023-11-15/.

[153] *Id.*

4

Laura A. Dickinson

Abu Ghraib: The Battle over Institutional Culture and Respect for International Law Within the U.S. Military

In the spring of 2004, news that U.S. troops in Iraq had brutally tortured and abused detainees at Abu Ghraib prison sent shock waves around the world. Newspapers, magazines, and internet sites displayed gruesome photographs of naked prisoners cowering behind attack dogs, while grinning uniformed U.S. soldiers looked on. One instantly iconic photograph depicted a hooded detainee, arms outstretched, standing on a black box with wires attached to his body, apparently being threatened with electric shocks. As public outcry erupted both at home and abroad, Bush administration officials rushed to condemn the behavior of the interrogators, to reaffirm their purported commitment to the Convention Against Torture and Cruel, Inhuman and Degrading Treatment,[1] and to characterize the events at Abu Ghraib as the actions of a few "bad apples." Subsequent investigations, however, suggested that Abu Ghraib cannot be seen as merely an isolated incident, divorced from broader governmental policies and practices. Yet, while a few individuals who committed abuses stood trial, broader accountability remained elusive.

The Abu Ghraib incidents thus raise important questions about the ability of international law to constrain the actions of those engaged in military detention and interrogation activities. In light of U.S. obligations both under the Torture Convention and under the Geneva Conventions' prohibitions of cruel treatment during wartime,[2] commentators have asked how such abuses could have occurred and why so few have been punished. Among the many stories one could tell about Abu Ghraib is the

---

1 Convention Against Torture and Other Cruel, Inhuman or Degrading Treatment or Punishment, Dec. 10, 1984, S. TREATY DOC. NO. 100–20, 1465 U.N.T.S. 113 [hereinafter Torture Convention].

2 Geneva Convention for the Amelioration of the Condition of the Wounded and Sick in Armed Forces in the Field, Aug. 12, 1949, 6 U.S.T. 3114, 75 U.N.T.S. 31; Geneva Convention for the Amelioration of the Condition of Wounded, Sick and Shipwrecked Members of Armed Forces at Sea, Aug. 12, 1949, 6 U.S.T. 3217, 75 U.N.T.S. 85; Geneva Convention Relative to the Treatment of Prisoners of War, Aug. 12, 1949, 6 U.S.T. 3316, 75 U.N.T.S. 135; Geneva Convention Relative to the Protection of Civilian Persons in Time of War, Aug. 12, 1949, 6 U.S.T. 3516, 75 U.N.T.S. 287 [hereinafter Geneva Convention IV].

tale of how, if at all, international law operates on the ground and whether (and under what circumstances) it can act as any sort of check on abuse.[3]

Such a tale requires consideration of how international norms are either internalized or undermined within the institutional culture of those organizations, such as the military, that are charged with implementing international law. In the months preceding the abuses at Abu Ghraib, Bush administration officials took a series of steps that weakened long-standing commitments within the military to the norms and values of the law of war, and in particular norms regarding the treatment of detainees. Administration authorities circulated statements and memoranda suggesting that the law of war might not apply to certain categories of detainees; issued multiple, confusing directives to troops on the ground regarding permissible interrogation practices; allowed civilian intelligence personnel, special forces, uniformed troops, and private contractors to co-mingle without clear lines of authority or divisions of responsibility; and greatly expanded the role of private contractors. Together, these practices helped set the stage for the abuses that took place.

Yet at the same time, Abu Ghraib is not only a story of how international law norms are sometimes undermined. Significantly, the commitment of many within the military to the values of international law, and the organizational structures that the military had constructed over many decades to maintain those commitments, proved difficult to dislodge. For it was, primarily, the *civilian* political employees who sought to change long-standing military practices. Uniformed military personnel and military lawyers, by contrast, in many cases took the lead in criticizing the administration and sought to tame the effect of administration policies, while reaffirming (and perhaps even re-institutionalizing) the military's respect for international law.

Thus, the Abu Ghraib case contains within it an important story about the role that organizational culture can play either in weakening, or giving effect to, international law. To the extent that international law failed to constrain troops on the ground from committing abuses, it was at least in part because Bush administration political appointees took steps that effectively undermined a bureaucratic culture that had institutionalized respect for that law. Yet that culture—a military committed to the law of war and the fair treatment of detainees—also

[3] For other stories, see, *e.g.*, THE TORTURE PAPERS: THE ROAD TO ABU GHRAIB (Karen J. Greenberg & Joshua L. Dratel eds., 2005); Diane Marie Amann, *Abu Ghraib*, 153 U. PA. L. REV. 2085 (2005); John T. Parry, *"Just for Fun": Understanding Torture and Understanding Abu Ghraib*, 1 J. NAT'L SEC. L. & POL'Y 253 (2005); Deborah N. Pearlstein, *Finding Effective Constraints on Executive Power: Interrogation, Detention, and Torture*, 81 IND. L.J. 1255 (2006); Steven L. Schooner, *Contractor Atrocities at Abu Ghraib: Compromised Accountability in a Streamlined, Outsourced Government*, 16 STAN. L. & POL'Y REV. 549 (2005); Marcy Strauss, *The Lessons of Abu Ghraib*, 66 OHIO ST. L.J. 1269 (2005).

proved to be "sticky."[4] Organizational practices and values remained resilient and served as the origin for much of the critique of, and resistance to, these changes.

Finally, we need to recognize the lasting effects of the U.S. use of torture in the counter-terrorism context, not only at Abu Ghraib, but also at Guantánamo Bay, in Afghanistan, and in so-called CIA "black sites" around the world. On the one hand, the institutional commitment to international law norms has continued to be resilient.[5] A series of statutes and presidential policies have reaffirmed the U.S. commitment against torture and cruel, inhuman, and degrading treatment.[6] Moreover, although Donald Trump said during the 2016 campaign that he would "load up" the U.S. military facility at Guantánamo[7] and reinstate the practice of torture,[8] no new prisoners were sent to Guantánamo during his first administration, and it does not appear that any new instances of extreme interrogation techniques were in fact authorized, either at Guantánamo or elsewhere.

On the other hand, the legacies of torture in the war on terror remain. More than two decades later, as of January 2025, fifteen terrorism suspects were still at Guantánamo Bay.[9] Some of those detainees have been brought before military commissions, but there have been protracted legal battles over whether evidence obtained through the use of past torture or cruel, inhuman, or degrading treatment can be used in those proceedings.[10] Others remain in detention without any charges having been brought at all, even in the military commissions. Such extended detention without charge may itself qualify as cruel, inhuman, and degrading treatment under international law, although such a determination depends on whether those detainees are classified as criminal defendants—with protections from indefinite detention under international human rights law—or instead as detainees in an ongoing global war on terror, and therefore subject only to the requirements of the international law of armed conflict.[11]

---

4 For an argument about the role that military culture can play in deterring war crimes, see generally MARK J. OSIEL, OBEYING ORDERS: ATROCITY, MILITARY DISCIPLINE, AND THE LAW OF WAR (1999).

5 For further discussion of the role policymaking plays in creating national security norms that can prove durable over time, see generally Laura A. Dickinson, *National Security Policymaking in the Shadow of International Law*, 2021 UTAH L. REV. 629 (2021).

6 *See infra* text accompanying notes 150–158.

7 Charlie Savage, *Donald Trump 'Fine' with Prosecuting U.S. Citizens at Guantánamo*, N.Y. TIMES (Aug. 12, 2016, 5:18 PM), https://www.nytimes.com/2016/08/13/us/politics/donald-trump-american-citizens-guantanamo.html [https://perma.cc/Q62E-MY4Y].

8 James Risen & Sheri Fink, *Trump Said 'Torture Works.' An Echo Is Feared Worldwide*, N.Y. TIMES (Jan. 5, 2017), https://www.nytimes.com/2017/01/05/us/politics/trump-torture-guantanamo.html [https://perma.cc/56DX-WK3H].

9 *The Guantánamo Docket*, N.Y. TIMES, https://www.nytimes.com/interactive/2021/us/guantanamo-bay-detainees.html (last updated Jan. 11, 2025).

10 *See infra* text accompanying notes 161–165.

11 *See infra* text accompanying notes 182–183.

I. THE ABU GHRAIB ABUSES: DISCOVERY AND RESPONSE

The Discovery of Abuse. In April 2004, news broke that U.S. soldiers had abused detainees at Abu Ghraib prison.[12] A notorious site near Baghdad during the brutal Hussein regime, the jail had long housed political prisoners who were confined in squalid conditions, tortured, and summarily executed at the hands of Hussein's henchmen.[13] The U.S. Army gutted the facility and turned it into a military prison during the early days of the Iraq conflict.[14] Detainees fell into three loosely defined categories: common criminals; security detainees suspected of "crimes against the coalition" (of U.S. and allied forces); and a small number of suspected "high-value" insurgency leaders.[15]

Subsequent reports added to the portrait of abuse.[16] Seymour Hersh, in the *New Yorker*, quoted an internal U.S. Army report to describe the specific incidents of wrongdoing:

> Pouring . . . phosphoric liquid on detainees; pouring cold water on naked detainees; beating detainees with a broom handle and a chair; threatening male detainees with rape; allowing a military police guard to stitch the wound of a detainee who was injured after being slammed against the wall in his cell; sodomizing a detainee with a chemical light and perhaps a broom stick, and using military working dogs to frighten and intimidate detainees with threats of attack, and . . . biting a detainee.[17]

Several news organizations obtained the report, authorized by Lieutenant General Ricardo S. Sanchez, the senior commander in Iraq, and written by Major General Antonio M. Taguba, even though it had not originally been meant for public release.[18] According to the report, soldiers of the 372d Military Police Company, as well as members of the American intelligence community, had committed systemic and "criminal" abuses of detainees that were "sadistic, blatant, and wanton.[19]

---

12 *Abuse of Iraqi POWs by GIs probed,* CBS NEWS (Apr. 28, 2004, 4:37 PM EDT), https://www.cbsnews.com/news/abuse-of-iraqi-pows-by-gis-probed/ [https://perma.cc/7WD7-D3GB] [hereinafter *Abuse of Iraqi POWs*].

13 *Id.; see also* Seymour Hersh, *Torture at Abu Ghraib*, NEW YORKER, May 10, 2004, at 42.

14 Hersh, *supra* note 13, at 42.

15 *Id.*

16 *See, e.g., id.*; James Risen, *G.I.'s Are Accused of Abusing Iraqi Captives*, N.Y. TIMES, Apr. 29, 2004, at A15.

17 Hersh, *supra* note 13, at 43.

18 *Id.*

19 *Id.*

U.S. Detainee at Abu Ghraib

The report revealed that U.S. soldiers had kicked and punched detainees, intimidated them with dogs, threatened them with electric shocks, coerced them to masturbate, sexually humiliated them, and forced them to pose naked for photographs.[20] Indeed, the abuse had originally surfaced in part because soldiers were widely circulating

[20] *Abuse of Iraqi POWs*, *supra* note 12.

numerous gruesome photographs among themselves.[21] One picture was of an Iraqi prisoner standing on a box, his head covered, with wires attached to his hands. He was apparently told that if he fell off the box, he would be electrocuted. Another photograph depicted a detainee with wires connected to his genitals.[22] In another, a dog attacked a detainee. And another showed a dead Iraqi man who appeared to have been badly beaten.[23] The report also included a detainee's statement charging that an Army translator had raped a male juvenile prisoner.[24]

By the time General Taguba completed the report, the Army official in charge of the prison, Army Reserve Brigadier General Janis Karpinski, along with her staff, confronted the end of long military careers. And six soldiers—Staff Sergeant Ivan L. Frederick II, Specialist Charles A. Graner, Sergeant Javal Davis, Specialist Megan Ambuhl, Specialist Sabrina Harman, and Private Jeremy Sivits—were facing courts-martial in Iraq on charges that included conspiracy, dereliction of duty, cruelty toward prisoners, maltreatment, assault, and indecent acts. A seventh suspect, Private Lynndie England, after becoming pregnant, was reassigned to what is now Fort Liberty, North Carolina.

World Outcry and Bush Administration Response. The Abu Ghraib story (and the shocking pictures that accompanied it) quickly circulated around the world, and many leaders rushed to condemn the abuses. Prime Minister Tony Blair of Great Britain, the leading ally of the United States in Iraq, emphasized that "the abuse of prisoners, the torture of prisoners, degrading treatment of people in the custody of coalition forces, these things are completely and totally unacceptable."[25] He added, "We went to Iraq to stop that kind of thing, not to do it ourselves."[26] Other U.S. allies also condemned the abuses.[27]

Outrage in the Arab and Muslim world was particularly fierce. The Arab Al-Jazeera news agency described the conduct of the U.S. soldiers as "unethical and inhuman."[28] Abdelbari Atwan, writing in *Al Quds al Arab*, asserted that the "torture is not the work of a few American soldiers. It is the result of an official American culture that deliberately

---

[21] *Id.; see also* Hersh, *supra* note 13, at 43. Reports also suggest that the Army decided to investigate after an Army reservist came forward to report on the abuse. *See* Risen, *supra* note 16.

[22] *Abuse of Iraqi POWs, supra* note 12.

[23] *Id.*

[24] *Id.*

[25] *Quoted in* Alan Cowell, *Bush's Words Do Little to Ease Horror at Prison Deeds*, N.Y. TIMES, May 7, 2004, at A12, https://www.nytimes.com/2004/05/07/world/struggle-for-iraq-reaction-bush-s-words-little-ease-horror-prison-deeds.html.

[26] *Quoted in id.*

[27] *See, e.g.*, Brian Knowlton, *7 Penalized for Iraq Prison Abuse; U.S. Review Faults Commanders; Muslim Outrage Growing*, INT'L HERALD TRIB., May 4, 2004, at A1.

[28] Thom Shanker & Jacques Steinberg, *Bush Voices "Disgust" at Abuse of Iraqi Prisoners*, N.Y. TIMES, May 1, 2004, at A1, https://www.nytimes.com/2004/05/01/world/the-struggle-for-iraq-captives-bush-voices-disgust-at-abuse-of-iraqi-prisoners.html.

insults and humiliates Muslims."[29] In predominantly Muslim Indonesia, thousands rallied to protest.[30]

President Bush swiftly spoke out against the acts committed at Abu Ghraib, expressing "deep disgust" at the prisoners' treatment and asserting that it "does not reflect the nature of the American people."[31] He vowed that any soldier found to be at fault would be punished.[32] Seeking to stem the tide of complaints across the Arab world, the President appeared on Arab-language television, assuring viewers that the abuses "represent the actions of a few people," and emphasizing that "in a democracy there will be a full investigation."[33] Meanwhile, Defense Secretary Donald Rumsfeld assigned responsibility for the abuse to a "very small minority" of soldiers in Iraq.[34]

Initial Investigations. Over the course of the year, the Bush administration ordered nine different investigations into the events at Abu Ghraib.[35] The initial report, prepared by Major General Taguba, defined the abuse as "systematic," and attributed the actions to "several members of the military police guard force,"[36] working alongside "other U.S. Government Agency's (OGA) interrogators" (a reference to the

---

[29] *Quoted in* Cowell, *supra* note 25, at A12.

[30] *Thousands Rally Against U.S. Abuses*, JAKARTA POST, May 17, 2004, at 4.

[31] *Quoted in* Shanker & Steinberg, *supra* note 28, at A1.

[32] *Id.*

[33] *Quoted in* Christine Hauser, *Many Iraqis Are Skeptical of Bush TV Appeal*, N.Y. TIMES, May 6, 2004, at A16, https://www.nytimes.com/2004/05/06/world/the-struggle-for-iraq-reaction-many-iraqis-are-skeptical-of-bush-tv-appeal.html.

[34] *Review of Department of Defense Detention and Interrogation Operations Before the S. Armed Forces Comm.*, 108th Cong. 10 (2004) (statement of Donald Rumsfeld, Sec'y of Def.) [hereinafter Rumsfeld Testimony].

[35] *See* DEP'T OF THE ARMY, ARTICLE 15–6 INVESTIGATION OF THE 800TH MILITARY POLICE BRIGADE 16–17 (May 27, 2004) (prepared by Major General Antonio M. Taguba, Investigating Officer), http://www.globalsecurity.org/intell/library/reports/2004/800–mp–bde.htm [hereinafter Taguba Report]; DEP'T OF THE ARMY, CID, CID REPORT OF INVESTIGATION (Jan. 30, 2004), https://irp.fas.org/agency/dod/taguba.pdf [https://perma.cc/HCL8-DHQX]; GEN. ANTHONY R. JONES, AR 15–6 INVESTIGATION OF THE ABU GHRAIB PRISON AND 205TH MILITARY INTELLIGENCE BRIGADE (Aug. 2004), https://perma.cc/C69D-LLZM [hereinafter Jones Report]; VICE ADM. ALBERT T. CHURCH, REVIEW OF DEPARTMENT OF DEFENSE INTERROGATION OPERATIONS (2005), https://www.esd.whs.mil/Portals/54/Documents/FOID/Reading%20Room/Detainne_Related/church_report_1.pdf [https://perma.cc/5MXN-MVCU] [hereinafter Church Report]; LT. GEN. PAUL T. MIKOLASHEK, DEPARTMENT OF THE ARMY DETAINEE OPERATIONS INSPECTION (2004), http://www.washingtonpost.com/wp-srv/world/iraq/abughraib/detaineereport.pdf [hereinafter DAIG Report]; MAJ. GEN. GEOFFREY MILLER, ASSESSMENT OF DOD COUNTERTERRORISM INTERROGATION AND DETENTION OPERATIONS IN IRAQ (2003), https://perma.cc/F92Q-8QYE [hereinafter Miller Report]; JAMES R. SCHLESINGER, FORMER SEC'Y OF DEF., FINAL REPORT OF THE INDEPENDENT PANEL TO REVIEW DOD DETENTION OPERATIONS (2004), http://www.isn.ethz.ch/pubs/ph/details.cfm?id=10157 [hereinafter Schlesinger Report]; LT. GEN. RANDALL MARK SCHMIDT & BRIG. GEN. JOHN T. FURLOW, INVESTIGATION INTO FBI ALLEGATIONS OF DETAINEE ABUSE AT GUANTÁNAMO BAY, CUBA DETENTION FACILITY (2005), https://perma.cc/9SPU-PWZP [hereinafter Schmidt Report]; MAJ. GEN. GEORGE R. FAY, AR–15–6 INVESTIGATION OF THE ABU GHRAIB DETENTION FACILITY AND 205TH MILITARY INTELLIGENCE BRIGADE (2004), https://www.thetorturedatabase.org/files/foia_subsite/pdfs/fay_jones_kern_report.pdf [https://perma.cc/PGF7-57BP] [hereinafter Fay Report].

[36] Taguba Report, *supra* note 35, at 16.

Central Intelligence Agency (CIA)).[37] At the behest of OGA interrogators, guards "routinely" hid captives from the International Committee of the Red Cross, the body charged with monitoring compliance with the Geneva Conventions.[38] In Taguba's view, the abusers violated two pertinent bodies of law: the Army's own regulations and the Third Geneva Convention.

Two additional military reports released in August 2004 concluded that CIA interrogation abuses had influenced the military. A panel headed by former Defense Secretary James R. Schlesinger concluded that CIA practices such as waterboarding and other "harsher techniques than allowed" under Army rules fostered "the belief that such methods were condoned."[39] A report prepared by Major General George F. Fay similarly concluded that CIA officers who had conducted interrogations inside the prison, flouting military procedures, had "eroded the necessity in the minds of Soldiers and civilians for them to follow Army rules."[40]

Meanwhile, Congress also held numerous hearings on the subject. General John P. Abizaid, the top commander in the Middle East, acknowledged in testimony to the Senate Armed Forces Committee that "systemic problems" at Abu Ghraib contributed to the prisoner abuse there and that the abuse was criminal, and he accepted responsibility for some problems, such as breakdowns in procedures.[41] Nevertheless, he said the abuse was "isolated" and insisted, "I do not believe that a culture of abuse existed in my command. . . . I believe that we have isolated incidents that have taken place."[42]

Critics charged that the military and congressional investigations were inadequate. Reed Brody of Human Rights Watch, for example, complained that the military inquiries lacked the mandate and the independence to give a full picture of abuse.[43] Though numerous, the investigations were often piecemeal, focusing in some instances only on narrow questions, such as the role of military intelligence officers.[44] Moreover, those assigned to prepare reports often lacked authority to question military brass above their rank. Some commentators contended

---

37 *Id.* at 18.

38 *Id.* at 26–27.

39 Schlesinger Report, *supra* note 35, at 16.

40 Fay Report, *supra* note 35, at 44–45.

41 *Review of Department of Defense Detention and Interrogation Operations Before the S. Armed Forces Comm.*, 108th Cong. 566 (2004) (statement of Gen. John P. Abizaid, Commander, U.S. Central Command) [hereinafter Abizaid SASC Testimony]; *see also* Eric Schmitt, *Two U.S. Generals Outline a Lag in Notification on Reports of Abuse in Iraqi Prison*, N.Y. TIMES, May 20, 2004, at A12, https://www.nytimes.com/2004/05/20/world/struggle-for-iraq-testimony-two-us-generals-outline-lag-notification-reports.html.

42 Abizaid SASC Testimony, *supra* note 41, at 588.

43 Reed Brody, *Justice for Abu Ghraib*, N.Y. TIMES, Jan. 19, 2005, https://www.nytimes.com/2005/01/19/opinion/justice-for-abu-ghraib.html.

44 *See* MARK DANNER, TORTURE AND TRUTH: AMERICA, ABU GHRAIB AND THE WAR ON TERROR (2005); Mark Danner, *We Are All Torturers Now*, N.Y. TIMES, Jan. 6, 2005, at A27, https://www.nytimes.com/2005/01/06/opinion/we-are-all-torturers-now.html.

that Congress fell short by refusing to examine the role of more senior authorities[45] and by limiting oversight largely to military, rather than CIA, activities.[46]

Initial Legislation. In response to the abuses at Abu Ghraib and Guantánamo Naval Base, some members of Congress sought to enact legislation that would enhance protections for detainees. Yet, this early legislation had significant gaps. Senator John McCain of Arizona introduced a bill in the fall of 2005 that promised to prohibit inhumane treatment of detainees held by the United States wherever they are located, and, for detainees in DOD custody, to limit interrogation techniques to those listed in the *Army Field Manual.* However, in part due to administration pressure, the bill that was ultimately enacted, the Detainee Treatment Act,[47] significantly "stripped" federal court jurisdiction over cases detainees might bring. A subsequent legislative effort culminated in the Military Commissions Act of 2006,[48] which expanded on the jurisdiction-stripping provisions of the DTA and prevented U.S. courts from relying on international or foreign law.[49]

Violations of International Law. The acts committed at Abu Ghraib constituted serious violations of international law. The Convention Against Torture and Cruel, Inhuman and Degrading Treatment defines torture as "any act by which severe pain or suffering, whether physical or mental, is intentionally inflicted on a person for such purposes as obtaining from him or a third person information or a confession" when "inflicted by or at the instigation of or with the consent or acquiescence of a public official or other person acting in an official capacity."[50] A very strong case could be made that many of the abuses committed at Abu Ghraib—including the reported sodomizing of a detainee with a broomstick and threatening detainees with electric shocks in order to set "conditions for favorable interrogation"[51]—constituted torture. And while the Torture Convention does not define cruel, inhuman, or degrading treatment, virtually all of the acts alleged would qualify as cruel treatment as interpreted by the many courts that

45 *See Abu Ghraib Unresolved*, N.Y. TIMES, Sept. 10, 2005, at A16, https://www.nytimes.com/2005/09/10/opinion/abu-ghraib-unresolved.html.

46 Douglas Jehl, *White House Has Tightly Restricted Oversight of C.I.A. Detentions, Officials Say*, N.Y. TIMES, Apr. 6, 2005, at A21, https://www.nytimes.com/2005/04/06/us/white-house-has-tightly-restricted-oversight-of-cia-detentions-officials.html.

47 Detainee Treatment Act of 2005, Pub. L. No. 109–148, 119 Stat. 2739 (2005) [hereinafter DTA].

48 Military Commissions Act of 2006, Pub. L. No. 109–366, 120 Stat. 2600 (2006).

49 *Id.* The MCA's jurisdiction-stripping provision was subsequently invalidated by the U.S. Supreme Court. Boumediene v. Bush, 553 U.S. 723, 792 (2008).

50 Torture Convention, *supra* note 1. The Convention further defines as torture "punishing him for an act he or a third person has committed or is suspected of having committed, or intimidating or coercing him or a third person, or for any reason based on discrimination of any kind." *Id.* art. 1.

51 Taguba Report, *supra* note 35, at 18.

have addressed the issue.[52] Moreover, the Convention admits of no exceptions to the ban on torture even in times of war or national emergency,[53] and it obligates all states parties to criminalize torture[54] and extradite or prosecute those suspected of committing torture.[55] At the time of the conflict in Iraq, the United States had ratified the Torture Convention and had enacted domestic legislation criminalizing the practice.[56]

Similarly, the acts in question likely violated the Geneva Conventions.[57] Under the Conventions, "grave breaches" include "torture or inhuman treatment . . ., willfully causing great suffering and serious injury to body or health," and such acts are war crimes.[58] The 1949 Geneva Convention Relative to the Protection of Civilian Persons in Time of War also contains numerous additional provisions prohibiting cruel and inhumane treatment.[59] As with the Torture Convention, the United States has ratified the Geneva Conventions and enacted domestic legislation conferring jurisdiction on U.S. courts to criminally punish offenders. The Uniform Code of Military Justice (UCMJ) confers jurisdiction on military courts to try and punish uniformed personnel for engaging in acts that would constitute war crimes.[60] In addition, the War Crimes Act gives jurisdiction to U.S. courts to criminally punish anyone who has committed war crimes overseas,[61] and the Military

---

52 *See, e.g.*, Ireland v. United Kingdom, 25 Eur. Ct. H.R. (ser. A) ¶ 246 (1978) (concluding that hooding, wall-standing, deprivation of food and drink, deprivation of sleep and subjection to loud noise, in combination, but for less than twenty-four hours, constituted cruel, inhuman, and degrading treatment, but not torture).

53 Torture Convention, *supra* note 1, art. 2.

54 *Id.* art. 4.

55 *Id.* arts. 6–8.

56 18 U.S.C. § 2340A.

57 *See* Geneva Convention IV, *supra* note 2.

58 *Id.* art. 147.

59 Article 3, which applies to both international and internal armed conflicts, provides that "[p]ersons taking no active part in hostilities . . . shall in all circumstances be treated humanely." *Id.* art. 3. In addition, Article 3 prohibits "mutilation, cruel treatment and torture," and "outrages upon personal dignity, in particular humiliating and degrading treatment" are proscribed. *Id.* Article 5 specifies that persons detained without trial have the right to be "treated with humanity." *Id.* art. 5. With respect to most civilians and others who are no longer taking an active part in hostilities, there shall be "respect for their persons, their honor. . . . They shall at all times be humanely treated, and shall be protected especially against all acts of violence or threats thereof and against insults and public curiosity." *Id.* art. 27. Furthermore, "No physical or moral coercion shall be exercised against protected persons, in particular to obtain information from them." *Id.* art. 31. Persons in control are "prohibited from taking any measure of such a character as to cause the physical suffering . . . of protected persons in their hands. This prohibition applies not only to murder, torture, corporal punishment, mutilation . . ., but also to any other measures of brutality whether applied by civilian or military agents." *Id.* art. 32. And "all measures of intimidation" are outlawed. *Id.* art. 33. *See generally* Jordan Paust, *Abuse of Iraqi Detainees at Abu Ghraib: Will Prosecution and Cashiering of a Few Soldiers Comply With International Law?*, JURIST (May 10, 2004), https://www.jurist.org/commentary/2004/05/abuse-of-iraqi-detainees-at-abu-ghraib/ [https://perma.cc/5U6C-MRFA].

60 10 U.S.C. §§ 801–946a.

61 18 U.S.C. § 2441.

Extraterritorial Jurisdiction Act extends the jurisdiction of federal courts to prosecute civilians working with the Armed Forces for violations of the UCMJ and other federal criminal law.[62]

Some scholars have argued that the acts at Abu Ghraib also constitute crimes against humanity.[63] While the Statute of the International Criminal Court (ICC) defines and prohibits such crimes,[64] neither the United States nor Iraq has ratified this treaty. The ICC is therefore unavailable as an enforcement mechanism for such abuses.[65] It is true that Afghanistan has ratified the treaty, and the ICC did assert jurisdiction over war crimes and crimes against humanity there, potentially including acts of torture committed by U.S. persons.[66] Yet, even with regard to potential violations in Afghanistan, the ICC Prosecutor has chosen to deprioritize investigation of cases of alleged detainee abuse by U.S. persons, and so prosecution in the ICC is unlikely.[67]

Accountability. The U.S. military tried and punished the soldiers depicted in the Abu Ghraib pictures, but few sanctions were imposed on civilians and others who may have been responsible higher up the chain of command. Indeed, although more than eighty members of the military were ordered to face court-martial on charges of abusing prisoners at Abu Ghraib and elsewhere, and more than fifty were convicted,[68] very few higher-ranked soldiers faced criminal penalties. Moreover, only one military intelligence soldier, Specialist Armin Cruz, was convicted.[69] Perhaps just as troubling, those convicted received light sentences. Of the

---

[62] Pub. L. No. 106–523, 114 Stat. 2488 (2000) (codified as amended at 18 U.S.C. §§ 3261–3267).

[63] *See, e.g.*, Paust, *supra* note 59.

[64] Rome Statute of the International Court art. 7, July 17, 1998, 2187 U.N.T.S. 3.

[65] *Id.* art. 12. Even if the United States or Iraq had ratified the ICC, under the complementarity principle the tribunal would not have the authority to hear such a case unless domestic authorities were "unable" or "unwilling" to investigate or prosecute the abuses. *Id.* art. 17.

[66] Situation in the Islamic Republic of Afghanistan, ICC-02/17-138, Judgment on the Appeal Against the Decision on the Authorisation of an Investigation into the Situation in the Islamic Republic of Afghanistan (Mar. 5, 2020), https://www.icc-cpi.int/sites/default/files/CourtRecords/CR2020_00828.PDF.

[67] *Statement of the Prosecutor of the International Criminal Court, Karim A. A. Khan QC, following the application for an expedited order under article 18(2) seeking authorisation to resume investigations in the Situation in Afghanistan*, INT'L CRIM. CT. (Sept. 27, 2021), https://www.icc-cpi.int/news/statement-prosecutor-international-criminal-court-karim-khan-qc-following-application.

[68] Scott Shane, *C.I.A. Contractor Guilty in Beating of Afghan Who Later Died*, N.Y. TIMES, Aug. 18, 2006, at A8, https://www.nytimes.com/2006/08/18/washington/18detain.html.

[69] After a plea deal, he received a sentence of eight months in prison. Norimitsu Onishi, *Military Specialist Pleads Guilty to Abuse and Is Jailed*, N.Y. TIMES (Sept. 12, 2004), https://www.nytimes.com/2004/09/12/world/middleeast/military-specialist-pleads-guilty-to-abuse-and-is-jailed.html.

forty who were sentenced to jail time, fewer than ten served more than a year.[70]

Outside the military justice system, few of those involved in the Abu Ghraib scandal have faced either criminal punishment or civil liability. Despite the existence of two statutes allowing federal prosecutions for war crimes[71] and torture[72] committed outside the United States, no one has stood trial under these statutes for acts at Abu Ghraib or elsewhere. Indeed, David Passaro, a contractor for the CIA, is the only civilian who has faced prosecution at all, for abuses committed against detainees in Afghanistan. Federal authorities brought charges against him for assault, and a jury convicted him in August of 2006.[73] Likewise, while the CIA and Defense Department reportedly referred twenty prison abuse cases to the Justice Department, these were primarily for actions undertaken by civilian contractors.[74] President Obama subsequently launched a formal investigation into whether certain "federal laws were violated in connection with the interrogation of specific detainees at overseas locations."[75] However, the ultimate report of that investigation, issued in 2011, "determined that an expanded criminal investigation . . . is not warranted," due to insufficient evidence.[76]

Although transnational criminal prosecution in a third-party state under principles of universal jurisdiction was theoretically a possibility,

70 *Id.*

71 18 U.S.C. § 2441.

72 *Id.* § 2340A.

73 Shane, *supra* note 68.

74 *Id.*

75 Press Release, Eric H. Holder, Jr., Att'y Gen., *Statement of the Attorney General Regarding Investigation into the Interrogation of Certain Detainees* (June 30, 2011), https://www.justice.gov/opa/pr/statement-attorney-general-regarding-investigation-interrogation-certain-detainees [https://perma.cc/H5WH-TVY2].

76 *Id.* Three years later, the Senate Intelligence Committee issued its report on the CIA's detention and interrogation program. SENATE SELECT COMM. ON INTELLIGENCE, COMMITTEE STUDY OF THE CENTRAL INTELLIGENCE AGENCY'S DETENTION AND INTERROGATION PROGRAM, S. REP. NO. 113–288, at xii (2014). The Report concluded that the CIA's use of enhanced interrogation techniques "was not an effective means of acquiring intelligence or gaining cooperation from detainees," and that the CIA deliberately obscured the extent and brutality of the program to policymakers—including Congress and the President himself. *Id.* at xi–xxviii. The Report also noted that those interrogation techniques were coercive and unauthorized, and that the CIA had no internal accountability measures. *Id.* at xxi, xxiii. Several advocacy organizations, led by the Human Rights Watch, subsequently called for the full Senate Intelligence Report to be declassified. *UN Human Rights Council: Joint NGO statement demanding full transparency and accountability for the U.S. CIA torture program*, Hum. Rts. Watch (Mar. 17, 2015), https://www.hrw.org/news/2015/03/17/un-human-rights-council-joint-ngo-statement-demanding-full-transparency-and [https://perma.cc/LP9Q-RH2M]. Likewise, advocacy groups have called for the declassification of the underlying findings contained in a separate Justice Department criminal investigation conducted by John Durham because the information from that investigation could be helpful in understanding the extent of the torture program, given the classification of the full Senate Intelligence Report. *See, e.g.*, Brian Tashman, *The Government Has Information on Gina Haspel's Torture Record. The Senate Can't See It.*, ACLU (May 15, 2018), https://www.aclu.org/news/national-security/government-has-information-gina-haspels-torture-record-senate-cant [https://perma.cc/9P3E-ZF98].

such suits never came to fruition. For example, although a group of Abu Ghraib victims filed an action for war crimes in Germany under that country's universal jurisdiction statute,[77] the statute requires approval from the chief German prosecutor before jurisdiction can be exercised. The prosecutor declined to move forward with the case,[78] most likely because of its politically sensitive nature.

Few of those implicated in the abuse faced civil sanctions either. Lawyers filed two federal suits against the companies that provided contract interrogators and translators implicated in the Abu Ghraib abuses. Relying in part on the Alien Tort Claims Act (ATCA),[79] which authorizes federal court jurisdiction over lawsuits "where an alien sues for a tort only [committed] in violation of the law of nations," plaintiffs alleged violations of international law, including extrajudicial killing, torture, war crimes, and crimes against humanity, as well as related domestic torts of assault, battery, sexual assault and battery, wrongful death, intentional and negligent infliction of emotional distress, and negligent hiring.[80] These claims were all subsequently dismissed by the D.C. Circuit.[81] However, a separate ATCA case against CACI in the Fourth Circuit was allowed to proceed and finally reached a verdict in November 2024, with a jury awarding the victims $42 million in damages.[82] And a third suit, brought against two CIA-contracted psychologists who allegedly developed many of the torture methods, ended in a confidential settlement on the eve of trial.[83]

To be sure, the military did subject many uniformed personnel to non-criminal sanctions. Army spokesman Major Wayne Marotto asserted

---

[77] *See, e.g.*, Scott Lyons, *German Criminal Complaint Against Donald Rumsfeld and Others*, 10 ASIL INSIGHTS, Issue 33 (2006), https://www.asil.org/insights/volume/10/issue/33/german-criminal-complaint-against-donald-rumsfeld-and-others#_edn1 [https://perma.cc/P7UE-JGSX].

[78] Opinion of the Prosecutor General at the Federal Supreme Court, Apr. 5, 2007 (English translation), http://www.fidh.org/IMG/pdf/ProsecutorsDecisionApril2007ENGLISH.pdf [https://perma.cc/5CM4-D8GV].

[79] 28 U.S.C. § 1350. For further discussion of the ATCA, see Harold Koh's chapter in this volume. Harold Hongju Koh, Filártiga v. Peña-Irala*: Judicial Internalization of the Customary International Law Norm Against Torture, in* INTERNATIONAL LAW STORIES (John E. Noyes, Laura A. Dickinson, Mark Weston Janis & Carlos M. Vázquez eds., 2d ed., 2025).

[80] Ibrahim v. Titan Corp., 391 F. Supp. 2d 10 (D.D.C. 2005); Saleh v. Titan Corp., 436 F. Supp. 2d 55 (D.D.C. 2006).

[81] Saleh v. Titan Corp., 580 F.3d 1 (D.C. Cir. 2009).

[82] *See* Al Shimari v. CACI Premier Technology, Judgment (E.D. Va., Nov. 12, 2024), https://ccrjustice.org/sites/default/files/attach/2024/11/VERDICT_in_Al_Shimari_trial.pdf [https://perma.cc/4KY5-ARBL]; *see also* Matthew Barakat, *Judge rejects military contractor's bid to end Abu Ghraib torture suit,* FED. TIMES (Aug. 2, 2023), https://www.federaltimes.com/federal-oversight/doj-fbi/2023/08/02/judge-rejects-military-contractors-bid-to-end-abu-ghraib-torture-suit/ [https://perma.cc/R6GZ-3Q4A] ("In a previous hearing, [Judge Leonie] Brinkema said there is evidence implicating CACI in the torture regime at Abu Ghraib, including an email from a CACI employee assigned to Abu Ghraib that she described as a potential 'smoking gun.' ").

[83] *CIA Torture Psychologists Settle Lawsuit,* ACLU (Aug. 17, 2017), https://www.aclu.org/press-releases/cia-torture-psychologists-settle-lawsuit [https://perma.cc/2EGM-HL3V].

in the spring of 2006 that the Army had investigated more than 600 accusations of detainee abuse in Iraq and Afghanistan since October 2001, and had punished 251 officers and enlisted soldiers for misconduct related to prisoners.[84] In addition, several generals and colonels received career-ending reprimands and were stripped of their commands. Nevertheless, there is little indication that other senior-level officers and civilian officials will ever be held accountable in any form. For example, although Brigadier General Karpinski was reassigned and demoted after the Abu Ghraib abuse, and Colonel Pappas was reprimanded and relieved of his command,[85] Defense Secretary Rumsfeld received only a relatively mild admonishment in August 2004 from the Schlesinger panel, which faulted him only for not exercising sufficient oversight. Moreover, when asked if Rumsfeld or other high-ranking officials should resign as a way of taking responsibility for the abuses, Schlesinger said no, opining that the Secretary's "resignation would be a boon to all of America's enemies."[86] In the end, Secretary Rumsfeld remained in office until after the November 2006 congressional elections.

II. THE ROLE OF MILITARY CULTURE

The story of abuse at Abu Ghraib is in many respects a story about the power of organizational culture within the U.S. military. The violations of international law committed at Abu Ghraib are at odds with a deeply entrenched commitment, within the military, to the international law of war. In the months preceding the abuse, administration authorities took a series of actions that undermined that culture: making statements of policy that emphasized the gaps and ambiguities in the law of war; issuing multiple, confusing directives on permissible interrogation practices for troops on the ground; failing to ensure adequate training; permitting multiple different groups—uniformed troops, civilian intelligence personnel, special operations forces, and private contractors—to co-mingle without clear division of roles and lines of authority; and greatly expanding the role of private contractors.[87] Yet at the same time, the long-standing organizational culture of respect for the law of war within the military proved to be at least somewhat resistant to these interventions by predominantly civilian political appointees. Uniformed officers and military lawyers, concerned about the administration's changes, helped to roll back many of them and implemented reforms designed to prevent further abuse.

A Tradition of Respect for the Rule of Law. The U.S. military has a long tradition of respect for the rule of law and the limits that the

---

[84] Schmitt, *supra* note 41.

[85] *Id.*

[86] *Quoted in Pentagon Panel: Top Brass Was Lax in Abu Ghraib Oversight*, NBCNEWS.COM (Aug. 24, 2004, 11:03 AM), https://www.nbcnews.com/id/wbna5807013 [https://perma.cc/E6CH-E9RR].

[87] For excellent, in-depth discussions of many of these practices, see Amann, *supra* note 3; Pearlstein, *supra* note 3.

law of war places on soldiers. As long ago as the U.S. Civil War, the U.S. Army published the *Instruction for Government of Armies of the United States in the Field* of 1863,[88] also known as the Lieber Code (because it was prepared by Francis Lieber). The Code set forth rules of conduct for U.S. forces that included humane treatment of detainees. Specifically, the Lieber Code states that "[m]ilitary necessity does not admit of cruelty—that is, the infliction of suffering for the sake of suffering or for revenge, nor of maiming or wounding except in fight, nor of torture to extort confessions."[89] Indeed, the Lieber Code helped spawn the branch of international humanitarian law that governs the law of hostilities, commonly known as Hague law.[90]

Following the Civil War, the U.S. Armed Forces embraced a culture of professionalism and respect for law.[91] The United States also played an active role in furthering the evolution of international humanitarian law from the Civil War to the period after World War II, which culminated in the adoption of the four Geneva Conventions and the enactment of the Uniform Code of Military Justice. Throughout this period, the U.S. Armed Forces trained troops in this emerging law of war. Indeed, the U.S. Military Academy began offering courses in the subject as early as 1863.[92] At the same time, lawyers within the military played a significant role in interpreting and applying these developing laws. The Army, for example, has maintained a permanent Judge Advocate General's (JAG) Corps of military lawyers since 1862.[93]

Nevertheless, the aftermath of the Vietnam war marked a turning point in the uniformed military's relationship to the law of war. The existence of such law obviously had not prevented U.S. troops from committing widespread atrocities at My Lai and elsewhere. After My Lai, a high-level Army investigation blamed the military's failure both to adequately train troops in war crimes law and to provide procedures for reporting abuses.[94] In response, the U.S. military strengthened its internal codes of conduct, updating the *U.S. Army Field Manual* so that, in addition to specifying prohibited acts, it emphasized that the main objective of wartime detention operations is "the implementation of the

---

[88] Instructions for the Government of Armies of the United States in the Field, General Orders No. 100 (Apr. 24, 1963), https://tile.loc.gov/storage-services/service/ll/llmlp/Instructions-gov-armies/Instructions-gov-armies.pdf [https://perma.cc/S9DZ-F89U].

[89] *Id.* ¶ 16.

[90] *See* Theodor Meron, *Francis Lieber's Code and the Principles of Humanity, in* POLITICS, VALUES, AND FUNCTIONS: INTERNATIONAL LAW IN THE 21ST CENTURY 249 (Jonathan I. Charney et al. eds., 1997). *See also* Thomas G. Barnes, *Introduction, in* RICHARD SHELLY HARTIGAN, LIEBER'S CODE AND THE LAW OF WAR 3 (1995); Theodor Meron, *The Humanization of Humanitarian Law*, 94 AM. J. INT'L L. 239 (2000).

[91] *See generally* SAMUEL P. HUNTINGTON, THE SOLDIER AND THE STATE (1957).

[92] *See* Patrick Finnegan, *The Study of Law as a Foundation of Leadership and Command: The History of Law Instruction at the United States Military Academy at West Point*, 181 MIL. L. REV. 112 (2004).

[93] *Id.*

[94] DEP'T OF THE ARMY, REPORT OF THE DEPARTMENT OF THE ARMY REVIEW OF THE PRELIMINARY INVESTIGATIONS INTO THE MY LAI INCIDENT (1970).

Geneva Conventions."[95] At the same time, the Department of Defense (DOD) dramatically stepped up training activities and gave military lawyers a greater role[96] by initiating a "law of war program," run primarily by the JAG Corps, designed to educate troops from all services in the law of war.[97] The JAG Corps also was given responsibility for helping to develop and review operations plans to ensure compliance with the law of war.[98] Such actions helped institutionalize the central role of these lawyers in vetting operational activities, often while embedded on the battlefield along with combat troops.[99] Thus, the military as a whole deepened its commitment to the laws of war, and, just as significantly, it put in place a group of lawyers with a clear mission to enforce adherence to that law.

Policies that Undermined the Military's Commitment to the Law of War. Following the terrorist attacks on the United States in September 2001, Bush administration officials took many steps that effectively undermined this long-standing military culture of commitment to the law of war. Indeed, some accounts suggest that a number of senior officials did so deliberately, in an effort to deconstruct what they perceived to be a pervasive culture of legalism and rule-following that they deemed to be outmoded in an era of terrorist threat.[100]

Policy Statements Narrowing Reach of Geneva Conventions. First, senior administration political appointees made many statements, both public and private, that at the very least sowed confusion about the precise legal rules that should apply to particular categories of detainees, and even went so far as to purport to exempt many detainees from any

---

[95] James F. Gebhardt, *The Road to Abu Ghraib: U.S. Army Detainee Doctrine and Experience*, MIL. REV., Jan.–Feb. 2005, at 44, 50.

[96] FREDERIC L. BORCH, JUDGE ADVOCATES IN COMBAT: ARMY LAWYERS IN MILITARY OPERATIONS FROM VIETNAM TO HAITI 30 (2001).

[97] *Id.* at 37; U.S. DEP'T OF DEF., DIRECTIVE 5100.77, DOD LAW OF WAR PROGRAM (Nov. 5, 1974), *cancelled by* U.S. DEP'T OF DEF., DIRECTIVE 5100.77, DOD LAW OF WAR PROGRAM (Dec. 9, 1998), https://ihl-databases.icrc.org/en/national-practice/directive-no-510077-dod-law-war-program-department-defense-1998 [https://perma.cc/6CMD-TMNP] (reissuing 1974 directive "to update policy and responsibilities in the Department of Defense").

[98] BORCH, *supra* note 96, at 31.

[99] For further discussion of the key role military lawyers play in inculcating international humanitarian law norms on the battlefield, see generally Laura A. Dickinson, *Military Lawyers on the Battlefield: An Empirical Account of International Law Compliance*, 104 AM. J. INT'L L. 1 (2010).

[100] *See, e.g.*, Seymour M. Hersh, *The General's Report*, NEW YORKER (June 25, 2007) (reporting Gen. Antonio Taguba's belief that he was forced to retire because he had been too thorough in reporting on abuses at Abu Ghraib as well as Taguba's statement that Secretary of Defense Rumsfeld knew about the damning Abu Ghraib photos before he said he did); *see also* U.S. DEP'T OF DEF., THE NATIONAL DEFENSE STRATEGY OF THE UNITED STATES OF AMERICA 5 (2005), https://history.defense.gov/Portals/70/Documents/nds/2005_NDS.pdf?ver=tFA4Qqo94ZB0x_S6uL0QEg%3D%3D [https://perma.cc/GV7L-9HKV] (calling the use of international "judicial process" a "strategy of the weak," akin to terrorism, that threatens "[o]ur strength as a nation state"); RICHARD A. CLARKE, AGAINST ALL ENEMIES (2004) (quoting President Bush saying, with regard to military intervention, "I don't care what the international lawyers say, we are going to kick some ass.").

legal protections whatsoever.[101] For example, a January 2002 memorandum issued by White House Counsel Alberto Gonzales asserted that "the war against terrorism is a new kind of war" that "renders obsolete Geneva's strict limitations on questioning of enemy prisoners and renders quaint" other provisions of the treaty.[102] In a memo written that same month, two lawyers from the Department of Justice's Office of Legal Counsel (OLC), Deputy Assistant Attorney General John Yoo and Special Counsel Robert Delahunty, argued that the Geneva Conventions did not protect members of Al Qaeda or Taliban militia captured in Afghanistan.[103] They reasoned that the "Al Qaeda organization . . . as a non-state actor cannot be a party to the international agreements governing war." Likewise, Defense Secretary Rumsfeld stated that "unlawful combatants do not have any rights under the Geneva Conventions,"[104] asserting that the United States would treat detainees in a manner "reasonably consistent with the Geneva Conventions," but only as a matter of policy and not because the treaties required it.[105]

In August 2002, the OLC produced a memorandum on the treatment of detainees that radically narrowed the prevailing understanding of prohibitions on torture and cruel treatment. Authored by John Yoo and signed by Jay S. Bybee, the memo concluded that, for coercive interrogation to amount to torture, the "victim must experience intense pain or suffering of the kind that is equivalent to the pain that would be associated with serious physical injury so severe that death, organ failure, or permanent damage resulting in a loss of significant bodily function will likely result."[106] In addition, the 2002 Yoo memo advised that the President not only had the authority to order any and all treatment falling short of such pain, but also that "even if an interrogation method arguably were to violate [the federal statute prohibiting war crimes], the statute would be unconstitutional if it

---

101 For an argument that ambiguities in the rules themselves enabled officials to make these arguments, see Amann, *supra* note 3.

102 Memorandum from Alberto R. Gonzales, White House Gen. Couns., to President George W. Bush, Re: Application of the Geneva Convention on Prisoners of War to the Conflict with Al Qaeda and the Taliban (Jan. 25, 2002), https://nsarchive2.gwu.edu/torturingdemocracy/documents/20020125.pdf [https://perma.cc/RDR7-WFYM]. The memorandum did not address whether Al Qaeda detainees would be entitled to protection against inhumane treatment under Geneva Convention IV, *supra* note 2, governing all others caught up in the scope of armed conflict.

103 Memorandum from John Yoo, Deputy Assistant Att'y Gen. & Robert J. Delahunty, Special Couns., to William J. Haynes II, Gen. Couns., Dep't of Def., Re: Application of Treaties and Laws to al Qaeda and Taliban Detainees (draft dated Jan. 9, 2002), https://nsarchive2.gwu.edu/torturingdemocracy/documents/20020109.pdf [https://perma.cc/X8R2-39HE].

104 *Defense Department Briefing: Donald Rumsfeld & Richard B. Myers*, at 8:56 (C-Span television broadcast Jan. 11, 2002), https://www.c-span.org/program/news-conference/defense-department-briefing/153229#!.

105 *Id.*

106 Memorandum from Jay S. Bybee, Assistant Att'y Gen., Office of Legal Couns., to Alberto R. Gonzales, Couns. to the President, Re: Standards of Conduct for Interrogation under 18 U.S.C. §§ 2340–2340A (Aug. 1, 2002), https://nsarchive2.gwu.edu/torturingdemocracy/documents/20020801-1.pdf [https://perma.cc/Q3TD-ZKN4].

impermissibly encroached on the President's constitutional power to conduct a military campaign."[107] Thus, the memo argued that any congressional legislation that interfered with the President's authority as Commander-in-Chief would be unconstitutional.

After the United States invaded Iraq in April 2003, the Bush administration stated publicly that it would treat detainees held in that conflict in accordance with the Geneva Conventions,[108] but in practice both its earlier statements regarding Al Qaeda and its policy guidance on the ground undermined that position. For example, under the established Geneva regime set forth in the two most applicable Conventions—those regarding prisoners of war and civilians picked up during armed conflict—military doctrine had long recognized four categories of detainees: enemy prisoners of war, retained personnel, civilian internees, and a residual category for other detainees. Yet, the United States "began housing thousands of detainees whose non-doctrinal identification brought with it indeterminate legal status: enemy combatants, unprivileged enemy combatants, security internees, criminal detainees, military intelligence holds, persons under U.S. forces control, and low-level enemy combatants."[109] Moreover, as troops transferred from Afghanistan to Iraq, the "shifting set of apparently applicable rules—including what kind of treatment attached to what kind of detainee—became increasingly difficult to follow."[110]

Confusing Directives to Troops on the Ground. Department of Defense directives to front-line forces on specific practices also sowed confusion. For example, in November 2002, shortly after OLC issued its policy guidance on torture, a memorandum from William J. Haynes II, the Legal Adviser to the Secretary of Defense, authorized specific so-called "counter-resistance" techniques for the interrogation of detainees at Guantánamo.[111] Approved by Secretary Rumsfeld, these techniques included both somewhat milder practices—such as sensory deprivation, hooding, forced nudity, removal of religious items, "use of stress positions (like standing), for a maximum of four hours," and claiming that the interrogator came "from a country with a reputation for harsh treatment"[112]—and more severe techniques, such as the use of military

---

[107] *Id.*

[108] *See* Dep't of Def., Briefing on Geneva Convention, EPWs and War Crimes (Apr. 7, 2003), https://www.thetorturedatabase.org/files/foia_subsite/c05951412.pdf [https://perma.cc/XF54-XGZ5].

[109] Pearlstein, *supra* note 3, at 1262 (citing DAIG Report, *supra* note 35, at 44–47; Fay Report, *supra* note 35, at 11–12).

[110] *Id.*

[111] Memorandum from William J. Haynes II, Gen. Couns., to Sec'y of Def., Re: Counter-Resistance Techniques (Nov. 27, 2002), https://library.rumsfeld.com/doclib/sp/380/2002-11-27%20from%20Haynes%20re%20Counter-Resistance%20Techniques.pdf [https://perma.cc/W9FC-FEP5]; *see also* Schmidt Report, *supra* note 35, at 14.

[112] Memorandum from William J. Haynes II, *supra* note 111 (approved by Rumsfeld on Dec. 2, 2002, with handwritten comment: "However, I stand for 8–10 hours a day. Why is standing limited to 4 hours?").

dogs to induce fear and exploit "individual phobias," the "use of scenarios designed to convince the detainee that death or severely painful consequences are imminent for him and/or his family," the "use of mild, non-injurious physical contact," and the "use of a wet towel and dripping water to induce the misperception of suffocation."[113] In December, Rumsfeld expanded the directive to include all detainees at Guantánamo and to authorize "stress positions," twenty-hour interrogations, the removal of clothing, isolation for up to thirty days, and sensory deprivation.[114] Meanwhile, a Pentagon "Working Group" on interrogation techniques, established by Secretary Rumsfeld, first issued guidance in March 2003 that tracked the earlier OLC torture memo, and then in April 2003 approved a list of harsh interrogation tactics that included stress positions, environmental manipulation, removal of clothing, prolonged isolation, and the use of dogs.[115]

These techniques then migrated from Guantánamo to Afghanistan[116] and Iraq.[117] For example, as discussed previously, Secretary Rumsfeld sent Major General Miller—in charge of detainee operations at Guantánamo—to Iraq to jump start what were perceived to be inadequate interrogation operations there. Miller then instructed the field commanders in Iraq on the techniques approved initially only for limited use at Guantánamo Bay,[118] and used the Working Group techniques as a "baseline" for his recommendations.[119] In September 2003, following Miller's visit to Iraq, Lieutenant General Ricardo Sanchez, then U.S. Army Commander of the coalition Joint Task Force in Iraq, authorized the use of twenty-nine controversial interrogation techniques, including the use of dogs to exploit "Arab fear of dogs," isolation, stress positions, sensory and sleep deprivation, and environmental manipulation.[120] Less than a month later, following objections by military lawyers who found the techniques "overly aggressive,"[121] General Sanchez modified the previous order but continued to authorize interrogators to control lighting, heating, food, shelter, and clothing given to detainees.[122]

Given these circumstances, it is evident that the rules and procedures for troops on the ground were murky at best. As one Army

113 *Id.*

114 *Id.*

115 Memorandum from Gen. Couns. for the Dep't of Def., to the Commander, U.S. S. Command, Re: Counter-Resistance Techniques in the War on Terrorism (Apr. 16, 2003), https://nsarchive2.gwu.edu/torturingdemocracy/documents/20030416.pdf [https://perma.cc/4S3X-ELLG].

116 Church Report, *supra* note 35, at 6.

117 Fay Report, *supra* note 35, at 24–25; Miller Report, *supra* note 35, at 2.

118 Fay Report, *supra* note 35, at 24–25; Miller Report, *supra* note 35, at 2.

119 Miller Report, *supra* note 35, at 2.

120 Fay Report, *supra* note 35, at 25.

121 Church Report, *supra* note 35, at 8.

122 Fay Report, *supra* note 35, at 16, 26; Schlesinger Report, *supra* note 35, at 10, 14–15, 37–38.

general noted, "[b]y October 2003, interrogation policy in Iraq had changed three times in less than thirty days and it became very confusing as to what techniques could be employed and at what level non-doctrinal approaches had to be approved."[123] Different agencies and units were effectively operating side by side using different interrogation techniques drawn from different theaters of operation, influenced by general policy directives that muddied the waters still further.[124] Not surprisingly, this period saw some of the worst abuses.

Commingling of Different Units and Lack of Clear Lines of Authority. Meanwhile, the Bush administration allowed several organizational changes on the ground that further contributed to the confusion and the resulting abuse. The CIA and other special operations forces mingled with the military police reservists in charge of detentions at Abu Ghraib, creating a climate in which abuse could more readily occur. The CIA and special operations forces reportedly employed waterboarding and other techniques that were "harsher . . . than allowed" under typical Army rules. The use of these techniques fostered "the belief that such methods were condoned," according to the Schlesinger Report.[125] And, as discussed previously, the Fay Report similarly concluded that flouting of military procedures by CIA officers who had conducted interrogations inside the prison "eroded the necessity in the minds of Soldiers and civilians for them to follow Army rules."[126]

An Expanded Role for Private Contractors. At the same time, the expanded role of private military contractors exacerbated the abuse. At Abu Ghraib, interrogators hired under a contract between the U.S. Department of the Interior and CACI Inc. reportedly supervised uniformed personnel during interrogations.[127] Translators hired under a similar contract with Titan Inc. were also present.[128] Yet, these interrogators and translators rarely had received any training in interrogation tactics or the permissible use of force during interrogation as a matter of international and U.S. law.[129] The contractual agreements themselves said little or nothing about whether contractors would receive education in international humanitarian and human rights law, training

---

123 *Quoted in* Fay Report, *supra* note 35, at 8.

124 Schlesinger Report, *supra* note 35, at 14, 33–38, 70, 81; Fay Report, *supra* note 35, at 16, 21–30, 42–44, 52–55, 118–19; Jones Report, *supra* note 35, at 14–15.

125 Jones Report, *supra* note 35, at 25.

126 Fay Report, *supra* note 35, at 44–45.

127 *See* Taguba Report, *supra* note 35, at 26, 36, 48; SEYMOUR M. HERSH, CHAIN OF COMMAND 32–34, 61 (2004); Joel Brinkley & James Glanz, *Contractors in Sensitive Roles, Unchecked*, N.Y. TIMES, May 7, 2004, at A15, https://www.nytimes.com/2004/05/07/world/struggle-for-iraq-civilian-employees-contractors-sensitive-roles-unchecked.html; *see also* Hersh, *supra* note 13, at 61.

128 *See* Taguba Report, *supra* note 35, at 26, 36, 48; Brinkley & Glanz, *supra* note 127.

129 Fay Report, *supra* note 35, at 50–51.

that U.S. military interrogators would normally receive.[130] Not surprisingly then, an Army Inspector General report on the conditions that led to the Abu Ghraib scandal concluded that thirty-five percent of CACI's Iraq interrogators did not even have any "formal training in military interrogation policies and techniques," let alone training in international law norms. Indeed, Torin Nelson, one of the thirty CACI interrogators at Abu Ghraib, asserted that CACI employed people with experience only as "cooks and truck drivers" to conduct interrogations.[131]

The use of contractors contributed to abuse not only because of the contractors' lack of training, but also because supervision of contractors was weak, and their role within the theater was often uncertain. General Fay, for example, emphasized that "no doctrine exists to guide interrogators and their intelligence leaders . . . in the contract management or command and control of contractors in a wartime environment. These interrogators and leaders faced numerous issues involving contract management," including the "roles, relationships, and responsibilities of contract linguists and contract interrogators with military personnel" and the "methods of disciplining contractor personnel."[132]

Contractors also committed abuses directly. For example, according to the Fay Report, one contractor, while interrogating an Iraqi policeman, prevented him from breathing for several seconds during interrogation.[133] In another incident, a contractor reportedly grabbed a detainee from the back of a truck, dropped him on the ground, and dragged him to an interrogation booth.[134] When the detainee attempted to rise to his knees, the contractor forced him to fall again on the ground.[135]

The Embeddedness of Organizational Norms and Values: The Role of Military Lawyers and Other Uniformed Personnel. Despite the undeniable influence of these policies, what is perhaps most striking in the story of Abu Ghraib and its aftermath is the significant role that uniformed military personnel, and in particular military lawyers, played in *resisting* these efforts. Indeed, although senior administration officials seeking to narrow the reach of international law in the fight against terrorism often deliberately excluded military lawyers from the conversation, those lawyers, both active and retired, worked in public and behind the scenes to try to thwart or tame administration policies.

---

130 *See generally* LAURA A. DICKINSON, OUTSOURCING WAR AND PEACE (2011); *see also* Laura A. Dickinson, *Public Law Values in a Privatized World*, 31 YALE J. INT'L L. 383 (2006); Fay Report, *supra* note 35, at 50–51.

131 Julian Borger, *Private Contractor Lifts the Lid on Systematic Failures at Abu Ghraib Jail*, GUARDIAN, May 7, 2004, at 4.

132 Fay Report, *supra* note 35, at 19.

133 *Id.* at 79.

134 *Id.*

135 *Id.*

For example, during the debate that followed the President's initial order establishing the use of military commissions to try terrorism suspects, military lawyers were particularly vocal. A team of administration political appointees from the White House, the Office of Legal Counsel, and Vice President Dick Cheney's office worked largely in secret to prepare the order, and they excluded military lawyers (as well as lawyers from the State Department) from the process.[136] Immediately following the release of the order, however, military lawyers strongly criticized the plan, in particular the denial of important procedural protections to defendants, including the lack of any right to choose a lawyer or to receive a unanimous death sentence.[137] These lawyers also expressed concern that the lack of protections in the proposed military commissions would, over time, undermine perceptions of the fairness of military justice more broadly, even though the UCMJ includes strong protections for the rights of the accused.[138]

Partly in response to such criticisms, the Bush administration developed regulations that softened some of the most disputed provisions and required, for example, unanimity before the death penalty could be imposed, a presumption of innocence, proof beyond a reasonable doubt, and a military appeals process.[139] Yet, as the commissions began their work, the military lawyers appointed to defend the accused continued to challenge the process, particularly because of the lack of judicial review in civilian courts.[140] And after the U.S. Supreme Court struck down the use of commissions as originally constituted (see Oona Hathaway's account elsewhere in this volume), military lawyers again asserted themselves as vocal opponents of the administration's efforts to resurrect the commissions.[141] Lawyers objected, in particular, to the new commissions' rules that would allow the admission of evidence defendants had not seen.[142]

---

136 Tim Golden, *After Terror, a Secret Rewriting of Military Law*, N.Y. TIMES, Oct. 24, 2004, at A1, https://www.nytimes.com/2004/10/24/us/threats-and-responses-tough-justice-after-terror-a-secret-rewriting-of.html.

137 William Glaberson, *Tribunal v. Court-Martial: A Matter of Perception*, N.Y. TIMES, Dec. 2, 2001, at A6, https://www.nytimes.com/2001/12/02/us/a-nation-challenged-the-law-tribunal-v-court-martial-matter-of-perception.html (citing Edward Sherman, former Army lawyer and former dean of Tulane Law School); *see also* Golden, *supra* note 136.

138 Glaberson, *supra* note 137 (citing John S. Cooke, a retired Army judge who was chair of the American Bar Association Section on Armed Forces Law); Golden, *supra* note 136.

139 Neil A. Lewis, *Rules on Tribunal Require Unanimity on Death Penalty*, N.Y. TIMES, Dec. 28, 2001, at A1, https://www.nytimes.com/2001/12/28/us/nation-challenged-military-tribunals-rules-tribunal-require-unanimity-death.html.

140 Neil A. Lewis, *Lawyer Says Detainees Face Unfair System*, N.Y. TIMES, Jan. 22, 2004, at A25, https://www.nytimes.com/2004/01/22/us/lawyer-says-detainees-face-unfair-system.html; Jonathan Mahler, *Commander Swift Objects*, N.Y. TIMES MAG., June 13, 2004, at 42, https://www.nytimes.com/2004/06/13/magazine/commander-swift-objects.html.

141 Mark Mazzetti & Neil A. Lewis, *Military Lawyers Caught in Middle on Tribunals*, N.Y. TIMES, Sept. 16, 2006, at A1, https://www.nytimes.com/2006/09/16/washington/16jags.html.

142 *Id.*

Military lawyers also repeatedly criticized the broad policy guidance and field directives issued regarding interrogation practices. Indeed, military lawyers strenuously resisted the recommendations contained in the OLC and Defense Department Working Group memos that largely adopted a very narrow definition of torture and a broad definition of presidential authority. For example, Brigadier General Kevin M. Sandkuhler, a senior Marine lawyer, wrote in a February 27, 2003, memorandum that the harsh interrogation regime could ultimately have adverse consequences for American service members.[143] In a pointed statement the memo declares that the Justice Department "does not represent the services; thus, understandably, concern for service members is not reflected in their opinion."[144] Likewise, Major General Thomas J. Romig, the Army's top-ranking uniformed lawyer, wrote in a March 3, 2003, memorandum that the approach recommended by the Justice Department "will open us up to criticism that the U.S. is a law unto itself."[145] Criticism of the field directives regarding specific interrogation practices was similarly strong. Deputy Judge Advocate General of the Air Force, Major General Jack L. Rives, advised that many of "the more extreme interrogation techniques, on their face, amount to violations of domestic criminal law" as well as military law.[146] Rives argued that the use of many of these techniques "puts the interrogators and the chain of command at risk of criminal accusations abroad" in other countries' domestic courts or in international tribunals.[147] And in September 2003, military lawyers objected to General Sanchez's authorization of the controversial interrogation techniques in Iraq discussed previously. The lawyers argued that these techniques were "overly aggressive," presumably because they would run afoul of the UCMJ and international law.[148] Finally, military lawyers pushed for significant revisions to the *U.S. Army Field Manual on Intelligence Interrogations*. The new *Manual*, released in September 2006, specifies that the Geneva Conventions apply to all detainees and eliminates distinctions between prisoners of war and enemy combatants.[149] Thus, throughout the period of 2002–2006, we see a military legal culture fighting back against efforts by political appointees to weaken or muddy U.S. commitment to the law of war.

---

[143] Neil A. Lewis, *Military's Opposition to Harsh Interrogation Is Outlined*, N.Y. TIMES, July 28, 2005, at A21, https://www.nytimes.com/2005/07/28/politics/militarys-opposition-to-harsh-interrogation-is-outlined.html.

[144] *Quoted in id.*

[145] *Quoted in id.*

[146] *Quoted in id.*

[147] *Quoted in id.*

[148] Church Report, *supra* note 35, at 8.

[149] *See* Jeannie Shawl, *New US Army interrogation manual mandates Geneva Rules*, JURIST (Sept. 6, 2006), https://www.jurist.org/news/2006/09/new-us-army-interrogation-manual/ [https://perma.cc/Q7XV-AL6A]. Congress, however, failed to explicitly include the CIA in its prohibition on torture and cruel treatment. *See* DTA, *supra* note 47, § 1002(a). This gap was subsequently closed as part of the 2016 National Defense Authorization Act (NDAA), *see infra* text accompanying notes 154–155.

III. THE LEGACIES OF TORTURE: GUANTÁNAMO AND BEYOND

The use of torture in the U.S. war on terror, both at Abu Ghraib and elsewhere, has had lasting effects on U.S. law, military policy, and judicial proceedings. Indeed, since Abu Ghraib, in a series of statutes and policies, the U.S. government has consistently repudiated the use of torture and cruel, inhuman, and degrading treatment. First, as noted above, the Detainee Treatment Act of 2005 (DTA) explicitly prohibited "cruel, inhuman, or degrading treatment or punishment" of any prisoner of the U.S. Government and also required military interrogations to be performed according to the *U.S. Army Field Manual*.[150] Second, the Military Commissions Act of 2006, which authorized the President to create military commissions to try "unlawful enemy combatants" for "violations of the law of war,"[151] specifically banned the use of evidence obtained through torture during trials before military commissions.[152] Third, the Military Commissions Act of 2009 (MCA) replaced that prohibition with a broader exclusion of any evidence obtained through cruel, inhuman, and degrading treatment, as well as torture.[153] Fourth, the 2016 National Defense Authorization Act (NDAA) included a provision[154] that closed a gap in the DTA, prohibiting any interrogation techniques not explicitly authorized by the *Army Field Manual* by all government officials, not just the military. The DTA had not specified what constituted torture or cruel treatment, thus leaving open to interpretation whether certain harsh interrogation techniques such as waterboarding were prohibited. But the *Army Field Manual*[155] does not permit waterboarding; therefore, the NDAA effectively prohibited it, including by the CIA. Fifth, OLC replaced or repudiated several of the notorious memos that had been used to justify torture of detainees.[156] Finally, DOD contractors are now barred from participating in interrogations except in limited circumstances,[157] and all contractors are barred from committing torture and cruel treatment.[158]

---

150 DTA, *supra* note 47, § 1002(a).

151 10 U.S.C. § 948b(a)–(b).

152 *Id.* § 948r(b).

153 10 U.S.C. § 948r.

154 National Defense Authorization Act (NDAA) for FY 2016, § 1045(a), 129 Stat. 726, 977–79 (2015) (current version at 42 U.S.C. § 2000dd–2).

155 U.S. DEP'T OF ARMY, FIELD MANUAL § 2–22.3.

156 *See, e.g.*, Memorandum from Daniel Levin, Acting Assistant Att'y Gen., Off. of Legal Couns., Re: Definition of Torture Under 18 U.S.C. §§ 2340–2340A (Dec. 30, 2004), https://www.justice.gov/sites/default/files/olc/opinions/2004/12/31/op-olc-v028-p0297_0.pdf [https://perma.cc/7CM5-VPVM]; Press Release, U.S. Dep't of Justice, Department of Justice Releases Nine Office of Legal Counsel Memoranda and Opinions (Mar. 9, 2009), https://www.justice.gov/opa/pr/department-justice-releases-nine-office-legal-counsel-memoranda-and-opinions [https://perma.cc/44PY-9SFD].

157 NDAA for FY 2010, § 1038, 123 Stat. 2190, 2451–52 (2010).

158 REPORT ON THE LEGAL AND POLICY FRAMEWORKS GUIDING THE UNITED STATES' USE OF MILITARY FORCE AND RELATED NATIONAL SECURITY OPERATIONS 35 (2016),

Significantly, these various statutes and policies survived even during the first Trump administration. Trump had campaigned on bringing back torture and "loading up" Guantánamo Naval Base with more counterterrorism detainees. For example, Trump said that "torture works" and promised to "immediately" reinstate waterboarding and other forms of torture when he became President "because 'we have to beat the savages' of the Islamic State."[159] Similarly, on the campaign trail, Trump vowed to keep the wartime prison at Guantánamo Naval Base open, offered to "load it up with some bad dudes," and said he would support prosecuting U.S. citizens accused of terrorism in the military commissions there.[160] However, the cultural norms against torture within DOD and the U.S. government more broadly appear to have held. The Trump administration did not, in fact, reinstate torture (as far as we know) or bring a single new detainee to Guantánamo Naval Base.

Despite these advances, the period of torture continues to cast a cloud over U.S. detention policy. Indeed, the military commission proceedings have repeatedly bogged down over how to deal with evidence obtained during this period. The MCA provides in relevant part that "[n]o statement obtained by the use of torture or by cruel, inhuman, or degrading treatment . . . whether or not under color of law, shall be admissible in a military commission."[161] However, the Department of Justice and members of the military commissions have at times taken the position that this prohibition only applies to evidence at trial, and that evidence gleaned from torture could still be used during pre-trial proceedings.[162] Their chief argument is that the phrase "admissible in a military commission" narrows the scope of the exclusion to trials "on the merits or during presentencing proceedings," and does *not* serve as a blanket prohibition on the use of those statements in other types of proceedings.[163]

Nevertheless in 2022, as part of a filing before a military commission, the Biden administration reversed course, stating that it had "reconsidered" its original interpretation of the statute and now agreed that the MCA prohibition "applies to all stages of a military commission

---

https://www.state.gov/wp-content/uploads/2019/10/Report-to-Congress-on-legal-and-policy-frameworks-guiding-use-of-military-force-.pdf [https://perma.cc/U67S-VZ27].

159 Risen & Fink, *supra* note 8.

160 Savage, *supra* note 7.

161 10 U.S.C. § 948r(a).

162 *See, e.g.*, Government Response to Defense Motion to Strike AE353V, at 14–25, United States v. Al-Nashiri (Apr. 14, 2021) https://www.mc.mil/Portals/0/pdfs/alNashiri2/Al%20Nashiri%20II%20(AE353Y(PH)).pdf [https://perma.cc/FUN8-E88M]; David Luban, *Torture Evidence and the Guantanamo Military Commissions*, JUST SECURITY (May 26, 2021), https://www.justsecurity.org/76640/torture-evidence-and-the-guantanamo-military-commissions/ [https://perma.cc/Q86G-5TQ5]; *see also* David Luban, *Lawfare and Legal Ethics in Guantánamo*, 60 STAN. L. REV. 1981 (2008).

163 *Al-Nashiri*, AE 353AA, at 3; *see also In re* Al-Nashiri, 47 F.4th 820 (D.C. Cir. 2022).

case, including pretrial proceedings."[164] The administration also sought plea deals in the cases of five terrorism suspects held at Guantánamo Bay, in no small part because of protracted disputes regarding evidence gleaned from torture or by cruel, inhuman, or degrading treatment.[165]

Finally, there are still concerns that the continued detention of suspects at Guantánamo Bay itself constitutes cruel, inhuman, and degrading treatment in violation of international law. For example, in 2023 the United Nations Special Rapporteur for Counterterrorism issued a report on conditions at the facility based on her visit there.[166] The Special Rapporteur found that several procedures at Guantánamo Bay constituted "without doubt" cruel, inhuman, and degrading treatment, and "may also meet the legal definition for torture."[167] Those conditions included the use of solitary confinement and restraints,[168] inadequate access to family,[169] ongoing and arbitrary detention without due process,[170] and inadequate access to independent healthcare professionals.[171] While acknowledging the "positive" steps the United States had taken to improve conditions at the facility, the Special Rapporteur decried the lack of "adequate accounting of the international law violations including violations of the opening of the facility."[172] Such norms are defined as those that are fundamental, non-derogable, and peremptory. The United States responded to the report by indicating that it disagreed with her findings "in significant respects," but would carefully review the report and "take any appropriate actions."[173] It also

---

[164] *See* Brief of the United States in Opposition, at 3, *In re* Al-Nashiri, 47 F.4th 820 (D.C. Cir. 2022) (No. 21-1208), https://www.justsecurity.org/wp-content/uploads/2022/01/Document.pdf [https://perma.cc/264M-96PX].

[165] Ben Fox, *Plea discussions launched in stalled 9/11 case at Guantánamo*, ASSOCIATED PRESS (Mar. 15, 2022), https://apnews.com/article/cuba-terrorist-attacks-2634cf67b7543f7b13ba4fbd48c08010. Plea agreements were reached, and although Secretary of Defense Austin attempted to rescind them, the United States Court of Military Commission Review concluded that he lacked the authority to do so. *See* Carol Rosenberg, *Pentagon Appeals Court Upholds Plea Deals in Sept. 11 Case*, N.Y. TIMES, Dec. 30, 2024, https://www.nytimes.com/2024/12/30/us/politics/911-case-plea-deals.html.

[166] *See* U.N. Special Rapporteur for Counterterrorism, Technical Visit to the United States and Guantánamo Detention Facility by the Special Rapporteur on the Promotion and Protection of Human Rights and Fundamental Freedoms while Countering Terrorism (June 14, 2023), https://www.ohchr.org/sites/default/files/documents/issues/terrorism/sr/2023-06-26-SR-terrorism-technical-visit-US-guantanamo-detention-facility.pdf [https://perma.cc/6ZQW-UM7C].

[167] *Id.* ¶ 49.

[168] *Id.* ¶ 18.

[169] *Id.* ¶¶ 30–35.

[170] *Id.* ¶¶ 36–47.

[171] *Id.* ¶ 24.

[172] *Id.* ¶¶ 2–3.

[173] U.S. Mission Geneva, *U.S. Response to the UN Special Rapporteur on Countering Terrorism*, U.S. MISSION TO INT'L ORGS. IN GENEVA (June 26, 2023), https://geneva.usmission.gov/2023/06/26/u-s-response-to-the-un-special-rapporteur-on-countering-terrorism/ [https://perma.cc/B4Y5-MGVW] (transmitted June 22, 2023).

acknowledged that U.N. member states "must be willing to open themselves to the scrutiny of outside observers."[174]

The United States also appeared before the United Nations Human Rights Committee in 2023, as part of a periodic review of human rights conditions mandated by the International Covenant on Civil and Political Rights.[175] The Committee asked about the specific timeline for closing the Guantánamo Bay detention facility,[176] the availability of legal remedies for detained individuals without due process,[177] the admissibility of evidence gleaned from torture,[178] concerns over future use of military commission trials,[179] the United States' response to the Special Rapporteur Report,[180] and the process for transferring detainees to other facilities.[181] The U.S. delegation was forthright that its ultimate goal was to close the facility, but reiterated that in the meantime, it would try to transfer eligible detainees either to their home countries or to third-party countries, with assurances that the detainees would be treated humanely.[182] However, the delegation did not address the other questions raised by the Committee.

The United States has an obligation, under either international humanitarian law (sometimes called the law of armed conflict) or international human rights law to treat detainees humanely. Thus, to the extent that the Special Rapporteur Report and the Human Rights Committee review concerned the treatment of detainees at Guantánamo, they were focusing on issues that would be relevant regardless of the applicable legal paradigm.

However, to the extent that those reviews focused only on the fact of continued detention itself, the applicable law matters. This is because the law of armed conflict permits detention of prisoners of war until the cessation of hostilities. Thus, if, as successive U.S. administrations have insisted, the war on terror is still ongoing and is global, then continued detention is potentially justifiable. In contrast, many insist that the war should be treated as having ended, particularly given the U.S. withdrawal from Afghanistan in 2021. If so, then the law of armed conflict

---

[174] *Id.*

[175] International Covenant on Civil and Political Rights, Dec. 19, 1966, 999 U.N.T.S. 171.

[176] United Nations, *4051st Meeting, 139th Session, Human Rights Committee (CCPR)*, UN WEB TV, at 21:30–21:44 (Oct. 18, 2023), https://webtv.un.org/en/asset/k1e/k1e80otbb4 [https://perma.cc/4DHC-FG7R].

[177] *Id.* at 21:48–22:03.

[178] *Id.* at 19:27–19:56.

[179] *Id.* at 22:31–23:00.

[180] *Id.* at 23:00–23:41.

[181] *Id.* at 23:47–24:41.

[182] United Nations, *4050th Meeting, 139th Session, Human Rights Committee (CCPR)*, UN WEB TV, at 2:14:23–2:14:40, 2:15:00 (Oct. 17, 2023), https://webtv.un.org/en/asset/k1t/k1tu2vqwgo [https://perma.cc/ZZ5B-LU8B].

no longer applies to the detainees, and international human rights law prohibits indefinite detention without trial.[183]

IV. CONCLUSION

Although many stories can be told about the shocking abuses at Abu Ghraib, one of the most important stories concerns the role that institutional culture plays in the implementation of international law norms. It is, of course, a truism to observe that most international law norms are not backed by coercive sanctions. As a result, such norms will only be effective because groups of people internalize those norms and adopt them as their own. For this reason, the Bush administration's many statements about enemy combatants and the law of war, though often "only" rhetorical, likely played a crucial role in complicating, diluting, and ultimately undermining on-the-ground adherence to basic humanitarian law standards. Moreover, contradictory directives, complicated chains of command, and the comingling of military personnel, intelligence operatives, and civilian contractors further muddied the waters at precisely the worst moment: during the sort of high stress period after the Iraq invasion when abuses were most likely to occur. Thus, there can be little doubt that the abuses at Abu Ghraib can be linked to the weakening of the military's traditional commitment to the law of war. Yet, at the same time the story of Abu Ghraib's aftermath indicates that adherence to international law can, over time, become sufficiently internalized that it is not so easy to dislodge. Indeed, even as top administration officials weakened military adherence to rule-of-law norms, many members of the military, particularly those versed in military law, fought back.

The broader lesson is that, because international law relies in part on institutional internalization, we must take account of the ways in which weakening that institutional commitment can create the conditions where abuses are more likely to occur. But we must also recognize that, if a culture of internalization is nurtured over a long period of time, it can respond and reclaim a role for international law going forward. As the Army's response to the My Lai massacres indicates, revulsion concerning abuses such as those committed at Abu Ghraib can themselves inspire a new generation committed to preventing such abuses in the future. Institutional culture, it turns out, is a key site where battles over international law are fought, and Abu Ghraib has already become an iconic touchstone in that crucial, though sometimes invisible, internal struggle.

---

[183] For further discussion of the importance of these two paradigms with regard to counterterrorism activities, see generally Laura A. Dickinson, *Towards a New Framework for Direct Action, in* PERPETUAL WAR AND INTERNATIONAL LAW: LEGACIES OF THE WAR ON TERROR (Brianna Rosen ed., Oxford Univ. Press, forthcoming).

5

Yuval Shany

Mellet v. Ireland: Constitutional Limits on Abortion Before the Human Rights Committee

Do human rights treaties make a difference? In a 2002 article with that title,[1] Oona Hathaway suggested that ratification of human rights treaties is not necessarily correlated with higher levels of compliance with international human rights law (IHRL) norms. In fact, she stipulated that the expressive function of joining human rights treaties—that is, the public acceptance of the norms provided in such treaties—might "serve to relieve pressure for real change in performance."[2] *Mellet v. Ireland*, a case decided in 2016 by the Human Rights Committee—a body of experts monitoring the implementation of the International Covenant on Civil and Political Rights by states that have accepted this major human rights treaty—provides a dramatic focal point for exploring the impact of human rights treaties and identifying possible explanations for such an impact.[3]

One factor that Hathaway identified in support of her counterintuitive conclusion was the weakness of the global treaty-monitoring mechanisms.[4] Indeed, the international treaty-monitoring bodies established, on a global level, to monitor the implementation of IHRL do not have the power to issue binding decisions (unlike regional courts, such as the European or Inter-American Courts of Human Rights, which can issue binding judgments). Rather, they generate non-binding normative outputs: recommendations to states concerning their IHRL practices in the form of concluding observations following periodic

---

1 Oona A. Hathaway, *Do Human Rights Treaties Make a Difference?*, 111 YALE L.J. 1935 (2002).

2 *Id.* at 2007. This assertion was questioned by Goodman and Jinks. *See* Ryan Goodman & Derek Jinks, *Measuring the Effects of Human Rights Treaties*, 14 EUR. J. INT'L L. 171 (2003).

3 Human Rights Comm., Views adopted by the Committee under article 5(4) of the Optional Protocol, concerning communication No. 2324/2013, U.N. Doc. CCPR/C/116/D/2324/2013 (2016) [hereinafter *Mellet*]. For the treaty provisions establishing and governing the Human Rights Committee, see International Covenant on Civil and Political Rights arts. 28–45, Dec. 16, 1966, 999 U.N.T.S. 171 [hereinafter ICCPR].

4 Hathaway, *supra* note 1, at 2022–23.

reviews of state reports,[5] non-binding "views" about individual communications alleging IHRL violations,[6] broad legal standards expounded through general comments,[7] and other committee documents (such as inquiry reports[8] and declarations[9]). Whereas the decisions of some international courts can be enforced through the operation of political organs of inter-governmental organizations, such as the Council of Europe Committee of Ministers[10] or the U.N. Security Council,[11] the normative outputs of global IHRL treaty bodies do not enjoy the support of such enforcement mechanisms, and are therefore mostly unenforceable as a formal matter.[12]

Still, despite the non-binding status of treaty body decisions, and the scarcity of formal enforcement powers attached to them, some decisions are being implemented. In fact, research conducted by the former secretary of the Human Rights Committee found that twenty-three percent of the Committee's views have generated meaningful implementation measures.[13] Such instances of implementation can be explained through traditional theories of international relations, for example, (a) a realistic cost-benefit analysis conducted by states, which leads to implementation when the reputational dividends of compliance with non-binding decisions outweigh the costs of the policy change;[14] (b) the tendency of liberal states to embrace judicial or quasi-judicial IHRL

---

[5] *See, e.g.*, ICCPR, *supra* note 3, art. 40. For a discussion of periodic review of state reports to treaty bodies, see Walter Kälin, *Examination of state reports*, *in* UN HUMAN RIGHTS TREATY BODIES: LAW AND LEGITIMACY 16 (Helen Keller & Geir Ulfstein eds., 2012).

[6] *See, e.g.*, ICCPR, *supra* note 3. For a discussion of review of individual communications by treaty bodies, see Geir Ulfstein, *Individual complaints*, *in* UN HUMAN RIGHTS TREATY BODIES, *supra* note 5, at 73.

[7] *See, e.g.*, Helen Keller & Leena Grover, *General Comments of the Human Rights Committee and their legitimacy*, *in* UN HUMAN RIGHTS TREATY BODIES, *supra* note 5, at 116.

[8] *See, e.g.*, Optional Protocol to the Convention on the Elimination of All Forms of Discrimination against Women, Oct. 6, 1999, 2131 U.N.T.S. 83 (entered into force Dec. 22, 2000).

[9] *See, e.g.*, Comm. on the Elimination of Racial Discrimination, Prevention of Racial Discrimination, including Early Warning and Urgent Action Procedures: Statement 3: France (2023), https://www.ohchr.org/en/press-releases/2023/07/statement-france-un-committee-elimination-racial-discrimination?sub-site=HRC.

[10] Convention on the Protection of Human Rights and Fundamental Freedoms art. 46, Nov. 4, 1950, E.T.S. No. 5, 213 U.N.T.S. 221.

[11] *See* U.N. Charter art. 94.

[12] Note, however, that some state parties to IHRL treaties have stipulated in their domestic laws or domestic court decisions that all or some treaty body views would be treated as binding. *See, e.g.*, Koldo Casla, *Supreme Court of Spain: UN Treaty Body individual decisions are legally binding*, EJIL TALK! (Aug. 1, 2018), https://www.ejiltalk.org/supreme-court-of-spain-un-treaty-body-individual-decisions-are-legally-binding/; L. 288/96, julio 5, 1996, DIARIO OFICIAL [D.O.] (Colom.).

[13] Kate Fox Principi, *Implementation of Decisions under UN Treaty Body Complaint Procedures—How Do States Comply?*, 37 HUM. RTS. L.J. 1 (2017).

[14] *See, e.g.*, Andrew T. Guzman, *A Compliance-Based Theory of International Law*, 90 CAL. L. REV. 1823, 1846 (2002).

decisions, barring strong reasons not to do so;[15] and (c) the persuasive impact of engaging in repeat interactions in international fora.[16]

A different explanation for compliance in the human rights law context has been offered by Beth Simmons. She has suggested that IHRL norms tend to have an impact when they are mobilized by domestic change actors, such as civil society groups or political elites.[17] The dramatic story of implementation of the Human Rights Committee's decision in *Mellet v. Ireland* generates interesting insights about compliance incentives, and operates to reinforce Simmons's theoretic claims. Indeed, the story of *Mellet v. Ireland* suggests that, in certain socio-political contexts, effective domestic mobilization can compensate for the lack of a binding effect and the weakness of formal enforcement avenues. It also suggests that, to the extent human rights treaty bodies are keen to enhance compliance with their decisions, they should be attuned to the ways in which such decisions are perceived by domestic audiences. The *Mellet* story thus suggests that treaty bodies' choices pertaining to the framing of decisions can increase their decisions' mobilization potential. The *Mellet* case illustrates some of these design choices.

I. THE DEBATE OVER IRELAND'S ABORTION LAWS

A fierce debate over the legal regulation of abortion has been going on in Ireland for many decades. In a 1983 referendum, two-thirds of Irish voters supported the eighth amendment to the Irish Constitution (which became section 40.3.3. of the Constitution).[18] The amendment provided: "The State acknowledges the right of life of the unborn and, with due regard to the equal right to life of the mother, guarantees in its laws to respect, and, as far as practicable, by its laws to defend and vindicate that right." The law giving practical effect to the eighth constitutional amendment when the *Mellet* case was considered was the Protection of Life During Pregnancy Act 2013,[19] which repealed and replaced provisions on abortion found in the Offences Against the Person Act 1861.[20] The 2013 Act provided that abortion could only take place following medical certification that abortion is needed to avert "real and

[15] *See, e.g.*, Benedict Kingsbury, *The Concept of Compliance as a Function of Competing Conceptions of International Law*, 19 MICH. J. INT'L L. 345, 356–57 (1998).

[16] *See, e.g.*, RYAN GOODMAN & DEREK JINKS, SOCIALIZING STATES: PROMOTING HUMAN RIGHTS THROUGH INTERNATIONAL LAW 24–26 (2013).

[17] *See* BETH A. SIMMONS, MOBILIZING FOR HUMAN RIGHTS: INTERNATIONAL LAW IN DOMESTIC POLITICS (2012).

[18] Eighth Amendment to the Constitution Act 1983 (1983) (Ir.), https://www.irishstatutebook.ie/eli/1983/ca/8/enacted/en/print.

[19] Protection of Life During Pregnancy Act 2013 (Act No. 13/2013) (Ir.), https://www.irishstatutebook.ie/eli/2013/act/35/enacted/en/pdf.

[20] Offences Against the Person Act 1861 (Act No. 100/1861) (Ir.), https://www.irishstatutebook.ie/eli/1861/act/100/enacted/en/print.html.

substantial risk of loss of the woman's life" from illness, medical emergency, or suicide. Abortion undertaken in Ireland in violation of these conditions constituted a crime entailing a prison sentence (up to fourteen years).

Another relevant law, comprising the Irish abortion law regime, was the Regulation of Information (Services Outside the State for the Termination of Pregnancies) Act, 1995,[21] which was passed pursuant to the thirteenth and fourteenth amendments to the Constitution, enacted in 1992.[22] This Act affirmed the right to travel outside Ireland in order to have an abortion and the right to obtain information about this option. The 1992 constitutional amendments and the 1995 Act were passed after a 1992 ruling from the European Court of Human Rights (ECtHR) that found Ireland to be in violation of the European Convention on Human Rights (ECHR) for restricting the provision of information to pregnant women about the option of travelling abroad to obtain an abortion.[23]

The conformity of the legal abortion regime in Ireland with the ECHR, following the eighth, thirteenth, and fourteenth amendments, was challenged directly in the 2010 ECtHR case of *A, B and C v. Ireland.* The case involved applications by three Irish women who travelled to the United Kingdom during the first trimester of their pregnancies, citing reasons of health and personal well-being for their decision to undergo an abortion. With respect to the first two applicants, the Court held that there had been no violation of their rights under the Convention because the legal regulation of abortion came within Ireland's margin of appreciation regarding the implementation of its obligations under article 8 of the ECHR (regarding right to privacy):

> [H]aving regard to the right to lawfully travel abroad for an abortion with access to appropriate information and medical care in Ireland, the Court does not consider that the prohibition in Ireland of abortion for health and well-being reasons, based as it is on the profound moral views of the Irish people as to the nature of life . . . and as to the consequent protection to be accorded to the right to life of the unborn, exceeds the margin of appreciation accorded in that respect to the Irish State. In such circumstances, the Court finds that the impugned prohibition in Ireland struck a fair balance between the right of the first and

[21] Regulation of Information (Services Outside the State for the Termination of Pregnancies) Act, 1995 (Act No. 5/1995) (Ir.), https://www.irishstatutebook.ie/eli/1995/act/5/enacted/en/html.

[22] Thirteenth Amendment to the Constitution Act, 1992 (1992) (Ir.), https://www.irishstatutebook.ie/eli/1992/ca/13/enacted/en/print; Fourteenth Amendment to the Constitution Act, 1992 (1992) (Ir.), https://www.irishstatutebook.ie/eli/1992/ca/14/enacted/en/html.

[23] Open Door and Dublin Well Woman v. Ireland, App. No. 14234/88, 246 Eur. Ct. H.R. (ser. A) (1992).

> second applicants to respect for their private lives and the rights invoked on behalf of the unborn.[24]

With respect to the third applicant, the Court found a violation due to the lack of a clear procedure for determining whether she was or was not eligible for abortion in Ireland because of her specific medical condition. This legal determination led Ireland to pass the aforementioned Protection of Life During Pregnancy Act 2013, which introduced clearer procedures and criteria for establishing medical eligibility for abortion.

Although the Court's decision appeared to have given an IHRL stamp of approval to the Irish abortion regime, the regime remained highly controversial both domestically and internationally. Domestically, there was a public uproar following the death from infection and sepsis of Savita Halappanavar, who was denied timely medical intervention because physicians refused to perform an abortion as long as there was fetal heartbeat.[25] In the aftermath of the Halappanavar tragedy, a number of attempts to introduce legislation repealing the eighth amendment or introducing new exceptions to the ban on abortion failed in the Irish Oireachtas (i.e., the bicameral Irish parliament).[26]

At the international level, IHRL bodies operating under U.N. auspices and under global IHRL treaties expressed their concern about the over-restrictive nature of Ireland's abortion laws, notwithstanding the judgment in *A, B and C v. Ireland*. In 2011, during the first cycle of Universal Periodic Review of Ireland before the Human Rights Council, a number of European countries called on Ireland to liberalize its abortion laws.[27]

In 2014, the Human Rights Committee—a body of eighteen independent human rights experts elected by the state parties to one of the most important IHRL treaties, the 1966 International Covenant on Civil and Political Rights (ICCPR), to monitor its implementation by states—conducted its fourth periodic review of Ireland's implementation of the ICCPR. The Committee expressed its concerns about the restrictive access in Ireland to abortion services, especially for women who fell victim to sexual offences (e.g., rape or incest), women whose health was seriously jeopardized by continuation of the pregnancy, and those women carrying fetuses suffering from fatal fetal abnormality. At the end of its review process, the Committee recommended that Ireland:

---

[24] A, B and C v. Ireland, App. No. 25579/05, ¶ 241 (Dec. 16, 2010), https://hudoc.echr.coe.int/eng#{ècli%22:[ÈCLI:CE:ECHR:2010:1216JUD002557905%22],ìtemid%22:[%22001-102332%22]}.

[25] Megan Specia, *How Savita Halappanavar's Death Spurred Ireland's Abortion Rights Campaign,* N.Y. TIMES (May 27, 2018), https://www.nytimes.com/2018/05/27/world/europe/savita-halappanavar-ireland-abortion.html.

[26] *See, e.g.*, 877 Dáil Deb. (May 8, 2015) No. 3 (Ir.); 866 Dáil Deb. (Feb. 6, 2015) No. 4 (Ir.).

[27] Hum. Rts. Council, Report of the Working Group on the Universal Periodic Review: Ireland, U.N. Doc. A/HRC/19/9, ¶¶ 108.4–.9 (2011).

> (a) Revise its legislation on abortion, including its Constitution, to provide for additional exceptions in cases of rape, incest, serious risks to the health of the mother, or fatal foetal abnormality;
>
> (b) Swiftly adopt a guidance document to clarify what constitutes a "real and substantive risk" to the life of the pregnant woman;
>
> (c) Consider making more information on crisis pregnancy options available through a variety of channels, and ensure that health-care providers who supply information on safe abortion services abroad are not subject to criminal sanctions.[28]

The dialogue between the Committee and the high-level Irish delegation, headed by Minister of Justice Frances Fitzgerald, received relatively wide coverage in the Irish media, as did the Committee's recommendation to amend the Irish Constitution.[29] Both the media and civil society groups drew particular attention to a comment made during the dialogue by the Chair of the Committee, Sir Nigel Rodley, who asserted that pregnant women were being treated by Irish abortion law as mere "vessels."[30] This comment was presented by critics of the abortion regime as proof that Irish abortion law shamed the country on the international plane.[31]

International criticism of the Irish abortion regime continued in the years that followed. In 2015 and 2016, other human rights treaty bodies adopted concluding observations critical of the compatibility of the Irish abortion laws with IHRL,[32] and the matter received much more attention during Ireland's second Universal Periodic Review cycle than it had received during the first cycle.[33] This process of international expressions of concern culminated in the Human Rights Committee's 2016 decision in

---

[28] Hum. Rts. Comm., Concluding observations on the fourth periodic report of Ireland, U.N. Doc. CCPR/C/IRL/CO/4, ¶ 9 (2014).

[29] *See, e.g.*, Kitty Holland, *Irish women are being denied human rights, says UN report*, IRISH TIMES (July 25, 2014), https://www.irishtimes.com/news/crime-and-law/courts/irish-women-are-being-denied-human-rights-says-un-report-1.1877329; Niall Behan, *State must respond to UN committee's concerns*, IRISH TIMES (July 25, 2014), https://www.irishtimes.com/news/health/state-must-respond-to-un-committee-s-concerns-1.1877078; *UN human rights panel criticises 'restrictive' Irish abortion law*, BBC NEWS (July 24 2014), https://www.bbc.co.uk/news/world-europe-28464086.

[30] *See, e.g.*, Ann Cahill, *UN: Irish abortion law treats women as 'vessels,'* IRISH EXAMINER (July 16, 2014), https://www.irishexaminer.com/news/arid-20275578.html; Amnesty Int'l, *She is not a Criminal: The Impact of Ireland's Abortion Law*, at 15, AI Index EUR 29/1597/2015 (June 9, 2015).

[31] *See, e.g.*, Peadar Ogrady, *Ireland's refusal to provide a safe abortion to a suicidal rape victim is a national shame*, INDEPENDENT (Aug. 20, 2014), https://www.independent.co.uk/voices/comment/ireland-s-refusal-to-provide-a-safe-abortion-to-a-suicidal-rape-victim-is-a-national-shame-9678858.html.

[32] Comm. on Econ., Soc. & Cultural Rts., Concluding observations on the third periodic report of Ireland, U.N. Doc. E/C.12/IRL/CO/3, ¶ 30 (2015); Comm. on the Rts. of the Child, Concluding observations on the combined third and fourth periodic reports of Ireland, U.N. Doc. CRC/C/IRL/CO/3–4, ¶ 57 (2016).

[33] Hum. Rts. Council, Report of the Working Group on the Universal Periodic Review: Ireland, U.N. Doc. A/HRC/33/17, ¶¶ 136.11, .15–.19, .64–.73 (2016).

the *Mellet* case discussed below. The growing domestic and international pressure to review existing abortion laws led the new Irish government, elected in 2016, to agree to convene within six months a Citizens' Assembly to look into a number of possible constitutional reforms, including possible changes in the eighth amendment.[34]

II. THE VIEWS OF THE HUMAN RIGHTS COMMITTEE IN *MELLET*

The *Mellet* case centered around the traumatic hardships encountered in 2011 by Amanda Jane Mellet, a married woman who was thirty-seven years old at the time. During the twenty-first week of her pregnancy (which she regarded as "much-wanted"), her fetus was diagnosed as suffering from congenital heart defects. A week later, following further tests, it was determined that the defects caused by a genetic disorder—trisomy 18—would cause the fetus to die in womb or shortly after birth. As Irish law precluded abortion even in cases involving fatal fetal abnormality, Mellet was advised that she could "travel," and indeed she did travel overseas, at her own expense, to have an abortion in Liverpool. Upon returning to Ireland, she did not receive any bereavement counselling. (Such services were not available, at the time, to women who had undergone abortion overseas.)

Mellet claimed before the Committee that her treatment by the Irish state amounted to cruel, inhuman, or degrading treatment, that her privacy rights and right to access information about abortion services abroad had been violated, and that she had been subjected to discrimination. Her discrimination claims were based on her gender vis-à-vis men (due to the state's refusal to support all of the reproductive health needs of women, while supporting the comparable reproductive needs of men) and vis-à-vis other women carrying fatally impaired fetuses to term (because aftercare services were provided to them by the Irish state, but not to women who underwent abortions overseas; Mellet claimed that this disparate treatment relied on a gender-based stereotype that women should continue pregnancies under all circumstances in order to fulfill their social role of mothers). Ireland, for its part, asserted that the eighth amendment "represents the profound moral choice of the Irish people,"[35] and that the legal regime in place represented a "nuanced and proportionate approach" to balancing the rights of the fetus against those of the woman.[36] It noted, in this regard, the holding of the ECtHR in *A, B and C v. Ireland* that the legal regime in place in Ireland struck a fair balance between the competing rights and interests. That holding supports the conclusion that it had not arbitrarily interfered with Mellet's

---

[34] MERRION STREET, A PROGRAMME FOR A PARTNERSHIP GOVERNMENT 153 (2016), https://www.merrionstreet.ie/merrionstreet/en/imagelibrary/programme_for_partnership_government.pdf.

[35] *Mellet*, *supra* note 3, ¶ 4.2.

[36] *Id.*

rights, nor subjected her to cruel, inhuman, or degrading treatment. It also asserted that her claims concerning lack of access to necessary information were unsubstantiated, and that the claims regarding gender discrimination must fail given the inherent differences between men and women relating to the capacity to become pregnant and in view of the overriding importance of the governmental interest in protecting fetal life.

In March of 2016, the Committee found that Ireland had violated the rights of Amanda Mellet under the ICCPR. On the claim regarding cruel, inhuman, or degrading treatment (article 7 of the ICCPR), it held that "[b]y virtue of the existing legislative framework, the State party subjected the author to conditions of intense physical and mental suffering."[37] The Committee held that the state could not rely on its own laws to justify its violation of the Covenant. In particular, the Committee noted the vulnerable position in which Mellet found herself after learning that her much-wanted pregnancy became unviable, and the negative experiences she suffered later on, including the stigma associated with having an abortion outside Ireland in circumstances that are criminalized inside Ireland. Such negative experiences could have been avoided had she been allowed to undergo a legal abortion in Ireland. Her suffering was further aggravated by the obstacles placed by the 1995 Regulation of Information Act (which criminalized advocating or promoting abortion) on provision of detailed information about abortion options inside and outside Ireland. According to the Committee, this combination of factors constituted cruel, inhuman, or degrading treatment. Under the Covenant, the right to be free from such treatment is an absolute right that cannot be justified by any limitation, justification, or attenuating circumstance.

With respect to the right to privacy (article 17), the Committee held that the non-viable nature of the pregnancy rendered the state's interference in Mellet's private decision to terminate the pregnancy "unreasonable and arbitrary" in light of the intense suffering it caused her.[38] With respect to her discrimination claims (article 26), the Committee held that the state's failure to provide support to women who choose to terminate an unviable pregnancy at their own expense while providing support to women who choose to carry such pregnancy to term, did not fully reflect health needs and socioeconomic circumstances, and "did not meet the requirements of reasonableness, objectivity and legitimacy of purpose."[39] As a result, it found that Mellet was also a victim of discrimination.

As the Committee often does in cases in which it finds a violation on some grounds, it declined to reach Mellet's remaining claims under articles 19 (access to information) and 2 and 3(1) of the Covenant

---

[37] *Id.* ¶ 7.4.

[38] *Id.* ¶ 7.8.

[39] *Id.* ¶ 7.11.

(equality in right protection). It is particularly noteworthy that the Committee did not embrace Mellet's claims of gender-based stereotyping and discrimination between men and women. Perhaps some members agreed with Ireland's view that the Covenant embraces a formal concept of discrimination, which prohibits "like" things being treated differently. Based on this view, these members may have believed that the legal regulation of pregnancies is not a form of sex-based discrimination, rather than a form of disparate treatment emanating from biological differences between the two sexes. It can also be speculated that some members felt uneasy about explicitly aligning the Committee's views with progressive feminist theories regarding the social institution of motherhood, which have limited resonance in many state parties.

With respect to remedies, the Committee concluded that the Covenant required the state to provide Mellet with adequate compensation and make available to her any psychological treatment she needed. Significantly, the Committee also specified the non-repetition remedies that Ireland should provide. It wrote:

> [T]he State party should amend its law on the voluntary termination of pregnancy, including if necessary its Constitution, to ensure compliance with the Covenant, ensuring effective, timely and accessible procedures for pregnancy termination in Ireland, and take measures to ensure that health-care providers are in a position to supply full information on safe abortion services without fearing they will be subjected to criminal sanctions, as indicated in the present Views of the Committee.[40]

The outcome of the *Mellet* case underscores the significance of case selection for an effective public litigation strategy. The *Mellet* case differed in its outcome from the *A, B and C v. Ireland* case not only because of the change in venue; the facts of these two "test cases" were also different. The litigation in *Mellet* focused on the application of the abortion legal regime to fatal fetal abnormality, the part of the regime that is hardest to justify from a "pro-life" point of view, since it involves the protection of a dying fetus that cannot be saved. In contrast, in *A, B and C v. Ireland*, the Court was asked to review the legal reaction to personal decisions to discontinue viable pregnancies for reasons that the state considered to be morally unjustified.[41] Furthermore, the civil society group responsible for representing Mellet—the Center for Reproductive Rights—timed the litigation well. Although proceedings before the Committee take place in writing, and thus lack some of the human drama

---

[40] *Id.* ¶ 9.

[41] *But see* Sissy Katsoni, *How to Maneuver Around Acknowledging the Right to Access Abortion: Some Thoughts on the ECtHR's judgment in M.L. v. Poland*, EJIL TALK! (Jan. 11, 2024), https://www.ejiltalk.org/how-to-maneuver-around-acknowledging-the-right-to-access-abortion-some-thoughts-on-the-ecthrs-judgment-in-m-l-v-poland/ (discussing a recent ECtHR case that found an abortion due to fatal fetal anomaly unlawful on procedural, not principled, grounds).

normally associated with court hearings, the fact that the *Mellet* case took place only two years after the periodic review of Ireland, during which Committee members met with women who had to travel to the United Kingdom for abortion for reasons of fatal fetal abnormalities, resulted in greater empathy of Committee member toward Amanda Mellet and her plight. The economic difficulties experienced by Mellet (which resulted in a very short duration of stay at the hospital, which in turn put her health at risk), the gruesome way in which she received the fetus's remains (it arrived to her house unexpectedly from Liverpool via courier), and the state's failure to explain the logic underlying the abortion ban of unviable pregnancies, all contributed to painting a picture of extremely harsh and gratuitous treatment of the victim by the state that crossed the article 7 threshold. In short, the case of Amanda Mellet powerfully illustrated the cruelty and irrationality of certain aspects of the Irish abortion regime.

Some Committee members added separate opinions to the collective views of the Committee, highlighting further normative considerations. (Appending separate opinions is not exceptional in landmark cases in which the Committee breaks new ground.) For some members the decision went too far; for others, it did not go far enough. And one member felt a need to provide an additional explanation for the Committee's conclusions.

According to Yadh Ben Achour, the Committee should have also pronounced itself on the gender discrimination claim and should have found a violation of articles 2(1) and 3 of the Covenant, read in conjunction with article 26. Ben Achour took the view that Irish abortion laws perpetuated a sexist stereotype, which limited the social role of women to the role of procreation instruments. In the same vein, Sarah Cleveland regarded the ban on abortion as applied to non-viable pregnancies as "*reductio ad absurdum*" of the prioritization given in Ireland to the reproductive role of women.[42] She also opined that article 26 requires " 'equal and effective protection against discrimination on the basis of sex,"[43] and that Ireland's laws denied access to reproductive medical needs that only women need, without placing equivalent burdens on men's access to reproductive health care. In her view, such differentiated treatment was not justified on grounds that were reasonable and "objective to a legitimate purpose under the Covenant,"[44] and were therefore based on gender stereotyping.

Three other members of the Committee, Victor Rodriguez-Rescia, Olivier de Frouville, and Fabian Salvioli, wrote separately on the claims under article 19. They took issue with the refusal of the public health authorities, based on the chilling effect of the 1995 Act, to provide Mellet with clear information about her options for terminating her pregnancy.

---

[42] *Mellet, supra* note 3, at 20, 23, ¶ 14 (concurring opinion of Committee member Sarah Cleveland).

[43] *Id.* at 21, ¶ 8.

[44] *Id.* at 23, ¶ 13.

In the view of these Committee members, the 1995 Act for this reason disproportionately limited the right to seek and obtain information about pregnancy termination, a complex and important personal matter. They also associated themselves with the positions of Ben Achour and Cleveland regarding the application of the right to equality to the gender discrimination aspects of the case (articles 2(1), 3, and 26).

In his short separate opinion, Nigel Rodley expressed the position that the state's violation of article 7 was based on the legal requirement that women carry a "doomed foetus" to term, with the anguish this entails.[45] Rodley's opinion thus underscores the critical role played by the specific facts of the *Mellet* case in producing the legal outcome.

The one member who took a narrower position than the majority on the legal findings in the *Mellet* case was Anja Seibert-Fohr, who criticized the Committee's holding on article 26. According to Seibert-Fohr, there is a reasonable distinction between providing support to women who carry an unviable pregnancy to term and providing support to women who seek abortion (except possibly with respect to bereavement support, but Siebert-Fohr maintained that domestic remedies were not exhausted with respect to this form of support). Seibert-Fohr was also critical of the Committee's failure to clearly identify the relevant category under article 26 for its legal discrimination holding. (The Committee relied only implicitly on health and socioeconomic grounds.)

III. AFTERMATH OF THE CASE

The views of the Committee in *Mellet* received much media attention, especially in Ireland,[46] and they were much welcomed by Irish civil society groups campaigning for repeal of the eighth amendment.[47] In its follow-up report on its implementation of the Committee's views, the Irish government informed the Committee that it had made an *ex gratia* payment to Amanda Mellet in November of 2016 and that it had expanded the availability of bereavement care services in pregnancy loss cases involving overseas abortions due to fetal abnormality.[48] The state also updated the Committee on the progress made toward a new

---

[45] *Id.* at 25, ¶ 1 (concurring opinion of Committee member Sir Nigel Rodley).

[46] *See, e.g.*, *Irish abortion laws caused inhuman treatment—UN*, RTE NEWS (June 9, 2016), https://www.rte.ie/news/2016/0609/794304-abortion-law-un/; Caroline O'Doherty, *Amanda Mellet: I still suffer from grief and trauma*, IRISH EXAMINER (June 10, 2016), https://www.irishexaminer.com/news/arid-20404151.html.

[47] *See, e.g.*, CTR. FOR REPROD. RTS., MELLET V. IRELAND: IRELAND MUST LEGALIZE ABORTION TO END VIOLATIONS OF WOMEN'S HUMAN RIGHTS (2016), https://reproductiverights.org/sites/default/files/documents/GLP_Europe_MelletvIreland_FS_09%2006_Web.pdf; *Ireland's ban on abortion violates human rights—ground-breaking UN ruling*, AMNESTY INT'L (June 9, 2016), https://www.amnesty.org/en/latest/news/2016/06/irelands-ban-on-abortion-violates-human-rights/.

[48] Hum. Rts. Comm., Follow-up progress report on individual communications, at 11–15, U.N. Doc. CCPR/C/122/3 (2022); *see also* Henry McDonald, *Ireland compensates woman forced to travel to Britain for an abortion*, GUARDIAN (Nov. 30, 2016), https://www.theguardian.com/world/2016/nov/30/ireland-compensates-abortion-amanda-mellet-britain.

constitutional referendum. In response, the Committee noted with satisfaction the progress made toward implementation of its views in the case, but decided to continue to monitor the implementation process.[49]

In the meantime, international criticism of the Irish abortion laws continued to accumulate. In 2017, the concluding observations of the Committee on the Elimination of Discrimination against Women[50] and the Committee against Torture expressed concern about these laws,[51] and called on Ireland to revise them. Furthermore, in 2017, the Human Rights Committee decided a case comparable in its facts to the *Mellet* case and involving another victim of the broad Irish ban on abortion (*Siobhan Whelan*)—finding again against Ireland.[52]

The extensive practice of the Human Rights Committee and other treaty bodies on the applicability of IHRL to abortion regulation facilitated the consolidation of the Committee's position on the matter as part of its 2018 General Comment on the Right to Life (General Comment No. 36). Paragraph 8 of the Comment, which like other General Comment paragraphs was adopted by way of consensus, set forth the following legal standards concerning the regulation of abortion:

> Although States parties may adopt measures designed to regulate voluntary termination of pregnancy, those measures must not result in violation of the right to life of a pregnant woman or girl, or her other rights under the Covenant. Thus, restrictions on the ability of women or girls to seek abortion must not, inter alia, jeopardize their lives, subject them to physical or mental pain or suffering that violates article 7 of the Covenant, discriminate against them or arbitrarily interfere with their privacy. States parties must provide safe, legal and effective access to abortion where the life and health of the pregnant woman or girl is at risk, or where carrying a pregnancy to term would cause the pregnant woman or girl substantial pain or suffering, most notably where the pregnancy is the result of rape or incest or where the pregnancy is not viable. In addition, States parties may not regulate pregnancy or abortion in all other cases in a manner that runs contrary to their duty to ensure that women and girls do not have to resort to unsafe abortions, and they should revise their abortion laws accordingly. For example, they should not take measures such as criminalizing pregnancy of unmarried women or applying

---

[49] Hum. Rts. Comm., *supra* note 48, at 14.

[50] Comm. on the Elimination of All Forms of Discrimination against Women, Concluding observations on the combined sixth and seventh periodic reports of Ireland, ¶¶ 10–11, 42–43, U.N. Doc. CEDAW/C/IRL/CO/6–7 (2017).

[51] Comm. against Torture, Concluding observations on the second periodic report of Ireland, ¶¶ 31–32, U.N. Doc. CAT/C/IRL/CO/2 (2017).

[52] Hum. Rts. Comm., Views adopted by the Committee under article 5(4) of the Optional Protocol, concerning communication No. 2425/2014, U.N. Doc. CCPR/C/119/D/2425/2014 (2017).

> criminal sanctions to women and girls who undergo abortion or to medical service providers who assist them in doing so, since taking such measures compels women and girls to resort to unsafe abortion. States parties should remove existing barriers to effective access by women and girls to safe and legal abortion, including barriers caused as a result of the exercise of conscientious objection by individual medical providers, and should not introduce new barriers. States parties should also effectively protect the lives of women and girls against the mental and physical health risks associated with unsafe abortions. In particular, they should ensure access for women and men, and especially girls and boys, to quality and evidence-based information and education on sexual and reproductive health and to a wide range of affordable contraceptive methods, and prevent the stigmatization of women and girls who seek abortion. States parties should ensure the availability of, and effective access to, quality prenatal and post-abortion health care for women and girls, in all circumstances and on a confidential basis.[53]

On the domestic front, the work of the Citizens' Assembly, which started after the *Mellet* case was decided, concluded in June 2017 with a report calling for amendment of the eighth amendment and for the introduction of legislation authorizing abortion without restriction during the first stages of pregnancy, as well as for abortion for specific reasons within certain gestational limits.[54] In that regard, the Assembly was briefed during its proceedings by experts who discussed the recent case law of the ECtHR and the Human Rights Committee. The Assembly's report was forwarded to a special joint committee of the Houses of the Oireachtas, which published its own recommendations in December of 2017.[55] The joint committee recommended repealing the eighth amendment and introducing legislation to prescribe grounds and gestational limits for pregnancy termination. Like the Citizens' Assembly, the joint committee was briefed by human rights experts, including one with experience in working in the U.N. and the ECtHR, and noted in its report Ireland's continuing violation of its international

---

53 Hum. Rts. Comm., General comment No. 36: Article 6: right to life, U.N. Doc. CCPR/C/GC/36 (2019).

54 THE CITIZENS' ASSEMBLY, FIRST REPORT AND RECOMMENDATIONS OF THE CITIZENS' ASSEMBLY, THE EIGHTH AMENDMENT OF THE CONSTITUTION (2017), https://citizensassembly.ie/wp-content/uploads/2023/02/FirstReport_EIGHTAMENDMENT.pdf.

55 GOV'T OF IR., HOUSE OF OIREACHTAS, REPORT OF THE JOINT COMMITTEE ON THE EIGHTH AMENDMENT OF THE CONSTITUTION (2017), https://data.oireachtas.ie/ie/oireachtas/committee/dail/32/joint_committee_on_the_eighth_amendment_of_the_constitution/reports/2017/2017-12-20_report-of-the-joint-committee-on-the-eighth-amendment-of-the-constitution_en.pdf.

obligations, as evidenced in the *Mellet* and *Whelan* decisions, as one of the critical factors warranting reform.[56]

Acting upon this recommendation, the Irish Cabinet approved the holding of a referendum on repealing the eighth amendment. The repeal motion passed in the May 2018 referendum by a large majority (with sixty-six percent of the voters in favor). Following the vote, the Oireachtas passed the Health (Regulation of Termination of Pregnancy) Act 2018, which legalized abortion in the first twelve weeks of a pregnancy, and introduced risk to life and health and fatal fetal abnormality as grounds for abortions beyond the first twelve weeks.

The civil society campaign leading to the referendum vote made use of IHRL arguments, alongside other arguments. The campaign was facilitated by a broad coalition of seventy civil society organizations, operating under the umbrella organization "Together for Yes" and comprised mainly of three sub-groups: the National Women's Council, the Coalition to Repeal the Eighth, and the Abortion Rights Campaign. While the messaging of the campaign centered mostly around abortion as a personal decision and a matter of health care,[57] parts of the campaign also dealt with the human rights dimensions of the issues at hand. For example, the Irish Council for Civil Liberties (ICCL), which participated in multiple proceedings before the Human Rights Committee and other treaty bodies, ran a campaign titled "Her Rights," which highlighted a number of case studies, including those of Mellet and Whelan.[58] The position of the Irish Human Rights and Equality Commission on the need to repeal the eighth amendment was also heavily influenced by the *Mellet* and *Whelan* decisions.[59]

---

[56] *Id.* ¶ 1.8 ("In arriving at this decision, the Joint Committee took into consideration expert legal and medical evidence provided to the Committee relating to . . . [t]he continuing and ongoing breach of Ireland's international human rights obligations as evidenced in the cases of *Mellet v. Ireland* and *Whelan v. Ireland*, in which the United Nations Human Rights Committee found Ireland to be in violation of the International Covenant on Civil and Political Rights (ICCPR). As well as directing compensation and counselling for the women concerned, the Human Rights Committee has called for Ireland to change its laws to allow for termination in cases of fatal foetal abnormality.").

[57] *See, e.g.*, NAT'L WOMEN'S COUNCIL FOR IR., LEARNING FROM THE 2018 TOGETHER FOR YES CAMPAIGN 14 (2018), https://www.nwci.ie/images/uploads/15089_TFY_Review_WEB.pdf.

[58] Irish Council for Civ. Liberties, *Her Rights: ICCL is calling for a YES vote to repeal the 8th Amendment*, https://www.iccl.ie/her-rights/ (last visited Oct. 2, 2024).

[59] IRISH HUM. RTS. AND EQUAL. COMM., HUMAN RIGHTS AND EQUALITY CONSIDERATIONS IN THE DEVELOPMENT OF A NEW LEGISLATIVE AND REGULATORY FRAMEWORK ON ABORTION 12–13 (2017), https://www.ihrec.ie/app/uploads/2017/10/Human-rights-and-equality-considerations-in-the-development-of-a-new-legislative-and-regulatory-framework-on-abortion.pdf.

Lampposts with Yes and No Posters Simultaneously

While the views of the Committee were not at the front and center of the repeal campaign, commentators and major media outlets covering the referendum described them as an important background development leading up to the vote.[60] Some supporters of the repeal were clearly motivated, in part, by the "national embarrassment" of Ireland being viewed by international bodies as an outlier on abortion rights.[61] Finally, the international attention given to the arguments raised in these cases appears to have played a part, along the way, in influencing key political actors to reconsider their position regarding the desirability of maintaining a broad ban on abortion.[62]

---

[60] *See, e.g.*, Jon Henley, *What you need to know: the Irish abortion referendum explained*, GUARDIAN May 25, 2018), https://www.theguardian.com/world/2018/may/25/irish-abortion-referendum-explained-what-you-need-to-know; *Timeline: Ireland and abortion*, BBC (May 26, 2018), https://www.bbc.co.uk/news/world-europe-43962738; *Referendum announced for 2018 on ending Ireland's strict abortion laws*, HUMANIST (June 16, 2017), https://humanists.uk/2017/06/16/referendum-announced-for-2018-on-ending-irelands-strict-abortion-laws/.

[61] *See, e.g.*, Anna Carnegie & Rachel Roth, *From the Grassroots to the Oireachtas: Abortion Law Reform in the Republic of Ireland*, 21 HEALTH & HUM. RTS. J. 109, 112–13 (2019); Brian O'Flynn, *Thousands March for Abortion Rights in Ireland*, VICE (Oct. 2, 2017), https://www.vice.com/en/article/59djj3/ireland-abortion-referendum-march-for-choice; Ciara Kenny, *Why we're flying home to vote: 'I want to be proud of my nation,'* IRISH TIMES (May 24, 2018), https://www.irishtimes.com/life-and-style/abroad/why-we-re-flying-home-to-vote-i-want-to-be-proud-of-my-nation-1.3506118.

[62] Amelia Gentleman, *UN calls on Ireland to reform abortion laws after landmark ruling*, GUARDIAN (June 9, 2016), https://www.theguardian.com/world/2016/jun/09/ireland-abortion-laws-violated-human-rights-says-un; Máiréad Enright, Kathryn McNeilly & Fiona de Londras, *Abortion activism, legal change, and taking feminist law work seriously*, 71 N. IR. LEGAL Q., no. 3, 2020, at 7, 19.

IV. CONCLUSIONS

The aftermath of the Human Rights Committee's decision in the *Mellet* case can be described, in some sense, as a story of successful implementation of human rights obligations. Within two years from the date of issuance of a non-binding decision calling for constitutional reform, Ireland changed its constitution and aligned its abortion laws with many of the international standards identified by the Committee.[63] Remarkably, this fast development transpired only a few years after the ECtHR had rejected the frontal challenge to the Irish abortion regime in *A, B and C*, generally accepting the IHRL-compatibility of the eighth amendment.[64]

The accumulation of criticism by IHRL bodies and in IHRL venues might have created some international pressure and "public shaming," and invited a reassessment of long-held positions on the question of appropriate abortion regulation. It also underscored the dissonance between how liberal and human rights friendly the Irish perceived themselves, and how they were perceived by outside observers. Still, a review of the *Mellet* litigation and its aftermath underscores the dramatic role played by civil society groups in initiating the submission of the case to the Human Rights Committee, in parallel to other IHRL advocacy work, and in building on the Committee's decision in order to facilitate a political and legal change back home in Ireland.

The foregrounding and backgrounding of different sets of arguments used in domestic and international discourse (e.g., empathy, trust, and quality health care domestically versus human rights violations internationally) further illustrates the key role played by civil society groups in orchestrating the repeal campaign and in using selectively and strategically at the domestic realm the outputs generated through IHRL processes such as the *Mellet* case. This chain of events vindicates the approach of Simmons regarding the centrality of civil society mobilization in facilitating domestic change directed toward implementing IHRL norms. In her words:

> [T]reaties can be used by stakeholders to improve human rights practices. . . . [T]reaties influence outcomes by altering the political calculations of domestic actors. . . . The most "top-down" mechanism involves the effect an international treaty can have on the political agenda of governing elites. Individual governments simply cannot control the international agenda;

---

[63] Note, however, that Irish abortion rights activists remain critical of certain aspects of the post-referendum legislation and its manner of implementation. *See, e.g.*, Sydney Calkin & Ella Berny, *Legal and non-legal barriers to abortion in Ireland and the United Kingdom*, 5 J. MED. ACCESS (2021), https://journals.sagepub.com/doi/epub/10.1177/23992026211040023.

[64] Éidín Ní Shé, *Systematic failure and grey areas: abortion in Ireland*, CONVERSATION (Dec. 5, 2012), https://theconversation.com/systematic-failure-and-grey-areas-abortion-in-ireland-11074.

> for many governments, treaties are an exogenous shock to their national priorities, which many (though certainly not all) are willing to accommodate. Second, treaty commitments can inspire and facilitate litigation. A few citizens can leverage law in legal proceedings, and when they are successful, these actions can change the calculus of important political actors, including, potentially, the government itself. Third, treaties can provide resources and galvanize social mobilization. Unless a government is so firmly ensconced that it can ignore social movements, or so democratic that such movements barely have a motive to form in the first place, international human rights treaties can give rights movements a unique form of political ammunition that can help legitimate group demands.[65]

Indeed, civil society groups initiated the *Mellet* litigation on the basis of the ICCPR. The views of the Human Rights Committee, together with outputs generated through other IHRL procedures that were equally critical of Ireland's abortion laws, raised the costs for the government of maintaining the existing abortion regime and put the repeal of the eighth amendment back on the domestic agenda. Once it was there, domestic civil society organizations were able to use IHRL as part of their political change strategy. The upshot is that *Mellet* was a relative success story not because of its underlying facts and the persuasive language of the views—although the article 7 framing that the facts of the case facilitated and the narrow article 26 holding might have helped increase its domestic effect—but rather because it fit well into a change campaign arranged by a well-organized and popular domestic social movement.[66] The story of *Mellet v. Ireland* shows that sometimes, when domestic mobilization conditions are suitable, human rights treaties do make a difference.

---

[65] SIMMONS, *supra* note 17, at 18–19.

[66] In 2024, another constitutional referendum was held in Ireland. It was designed to modernize the language of the Constitution, with a view to rejecting outdated language reflecting stereotypes concerning the role of women in society. The changes in the Constitution were not approved, however. Rory Carroll, *Ireland's referendums: what went wrong, and what happens now?*, GUARDIAN (Oct. 3, 2024), https://www.theguardian.com/world/2024/mar/10/ireland-referendums-what-went-wrong-and-what-happens-now. That outcome may have been due to confusing messages from the government and lack of focus of civil society groups. *See Ireland: 'The referendums failed because the government overlooked the need to engage affected communities,'* CIVICUS (Apr. 15, 2024), https://www.civicus.org/index.php/media-resources/news/interviews/6964-ireland-the-referendums-failed-because-the-government-overlooked-the-need-to-engage-affected-communities.

II. REGIONAL INTERNATIONAL LAW

6

Claudio Grossman and Nienke Grossman

The *Velásquez Rodríguez* Case: Its Role in the Development of the Inter-American Human Rights System and Its Impact

Angel Manfredo Velásquez Rodríguez disappeared on September 12, 1981, in broad daylight in downtown Tegucigalpa, Honduras. His friends and family never saw him again. The Honduran government denied any knowledge or involvement in his disappearance, and the Honduran courts would not hear the family's case.

For Manfredo Velásquez's family, along with the families of many other victims, disappearances were a grim political and legal reality in Latin America during the 1970s and 1980s, a period marked by authoritarianism and state-sponsored violence. Disappearances constitute one of the most egregious violations of human rights because state authorities perpetrate or acquiesce in the systematic extermination of individuals, which typically includes torture and killing, while denying any knowledge of the situation.

The desire for justice, along with the need to uncover and share Manfredo Velásquez's fate, motivated his family to bring the case to the Inter-American Commission on Human Rights (the Commission). Later, *Velásquez Rodríguez v. Honduras* became the first contested case to reach the Inter-American Court of Human Rights (the Court), giving the case great significance.[1]

As the first contentious case to reach both the Commission and the Court, the *Velásquez Rodríguez* case presented these bodies with many novel issues and important choices. Not only were they required to find facts and to interpret and apply norms in relevant legal instruments, but they also had to decide the level and type of proof required, the role of the petitioners in the proceedings, the nature of state responsibility, and the type of reparations available to victims of human rights abuses, among other issues. The Court had to determine whether it would engage in factfinding, as a trial court, or limit itself to legal questions, as an

[1] Velásquez Rodríguez v. Honduras, Merits, Judgment, Inter-Am. Ct. H.R. (ser. C) No. 4 (July 29, 1988).

appellate body. The judges had to establish the Court's legitimacy and satisfy the petitioners' claim for justice, while also depriving Honduras of any excuse to withdraw from the proceedings. The Court's choices would greatly influence the Inter-American system, and the case of Manfredo Velásquez became a departure point for much of the Court's future jurisprudence. This chapter provides both a social and legal history of the case, and it provides some insights into the case's impact on the development of the Inter-American system and international human rights law.

I. THE SOCIAL AND LEGAL BACKGROUND

Disappearances. The term "desaparecidos" (disappeared persons) emerged during the 1960s to describe the government practice of eliminating political dissidents while denying any responsibility for the crime.[2] A state policy of disappearances became systematic in the Chilean and Argentinean military dictatorships of the 1970s, and in El Salvador and Honduras in the 1980s.[3] The practice flourished in regimes where the military existed independently from any civilian control. A special branch of the military usually carried out forced disappearances, without any effective protection accorded to the victims by the judiciary.[4] Although the duty to prevent and punish forced disappearances in the region can be traced back to 1969 and the American Convention on Human Rights, which recognized a duty to enforce the rights enshrined in the Convention,[5] the Convention does not use the term "disappearances," and few legal remedies existed for victims of enforced disappearances.

The practice of disappearances began in Honduras as the conflict in Nicaragua escalated in the 1980s and spilled over into Honduras. In response to growing social tension and the government's concern for national security, General Gustavo Alvarez Martinez, head of the armed forces and de facto ruler of Honduras, resorted to the systematic use of disappearances to purge "the insurgency" from the country.[6] Between

---

2 *See* Juan E. Méndez & José Miguel Vivanco, *Disappearances and the Inter-American Court: Reflections on a Litigation Experience*, 13 HAMLINE L. REV. 507, 510 (1990) (noting that the label of disappearances is really a euphemism for a practice that includes arbitrary arrest, kidnapping, torture, and murder).

3 *Id.* at 509–10; *see id.* at 511 (observing that democratically elected governments in Peru and Colombia also practiced disappearances).

4 *See id.* at 511 (reporting that the secretive nature of disappearances meant that habeas corpus petitions were ineffective).

5 *See* American Convention on Human Rights art. 3, Nov. 22, 1969, 1144 U.N.T.S. 123 (entered into force July 18, 1978, after ratification by its eleventh member state) [hereinafter American Convention or Convention].

6 Disappearances were part of a strategy to contain the Nicaraguan Sandinistas regime and a means to annihilate those opposing the presence of the anti-Sandinista Contra troops in Honduras. Death squads from the armed forces captured suspects, and then interrogated, tortured, and executed those believed to be political opponents before dumping their bodies into unidentified graves.

1980 and 1992, approximately 150 people disappeared in Honduras.[7] Victims were typically teachers, students, labor organizers, peasant leaders, and human rights defenders.[8]

Angel Manfredo Velásquez Rodríguez was one of these victims. According to eyewitness accounts, unidentified men forced him into a small van in the parking lot of the Palace and Lido Theaters in Tegucigalpa and took him to the Public Security Forces station, where he was interrogated and tortured.[9] At the time of his disappearance, Manfredo taught at a local high school, attended graduate school in economics, and served as Secretary General of the Student Union at the National Autonomous University of Honduras. He was thirty-five years old, with a wife and three children.[10]

The primary defenders of human rights victims were families of the disappeared, churches, and non-governmental organizations. Honduras's repressive regime wanted to silence every voice that opposed its policies. Newspapers denied disappearances were taking place by blaming "family conflicts" or stating that people ran away to join political movements abroad. The President of the Supreme Court of Honduras characterized claims of disappearances as conspiracies to destroy the good name of Honduras. In the face of these state denials, non-governmental organizations and human rights defenders faced significant dangers and challenges in gathering evidence, developing public opinion campaigns, and identifying fora in which to present their claims. Despite these obstacles, the families presented writs of habeas corpus, brought criminal complaints, contacted embassies and international organizations, and pressured internal and external political parties in an effort to prosecute those responsible and learn the location of their loved ones.[11] Zenaida Velásquez, Manfredo's sister, filed two habeas corpus petitions in Tegucigalpa in 1981 and 1982, which the courts simply ignored. A third habeas petition, naming Manfredo and other victims, was filed on July 4, 1983, and was denied on September 11, 1984. Zenaida and other family members also filed criminal complaints in 1982 and 1984.[12]

Cases and complaints achieved no results in the domestic setting. Little information was gained about the fate of the disappeared, and those responsible for the violations were not brought to justice because, in most situations, the disappearances resulted from state policy and occurred with the judiciary's active collusion or tacit acceptance. While there were a few courageous judges, they were the absolute exception.

---

7 *See* Velásquez Rodríguez v. Honduras, Merits, Judgment, Inter-Am. Ct. H.R. (ser. C) No. 4, ¶ 147(a) (July 29, 1988) (finding that the number of disappeared in Honduras between 1981 and 1984 was between 100 and 150).

8 Méndez & Vivanco, *supra* note 2, at 511.

9 *See id.* at 517; *Velásquez Rodríguez*, Inter-Am. Ct. H.R. (ser. C) No. 4, ¶¶ 3, 147(e).

10 *See Velásquez Rodríguez*, Inter-Am. Ct. H.R. (ser. C) No. 4, ¶ 147(g)(i).

11 *See* Méndez & Vivanco, *supra* note 2, at 508–09.

12 *See infra* note 58.

Although the efforts of national human rights organizers helped bring attention to disappearances, the victims had no effective domestic legal remedy. With no avenues to pursue internally, victims turned to the international community, seeking to learn the fate of their loved ones and to achieve justice. The Inter-American system offered a venue whose importance and utility had yet to be tested.

The Inter-American System: The Commission and the Court. In 1948, the nations of the Western hemisphere established the Organization of American States and adopted the American Declaration of the Rights and Duties of Man.[13] In 1959, the Inter-American Commission on Human Rights was created and charged with a limited diplomatic and political mandate to study the human rights delineated in the American Declaration.[14] The revised OAS Charter transformed the Commission into a treaty-based organ.[15]

To enhance its efficacy, the members of the OAS adopted the American Convention on Human Rights during the specialized Conference on Human Rights in Costa Rica in 1969.[16] The Convention expanded the Commission's mechanisms for protecting human rights and established the Inter-American Court of Human Rights. The treaty also institutionalized activities already undertaken by the Commission, such as preparing country reports, conducting *in loco* visits, and providing advisory services to the OAS and member states.

The Commission's primary function is to advise the OAS on promoting and protecting human rights and ensuring compliance by member states. It operates at three levels: assessing the human rights conditions of member states, analyzing general thematic areas, and addressing individual complaints. Through the publication of country reports and on-site visits, the Commission has assessed human rights conditions in twenty-three member states and published over seventy reports.[17] Furthermore, the Commission established Rapporteurships on various themes, including freedom of expression, the rights of indigenous

---

13 American Declaration of the Rights and Duties of Man, Org. Am. States [OAS] Res. XXX, International Conference of American States, 9th Conf., OAS Doc. OEA/Ser.L./V/I.4 rev. XX (1948) [hereinafter American Declaration]; *see generally* THOMAS BUERGENTHAL & DINAH SHELTON, PROTECTING HUMAN RIGHTS IN THE AMERICAS 37 (4th ed. 1995) (noting that the inter-American system predates the OAS Charter and can be traced to the 1826 Congress of Panama).

14 *See* American Declaration, *supra* note 13, art. 52; OAS Res. VIII, 5th Meeting of Consultation of Ministers of Foreign Affairs, OEA/Ser.L./V/1.4, at 35–36 (1960) (establishing the Commission, composed of seven members elected in their individual capacity, ten years after the Declaration); Cecilia Medina, *The Inter-American Commission on Human Rights and the Inter-American Court of Human Rights: Reflections on a Joint Venture*, 12 HUM. RTS. Q. 440, 441 (1990).

15 *See* OAS Res. XXII, Inter-Am. Conference, OEA/Ser.E./XIII.I, doc. 150 rev. (1965).

16 American Convention, *supra* note 5, art. 3.

17 Claudio M. Grossman, *Inter-American Commission on Human Rights (IACommHR)*, *in* MAX PLANCK ENCYCLOPEDIA ON PUBLIC INTERNATIONAL LAW (Dec. 2021), https://opil-ouplaw-com.proxygt-law.wrlc.org/display/10.1093/law:epil/9780199231690/law-9780199231690-e831.

peoples, women, LGBTQ persons, migrants, afro-descendants, and other marginalized groups.

The Commission also processes individual complaints alleging violations of the Convention.[18] In cases where the offending state has not ratified the Convention, the American Declaration is used for individual petitions. While the Commission and the Court are involved in handling petitions, individuals can only petition the Commission. It decides on admissibility, engages parties in friendly settlements,[19] decides requests for precautionary measures,[20] and makes a final recommendation on the merits of petitions.[21] In cases where its recommendations are not implemented, the Commission may publish reports or refer the case to the Court, subject to the country's acceptance of the Court's compulsory jurisdiction.

The Commission played a crucial role in documenting and denouncing the scope and gravity of human rights violations through its country reports during the period of dictatorships and mass human rights violations in the 1980s. These reports were instrumental tools for the international community to exert pressure, support victims, and condemn dictatorial regimes. By exposing violations such as forced disappearances, torture, and rejection of due process, the Commission contributed to the isolation of these regimes, the support of domestic opponents, and the eventual collapse of authoritarian governments. The Commission's evolution, broad mandate, and mechanisms for addressing human rights violations have established it as a vital actor in the regional human rights system, facilitating promotion, protection, and accountability for human rights across the Americas.

The Inter-American Court, established in 1979 in San José, Costa Rica, is an autonomous judicial institution of the Inter-American system.[22] The Court has both advisory and contentious jurisdiction.[23] Under its advisory jurisdiction, the Convention authorizes the Court to

---

[18] American Convention, *supra* note 5, art. 41(f).

[19] *See id.* art. 46 (listing the admissibility requirements, namely, that remedies under domestic law have been pursued and exhausted, that the petition was lodged within six months of the final judgment, that the subject of the petition is not pending in another international proceeding, and that the petition contains the name, nationality, profession, domicile, and signature of the person filing the petition); *see id.* art. 48(f); Inter-Am. Comm'n H.R., Rules of Procedure art. 41 [hereinafter Commission's Rules of Procedure] ("On its own initiative or at the request of any of the parties, the Commission shall place itself at the disposal of the parties concerned, at any stage of the examination of a petition or case, with a view to reaching a friendly settlement of the matter.").

[20] *See* Commission's Rules of Procedure, *supra* note 19, art. 25(1) ("In serious and urgent cases, and whenever necessary according to the information available, the Commission may, on its own initiative or at the request of a party, request that the State concerned adopt precautionary measures to prevent irreparable harm to persons.").

[21] *See* American Convention, *supra* note 5, art. 50.

[22] In accordance with Article 74(2), the American Convention entered into force on July 18, 1978, after the eleventh state party ratified it.

[23] Inter-Am. Court H.R. Annual Report 2023, at 7. In 2023, the Court delivered thirty-three judgments, and two advisory opinions were submitted.

interpret the American Convention as well as any other Inter-American regional human rights treaty.[24] The Court may also issue provisional measures.[25] The Convention permits the Court to assess the compatibility of domestic law with other human rights treaties ratified by the member states.[26] Both OAS member states and organs of the OAS may request advisory opinions from the Court.[27]

The Court's contentious jurisdiction is limited to interpreting and applying the American Convention.[28] In interpreting the scope of the American Convention, the Court has resorted to other human rights treaties.[29] A state party may generally accept the contentious jurisdiction of the Court, or agree to be bound by the Court's decision for a specific case or a limited period of time.[30] The Court's judgments in contentious cases are binding on the parties and cannot be appealed.[31] The Court also retains jurisdiction over cases to monitor compliance.[32]

Proceedings Before the Inter-American Commission. Lacking any legal remedies in Honduras or effective diplomatic means to obtain information and redress, Manfredo Velásquez's family, supported by Honduran human rights organizations, filed a petition with the Inter-American Commission in October 1981.[33] The petition alleged that the Honduran government was responsible for Manfredo's disappearance.[34]

---

24 *See* American Convention, *supra* note 5, art. 64.

25 *See id.* art. 63(2) ("In cases of extreme gravity and urgency, and when necessary to avoid irreparable damage to persons, the Court shall adopt such provisional measures as it deems pertinent in matters it has under consideration.").

26 *See id.*; *see also* The Right to Information on Consular Assistance in the Framework of the Guarantees of the Due Process of Law, Advisory Opinion OC-16/99, Inter-Am. Ct. H.R. (ser. A) No. 16 (Oct. 1, 1999). Mexico requested an advisory opinion on the rights, under the International Covenant on Civil and Political Rights, Dec. 16, 1966, 999 U.N.T.S. 171, and the Vienna Convention on Consular Relations, Apr. 24, 1963, 596 U.N.T.S. 261, of Mexican nationals condemned to death by courts in the United States.

27 *See* American Convention, *supra* note 5, art. 64(2).

28 *See id.* arts. 61–63.

29 *See, e.g.*, Pueblo Bello v. Colombia, Merits, Reparations and Costs, Judgment, Inter-Am. Ct. H.R. (ser. C) No. 140, ¶ 124 (Jan. 31, 2006).

30 *See* American Convention, *supra* note 5, art. 61(2).

31 *Id.* art. 67.

32 *See id.* art. 65 ("[s]hall specify, in particular, the cases in which a State has not complied with its judgments").

33 *See* Velásquez Rodríguez v. Honduras, Case 7920, Inter-Am. Comm'n H.R., Report No. 22/86, OEA/Ser.L./V/II.68, doc. 8, rev. ¶ XXX (1986) (reporting that the Commission received the petition on Oct. 7, 1981, and noting that the petition maintained that Manfredo Velásquez and other missing political prisoners were being held by the First Battalion of Infantry in Tegucigalpa).

34 *See id.* ¶ 1 (reporting that the petition stated that "[w]e assign responsibility for that action to Colonels Leonidas Torres Arias (G–2), Gustavo Alvarez (FUSEP), Juan Lopez Grijalba (National Investigation Department) and Hubbert Bodden (Commander, First Battalion of Infantry, Tegucigalpa)").

The government of Honduras provided the Commission with no evidence or information about the disappearance.[35] While the credibility of the Commission's findings increases when all parties participate in the proceedings and the Commissioners decide the case on its merits, if the defendant refuses to participate in the proceedings, the Commission, in accordance with its regulations, can presume the validity of the facts as alleged by the petitioner.[36] Honduras's lack of cooperation left the Commission with no option but to apply this presumption. The Commission decided to refer the petition to the Inter-American Court to decide whether his disappearance violated his right to life (Article 4) and to personal liberty (Article 7) under the American Convention.[37] The Commission recommended that the government undertake a complete and impartial investigation, punish those responsible for the disappearance, and then inform the Commission about the measures enacted to comply with the Commission's recommendations.[38]

In response, the government requested that the Commission reconsider its decision because the petitioners had not exhausted all domestic remedies, and there were rumors that he was alive and participating in guerilla activities.[39] The government claimed that it was making efforts to establish the whereabouts of Manfredo Velásquez.[40] The Commission agreed to postpone the final decision.[41]

After General Alvarez was ousted from power in 1985, the new government of Honduras requested additional time to conduct an internal investigation.[42] A special national commission, composed of six Honduran colonels, issued a report consisting of four sentences, concluding that no evidence existed connecting anyone in the military to the disappearances.[43] The report claimed that those who had disappeared had never been in government custody.[44]

In April of 1986, the Commission ruled that the government's investigation was insufficient to warrant a reconsideration of its former

---

35 *See id.* ¶¶ 4–6 (noting that the Commission did not receive the requested information from the Honduran government despite the requests sent on Oct. 14, 1981, Nov. 24, 1981, Oct. 6, 1982, Mar. 23, 1983, and Aug. 9, 1983).

36 *See* Commission's Rules of Procedure, *supra* note 19, art. 39.

37 *See* Velásquez Rodríguez v. Honduras, *supra* note 33.

38 *Id.*

39 *Id.*

40 *See id.* (noting that the government claimed that Manfredo Velásquez was hiding and that he had been seen with groups of guerrillas from El Salvador).

41 *See id.* ¶ 12 (deciding to continue studying the case at its 62nd Session in May 1984, and requesting that the government provide information concerning the status of the case under domestic law, including the habeas corpus petition). The Commission continued studying the case for two-and-one-half years. *Id.*

42 *See id.* ¶ 16 (reporting that Honduras requested postponement of consideration of the case in its cablegram of Mar. 1, 1985, and informed that it had set up an Investigating Commission to examine the complaints and identify those responsible so they could be punished).

43 *See* Grossman, *supra* note 17.

44 *See* Velásquez Rodríguez v. Honduras, *supra* note 33.

Recommendation, partly because of the "unjustifiable delay in the administration of justice," and it resolved to confirm its earlier Recommendation in its entirety.[45] At the request of the family's lawyers, the Commission referred the case to the Inter-American Court of Human Rights on April 24, 1986, almost five years after the filing of the initial petition.[46] In addition to the Commission's lawyers, four lawyers, including one author of this chapter, represented Manfredo's family in the Court's proceedings.[47]

Proceedings Before the Inter-American Court of Human Rights. The Court accepted jurisdiction of the *Velásquez Rodríguez* case under Articles 61 and 62 of the American Convention.[48] At the time, Honduras was one of eight countries that had accepted the Court's contentious jurisdiction.[49] Honduras's 1981 decision to accept the Court's contentious jurisdiction was influenced by the policy of the United States, a close Honduran ally. Under the Carter administration, the United States actively promoted human rights initiatives and publicly condemned disappearances. In Honduras, domestic pressure to stop the most outrageous violations of human rights had grown. The Honduran government considered acceptance of the Court's contentious jurisdiction to be an important symbolic gesture.

Litigation of the case before the Court lasted over two years. The Court issued four separate decisions, one on Honduras's preliminary objections, one on the merits, and two on the issue of compensation.[50] Even though the government raised preliminary objections and initially resisted full compliance with the Court's judgment, Honduras actively participated throughout the process. The victim's lawyers and the Commission were concerned that Honduran military or government officials might attempt to withdraw Honduras from the Convention or the Court's jurisdiction, and, accordingly, they took steps to minimize that possibility. For example, the lawyers avoided focusing on politics and instead relied on technical legal arguments, playing on a formalistic legal tradition.

---

[45] *See id.* at 5–6.

[46] *See* Commission's Rules of Procedure, *supra* note 19, art. 50; American Convention, *supra* note 5, art. 63(1).

[47] In addition to Claudio Grossman, Juan Méndez, Hugo Muñoz, and José Miguel Vivanco represented the victims. Dr. Ramón Custodio López, director of the Committee for the Defense of Human Rights in Honduras, and relatives of the victims approached these lawyers because of their reputation and their engagement in the Inter-American human rights system. The attorneys performed their services pro bono.

[48] American Convention *supra* note 5, arts. 61–62.

[49] Honduras accepted the contentious jurisdiction of the Court on September 9, 1981.

[50] Velásquez Rodríguez v. Honduras, Preliminary Objections, Judgment, Inter-Am. Ct. H.R. (ser. C) No. 1 (June 26, 1987); Velásquez Rodríguez v. Honduras, Merits, Judgment, Inter-Am. Ct. H.R. (ser. C) No. 4 (July 29, 1988); Velásquez Rodríguez v. Honduras, Reparations and Costs, Judgment, Inter-Am. Ct. H.R. (ser. C) No. 7 (July 21, 1989); Velásquez Rodríguez v. Honduras, Interpretation of the Judgment of Reparations and Costs, Judgment, Inter-Am. Ct. H.R. (ser. C) No. 9 (Aug. 17, 1990).

Preliminary Objections. On October 31, 1986, the Honduran government presented the Court with several preliminary objections, arguing that the Commission's handling of the case violated the American Convention and seeking to avoid a hearing on the merits.[51] The government argued that the Commission failed to follow the procedure established for issuing a formal declaration of admissibility, and that it did not sufficiently explore a friendly settlement, conduct a preliminary hearing or an investigation in Honduras, issue a final report in a timely manner, or demand that petitioners exhaust available domestic remedies. The Court unanimously rejected all but one of Honduras's objections,[52] ruling that the failure to exhaust available domestic remedies should be joined with the merits of the case.[53]

The Merits. On July 29, 1988, nearly seven years after Manfredo Velásquez disappeared, the Court held Honduras responsible for his disappearance. In its decision on the merits, the Court defined the petitioners' obligation to exhaust domestic remedies by articulating what constituted a domestic remedy, established the type and level of evidence admissible to prove disappearances, and defined the crime of disappearances. The judgment identified the articles of the Convention that were violated by the practice of disappearances, and it declared the state's duty to prevent, investigate, and punish those responsible for disappearances. The decision also interpreted the obligation to provide a remedy and offer fair compensation as required by the Convention.[54]

Both the Commission and the Court rejected Honduras's arguments on failure to exhaust domestic remedies as required by Article 46 of the Convention.[55] In the proceedings, Honduras argued that various remedies remained available to the petitioners, such as appeals, cassations, extraordinary writs of *amparo*, civil remedies of a presumptive finding of death, and criminal proceedings,[56] and that the courts granted writs of habeas corpus during that period but had not reached a final decision on either the habeas petition or the criminal cases

---

[51] *See Velásquez Rodríguez*, Inter-Am. Ct. H.R. (ser. C) No. 1, ¶ 25.

[52] *Id.* Interpreting the friendly settlement provisions of Article 48(1)(f) of the American Convention and Article 45(2) of the Commission's Regulations, the Court concluded that the Commission has discretion to decide whether the circumstances would be conducive to a friendly settlement negotiation. *See id.* ¶¶ 44–46 (concluding that friendly settlement would not be possible in these circumstances because state authorities had been involved in Manfredo Velásquez's disappearance and denied that it had occurred). The Court also found that the Commission has discretion to conduct on-site investigations or hearings, as well as declarations of admissibility and issuance of reports. *See id.* ¶¶ 49–50, 77–78.

[53] *See id.* ¶¶ 91–96 (concluding that a decision on the issue of domestic remedies would be a prejudgment on the merits and prejudicial to one side).

[54] *See* American Convention, *supra* note 5, art. 63.

[55] *See id.* art. 46(1)(a) (requiring that admission by the Commission of a petition must demonstrate "that the remedies under domestic law have been pursued and exhausted in accordance with generally recognized principles of international law").

[56] *See* Velásquez Rodríguez v. Honduras, Merits, Judgment, Inter-Am. Ct. H.R. (ser. C) No. 4, ¶ 53 (July 29, 1988).

associated with Manfredo Velásquez's case because the perpetrators had not been identified.[57] The Commission, however, determined that the Honduran courts never processed the three habeas corpus petitions filed by the family,[58] and the courts dismissed the two criminal complaints against military officers for lack of evidence. It concluded that the petitioners had effectively exhausted domestic remedies because the internal situation in Honduras at the time meant there was no hope the cases would be favorably resolved.[59]

The Court agreed with the Commission, holding that the government of Honduras had the burden to prove that the petitioners failed to exhaust domestic remedies.[60] The Court found that a remedy must be effective, adequate, and at least capable of producing the intended result.[61] States cannot avoid liability by demonstrating the mere existence of a formal legal system. Instead, the domestic legal system must be effective at ensuring "the free and full enjoyment of human rights."[62] The Court rejected the government's argument that the petitioners were required to seek a presumptive finding of death from the courts because a presumptive finding of death is a civil remedy allowing disposition of the estate and permitting a spouse to remarry, and it could never involve punishment of the perpetrators or disclosure to the families of what had actually happened.[63] Although legal remedies technically existed in Honduras, the Court found that the habeas corpus petitions and criminal complaints were ineffective in cases of disappearances because imprisonment occurred in secret, formal procedural requirements precluded effective relief, and officials ignored the petitions.[64] The Court also pointed to threats and intimidation received by judicial officials if they pursued these types of cases.[65] Therefore, the Court found that the petitioners had exhausted available domestic remedies, satisfying that admissibility requirement,[66] and it turned to proof of disappearances.

---

57 *See id.* ¶¶ 68–70, 75.

58 *See id.* ¶ 74 (noting that Zenaida Velásquez brought habeas corpus petitions against the Public Security Forces on Sept. 17, 1981, and on Feb. 6, 1982, without result). On July 4, 1983, relatives of the disappeared brought a habeas petition, which was denied that September. Zenaida and other family members filed the criminal complaints in 1982 and 1984 without result. *Id.*

59 *See id.* ¶ 55.

60 *See id.* ¶ 59; Velásquez Rodríguez v. Honduras, Preliminary Objections, Judgment, Inter-Am. Ct. H.R. (ser. C) No. 1, ¶ 88 (June 26, 1987) (stating that a country expressly or implicitly waives its right to object that domestic remedies have not been exhausted, if it fails to raise the objection early in the proceedings).

61 *Velásquez Rodríguez*, Inter-Am. Ct. H.R. (ser. C) No. 4, ¶¶ 63, 66; *see id.* ¶ 67 (disagreeing with the Commission's argument that a domestic remedy is ineffective if it does not find in favor of the petitioner).

62 *Id.*

63 *Id.* ¶ 64.

64 *Id.* ¶¶ 80–81.

65 *Id.* ¶¶ 80, 118(b).

66 *Id.* ¶ 81.

The lack of forensic evidence makes it difficult to prove a disappearance case. In response to this problem of a lack of physical evidence, the Court held that an individual case of disappearance can be proven by circumstantial evidence and logical inference.[67] Before the Court will allow circumstantial evidence, however, the Commission must establish the existence of a pattern of disappearances by a high standard of proof, and it cannot rely solely on reasonable inferences or hearsay.[68] Petitioners satisfy their burden of proof when they properly establish a pattern of disappearances and link the individual case to the pattern through circumstantial evidence. The burden then shifts to the state to disprove the pattern or the link to the individual case. The Court allowed circumstantial evidence in disappearance cases because "this type of repression is characterized by an attempt to suppress all information about the kidnapping or the whereabouts and fate of the victim."[69] A functional legal system presumes that the state and its organs will investigate crimes and punish those responsible. If a state and its organs are responsible for committing the crimes, however, state officials will refuse to cooperate, and they will actively engage in a cover-up with all the resources at their disposal.[70] Additionally, the Court's judgment reflected that evidentiary standards in international human rights tribunals differ from those in criminal proceedings because the purpose is to protect victims and grant reparations where violations have occurred, rather than determine guilt.[71]

Reliance on witnesses to prove disappearances also poses challenges. Thirteen days before testifying at trial, José Isaías Vilorio, a former Honduran Army sergeant, was killed on a public street in Honduras.[72] Although a group of armed men draped his body with the banner of a leftist guerilla organization, human rights groups claimed that the organization was not active.[73] Human rights groups argued that the military carried out this assassination to silence Vilorio because he intended to testify about his activities as a former member of a Honduran death squad. Another trial witness, Miguel Angel Pavón Salazar, Vice Chairman of the Honduran Human Rights Committee and alternate Deputy to Congress, who testified before the Inter-American Court against the government of Honduras in September of 1987, was assassinated while sitting in a parked car.[74] The Honduran government has never investigated either case, and those responsible have never been punished.

67 *See id.* ¶¶ 124–126.

68 *Id.*

69 *Id.* ¶ 131.

70 *Id.* ¶¶ 135–136.

71 *See id.* ¶¶ 129–134.

72 *See id.* ¶ 40.

73 *See id.*

74 *See id.* ¶ 41.

Relying on the witness testimony that was presented at trial and on press clippings that confirmed the facts available to the Court, the Court concluded that between 1981 and 1984, the Honduran government carried out or tolerated a systematic practice of disappearances.[75] The evidence also tended to show that the perpetrators of the disappearances had a particular modus operandi.[76] The Court found that Battalion 316, the alleged perpetrators of the disappearances, used vehicles with tinted glass and with no license plates, guns unique to government agents, and disguises.[77] Military agents initiated surveillance of victims considered dangerous to state security before taking them into custody and transporting them to unofficial detention centers.[78] After hearing the testimony of disappearance victims who later regained their liberty and of former members of the armed forces, the Court held that many disappearance victims were also subjected to torture and other cruel, inhuman, and degrading treatment while in prison.[79] The Court held that the disappearances often involved clandestine executions without trial, followed by the disposal of all material evidence, including the body.[80] The Court also found that government officials denied any knowledge of the victims and pursued no investigations.[81]

The Court found that Manfredo Velásquez's disappearance followed this same pattern, occurred in this context, and thus created the reasonable presumption that he was dead.[82] The Court also determined that members of the armed forces or those operating by their orders carried out his disappearance.[83] By allowing circumstantial evidence in Manfredo's case, in the context of a practice of disappearances, the Court overcame an evidentiary hurdle that could have prevented the attribution of state responsibility in disappearance cases.[84]

Although the Convention does not list disappearance as a separate crime, the Court ruled that forced disappearances constitute multiple and continuous violations of the rights enshrined in the American Convention.[85] It concluded that the practice of disappearances violated four articles of the American Convention, specifically Articles 1, 4, 5, and 7.[86] It explained, "the kidnapping of a person is an arbitrary deprivation of liberty, an infringement of a detainee's right to be taken without delay before a judge and to invoke the appropriate procedures to review the

---

75 *Id.* ¶ 119.

76 *See id.* ¶ 99.

77 *Id.* ¶ 147.

78 *Id.* ¶¶ 103, 147.

79 *See id.* ¶ 147(d)(iii).

80 *See id.*

81 *See id.* ¶ 147(d)(iv)–(v).

82 *Id.* ¶ 147(e), (g).

83 *Id.* ¶ 147(f).

84 *See id.* ¶ 148.

85 *See id.* ¶ 155.

86 *Id.* pt. XIV.

legality of the arrest, all in violation of Article 7 of the Convention which recognizes the right to personal liberty."[87] The Court broadly interpreted Article 5's provisions against cruel and inhuman treatment by concluding that they prohibit incommunicado detention.[88] It found that prolonged and isolated imprisonment harms the "psychological and moral integrity of the person."[89] Finally, the Court acknowledged that disappearances involving clandestine executions and burials without trials violate the right to life under Article 4.[90] The Court concluded by stating that "[t]he practice of disappearances . . . constitutes a radical breach of the treaty in that it shows a crass abandonment of the values which emanate from the concept of human dignity and of the most basic principles of the Inter-American system and the Convention."[91] Once the Court established that Manfredo Velásquez's disappearance conformed to a widespread pattern of disappearances with the Honduran government's involvement or knowledge, and that the practice of disappearances in general violated the American Convention, the Court determined that Honduras violated the American Convention in Manfredo Velásquez's case.

The Court relied on the Convention's Article 1(1) to impute liability to the state, although the Commission did not argue that Honduras had violated it.[92] Article 1(1) obligates Honduras to "respect the rights and freedoms recognized herein and to ensure to all persons subject to their jurisdiction the free and full exercise of those rights and freedoms."[93] The Court in *Velásquez Rodríguez* held that the duty to "respect" applies to violations committed by state officials acting in their official capacity that can be directly attributed to the state.[94] The duty to "ensure" obligates the state "to organize the government in such a way as to guarantee rights recognized in the Convention"[95] and to protect individuals against violations of the Convention committed by non-state actors with the acquiescence of the state.[96] If human rights are violated by non-state actors and the state does not take measures to prevent or punish the perpetrators, then responsibility for the violations can be imputed to the state, even if the identity of the actor is unknown.[97] The Court applied a due diligence standard requiring states to affirmatively prevent, investigate, and punish human rights abuses, as well as compensate the

---

87 *Id.* ¶ 155.

88 *Id.* ¶ 156 (stating that "prolonged isolation and deprivation of communication are in themselves cruel and inhumane treatment, harmful to the psychological and moral integrity of the person").

89 *Id.*; American Convention, *supra* note 5, art. 5.

90 *Velásquez Rodríguez*, Inter-Am. Ct. H.R. (ser. C) No. 4, ¶ 157.

91 *Id.* ¶ 158.

92 *See id.* ¶¶ 163–164. The Court has the power and the duty to apply legal provisions relevant to the proceeding even when parties do not expressly invoke them. *Id.*

93 American Convention, *supra* note 5, art. 1(1).

94 *Velásquez Rodríguez*, Inter-Am. Ct. H.R. (ser. C) No. 4, ¶¶ 166, 169–171.

95 *Id.* ¶¶ 166, 169.

96 *See id.* ¶ 166.

97 *Id.* ¶¶ 172–173.

victims.[98] The Court defined due diligence as including political, legal, administrative, and cultural measures.[99]

The Court concluded that the Honduran government did not respect or ensure Manfredo Velásquez's human rights because the government had not investigated, punished, or paid compensation as required by Article 1(1).[100] The clandestine abductions violated Manfredo's right to personal liberty and legal recourse, and the Court concluded that Manfredo was probably detained and tortured.[101] Therefore, Honduras failed to guarantee Manfredo's right to life under Article 4, to liberty under Article 7, and to freedom from torture and other degrading or inhuman treatment under Article 5.[102] The Court held the government of Honduras liable for the disappearances and deaths of Manfredo Velásquez and the victims represented in three other cases,[103] and ordered the government to pay fair compensation to the next of kin.[104]

Reparations. The Court gave the Honduran government and the Commission an opportunity to agree on the amount and form of compensation to be paid. After six months, the parties had reached agreement only on the identity of the beneficiaries.[105] The Court ordered a public hearing on the issue of compensation.

The Commission submitted a request for payment that included a pension, title to "an adequate house," and compensation for the pain and suffering of Manfredo Velásquez's wife and children.[106] The victims' lawyers argued for moral reparations, loss of earnings, and emotional and punitive damages.[107] Under the technical supervision of the Commission, the lawyers requested an end to forced disappearances, a disbanding of the organizations that carried out torture and disappearances,[108] public condemnation of the disappearances, and exhaustive investigations, prosecutions, and punishments.[109] They asked that the work of the family

---

98 *Id.* ¶ 174.

99 *Id.* ¶ 175.

100 *Id.* ¶¶ 178–181.

101 *Id.* ¶ 187.

102 *Id.* ¶¶ 185–188.

103 *See, e.g.*, Godinez Cruz v. Honduras, Merits, Judgment, Inter-Am. Ct. H.R. (ser. C) No. 5 (Jan. 20, 1989) (finding that Honduras was also responsible for the disappearance of Saul Godinez Cruz, and ordering Honduras to pay an amount totaling 1,300,000 *lempiras* (approximately U.S. $232,000 at the time the decision was adopted) to the Godinez Cruz family as compensation).

104 *Id.*; *Velásquez Rodríguez*, Inter-Am. Ct. H.R. (ser. C) No. 4, ¶ 189.

105 *See* Velásquez Rodríguez v. Honduras, Reparations and Costs, Judgment, Inter-Am. Ct. H.R. (ser. C) No. 7, ¶¶ 20–21 (July 21, 1989) (noting that the parties agreed that the next of kin would include Manfredo's wife and three children).

106 *Id.* ¶ 8. The Commission did not specify an amount but argued that the monetary compensation should correspond to the benefits offered by the Institute of Military Pensions, as well as a cash amount. *Id.* ¶ 44.

107 *Id.*

108 *Id.* ¶ 7(7).

109 *Id.* ¶¶ 7(2), 9.

and humanitarian organizations be respected, as well as for the creation of an educational fund for the children of the disappeared.[110] Honduras, on the other hand, argued that the Court's order of just compensation did not require any explanation.[111] Rather, the state argued, as provided by the Law of Social Security for Teachers in the case of accidental death, the victim's family was entitled to 41,200 *lempiras*.[112] It offered to pay an additional 108,800 *lempiras*.[113]

The Court made several important statements in its decision on remedies. It held that full restitution should be understood broadly to encompass both material and moral damages. Material damages include "*daño emergente*," direct or immediate damages suffered by the victims and the costs incurred by the victims due to the violations, including their pursuit of justice, and "*lucro cesante*," the earnings he would have made over his lifetime. Moral damages include monetary compensation for pain and suffering caused by the violation. The Court held that Honduras had an obligation under international law to make adequate restitution to the victims, including reparation and indemnification.[114] "Fair compensation" under Article 63(1) of the Convention required Honduras to provide full restitution to victims or their families for the injuries suffered as a result of violations of the Convention.[115]

The Court rejected the petitioners' request for punitive damages because it fell outside of the scope of Article 63(1) and international law,[116] and the request for legal fees and costs because the lawyers had not argued for those expenses. It rejected the government's assertion that compensation should be based on an insurance calculation for accidental death, noting that Manfredo Velásquez did not die accidentally.[117] The Court set damages at 750,000 *lempiras*,[118] moral damages for the family's pain and suffering at 250,000 *lempiras*, and loss of earnings at 500,000 *lempiras*. The Court ordered the government, within ninety days of the judgment, to pay one-fourth of the damages directly to the victim's widow and directed the government to place the remaining three-fourths of the funds in a trust fund in the Central Bank for the victim's three children.[119]

---

110 *Id.* ¶ 7.

111 *Id.* ¶ 14.

112 This amount is equivalent to approximately U.S. $7360 at the time the decision was adopted.

113 *Velásquez Rodríguez*, Inter-Am. Ct. H.R. (ser. C) No. 7, ¶ 43. This amount is equivalent to approximately U.S. $26,800 at the time the decision was adopted.

114 *See id.* ¶¶ 25–26.

115 *See id.* ¶ 29; American Convention, *supra* note 5, art. 63 (stating that if there has been a violation, then the Court shall order that the breach be remedied).

116 *Velásquez Rodríguez*, Inter-Am. Ct. H.R. (ser. C) No. 7, ¶¶ 38–39.

117 *Id.* ¶ 46.

118 *Id.* ¶¶ 49, 52, 57. This amount is equivalent to approximately U.S. $134,000 at the time this decision was adopted.

119 *Id.* ¶ 58. The trust fund would be administered under the most favorable conditions permitted by Honduran banking practice. Under the decision, the children would

Eight months later, Honduras still had failed to comply, and the *lempira* had declined in value, reducing the value of the children's trust fund by fifty percent.[120] Due to hyperinflation of Honduran currency, the Commission requested a clarification of the Court's July 21, 1989, judgment,[121] urging it to protect the award against devaluation by tying the amount to an index to maintain its purchasing power.[122] If the government did not compensate for the decrease in value caused by its own delay, the money would lose all real value and become merely symbolic.[123] The government argued that the Court's judgment required no clarification, and the Court had implemented no other monetary guidelines.[124]

In a judgment issued on August 17, 1990, the Court found that it retained jurisdiction to hear the case under Article 67 because a contentious case remains open until the parties fully comply with the judgment.[125] The Court also found that the government should bear the consequences caused by Honduras's delay in making the payments, and it ordered Honduras to compensate the family for losses incurred by the government's delay,[126] and to pay the family the 750,000 *lempiras* as of October 21, 1989, as well as interest on the entire amount of the capital.[127]

In response to the Court's decision, Honduras initially agreed to pay the victims only the amount specified in the original compensation judgment, refusing to pay interest or compensate for the inflationary losses. Full compliance with the Court's decision occurred only after an international campaign to pressure the government, and after Roberto Reina, a former member of the Inter-American Court, became president of Honduras. The Honduran government ultimately paid the full compensation in 1995, fourteen years after Manfredo Velásquez's disappearance.[128]

---

receive monthly interest payments until the age of twenty-five, when they would receive their proportionate part. Honduras could either pay one lump sum or pay the amount in six consecutive monthly installments. *Id.* ¶ 57.

120 Velásquez Rodríguez v. Honduras, Interpretation of the Judgment of Reparations and Costs, Judgment, Inter-Am. Ct. H.R. (ser. C) No. 9, ¶ 18 (Aug. 17, 1990).

121 *Id.* ¶ 1.

122 *Id.* ¶ 19.

123 *Id.*

124 *Id.* ¶ 21.

125 *See* American Convention, *supra* note 5, art. 67 (stating that "[i]n the case of disagreement as to the meaning or scope of the judgment, the Court shall interpret it at the request of any of the parties, provided the request is made within ninety days from the date of notification of the judgment").

126 *Velásquez Rodríguez*, Inter-Am. Ct. H.R. (ser. C) No. 9, ¶ 23.

127 *Id.* ¶ 39. The Court held that the phrase "under the most favorable conditions" obligated the trustee of the trust fund to maintain and increase the value of the funds by selecting a diverse investment portfolio, such as U.S. dollars, real estate, and securities. *Id.* ¶¶ 30–31.

128 *See* David Harris, *Regional Protection of Human Rights: The Inter-American Achievement*, *in* THE INTER-AMERICAN SYSTEM OF HUMAN RIGHTS 1, 24–25 (David Harris &

II. IMPACT OF THE CASE

The Court's ruling in *Velásquez Rodríguez* has had significant immediate and long-term effects. These include helping to shape a new Inter-American Court of Human Rights as it began developing its contentious jurisdiction, strengthening the rights and role of the individual in the Inter-American System, and engendering several procedural innovations that affected later decisions and prompted changes in the Commission's and Court's Rules of Procedure. Through the *Velásquez Rodríguez* decision, the Inter-American Court also had a lasting impact on normative developments in international law, including on disappearances, reparations, and state responsibility for gender-based violence.

The Role of the Court. The Court in *Velásquez Rodríguez* for the first time exercised its compulsory jurisdiction in a contested case pursuant to Article 62 of the Convention.[129] The Convention, however, did not indicate whether the Court was a trial court, which would determine factual questions de novo, or an appeals court, limiting its jurisdiction to questions of legal interpretation only. In this case, the Court established itself as a court of first instance, with jurisdiction over all relevant issues, practically trying the case anew and considering all factual evidence.[130]

This had important legal and political ramifications for the Court's authority in this case, for its future, and for human rights in the region. First, if the Court, acting as an appellate chamber, had simply certified the Commission's finding of state responsibility rooted in Honduras's refusal to participate in the proceedings and the Commission's Rules of Procedure, the Court's decision would have been vulnerable to criticism that it lacked any grounding in a treaty.[131] Instead, the Court made its own factual findings and legal determinations concerning state responsibility for disappearances, grounded in the American Convention, and lent its weight to the factual findings.

Further, acting as a trial court, the Court could attract media or public attention to the horrible crime of disappearances. Witness testimony about Manfredo Velásquez's story served as powerful evidence and focused attention on systematic human rights abuses occurring in

---

Stephen Livingstone eds., 1998); Antonio Augusto Cançado Trindade, *The Operation of the Inter-American Court of Human Rights, in id.* at 133, 138–39.

[129] The Court exercised jurisdiction in an uncontested case previously. *See In re* Viviana Gallardo, Advisory Opinion, Inter-Am. Ct. H.R. (ser. A) No. 101, ¶ 3 (July 15, 1981). Costa Rica submitted the case against itself and agreed to be bound by the ruling, but the case was dismissed before a final ruling was reached.

[130] *See* Velásquez Rodríguez v. Honduras, Preliminary Objections, Judgment, Inter-Am. Ct. H.R. (ser. C) No. 1, ¶ 29 (June 26, 1987) (stating, "[i]n exercising these powers, the Court is not bound by what the Commission may have previously decided; rather its authority to render judgment is in no way restricted. The Court does not act as a court of review, of appeal or other similar court in its dealings with the Commission.").

[131] *See* Inter-Am. Ct. H.R., 2001 Rules of Procedure art. 42 [hereinafter Court's Rules of Procedure].

Honduras. It also assisted in mobilizing public shame for promoting compliance. Further, without the publicity generated by Court proceedings, the lawyers were concerned that Honduras might withdraw on a technicality, since the Court did not yet possess the legitimacy earned by an institution through successful adjudication of cases over time.[132] Publicity escalated the political stakes if Honduras attempted to withdraw. To its credit, the Honduran government appeared and actively participated throughout the proceedings. As a trial court, the Court garnered extra media attention, heightened awareness of the Court's existence and role in the region, and further strengthened the Court's credibility.

At the same time, concerns arose that treating the Court as a trial court meant every case would have to be proven twice: once before the Commission, and then again before the Court. This increased expenses because witnesses had to be brought before both tribunals, made the process less accurate as evidence became stale and memories faded over time, and potentially reduced incentives for member states to engage in proceedings before the Commission.

These concerns led the Court to adopt new Rules of Procedure in 2000 and again in 2009. Under these Rules, the Court, while retaining its right to "retry" a case, may give probative value to the Commission's proceedings if, in the Court's judgment, those proceedings satisfy the necessary standards.[133] The Court has applied these regulations in a number of cases.[134]

Individuals as Subjects of International Law. In the *Velásquez Rodríguez* decision, the Court applied and enforced the rights laid down in the Convention, helping to develop a new role for the individual in the Inter-American system. According to late nineteenth- and early twentieth-century conceptions, international law governed relationships and conflicts between states, and only states were considered proper subjects of international law.[135] International law generally ignored the individual, as well as other subjects such as international organizations, peoples, minority groups, other collective groups, and humankind.[136]

Human rights law generally, and the American Convention specifically, departed from state-centric conceptions of international law by according both substantive and procedural rights to the individual. From the human rights perspective, this progress was fueled by the

[132] *See, e.g.*, Anastasia Telesetsky, *The International Tribunal for the Law of the Sea: Seeking the Legitimacy of State Consent, in* LEGITIMACY AND INTERNATIONAL COURTS 174 (Nienke Grossman, Harlan Grant Cohen, Andreas Follesdal & Geir Ulstein eds., 2018) (discussing how legitimacy may accumulate over time in relation to the Law of the Sea Tribunal).

[133] *See id.*

[134] *See* Dinah Shelton, *Judicial Review of State Action by International Courts*, 12 FORDHAM INT'L L.J. 361 (1989).

[135] *See* LOUIS HENKIN, HOW NATIONS BEHAVE 15 (2d ed. 1979).

[136] *See* BUERGENTHAL & SHELTON, *supra* note 13, at 6.

atrocities committed during World War II; human rights defenders argued that the lack of internationally defined rights that individuals could assert against their own governments contributed to genocide and other mass and gross violations of human rights.[137]

The Inter-American Commission began processing individual petitions in the Western hemisphere in 1965 based on the American Declaration, an instrument that was viewed as establishing only ethical standards and not legal obligations. Most of the Commission's actions, however, were visits *in loco* and country reports designed to assess the overall human rights situation in a country, not legally reasoned findings in individual cases designed to establish truth and state responsibility.[138] When mass and gross human rights violations prevailed in the region, the Commission believed that visits *in loco* and country reports offered the most effective way to mobilize public opinion and shame governments into change, rather than painstakingly proving violations in individual cases. Undoubtedly, exposure of violations served a useful purpose, but a collective examination of disappearances or other human rights violations could not substitute for justice to each victim.[139]

As the sheer number of violations began to decrease, conditions improved for addressing violations on a case-by-case basis. For example, countries in the region began the transition from authoritarianism to democratically elected governments. In this new environment, the Commission gradually shifted away from *in loco* visits and country reports to individual petitions, which required the examination of evidence and reasoned decisions in accordance with accepted modes of legal analysis, ideas of justice, and remedies.[140] These changed circumstances created the opportunity for the Court to issue the *Velásquez Rodríguez* decision. Based on a binding treaty, the ruling helped fuel the development of individuals as subjects of international law in the Inter-American system, and to strengthen the use of the individual petition system.[141]

The Inter-American human rights system remains highly relevant. The workload of both the Commission and Court has grown dramatically.[142] In 1986, the Court had three on-going contentious cases; in 2023, the number of contentious cases before the Court climbed to fifty-

---

[137] *See* HENKIN, *supra* note 135, at 229.

[138] *See* Harris, *supra* note 128, at 21.

[139] The Commission also encountered limitations because it could only visit a country with the government's permission, and it did not have the same legitimacy as a court.

[140] *See* Claudio Grossman, *El Fortalecimiento de la democracia: el sistema interamericano de derechos humanos*, 1 FOREIGN AFF. EN ESPAÑOL, no. 3, at 115 (2001).

[141] *See generally* Grossman, *supra* note 17 (expanding on the role of the individual under international law).

[142] For example, in 1998 the Commission received 571 petitions, while in 2023, the Commission received 2692. *See* Inter-American Commission's Annual Report 2023, at 317, https://www.corteidh.or.cr/docs/informe2023/ingles.pdf.

five.[143] In 1987, the Court issued one judgment and no pronouncements on preliminary objections, merits, or reparations. In 2022, the Court issued judgments in thirty-four cases and pronouncements on preliminary objections, merits, or reparations in sixty-three cases.[144] The number of provisional measures ordered by the Court has also dramatically increased, amounting to over 700 provisional measures since its inception.[145] In 1980, the Court held thirty-eight days of sessions; by 2022, the Court was in session for 192 days.[146]

Procedural Developments. Changes in the Rules of Procedure of the Commission and the Court further strengthened the individual's position within the system.[147] While victims' lawyers participated in the *Velásquez Rodríguez* case, greatly benefitting the process as a whole, the lawyers' participation was theoretically under the supervision of the Commission.[148] Subsequently, the Court embarked on a process of change, ultimately allowing direct representation of the victims before the Court beyond just the reparations stage.[149]

---

143 *See Contentious Cases in Progress*, INTER-AM. CT. HUM. RTS., https://www.corteidh.or.cr/casos_en_tramite.cfm (last visited June 11, 2024).

144 *See Judgments*, INTER-AM. CT. HUM. RTS, https://www.corteidh.or.cr/casos_sentencias.cfm?lang=en (last visited June 11, 2024); Rep. Inter-Am. Comm'n H.R., OEA/Ser.L/V/II, doc. 50 rev. 1, ch. 2 ¶ 19 (Apr. 1, 2023) [hereinafter Annual Report 2022].

145 Annual Report 2022, *supra* note 144, at 76–77; *Provisional Measures Resolutions*, INTER-AM. CT. OF HUM. RTS., https://www.corteidh.or.cr/medidas_provisionales.cfm?lang=en (last visited June 11, 2024).

146 *See Session Dates*, INTER-AM. CT. HUM. RTS., https://www.corteidh.or.cr/periodo_de_sesiones.cfm?lang=en (last visited June 11, 2024). Recently, the Court has held special sessions in other countries, such as Brazil, Argentina, and El Salvador.

147 *See* Commission's Rules of Procedure, *supra* note 19 (approved by the Commission at its 109th special session held from Dec. 4 to 8, 2000, and amended at its 116th regular period of sessions, held from Oct. 7 to 25, 2002, and at its 118th regular sessions, held from Oct. 7 to 24, 2003); Court's Rules of Procedure, *supra* note 131 (modified in 1991, 1996, 2000, and 2003). *See generally* JO M. PASQUALUCCI, THE PRACTICE AND PROCEDURE OF THE INTER-AMERICAN COURT OF HUMAN RIGHTS 18–22 (2003).

148 The four lawyers for the victim's family joined the two lawyers from the Commission and expanded the expertise, resources, and time that could be brought to bear on the case. Through their lawyers, the families of the victims, and the non-governmental organizations supporting them, felt represented in a procedure that otherwise would have involved only the Honduran government and the Commission. *See generally* Grossman, *supra* note 17. Although the Convention does not allow the victim's lawyers to directly present cases to the Court, the Commission in *Velásquez Rodríguez* appointed them as legal advisors. *See* Commission's Rules of Procedure, *supra* note 19, art. 69(4). The Commission later modified its Rules of Procedure to allow the petitioner to be included as a delegate. *See id.* art. 69(2). The Commission's discretionary power to appoint delegates, however, did not guarantee adequate participation by the victims or their lawyers. In some cases, the Commission's political goals and its protection of the integrity of the system might diverge from the interest of the victims for justice in their case.

149 *See* Court's Rules of Procedure, *supra* note 131, art. 23; SERGIO GARCÍA RAMÍREZ, LA JURISDICCIÓN INTERAMERICANA DE DERECHOS HUMANOS 188 (2006). Despite these changes, the victims are not permitted to allege new facts. They are, however, permitted to clarify and allege new violations of articles based on the Commission's statement of fact. *See* Commission's Rules of Procedure, *supra* note 19, art. 71. The Commission also changed its Rules of Procedure to facilitate victims' access to the Court by reducing the number of votes required to send the case to the Court. Most cases are now referred to the Court. *See id.* art. 44.

The Court in *Velásquez Rodríguez* also defined what local remedies victims were required to exhaust before bringing their case to an international tribunal.[150] Although the failure to exhaust domestic remedies is a preliminary, procedural objection, the Court's later jurisprudence concerning this issue relied on the substantive right to judicial protection under Article 25 of the American Convention and the general obligation to respect and ensure rights under Article 1. The Court held member states must offer their citizens an effective domestic judicial remedy; the existence of formal domestic remedies on the books is insufficient.[151]

The Court's rulings concerning the burden of proof and lawyers' fees also influenced later procedural developments. By articulating a reasonableness standard for the evidence required to prove a case of disappearances, the Court provided valuable guidance for petitioners and governments. While the Court did not award lawyer's fees to the plaintiffs' lawyers,[152] its ruling opened the door for future lawyers to argue that the state should pay such fees. The Court currently awards legal fees and court costs based on issues of equity, the circumstances surrounding the case, the international jurisdiction, and reasonable expenses incurred by the parties.[153]

Disappearances. While it is impossible to quantify the precise impact of the *Velásquez Rodríguez* decision in combatting the practice of disappearances as a widespread tool of state repression, the decision undoubtedly played a role in the region and in the world. Prior to the Court's decision in *Velásquez Rodríguez*, international and regional bodies responded to disappearances by issuing resolutions and establishing working groups to address the state practice of disappearances.[154] The United Nations General Assembly would adopt

---

[150] *See* Velásquez Rodríguez v. Honduras, Merits, Judgment, Inter-Am. Ct. H.R. (ser. C) No. 4, ¶¶ 55 *et seq.* (July 29, 1988).

[151] *See* Castillo Páez v. Peru, Merits, Judgment, Inter-Am. Ct. H.R. (ser. C) No. 34, ¶ 90 (Nov. 3, 1997); Blake v. Guatemala, Merits, Judgment, Inter-Am. Ct. H.R. (ser. C) No. 36 (Jan. 24, 1998). Judge Cançado Trindade wrote that "[i]n the Court's own words, the provision of the right to an effective remedy before the competent national judges or tribunals 'constitutes one of the basic pillars, not only of the American Convention, but of the rule of law . . . itself in a democratic society . . . .' " Antonio Augusto Cançado Trindade, *The Inter-American Court of Human Rights at a Crossroads: Current Challenges and its Emerging Case Law on the Eve of the New Century*, *in* PROTECTING HUMAN RIGHTS: THE EUROPEAN PERSPECTIVE 167, 177 (Paul Mahoney & Rolv Ryssdal eds., 2000).

[152] *See* Velásquez Rodríguez v. Honduras, Reparations and Costs, Judgment, Inter-Am. Ct. H.R. (ser. C) No. 7 (July 21, 1989).

[153] *See, e.g.*, The "Street Children" (Villagrán-Morales) v. Guatemala, Reparations and Costs, Judgment, Inter-Am. Ct. H.R. (ser. C) No. 77, ¶ 9 (May 26, 2001) (ordering the state to reimburse expenses and costs of both the representatives of the victims' next of kin, in the domestic and international jurisdictions); 19 Merchants v. Colombia, Merits, Reparations and Costs, Judgment, Inter-Am. Ct. H.R. (ser. C) No. 109, ¶ 284 (July 5, 2004) (noting that legal assistance to the victim does not begin at the reparations stage, but starts in the cases before the domestic judicial bodies and continues through the proceedings before the Commission and before the Court); Ximenes-Lopes v. Brazil, Merits, Reparations and Costs, Judgment, Inter-Am. Ct. H.R. (ser. C) No. 149, ¶ 252 (July 4, 2006).

[154] *See Velásquez Rodríguez*, Inter-Am. Ct. H.R. (ser. C) No. 4, ¶¶ 151–153.

resolutions to condemn disappearances, and the U.N. Commission of Human Rights of the Economic and Social Council created the Working Group on Enforced and Involuntary Disappearances to assist families in determining the fate of their relatives and to establish channels of communication between the families and the governments.[155] The Inter-American Commission condemned the practice and urged that it be investigated and stopped.[156] The OAS General Assembly characterized the crime of disappearances as "an affront to the consciousness of the hemisphere" and a crime against humanity.[157] Most human rights instruments, however, did not address disappearances as a specific violation.

As the first contested case before the Inter-American Court of Human Rights, *Velásquez Rodríguez* received extensive media attention.[158] The case brought the inhumanity of the practice of disappearances to the attention of the international community. Journalists, local human rights organizations, and the OAS had denounced the practice of disappearances for years, but Manfredo Velásquez had the sad honor of being the first person recognized by a judicial body in the Americas as an "officially" disappeared person. Honduras accepted the Court's ruling, admitting to responsibility for the wrongful practice.[159]

The decision established forced disappearances as violations of basic principles enshrined in the Inter-American system and of the right to human dignity, and it challenged the culture of impunity and deniability that was pervasive in the region. By exposing the state's responsibility in this inhuman practice and confronting a status quo characterized by repression and authoritarianism, the case helped further the goals of human rights in the region. The Court, since then, has noted that family members of the disappeared are often direct victims of cruel, inhuman, and degrading treatment because they are denied access to justice and live with the uncertainty of not knowing the whereabouts of their loved ones.[160] Further, *Velásquez Rodríguez* was the impetus for the drafting and codification of the crime of disappearances in the Inter-American

---

155 *See* Méndez & Vivanco, *supra* note 2, at 515.

156 *See, e.g.,* Report on Argentina, Inter-Am. Comm'n H.R., OEA/Ser.L/V/II.49, doc. 19 rev.1 (1980); Report on Chile, Inter-Am. Comm'n H.R., OEA/Ser.L/V/II.66, doc. 17 (1985).

157 OAS G.A. Res. 666 (XIII–0/83) (Nov. 18, 1983); OAS G.A. Res. 742 (XIV–0/84) (Nov. 17, 1984).

158 *See, e.g.,* Stephen Kinzer, *O.A.S. Tribunal Finds Honduras Responsible for a Political Killing,* N.Y. TIMES, July 30, 1988, at A1; William Branigin, *Honduras on Trial in Rights Court,* WASH. POST, Jan. 21, 1988, at A28; *Rights Court Faults Honduras,* WASH. POST, July 30, 1988, at A19.

159 *See* Harris, *supra* note 128, at 24–25; Trindade, *supra* note 128, at 138–39.

160 *See* 19 Merchants v. Colombia, Merits, Reparations and Costs, Judgment, Inter-Am. Ct. H.R. (ser. C) No. 109, ¶ 229 (July 5, 2004); Juan Humberto Sánchez v. Honduras, Preliminary Objection, Merits, Reparations and Costs, Judgment, Inter-Am. Ct. H.R. (ser. C) No. 99, ¶ 101 (June 7, 2003); Blake v. Guatemala, Reparations and Costs, Judgment, Inter-Am. Ct. H.R. (ser. C) No. 48, ¶ 38 (Jan. 22, 1999); Bámaca-Velásquez v. Guatemala, Merits, Judgment, Inter-Am. Ct. H.R. (ser. C) No. 70, ¶ 160 (Nov. 25, 2000).

Convention on the Forced Disappearance of Persons, which incorporated the definition of disappearances used in the *Velásquez Rodríguez* case and encompasses the crimes of kidnapping, torture, and murder.[161] Fifteen countries in the hemisphere have currently accepted the Inter-American Convention on the Forced Disappearance of Persons.[162]

The international community recognized disappearances as an explicit violation of international law in 1992, four years after the July 1988 *Velásquez Rodriguez* judgment, in the U.N. Declaration on the Protection of all Persons from Enforced Disappearances.[163] The Declaration also cemented the role of the Working Group on Enforced or Involuntary Disappearances (WGEID) as the principal supervisory body responsible for monitoring states' compliance. Since its inception, the WGEID has registered a total of 61,626 cases of enforced disappearance. Of these cases, 48,619 remain active as of 2024.[164]

The International Convention for the Protection of All Persons from Enforced Disappearance followed in 2006, establishing the Committee on Enforced Disappearances (CED), a group of independent experts who serve as the Convention's monitoring mechanism.[165] Today, CED carries out a unique rapid response function through its "urgent action" program, which allows cases of enforced disappearance to be processed within forty-eight hours of receipt by the Committee, thus increasing the likelihood of locating the person concerned. CED may request that states provide information about the alleged victim and issue interim measures to ensure the person is quickly located. Since the creation of this mechanism in 2012, the CED has registered 1578 requests for urgent action.[166]

The *Velásquez Rodríguez* decision was also essential in the adoption of disappearances in the Rome Statute of the International Criminal Court. In the Rome Statute, the forced disappearance of persons constitutes a crime against humanity and is subject to the jurisdiction of the International Criminal Court. The crime is defined as the

> arrest, detention or abduction of persons by, or with the authorization, support or acquiescence of, a State or a political organization, followed by a refusal to acknowledge that deprivation of freedom or to give information on the fate or

---

[161] *See* Inter-American Convention on the Forced Disappearance of Persons, June 9, 1994, 33 I.L.M. 1529 (1994) (entered into force Mar. 28, 1996).

[162] Those countries are Argentina, Bolivia, Brazil, Chile, Colombia, Costa Rica, Ecuador, Guatemala, Honduras, Mexico, Nicaragua, Panama, Paraguay, Peru, Uruguay, and Venezuela.

[163] G.A. Res. 47/133 (Dec. 19, 1992).

[164] Comm'n. on Hum. Rights, Rep. of the Working Grp. on Enforced or Involuntary Disappearances, U.N. Doc. A/HRC/57/34 (2024).

[165] International Convention for the Protection of All Persons from Enforced Disappearance art. 26, Dec. 20, 2006, 2716 U.N.T.S. 3 (entered into force Dec. 23, 2010).

[166] *See* Report of the Committee on Enforced Disappearances, ch. X, at 16, U.N. Doc. A/78/56 (2023).

> whereabouts of those persons, with the intention of removing them from the protection of the law for a prolonged period of time.[167]

The development of the concept and definition of enforced disappearances in the jurisprudence of the Inter-American system and other universal and regional jurisdictions also brought about the recognition of other essential state duties, including the duty to investigate and punish. The Inter-American Court first derived this duty from its interpretation of Article 1 of the American Convention. Similarly, the European system recognizes a duty to guarantee the rights contained in the European Convention and indicates that the failure to diligently investigate an alleged enforced disappearance is a violation of the Convention.[168] Furthermore, amnesty laws preventing the investigation and punishment of the crime of enforced disappearance violate the duty to investigate and punish the violation.

Reparations. It is a well-established principle of international law that a violation of a right creates an obligation to adequately remedy that violation.[169] In *Velásquez Rodríguez*, the Inter-American Court for the first time elaborated on what measures constituted reparations for a human rights violation and what fair compensation may require. Significantly, the Court did not refer to Honduran domestic law on reparations, but rather, applied classic international law notions of reparations.[170] The judgments provided a precedent for awarding damages for both material and non-material harm.[171]

In subsequent cases, the Court elaborated and expanded upon the principle of full reparation, which was announced in *Velásquez Rodriguez*, in order to achieve an integral reparation, including measures

---

[167] Rome Statute of the International Criminal Court art. 7(2)(i), July 17, 1998, 2187 U.N.T.S. 90.

[168] *See* Convention for the Protection of Human Rights and Fundamental Freedoms art. 13, Nov. 4, 1950, 213 U.N.T.S. 221 (entered into force Sept. 3, 1953) (establishing a duty to provide effective domestic remedies for violations of rights enshrined in the Convention).

[169] *See, e.g.*, López-Álvarez v. Honduras, Merits, Reparations and Costs, Judgment, Inter-Am. Ct. H.R. (ser. C) No. 141, ¶ 190 (Feb. 1, 2006); Pueblo Bello Massacre v. Colombia, Merits, Reparations and Costs, Judgment, Inter-Am. Ct. H.R. (ser. C) No. 140, ¶ 227 (Jan. 31, 2006). Article 63 of the American Convention states that "[i]f the Court finds that there has been a violation of a right or freedom protected by this Convention, the Court shall rule that an injured party be ensured the enjoyment of his right or freedom that was violated." American Convention, *supra* note 5, art. 63(1). The Convention adds that the breach should "be remedied and fair compensation be paid to the injured party." *Id.*

[170] *See* Méndez & Vivanco, *supra* note 2, at 568. In contrast, the European Court of Human Rights regularly looks to domestic law for issues of reparations under Article 50 of the European Convention on Human Rights. However, the Inter-American Court does have flexibility to refer the case to domestic procedures for reparations due to the nature of the issue before it, such as the complex economic issues it faced in *Five Pensioners v. Peru*, Merits, Reparations and Costs, Judgment, Inter-Am. Ct. H.R. (ser. C) No. 98, ¶ 178 (Feb. 28, 2003). *See* RAMÍREZ, *supra* note 149, at 203 n.42.

[171] In 1988, the Commission first recommended reparations in addition to monetary compensation in Case 9755 against Chile, in addition to compensation for moral injury. Annual Report of the Inter-American Commission on Human Rights 1987–1988, Inter-Am. Comm'n H.R., OEA/Ser.L/V/II.74, doc. 10 rev. 1 (1988).

of satisfaction and non-repetition. Examples of such developments include the concept of damage to the life project and the expansion of remedial measures, such as investigation and punishment.[172] The classical calculation of material damages only included factors such as age, occupation, yearly salary, and probable increase in salary. Reparations to redress the disruption in a victim's aspirations, aptitudes, and circumstances recognize that the victim's potential was severely interrupted or permanently altered by the violation. For example, an individual's life project of studying may have resulted in dramatically altering the conditions of his or her existence. In such a case, the Court may order the state to create a scholarship for a victim to continue his interrupted studies.[173]

In addition, the Court in numerous cases since *Velásquez Rodríguez* ordered states to make reparations through symbolic measures, such as building monuments, publishing the Court's decision in the newspaper, or providing the resources for a proper burial.[174] The Court also required that states make reparations to a particular community to which the victim belongs by providing services lacking as a way to prevent future violations.[175] Also, the Court used Articles 1(1) and 2 to find that domestic

---

[172] *See* Loayza Tamayo v. Peru, Reparations and Costs, Judgment, Inter-Am. Ct. H.R. (ser. C) No. 42, ¶¶ 147–148 (Nov. 27, 1998); RAMÍREZ, *supra* note 149, at 218–19 nn.73–77.

[173] In other cases, the Court has ordered damages of measures of rehabilitation as a form of reparations. *See* Rodríguez Vera v. Colombia, Preliminary Objections, Merits, Reparations and Costs, Judgment, Inter-Am. Ct. H.R. (ser. C) No. 287, ¶¶ 194–195 (Nov. 14, 2014) (ordering the state to provide free, immediate, effective, and adequate medical, psychiatric, and psychological treatment to victims as well as training for security forces on respecting human rights).

[174] *See* Barrios Altos v. Peru, Merits, Judgment, Inter-Am. Ct. H.R. (ser. C) No. 75, at 16–17 (Mar. 14, 2001) (ordering the state to provide the beneficiaries with educational benefits, including scholarships, classroom materials, and uniforms, and to erect a monument commemorating the victims within sixty days of the signing of an agreement between the Commission and the state); The "Street Children" (Villagrán-Morales) v. Guatemala, Reparations and Costs, Judgment, Inter-Am. Ct. H.R. (ser. C) No. 77, at 6, 7 (May 26, 2001) (requiring that Guatemala provide the resources for a proper burial for one of the victims, and designate an educational center with a plaque dedicated to the victims); *see also* Masacre Plan de Sánchez v. Guatemala, Reparations, Judgment, Inter-Am. Ct. H.R. (ser. C) No. 116, at 59 (Nov. 19, 2004); Río Negro Massacres v. Guatemala, Preliminary Objection, Merits, Reparations and Costs, Judgment, Inter-Am. Ct. H.R. (ser. C) No. 250, at 93–100 (Sept. 4, 2012) (ordering the implementation of: a) study and dissemination of the culture and language of the affected communities; b) maintenance and improvements in the road communication system between the indicated communities and the municipal heads; c) sewer system and supply of drinking water; d) provision of trained teaching personnel in intercultural and bilingual teaching in primary, secondary, and diversified education of these communities; and e) establishment of a health center to provide medical and psychological care to affected people).

[175] *See, e.g.*, Aloeboeteo v. Suriname, Reparations and Costs, Judgment, Inter-Am. Ct. H.R. (ser. C) No. 15, ¶ 116.5 (Sept. 10, 1993) (ordering the opening of a school and pharmacy for the community as part of the reparations); Fermín Ramírez v. Guatemala, Merits, Reparations and Costs, Judgment, Inter-Am. Ct. H.R. (ser. C) No. 126, ¶ 138.12 (June 20, 2005) (ordering Guatemala to improve detention conditions to conform with international standards); Yakye Axa Indigenous Community v. Paraguay, Merits, Reparations and Costs, Judgment, Inter-Am. Ct. H.R. (ser. C) No. 125, ¶ 221 (June 17, 2005) (ordering the state to provide clean water and medical care for an indigenous community while the community is without their own land); Indigenous Communities of the Lhaka Honhat (Our Land) Association v. Argentina, Merits, Reparations, and Costs, Judgment,

legislation violated the American Convention, and it ordered states to change their legislation to protect human rights as part of the reparations. In later cases, it linked the duty to respect and ensure human rights under Article 1(1) with the duty under Article 2 to adopt legislative measures to "give effect" to the Convention's rights or freedoms.[176]

Relying on *Velásquez Rodríguez* and its interpretation of Article 1(1), the Court in later cases explicitly ordered the state to investigate and punish those who appear responsible for violating provisions of the Convention as a part of the required reparations.[177] Investigation and punishment are important because victims of human rights violations do not accept that "money cures all wrongs"; for them it is fundamental that the truth be told, and that those responsible be held accountable, in order to prevent repetition of these events in the future.[178]

This interpretation has been extremely valuable because it provided a valid legal basis to fight impunity and seek justice in the region.[179] Court cases building on the *Velásquez Rodríguez* decision required that states actively investigate and punish human rights abuses, and this interpretation provided a tool to attack amnesty laws in the region.[180]

Inter-Am. Ct. H.R. (ser. C) No. 400, ¶¶ 337–342 (Feb. 6, 2020) (ordering the creation of a "community development fund" to rectify a violation of the right to a healthy environment based on Article 26 of the Convention); *see also* CENTER FOR JUSTICE & INT'L LAW, GACETA: LAS REPARACIONES EN EL SISTEMA INTERAMERICANO DE PROTECCIÓN DE LOS DERECHOS HUMANOS No. 22 (2004), *available at* https://cejil.org/wp-content/uploads/pdfs/Gaceta_22_sp_0.pdf.

176 *See* Trindade, *supra* note 151. *See also* Maldonado Vargas v. Chile, Merits, Reparations and Costs, Judgment, Inter-Am. Ct. H.R. (ser. C) No. 300, ¶ 170 (Sept. 2, 2015) (ordering the state to adopt domestic legal provisions to "make available to persons convicted by the war councils during the Chilean military dictatorship an effective mechanism to review and annul the sentences of conviction that were handed down in proceedings that may have taken into account evidence and/or confessions obtained under torture").

177 *See* Castillo Páez v. Peru, Merits, Judgment, Inter-Am. Ct. H.R. (ser. C) No. 34, ¶ 90 (Nov. 3, 1997) (ordering the state to identify those responsible for the crimes, and to punish the perpetrators as part of the compensation); Garrido & Baigorria v. Argentina, Reparations and Costs, Judgment, Inter-Am. Ct. H.R. (ser. C) No. 39, at 4 (Aug. 27, 1998) (deciding that "the Argentine State shall investigate the facts leading to the disappearance of Adolfo Garrido and Raúl Baigorria and prosecute and punish their authors, accomplices, accessories after the fact and all those who may have had some part in these events").

178 *See* INT'L COMM'N OF JURISTS, JUSTICE NOT IMPUNITY: INTERNATIONAL MEETING ON IMPUNITY OF PERPETRATORS OF GROSS HUMAN RIGHTS VIOLATIONS (1992).

179 For example, in *Barrios Altos*, the Court stated that "all amnesty provisions . . . are intended to prevent the investigation and punishment of those responsible for serious human rights violations such as torture, extrajudicial, summary or arbitrary execution and forced disappearance" and that amnesty laws "are manifestly incompatible with the aims and spirits of the Convention." *Barrios Altos*, Inter-Am. Ct. H.R. (ser. C) No. 75, ¶¶ 41, 43.

180 During the transition to democracy in many Latin American countries, outgoing authoritarian regimes often passed amnesty laws protecting themselves and blocking later investigations or prosecutions. When amnesty laws could not be challenged directly, human rights defenders argued that gross violations, like disappearances, were continuous and ongoing crimes, and that neither amnesty laws nor statutes of limitations applied. *See, e.g.*, Corte de Apelaciones de Santiago, Inter-Am. Comm'n H.R., Report No. 11.821–03 (2004); Hermosilla v. Chile, Case 10.843, Inter-Am. Comm'n H.R., Report No. 36/96, OEA/Ser.L./

Even when states have not immediately applied the Court's decisions, investigation and punishment have taken place years later.[181] When criminal liability has not been established, the duty of the state to investigate and punish those responsible has meant the end of careers or untenable political consequences for those involved in violating human rights.[182]

The development of the law of reparations in the Inter-American system has been one of its most important contributions to international human rights law. One example of its wide-ranging influence is found in the Committee Against Torture's General Comment No. 3, which systematizes the concept of full or integral reparations.[183]

State Responsibility for Gender-Based Violence. Through its elaboration of the due diligence standard, holding states internationally responsible for failing to prevent, investigate, or punish violations of human rights when abuses are committed by non-state actors, the *Velásquez Rodríguez* decision also influenced the development of international law in relation to Gender-Based Violence (GBV) in the Inter-American system and beyond.[184]

Both the Commission and the Court utilized the *Velásquez Rodríguez* decision in establishing state responsibility and finding breaches of relevant legal instruments in relation to GBV. For example, in *Maria da Penha Maia Fernandes v. Brazil*, the Commission relied on the Court's interpretations of Article 1 in *Velásquez Rodríguez* in finding that Brazil breached various articles of the American Convention, American Declaration, and Convention of Belém do Pará, because of the "unwarranted delay and negligent processing" of a domestic violence case involving attempted murder and lasting seventeen years, with no domestic judicial resolution.[185] The Court similarly invoked *Velásquez*

V/II.95, doc. 7 rev. ¶ 73 (1996); *see also* Espinoza v. Chile, Case 11.725, Inter-Am. Comm'n H.R., Report No. 133/99, OEA/Ser.L./V/II.106, doc. 6 rev. ¶¶ 102–107.

181 *See, e.g.*, Thomas Catan, *The Sins of Montesinos*, FIN. TIMES MAG., July 26, 2003, at 15 (describing the trial of a Vladimir Montesino, the head of the secret police under the former Peruvian President Alberto Fujimori); Benavides-Cevallos v. Ecuador, Merits, Reparations and Costs, Judgment, Inter-Am. Ct. H.R. (ser. C.) No. 38, ¶¶ 12–13 (June 19, 1998) (ordering the state to investigate and punish human rights violations to fully satisfy the damages awarded by the Court).

182 *See supra* text accompanying note 177; Larry Rohter & Pascale Bonnefoy, *Peru Asks Chile to Extradite Fujimori to Face a Range of Charges*, N.Y. TIMES, Jan. 4, 2006, at A5 (noting that Fujimori was on his way to Peru to campaign for the presidential election when he was detained on charges of corruption and human rights violations).

183 U.N. Comm. Against Torture, General Comment No. 3: Implementation of article 14 by States parties, U.N. Doc. C/GC/3 (2012). Claudio Grossman, one author of this chapter, proposed the adoption of this General Comment while serving as Chair of the Committee.

184 Elizabeth A.H. Abi-Mershed, *Due Diligence and the Fight against Gender-based Violence in the Inter-American System*, *in* DUE DILIGENCE AND ITS APPLICATION TO PROTECT WOMEN FROM VIOLENCE 127 (Carin Benninger-Budel ed., 2009).

185 Inter-American Convention on the Prevention, Punishment and Eradication of Violence Against Women (Belém do Pará Convention), June 9, 1994, 33 I.L.M. 1049 (1994); María da Penha Maia Fernandes v. Brazil, Case 12.051, Inter-Am. Comm'n H.R., Report

Rodríguez in a case involving the disappearance of three women in a cotton field in Ciudad Juárez when it found Mexico breached its obligation to guarantee various rights in the American Convention and the Convention of Belém do Pará and to properly investigate their disappearances.[186]

The case's impact in this context transcends the Inter-American system. For example, the European Court of Human Rights cited *Velásquez Rodríguez* (and *Maria da Penha Maia Fernandez*) in *Opuz v. Turkey*, in relation to state responsibility for the acts of non-state actors when the state fails to act with due diligence to prevent or respond to human rights violations, including violence against women.[187] The Committee on the Elimination of Discrimination Against Women's General Recommendation No. 19 on Violence Against Women does not directly cite *Velásquez Rodríguez*, but it contains nearly identical language on the state's responsibility for private acts if it fails to act with due diligence to prevent violations of rights, to investigate, to punish perpetrators, or to compensate victims.[188] Several other U.N.-sponsored reports and scholars of GBV emphasize the case's importance in establishing the liability of states for the acts of private actors and the due diligence standard.[189]

III. CONCLUSION

The *Velásquez Rodriguez* petition was filed in the Inter-American Human Rights Commission over forty years ago. Its contributions and influence in the last four decades are remarkable and wide-ranging. The case brought a measure of justice to Manfredo Velásquez's family and exposed a pattern of mass and gross violations of human rights in Honduras, and it established a solid foundation for the Inter-American Court of Human Rights as a respected and important interpreter of

---

No. 54/01, OEA/Ser.L./V/II.111, doc. 20 ¶¶ 42, 60 (2001). *See also, e.g.*, Paola del Rosario Abarracín Guzmán and Relatives v. Ecuador, Case 12.678, Inter-Am. Comm'n H.R., Report No. 110/18, OEA/Ser.L/V/II.169 doc. 127 ¶¶ 134, 139, 142 (2018).

186 González ("Cotton Field") v. Mexico, Preliminary Objections, Merits, Reparations and Costs, Judgment, Inter-Am. Ct. H.R. (ser. C) No. 205, ¶¶ 236, 252, 288, 602 (Nov. 16, 2009); *see also, e.g.*, Fernández Ortega v. Mexico, Preliminary Objections, Merits, Reparations and Costs, Judgment, Inter-Am. Ct. H.R. (ser. C) No. 216, ¶¶ 191, 228 (Aug. 30, 2010) (discussing the due diligence standard and other aspects of *Velásquez-Rodriguez* in a case involving GBV).

187 Opuz v. Turkey, App. No. 33401/02, Eur. Ct. H.R. ¶¶ 83, 86, 169 (2009).

188 General Recommendation No. 19: Violence against women, U.N. Doc. A/47/38, ¶ 9 (1992),

189 *See, e.g.*, Report of the Special Rapporteur on Extrajudicial, Summary or Arbitrary Executions on a Gender-Sensitive Approach to Arbitrary Killings, U.N. Doc. A/HRC/25/23, ¶ 13 (June 6, 2017); Caroline Bettinger-Lopez, *The Challenge of Domestic Implementation of International Human Rights Law in the Cotton Field Case*, 15 CUNY L. REV. 315, 316 n.6, 320 (2012) (referring to the application of *Velásquez Rodríguez*'s due diligence standard to GBV); Paulina García del Moral & Megan Alexandra Dersnah, *A Feminist Challenge to the Gendered Politics of the Public/Private Divide: On Due Diligence, Domestic Violence, and Citizenship*, 18 CITIZENSHIP STUDS. 661, 665 (2014) (discussing the "feminist appropriation of the due diligence standard" after the *Velásquez Rodríguez* decision).

human rights law, strengthening the role of human rights and the rule of law in the region. The case opened the door to important procedural and normative developments, both in the Americas and beyond, including in relation to disappearances, reparations, and gender-based violence.

One of its most important legacies is its contribution to the depoliticization of human rights discourse in the hemisphere. Historically, Latin American countries adopted an absolute view of the principle of nonintervention, rejecting intervention for whatever purpose and by whatever means.[190] In addition, criticisms against a state for human rights violations were identified with either the right or the left, depending on the victims of human rights abuses and the ideological affiliation of the government. The Commission and the Court successfully grounded their decisions in *Velásquez Rodriguez* in human rights abuses and legal analysis on the basis of an existing treaty—not politics or foreign intervention—reinforcing the idea that human rights apply regardless of the political context or the regime in power.

At the same time, challenges persist. Resource constraints are a recurring theme in the Inter-American system. The increase in the number of cases in recent years has only increased the need for more resources. While the system has achieved some impressive results despite serious limitations, ensuring its viability continues to require adequately and consistently funding the Court and the Commission. Backlogs and delays remain significant, and compliance with the Court's and Commission's decisions can certainly be improved.

The United States and Canada, along with Trinidad and Tobago, remain outside the jurisdiction of the Inter-American Court, although as members of the OAS, they remain bound by the human rights provisions of the OAS Charter and subject to the jurisdiction of the Commission under the American Declaration. The failure of Canada, the United States, and Trinidad and Tobago to accede to the American Convention helps support the view that the Convention is mostly for Spanish and Portuguese-speaking Latin American countries, limiting its benefits. Nonetheless, the recent appointment of two Commissioners from the Caribbean, significantly increasing that region's representation within the Commission and bringing the total to three, is a step in the right direction.[191]

Populist leaders and authoritarian-leaning governments threaten to undermine the system and human rights protections.[192] For example, the Venezuelan government of Nicolás Maduro denounced the American

---

190 *See generally* EXPORTING DEMOCRACY: THE UNITED STATES AND LATIN AMERICA (Abraham F. Lowenthal ed., 1991).

191 Results of Elections of Members to Fill Vacancies in Organs, Agencies, and Entities, of the Organization, OEA/Ser.P AG/doc.5827/23 (June 23, 2023), *available at* https://www.oas.org/en/council/AG/regular/53RGA/documents.asp.

192 *See generally, e.g.*, Nienke Grossman, *Populism, International Courts, and Women's Human Rights*, 35 MD. J. INT'L L. 104 (2021) (discussing the potential impact of populist movements on women's human rights, as mediated by international courts).

Convention in 2012, although the OAS continues to consider Venezuela a state party since Interim President Juan Guaidó deposited an instrument of ratification in 2019.[193] In 2022, Nicaragua declared it had withdrawn from the OAS, following President Daniel Ortega's election to a fourth consecutive term, despite widespread criticism of human rights violations.[194]

Despite these challenges, the legacy of the *Velásquez Rodríguez* case and the legitimacy it provided to the human rights narrative and the Inter-American system live on. Never before had an international court in the Americas held a government accountable for violating an individual's human rights in this way. States continue to participate actively in the system. Petitioners and human rights defenders continue to look to the Inter-American system as a tool in their search for justice, when their domestic legal systems fail to provide it—just as Manfredo Velásquez's family did forty years ago. Their fight against impunity laid the groundwork for crucial normative and procedural developments in the Inter-American system and remains an inspiration.

193 *Status of Ratification: American Convention on Human Rights Pact of San Jose, Costa Rica*, ORG. AM. STATES, https://www.oas.org/dil/treaties_b-32_american_convention_on_human_rights_sign.htm (last visited Aug. 11, 2023).

194 *Nicaragua sparks backlash in quitting OAS over Ortega re-election criticism*, REUTERS (Apr. 25, 2022), https://www.reuters.com/world/americas/nicaragua-quits-oas-over-ortega-re-election-criticism-says-it-is-not-colony-2022-04-25/.

7

Natasha Holcroft-Emmess

Hassan v. United Kingdom: A Harbinger of the Fate of International Human Rights Law?

A merchant saw a stranger in the marketplace at Baghdad and he knew that the stranger was Death. Death looked perplexed, as if the encounter was unexpected. The merchant fled many miles for the city of Samarra, where he was sure that Death could not find him. But when at last he came to Samarra, the merchant saw that Death was waiting for him.

"Very well," said the merchant, "I give in. . . . But tell me, why did you look surprised to see me this morning in Baghdad?" "Because," said Death, "I knew that I had an appointment with you tonight, in Samarra."[1]

I. INTRODUCTION

The case of *Hassan v. United Kingdom*[2] is about a death in Samarra. It was not a death that was inevitable, unlike that in the epigraph quote, which is a short parable about fate. While I do not believe that fate played a role in the death of Tarek Hassan, fate perhaps played a role in the workings of the legal case that followed his death. I will suggest that it is, perhaps, the fate of international human rights legal systems, like that created by the European Convention on Human Rights (the ECHR or the Convention)[3]—that, on several metrics, can be viewed as having a degree of success—to be overly cautious when approaching hard cases like

---

1 Paraphrase of W. Somerset Maugham's retelling of an ancient Mesopotamian tale, *An Appointment in Samarra*. Somerset Maugham's retelling is found in his play, *Sheppey*. SOMERSET MAUGHAM, SHEPPEY: A PLAY IN THREE ACTS (William Heinemann, 1st ed. 1933). The paraphrase text is adapted from the script of The Six Thatchers, from the BBC series "Sherlock" written by Mark Gatiss and Steven Moffat. *Sherlock: The Six Thatchers* (British Broadcasting Corporation Jan. 1, 2017). Part of ancient Mesopotamia now constitutes territory in modern-day Iraq.

2 Hassan v. United Kingdom, App. No. 29750/09 (Sept. 16, 2014), https://hudoc.echr.coe.int/fre?i=001-146501.

3 Convention for the Protection of Human Rights and Fundamental Freedoms, Nov. 4, 1950, E.T.S. No. 5, 213 U.N.T.S. 221 [hereinafter ECHR].

Hassan v. U.K. in the current political climate of pushback against international human rights law. Under present conditions, the more successful an international human rights regime is, the more likely it is to be criticized for activism and mission creep. In such times, judicial decision-makers can hardly be blamed for adopting a cautious approach to difficult cases, but I am concerned that this caution comes at a cost. It risks the achievement of the core aim of the system: the effective protection of human rights.

The precise circumstances of Tarek Hassan's death are unknown. On September 1, 2003, his family received a phone call from a person they did not know, informing them that a body had been discovered in the outskirts of Samarra, a city north of Baghdad, the capital of Iraq. Their phone number had been written on a piece of paper, concealed in the pocket of the deceased person. Two sons of the family travelled to Samarra. There they found the body of their brother, Tarek Hassan, his hands tied with plastic wire, with eight bullet wounds from an AK-47 machine gun in his chest. He was twenty-two years old.

We do not know all of the events leading up to Tarek Hassan's death, but we do know the prologue and the epilogue. The prologue was the invasion of Iraq by a military coalition led by the United States of America in 2003, in an international armed conflict known as the "Iraq War." It extends to Tarek Hassan's being taken into custody by British Armed Forces, the confirmation of his civilian status, and his being released from the internment facility, Camp Bucca, before his death in unexplained circumstances. The epilogue to his death was a legal controversy that reached the European Court of Human Rights in Strasbourg (the ECtHR or the Court).

The ECtHR is an international court established under the European Convention on Human Rights.[4] The ECHR is a treaty drafted following the Second World War with the aim of securing the realization of human rights. States parties to the ECHR pledge to uphold the various rights set out in the Convention for all persons within their jurisdiction, and to abide by the judgments of the ECtHR. The ECtHR rules on applications by individuals or states party to the ECHR alleging a violation of one or more of the rights listed in the Convention. The central question for the ECtHR in the case of *Hassan* was whether the internment (i.e., the indefinite detention) of Tarek Hassan could be accommodated as a limitation to the right to liberty under Article 5 of the Convention, or whether a notified derogation under Article 15 was required for the relevant state—the United Kingdom—to carry out the internment without violating its obligations under the Convention.

---

[4] *Id.* art. 19.

The term "derogation" has a general meaning: it is defined in the *Oxford English Dictionary* as the "partial abrogation or repeal of a law."[5] However, in international human rights treaty law, "derogation" is a term of art. It pertains to states' ability to rely on a derogation clause—a provision found in some human rights treaties—as a special kind of justification for measures that, if adopted in normal circumstances, would violate obligations to protect human rights. Derogation clauses allow states, subject to certain conditions, effectively to suspend some obligations to protect human rights in times of war or emergency.

The ECHR's derogation clause—Article 15—reads:

> 1. In time of war or other public emergency threatening the life of the nation any High Contracting Party may take measures derogating from its obligations under this Convention to the extent strictly required by the exigencies of the situation, provided that such measures are not inconsistent with its other obligations under international law.
>
> 2. No derogation from Article 2 [the right to life], except in respect of deaths resulting from lawful acts of war, or from Articles 3 [freedom from torture and inhuman or degrading treatment and punishment], 4 (paragraph 1) [freedom from slavery and servitude] and 7 [no punishment without law] shall be made under this provision.
>
> 3. Any High Contracting Party availing itself of this right of derogation shall keep the Secretary General of the Council of Europe fully informed of the measures which it has taken and the reasons therefor. It shall also inform the Secretary General of the Council of Europe when such measures have ceased to operate and the provisions of the Convention are again being fully executed.

Derogation clauses have some domestic analogues: for example, the Suspension Clause in the U.S. Constitution performs a slightly similar function to the derogation clause. It states: "The Privilege of the Writ of Habeas Corpus shall not be suspended, unless when in Cases of Rebellion or Invasion the public Safety may require it."[6] This provision allows for some flexibility of executive action when circumstances require, while seeking to ensure that fidelity to the Constitution is maintained overall.[7]

---

5 1 SHORTER OXFORD ENGLISH DICTIONARY 650 (5th ed. 2002).

6 U.S. CONST. art. I, § 9, cl. 2.

7 On the suspension clause, see, *e.g.*, WILLIAM REHNQUIST, ALL THE LAWS BUT ONE: CIVIL LIBERTIES IN WARTIME (2000); Jonathan N. Katz & Mathew D. McCubbins, *Constitutions of Exception: The Constitutional Foundations of the Interruption of Executive and Legislative Function*, 174 J. INST. & THEORETICAL ECON. 77 (2018); Paige Tapp, Student Paper, *To Derogate or Not to Derogate, that Is the Question: a Comparison of Derogation Provisions, Alternative Mechanisms and Their Implications for Human Rights* (Univ. Chi. L. Sch. Int'l Program, Working Paper No. 116, 2019), https://chicagounbound.uchicago.edu/international_immersion_program_papers/116.

The requirement of notification in Article 15(3) of the ECHR is designed to enhance the transparency of very restrictive measures. It also signals to courts that a heightened standard of review of those measures is warranted. These benefits would be lost if states were not required to notify derogations when they adopt exceptionally restrictive measures in times of war or emergency. This became an issue in *Hassan* because the United Kingdom had not notified a derogation under Article 15(3) of the ECHR in respect of internments carried out by British Armed Forces in Iraq. A key aspect of the case was whether a notified derogation was needed to intern Tarek Hassan lawfully, or whether his internment could be interpretatively accommodated as a limitation to the right to liberty.

Ultimately, a majority of the ECtHR Grand Chamber (thirteen judges)[8] concluded that it was possible to accommodate the internment of Tarek Hassan with the right to liberty. Consequently, the United Kingdom was found not to have violated Tarek Hassan's rights. The majority conceptualized internment in an international armed conflict as a limitation to Article 5 of the ECHR, rather than as a derogation measure. However, four judges could not agree with the majority's conclusion. The minority—led by Judge Spano, who subsequently became President of the ECtHR—penned a powerful dissenting opinion, expressing grave concerns about the implications of the majority decision. They rejected the idea that internment could be accommodated with the right to liberty. Instead, they would have required a notified derogation to make Tarek Hassan's internment compatible with the ECHR.

The *Hassan* case was undoubtedly a difficult one, with relatively strong arguments underlying both sides' reasoning. The majority decision rested upon a principle of international law known as systemic integration—the harmonious interpretation of different legal regimes (here, the laws of war and international human rights law). It also relied upon an interpretation of state practice that seemed to support the conclusion that states do not view themselves as obliged to notify derogations to intern people in international armed conflicts. The minority's opinion, by contrast, advocated a narrower interpretation of limitations to the right to liberty, concerned that the majority's finding did not "reflect an accurate understanding of [the Convention's] purpose and its historical origins in the atrocities of the international armed conflicts of the Second World War."[9] The imperatives that underlie the respective conclusions demonstrate a tension that can be seen in respect of international human rights law more broadly.

---

[8] The Grand Chamber is a formation of seventeen ECtHR judges, the largest number that can decide a case. It can accept referral requests regarding cases already initially decided by a smaller formation (a Chamber). Jurisdiction to hear a case can also be relinquished by a Chamber to the Grand Chamber. Grand Chamber decisions are final. *See* ECHR, *supra* note 3, arts. 26, 30, 43–44.

[9] *Hassan*, App. No. 29750/09, ¶ 19 (Spano, J., dissenting, joined by Judges Nicolaou, Bianku, and Kalaydjieva).

On the one hand, international courts, like the ECtHR, must be attentive to state practices establishing the agreement of the parties regarding the interpretation of the treaty, and the wider context that includes attitudes toward human rights law. On the other hand, international courts must be alive to arguments about how the treaty ought to be interpreted to pay tribute to its historical origins and the need for effective protection of human rights. These values pulled the reasoning in *Hassan* in different directions. If, in hard cases like *Hassan*, an overly cautious interpretive approach is adopted, one that perhaps reflects cognizance of growing disaffection toward international human rights treaties among some states, then—although that caution is understandable—the cost will be weaker protection of human rights.

II. BACKGROUND TO *HASSAN*: PRELUDE TO THE IRAQ WAR

To understand the legal landscape in which coalition forces invaded Iraq and captured Tarek Hassan in 2003, it is necessary to go back to the 1990s. "Never before in American history was there a period quite like it. . . . [The] United States moved inexorably toward war, acting on authority granted by an international organization."[10] These words were written about the First Gulf War—an armed conflict between Iraq and a coalition led by the USA.[11] On August 2, 1990, Iraq—then governed by President Saddam Hussain, a leading member of the Ba'ath Party—invaded neighboring Kuwait. Within days of crossing the border, Iraqi forces rapidly occupied Kuwait and installed a puppet regime. The invasion was condemned around the world, including by the United Nations. The Security Council (UNSC) passed several resolutions calling for a swift end to the situation and imposing various sanctions on the Iraqi regime.

One resolution—Resolution 678—authorized member states "to use all necessary means" to bring about the withdrawal of Iraq from Kuwait.[12] The Resolution countenanced U.N. member states forcing Iraqi soldiers out of Kuwait if necessary. On January 16, 1991, U.S. President George H.W. Bush decided that there was "no choice but to drive Saddam from Kuwait by force."[13] This decision led to *Operation Desert Storm*, a multilateral military offensive in which U.S. Armed Forces, along with allies including the United Kingdom, ousted Iraqi forces from Kuwait. However, although coalition forces entered and occupied parts of Iraq,

---

10 Council on Foreign Relations, *The Road to War*, 70 FOREIGN AFF. 1, 1–4 (1992).

11 On the First Gulf War, see, *e.g.*, THE GULF WAR READER: HISTORY, DOCUMENTS, OPINIONS (Micah L. Sifry & Christopher Cerf eds., 1991); THE GULF WAR OF 1991 RECONSIDERED (Andrew J. Bacevich & Efraim Inbar eds., 2003); PHILIP SMITH, WHY WAR? THE CULTURAL LOGIC OF IRAQ, THE GULF WAR, AND SUEZ 99–153 (2010); INTO THE DESERT: REFLECTIONS ON THE GULF WAR (Jeffrey A. Engel ed., 2013).

12 S.C. Res. 678, U.N. Doc. S/RES/678 (Nov. 29, 1990).

13 George H. W. Bush, Address to the Nation Announcing Allied Military Action in the Persian Gulf, 27 WEEKLY COMP. PRES. DOC. 50 (Jan. 21, 1991).

they did not push on to its capital, and Saddam Hussain remained in power.

After the First Gulf War, the UNSC imposed or extended various sanctions on Saddam Hussain's regime, requiring Iraq to disarm itself of all chemical and biological weapons, and to cease any development of nuclear weapons capability. The Security Council set up a Special Commission on Iraq (UNSCOM) to monitor Iraq's cooperation.[14] However, even after several years, UNSCOM was not convinced that the Iraqi regime had fully complied with its disarmament obligations. Politicians and media in the West expressed concerns about Iraq's alleged capacity to operationalize "weapons of mass destruction" (or WMD). Such fears eventually played an important role in the ostensible justification for U.S. and U.K. forces returning to Iraq in 2003.

III. THE "WAR ON TERROR" AND SECURITY COUNCIL DEADLOCK

While U.N. weapons inspectors continued to investigate Iraq's munitions capabilities, several simultaneous, deadly attacks took place on U.S. soil on September 11, 2001. The 9/11 attacks were perpetrated by the al-Qaeda terrorist group. The United States' response was to declare a "Global War on Terror," announced by then-President George W. Bush (son of former President, and Commander-in-Chief during the First Gulf War, George H.W. Bush). Although al-Qaeda had no official link with Saddam Hussain's regime, President Bush referred to Iraq as one third of what he termed the "axis of evil," alongside Iran and North Korea, in his 2002 State of the Union Address.[15] The Bush administration was exploring the possibility of a military invasion of Iraq with the goal of regime change.[16]

The United Kingdom, one of the United States' closest allies, was initially strongly opposed to any use of force against Iraq without express authorization by the UNSC. The U.K. government, led by Prime Minister Tony Blair, did, however, conclude that Iraq had not fully complied with its disarmament obligations. It published a dossier outlining the threat thought to be posed by Saddam Hussain's regime, which included the claim that it possessed weapons of mass destruction and had the capability to utilize them within minutes of a decision to do so.[17]

---

[14] *See* S.C. Res. 687, U.N. Doc. S/RES/687 (Apr. 3, 1991).

[15] George W. Bush, President of the United States, President Delivers State of the Union Address (Jan. 29, 2002), https://georgewbush-whitehouse.archives.gov/news/releases/2002/01/20020129-11.html.

[16] DOMINIC MCGOLDRICK, FROM '9-11' TO THE 'IRAQ WAR 2003': INTERNATIONAL LAW IN AN AGE OF COMPLEXITY 11–12 (2004).

[17] Select Comm. on Foreign Affairs, *The September Dossier*, *in* HOUSE OF COMMONS, FOREIGN AFFAIRS—NINTH REPORT, SESSION 2002–03, ¶ 20 (July 3, 2003), https://publications.parliament.uk/pa/cm200203/cmselect/cmfaff/813/81306.htm.

The need for a new UNSC resolution authorizing the use of force against Iraq became a sticking point between the U.S. and U.K. governments throughout 2002. In November 2002, the UNSC passed Resolution 1441, which declared Iraq to be in material breach of its disarmament obligations and gave Iraq "a final opportunity to comply."[18] However, other UNSC member states would not agree to a resolution with the more strongly worded "all necessary means" formulation, as had appeared in Resolution 678, cited as the authorization for the use of force during the First Gulf War.

There thus was a marked contrast between the First Gulf War and the invasion of Iraq in 2003 in terms of the legal justification for the use of force: while Resolution 678 underlay the 1991 military operations in Kuwait and Iraq, it was not possible to secure a resolution with the "all necessary means" formulation in respect of the Iraq War. The "decision to use force [without a new, expressly authorizing resolution by the UNSC] . . . provoked profound controversy,"[19] contributing to the contested legality of the invasion of Iraq. Nonetheless, by March 2003 coalition forces had amassed on the border with Kuwait and were preparing to enter Iraqi territory.

IV. MARCH 2003: THE INVASION OF IRAQ

On March 17, 2003, President George W. Bush addressed U.S. citizens. He stated:

> For more than a decade, the United States and other nations have pursued patient and honorable efforts to disarm the Iraqi regime without war. . . .
>
> Today, no nation can possibly claim that Iraq has disarmed. And it will not disarm so long as Saddam Hussein holds power. . . . The United Nations Security Council has not lived up to its responsibilities, so we will rise to ours.[20]

President Bush gave Saddam Hussein forty-eight hours to leave Iraq. Failure to do so would "result in military conflict" with a "coalition of the willing": a multinational force with contributions from around forty states, including a large contingent from the United Kingdom, and a unified command led by the United States.

On March 19, 2003, coalition forces invaded Iraq.[21] One of the first objectives of the operation—code-named *Operation Iraqi Freedom*—was

---

[18] S.C. Res. 1441, S/RES/1441 (Nov. 8, 2002).

[19] THE REPORT OF THE IRAQ INQUIRY: EXECUTIVE SUMMARY ¶ 4 (2016) (inquiry led by Sir John Chilcot).

[20] George W. Bush, President of the United States, President Says Saddam Hussein Must Leave Iraq Within 48 Hours (Mar. 17, 2003), https://georgewbush-whitehouse.archives.gov/news/releases/2003/03/20030317-7.html.

[21] On the Iraq War, see, *e.g.*, MCGOLDRICK, *supra* note 16; THE IRAQ WAR READER: HISTORY, DOCUMENTS, OPINIONS (Micah L. Sifry & Christopher Cerf eds., 2003); WILLIAMSON MURRAY & ROBERT H. SCALES, JR., THE IRAQ WAR: A MILITARY HISTORY

to secure Umm Qasr, a port city within the province of Basra. British and American marines encountered some resistance, but ultimately gained control of the port. At a press conference on March 27, 2003, U.K. Prime Minister Tony Blair stated: "Our forces are now within 50 miles of Baghdad. They've surrounded Basra. They've secured the key port of Umm Qasr."[22] The port city was home to Tarek Hassan.

On April 9, 2003, U.S. forces took control of the capital city of Baghdad. Images of an iron statue of Saddam Hussain being toppled circulated widely in the media. On May 1, 2003, President Bush gave a televised speech declaring: "Major combat operations in Iraq have ended . . . [and] now our coalition is engaged in securing and reconstructing that country."[23]

It would, however, be a long time before coalition troops eventually withdrew from Iraq. Coalition forces established a transitional government for Iraq—the Coalition Provisional Authority—that remained in place until democratic elections later installed the Interim Iraqi Government. Insurgency and other security issues challenged coalition forces and the new government for years after the invasion. The United States achieved its stated aim of regime change in Iraq, but when WMD were not found, the U.K.'s involvement in the conflict was criticized afresh. Prime Minister Tony Blair's approval ratings tumbled, and he resigned from office. Withdrawal of most U.S. troops from Iraq was completed in 2011, almost a decade after the invasion.

The reason for recounting the history of the military operation is because the timeline matters for ascertaining the laws that applied to Tarek Hassan when he was detained. The laws applicable during an international armed conflict include the law of armed conflict (LOAC).[24] Despite some debate, it is now widely recognized that international human rights law, including the ECHR, applies (subject to the condition of jurisdiction) in a time of armed conflict alongside the LOAC. Aspects of both legal regimes were relevant in the case about Tarek Hassan. With the background explained, it is now possible to turn to the facts that gave rise to the legal dispute.

V. APRIL 2003: THE CAPTURE OF TAREK HASSAN

Early in the morning of April 23, 2003, a British Army unit, the 1st Battalion The Black Watch, went to the home of Tarek Hassan's brother,

---

(2003); THE IRAQ WAR AND INTERNATIONAL LAW (Philip Shiner & Andrew Williams eds., 2008); CHARLOTTE PEEVERS, THE POLITICS OF JUSTIFYING FORCE: THE SUEZ CRISIS, THE IRAQ WAR, AND INTERNATIONAL LAW 129–97 (2013).

[22] George W. Bush, President of the United States, President Bush, Prime Minister Blair Hold Press Availability (Mar. 27, 2003), https://georgewbush-whitehouse.archives.gov/infocus/iraq/news/20030327-3.html.

[23] George W. Bush, President of the United States, President Bush Announces Major Combat Operations in Iraq Have Ended (May 1, 2003), https://georgewbush-whitehouse.archives.gov/news/releases/2003/05/20030501-15.html.

[24] Also called the laws of war or international humanitarian law (IHL).

Khadim Resaan Hassan, seeking to arrest him. Khadim Resaan Hassan had been a general manager in the national secretariat of the Ba'ath Party and a general in the Al-Quds Army, the Party's military wing. After occupying Basra, U.K. forces started to arrest high-ranking members of the Ba'ath Party. Other Party members had been killed by Iraqi militia. Consequently, Khadim Resaan Hassan and his family went into hiding. They left Tarek Hassan to protect the family home. When British forces approached the house, there was no sign of Khadim Resaan Hassan, but army records indicated that there was a "gunman" on the roof of the house. He identified himself as Tarek Hassan. He was arrested and led away by British soldiers.[25]

Tarek Hassan's family made efforts to find out what had happened to him. They approached the British military authority for information, but were told that, before Tarek Hassan would be released, Khadim Resaan Hassan would have to surrender himself to the authorities.[26]

Following his arrest, Tarek Hassan was taken for detention at Camp Bucca. Although it was officially a U.S. facility, U.K. forces detained people they had captured there too. On arrival, detainees would be processed with the assistance of an interpreter. The database of detainee information showed that Tarek Hassan was initially deemed to be a soldier with allegiance to Iraq and identified as an "enemy prisoner of war." This designation is a legal status under the LOAC. But at the entry stage—when the status of a detained person was uncertain—all detainees were initially classified as prisoners of war, apart from those captured on suspicion of having committed crimes. There would then be an interview process to determine whether a detainee was a member of the Iraqi military or a paramilitary, or whether there were grounds to suspect them of posing a risk to security.[27] The status of detainees mattered because different rules apply to prisoners of war, civilians posing a threat to security, and civilians posing no threat to security under the LOAC.

The LOAC is a body of rules found in several different treaties. Among them are the four Geneva Conventions of 1949. Of relevance in *Hassan* were the Third Geneva Convention, relative to the treatment of prisoners of war, and the Fourth Geneva Convention, relative to the protection of civilian persons in time of war. Article 21 of the Third Geneva Convention states that a "Detaining Power may subject prisoners of war to internment."[28] Article 42 of the Fourth Geneva Convention states that the "internment . . . of protected persons may be ordered . . .

---

[25] Details in this paragraph are from *Hassan*, App. No. 29750/09, ¶¶ 9–13.

[26] *Id.* ¶ 12.

[27] Details in this paragraph are from *id.* ¶¶ 14–21.

[28] Geneva Convention Relative to the Treatment of Prisoners of War art. 21, Aug. 12, 1949, 6 U.S.T. 3116, 75 U.N.T.S. 135.

if the security of the Detaining Power makes it absolutely necessary."[29] These articles provide for the internment of enemy combatants, captured and detained as prisoners of war, and of civilians posing a threat to security. As his status was initially unclear, Tarek Hassan was subjected twice to questioning.

His first interview recorded that Tarek Hassan lived at home with his parents and siblings. He had left school as a soccer recruit and played as an attacker/forward in the Basra Soccer Club. He was aware that his detention was connected with his brother. The interviewer said that Tarek Hassan "loves his family and soccer"; he seemed "to be innocent of anything himself" and to be "a good kid who was probably so involved with soccer that he didn't follow his brother's whereabouts all that much." The second round of questioning recorded Tarek Hassan stating that the gun found at the house where he was captured "was only kept for personal protection." He confirmed that his brother had fled, fearing reprisals against Ba'ath Party members, and claimed not to be aware of his brother's location. The interviewer commented that Tarek Hassan appeared "to be telling the truth and has been arrested as a result of mistaken identity." Thus, although he had been captured as a suspected combatant or civilian posing a threat to security, Tarek Hassan was ultimately classified as a civilian who posed no threat to security. He was transferred to the civilian compound pending his release.[30]

A friend of Tarek Hassan's family, Fouad Awdah Al-Saadoon, was also being detained at Camp Bucca. He was formerly the chairman of the Basra branch of the Iraqi Red Crescent, a limb of the world's largest volunteer-based humanitarian network: the International Federation of Red Cross and Red Crescent Societies. Mr. Al-Saadoon was in ill-health and stated that Tarek Hassan "brought him food and cared for him." Al-Saadoon was released on April 27, 2003, with around 200 other detainees, all of whom were fifty-five years old or older. After his release, Al-Saadoon informed Tarek Hassan's family that he had seen Tarek Hassan at Camp Bucca.[31]

By the beginning of May 2003, the decision was taken to release U.K.-captured detainees from Camp Bucca (save for those facing criminal charges or whose detention was continued for security reasons). The plan was for detainees to be loaded onto buses with a military escort and transported to specific repatriation points where they would be released. The U.K. government produced database records as evidence that Tarek Hassan had been released, with the place of his release recorded as "Umm Qasr," and the ground of release as "End of Hostilities." However, Tarek Hassan's family received no contact from him after his "purported

---

[29] Geneva Convention Relative to the Protection of Civilian Persons in Time of War art. 42, Aug. 12, 1949, 6 U.S.T. 3516, 75 U.N.T.S. 287.

[30] Details in this paragraph are from *Hassan*, App. No. 29750/09, ¶¶ 23–25 & 78.

[31] Details in this paragraph are from *id.* ¶ 25.

release."[32] Months passed, then they received the phone call informing them that a body had been found in the countryside near Samarra. Khadim Resaan Hassan and his brother travelled to Tekrit General Hospital and identified the body of Tarek Hassan.

Between 2003 and 2006, Khadim Resaan Hassan remained in hiding, before leaving Iraq for Syria. From there, he was able to contact lawyers in the United Kingdom, who commenced proceedings in the U.K. High Court, arguing that Tarek Hassan's ECHR rights had been violated. They sought an order requiring the U.K. government "to initiate an independent and public investigation into the fate of [Tarek Hassan] after he was detained by British forces . . . ."[33] However, Khadim Resaan Hassan's claim was not successful. The High Court's decision is explained below, but first, it is convenient briefly to outline relevant aspects of the treaty at the heart of the legal claim: the ECHR.

VI. THE ECHR AND THE JURISDICTION HURDLE

The ECHR was drafted in the aftermath of the Second World War and is commonly viewed as a response to the grave human rights abuses that led up to, and took place during, that conflict. First efforts to enshrine stronger protection for human rights in international law after the Second World War had resulted in the Universal Declaration of Human Rights (UDHR), adopted by the U.N. General Assembly on December 10, 1948. Its preamble alluded to the horrors of the Second World War and, in particular, to the Holocaust: the mass murder of Jewish people and other minorities perpetrated by the Nazi regime in Germany in the first half of the twentieth century. To see that such horrors would not be repeated, U.N. member states pledged "to achieve . . . the promotion of universal respect for and observance of human rights and fundamental freedoms."[34] The major weakness, though, of the UDHR was that it imposed no legally binding obligations. However, the U.N. Commission on Human Rights' next project was to draft legally binding instruments, to give the protection of human rights more than aspirational status.

Around the same time that the UDHR was drafted, several regional organizations set out to agree to their own legally binding treaties to protect human rights. One was the Council of Europe, a body that is distinct from the European Union (EU). There is some, but not complete, overlap in membership between the two organizations: at time of writing, the EU has twenty-seven member states, while the Council of Europe has forty-six. Although the EU has focused on achieving political and economic union among its member states—especially through harmonization of trade across borders—the Council of Europe's inaugural

---

[32] Hassan v. United Kingdom, App. No. 29750/09, ¶ 29 (Sept. 16, 2014), https://hudoc.echr.coe.int/fre?i=001-146501.

[33] *Id.* ¶ 31.

[34] G.A. Res. 217A (III), U.N. Doc. A/810, at 71, preamble, para. 6 (Dec. 10, 1948).

purpose and focus has been upholding "human rights, democracy and the rule of law."[35] The ECHR is a product of the Council of Europe. It was signed on November 4, 1950, and came into force on September 3, 1953.

Both before and after the ECHR was signed, the U.N. Commission on Human Rights continued to work toward legally binding treaties for the protection of human rights at the U.N. level. These efforts resulted in two treaties—the International Covenant on Civil and Political Rights[36] and the International Covenant on Economic, Social and Cultural Rights[37]—that were adopted by the U.N. General Assembly in 1966. Thus, the 1950s and 1960s saw an increase in the number of legally binding human rights treaties, both within and outside of Europe.

The ECHR incorporates a wide range of rights. They include, for example, the right to life (Article 2), the right to liberty (Article 5), freedom of religion and belief (Article 9), freedom of speech (Article 10), and more. Since its conclusion, the ECHR has also been supplemented by optional protocols that enshrine further rights.

Three ECHR provisions were of particular interest in *Hassan*. Two were the right to life (Article 2) and the right to liberty (Article 5).[38] We will return to the claims under these provisions below. First, however, it is pertinent to explain the importance of the other ECHR provision of special relevance in *Hassan*: Article 1, the Convention's jurisdiction clause.

Article 1 of the ECHR states:

> The High Contracting Parties shall secure to everyone within their jurisdiction the rights and freedoms defined in . . . this Convention.

The importance of this clause is difficult to overstate. Jurisdiction is the gateway to the rights enshrined in the ECHR. If no state has jurisdiction, there will be no scope to enquire into the merits of an alleged human rights violation. In other words, if no state party to the ECHR had jurisdiction over Tarek Hassan at the time of the impugned conduct, then there could be no claim for a violation of Article 2 or Article 5, and no remedy would lie in international human rights law. The scope of jurisdiction—how broadly or narrowly it is interpreted—is therefore an enormously important matter.

---

[35] The Council of Europe in Brief, https://www.coe.int/en/web/about-us/do-not-get-confused (last visited Oct. 4, 2024).

[36] International Covenant on Civil and Political Rights, Dec. 16, 1966, 999 U.N.T.S. 171.

[37] International Covenant on Economic, Social and Cultural Rights, Dec. 16, 1966, 993 U.N.T.S. 3.

[38] Khadim Resaan Hassan wanted British authorities to conduct an inquiry into the circumstances of the death of his brother and claimed that Tarek Hassan had been unlawfully detained by British forces.

In the overwhelming majority of ECHR cases, jurisdiction is not in dispute. This is because in most cases, the impugned state action takes place within the territory of that state. This means that, even though the "merits question"—whether a restriction on rights is justified in the circumstances—still needs to be answered, jurisdiction is not typically in doubt. However, jurisdiction was in dispute in *Hassan* because the impugned conduct took place in Iraq. Iraq is not a High Contracting Party to the ECHR. It is also not a part of the United Kingdom; these are separate sovereign nations. But the U.K. *is* a High Contracting Party to the ECHR, and its soldiers were taking action in Iraq in 2003. This conduct raised the question of whether Tarek Hassan fell within the U.K.'s extraterritorial jurisdiction for the purposes of human rights law.

VII. THE U.K. COURT'S ANSWER TO THE JURISDICTION QUESTION

In July 2007, Khadim Resaan Hassan lodged an application in the U.K. High Court for judicial review of the treatment of Tarek Hassan by British Armed Forces. The claim was brought against the relevant government minister: the Secretary of State for Defence. One ground on which a person can request judicial review is to bring a claim under the Human Rights Act 1998 (HRA),[39] which obliges certain public authorities not to act incompatibly with the "Convention rights" listed in Schedule 1. Strictly speaking, these rights exist in domestic, U.K. law, but in the language of their drafting, they mirror the rights set out in the ECHR. The United Kingdom has a "dualist" approach to international law, meaning that international law (even international treaties, like the ECHR, that the U.K. has accepted) does not automatically form part of domestic law. Such instruments bind the United Kingdom in international law, but do not have any legal effect at the domestic level unless legislation provides for such effect. This was the purpose of the HRA—to enable individuals to bring claims concerning Convention rights in British courts, with the aim of sparing litigants the time and expense of taking a case to the ECtHR.

On February 25, 2009, High Court Justice Walker handed down his judgment in *Hassan v. Secretary of State for Defence*.[40] Khadim Resaan Hassan's claims were brought under Articles 2, 3, and 5 of the ECHR: the right to life (encompassing the right to an effective investigation into deaths involving state agents), freedom from torture and inhuman and degrading treatment, and the right to liberty. But ultimately the High Court did not adjudicate any of these claims. This was because it first had to be established that the United Kingdom had jurisdiction over Tarek Hassan, and the High Court decided that the U.K. did not have jurisdiction over him at the time of the impugned conduct. The claim before the High Court could not get over the jurisdiction hurdle, and

39 Human Rights Act, 1998, c. 42.

40 Hassan v. Sec'y of State for Def. [2009] EWHC 309 (Admin).

consequently it was rejected in its entirety. Walker was, in fact, obliged to reach this conclusion because of the doctrine of precedent in U.K. law. The High Court was bound by an earlier decision of the House of Lords, then the U.K.'s most senior court, in *Al-Skeini v. Secretary of State for Defence*.[41]

The latter case concerned six linked claims, brought by relatives of Iraqi civilians who had been killed following the completion of major combat operations, and prior to the installation of the Interim Iraqi Government. In five cases, those killed had been injured in incidents involving British troops. Hazim Jum'aa Gatteh Al-Skeini, for example, had been shot dead by a member of a British military patrol in Basra. The claimant was his brother. The sixth case concerned a man named Baha Mousa. He was a receptionist at a hotel in Basra and had been working one morning when British troops entered the hotel. He was taken to, and detained at, a British military base. He died in British military custody, allegedly as a result of torture carried out by soldiers at the base. The claimant was his father. The families of the deceased persons all sought judicial review of the failure by the Secretary of State for Defence to conduct independent inquiries into the deaths, but the success of their claims depended on whether the deceased were within the U.K.'s jurisdiction.

The House of Lords opined that the domestic courts "ought not to construe article 1 as reaching any further than the existing Strasbourg jurisprudence clearly shows it to reach."[42] It noted that the latter's jurisprudence on Article 1 was not always consistent, and in such circumstances, the case law of the Grand Chamber was to be regarded as authoritative. The House of Lords made particular reference to a decision of the ECtHR Grand Chamber: *Banković v. Belgium*.[43]

Banković concerned the NATO bombing of radio and television stations in Belgrade, in the former Republic of Yugoslavia. The families of people killed sought remedies from Belgium and other NATO member states that were parties to the ECHR. As a preliminary matter, the ECtHR had to decide whether the states defending the claims had jurisdiction over the individuals killed. The Grand Chamber declared that jurisdiction under Article 1 ECHR was "primarily territorial." Extraterritorial bases of jurisdiction were "exceptional and [required] special justification." Extraterritorial jurisdiction would exceptionally be recognized, for instance, in respect of embassies, and with regards to certain acts of diplomatic and consular agents. Another exception was

41 Al-Skeini v. Sec'y of State for Def. [2007] UKHL 26, [2008] 1 AC 153. In 2009, the judicial functions of the House of Lords as the most senior appellate court were taken over by the newly established U.K. Supreme Court.

42 Al-Skeini v. Sec'y of State for Def. [2007] UKHL 26, [2008] 1 AC 153, ¶ 107.

43 Banković v. Belgium (Admissibility), App. No. 52207/99 (Dec. 12, 2001), https://hudoc.echr.coe.int/eng?i=001-22099. The quotations in the next paragraph are from *id.* ¶¶ 57, 59, 71 & 75, and *Al-Skeini*, [2007] UKHL 26, [2008] 1 AC 153, headnote and ¶¶ 79, 109.

where a state "through effective control of another territory exercised powers normally exercised by the government of that territory," provided that the relevant state had "such effective control over an area as to enable it to provide the full package of human rights and freedoms . . . to everyone within that area."

The House of Lords applied these principles from *Banković* to the facts of *Al-Skeini v. Secretary of State for Defence*. In the case of Baha Mousa, it had been conceded that the exceptional ground concerning embassies could be applied by analogy to him, as he was detained in a British military base—the equivalent, essentially, of an area of British soil in otherwise foreign territory. As regards the other five deceased persons, however, the House of Lords concluded that this exception could not apply, and that the U.K.'s "presence in Iraq [fell] well short" of the requisite level of control over an area to secure to everyone the full gamut of Convention rights.[44] This decision was binding on Justice Walker when he came to consider whether the United Kingdom had jurisdiction over Tarek Hassan.

Applying the House of Lords' reasoning from *Al-Skeini v. Secretary of State for Defence*, Walker concluded that the United Kingdom did not have jurisdiction over Tarek Hassan.[45] This was for, essentially, two reasons. First, the U.K. did not have effective territorial control over Southern Iraq. Second, it had been argued by his family that, even absent effective control over territory, Tarek Hassan fell within the U.K.'s jurisdiction because its agents had effective control over him as an individual. Walker was "[a]t first . . . attracted by these submissions," but ultimately concluded that they were out of line with the House of Lords' decision in *Al-Skeini v. Secretary of State for Defence*, reached on the basis of *Banković*. Tarek Hassan could not, therefore, be regarded as within the U.K.'s extraterritorial jurisdiction at any time prior to his detention, nor could Camp Bucca be regarded as akin to a U.K. "embassy or ship or aircraft." The upshot was that the ECHR did not apply to Tarek Hassan, and his family's claim was dismissed by Justice Walker.

This was the U.K.'s answer to the jurisdiction question: Tarek Hassan was not within the jurisdiction of the United Kingdom. Since that answer flowed from a decision of the House of Lords, a domestic appeal was unlikely to have any prospect of success. Consequently, the family of Tarek Hassan applied to the ECtHR. Although the U.K.'s House of Lords had given its answer to the jurisdiction question, the ECtHR had not yet done so. However, around the same time as *Hassan* was lodged with the ECtHR, another case was progressing in Strasbourg to address precisely that question: namely, whether the United Kingdom had jurisdiction over people in Iraq during the Iraq War. That case was *Al-Skeini v. U.K.—Al-*

---

44 *Al-Skeini*, [2007] UKHL 26, [2008] 1 AC 153, ¶ 97.

45 The quotations in this paragraph are from *Hassan*, [2009] EWHC 309, ¶¶ 22, 33.

Skeini v. Secretary of State for Defence, brought before the ECtHR.[46] Examination of *Hassan* was consequently adjourned pending the outcome of *Al-Skeini v. U.K.*, which gave the ECtHR opportunity to provide its own answer to the jurisdiction question. In a judgment that pleased some commentators and appalled others, the ECtHR's answer to the jurisdiction question differed from that which had been given by the U.K.'s House of Lords.

VIII. THE ECTHR'S ANSWER TO THE JURISDICTION QUESTION

Al-Skeini v. U.K. gave the ECtHR occasion to reassess its case law on jurisdiction. It reiterated that jurisdiction under Article 1 ECHR is "primarily territorial" and that acts of contracting states performed or having effect outside their territories "can constitute an exercise of jurisdiction . . . only in exceptional cases."[47] It accepted that effective control over an area outside the state's territorial borders constituted such an exception. It considered that *Banković* stood for the proposition that where a contracting state, with the consent, invitation, or acquiescence of the government of a foreign territory, exercised public powers in that territory, that too could be a basis for exceptional, extraterritorial jurisdiction. But in addition, the ECtHR held that there were certain circumstances where a contracting state exercised authority and control over persons in which the use of force by state agents could bring individuals within a state's extraterritorial jurisdiction. This move has been termed a shift from the spatial model of jurisdiction, based on control over territory, to a personal model, allowing for jurisdiction in certain cases of control over persons, even in the absence of control over territory.[48] The personal model of jurisdiction sat uncomfortably with the central holding in *Banković* and the decision in *Al-Skeini v. Secretary of State for Defence*.

Part of the trouble with *Banković* was that its restrictive interpretation of Article 1 seemed to be inconsistent with a number of other ECtHR decisions regarding jurisdiction. These included *Öcalan v. Turkey*,[49] *Issa v. Turkey*,[50] *Al-Saadoon v. U.K.*,[51] and *Medvedyev v.*

---

46 Al-Skeini v. United Kingdom, App. No. 55721/07 (July 7, 2011), https://hudoc.echr.coe.int/fre?i=001-105606.

47 *Id.* ¶ 131.

48 Marko Milanovic, *Extraterritorial Derogations from Human Rights Treaties in Armed Conflict, in* THE FRONTIERS OF HUMAN RIGHTS 55 (Nehal Bhuta ed., 2016) [hereinafter Milanovic, *Extraterritorial Derogations*].

49 Öcalan v. Turkey, App. No. 46221/99 (May 12, 2005), https://hudoc.echr.coe.int/eng?i=001-69022.

50 Issa v. Turkey, App. No. 31821/96 (Mar. 30, 2005), https://hudoc.echr.coe.int/eng?i=001-67460.

51 Al-Saadoon v. United Kingdom, App. No. 61498/08 (Oct. 4, 2010), https://hudoc.echr.coe.int/eng?i=001-97575.

France.[52] For example, in *Öcalan*, the applicant had been handed over to Turkish officials by Kenyan officials, and was held to fall within Turkey's jurisdiction, even though Turkey was exercising authority outside of its own territory in an area where it did not have effective control. In *Medvedyev*, the applicants fell within France's jurisdiction because of the control that French agents had over a ship in international waters. These cases were out of step with the focus on control over territory, as opposed to control over persons, in the concept of jurisdiction as articulated in *Banković*.

The ECtHR in *Al-Skeini v. U.K.* placed a stronger emphasis on control over persons as being a possible avenue of extraterritorial jurisdiction. It stated that "whenever the State through its agents exercises authority and control over an individual, and thus jurisdiction, the State is under an obligation under Article 1 to secure to that individual the rights and freedoms [in] the Convention that are relevant to the situation of that individual."[53] This allowed for the application of Convention rights to be "divided and tailored" to the extent of state control.[54] This was a different approach from *Banković*, where it was held that, as regards effective control over territory, the contracting state had to be able to give effect to the entire range of Convention rights. In a more recent case, *Ukraine and the Netherlands v. Russia*, the ECtHR strengthened its rejection of this point in *Banković*, stating that the argument that Convention rights could not be divided and tailored was "no longer an accurate statement of the Court's approach under Article 1."[55]

The upshot of the Court's reasoning in *Al-Skeini v. U.K.* was that the applicants' relatives—who had been killed in incidents involving British Armed Forces—were all within the U.K.'s jurisdiction for the purposes of Article 1 ECHR. While the House of Lords' answer to the jurisdiction question had been "no,"[56] the ECtHR's answer was "yes."

Al-Skeini v. U.K.'s answer to the jurisdiction question provoked mixed reactions. Some commentators were pleased with certain aspects of the decision. For example, Marko Milanovic wrote: "[T]his is as close as we've ever come to the European Court overruling *Banković*. And good riddance."[57] However, *Al-Skeini* has also been seriously criticized. In 2023, a former Justice of the U.K. Supreme Court, Lord Sumption, argued

---

52 Medvedyev v. France, App. No. 3394/03 (Mar. 29, 2010), https://hudoc.echr.coe.int/eng?i=001-97979.

53 Al-Skeini v. United Kingdom, App. No. 55721/07, ¶ 137 (July 7, 2011), https://hudoc.echr.coe.int/fre?i=001-105606.

54 *Id.*

55 Ukr. and Neth. v. Russ., App. Nos. 8019/16, 43800/14, 28525/20, ¶ 571 (Nov. 30, 2022), https://hudoc.echr.coe.int/eng?i=002-13989.

56 In each case except Baha Mousa's, where jurisdiction was conceded.

57 Marko Milanovic, *European Court Decides Al-Skeini and Al-Jedda*, EJIL:TALK! (July 7, 2011), https://www.ejiltalk.org/european-court-decides-al-skeini-and-al-jedda/ [hereinafter Milanovic, *Al-Skeini and Al-Jedda*].

that, because of the way in which the ECtHR was interpreting the Convention, withdrawal from the Convention was "now the least bad option" for the United Kingdom, apparently referring to *Al-Skeini* as justification:

> [I]n 1975 the Strasbourg court impermissibly extended the Convention to military operations by one Convention state in the territory of another. In 2001, the Court was invited to apply the Convention to the participation by European states in Nato's bombing of Belgrade. It refused to do so. . . .[58] Then, without any explanation, the court abruptly reversed its position in 2011 and gave a series of judgments on UN-sponsored peacekeeping operations in Iraq and Afghanistan.[59] Some of these decisions have hamstrung European armies. . . . This has caused dismay not only in European defence ministries but at the United Nations. . . . It is one of the worst and most damaging decisions in Strasbourg's history.[60]

To summarize: the ECtHR's approach to jurisdiction was clarified in *Al-Skeini v. U.K.*, attracting a mixed reception. The relevance of that case for *Hassan v. U.K.* was that contracting states could (subject to some conditions) have extraterritorial jurisdiction where they did not have effective control over territory, but did have effective control over individuals. Although this had "human rights-friendly end results,"[61] *Al-Skeini v. U.K.* has been sharply criticized as the ECtHR exceeding its mandate and "impermissibly extend[ing]" the Convention. Once *Al-Skeini* had been handed down, the *Hassan* case could once again proceed for consideration by the ECtHR.

IX. 2014: *HASSAN* IN THE ECTHR

On September 16, 2014, the ECtHR Grand Chamber handed down its judgment in *Hassan v. U.K.*[62] It was initially pleaded that the United Kingdom had violated Articles 2 and 3 of the ECHR (the right to life, and freedom from torture and inhuman and degrading treatment), as well as Article 5 ECHR (the right to liberty). The Court held that there was "no evidence to suggest that Tarek Hassan was ill-treated while in detention." Similarly, it held that "in the absence of any evidence of the involvement of [U.K.] State agents in the death [of Tarek Hassan] . . . no

---

[58] This is presumably a reference to *Banković*.

[59] This sentence appears to allude to *Al-Skeini v. U.K.*

[60] Jonathan Sumption, *Jessica Simor's misguided defence of the ECHR*, PROSPECT (Oct. 5, 2023), https://www.prospectmagazine.co.uk/ideas/law/63392/jonathan-sumption-response-to-jessica-simor-european-convention-human-rights.

[61] Milanovic, *Al-Skeini and Al-Jedda*, *supra* note 57.

[62] The quotations in this and the next paragraph are from *Hassan v. United Kingdom*, App. No. 29750/09, ¶¶ 63, 76 & 80 (Sept. 16, 2014), https://hudoc.echr.coe.int/fre?i=001-146501.

obligation . . . under Article 2 can arise." Consequently, the Court held the claims under Articles 2 and 3 to be manifestly ill-founded.

However, the Court did not reject the claims under Article 5 ECHR (the right to liberty) as manifestly ill-founded. This meant that it had to consider the question of jurisdiction under Article 1 ECHR. Applying *Al-Skeini v. U.K.*, the Grand Chamber unanimously concluded that Tarek Hassan "fell within the jurisdiction of the [U.K.] from the moment of his capture by [U.K.] troops . . . on 23 April 2003 until his release." This was because Tarek Hassan "was within the physical power and control of the United Kingdom soldiers." It was an example of the exceptional, personal model of jurisdiction described in *Al-Skeini* applying to the facts of *Hassan*.

There is a very interesting question about whether the jurisdiction issue in *Hassan* would be decided the same way today. In 2021, the ECtHR Grand Chamber decided *Georgia v. Russia (II)*,[63] which seemed to narrow the interpretation of jurisdiction under Article 1 ECHR. According to the ECtHR in that case, states cannot have jurisdiction during the "active hostilities phase" of an armed conflict.[64] There was a dispute in *Hassan* as to whether the arrest and detention took place in the active hostilities phase. If so, this could potentially exclude jurisdiction, applying *Georgia v. Russia (II)*. However, there are still questions about how *Georgia v. Russia (II)* would apply to *Hassan*. This is because, first, the ECtHR did not expressly disapprove *Hassan* on the jurisdiction point in *Georgia v. Russia (II)*, and, second, the ECtHR has since appeared to renege somewhat on the "active hostilities" exclusion, in its more recent decision of *Ukraine and the Netherlands v. Russia*. In the latter case, "the Court left the door open to applying the personal model of jurisdiction, even though this was precisely the type of activity it had excluded from the Convention's coverage in [*Georgia v. Russia (II)* under the 'active hostilities' exclusion]."[65] However, this uncertainty aside, the unanimous decision of the Grand Chamber in *Hassan* was that the United Kingdom had jurisdiction over Tarek Hassan throughout his detention by British Armed Forces.

Once jurisdiction was determined, the Grand Chamber went about deciding the merits of the Article 5 claim.[66] Here the judges split, thirteen to four. Tarek Hassan's family argued (among other things)[67] that he had

---

[63] Georgia v. Russia (II), App. No. 38263/08 (Jan. 21, 2021), https://hudoc.echr.coe.int/fre?i=001-207757.

[64] *Id.* ¶¶ 138–144.

[65] Marko Milanovic, *The European Court's Admissibility Decision in Ukraine and the Netherlands v Russia: The Good, the Bad and the Ugly—Part I*, EJIL:TALK! (Jan. 26, 2023), https://www.ejiltalk.org/the-european-courts-admissibility-decision-in-ukraine-and-the-netherlands-v-russia-the-good-the-bad-and-the-ugly-part-i/.

[66] Unless otherwise noted, the quotes in this and the following three paragraphs are from *Hassan*, App. No. 29750/09, ¶¶ 65, 99, 100 & 103–104.

[67] The applicant also claimed violations of Article 5(2)–(4) of the ECHR. Space precludes detailed consideration of these claims; none were successful.

been unlawfully deprived of liberty, claiming that his detention fell outside the scope of any limitations to Article 5(1) ECHR. That provision has a particular structure, stating that "[everyone] has the right to liberty and security of person [and no] one shall be deprived of his liberty save in the following cases." The provision then lists several forms of permissible deprivation of liberty, including, for example, detention after criminal conviction by a court, and detention with a view to deportation. On the face of the provision, none of the listed exceptions encompasses internment in an international armed conflict. However, despite this, a majority of the Grand Chamber—thirteen judges—ultimately concluded that such an exception could be read into Article 5(1).

The majority reached its conclusion through several steps. First, it grappled with the U.K. government's argument that the Convention should be interpreted differently in wartime, in the absence of a notified derogation. (This mattered, it will be recalled, because the United Kingdom had not notified a derogation under Article 15(3) of the ECHR.) The Grand Chamber noted that this was the first occasion on which the Court had the opportunity to consider whether "it was compatible with [Article 5(1)] to detain a person under the Third and Fourth Geneva Conventions in the absence of a valid derogation under Article 15." The majority ultimately concluded that the "lack of a formal derogation under Article 15" did not prevent the Court from interpretatively accommodating internment under the LOAC with Article 5 ECHR. Reaching this conclusion, the majority referred to Article 31(3)(b) and 31(3)(c) of the Vienna Convention on the Law of Treaties (VCLT).[68]

Article 31(3)(b) states that, under the general rule of interpretation, treaty bodies (like the ECtHR) shall take into account "any subsequent practice in the application of the treaty which establishes the agreement of the parties regarding its interpretation." The Court looked at several instances in which states had not notified a derogation while interning people in international armed conflicts. This was not a unanimous practice, but the Court concluded that it was sufficient to establish the agreement of the parties as to the interpretation of the treaty. This part of the Court's reasoning has been criticized by some commentators. For example, Marko Milanovic has queried whether a negative practice (*not notifying* a derogation), even if widespread, is sufficient to establish the agreement of the parties regarding the treaty's interpretation.[69]

The Grand Chamber majority also referred to Article 31(3)(c) of the VCLT, which requires treaty bodies to take into account "any relevant rules of international law applicable in the relations between the parties." This provides for systemic integration or harmonization of legal rules, suggesting that the ECtHR should find a way to avoid a clash between the regimes of the LOAC and the ECHR. The ECtHR did this by accepting that it should interpretatively accommodate internment in an

68 Vienna Convention on the Law of Treaties, May 23, 1969, 1155 U.N.T.S. 331.

69 Milanovic, *Extraterritorial Derogations*, *supra* note 48, at 57.

international armed conflict under the LOAC with the right to liberty under Article 5 of the ECHR, despite the lack of any notified derogation. The majority stated:

> By reason of the co-existence of [the LOAC and the ECHR] in time of armed conflict, the grounds of permitted deprivation of liberty [under Article 5(1)] should be accommodated, as far as possible, with the taking of prisoners of war and the detention of civilians who pose a risk to security under the Third and Fourth Geneva Conventions.

Under this reasoning, detention in line with the LOAC was deemed a permissible deprivation of liberty under Article 5 of the ECHR, and the ECtHR found no violation of Article 5(1) ECHR in Tarek Hassan's case. However, the decision in *Hassan* was not unanimous. The minority was quite vocal in its objections. It considered that important issues were at stake regarding the Convention's application to armed conflicts and was clearly concerned about the impact on the protection of human rights.

The dissenting opinion—given by Judge Spano, joined by Judges Nicolaou, Bianku, and Kalaydjieva—concluded that it was not possible interpretatively to accommodate internment under the LOAC in an international armed conflict with the narrowly-worded limitations to Article 5 ECHR in the absence of a notified derogation.[70] The majority's reasoning, the minority posited, meant that civilians could be "interned indefinitely," until the cessation of hostilities. The minority was concerned that this could take place "without the State having derogated [i.e., without it having notified a derogation] under Article 15," even though Article 15 is the provision that allows states to take measures that are more restrictive of rights than are usually permitted under the Convention. The majority's approach was a "novel understanding of the exhaustive grounds of detention under Article 5(1)," relieving states of the need to go through the "openly transparent . . . process of lodging a derogation" to intern people in international armed conflicts. The minority held that the majority judgment did not "conform with the text . . . or purpose of Article 5(1) [of the ECHR] . . . [nor] the structural mechanism for derogation in times of war provided by Article 15."

The minority urged caution in using the "subsequent practice" rule under Article 31(3)(b) of the VCLT, especially regarding practice that "limits or restricts" Convention rights. It stated that the majority's interpretative approach "effectively disapplies or displaces the fundamental safeguards . . . by creating a new, unwritten ground for deprivation of liberty." The minority was emphatic about its rejection of this approach, stating "[w]hatever *accommodation* means, it cannot mean this!" Its conclusion was framed as follows:

---

[70] The quotes in this and the following paragraph are from *Hassan*, App. No. 29750/09, ¶¶ 5, 6, 8–9, 13 & 18 (Spano, J., dissenting) (emphasis in original).

> The Convention applies . . . in both peacetime and wartime. That is the whole point of the mechanism of derogation provided by Article 15. . . . There would have been no reason to include this structural feature if, when war rages, the Convention's fundamental guarantees automatically became silent or were displaced in substance. . . . It follows that if the [U.K.] considered it likely that it would be "required by the exigencies of the situation" during the invasion of Iraq to detain prisoners of war or civilians posing a threat to security . . . a derogation under Article 15 was the only legally available mechanism [to do so].

In summary: while the majority in *Hassan* was prepared to interpretatively accommodate internment under the LOAC in the absence of a notified derogation, the minority was of the view that such accommodation could not be reached without a notified derogation. The minority was concerned about the implications of the majority's reasoning on human rights protection. In their view, it sidelined the derogation clause as a structural mechanism for protecting human rights.

X. NO NEED FOR A NOTIFIED DEROGATION?

When I first read the case of *Hassan* in 2014, it puzzled me. I could certainly see the virtue in harmonizing the regimes of the LOAC and the ECHR, to avoid any conflicts of rules. However, the majority's reasoning troubled me. Like the minority, my view was that the facts of *Hassan* fell within "derogation territory." The measure—internment—looked like the epitome of a derogation measure: a measure exceptionally restrictive of rights, adopted in the exceptional circumstance of armed conflict. In fact, I struggled to think of a measure more restrictive of liberty than internment. Internment is indefinite deprivation of liberty. If this was not a derogation measure, it was difficult to conceive of what would be. I was also rather skeptical of the conclusion based on state practice. The practice was a negative one, it was not universal, and, as the minority pointed out, the absence of notifications of derogation was likely based on an assumption about extraterritorial jurisdiction that derived from *Banković*. But, by the time *Hassan* was decided, *Banković* had been all but overturned.

It further seemed to me that the minority's claim, that interpretative accommodation would render the derogation clause effectively obsolete regarding internment in international armed conflicts, had merit. Why would that matter? The derogation clause had, in fact, been carefully debated during the drafting of the ECHR, and it was included to provide safeguards when states adopt exceptional measures in exceptional times.[71] It seemed to me that the derogation clause performed an

[71] European Comm'n of Human Rights, Preparatory Work on Article 15 of the European Convention on Human Rights (May 22, 1956), https://www.echr.coe.int/documents/d/echr/echrtravaux-art15-dh-56-4-en1675477.

important role within the structure of the Convention. Consequently, I came to the view that, rather than shoehorning an apparently novel permissible deprivation of liberty into Article 5(1), the better approach would be to say that internment in an international armed conflict was only compatible with Article 5 *if there had been a notified derogation*. Such notifications are designed to enhance transparency around measures very restrictive of rights and can also signal courts to apply a heightened standard of review to such measures. But these safeguards will be lost if states are not required to notify derogations when they adopt exceptionally restrictive measures in times of war or emergency.

These thoughts made *Hassan* perplexing to me. However, there were at least two "elephants in the room" that may have inclined the majority to its reasoning. One was the issue of remedy. If Tarek Hassan had been unlawfully detained, then presumably thousands of people in the same situation would also have been unlawfully detained and could potentially start seeking financial remedies for ECHR violations. The potential to open the floodgates for similar claims must have been apparent to the Court. Another possible "elephant in the room" was the context in which the Court made its decision, one of vocal political pushback to the Convention system and international human rights law in general.

Although I am sympathetic to the difficult position that the Court was in, I would ultimately have reached the same conclusion as the minority. This may have entailed a finding that Article 5(1) had been violated, but it would also have sent a message to states that there was a clear way to avoid such violations in the future: namely, to notify derogations in respect of measures exceptionally restrictive of rights, adopted in times of war or emergency. Such an approach would have restored the derogation clause to its appropriate role, rather than rendering it practically obsolete as regards internment in international armed conflicts, and potentially other very serious rights-restrictions. Since the minority's reasoning did not succeed, however, this message was not communicated to states, and as a consequence, *Hassan*-type reasoning has cropped up in a number of other circumstances.[72]

XI. *HASSAN*: A PARABLE ABOUT THE FATE OF INTERNATIONAL HUMAN RIGHTS LAW?

My concern about *Hassan* is that it is the thin end of the wedge. The United Kingdom adopted a measure that seemed exceptionally restrictive of rights, in an exceptional context, and yet it was not obliged to go

[72] Space precludes detailed discussion of these circumstances, though the following are worthy of note: (i) one prominent extension of *Hassan* is the case of *Serdar Mohammed v. Secretary of State for Defence*, [2017] UKSC 2, [2017] AC 821, where the U.K. Supreme Court applied *Hassan*-type accommodation reasoning to a case concerning a non-international armed conflict; (ii) *Hassan* is labelled a "key case" on the ECtHR's HUDOC database; (iii) *Hassan* has been cited with apparent approval in subsequent ECtHR cases, including the Grand Chamber case of *Georgia v. Russia (II)*, App. No. 38263/08 (Jan. 21, 2021), https://hudoc.echr.coe.int/fre?i=001-207757.

through the process of notifying a derogation. The Grand Chamber majority's acceptance of this result has made it more likely that states will feel assured going forward that they can adopt exceptionally restrictive measures without notifying them as derogation measures. Consequently, the derogation clause—which is designed to bring into play a number of safeguards for human rights—may become redundant in a variety of circumstances. The risk is one of watering down human rights protection in times of war or emergency.

Perhaps, though, decisions like *Hassan* are inevitable in a system like the ECHR. The ECtHR does not decide cases in a vacuum. One wonders whether the Court is more inclined—whether it is more prudent, even—to adopt a cautious approach in cases touching, as *Hassan* did, on international relations and armed conflict: traditionally the domain of states and their sovereignty. To be clear, I am not suggesting that there was no legal basis for the majority's decision in *Hassan*. My claim is not that the ECtHR eschewed the law for politics. But the ECtHR cannot but take notice of the context in which it is making decisions, and that includes various criticisms levelled at the ECtHR and its previous decisions concerning armed conflicts.

Although the ECHR system has grown in strength and influence, that very success has engendered strong disaffection among an array of national governments. It is no secret that several prominent British politicians—including recent Prime Ministers—have found a number of ECtHR decisions distasteful.[73] Shortly before her selection to be Prime Minister, Theresa May stated that she would consider withdrawing the United Kingdom from the ECHR altogether.[74] As noted above, further calls for withdrawal have come from a former Justice of the Supreme Court, Lord Sumption.[75] There is little warmth for the ECHR, or the ECtHR, in some corners of the United Kingdom.

While several British politicians have (only) threatened withdrawal from the Convention, another state—Russia—has already withdrawn. On February 25, 2022, the day after Russia's invasion of Ukraine, the Committee of Ministers of the Council of Europe agreed to suspend Russia's rights of representation.[76] In March 2022, as the Parliamentary Assembly was reaching the conclusion that Russia's actions were not

---

[73] Prime Minister David Cameron was said to be "sickened" when the ECtHR found a blanket ban on prisoner voting unlawful. *See* Hirst v. United Kingdom (No. 2), App. No 74025/01 (Oct. 6, 2005), https://hudoc.echr.coe.int/eng?i=001-70442; *Cameron Sickened by Prisoner Vote*, TIMES (Nov. 3, 2010, 2:11pm GMT), https://www.thetimes.co.uk/article/cameron-sickened-by-prisoner-vote-j3zf67bbm2t.

[74] Anushka Asthana & Rowena Mason, *UK must leave European convention on human rights, says Theresa May*, GUARDIAN (Apr. 25, 2016, 14:54 EDT), https://www.theguardian.com/politics/2016/apr/25/uk-must-leave-european-convention-on-human-rights-theresa-may-eu-referendum.

[75] *See supra* text accompanying note 60.

[76] Comm. of Ministers, *The Russian Federation is excluded from the Council of Europe*, COUNCIL OF EUROPE (Mar. 16, 2022), https://www.coe.int/en/web/portal/-/the-russian-federation-is-excluded-from-the-council-of-europe.

compatible with membership in the Council of Europe, the Russian government informed the Secretary General that it was withdrawing from the organization and intended to denounce the ECHR.[77]

Is the price of avoiding political controversy the making of decisions like *Hassan*? Perhaps the re-interpreted concept of jurisdiction had to be matched by a broader interpretation of permissible deprivations of liberty, or by a restrictive interpretation of the notification requirement under the derogation clause, to avoid fueling further backlash. Perhaps it is the fate of institutionalized systems of human rights protection that once they make some gains for human rights, the tide must be stemmed, lest the realization of the ambitions of the system alienate those who set it up in the first place.

These developments come at a time of questioning, challenge, and backlash to international human rights law more generally. The idealism that underlay the establishment of that system in the 1950s has been questioned by the emergence of realist and skeptical critiques. For example, in *The Endtimes of Human Rights*, Stephen Hopgood argues that "we are on the verge of the imminent decay of the Global Human Rights Regime."[78] In *The Last Utopia*, Samuel Moyn has sought to challenge the historical basis of the idea of human rights as a noble project responding to the Second World War and the Holocaust. Instead, he posits that a "minimalist" utopia has emerged.[79] Global backlash against human rights law, coupled with rising nationalism and populism, has even seen some commentators suggesting that we are now in a "post-human rights world."[80]

Can international human rights law weather these storms? In her book, *Evidence for Hope: Making Human Rights Work in the 21st Century*, Katherine Sikkink offers an optimistic view.[81] She cautions against the view that the landscape for protection of human rights is worsening. In fact, she suggests, human rights skeptics engage in measurement errors; in reality (she claims) there are good reasons to believe that human rights law has advanced toward success in its goals.[82]

As these texts draw out, a key challenge for human rights law is balancing the achievement of its aims with changing attitudes toward international law and courts. The discipline of human rights law has had to shift from one that sought to establish agreement on a range of rights, to one that is now navigating a terrain of pushback. Given their

---

77 *Id.*

78 STEPHAN HOPGOOD, THE ENDTIMES OF HUMAN RIGHTS ix (2013).

79 SAMUEL MOYN, THE LAST UTOPIA 1–10, 121 (2010).

80 Sebastian Strangio, *Welcome to the Post-Human Rights World*, FOREIGN POL'Y (Mar. 7, 2017, 8:00 AM), https://foreignpolicy.com/2017/03/07/welcome-to-the-post-human-rights-world.

81 KATHRYN SIKKINK, EVIDENCE FOR HOPE: MAKING HUMAN RIGHTS WORK IN THE 21ST CENTURY (2017).

82 *Id.* at 11, 229.

dependence on the continued commitment of national authorities, human rights treaty regimes remain somewhat fragile. Russia's denunciation of the ECHR is a clear example of fracture within the system. But it is perhaps the repeated rumblings about the United Kingdom potentially leaving the Convention that really hint at a thinning of the political will for unity around tackling human rights violations. If the U.K. were to denounce the ECHR, the impact would reverberate beyond the European system. If one of the earliest sponsors and advocates of the ECHR—a state that played a crucial role in its drafting—no longer wished to pledge itself to those commitments, might other states reassess the idea that human rights protection ought to be a collective project?

While not a perfect system, the ECHR regime can be viewed as successful on several metrics. It has engendered real change in domestic laws. Headline examples include cases that have either led directly to, or supported, the decriminalization of homosexuality,[83] the legal recognition of same-sex couples,[84] the protection of children from corporal punishment,[85] and the recognition of certain obligations owed, in the planning and conduct of military operations, to protect soldiers.[86] By and large, states tend to comply with ECtHR judgments. It seems that the questioning of human rights law has developed, in part, *because* the project has proved to be successful in many ways. There is a danger, though, that the regime could become a victim of its own success. One symptom of this risk is the adoption of an overly cautious approach to hard cases, and I argue that *Hassan* is a good example. Although I am sympathetic to the difficulties of deciding a case like *Hassan*, I fear that the majority's reasoning has the potential to subvert the effective protection of human rights.

XII. CONCLUSION

My aim has been to question whether it is the fate of international systems for the legal protection of human rights to take steps backwards, after they have taken steps forward, to insulate themselves against the backlash to internationalization. I have argued that *Hassan* could be seen as part of this phenomenon. After clarifying the scope of extraterritorial jurisdiction under the ECHR, the ECtHR was called upon to articulate its consequences. The Grand Chamber majority in *Hassan* interpretatively accommodated internment in an international armed conflict with the right to liberty, in the absence of a notified derogation. In some ways, the majority appears to have taken the path of least

[83] Dudgeon v. United Kingdom, App. No. 7526/76 (Oct. 22, 1981), https://hudoc.echr.coe.int/eng?i=001-57473.

[84] Buhuceanu v. Romania, App. No. 20081/19 (Sept. 25, 2023), https://hudoc.echr.coe.int/fre?i=001-224774.

[85] Tyrer v. United Kingdom, App. No. 5856/72 (Apr. 25, 1978), https://hudoc.echr.coe.int/fre?i=001-57587; Campbell v. United Kingdom, App Nos. 7511/76, 7743/76 (Feb. 25, 1982), https://hudoc.echr.coe.int/fre?i=001-57455.

[86] Smith v. Ministry of Def. [2013] UKSC 41, [2014] AC 52.

resistance, and while I am sympathetic to the reasons that might underlie that approach, I am concerned about its impact on human rights.

Might the minority's approach—if it had been successful—have engendered backlash from certain states? I suspect so. Would it have fueled increased calls for withdrawal from the system? Possibly. Does that mean, then, that it is, perhaps, the fate of institutions set up to protect human rights to take an overly cautious approach to reasoning in hard cases? I think *Hassan* might be a case in point. If so, what is the solution? After all, international courts can do relatively little to defend themselves in the difficult position of having to decide hard cases like *Hassan*. I think that more and better education at a societal level about the history, aims, and successes of international human rights law can provide the antidote to the backlash. The institutions in the international legal system must have confidence that their treaty system can weather the storms of pushback. That confidence can come from the knowledge of popular support for international human rights law, but, in the current climate, a much deeper and richer understanding of that law within society is a necessary precondition for such development.

8

James Thuo Gathii

Saving the Serengeti Before the East African Court of Justice

This chapter tells the story of the *Serengeti* case, filed in an African international court, the East African Court of Justice (EACJ). In this case, *African Network for Animal Welfare v. Tanzania* (the *Serengeti* case), the EACJ issued a remarkable ruling in 2014: a permanent injunction barring the government of Tanzania from building a road across the Serengeti National Park, a United Nations Educational, Scientific and Cultural Organization (UNESCO) World Heritage Site.[1] On appeal, in July, 2015, the Appellate Division of the EACJ upheld that decision.[2] The case was not an isolated example of an international court standing up to governmental abuse. Rather, it joined a string of pathbreaking decisions issued by Africa's fledgling international courts to protect the environment, highlighting the importance of these courts in this crucial domain.

The *Serengeti* case is significant for several reasons. First, the case illustrates how decisions of African governments to pursue mega-development projects such as the Serengeti superhighway, without regard to the environment or local populations, may spur litigation in an international court. Second, the case shows how resistance through judicial processes against such mega-development projects can unfold. Specifically, resistance builds through alliances of those directly affected by these projects at the grassroots level together with global environmental movements. Third, and more broadly, *Seregenti* illustrates how international courts in Africa are issuing unprecedented decisions to protect the environment when government conduct violates treaty-protected environmental rights. Litigation seeking to enforce environmental rights has repurposed many of Africa's international

1 African Network for Animal Welfare (ANAW) v. Att'y Gen. of the United Republic of Tanz., Ref. No. 9 of 2010, Judgment, ¶ 64 (East African Court of Justice at Arusha First Instance Div. June 20, 2014), https://eacj.org/wp-content/uploads/2014/06/Judgement-Ref.-No.9-of-2010-Final.pdf.

2 Att'y Gen. of the United Republic of Tanz. v. African Network for Animal Welfare (ANAW), Appeal No. 3 of 2014, Appeal Judgment (East African Court of Justice at Arusha App. Div. July 29, 2015), https://eacj.org/?cases=the-attorney-general-of-the-united-republic-of-tanzania-vs-african-network-for-animal-welfare.

courts from their original mandate as trade courts to become enforcers of environmental rights as well.

This chapter proceeds as follows: Part II reviews the establishment of Africa's regional trade integration systems and discusses these systems' multiple objectives, including those relating to environmental protection. While these integration systems were intended primarily to open up regional trade, the courts established within them have been redeployed, first to become human rights courts and more recently to protect the environment. Part III discusses the *Serengeti* case, which, of all the cases in this area, best exemplifies Africa's growing judicial environmentalism. It begins by discussing how local and international alliances mobilized to save the Serengeti through litigation in the EACJ. It then discusses how the government of Tanzania responded to the litigation. Finally, Part IV highlights how litigation on environmental rights represents yet another repurposing of African international courts, following their earlier redeployment from trade to human rights cases. This part also critically assesses the prospects of this environmental judicialism for Africa's fledgling international courts and for the enforcement of international environmental law.

I. THE RISE OF AFRICA'S INTERNATIONAL COURTS AND THEIR RE-REPURPOSED MANDATES

Africa has eight functioning international courts. These include (1) the African Court of the Human and Peoples Rights (ACHPR),[3] (2) the East African Court of Justice (EACJ),[4] (3) the Southern African Development Community Tribunal (SADC Tribunal), which is currently suspended but in the process of reconstitution,[5] (4) the Economic Community of West Africa Court of Justice (ECOWAS Court),[6] (5) the Common Market for Eastern and Southern Africa Court of Justice,[7] (6) the Organisation pour l'Harmonisation du Droit des Affaires en Afrique

---

3 *See* Protocol to the African Charter on Human and Peoples' Rights on the Establishment of an African Court on Human and Peoples' Rights, June 10, 1998, Org. of African Unity [OAU], https://au.int/sites/default/files/treaties/36393-treaty-0019_-_protocol_to_the_african_charter_on_human_and_peoplesrights_on_the_establishment_of_an_african_court_on_human_and_peoples_rights_e.pdf. (last visited Feb. 3, 2025).

4 *See* Treaty for the Establishment of the East African Community arts. 23–47, Nov. 30, 1999, 2144 U.N.T.S. 255 (providing at Article 9(1)(e) for the establishment of the EACJ) [hereinafter EAC Establishment Treaty].

5 *See* Southern African Development Community, Agreement Amending the Protocol on Tribunal, signed on Aug. 18, 2014, https://ijrcenter.org/wp-content/uploads/2016/11/New-SADC-Tribunal-Protocol-Signed.pdf (last visited Feb. 3, 2025).

6 *See* Supplementary Protocol A/SP1/01/05 Amending the Preamble and Articles 1, 2, 9, and 30 of Protocol (A/P.1/7/91) and Article 4 of the English Version of the Said Article, Jan. 19, 2005, https://www.courtecowas.org/wp-content/uploads/2018/11/Supplementary_Protocol_ASP.10105_ENG.pdf (last visited Feb. 3, 2025).

7 *See* Treaty Establishing the Common Market of Eastern and Southern Africa art. 7, Dec. 8, 1993, 2314 U.N.T.S. 265, https://www.comesa.int/wp-content/uploads/2019/02/comesa-treaty-revised-20092012_with-zaire_final.pdf (last visited Feb. 3, 2025).

(OHADA) Common Court of Justice and Arbitration,[8] (7) the Common Market for Central Africa Court of Justice,[9] and (8) the Court of Justice of the West African Economic and Monetary Union.[10] Every African country except two, Somalia and São Tóme and Príncipe, falls under the jurisdiction of at least one of these courts. The courts are historically recent, especially relative to international courts in other regions: all became operational in the first decade of the twenty-first century. With the exception of the ACHPR, which was constructed as a human rights court, each of these courts was established as a trade court to oversee the implementation of regional trade commitments.

Incorporated in African regional integration treaties, these courts were created to resolve interstate trade disputes. As originally envisaged, a central mandate of these trade courts was to resolve disputes in the respective regional trade integration agendas. In East Africa, for example, the integration agenda is sequenced from a customs union, towards a common market, and on to a monetary union, with a political federation as the final integration stage. As it turns out, trade cases are rarely judicialized, and so these courts have for the most part not decided as many trade cases as human rights cases and, increasingly, environmental cases.

In their design, these courts mimic the Court of Justice of the European Union (CJEU) in many respects.[11] To begin with, the jurisdictional mandates of these African courts were designed as carbon

---

[8] *See* Traité portant révision du Traité relatif à l'Harmonisation du Droit des Affaires en Afrique, [Treaty revising the Treaty on the Harmonization of Business Law in Africa], Oct. 17, 2008, https://www.ohada.com/textes-ohada/traite-ohada.html (last visited Feb. 3, 2025).

[9] *See* Traité Instituant la Communauté Economique et Monetaire de l'Afrique Centrale [Treaty Establishing the Economic and Monetary Community of Central Africa], Mar. 16, 1994, https://www.beac.int/wp-content/uploads/2016/11/TrCemac-rev.pdf (last visited Feb. 3, 2025).

[10] *See* Traité de l'Union Economique et Monétaire Ouest-Africaine [Treaty on the West African Economic and Monetary Union], Jan. 10, 1994, https://www.banque-france.fr/system/files/2023-08/Banque%20de%20France%20%E2%80%93%20uemoa.pdf (last visited Feb. 3, 2025). The Arab Maghreb Union does not yet have a functional court. *See* KAREN J. ALTER, THE NEW TERRAIN OF INTERNATIONAL LAW: COURTS, POLITICS, RIGHTS 99 (2014); Harrison Otieno Mbori, *Resolving Economic Disputes in Africa: Assessing the Role of International Courts and Arbitral Tribunals*, Thesis Submitted to Loyola University Chicago School of Law in Partial Fulfillment of the Requirements for the Degree Doctor of Juridical Science (SJD) in International and Comparative Law 84–85 (2023) (on file with author). This list excludes the African Commission on Human and Peoples' Rights, *see generally* African Commission on Human and Peoples' Rights, https://achpr.au.int/en (last visited Sept. 27, 2024), which, though not formally a court, exercises quasi-judicial functions and issues decisions heavily relied upon by African sub-regional courts. The list also excludes both the International Criminal Tribunal for Rwanda, which was established in 1994 under a U.N. Security Council mandate and closed in 2015, *see* United Nations International Residual Mechanism for Criminal Tribunals, https://unictr.irmct.org/ (last visited Sept. 27, 2024); and the Special Court for Sierra Leone, which was established in 2002 and closed in 2013, *see* Residual Special Court for Sierra Leone, https://rscsl.org/ (last visited Sept. 27, 2024).

[11] *See generally* Francesco Duina, *Frames, Scripts, and the Making of Regional Trade Agreements, in* CONSTRUCTING THE INTERNATIONAL ECONOMY 109 (Rawi Abdelal et al. eds., 2010).

copies of the CJEU.[12] The African courts borrow another design feature of the CJEU in allowing suits to be initiated by non-state actors with very liberal access and admissibility rules.[13] In addition, like the CJEU, these African courts were created on the promise that they would contribute to realizing the benefits of liberal economics, democracy, and the rule of law.[14] Many of these courts are ensconced within trade integration plans like the European Union that evolve from free trade areas, to customs unions, to common markets, and ultimately to political unions.

Although these courts were originally established as regional trade courts, three of them primarily have decided human rights cases—the East African Court of Justice (EACJ), the Southern African Development Community Tribunal (SADC Tribunal), and the West African Community Court of Justice (ECOWAS Court). This development is particularly remarkable for the EACJ and the SADC Tribunal. The ECOWAS Court has an explicit jurisdictional mandate to decide human rights cases.[15] By contrast, the EACJ and the SADC Tribunal have pursued a broad interpretive strategy to justify assuming jurisdiction over human rights by invoking human rights provisions contained in the preambles of the treaties that establish them.[16] Thus, a major feature of these courts is the manner in which they have repurposed their original mandates over trade disputes to become bold adjudicators of human rights cases and disputes of a political nature. Scholars have argued that that these courts became adjudicators of human rights cases in response to the failure of domestic mechanisms to redress human rights violations and the threats posed to the rule of law in the absence of any checks at the national level.[17]

These courts have also issued an increasing number of environmental decisions, reflecting a second repurposing of Africa's international courts. Thus, initially repurposed from trade to human rights courts, they are now evolving to serve the additional function of adjudicating environmental cases. Decisions such as the *Serengeti* case show that environmental interest groups have learned from human rights lawyers who successfully transformed these courts from their

---

12 *See generally id.*

13 *See, e.g.*, James Thuo Gathii, *Mission Creep or a Search for Relevance: The East African Court of Justice's Human Rights Strategy*, 24 DUKE J. COMP. & INT'L L. 249 (2013).

14 ALTER, *supra* note 10, at 160.

15 Karen J. Alter et al., *A New International Human Rights Court for West Africa: The ECOWAS Community Court of Justice*, 107 AM. J. INT'L L. 737, 776–77 (2013); *see also* Solomon T. Eboborah, *The Role of the ECOWAS Community Court of Justice in the Integration of West Africa: Small Strides in the Wrong Direction?* (iCourts Working Paper Series No. 27, 2015), http://papers.ssrn.com/sol3/papers.cfm?abstract_id=2621453.

16 *See* James Thuo Gathii, *The COMESA Court of Justice*, *in* THE LEGITIMACY OF INTERNATIONAL TRADE COURTS AND TRIBUNALS 314 (Robert Howse et al. eds., 2018).

17 Alter et. al., *supra* note 15, at 778 (arguing that litigation in sub-regional courts "provides a corrective to the limited avenues of legal recourse available to victims of human rights abuses in Africa"). For a more recent analysis, see THE PERFORMANCE OF AFRICA'S INTERNATIONAL COURTS: USING LITIGATION FOR POLITICAL, LEGAL, AND SOCIAL CHANGE (James Thuo Gathii ed., 2020).

original mission of adjudicating trade to deciding human rights cases. This chapter illustrates how domestic and international environmental interest groups worked together on a litigation and publicity campaign that has mimicked that of human rights activists in persuading these courts to decide environmental cases.

A notable structural feature of these courts has helped pave the way for this evolution. Africa's international courts are not the traditional international courts in which only states can sue states, based on their mutual consent to jurisdiction.[18] These new courts exercise jurisdiction to decide whether particular national law or conduct is consistent with the applicable treaty, and they allow private litigants (whether individuals or non-governmental organizations (NGOs)) to initiate litigation.[19] Furthermore, these new-style courts in Africa allow private actors to bring cases against states without requiring states to consent in each specific case.[20] Private litigants have been more willing than states to file cases, which in turn have kept these courts busy. This experience accords with that of courts in other regions of the world where direct private access is permitted, fueling a relatively high level of judicial activity.[21] Since many of Africa's international courts are carbon copies of the Court of Justice of the European Communities, there was not much discussion, when the treaties establishing them were ratified, about whether or not to permit NGOs or individuals to bring suit. It is only after governments were successfully sued by NGOs and individuals in these courts that there was a discussion and some backlash against this type of access.[22]

II. THE *SERENGETI* CASE

In June 2014, the first Instance Division of the EACJ delivered an audacious and unprecedented decision. It was audacious because the EACJ, as a regional court, was exercising authority to essentially reverse the decision of a sovereign government to build a road within its own borders. It was unprecedented because it was the first decision, as far as

---

18 *See generally* ALTER, *supra* note 10 (discussing the features of new-style courts).

19 *Id.* at 5.

20 For example, in the ECOWAS Court since 2005, individuals have been able to bring cases challenging human rights violations under the African Charter on Human and Peoples' Rights. *See* Alter et al., *supra* note 15, at 753–58. However, individuals do not have a direct right of access to the court to file cases of violation of ECOWAS trade rules. *Id.* Only a preliminary reference by a national court, by the ECOWAS Commission, or by a member state can initiate such a case. *Id.* In this chapter, the terms "member states" and "partner states" are used interchangeably. In the practice of the East African Community, the term "partner states" refers to the member states of the Community. The East African Court of Justice often refers to "member states" as opposed to "partner states" in its decisions.

21 One of the most successful of these courts is the European Court of Justice, which in 2022 received 45,500 applications and in 2023 received 34,650 applications. *See* REGISTRY OF THE EUR. CT. OF HUM. RTS., ANNUAL REPORT 2023, at 108 (2024), https://www.echr.coe.int/documents/d/echr/annual-report-2023-eng.

22 For an extensive analysis, see Karen Alter, James Gathii & Laurence Helfer, *Backlash Against International Courts in West, East and Southern Africa: Cases and Consequences*, 27 EUR. J. INT'L L. 293 (2016).

I can tell, in which an international court invoked international environmental rules to prohibit a government from undertaking a project because proceeding with the project would be inconsistent with those rules. To fully appreciate the significance of that decision, this part of the chapter will begin by discussing how Tanzania transformed from a socialist country that valued its environment and eschewed big development projects to a market-oriented economy in which big development projects that have or are likely to have large adverse impacts on the environment are now the norm. It is this turn from a commitment to environmental conservation towards neo-liberal market reforms that brought local communities opposed to the road across the Serengeti National Park together with international environmental groups. One of their key strategies was using the EACJ in their opposition to the road project. After describing this transformation in Tanzania and the activism it catalyzed, the chapter then turns to discuss the various phases of the *Serengeti* case in the EACJ.

Tanzania: From Environmental Conservationism to Big Development Projects. The Serengeti National Park, located in Tanzania, is a one and one-half million-hectare park designated by UNESCO as a World Heritage Site because of its pristine natural habitats, wildlife populations, rich biodiversity, and status as a critical ecosystem in East Africa.[23] The populations that live in the Serengeti National Park are mostly indigenous people who depend on the Serengeti for their livelihood and who have subsisted sustainably in the park for thousands of years.

The effort to build a road across the Serengeti, first proposed in 2005, reflected a tension between two discordant modern Tanzanian identities. The first was as the nation of post-colonial African socialism, idealized by its "founding father" and first President, Julius Nyerere, from 1962 to 1985, as free from corrupting foreign investment and centered on agricultural production and environmental protection.[24] Nyerere's notion of African socialism was reflected in what he called Ujamaa—which was founded on three values: mutual respect, common ownership of property, and a work obligation for all citizens. It was also based on the principles of equality, freedom, and unity.[25] Tanzania's second identity was as a nation of Western-friendly capitalism and free markets, as envisioned by President Jakaye Kikwete, whose tenure ran from 2005–2015. This

---

23 The United Nations Educational, Scientific and Cultural Organization (UNESCO) designates a place a World Heritage Site because of its cultural or natural significance as defined under the 1972 Convention Concerning the Protection of World Cultural and Natural Heritage, Nov. 16, 1972, 1037 U.N.T.S. 151. *See generally Serengeti National Park*, UNESCO WORLD HERITAGE CONVENTION, http://whc.unesco.org/en/list/156 [hereinafter UNESCO Designation].

24 *Tanzania: Kikwete Support Will Spur Serengeti Road*, OXFORD ANALYTICA DAILY BRIEF (Oct. 1, 2010), https://dailybrief.oxan.com/Analysis/DB163089/TANZANIA-Kikwete-support-will-spur-Serengeti-Road.

25 Olusegun Gbadegesinm, *Ujamaa: Julius Nyerere on the Meaning of Human Existence*, 17 ULTIMATE REALITY AND MEANING 51 (1994).

capitalist model partially relied on foreign investment for industrial expansion and economic growth, without much regard for the environment.[26]

Tanzania became independent from British colonial rule in 1962 as a socialist country dedicated to preserving and protecting its environment. One of the principal objectives of President Nyerere's platform was to ensure that the government exercised "effective control over the principal means of production and [pursued] policies which facilitate the way to collective ownership of [Tanzania's] resources."[27] Nyerere posited that increased agricultural production and pastoral farming would ignite Tanzania's development.[28] He warned against investment in a large foreign-owned industrial sector[29] because such development would have to rely on foreign aid and corporate investment that would result in the cession of its freedom to such investors.[30] In addition, Nyerere was committed to conservation and wildlife preservation, as he set out in his important Arusha Manifesto in 1961.[31] Nyerere argued that Tanzania would "do everything in our power to make sure that our children's grandchildren will be able to enjoy this rich and precious inheritance" of Tanzania's wildlife and wild places.[32] He believed Tanzania's success or failure in this task "would not only [affect] the continent of Africa but the rest of the world as well."[33]

Yet, however well intended Nyerere's commitment was to development through socialism, Tanzania's economy stagnated, with only 0.2% growth in real per capita GDP between 1976 and 1984.[34] The nationalization of Tanzania's major commodities led to a sharp decline in production, and the large bureaucracy in Dar es Salaam, Tanzania's capital, led to corruption, patronage, and high import and export taxes.[35] In addition, contradictory and arbitrary government policies relating to the importance of conservation under Ujamaa undermined traditional

---

[26] For an account of President Kikwete's development plans, see UNITED REPUBLIC OF TANZ. PRESIDENT'S OFF., PLAN. COMM'N, THE TANZANIA FIVE YEAR DEVELOPMENT PLAN 2011/2012–2015/2016: UNLEASHING TANZANIA'S GROWTH POTENTIALS 7–8 (2011), https://faolex.fao.org/docs/pdf/tan151051.pdf.

[27] JULIUS K. NYERERE, *The Arusha Declaration*, *in* UJAMAA—ESSAYS ON SOCIALISM 13, 15 (1968).

[28] *Id.* at 29.

[29] JULIUS K. NYERERE, *The Purpose is Man*, *in* UJAMAA—ESSAYS ON SOCIALISM 91, 96 (1968).

[30] NYERERE, *The Arusha Declaration*, *supra* note 27, at 25–26.

[31] UNITED REPUBLIC OF TANZ., NAT'L ENV'T MGMT. COUNCIL (NEMC), THE ARUSHA MANIFESTO (2022), https://www.nemc.or.tz/uploads/publications/sw-1646119411-BROCHURE%20-%20THE%20ARUSHA%20MANIFESTO%202.pdf.

[32] *Id.*

[33] *Id.*

[34] *See* Michael Chege, *Swapping Development Strategies: Kenya and Tanzania After Their Founding Presidents*, *in* POLITICAL DEVELOPMENT AND THE NEW REALISM IN SUB-SAHARAN AFRICA 247, 247–50 (David E. Apter & Carl G. Rosberg eds., 1994).

[35] *Id.* at 268–69, 272–73.

and indigenous structures that had built-in conservation systems and practices.[36]

These contradictions and their often adverse consequences eventually led Tanzania to abandon its socialist experiment. Finally, in June of 1986, a gathering of Tanzania's leading donors in Paris, under the leadership of the World Bank, adopted an economic recovery program for Tanzania with market-production priorities.[37] While the program may have caused positive GDP growth, it also led to rising income inequality and a collapse of government-provided services.[38]

In the 1990s, Tanzania's commitment to environmental conservation and preservation ended as its political leadership abandoned the socialist commitment to central planning and environmental conservation and adopted a market-centered, neo-liberal development agenda.[39] In addition, once the government adopted a multi-party system of government in the 1990s, it began seeing the indigenous populations of the Serengeti as a potential voting block.[40] Thus, in 2005 during his presidential election campaign for the Tanzanian presidency, Jakaya Kikwete, promised the inhabitants of the Mara Region, the area west of the Serengeti National Park, that the government would build a road connecting them with eastern Tanzania's markets, hospitals, and other services.[41] From Kikwete's perspective, building a road across the Serengeti was consistent with Tanzania's new commitment to stimulating economic growth through large infrastructural projects, and in the process gaining political support for the ruling party from the region's 2.3 million residents.[42] Unlike neighboring Kenya, whose nationalist ruling party was ousted from power more than a decade earlier, Tanzania's nationalist party—initially the Tanganyika African National Union (TANU) and, since 1977, the Chama Cha Mapinduzi—to date still wields the reins of government and has a much weaker opposition political movement than does Kenya.[43]

---

[36] Michael J. Sheridan, *The Environmental Consequences of Independence and Socialism in North Pare, Tanzania, 1961–88*, 45 J. AFR. HIST. 98 (2004).

[37] Chege, *supra* note 34, at 273.

[38] *Id.*

[39] *Id.* at 250.

[40] UNESCO Designation, *supra* note 23.

[41] Jeffrey Gettleman, *Serengeti Road Plan Offers Prospects and Fears*, N.Y. TIMES (Oct. 30, 2010), http://www.nytimes.com/2010/10/31/world/africa/31serengeti.html.

[42] African Network for Animal Welfare (ANAW) v. Att'y Gen. of the United Republic of Tanz., Ref. No. 9 of 2010, Judgment, ¶ 22 (East African Court of Justice at Arusha First Instance Div. June 20, 2014), https://eacj.org/wp-content/uploads/2014/06/Judgement-Ref.-No.9-of-2010-Final.pdf. Among the ideas the government invoked in building the road was the argument that it would lower transportation costs between Mugumu and Loniondo Centers. *Id.*

[43] On Tanzania's opposition, see generally Barak Hoffman & Lindsay Robinson, *Tanzania's Missing Opposition*, 20 J. DEMOCRACY 123 (2009) (discussing how Chama Cha Mapinduzi suppresses any opposition to its near-monopoly of power over Tanzanians). For a more recent view, see Aikande Clement Kwayu, *Tanzania's Election Laws Make it Hard to Build Political Opposition*, CONVERSATION (July 14, 2024), https://theconversation.com/

In contrast to Nyerere's ideal of a socialist Tanzania, Kikwete continued the transition towards market-oriented economy that relies on foreign government borrowing and assistance as well as on foreign investors to develop Tanzania's infrastructure, exploit its natural resources, and spur its economy.[44] Kikwete's economic vision included a reliable and extensive road network to connect the remote regions of Tanzania to its capital, Dar es Salaam.[45] This road network, including the Serengeti road, would, according to this vision, lower the cost of business in the country and attract investment.[46] Some of the residents of the Serengeti National Park and its environs supported the road project because the Mara region is not connected with the large urban markets in eastern Tanzania.[47] For example, Edward Porokwa, the head of the Pastoralists Indigenous Non-Government Organizations, argued that Kenya benefited from cheap Tanzanian cattle at the expense of Tanzanian cattle herders west of the Serengeti who have no access to eastern Tanzania's urban markets.[48]

Yet, President Kikwete's vision of development was exactly what Nyerere feared—that Tanzania would lose its economic freedom to external forces. This economic model, which included building a road through the Serengeti, also posed a threat to the spectacular wildebeest migration from Kenya's Maasai Mara to Tanzania's Serengeti National Park—a migration considered to be a modern "wonder of the world."[49] In addition, in 2012, President Kikwete attempted to evict the Maasai, an indigenous group of pastoral herders whose ancestral land spans the Maasai Mara Game Reserve in southern Kenya into the Serengeti and surrounding regions in Tanzania,[50] from the Loliondo region.[51] While Nyerere believed the Tanzanian identity resided with these small-scale pastoral herders and farmers, President Kikwete argued that a "nomadic

---

tanzanias-election-laws-make-it-hard-to-build-political-opposition-what-needs-to-change-233995.

44 Paul Kibuuka, *Gov't Now Views Private Sector as Engine for Growth*, ALLAFRICA.COM (Aug. 7, 2014), https://allafrica.com/stories/201408070465.html (originally published in the *Tanzania Daily News*).

45 Deogratias Mushi, *Tanzania: Reflecting on Kikwete's Five Year Development Plan*, ALLAFRICA.COM (Dec. 22, 2011), https://allafrica.com/stories/201112230262.html (originally published in the *Tanzania Daily News*).

46 *Tanzania: Kikwete Talks Tough on Roadblocks*, ALLAFRICA.COM (Mar. 22, 2015), https://allafrica.com/stories/201503232142.html (originally printed in *East African Business Week*).

47 George Omondi, *Kenya, Tanzania Experts Differ on Serengeti Road Plan*, BUS. DAILY (Dec. 24, 2020), https://www.businessdailyafrica.com/Kenya-and-Tanzania-experts-differ-on-Serengeti-road-plan/-/539546/1962852/-/11njmi3z/-/index.html.

48 Marc Nkwame, *East Africa: NGOs Attack Kenya Over Serengeti Highway*, ALLAFRICA.COM (Apr. 30, 2012), https://allafrica.com/stories/201204300003.html (originally published in the *Tanzania Daily News*).

49 *Id.*

50 *See Maasai Tribe,* ATLAS OF HUMANITY, https://www.atlasofhumanity.com/maasai (last visited May 7, 2025).

51 Jason Patinkin, *Maasai Fury as Plan to Lure Arabian Gulf Tourists Threatens Their Ancestral Land*, GUARDIAN (Mar. 30, 2013, 10:00 AM), http://www.theguardian.com/world/2013/mar/30/maasai-game-hunting-tanzania.

lifestyle is unproductive" and sought to remove the Maasai to make way for efficient agricultural production.[52]

Additionally, Tanzania's development plans directly challenged those of the regional economic powerhouse, Kenya. For example, a planned development of the Dar es Salaam port would have competed with the port at Mombasa, "East Africa's main gateway," and Kenya's plans to construct a new port at Lamu to transport goods from its own landlocked neighbors to the world.[53] It is very plausible, therefore, that another motivation for building the road was to challenge Kenya's economic dominance in the region so that Tanzania could become an alternative to Kenya as the "main gateway" to east Africa.[54] It is notable that Kenya, Uganda, and Rwanda initially excluded Tanzania from the "Coalition of the Willing," a coalition intent on quickly collaborating to implement regional infrastructural projects to quicken the pace of the East African Community integration agenda.[55] The Coalition eventually included Tanzania, but the snub caused political friction between itself and Tanzania.[56]

ANAW and the Filing of the* Serengeti *Case. The *Serengeti* litigation emerged from a partnership of NGOs that are embedded in communities within Tanzania but also engaged in forging connections across Africa and globally. It is a story of both highly local grassroots activism and global networks. The actors in this story drew on past experiences with impact litigation to leverage Africa's fledgling supranational courts to protect environmental norms.

Founded in 2006, the Africa Network for Animal Welfare (ANAW) is a pan-African non-profit environmental conservation organization based in Nairobi, Kenya.[57] ANAW is dedicated to promoting the humane treatment of wild, farm, working, and companion animals and the well-being of communities that live in proximity to these animals.[58] For ANAW, wild animals are sentient beings and have "feelings, emotions and respond to psychological and physiological changes in the

---

52 *Id.*

53 Edmund Blair & Fumbuka Ng'Wanakilala, *Tanzania President Maps Out Plans for Transport Hub*, REUTERS (Apr. 11, 2014, 2:18 PM), https://www.reuters.com/article/2014/04/11/africa-summit-tanzania-transportation-re-idUSL6N0N346U20140411/.

54 *Id.*

55 Muthoki Mumo, *Tanzania, Burundi to Join 'Coalition of the Willing,'* DAILY NATION (July 5, 2020), https://nation.africa/kenya/life-and-style/smart-company/tanzania-burundi-to-join-coalition-of-the-willing—954032#google_vignette. For an analysis of the Coalition of the Willing in the context of East African integration, see TIMOTHY MASIKO, FLEXIBLE REGIONAL INTEGRATION IN AFRICA: LESSONS AND IMPLICATIONS FOR THE MULTILATERAL TRADING SYSTEM 138 (2022).

56 Mumo, *supra* note 55.

57 *See* African Network for Animal Welfare [ANAW], *About*, FACEBOOK, https://www.facebook.com/pages/Africa-Network-for-Animal-Welfare-ANAW/104162487424?sk=info&tab=page_info (last visited Oct. 8, 2024).

58 *Our Profile*, AFRICAN NETWORK FOR ANIMAL WELFARE [ANAW], https://www.anaw.org/index.php/about-us/our-profile (last visited Apr. 14, 2024).

environment."[59] ANAW's work has a grassroots focus. This means that it is engaged in efforts with the communities that are in most direct contact with animals with a view to enhancing the mutual welfare of these human communities and animals.[60] In addition, ANAW aims to build partnerships and networks with "other animal welfare organizations and governments in Kenya and across Africa."[61]

Saitabao Ole Kanchory, the attorney ANAW hired to bring the *Serengeti* case against the government of Tanzania, had, prior to being instructed to file the case, provided legal advice to ANAW.[62] He initially wrote a legal opinion for ANAW about the feasibility of bringing the case against the government of Tanzania in the EACJ.[63] ANAW was guided by this legal opinion in deciding to instruct him to file the case.[64] ANAW's executive director argued that his organization's mission in bringing the case was designed to "be of future benefit not only to Tanzanians or East Africans but also the entire humanity [sic]."[65]

Serengeti Watch, which I discuss more extensively below, partnered with ANAW in part by providing funding through its Serengeti Legal Defense Fund for legal fees and research trips.[66] The Friends of the Serengeti also provided funds for the Serengeti Legal Defense Fund.[67] ANAW-USA, ANAW's American counterpart, also launched an online campaign to help finance the case.[68]

---

59 *Id.*

60 *Id.*

61 *Id.*

62 Interview with Saitabao Ole Kanchory, Attorney for ANAW, in Nairobi, Kenya (Sept. 27, 2015).

63 *Id.*

64 *See* John Mbaria & Erick Kabendera, *Win for Conservationists as East African Court Stops Serengeti Road*, EAST AFR. (June 21, 2014), https://www.theeastafrican.co.ke/tea/news/east-africa/win-for-conservationists-as-east-african-court-stops-serengeti-road—1325590.

65 Jeremy Hance, *Regional Court Kills Controversial Serengeti Highway*, MONGABAY (June 23, 2014), https://news.mongabay.com/2014/06/regional-court-kills-controversial-serengeti-highway/.

66 Friends of the Serengeti, *The Serengeti Highway Battle Won, the War with the Courts Continues*, AFR. GEOGRAPHIC (July 30, 2014), http://africageographic.com/blog/the-serengeti-highway-battle-won-the-war-with-the-courts-continue/; Boyd Norton, *Serengeti Watch—The Serengeti Highway*, EARTH ISLAND J. (May 2012), https://www.earthisland.org/journal/index.php/magazine/entry/serengeti-watch/ ("Serengeti Watch has raised funds to give a substantial grant to ANAW to help in the legal costs.").

67 Wouter Vergeer, *Travel Association Seek to Save the Serengeti*, SAFARI BOOKINGS BLOG (June 27, 2014), https://web.archive.org/web/20140628210738/https://www.safaribookings.com/blog/158.

68 Contributors were asked to donate to the organization through its website *See generally* Africa Network for Animal Welfare (ANAW)-USA, https://www.anaw.org/index.php?option=com_content&view=article&id=48&Itemid=37 (last visited May 12, 2025); *see also Africa Network for Animal Welfare-USA*, COLO. GIVES FOUND., https://www.coloradogives.org/organization/ANAW (last visited Apr. 14, 2024) ("As a result of ANAW's advocacy . . . in 2014 ANAW and partners stopped the government from building a road that would bi-sect the Serengeti, a World heritage site and migration corridor for millions of animals . . . .").

The international alliance that ANAW brought together in the *Serengeti* case must be understood as a counterpart to the grassroots organizing around animal welfare issues in Africa that ANAW had helped coordinate. In addition, ANAW's attorney, Saitabao Ole Kanchory, had been involved in filing cases in the Kenyan High Court on environmental conservation on behalf of Maasai communities affected by development projects.[69] For example, he had represented the Maa Community in its challenge of appointments to the Kenyan National Land Commission,[70] indicating his prior commitment to issues surrounding the Maasai community and its land rights. ANAW and perhaps the Serengeti Legal Defense Fund, insofar as I can tell, provided funding for John Kuloba, the Kenyan environmental impact assessment specialist[71] who evaluated the impact of the Serengeti road and concluded that the project should be abandoned due to its negative impacts on the ecosystem. He testified on behalf of ANAW in the case.[72]

ANAW was therefore the glue that brought together and mobilized grassroots indigenous communities, on the one hand, and international environmental and conservation groups, on the other, in their efforts to defeat the building of the road.

International NGO Opposition to the Serengeti Road. Although President Kikwete promised to build the Serengeti road in his 2005 election campaign, international mobilization against it did not begin until 2010.[73] An article published in 2013 in *Departures*, a travel magazine, reported that Dr. Dennis Rentsch of the Frankfurt Zoological Association had uncovered Tanzania's plan to pave the road in May of 2010.[74] Dr. Rentsch inferred from tiny red flags dotting the trees along the current road that a construction project through the Serengeti would soon begin.[75] He quickly conveyed this information to his boss, Dr. Markus Bonner, who then attempted to use the agency's influence to stop the construction of the road.[76] When this effort proved unsuccessful, Dr. Christof Schenck, the director of the Frankfurt Zoological Society, sent a letter dated May 31, 2010, to President Kikwete urging him to halt the

---

69 *See* Ben Ole Koissaba, *Elusive Justice: The Maasai Contestation of Land Appropriation in Kenya; A Historical and Contemporary Perspective*, INTERCONTINENTAL CRY (Jan. 28, 2015), https://intercontinentalcry.org/elusive-justice-maasai-contestestation-land-kenya/ (citing S.O. Kanchory, *The Proposed Maasai Land Case Brief: Report Prepared with the Authority upon Commissioning by the Maa Civil Society Forum* (2006)).

70 Munei v. Nat'l Land Comm'n Selection Panel and the Att'y Gen., Petition 266 of 2012 (High Court of Kenya at Nairobi (Milimani Law Courts) July 31, 2012).

71 Omondi, *supra* note 47.

72 *Id.*

73 Gettleman, *supra* note 41; Mark Seal, *The Fight Over the Serengeti Highway*, DEPARTURES (Sept. 19, 2013), https://web.archive.org/web/20150310222956/http:/www.departures.com/travel/travel/fight-over-serengeti-highway.

74 Seal, *supra* note 73.

75 *Id.*

76 *Id.*

construction.[77] Dr. Schenck also sent a copy of the letter to a *New York Times* "Opinionator" writer, Olivia Judson.[78] Judson then published an opinion piece on June 15, 2010, expressing the concerns of the international community that the proposed road would bisect the annual wildebeest migration route, now designated as an additional "wonder of the world," and provide greater accessibility to poachers.[79] In addition, Dr. Bonner, along with other conservationists and scientists, published an article in *Nature* on September 16, 2010, that decried the planned construction of the road.[80] These publications enhanced international awareness about the planned road and its potential environmental impact.[81]

Several NGOs became aware of the construction project and began to organize an international response to it.[82] In May 2010, Boyd Norton learned from his Maasai friends of the Tanzanian government's Serengeti highway construction plan.[83] Within a few days, Norton created the "Stop the Serengeti Highway" Facebook page that quickly drew international attention to the issue and began to organize opposition to the road.[84] In the fall of 2010, Norton and Dave Blanton, along with the Earth Island Institute, a U.S. conservation-focused NGO based in Berkeley, CA,[85] created a project named Serengeti Watch.[86] The Serengeti Watch's social media campaigns, outreach with other international NGOs and governments, and organization of Serengeti tourism companies created a diverse and extensive movement opposed to the road.[87] For example, Serengeti Watch formed the Friends of Serengeti to protect the Serengeti from environmental degradation through sustainable tourism and activism.[88] The Friends of Serengeti believe that building the road across

---

77 *Id.*

78 Olivia Judson, Opinion, *Road Kill in the Serengeti?*, N.Y. TIMES (June 15, 2010, 6:53 PM), http://opinionator.blogs.nytimes.com/2010/06/15/road-kill-in-the-serengeti/?_r=0.

79 *Id.*

80 Andrew P. Dobson et al., Opinion, *Road Will Ruin Serengeti*, 467 NATURE 272, 272–73 (2010).

81 *Id.*

82 *Id.*

83 Boyd Norton, *Protecting One of the Great Wildlife Reserves on Earth*, 30 EARTH ISLAND J., Summer 2015, at 15, https://www.earthisland.org/journal/index.php/magazine/entry/protecting_one_of_the_great_wildlife_reserves_on_earth/.

84 *Id.*

85 *About Earth Island*, EARTH ISLAND INST. http://www.earthisland.org/index.php/aboutUs/ (last visited Apr. 14, 2024).

86 *About Serengeti Watch*, SERENGETI WATCH, https://serengetiwatch.org/about-2/ (last visited Apr. 14, 2024).

87 *Id.*

88 Vergeer, *supra* note 67; *see also Friends of Serengeti*, SERENGETI WATCH, https://serengetiwatch.org/friends-of-serengeti/ (last visited Apr. 14, 2024); Christopher Doyle, *Save the Serengeti: An ATTA Call to Action*, ADVENTURE TRAVEL TRADE ASS'N (June 25, 2010), http://www.adventuretravelnews.com/save-the-serengeti-an-atta-call-to-action.

the Serengeti National Park would decrease the flow of tourists and could lead to major economic losses in an already poor region.[89]

Once the road gained international attention, the African Wildlife Foundation, as well as the German government and the World Bank,[90] opposed the plan and supported the road's construction further south.[91] Both the World Bank and the German government had made financial commitments to build the road. The World Bank argued that building the road farther south would "meet the development needs of northern Tanzania, while preserving he unique character of the Serengeti."[92] The World Bank's rejection of the route through the Serengeti was based on its desire not to fund a project that would disrupt the annual wildebeest migration.[93] Similarly, the German government opposed building the road through the Serengeti on environmental grounds.[94] At the time, the German government offered funding if the road was built elsewhere.[95]

The* Serengeti *Case in the East African Court of Justice. The opposition to the road that had coalesced around ANAW's opposition now included international partners. That was the backdrop against which ANAW filed its case against Tanzania in 2010 in the EACJ seeking a permanent injunction against the government of Tanzania's proposed construction and maintenance of a fifty-three-kilometer section of the Natta-Mugumu-Tabora B-Kliens Gate-Loliondo Road across the Serengeti National Park.[96] According to the Tanzanian government, the primary users of this road would be tourists and officials of the Tanzania National Park Authority (TNPA).[97] Anyone who wished to use the road other than tourists or TNPA officials would be required to obtain authorization from the park's management.[98] ANAW's suit sought an injunction against the government of Tanzania with respect to its plans

---

89 *Friends of Serengeti*, *supra* note 88.

90 Tracy McVeigh, *Serengeti Highway Threatens National Park's Wildebeest Migration*, GUARDIAN (Mar. 26, 2011), https://www.theguardian.com/world/2011/mar/27/serengeti-highway-national-park.

91 *Worldwide Opposition to Serengeti Road Has Yet to Sway Tanzanian Government*, AFR. WILDLIFE FOUND. (Mar. 15, 2011), http://www.awf.org/news/worldwide-opposition-serengeti-road-has-yet-sway-tanzanian-government.

92 William McLennan, *Tanzania Urged to Accept World Bank Funding of Alternative Serengeti Highway Route*, ECOLOGIST (Mar. 3, 2001), https://theecologist.org/2011/mar/03/tanzania-urged-accept-world-bank-funding-alternative-serengeti-highway-route.

93 *See* Gettleman, *supra* note 41; Ng'Wanakilala, *supra* note 53.

94 *See* McVeigh, *supra* note 90.

95 Appolinari Tairo, *Tanzania Revives Plan to Tarmac Highway Through Serengeti*, EAST AFR. (Mar. 17, 2024), https://www.theeastafrican.co.ke/tea/news/east-africa/tanzania-revives-plan-to-tarmac-highway-through-serengeti-4558236.

96 African Network for Animal Welfare (ANAW) v. Att'y Gen. of the United Republic of Tanz., Ref. No. 9 of 2010, Judgment, ¶¶ 1–2, 5, 17 (East African Court of Justice at Arusha First Instance Div. June 20, 2014), https://eacj.org/wp-content/uploads/2014/06/Judgement-Ref.-No.9-of-2010-Final.pdf.

97 *Id.* ¶ 9.

98 *Id.*

to "upgrade, tarmac, pave, realign, construct, create, and/or commission a trunk road across the northern wilderness of the park."[99]

ANAW asked the court for a number of remedies: first, to permanently prevent the Tanzanian government from "maintaining any road or highway across any part of the Serengeti National Park";[100] second, to declare that construction of the road would violate Tanzania's obligations under the Treaty for the Establishment of the East African Community (EACT or EAC Establishment Treaty); and third, to find the government of Tanzania accountable for violating its obligations under the EACT.[101]

Even at the outset, opposition to the road and the litigation prompted a key change in the Tanzanian government's behavior. Notably, the government had initially planned to upgrade the entire 239-kilometer road to asphalt.[102] However, after local and international opposition from NGOs and UNESCO,[103] and after a government-hired consultant firm advised against paving the road through the Serengeti,[104] the government decided to upgrade the fifty-three-kilometer section passing through the Serengeti "to gravel status only."[105] The Tanzanian government abandoned its plan to construct a paved road through the Serengeti after it was advised a paved road would likely cause environmental damage and disrupt the annual wildebeest migration—regarded by many as a spectacular wildlife event.[106] Nonetheless, the litigation continued to challenge the unpaved road.

Proceedings in the EACJ's First Instance Division. At the outset of proceedings in the EACJ's First Instance Division, the Tanzanian government filed a jurisdictional challenge and argued that the case was time-barred.[107] On August 26, 2011, the court overruled Tanzania's objections.[108] The First Instance Division determined that it had jurisdiction over environmental cases brought by any resident of the East African Community and that it had the power to issue a permanent injunction preventing member states from engaging in any conduct that may "affect the well-being of a shared resource."[109] However, in October 2011 Tanzania appealed this ruling, arguing that the court did not have

---

[99] *Id.* ¶¶ 10, 17.

[100] *Id.* ¶ 17.

[101] *Id.* ¶ 17(i).

[102] *Id.* ¶ 12.

[103] *Id.* ¶ 27.

[104] *Id.* ¶ 19.

[105] *Id.* ¶ 28.

[106] *Id.*

[107] *Id.* ¶ 6.

[108] *Id.*

[109] Save the Serengeti, *Chronology of ANAW Lawsuit to Block the Highway*, FACEBOOK (May 5, 2021), https://www.facebook.com/notes/stop-the-serengeti-highway/chronology-of-anaw-lawsuit-to-block-the-highway/344571812240687 [hereinafter *ANAW Litigation Chronology*].

jurisdiction.[110] As a result, the case was sent to the appellate court on the question of jurisdiction.[111] On March 15, 2012, the EACJ Appellate Division ruled in ANAW's favor and dismissed the government's appeal.[112]

The proceedings in the First Instance Division then turned to the merits. In Tanzania's reply to the reference filed in the merits hearing, it made several arguments. First, Tanzania contended that the road as it currently existed had been in use without any negative impact on the park.[113] Second, the government argued that the road was not the first of its kind.[114] Third, Tanzania further argued that the case should be dismissed because a Protocol on the Environment envisaged in the EAC Establishment Treaty had not yet been enacted.[115] Finally, Tanzania argued that the EACJ did not have jurisdiction to determine if there were violations of non-EACJ international conventions and declarations on environment and natural resources.[116]

The First Instance Division ruled in favor of ANAW and against Tanzania on June 20, 2014.[117] According to the court, the applicant had demonstrated that Tanzania intended to upgrade, tarmac, pave, realign, create and/or commission a trunk road across the northern wilderness of the world-famous Serengeti.[118] Further, the court held that the provisions relating to the environment in the EAC Establishment Treaty were in force as they were properly ratified, notwithstanding the fact that a Protocol on the Environment had yet to enter into force.[119] According to the First Instance Division, although protocols to the EACT "shall form an integral part" of the Establishment Treaty, "failure to enact a protocol does not oust the obligations placed on a Partner State by clear and unambiguous provisions in the body of the Treaty. . . . Chapter Nineteen [titled "Co-operation in Environment and Natural Resources"] is as binding on Tanzania as to other Partner States with or without a protocol in that regard."[120] Further, citing to Article 130(1) and (4) of the EAC Establishment Treaty, the First Instance Division held that Tanzania was also required to comply with non-East African Community

---

110 *Id.*

111 *Id.*

112 Att'y Gen. of the United Republic of Tanz. v. African Network for Animal Welfare (ANAW), Appeal No. 3 of 2014, Appeal Judgment, ¶ 59 (East African Court of Justice at Arusha App. Div. July 29, 2015), https://eacj.org/?cases=the-attorney-general-of-the-united-republic-of-tanzania-vs-african-network-for-animal-welfare.

113 *ANAW v. Tanz.*, Ref. No. 9, ¶ 19.

114 *Id.*

115 *Id.* ¶ 29.

116 *Id.* ¶ 44.

117 *ANAW Litigation Chronology*, *supra* note 109.

118 *Tanz. v. ANAW*, Appeal No. 3 of 2014 (summarizing the lower court's findings).

119 *ANAW v. Tanz.*, Ref. No. 9, ¶¶ 22–29. The court cited Article 151, which provides that the "non-conclusion of a protocol does not oust obligations placed on a Partner State by the Treaty itself."

120 *Id.* ¶ 42.

environmental treaties and rules of international law to which Tanzania was bound.[121] These were the 2003 African Convention on Conservation of Nature and Natural Resources,[122] the 1992 Rio Declaration,[123] the 1972 Stockholm Declaration,[124] and the 1992 United Nations Convention on Biodiversity.[125] According to the First Instance Division, since these non-East African Community treaties and rules of international law were incorporated into East African Community law by Chapter 19 of the EAC Establishment Treaty, the alleged violations in the case were those of Chapter 19, which fell within the mandate of the EACJ.[126]

In effect, the First Instance Division was arguing that by virtue of the incorporation of these non-East African Community treaties and rules of international law into the EAC Establishment Treaty, it had jurisdiction to decide whether these treaty provisions and rules had or had not been violated. As we shall see below, the Appellate Division went much further than the First Instance Division in relying on these treaties and rules in its decision.

On whether the applicants were entitled to permanently bar the government of Tanzania from building the road, the court held that if the road project was implemented as originally planned, the effects would be devastating both for the park and neighboring parks, and therefore concluded it could not be built.[127] The court was nonetheless sensitive to the arguments of the government of Tanzania, observing in part that while the aim of its decision was to prevent future degradation of an ecosystem, this must be done without taking away the government's ability to develop the economy of the region.[128]

Proceedings in the Appellate Division of the EACJ. The government of Tanzania then appealed this decision of the First Instance Division to the Appellate Division, which is the highest level of the EACJ.[129] In the Memorandum of Appeal, the Tanzanian Attorney General asked the court to set aside the judgment of the First Instance Division, allow its appeal with costs, and make any other orders the court deemed just and equitable.[130] Tanzania argued the following multiple grounds for the appeal: first, that the First Instance Court erred in law and fact by issuing a judgment on the Tanzanian government's proposal to upgrade

---

[121] *Id.* ¶ 48.

[122] African Convention on Conservation of Nature and Natural Resources, July 11, 2003, 1001 U.N.T.S. 3.

[123] Rio Declaration on Environment and Development, June 3–14, 1992, U.N. Doc. A/CONF.151/26 (Vol. I).

[124] Rep. of the United Nations Conference on the Human Environment, Stockholm, June 5–16, 1972, U.N. Doc. A/CONF.48/14/Rev.1.

[125] Convention on Biological Diversity, June 5, 1992, 1760 U.N.T.S. 79 (1992)

[126] *Tanz. v. ANAW*, Appeal No. 3 of 2014, ¶ 49.

[127] *Id.* ¶ 82.

[128] *Id.*

[129] *Id.* ¶ 3.

[130] *Id.* ¶ 4.

the road to asphalt, because the government had abandoned that plan;[131] second, that the First Instance Court erred in law and fact in its enforcement of Articles 111–114 of the EAC Establishment Treaty, because no implementing protocol had yet been negotiated, agreed, signed, and ratified by all of the partner states;[132] third, that the lower court incorrectly concluded that it had jurisdiction to settle disputes based on other international declarations and conventions outside of the EACT;[133] and finally, that the First Instance Court wrongfully granted a permanent injunction against Tanzania as it lacked the power to do so under the EACT.[134] In the scheduling conference on September 8, 2014, the parties agreed that the appellant's four grounds for appeal would comprise the agreed issues for the court's consideration along with a fifth issue of whether the parties were entitled to the remedies sought.[135] Both the appellant and the respondent, ANAW, filed submissions.

The Appellate Division decided the case on July 29, 2015.[136] On the question whether the First Instance Division erred in law by enforcing Articles 111–114 of the EACT when those articles had yet to be fleshed out by all EACT parties through a protocol, Tanzania lost the appeal.[137] The court concluded that those articles imposed obligations, duties, and undertakings on EACT member states with regard to their mutual cooperation on environmental issues, even though EACT partner states had not yet negotiated a protocol.[138] Indeed, the Appellate Division held that all provisions of the EACT (Articles 5(3)(c)–114(1)) are "live and vibrant" provisions of the treaty and, as such, are subject to the Court's interpretation and application pursuant to its Article 27(1) power and its Article 23(1) power to ensure compliance with the EACT.[139] The Appellate Division held that the failure of EACT partner states to ratify a Protocol on the Environment and Natural Resources did not void the obligation of those states to be bound by the EACT and had nothing to do with the Court's ability to interpret and apply Articles 111–114.[140]

---

131 *Id.* ¶ 3.1.

132 *Id.* ¶ 3. Article 111(1)(b) of the EAC Establishment Treaty, *supra* note 4, provides in part that the partner states shall undertake to take actions "for the protection and conservation of the natural resources and environment against all forms of degradation and pollution arising from developmental activities"; Article 112(1)(e) commits the partner states to "integrate environmental management and conservation measures in all development activities such as trade, transport, agriculture, industrial development, mining and tourism in the Community"; Article 113 contains commitments on preventing the illegal trade in and movement of toxic chemicals, substances, and hazardous wastes; and Article 114(1)(a) obliges partner states to "take necessary measures to conserve their natural resources."

133 *Tanz. v. ANAW*, Appeal No. 3 of 2014, ¶ 3.

134 *Id.*

135 *Id.* ¶ 5.

136 *Id.*

137 *Id.* ¶¶ 33–39.

138 *Id.* ¶ 22.

139 *Id.* ¶ 23.

140 *Id.* ¶ 24.

The Appellate Division also held that Articles 111–114 of the EAC Establishment Treaty, which relate to environmental obligations, responsibilities, and standards of EAC states, are self-executing and do not require a protocol or other special act, process, procedure, or proceeding to establish their enforcement.[141] In a very important finding, the Appellate Division affirmed that these provisions are not only obligations of the partner states, but also causes of action allowing an injured party to seek a remedy against the state for their breach without having to demonstrate "a personal tort, right, infringement, injury or damage specific to himself."[142] The Appellate Division held that the EAC Establishment Treaty does not require the partner states to ratify a Protocol on the Management of the Environment and Natural Resources in order for Articles 111–114 to become enforceable.[143]

ANAW also prevailed on the question of whether the First Instance Division had erred in law by considering whether Tanzania had violated non-EAC international environmental treaties and declarations such as the African Convention on the Conservation of Nature and Natural Resources of 2003, the Rio Declaration of 1992, the Stockholm Declaration and Action Plan for the Human Environment of 1972, the U.N. Convention on Migratory Species of Wild Animals of 1979, and the U.N. Convention on Biodiversity of 1992.[144] The Appellate Division found that the First Instance Court's decision did not rely on these non-EAC international conventions and declarations regarding environmental protection.[145] Rather, the Appellate Division noted that, even if the First Instance Division had considered aspects of these international instruments, it would not "have been unduly alarmed" because EAC member states "do subscribe to the various standards, norms and values of these Conventions."[146] Drawing an analogy to another of its decisions on human rights, the Appellate Division reasoned that nothing precludes it from referring to relevant provisions of non-EAC treaties "in order to interpret the EAC Treaty."[147] It further ruled that references to non-EAC treaties are relevant where they are recognized in the text of the EAC treaties. Such treaties, the court held, become "*ipso jure* obligations" of EAC member states.[148]

On the question whether the court had jurisdiction to grant permanent injunctions against sovereign EAC partner states, the Appellate Division held that the court did in fact have such jurisdiction.[149]

---

141 *Id.* ¶ 25.

142 *Id.*

143 *Id.*

144 *Id.* ¶ 40; *see supra* notes 122–125 and Convention on the Conservation of Migratory Species of Wild Animals, June 23, 1979, 1651 U.N.T.S. 333.

145 *Id.* ¶ 47.

146 *Id.* ¶ 48.

147 *Id.* ¶ 49.

148 *Id.*

149 *Id.* ¶¶ 50–56.

It held that a permanent injunction is an equitable remedy "encapsulated" within Article 23(1) of the EACT as well as Rule 1(2) of the court's Rules of Procedure derived from Article 42 of that treaty.[150] The Appellate Division concluded that the EACJ's power to grant a permanent injunction is an inherent right available to every court of law in order to adjudicate cases.[151]

In short, Tanzania's appeal failed, and ANAW prevailed. Yet even though the Appellate Division upheld the power of the First Instance Division to issue a permanent injunction, the Appellate Division's judgment was far from clear on other issues. For example, consider the question of whether the First Instance Division properly considered Tanzania's argument on appeal that the ANAW was challenging a "mere proposal" to construct the Serengeti road.[152] Here, the court concluded that, because the road was a "mere proposal," it could not be the basis for suit. The Appellate Division's judgment on this point is murky for several reasons, and it is notable that notwithstanding this lack of clarity, it did not dismiss the case as Tanzania wanted.

First, the First Instance Division had not considered the question whether what ANAW was challenging was a "mere proposal" or not. Tanzania raised the question for the first time in the appeal against the merits decision of the First Instance Division.[153] Notwithstanding the fact that this issue was being raised for the first time, the Appellate Division curiously held that the First Instance Division Court had the obligation to confirm that ANAW's case centered on a "real live dispute," and not a mere proposal to build a road.[154] Relying on cases it had decided earlier on the question of mootness,[155] the Appellate Division held that the function of the EACJ courts is to rule on concrete disputes between adverse parties, not to entertain hypothetical questions.[156] It held that under Article 30 of the EACT, parties may only "challenge the legality of an 'act, regulation, directive, decision, or action' of a Partner State" that they allege violates the EACT.[157] Actions of Tanzania that may have

---

150 *Id.* ¶ 51. According to the court, Article 23(1) names the EACJ a "judicial body" with the ability to "ensure" the partner states adhere to their EACT obligations. *Id.* ¶ 53. In order to be a judicial body and fulfill this role, the court must have the attributes of other judicial bodies, such as the ability to grant permanent injunctions. *Id.* Additionally, Rule 1(2) of the court's Rules of Procedure provides that nothing in the Rules may "limit or otherwise affect the inherent power of the Court to make such orders as may be necessary for the ends of justice," including orders granting permanent injunctions against partner states. *Id.* ¶ 54.

151 *Id.* ¶ 55.

152 *Id.* ¶¶ 58–80.

153 *Id.* ¶ 64.

154 *Id.* ¶ 67.

155 *Id.* ¶¶ 68–70. These cases are Alcon Int'l Ltd. vs. Standard Chartered Bank of Uganda, Appeal No. 3 of 2013, Judgment (East African Court of Justice July, 27, 2015), and Legal Brains Trust (LBT) vs. Att'y Gen. of Uganda, Appeal No. 4 of 2012, Judgment (East African Court of Justice May, 19, 2012).

156 *Tanz. v. ANAW*, Appeal No. 3 of 2014, ¶ 71.

157 *Id.* ¶ 75.

constituted a disputable action included agreed-upon architectural plans and drawings and/or bills of quantities.[158] The Appellate Division relied on a statement made by the First Instance Division Court to the effect that "all parties now agree that if the initial plan were implemented," its negative impacts on the Serengeti would not outweigh the benefit of connecting the residents of Mugumu-Loliondo to Dar es Salaam.[159] This statement, according to the Appellate Division, demonstrated that Tanzania had abandoned its proposal to construct a paved road across the Serengeti. According to the court, such inaction or omission by a partner state could not constitute a cause of action under Article 30 of the EACT because challenging a proposal as opposed to conduct would not suffice to be a case in controversy.[160]

These findings, that ANAW's case challenged a "mere proposal" to build a road and that it was therefore not actionable, sit in sharp contrast to the Appellate Division's failure to dismiss the case and its endorsement of ANAW's case in other respects. For example, in ordering that each party to the case bear its own costs, the Appellate Division noted that ANAW had "partially triumphed in their quest . . . in this, the first Environmental Case of its kind to be brought before this Court. . . . They brought the Reference and have prosecuted it not out of any wish for personal, corporate, or private gain; but out of the public-spirited interest of the noblest kind—namely preservation of a natural resource which . . . is truly a gem of a heritage, one-of-a-kind for all mankind."[161]

The Appellate Division's judgment is also murky because it did not explicitly lift the permanent injunction that was imposed by the First Instance Division.[162] This lack of clarity thus seems purposeful. The Appellate Division may well have realized that a clear refusal of jurisdiction in the case at this late stage in the litigation would have clipped the expanding wings of the EACJ to cover environmental disputes. Yet, the court also realized that it had to please the government of Tanzania so that it would not suffer a backlash.[163] The judgment was confusing enough that in September 2015, when I interviewed ANAW's lawyer who had litigated the case, he too was unsure what the Appellate Division intended by not lifting the permanent injunction.[164] Clearly, getting an order that could be served on the government of Tanzania pursuant to the judgment was out of the question because of this lack of clarity. Yet, Tanzania on its part could see the writing on the wall. Should it decide to make concrete plans to build the road, ANAW could

158 *Id.* ¶ 76.

159 *Id.* ¶ 74.

160 *Id.* ¶¶ 75, 79–80.

161 *Id.* ¶ 81.

162 *Id.* ¶ 82.

163 On the backlash against Africa's international courts, see Alter, Gathii & Helfer, *supra* note 22.

164 Interview with Saitabao Ole Kanchory, *supra* note 62.

potentially have gone back to the court and obtained orders to permanently bar Tanzania from building the road.

The final decision of the Appellate Division is thus less emphatic than its earlier decision affirming that the First Instance Division had jurisdiction and therefore dismissing Tanzania's jurisdictional challenges.[165] As noted above, in that decision affirming that the First Instance Division had jurisdiction in the case, the Appellate Division announced that the EAC Establishment Treaty binds member states "to observe a variety of express undertakings and obligations concerning the promotion, preservation, conservation and protection of the environment" that are "clearly and emphatically" within the court's purview.[166] Since that earlier decision, major changes had occurred on the court; in particular, Harold Nsekela, a member of the court from its inception, had retired as Judge and President of the court.[167] He and some of the more senior and seasoned judges on the Appellate Division had been replaced by a younger group of judges on the Appellate Division. Based on the final *Serengeti* decision, it could be surmised that these younger judges were less likely to use the jurisdiction of the EACJ to directly challenge EAC member state prerogatives as the original members of the Court had.[168]

III. SIGNIFICANCE OF THE *SERENGETI* CASE

Although Africa's international courts are established within sub-regional trade integration schemes, the *Serengeti* case illustrates how they interpret and apply environmental law in the broader context both under African international law and under multilateral environmental treaties. In effect, these courts apply and interpret rules of international law outside their immediate sub-regional treaty system. The East Africa Court of Justice's First Instance Division *Serengeti* decision on the merits,[169] which stopped the government of Tanzania from building a road through a UNESCO World Heritage Site, illustrates this point. The court invoked a rule of systemic integration contained in Article 130(1) of

---

[165] Att'y Gen. of the United Republic of Tanz. v. African Network for Animal Welfare (ANAW), Appeal No. 3 of 2011, Appeal Judgment (East African Court of Justice at Arusha, App. Div. Mar. 15, 2012).

[166] *Tanz. v. ANAW*, Appeal No. 3 of 2014, ¶ 11.

[167] *President of East Africa Court of Justice Signs Out*, IGIHE (May 29, 2014), https://en.igihe.com/news/president-of-east-africa-court-of-justice-signs.

[168] This trend may have begun on the human rights side with the Appellate Division cutting back against the expansive holdings of the First Instance Division. *See* Awadh v. Att'y Gen. of Uganda, Appeal No. 2 of 2012, Appeal Judgment, ¶ 15 (East African Court of Justice App. Div. Apr. 15, 2013), https://www.eacj.org/?cases=omar-awadh-and-6-others-vs-attorney-general-of-uganda (strictly construing the two-month limitation for bringing cases and reversing the invocation of the doctrine of continuing violations adopted by the First Instance Division).

[169] African Network for Animal Welfare (ANAW) v. Att'y Gen. of the United Republic of Tanz., Ref. No. 9 of 2010, Judgment (East African Court of Justice at Arusha First Instance Div. June 20, 2014), https://eacj.org/wp-content/uploads/2014/06/Judgement-Ref.-No.9-of-2010-Final.pdf.

the EAC Establishment Treaty,[170] which serves an equivalent role to that of Article 31(3)(c) of the Vienna Convention of the Law of Treaties,[171] and concluded that East African Community treaties should not be interpreted in isolation from other treaties such as the African Convention on Conservation of Nature and Natural Resources, the Rio Declaration, the Stockholm Declaration, and the U.N. Convention on Biodiversity.[172] As interpreted by the EACJ, Article 130(1) of the Treaty for the Establishment of the East African Community strongly suggests that EAC treaties should be interpreted in a manner that furthers the objectives of these other treaties.[173] In this manner, the EACJ was in effect promoting coherence within a fragmented system of international law by applying and interpreting rules of international law that fell outside East African Community law.[174]

Cases such as *Serengeti* evidence that African international courts have been evolving incrementally as a result of new rules in second generation regional trade agreements that include goals such as human rights and environmental protection. New players, including NGOs, have a vested interest in mobilizing these rules and evolving contexts in which regional cooperation has slowly but surely come to be accepted by states as putting constraints on their sovereignty.[175] The emergence of judicial environmentalism in Africa's international courts is nevertheless surprising. This is because many commentators have long assumed that there should be a more structured, organized, and coordinated model of claiming environmental violations, particularly through international courts.[176] Others have argued that the best way to promote transnational environmental values is to have an international environmental court.[177] Still others have argued for coordinated efforts in litigation strategies, so that environmental cases around the world are not brought individually. Rather, these commentators contend that litigants should cooperate and learn from each other so that they can build more effective jurisprudence

---

170 EAC Establishment Treaty, *supra* note 4.

171 Vienna Convention on the Law or Treaties art. 31(3)(c), May 23, 1969, 1155 U.N.T.S. 331 (providing that "any relevant rules of international law applicable in the relations between the parties" shall be taken into account as part of the context in interpreting a treaty).

172 *ANAW v. Tanzania*, Ref. No. 9, ¶ 48.

173 *Id.*

174 For more analysis of this issue, see James Thuo Gathii, *The Promise of International Law: A Third World View*, 36 AM. U. INT'L L. REV. 377 (2021) [hereinafter Gathii, *The Promise of International Law*].

175 For a similar analysis in the context of the ECOWAS Court, see Alter et. al., *supra* note 15.

176 *See* Hari M. Osofsky, *Learning from Environmental Justice: A New Model for International Environmental Rights*, 24 STAN. ENV'T. L.J. 71 (2005).

177 Alfred Rest, *The Need for an International Court for the Environment?—Underdeveloped Legal Protection for the Individual in Transnational Litigation*, 24 ENV'T POL'Y & L. 173 (1994). For a review of the 1992 effort of the International Court of the Environment Foundation, see Ole W. Pedersen, *An International Environmental Court and International Legalism*, 24 J. ENV'T L. 547, 547–58 (2012).

that gives victims of environmental harm the greatest chance of redress.[178]

There is a consensus view that preambular provisions in trade agreements such as those relating to human rights, the rule of law and democracy, and the protection of the environment[179] are merely hortatory or non-binding.[180] However, African international courts are showing that these provisions are not merely lofty aspirations that cannot be enforced.

Even more, African international courts are working to counteract what many international lawyers have referred to as fragmentation in international law.[181] Fragmentation in this context refers to the growth of and existence of many separate legal regimes or systems and new types of international norms "outside the acknowledged sources."[182] There was an ill-founded fear that specialized courts established under these new international norms, especially after the Cold War, would "damage the coherence of the international legal system."[183] The *Seregenti* case, however, demonstrates that far from damaging the coherence of the international legal system, the East African Court of Justice has developed important jurisprudence that brings these disparate norms of international law together.[184]

These African courts have decided not to behave like the WTO's Dispute Settlement Body, which confines its mandates to decide only cases that raise trade issues.[185] And, the fact that Africa's international courts have decided not to confine their role merely to trade issues shows that African regional trade agreements are focused on more than

---

178 *See* Osofsky, *supra* note 176.

179 Such "soft" commitments to human rights are included in trade treaties in the context of West, East, and Southern Africa. *See* Alter, Gathii & Helfer, *supra* note 22.

180 For example, in the World Trade Organization (WTO), preambular provisions have been held by the Appellate Body as only capable of adding color and texture (rather than a different interpretation than that found in the substantive provisions), *see* Appellate Body Report, *US—Import Prohibition of Certain Shrimp and Shrimp Products* ¶ 153 (WT/DS58/AB/R) (adopted Oct. 12, 1998), in which the Appellate Body held that the language of the Preamble of the WTO Agreement "demonstrates a recognition by WTO negotiators that optimal use of the world's resources should be made in accordance with the objective of sustainable development. As this preambular language reflects the intentions of negotiators of the *WTO Agreement*, we believe it must add colour, texture and shading to our interpretation of the agreements annexed to the *WTO Agreement*, in this case, the GATT 1994." *Id. See also* James Thuo Gathii, *The Legal Status of the Doha Declaration on TRIPS and Public Health Under the Vienna Convention of the Law of Treaties*, 15 HARV. J. L. & TECH. 291 (2002).

181 *See, e.g.*, Anne Peters, *The Refinement of International Law: From Fragmentation to Regime Interaction and Politicization*, 15 INT'L J. CONST. L. 671 (2017) (exploring the techniques that courts and tribunals use to coordinate the various subfields of international law).

182 *Id.* at 672.

183 Jonathan I. Charney, *Is International Law Threatened by Multiple International Tribunals?*, 271 RECUEIL DES COURS 101, 347 (1998).

184 *See also* Gathii, *The Promise of International Law*, *supra* note 174.

185 James Thuo Gathii, *Saving the Serengeti: Africa's New International Judicial Environmentalism*, 16 CHI. J. INT'L L. 393, 393–94 (2016).

achieving market liberalization. After all, these agreements establish commitments in a broad variety of areas.[186] The interpretive approach of African regional trade courts is therefore consistent with these multiple objectives to the extent that this approach does not give priority to one set of objectives (for example, trade) over another (for example, human rights).[187] In fact, as the case law that I have discussed in this chapter shows, there is nothing to suggest that these courts cannot simultaneously decide trade cases while deciding environmental and human rights cases. As these courts grow, as their legitimacy spreads, and as people get to know how to use them, treaty reforms could authorize the creation of separate chambers within the courts to decide cases of different genres. For example, one chamber could decide trade cases, another chamber could decide human rights cases, and another could decide environmental cases. Separate chambers could give parties the ability to control the composition of a chamber and provide special expertise in the subject matter of the dispute, as has been the case at the International Court of Justice.[188]

Ultimately, this chapter has demonstrated the expanding role of Africa's international courts in implementing, applying, and enforcing environmental laws and policies. This role, in turn, is part of a broader movement that includes national courts.[189] Together, national and international courts have increasingly played an important part in giving content to environmental rights; facilitating administrative justice in environmental law; promoting judicial access to enforcing environmental obligations; examining the validity of governmental conduct in the area of the environment; and linking rights of indigenous peoples to environmental rights.[190] These new roles assumed by African international courts are a far cry from the excessive reliance on common law concepts such as nuisance and negligence that existed prior to the enactment of modern environmental statutes at the national, regional, and sub-regional levels, especially in the 1990s after the end of the Cold War.[191] It is this expanded landscape of environmental law, along with broadened standing and active involvement of civil society groups, that has resulted in Africa's judicial environmentalism.

---

[186] *See generally* JAMES THUO GATHII, AFRICAN REGIONAL TRADE AGREEMENTS AS LEGAL REGIMES 1–33 (2011).

[187] *See also* Gathii, *The Promise of International Law*, *supra* note 174.

[188] Andreas Zimmerman, *Ad Hoc Chambers of the International Court of Justice*, 8 DICK. L. REV. 1, 2–3 (1989) (also noting that rules giving parties a role in selecting members of a chamber have caused considerable controversy).

[189] *See generally* GATHII, *supra* note 186.

[190] For an exhaustive evaluation of these roles, see THE PERFORMANCE OF AFRICA'S INTERNATIONAL COURTS, *supra* note 17.

[191] For a Kenyan case study of this earlier period, see CELESTINE NYAMU & JAMES GATHII, INT'L DEV. RESEARCH CENTRE, DEVELOPING SOUND APPROACHES TO SUSTAINABLE ENVIRONMENTAL MANAGEMENT IN KENYA: CONSTRAINTS AND PROSPECTS (1996) (available through the International Development Research Centre's repository).

IV. CONCLUSION

The *Serengeti* case shows how the case law of Africa's international courts has been shaped by treaty provisions that oblige African countries to have regard for the environment. Key to this developing case law is the growing role that non-state actors have played in mobilizing these courts to hold governments accountable, particularly for undertaking infrastructural activities or endorsing extractive initiatives inconsistent with the protections embodied in these provisions. If the courts continue to remain as receptive and responsive as the courts were in the *Serengeti* case, the trend may continue.

The case also illustrates the growing importance of environmental concerns in the docket of a court initially established as a trade court. By issuing the unprecedented remedy of a permanent injunction and invoking environmental treaties and rules beyond those within the regime of East African Community law, the EACJ has demonstrated that it is possible to offer significant relief in an environmental case while integrating disparate regimes of international environmental law.

III. INTERNATIONAL LAW: THE DOMESTIC IMPACT

9

Roger P. Alford

Charming Betsy: International Law as a Rule of Statutory Construction

The facts of *Charming Betsy* amply illustrate the importance that foreign relations and international law have played in statutory interpretation. A detailed portrait of the case is required to fully appreciate these concerns.[1] This portrait reveals a naval officer loosely interpreting congressional authorization to seize a neutral vessel in violation of international law, resulting in an international imbroglio that threatened the young republic's relations with neutral European countries critically important to its future. The Supreme Court interpreted the ambiguous statute consistent with requirements of the law of nations, and in so doing displayed both great deference to the importance of executive performance in foreign affairs and great sensitivity to the fledgling nation's need and desire to comply with international maritime law.[2]

I. THE BIRTH OF THE UNITED STATES NAVY

Almost a year before the signing of the Declaration of Independence, delegates from Rhode Island traveled to the Continental Congress in Philadelphia to request the establishment of "a fleet of sufficient force for the protection of [the] colonies."[3] At this point in the summer of 1775, the fleet's main intended purpose would have been to protect commercial ships from British blockades. John Langdon of New Hampshire, Silas Deane of Connecticut, and John Adams of Massachusetts oversaw this proposal.[4] This three-man committee then recommended that the fleet expand its mission to include the interception of British supply ships en route to the colonies. The Continental Congress adopted these provisions

---

1 Roger P. Alford, *Foreign Relations as a Matter of Interpretation: The Use and Abuse of* Charming Betsy, 67 OHIO ST. L.J. 1339, 1344 (2006).

2 *Id.*

3 Adam Bisno, *The Birth of the U.S. Navy*, NAVAL HIST. & HERITAGE COMMAND (Dec. 19, 2019), https://www.history.navy.mil/browse-by-topic/heritage/origins-of-the-navy/birth-of-the-us-navy.html; *see also* RAYMOND G. O'CONNOR, ORIGINS OF THE AMERICAN NAVY: SEA POWER IN THE COLONIES AND THE NEW NATIONS 15 (1993).

4 *Id.*

and authorized the purchase of a schooner and sloop for use by General George Washington. Additionally, the Continental Congress authorized Connecticut and Rhode Island to arm merchant vessels. By the end of October, this committee had grown to seven, and the naval force under their command launched four more ships to patrol the Eastern seaboard.[5] These months of 1775 served to establish the "American Navy," primarily tasked with capturing British vessels working to suppress the colonial revolt.[6]

Following the Revolutionary War, the 1781 Articles of Confederation stopped short of authorizing the newly independent nation to establish a navy. The 1789 Constitution did, however, provide in Article I, Section 8 that Congress could "provide and maintain a Navy."[7] By 1793, the Barbary pirates of North Africa began to seize American ships, hold Americans captive, and demand tribute.[8] In response to the "depredations committed by the Algerine corsairs on the commerce of the United States," Congress passed, and President George Washington signed, the "Act to provide a Naval Armament of 1794."[9] This act authorized the construction of six naval frigates. When Congress approved their construction, it made sure no two ships were built in the same port to incentivize competing ports to construct ships that were "the best, cheapest, and most expeditiously built."[10] Among these ships was the Baltimore-built *Constellation*, the future instigator in the *Charming Betsy* matter.[11]

On August 30, 1798, President John Adams signed a bill establishing the Department of the Navy. The Secretary of the Navy would head the department, responsible for "execut[ing] such orders as he shall receive from the President of the United States, relative to the procurement of naval forces and materials and the construction, armament, equipment and employment of vessels of war."[12] Prior to the Adams administration, only the *Constellation*, *United States*, and *Constitution* had been completed. In support of his cause, President Adams ensured the completion of the *Congress*, *Chesapeake*, and *President*. Each ship would prove crucial in executing U.S. security goals in the face of the French

---

5 *Id.*

6 *Id.*; *see also* Adams Paper Project, *VIII. Rules for the Regulation of the Navy of the United Colonies, 28 November–December 1775*, NAT'L ARCHIVES, https://founders.archives.gov/documents/Adams/06-03-02-0076-0009 (last visited Jan. 14, 2024) (making several mentions of prize law).

7 U.S. CONST. art. I, § 8, cl. 13.

8 GREGORY FREMONT-BARNES, THE WARS OF THE BARBARY PIRATES: TO THE SHORES OF TRIPOLI: THE RISE OF THE US NAVY AND MARINES (2006).

9 An Act to Provide a Naval Armament, ch. 12, 1 Stat. 350 (1794).

10 *Navy Department Appropriation Bill, 1929: Hearing on H.R. 12286 Before the Subcomm. on Navy of the H. Comm. on Appropriations*, 70th Cong. 76 (1929) (quoting Secretary of War James McHenry, explaining in 1798 why the construction of the frigates occurred in different locations).

11 Bisno, *supra* note 3.

12 Robert G. Albion, *The First Days of the Navy Department*, 12 MIL. AFF. 1, 5 (1948).

hostilities at sea. As President Adams stated in his 1798 State of the Union Address,

> [p]erhaps no country ever experienced more sudden and remarkable advantages from any measure of policy than we have derived from the arming for our maritime protection and defense. We ought without loss of time to lay the foundation for an increase of our Navy to a size sufficient to guard our coast and protect our trade.[13]

As a formal sea-faring force, the Navy was now prepared to protect U.S. interests at sea.

II. ADMIRALTY LAW: PRIZE AND SALVAGE

Alongside the growing U.S. Navy, the U.S. government also authorized private ships to protect American interests at sea. Privateers "were privately owned vessels awarded a license by the government, and legally permitted—subject to certain restrictions—to sell seized ships and cargo to the highest bidder and keep any resulting profit."[14] When either a public or an authorized private ship seized an enemy vessel, the crew's efforts entitled them to the "prize." A prize is a ship and her cargo forcibly taken through conflict at sea. After a capture, a victorious crew would raise its flag and sail the captured ship into a friendly or neutral port, whereupon a prize court would adjudicate whether it was a lawful prize.[15] If the crew had captured a neutral vessel or cargo, the court would deem the seizure illegal and not offer compensation. These adjudicative processes also benefited the United States in that every moment a hostile ship spent docked in deliberation was one moment it could not harass U.S. ships.

A "salvage," unlike a "prize," relates to the rescue of a ship or her contents from peril.[16] As the Supreme Court wrote in 1869, "[s]alvage is the compensation allowed to persons by whose assistance a ship or her cargo has been saved, in whole or in part, from impending peril on the sea, or in recovering such property from actual loss, as in cases of shipwreck, derelict, or recapture."[17] Beyond mere compensation for services via *quantum meruit*, salvage rewards a captain and crew for the risk they may have experienced in the rescue of another's ship from peril. Indeed, in the name of public policy, courts historically rewarded salvage to encourage the rescue of life and property.[18] Furthermore, through

---

[13] John Adams, Second Annual Message of John Adams (Dec. 8, 1798), *available at* https://avalon.law.yale.edu/18th_century/adamsme2.asp (last visited Oct. 1, 2024).

[14] Gary M. Anderson & Adam Gifford Jr., *Privateering and the Private Production of Naval Power*, 11 CATO J. 99, 100 (1991); *see also* H.H. Buckman, *The Obligation of Neutrality and the Alabama Case*, 32 AM. L. REV. 945, 947 (1898).

[15] *See generally* Frank E. Hodgins, *Maritime War Rights*, 16 CAN. L. TIMES 77 (1896).

[16] G.H. Robinson, *Admiralty Law of Salvage*, 23 CORNELL L. REV. 229, 229 (1938).

[17] The Blackwall, 77 U.S. (10 Wall.) 1, 12 (1869).

[18] Robinson, *supra* note 16, at 230.

rewarding the heroics of a rescuing sailor, salvage removed the incentive to plunder and exploit an imperiled ship.[19] In the case of hostilities, recapturing a neutral vessel from a belligerent entitled the rescuing crew to a salvage claim for the risk associated with retaking the vessel.[20]

III. THE QUASI-WAR WITH FRANCE

During the American Revolutionary War, France proved to be a critical ally to the United States. But the United States wished to remain neutral in the French Revolutionary Wars. In the Neutrality Proclamation of 1793, President George Washington promulgated American non-interventionism on the world stage, committing the United States to "adopt and pursue a conduct friendly and impartial toward the belligerent Powers."[21] The French deemed the U.S. signing of the 1794 Jay Treaty with Great Britain as a betrayal[22] and a "clear violation" of previous Franco-American alliance and commerce treaties, and reacted in kind.[23]

In 1796, France "severed diplomatic relations with the United States at the ministerial level" and then "unleashed its warships and privateers on American commerce."[24] France's goal was "to force the United States to repudiate the Jay Treaty and to loot American trade in the process."[25] In particular, France encouraged French privateers to openly plunder U.S. commercial ships in the Caribbean.[26] France operated under the misguided assumption it could "bully" the young United States, an old habit with respect to "the lesser powers of Europe."[27] The French miscalculated the will and capacity of the U.S. government.

Beginning in 1798, the previously undeclared Quasi-War with France officially began when Congress passed "retaliatory legislation authorizing American vessels to seize French vessels hovering off the American coast."[28] Congress then abrogated all treaties with France, expanded the U.S. army, appropriated funds for new warships, suspended commercial intercourse between the two nations, and actively patrolled the Caribbean Sea to protect U.S. ships from French capture.[29]

---

19 *Id.*

20 *See generally* Talbot v. Seeman, 5 U.S. (1 Cranch) 1 (1801).

21 Robert D. Sloane, *The Scope of Executive Power in the Twenty-First Century: An Introduction*, 88 B.U. L. REV. 341, 348 (2008).

22 Donald R. Hickey, *The Quasi-War: America's First Limited War, 1798–1801*, 18 N. MARINER 67, 68–69 (2008).

23 Alford, *supra* note 1, at 1345.

24 Hickey, *supra* note 22, at 69.

25 *Id.*

26 *Id.*

27 *Id.*

28 Alford, *supra* note 1, at 1345.

29 SAMUEL FLAGG BEMIS, A DIPLOMATIC HISTORY OF THE UNITED STATES 111–25 (Holt, Rinehart & Winston, 5th ed. 1965); *see also* Hickey, *supra* note 22, at 74–75.

Most relevant here, Congress passed the Nonintercourse Act of 1800, which suspended commercial dealing between American vessels and France. The Nonintercourse Act sparked immediate controversy and became the legislation at issue in the *Charming Betsy* case. The Act provided in relevant part:

> [I]t shall be lawful for the President . . . to give instructions to the public armed vessels of the United States, to stop and examine any ship or vessel of the United States on the high sea, which there may be reason to suspect to be engaged in any traffic or commerce contrary to this act, and if upon examination, it shall appear that such ship or vessel is bound or sailing to, or from any port or place, contrary to the true intent and meaning of this act, it shall be the duty of the commander of such public armed vessel, *to seize every ship or vessel engaged in such illicit commerce*, and send the same to the nearest convenient port of the United States, to be there prosecuted in due course of law, and held liable to the penalties and forfeitures[.][30]

The President instructed commanding officers of armed vessels to "be vigilant that vessels or cargoes really American, but covered by Danish [(neutral)] or other foreign papers, and bound to, or from, French ports, do not escape you."[31] He also emphasized that commanders be "extremely careful not to harass or injure the trade of foreign nations with whom we are at peace," setting up a decision-making quandary.[32] These instructions to avoid seizing neutral vessels but be vigilant against those U.S. vessels posing as neutrals foreshadowed the exact situation that arose in the *Charming Betsy* incident in the summer of 1800.

IV. THE *CHARMING BETSY* INCIDENT

In the early morning of July 3, 1800, the U.S. naval frigate *Constellation* was patrolling the Caribbean Sea when it spotted two suspicious ships in the distance and gave chase. Captain Alexander Murray launched a cannonball over the first ship and overtook it.[33] The master of the captured vessel, named the *Charming Betsy,* called for help, explaining that she had been seized by a French vessel and was headed to the French island of Guadeloupe under the command of a French crew for sale as prize.[34]

---

[30] An Act Further to Suspend the Commercial Intercourse between the United States and France, and the Dependencies Thereof, ch. 10, § 8, 2 Stat. 7, 10 (1800) [hereinafter the Nonintercourse Act] (expired 1801) (emphasis added).

[31] *Quoted in* Little v. Barreme, 6 U.S. (2 Cranch) 170, 171 (1804).

[32] *Quoted in id.* at 172.

[33] Frederick C. Leiner, *The* Charming Betsy *and the Marshall Court,* 45 AM. J. LEGAL HIST. 1, 2 (2001).

[34] *Id.* at 3.

While the *Charming Betsy* was a Danish vessel when captured by French belligerents in the Caribbean, it originally was a U.S. vessel owned by one Jared Shattuck, an American who had become a naturalized Danish citizen living in St. Thomas. Shattuck flagged the *Charming Betsy* as a Danish vessel, and such was the state of the schooner when French privateers captured her shortly before its confrontation with the U.S. naval vessel *Constellation*. The French disregarded all indications of its Danish status, however, believing she was merely masquerading as a neutral vessel. They subsequently captured the ship "upon strong grounds of her being an American[.]"[35] Due to the Nonintercourse Act, it was illegal for American vessels to engage in commercial intercourse with France. Captain Murray of the *Constellation* sent a boarding party to inspect the ship for a potential violation of the Act.

Like his French counterparts, Captain Murray was unconvinced that the *Charming Betsy* was a Danish schooner. He had examined many vessels before and had several compelling reasons to think the *Charming Betsy* was only masquerading as neutral. First, the vessel was low, sleek, and featured raked-back masts and an "unmistakable look of a *Baltimore*-built pilot-boat schooner[.]"[36] The Baltimore schooners predated the more noteworthy Baltimore clippers, yet both ships possessed distinctive features making them readily identifiable.[37] Their sharp bows and black, V-shaped hulls, which allowed these ships to move quickly and avoid tipping, were tell-tale signs they were constructed in Baltimore.[38] Second, illegal U.S. trade frequently occurred under neutral, Danish colors, suggesting the ship was sailing under fictitious Danish registration.[39] Third, the *Charming Betsy*'s suspicious response indicated she could not have been of a neutral nation.[40] Murray hypothesized that if the vessel were truly neutral, she "would not have run [before the wind] many hours direct to leeward and out of her tract from any Vessel when chased by the Privateer & nearly in sight of Martinique which was out of her route to Guadeloupe."[41]

---

[35] Letter from Captain Alexander Murray, U.S. Navy, to Benjamin Stoddart, Sec'y of the Navy (Nov. 29, 1800), *in* 6 NAVAL DOCUMENTS RELATED TO THE QUASI-WAR BETWEEN THE UNITED STATES AND FRANCE: NAVAL OPERATIONS FROM JUNE 1800 TO NOVEMBER 1800, at 561, 562 (1938) [hereinafter 6 NAVAL DOCUMENTS].

[36] Leiner, *supra* note 33, at 3 (emphasis added).

[37] Jennifer Klima, *The Baltimore Clipper*, MD. ST. ARCHIVES (Dec. 9, 1998), https://msa.maryland.gov/msa/stagser/s1259/121/6771/html/essay95.html. The Maryland State Archives document that Baltimore schooners were "sharp built," well suited for prize taking. As for the related Baltimore clippers, they had "heart-shaped midsections with short keels and raking sterns" with black hulls and sharp bows amongst other features.

[38] *Baltimore Clippers*, PRIDE OF BALTIMORE, https://pride2.org/education/baltimore-clippers/ (last visited May 28, 2024).

[39] Leiner, *supra* note 33, at 3.

[40] *Id.*

[41] *Id.*

Captain Murray thus resolved to take the *Charming Betsy* to Martinique for adjudication as a U.S. vessel engaged in illegal commercial intercourse with the French, thinking he "had no alternative" per the Nonintercourse Act.[42] Murray further reasoned that, no matter the true nationality of the vessel, he and his men would likely gain financially. If the *Charming Betsy* was Danish, Captain Murray and his crew would earn a salvage payment for recapturing the ship from the French privateers. On the other hand, if the *Charming Betsy* was American, it was engaged in illegal trade, and the court would presumably recognize the trading schooner "as a valid prize in that the *Constellation* had stopped illegal trade[.]"[43]

After the provisions aboard the *Charming Betsy* were sold in Martinique, and its proceeds remitted to the Bank of the United States pending resolution of the proceeding, the ship sailed to Philadelphia for trial. There, Captain Murray's prize lawyers, William Lewis and Jared Ingersoll, pressed their case.[44] Both Lewis and Ingersoll were prominent in the early Republic, President Washington having appointed Lewis as the first U.S. Attorney for Pennsylvania and Ingersoll being a delegate to the Continental Congress and signer of the Constitution.[45] In the initial case plea for *Murray v. The Schooner Charming Betsy*, Murray's lawyers alleged that the *Charming Betsy*'s owner, Jared Shattuck, was a U.S. citizen and the ship a U.S. vessel. Therefore, under this theory, the vessel engaged in trade in violation of the Nonintercourse Act.[46]

Opposing counsel pointed out, however, that Jared Shattuck had been a naturalized Danish subject for years, and the *Charming Betsy* schooner was now a Danish vessel. Under these facts, the Nonintercourse Act was never violated, and Captain Murray had no authorization to stop the neutral vessel.[47] If this were proved in court, they claimed that Murray would be subject to "damages for the detention of the vessel and the loss to her cargo."[48] Under their view, Murray's hope for financial gain might have been ill-placed.

The trial court judge agreed with opposing counsel, finding that Shattuck and the *Charming Betsy* were, in fact, Danish and, unfortunately for Captain Murray, warship commanders acted at their own risk in such conflagrations. As stated by Chief Justice Marshall in a related case, "[a] commander of a ship of war of the United States, in obeying his instructions from the President of the United States, acts at

---

42 Alford, *supra* note 1, at 1348 (quoting Letter from Captain Alexander Murray, U.S. Navy, to Benjamin Stoddart, Sec'y of the Navy (Nov. 29, 1800), *reprinted in* 6 NAVAL DOCUMENTS, *supra* note 35, at 562).

43 Leiner, *supra* note 33, at 4.

44 *Id.* at 6.

45 *Id.*

46 *Id.* at 7.

47 *Id.*

48 *Id.* at 7.

his peril."[49] Shattuck accordingly was awarded $20,594 in damages, an exceedingly large sum for the time.[50] After accounting for previous payments already made to Shattuck, Captain Murray was personally responsible for damages bill totaling $14,930.50, "an enormous amount of money [that amounted to] many times the annual compensation a naval captain earned."[51] Saddled with damages over ten times his approximate annual salary, Murray naturally felt the decree unjust, and could not afford to post the bond in order to appeal.[52] His lifeline would later arrive via an appeal to the Secretary of the Navy, who after much hesitation agreed to post the bond on Captain Murray's behalf.[53]

While the Treaty of Mortefontaine brought the Quasi-War between the United States and France to an end in 1800, the state of international affairs remained dire.[54] Just days after Murray's loss in trial court, the Pasha of Tripoli declared war against the United States, sparking a conflict known today as the Barbary Coast War.[55] Tripoli's declaration of war directly resulted from President Jefferson's refusal to pay the growing ransom for safe passage through North African waters.[56] Thus, "[a]t the same time the Jefferson Administration was deciding whether to defend Captain Murray's mistreatment of the neutral vessel *Charming Betsy*, it was fighting a war in Northern Africa to defend the principle of safe passage of neutral vessels from Barbary pirates."[57] Moreover, the United States had the second largest merchant marine presence on the high seas at the time. Therefore, the young United States could not afford to appear to disregard the international law norms protecting freedom for neutral commerce on the high seas.

---

49 Little v. Barreme, 6 U.S. (2 Cranch) 170, 170 (1804).

50 Leiner, *supra* note 33, at 10. Shattuck's damages totaled about $545,000 when adjusted to the 2024 inflation rate.

51 *Id.* Captains commanding vessels sized comparatively to the *Constellation* earned $1200 per year, which adjusted to the 2024 inflation rate would equal about $32,000. At the same time, personal damages billed to Murray totaled about $380,000 when adjusted to the 2024 inflation rate.

52 *Id.*

53 Letter from Captain Alexander Murray, U.S. Navy, to the Sec'y of the Navy (Sept. 1, 1801), *reprinted in* 7 NAVAL DOCUMENTS RELATED TO THE QUASI-WAR BETWEEN THE UNITED STATES AND FRANCE: NAVAL OPERATIONS FROM DECEMBER 1800 TO DECEMBER 1801, at 280 (1938).

54 Hickey, *supra* note 22, at 76 (citing Convention between the French Republic, and the United States of America, Fr.-U.S., Dec. 30, 1800, *available at* https://avalon.law.yale.edu/19th_century/fr1800.asp) (last visited Oct. 2, 2024).

55 *U.S. Marines attacked Derna, Tripoli*, NAT'L MUSEUM OF THE U.S. NAVY (Feb. 12, 2021, 1:17 PM), https://www.history.navy.mil/content/history/museums/nmusn/explore/photography/forgotten-wars-19th-century/barbary-war-1801-1805/marines-derna.html. Later during the war, the U.S. Marines made their first incursion onto foreign soil at the Battle of Derna. The first verse of the Marines' Hymn proclaims: "From the Halls of Montezuma to the shores of Tripoli, we fight our country's battles in the air, on land, and sea."

56 *Barbary Wars*, NAVAL HIST. & HERITAGE COMMAND (July 28, 2023, 8:37 AM), https://www.history.navy.mil/browse-by-topic/wars-conflicts-and-operations/barbary-wars.html.

57 Alford, *supra* note 1, at 1349.

These commercial and national security considerations did not escape Chief Justice Marshall when the case reached the Supreme Court in 1803. The circuit court affirmed the district court in returning the *Charming Betsy* to Shattuck, but reversed on every other issue, clearing Murray of all personal damages. On appeal, the central question was whether the U.S.-born Jared Shattuck, now living in St. Thomas as a Danish citizen, and his U.S.-built *Charming Betsy*, now a documented Danish vessel, were American under the Non-Intercourse Act.

If the Court declared Shattuck and his vessel to be American, and thus found them to have violated the statute, the Court risked offending the Danish right to engage in neutral commerce on the high seas. Wary of such ramifications, Marshall interpreted the Nonintercourse Act under the following rule:

> [A]n act of Congress ought never to be construed to violate the *law of nations* if any other possible construction remains, and consequently can never be construed to violate neutral rights, or to affect neutral commerce, further than is warranted by the law of nations as understood in this country.[58]

Writing for a unanimous court, Justice Marshall laid down a rule of statutory interpretation that forever changed international law in U.S. courts. In the face of ambiguity on questions involving international maritime custom, Marshall deferred to the law of nations. He cited no authority for this proposition. According to Marshall, in order for a vessel to fall under the Nonintercourse Act, the ship must have been owned by a United States citizen "not at the time of the passage of the law, but at the time when the act of forfeiture [was] committed."[59] Marshall continued: "If it was intended [by Congress] that any American vessel sold to a neutral should, in the possession of that neutral, be liable to the commercial disabilities imposed on her while she belonged to citizens of the United States, such extraordinary intent ought to have been *plainly expressed*."[60] In other words, if Congress intended to subject U.S.-made vessels to trade restrictions even after they were sold to foreign neutrals, this intent should have been explicitly stated. Here, Congress had not so stated.

Nevertheless, the question of Shattuck's nationality remained "a dicey issue loaded with politics."[61] President Jefferson "believed that the ability to renounce the citizenship of one's birth and make allegiance to a different sovereign was a natural right of man."[62] Most Federalists, however, "believed that citizenship was inalienable, or at least

---

[58] Murray v. Schooner Charming Betsy, 6 U.S. (2 Cranch) 64, 118 (1804) (emphasis added).

[59] *Id.* at 119.

[60] *Id.* (emphasis added).

[61] Leiner, *supra* note 33, at 12.

[62] *Id.*

changeable only upon the rules of the sovereign."[63] As he often did, the Chief Justice threaded the needle, never addressing the question directly. Marshall stated: "[A]n American citizen may acquire in a foreign country, the commercial privileges attached to his domicile, and be exempted from the operation of an act expressed in such general terms as that now under consideration."[64] In other words, if a U.S. citizen is abroad in Rome, he may be considered Roman, and thus exempt from the Nonintercourse Act.[65]

Applied to the case at bar, given Shattuck was a foreign domiciliary who swore allegiance to the Danish crown, Marshall found that he had taken himself "out of the description of the act."[66] It followed that "the *Charming Betsy*, . . . being at the time of her recapture the *bona fide* property of a *Danish* burgher, [was] not forfeitable in consequence of her being employed in carrying on trade and commerce with a *French* island."[67] Therefore, the offense of French commercial intercourse was committed by a Danish vessel owned by a Danish citizen, which was no offense at all. The fact that Shattuck and his vessel were originally American was a nonissue.

Although Murray failed to secure a full reversal on appeal, Marshall made sure to pay due respect to the captain:

> Although there does not appear to have been such cause to suspect the *Charming Betsy* and her cargo to have been American, as would justify captain Murray in bringing her in for adjudication, yet many other circumstances combine with the fairness of his character to produce a conviction that he acted upon correct motives, from a sense of duty; for which reason this hard case ought not to be rendered still more so by a decision in any respect oppressive.[68]

Marshall further conceded that Murray's orders "were such as might well have induced him to consider [the *Charming Betsy*] as an armed vessel within the [Nonintercourse Act], sailing under authority from the French republic."[69] The Chief Justice concluded that the district court's damages calculation was "really greater than it ought to have been."[70] As such, the Supreme Court remanded the damages judgment for recalculation, but otherwise affirmed the district court's judgment in its entirety.[71]

---

63 JEAN EDWARD SMITH, JOHN MARSHALL: DEFINER OF A NATION 338 (1996) (quoted in Leiner, *supra* note 33, at 12).

64 *Schooner Charming Betsy*, 6 U.S. (2 Cranch) at 120.

65 Leiner, *supra* note 33, at 12.

66 *Schooner Charming Betsy*, 6 U.S. (2 Cranch) at 120.

67 *Id.* at 120–21.

68 *Id.* at 123–24.

69 *Id.* at 124.

70 *Id.* at 125.

71 *Id.* at 125–26.

V. THE *CHARMING BETSY* DOCTRINE AND LEGACY

The *Charming Betsy* incident, involving a small conflagration with a Danish trading schooner in the Caribbean, implicated the global law of nations and America's position on the world stage. In the interest of avoiding such conflagrations in the future, the Marshall Court relied upon a doctrine that, whenever possible, statutes should "never be construed to violate neutral rights, or to affect neutral commerce, further than is warranted by the law of nations as understood in this country."[72]

The *Charming Betsy* canon can be described as a separation of powers doctrine, encouraging the judiciary to steer clear of international affairs, a role traditionally reserved for the political branches of government. By eschewing potential international law violations through statutory interpretation, this interpretive rule enhances the United States' performance in foreign affairs.[73] What was Justice Marshall's intention in laying down this highly deferential canon of interpretation? And what constitutes the "law of nations" as used in his opinion? Justice Marshall's failure to cite precedent for the doctrine makes these inquiries difficult.

Integral to Chief Justice Marshall's opinion is an understanding of the "law of nations." During Marshall's time, the law of nations was understood as an encapsulation of the common maritime law shared among nations: a "set of principles that had established itself as a sort of consensus among judges, jurists, and lawmakers around the world."[74] It often served as "a set of background rules, not emanating from any particular sovereign source, that could be applied by courts in the absence of controlling positive law to the contrary."[75] As a fledgling nation in a precarious position in international affairs, the United States had a strong incentive to signal its compliance with the international order and the custom of nations. The Supreme Court's docket in the early days of the Republic demonstrates as much.

The Schooner Adeline, an 1815 case highly reminiscent of the *Charming Betsy* incident, demonstrates the level of deference in U.S. courts towards the law of nations at the time.[76] The vessel at issue, the *Adeline*, was a U.S. ship that sailed from Bordeaux for the United States with a cargo owned by both American and French citizens.[77] A British squadron captured the ship in the Bay of Biscay and placed a prize crew

---

[72] *Id.* at 118.

[73] Alford, *supra* note 1.

[74] Jeremy Waldron, *Foreign Law and the Modern* Ius Gentium, 119 HARV. L. REV. 129, 132 (2005).

[75] Curtis A. Bradley, *The* Charming Betsy *Canon and Separation of Powers: Rethinking the Interpretive Role of International Law*, 86 GEO. L.J. 479, 493 (1998).

[76] *See* The Schooner Adeline, 13 U.S. (9 Cranch) 244 (1815).

[77] *Id.* at 244–45.

on board, ordering her to sail for Gibraltar.[78] After just six days in British possession, a U.S. privateer expedition recaptured the vessel.[79] The Americans ordered the vessel for the United States, where she arrived and was libeled by the re-captors as a prize of war.[80] Here, because the crew rescued the ship from peril, the law of salvage applied. The central question at trial surrounded the allowable rate of salvage for the re-captors of the *Adeline*. Cognizant of the gravity of the case, the Supreme Court held: "The Court of prize is emphatically a Court of the law of nations; and it takes neither its character nor its rules from the mere municipal regulations of any country."[81] This highly deferential approach to the law of nations might surprise a modern audience, but was par for the course at the time, especially within the realm of prize law.[82]

A certain pragmatism on the part of U.S. courts explains this level of deference. That is, it would spell doom for the United States if it appeared to disregard the law of nations on the high seas. The Supreme Court thus sought to create rules of law that ensured United States courts respected the law of nations, mandating "that the political branches—rather than courts—made sensitive decisions either to abrogate another nation's rights under the law of nations or to take actions apt to trigger or escalate hostilities[.]"[83]

Talbot v. Jansen was another case emphasizing the central importance of the law of nations.[84] The May 1794 maritime incident in *Talbot*, also reminiscent of the *Charming Betsy*, nearly sparked war with the Netherlands. The United States considered the Netherlands an ally, as it was the second European nation to recognize American independence in 1781. However, when a U.S. citizen captured a private vessel owned by citizens of the Netherlands, an international crisis ensued.[85] At issue was whether the captors had unlawfully seized the vessel, and thus violated the Netherlands' right to neutral use of the high seas. If the Supreme Court failed to properly redress this "erroneous capture of a Dutch ship by a U.S. citizen," it would have violated the rights of the Netherlands "and given it just cause for war against the

---

[78] *Id.* at 244.

[79] *Id.*

[80] *Id.*

[81] *Id.* at 284.

[82] In 1795, the Supreme Court went so far as to state that "[a] prize court is, in effect, a court of all the nations in the world[.]" Penhallow v. Doane's Adm'rs, 3 U.S. (3 Dall.) 54, 91 (1795). The Continental Congress routinely authorized privateers to seize vessels provided they did so consistent with the law of nations. *See* 3 JOURNALS OF THE CONTINENTAL CONGRESS 1774–1789: SEPTEMBER 21–DECEMBER 30, 1775, at 439 (Worthington Chauncey Ford ed., Gov't Printing Off. 1905) ("Resolved, That the several vessels heretofore taken and carried into Massachusetts Bay, by the Armed Vessels in the service of the United Colonies, be proceeded against *by the rules of the law of Nations*, and libelled in the courts of admiralty erected in said colony.") (emphasis added)).

[83] Anthony J. Bellia & Bradford R. Clark, *The Law of Nations as Constitutional Law*, 98 VA. L. REV. 729, 792 (2012).

[84] Talbot v. Jansen, 3 U.S. (3 Dall.) 133 (1795).

[85] Bellia & Clark, *supra* note 83, at 785.

United States."[86] The Supreme Court disapproved of the capture by appealing to the law of nations, Justice Iredell writing that courts are required to "apply the law of nations to redress acts of hostility that the political branches have not authorized against foreign nations."[87]

As demonstrated by the Supreme Court's early docket, American deference to the law of nations was not a purely constitutional matter, but was also driven by a pragmatic concern for the precarious position of the United States in international affairs. When oral arguments began for the *Charming Betsy* case in 1803, the global implications were evident for Justice Marshall to see. In sum, the Barbary Coast War was roaring, the British and French were at war again, and the United States remained uniquely vulnerable on the high seas.[88] Global affairs necessitated due deference to the law of nations.

VI. *CHARMING BETSY* AFTERMATH

Although his efforts failed on appeal, Captain Murray remained unwavering in his pursuit of justice. He petitioned Congress for relief on November 23, 1804, and a private bill was introduced on his behalf.[89] Murray's bill was passed by the House and Senate, and on January 31, 1805, President Jefferson signed it into law.[90] The Treasury paid Murray pursuant to the bill, reflecting "the first time that Congress indemnified a public officer for a service-related judgment."[91] In the end, Murray's assumption that he and his crew would receive a payment for seizing the *Charming Betsy* was correct. However, it is reasonable to assume Murray never thought this payment would come in the form of congressional indemnification, one that merely canceled out his prior damages for seizing the vessel.

History has vindicated President Adams's decision to establish and expand a formal sea-faring force. James McHenry, Secretary of War to President Adams, in letters to Alexander Hamilton, revealed wariness of involving the Navy, and thus the country, in war.[92] From a statutory perspective, the concern centered upon the Executive's ability to issue orders to the Navy bordering on war.[93] Absent a declaration of war from Congress in the Quasi-War, President Adams's authority to issue orders was considered dubious. As history shows, however, the Navy is

---

86 *Id.*

87 *Id.*

88 Alford, *supra* note 1, at 1352.

89 Leiner, *supra* note 33, at 18.

90 An Act for Relief of Alexander Murray, ch. 12, 6 Stat. 56 (1805) (quoted in Leiner, *supra* note 33, at 19).

91 Leiner, *supra* note 33, at 19 (citing TREASURY DEP'T, AN ACCOUNT OF THE RECEIPTS AND EXPENDITURES OF THE UNITED STATES, FOR THE YEAR 1805, at 47 (1806)).

92 Jane Manners, *Executive Power and the Rule of Law in the Marshall Court: A Rereading of* Little v. Barreme *and* Murray v. Schooner Charming Betsy, 89 FORDHAM L. REV. 1941, 1955 (2021).

93 *Id.*

consistently employed as America's first response to conflict, even in the absence of war. This reflects President Adams's intuition to order the protection of U.S. vessels from French privateers through the use of the newborn Navy.

As for Jared Shattuck, the *Charming Betsy* dispute would not be his final foray with prominent disputes. *Maley v. Shattuck* concerned the libel of a schooner titled *Mercator*, another vessel owned by Shattuck. Perhaps having learned from *Charming Betsy*, his principal claim in his petition to Judge Richard Peters of the District of Pennsylvania was his status as a subject of the King of Denmark.[94] Shattuck further claimed that Lieutenant William Maley, commander of the U.S. Navy schooner *Experiment*, unlawfully seized $13,920 worth of his property aboard the *Mercator* in contravention of the law of nations.[95] Lieutenant Maley's defense rested upon the Nonintercourse Act, and ironically re-raised the issue of Jared Shattuck's citizenship.[96] Further complicating matters, the *Mercator* actually was seized by a British privateer while it was in Maley's possession.[97]

When the appeal reached the Supreme Court, Chief Justice Marshall delivered an opinion in which he cited the authority of *Charming Betsy* as decisive.[98] The Chief Justice applied the *Charming Betsy* rule and again found for Shattuck.[99] Secretary of State James Madison, in a letter to Congress, requested that as "the general policy of the United States [is] to favor the redress of wrongs on the high seas," a bill be passed to indemnify Jared Shattuck for his losses associated with the *Mercator*.[100]

VII. END OF PRIZE: THE POST-COLONIAL ERA THROUGH TODAY

Following the American and French Revolutions, privateering largely ceased with the adoption of the Declaration Respecting Maritime Law of April 16, 1856.[101] The Declaration was adopted in recognition of privateering as a recurring source of conflict due to privateers' disruption of maritime commerce. The operative provisions of the treaty are brief:

---

94 Maley v. Shattuck, 7 U.S. (3 Cranch) 458, 459 (1806).

95 *Id.*

96 *Id.* at 461–62.

97 *Id.* at 464–65.

98 *Id.* at 489.

99 *Id.* at 491.

100 Letter from James Madison to the Speaker of the House of Representatives, Apr. 9, 1806, *in* FOUNDERS ONLINE, NAT'L ARCHIVES, https://founders.archives.gov/documents/Madison/02-11-02-0402 (last visited Jan. 16, 2024).

101 Int'l Comm. of the Red Cross, *Declaration Respecting Maritime Law. Paris, 16 April 1856*, INT'L HUMANITARIAN L. DATABASES, https://ihl-databases.icrc.org/en/ihl-treaties/paris-decl-1856 (last visited May 30, 2024).

1. Privateering is, and remains, abolished;

2. The neutral flag covers enemy's goods, with the exception of contraband of war;

3. Neutral goods, with the exception of contraband of war, are not liable to capture under enemy's flag;

4. Blockades, in order to be binding, must be effective, that is to say, maintained by a force sufficient really to prevent access to the coast of the enemy.

Fifty-five nations accepted the document, including naval powers such as the United Kingdom and France.[102] The United States did not accede to the treaty because its proposed amendment to exempt all private property from capture at sea was not adopted.[103]

A half century later, the Hague Peace Conferences of 1899 and 1907 became the first international gatherings intended to preserve a present peace, as opposed to ending an on-going conflict.[104] The Second Hague Peace Conference in 1907 attempted to establish an international prize court considering that "prize law [had] been administered by national courts and [had] been given a specific character in each national jurisdiction, there exist[ed] no body of rules universally acknowledged which could be administered by such a general court."[105]

Germany and Great Britain both proposed a prize tribunal.[106] This International Prize Court was intended as a court of appeal, whereas the courts of the capturing nation would function as the trial courts.[107] Domestic courts were to be exhausted up to the highest level before resorting to the prize court.[108] Had the court been established, it would have been comprised of fifteen judges.[109] Indeed, the prize court treaty was lengthy, comprising of fifty-seven articles. The proposal never came to fruition, however, as the treaty failed to secure the necessary signatures for adoption.[110]

---

102 *Id.*

103 *Id.*; *see* Nicholas Parrillo, *The De-Privatization of American Warfare: How the U.S. Government Used, Regulated, and Ultimately Abandoned Privateering in the Nineteenth Century*, 19 YALE J. L. & HUMANITIES 1, 57–64 (2007) (discussing the United States' position on this Declaration and the demise of privateering in the United States).

104 CARNEGIE ENDOWMENT FOR INT'L PEACE, THE PROCEEDINGS OF THE HAGUE PEACE CONFERENCES: TRANSLATION OF THE OFFICIAL TEXTS, at v (Oxford Univ. Press 1920).

105 Paul S. Reinsch, *Failures and Successes at the Second Hague Conference*, 2 AM. POL. SCI. REV. 204, 208–09 (1908).

106 *Id.*

107 James Tryon, *The International Prize Court and Code*, 20 YALE L.J. 604, 605 (1911).

108 *Id.* at 606.

109 *See Convention Relative to the Establishment of an International Prize Court*, 2 AM. J. INT'L L., no. 1/2, Jan.–Apr. 1908, at 174 (Supp. 1908).

110 Eugene Kontorovich, *Three International Courts and Their Constitutional Problems*, 99 CORNELL L. REV. 1353, 1373–80 (2014); Int'l Comm. of the Red Cross, *Convention (XII) relative to the Creation of an International Prize Court, The Hague, 18*

Prize law is no longer a feature of U.S. law or practice. The United States has not adjudicated a prize case since the mid-twentieth century.[111] Instead, since the early twentieth century U.S. policy has been to avoid the use of prize procedure and resort to requisitioning ships and paying just compensation to the owner.[112] The incentive for mischief by personally profiting from the seizure of vessels has thus been removed. "[O]ur country has maintained its position of endeavoring to lead the world towards a general law or rule of immunity from capture or destruction of peaceful merchantmen and cargoes not contraband."[113]

VIII. CONCLUSION

What animated Marshall's deference in *Murray v. The Schooner Charming Betsy* to the law of nations? While the effect of deferring to maritime custom was to strengthen the separation of powers in international affairs, the Court's motivation went beyond purely constitutional concerns. To find that Shattuck and the *Charming Betsy* violated the Act would have infringed upon the Danish right to engage in neutral commerce on the high seas and ushered the United States into further international controversy. As stated by historian Frank Leiner:

> To the Marshall court, the importance of the *Charming Betsy* case was not the rule of construction generations of lawyers have come to cite . . . but the reinforcement of international law norms at a time when a militarily weak neutral nation with extensive mercantile interests at stake desperately wanted the law respected.[114]

Justice Marshall's genius in applying the law of nations in his interpretation of the Nonintercourse Act was avoiding another potential conflict with a major maritime power, one the newly created United States did not need.

Today, the *Charming Betsy* canon continues to influence U.S. courts in their approach to issues involving international law.[115] The origins of the often-cited doctrine reveal an extraordinary story of a nation at war and how a pragmatic Supreme Court responded. Yet little do most know,

---

October 1907, INT'L HUMANITARIAN L. DATABASES, https://ihl-databases.icrc.org/en/ihl-treaties/hague-conv-xii-1907 (last visited May 30, 2024).

111 Arnold W. Knauth, *Prize Law Reconsidered,* 46 COLUM. L. REV. 69, 69 n.3 (1946) (citing The Olinde Rodrigues, 174 U.S. 510 (1899) (released); The Pedro, 175 U.S. 354 (1899) (condemned); The Guido, 175 U.S. 382 (1899) (condemned); The Buena Ventura, 175 U.S. 384 (1899) (released); The Paquete Habana and The Lola, 175 U.S. 677 (1900) (released with award of damages); The Newfoundland, 176 U.S. 97 (1900) (released); The Adula, 176 U.S. 361 (1900) (condemned); The Panama, 176 U.S. 535 (1900) (condemned); The Benito Estenger, 176 U.S. 568 (1900) (condemned); The Carlos F. Roses (cargo), 177 U.S. 655 (1900) (condemned)); *see also* Parrillo, *supra* note 103.

112 Knauth, *supra* note 111, at 92.

113 *Id.* at 86.

114 Leiner, *supra* note 33, at 18.

115 *See generally* Alford, *supra* note 1, at 1352–57.

despite the grandeur of the high seas and the esteemed actors involved, that the doctrine sprung from a small conflagration with a Danish trading schooner on the high seas, a vessel named the *Charming Betsy*.

10

Carlos M. Vázquez

Foster v. Neilson, *United States v. Percheman*, and *Medellín v. Texas*: Judicial Enforcement of Treaties

Foster v. Neilson[1] is usually ranked among the most important cases on the constitutional law of foreign affairs. It is best known for having added an important gloss to the Constitution's statement that "all Treaties made, or which shall be made, under the authority of the United States, shall be the supreme Law of the Land; and the judges in every State shall be bound thereby, any Thing in the Constitution or the Laws of any State to the Contrary notwithstanding."[2] While that constitutional text explicitly provides that treaties have the status of federal law once "made" and are to be enforced by judges when they apply, *Foster* established that some treaties—those that have subsequently become known as "non-self-executing"—are not enforceable in the courts until implemented by the legislature. The decision is also sometimes cited for the proposition that the courts are to defer to the executive branch's interpretation of treaties.[3] With respect to both propositions, the *Foster* decision has been misunderstood.

Though *Foster*'s non-self-execution holding was important, many today hold an exaggerated understanding of the doctrine introduced by that decision. Some modern scholars and lower courts appear to view "non-self-execution" as the rule and supremacy as the exception. For these jurists, *Foster* has come to stand for far more than the Court held in the case. The Court did not hold, or even suggest, that U.S. treaties are presumptively non-self-executing. Any doubt on that score was removed by Chief Justice Marshall's subsequent brush with the issue in *United States v. Percheman*,[4] which is properly regarded as a companion case to *Foster*.

[1] Foster v. Neilson, 27 U.S. (2 Pet.) 253 (1829).

[2] U.S. CONST. art. VI, cl. 2.

[3] *See, e.g.*, David J. Bederman, *Revivalist Canons and Treaty Interpretation*, 41 U.C.L.A. L. REV. 953, 961–62 (1994) ("The origins of this judicial deference [to the executive's interpretations] can be traced to the early case of *Foster v. Neilson* . . . .").

[4] United States v. Percheman, 32 U.S. (7 Pet.) 51 (1833).

For a canonical foreign relations case, *Foster* produced remarkably few progeny during the nearly two centuries since it was decided. Indeed, until the Court's 2008 decision in *Medellín v. Texas*,[5] *Foster* itself remained the only case in which the Supreme Court unambiguously denied relief on the ground that the treaty being relied upon was not self-executing. Even that specific holding was overruled a few years later in *Percheman*.[6] Chief Justice Marshall's *Percheman* opinion reversing *Foster* suggests that the doctrine introduced in *Foster* should be approached with caution.

The Court's more recent opinion in *Medellín* is amenable to numerous and divergent interpretations,[7] but it cannot be denied that its interpretation of *Foster* was anything but cautious. The Court took as its point of departure its own broadest dicta concerning the doctrine of non-self-executing treaties. It recognized that *Percheman* had overruled *Foster*, but it described that overruling as being "on other grounds."[8] Closer attention to the story of *Foster* and *Percheman* as detailed in this chapter would have revealed that Chief Justice Marshall's second thoughts in *Percheman* actually went to the heart of the Court's reasoning in *Foster*.

This chapter begins by examining the complex factual background of the *Foster* case, which was the basis for the Court's principal holding in the case—that the treaty the plaintiff relied upon did not reach the parties' dispute. In reaching that decision, the Court addressed the obligation of the judiciary to defer to the political branches' interpretations of treaties under certain contexts, language that has been read overbroadly as counseling deference to the executive branch's treaty interpretations. The Court's conclusion that the treaty was inapplicable to the dispute made it unnecessary for the Court to determine whether the relevant treaty provision was self-executing, but Chief Justice Marshall ventured some thoughts on that question, rendered without the benefit of adversarial briefing. Those unnecessary musings eventually gave rise to the confounding doctrine of non-self-execution. A few years later, with the benefit of adversarial briefing, and with the treaty's Spanish language text before it for the first time, Chief Justice Marshall reversed the Court's conclusion that the relevant treaty was non-self-executing in an opinion that is best interpreted as establishing a presumption that treaties are self-executing. The chapter ends with some reflections on the *Medellín* decision. The current Chief Justice's muddled opinion in that case overlooked the lessons his predecessor learned in *Percheman*. Nevertheless, Chief Justice Roberts's opinion in *Medellín* can

---

5 Medellín v. Texas, 552 U.S. 491 (2008).

6 *See Percheman*, 32 U.S. (7 Pet.) at 88–89.

7 *See generally* Carlos M. Vázquez, *Treaties as Law of the Land: The Supremacy Clause and the Judicial Enforcement of Treaties*, 122 HARV. L. REV. 599, 646–67 (2008).

8 *Medellín*, 552 U.S. at 505.

be reconciled with the presumption of self-execution adopted by Chief Justice Marshall in *Percheman*.

I. BACKGROUND OF THE *FOSTER* CASE

Important questions of public law are frequently decided in the context of purely private disputes. *Foster v. Neilson* was a dispute between private parties about the ownership of 3000 arpents of land (approximately 2540 acres) located just east of the Mississippi River, in what is now eastern Louisiana.[9] James Foster and Pleasants Elam claimed to be the lawful owners of the land, having bought it in 1811 from Francoise Poinet, who had purchased it in 1805 from Joseph Maria de la Barba, who had purchased it from Jayme Joydra. The land was part of a larger parcel that Joydra had bought from the Spanish government in 1804.[10] Foster and Elam initiated an action in the nature of ejectment against David Neilson, who was in possession of the land. Neilson did not set forth the basis of his competing claim.[11] He defended the action on the ground that the Spanish government lacked the power to convey this land to Joydra in 1804 because sovereignty over that territory had been ceded by Spain to France in the Treaty of San Ildefonso in 1800[12] and then by France to the United States in the Treaty of Paris of 1803 (which effectuated the Louisiana Purchase).[13] The District Court for the Eastern District of Louisiana agreed with Neilson, and Foster and Elam appealed to the Supreme Court.[14]

Deciding whether the land in question belonged to Foster and Elam or Neilson required the Supreme Court to delve into a longstanding dispute between the United States and Spain over which of the two nations possessed sovereignty between 1803 and 1819 over the territory bordering the Gulf of Mexico between the Mississippi and Perdido Rivers. Spain maintained that only land west of the Mississippi had been ceded to France in 1800 and to the United States in 1803,[15] whereas the United States contended that the 1800 cession, and hence the 1803 Louisiana Purchase, extended to the Perdido.[16] That dispute, in turn, revolved

---

9 Foster v. Neilson, 27 U.S. (2 Pet.) 253, 254 (1829).

10 *Id.* Joydra had initially purchased 40,000 arpents on January 2, 1804. Though the King of Spain did not confirm the sale until February 20, 1805, the deed had been made effective as of 1804 by Juan Ventura Morales, the intendant of the Spanish government.

11 *Id.* at 256 (citing to Foster's and Elam's attorney's statement that "[n]o title has been exhibited by the defendant; but having acquired the possession, he has rested his defence [sic] on the single ground of denying the validity of the grant, which lies at the foundation of the plaintiff's title").

12 Treaty of St. Ildefonso, Fr.-Spain, Oct. 1, 1800, 55 Consol. T.S. 375.

13 Treaty Between the United States of America and the French Republic, U.S.-Fr., Apr. 30, 1803, 8 Stat. 200.

14 *Foster*, 27 U.S. (2 Pet.) at 255–56.

15 *See* ISAAC JOSLIN COX, THE WEST FLORIDA CONTROVERSY, 1789–1813: A STUDY IN AMERICAN DIPLOMACY 86 (1918).

16 *Foster*, 27 U.S. (2 Pet.) at 272–73. The United States had maintained this position since 1804, but "[t]his claim was . . . confined to diplomatic discussion; it was not made

around the construction of a succession of treaties between and among Spain, France, Great Britain, and the United States between 1763 and 1819. For present purposes, the following distillation of the dispute should suffice.

Until 1763, the territory between the Mississippi and the Perdido (the river that forms the western border of present-day Florida) was claimed by France as part of French Louisiana.[17] The territory east of the Perdido was Spanish Florida. In 1763, the French lost the French and Indian War (also known as the Seven Years' War), and in the Treaty of Paris they ceded to Great Britain the portion of Louisiana that lay east of the Mississippi.[18] In the same treaty, Spain ceded Florida to Great Britain. As compensation for fighting alongside it in the war, France ceded to Spain the rest of Louisiana (i.e., the portion west of the Mississippi).[19] Thus, as of 1763, Spain had sovereignty over the territory west of the Mississippi and Great Britain had sovereignty over the territory east of the Mississippi.

Great Britain divided its newly acquired territory into two administrative departments, East and West Florida,[20] with the Appalachicola River (well east of the Perdido) as the dividing line.[21] Thus, for the twenty years between the end of the French and Indian War and the end of the American War of Independence, the land at issue in *Foster* formed a part of British West Florida.

In 1783, the Treaty of Versailles[22] brought the American War of Independence to an end. Spain had aided the colonists and was rewarded with the Floridas.[23] Thus, between 1783 and 1800, Spain held Florida (East and West) and Louisiana.

public; no notice of it was communicated to the world, nor was it manifested by any *overt* act or proceeding." *Id.* (emphasis in original).

17 *Id.* at 258.

18 *Id.* at 261; Definitive Treaty of Peace between France, Great Britain and Spain, Feb. 10, 1763, 42 Consol. T.S. 279.

19 *Foster*, 27 U.S. (2 Pet.) at 261. All of the land ceded by France to Spain lay west of the Mississippi River except the island of Orleans.

20 *Id.*

21 *See* Howard v. Ingersoll, 54 U.S. (13 How.) 381, 406–07 (1852) (discussing the boundaries of West Florida under British rule). *See also* CECIL JOHNSON, BRITISH WEST FLORIDA 1763–1783 following index (1971) (map of West Florida under British rule).

22 Definitive Treaty of Peace Between the United States of America and his Britannic Majesty, U.S.-Gt. Brit., Sept. 3, 1783, 8 Stat. 80.

23 Treaty of Peace Between Great Britain and Spain art. 5, Gt. Brit.-Spain, Sept. 3, 1783, 48 Consol. T.S. 481. *See Foster*, 27 U.S. (2 Pet.) at 262.

Louisiana and East and West Florida, Showing Present-Day Boundaries of U.S. States

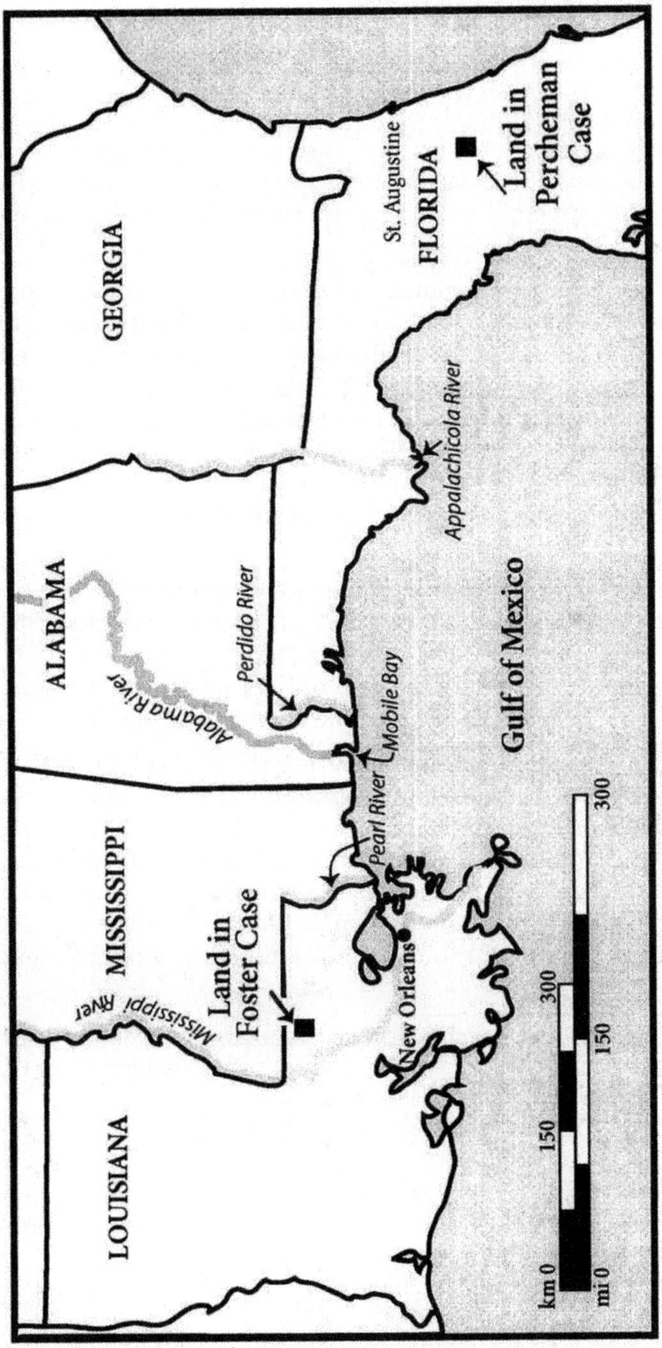

The status of the territory between the Mississippi and Perdido Rivers became murkier in 1800. As part of a broader scheme to establish a French empire in North America, Napoleon and his Foreign Minister Talleyrand sought the retrocession of Louisiana from Spain.[24] To induce Charles IV of Spain to give back Louisiana, they offered to install Charles's brother-in-law, the Duke of Parma, as king of a new Kingdom of Etruria, consisting mostly of Tuscany.[25] In the Treaty of San Ildefonso, initially kept secret, Charles "promise[d] and engage[d] on his part to retrocede [Louisiana] to the French Republic, six months after the full and entire execution of the . . . stipulations relative to his Royal Highness, the Duke of Parma."[26]

The treaty was ambiguous, however, concerning the boundary of the territory to be retroceded. In a provision that played a central role in the *Foster* decision, the treaty described the territory to be retroceded as "the Colony or Province of Louisiana, with the same extent that it now has in the hands of Spain, and that it had when France possessed it, and such as it should be after the treaties subsequently entered into between Spain and other states."[27] When France ceded Louisiana to the United States three years later in the Treaty of Paris, it quoted that language to describe the territory being ceded.[28]

The first question in *Foster* was whether the territory between the Mississippi and the Perdido was part of the territory that Spain agreed to retrocede to France in 1800 and that France in turn ceded to the United States in 1803. If it was, then Spain did not possess sovereignty over the land in 1804, the year that Spain sold it to Jayme Joydra.

Spain at the time took the position that it had agreed to retrocede only the territory west of the Mississippi. It had received the territory east of the Mississippi from Great Britain. The term "retrocede" means to cede back.[29] Because Spain had not received from France any territory east of the Mississippi, it could not "retrocede" any such territory to it. Moreover, Great Britain had denominated that territory "West Florida," and Spain had retained it under that name. Thus, only the territory west

---

24 E. WILSON LYON, LOUISIANA IN FRENCH DIPLOMACY, 1759–1804, at 109 (1934).

25 *Id.* at 110. *See also* THE LOUISIANA PURCHASE: A HISTORICAL AND GEOGRAPHICAL ENCYCLOPEDIA 306 (Junius P. Rodriguez ed., 2002).

26 Foster v. Neilson, 27 U.S. (2 Pet.) 253, 301 (1829) (citing "the third article" of the Oct. 1, 1800, "treaty . . . concluded between France and Spain, at St. Ildefonso"); Treaty of St. Ildefonso, *supra* note 12, art. 3.

27 *Quoted in Foster*, 27 U.S. (2 Pet.) at 301.

28 Treaty Between the United States of America and the French Republic, *supra* note 13, art. I.

29 *See Foster*, 27 U.S. (2 Pet.) at 271 (pointing out that the final act of delivery from Spain to France purported to transfer possession "*to the same extent* which [the Spanish] now possess, and which they had in the hands of France, *when she ceded them to the crown of Spain*" (emphasis added and internal quote marks omitted)). *See also id.* at 267 (citing the Supreme Court's decision in *Johnson v. McIntosh*, 21 U.S. (8 Wheat.) 543 (1823), to support the notion that "[t]he term retrocede would seem to limit it to what had been before ceded").

of the Mississippi could be said to constitute "the Colony or Province of Louisiana, with the same extent as it now has in the hands of Spain." On the other hand, the text of the treaty provided some support for a broader interpretation. The Colony or Province of Louisiana, "when France possessed it," extended east of the Mississippi to the Perdido. The "treaties subsequently entered into between Spain and other states" included the treaty with Great Britain ceding the Floridas to Spain and thus reuniting the land to the east of the Mississippi with the rest of Louisiana. There is evidence that Napoleon and Talleyrand had been purposely ambiguous in describing the territory being "retroceded."[30] In later ceding the same territory to the United States, Talleyrand encouraged Robert Livingston, the U.S. Ambassador in Paris, to "make the most" of the ambiguity.[31]

Although Livingston had earlier maintained that West Florida was not part of Louisiana, the United States followed Talleyrand's advice and interpreted the treaty to cede the land between the Mississippi and the Perdido.[32] Based on such an interpretation, Congress in 1804 passed the Mobile Act,[33] which authorized the President to establish a separate customs district to consist of the shores of the bay and river of Mobile, although, because of Spanish protests, President Jefferson refrained from taking control of the territory claimed by Spain at that time.[34] Later in 1804, Congress passed a law specifically nullifying Spanish grants in the ceded territory, with certain exceptions that did not cover the land at issue in *Foster*.[35]

In 1810, residents of West Florida revolted against Spanish rule and formed an independent government, hoping for eventual annexation by the United States.[36] To ward off the British, President Madison took control of West Florida to the Pearl River (the eastern border of present-day Louisiana).[37] In 1812, Congress enacted a statute providing that the territory containing the land at issue in *Foster* formed part of the state of

---

30 LYON, *supra* note 24, at 225; COX, *supra* note 15, at 81–82 ("Napoleon's cynical threat to render the territorial article obscure, if it were not already so [and] Talleyrand's mocking encouragement to make the best possible bargain out of the treaty . . . pointed to but one conclusion: the Americans might interpret the treaty to suit themselves."); PHILIP COOLIDGE BROOKS, DIPLOMACY AND THE BORDERLANDS: THE ADAMS-ONÍS TREATY OF 1819, at 4 (1939) ("[A] now-famous ambiguity in the treaty left uncertain whether West Florida was included in the retrocession."). *See also Foster*, 27 U.S. (2 Pet.) at 267 (argument of Foster's counsel) ("It will not be pretended that this language is free from ambiguity; and the probability is, from an anecdote related by one of the negotiators Barbé Marbois, in his recent work on the subject of Louisiana, that it was not accidental.").

31 LYON, *supra* note 24, at 225–26.

32 COX, *supra* note 15, at 83.

33 Act of Feb. 24, 1804, § 11, 2 Stat. 251, 254; *see Foster*, 27 U.S. (2 Pet.) at 303–04.

34 THE LOUISIANA PURCHASE, *supra* note 25, at 351. *See also* COX, *supra* note 15, at 95–100 (noting that Jefferson "expected to gain that part of West Florida [under dispute] bordering on the Mississippi through the voluntary action of its inhabitants" but that when resistance to that idea "proved unexpectedly strong, he wavered").

35 *Foster*, 27 U.S. (2 Pet.) at 304–05.

36 THE LOUISIANA PURCHASE, *supra* note 25, at 351.

37 *Id.*

Louisiana.[38] Subsequent statutes instructed the President to take control of the remainder of West Florida, and incorporated such territory into the new state of Alabama.[39]

Throughout this period, Spain maintained its claim to West Florida.[40] The competing claims to sovereignty over West Florida were resolved in the Adams-Onís Treaty of 1819,[41] in which Spain ceded East Florida to the United States and recognized American sovereignty over West Florida. Several provisions of this treaty were of central significance in *Foster v. Neilson*. Article 2 of the treaty provided that "his Catholic majesty cedes to the United States, in full property and sovereignty, all the territories which belong to him, . . . known by the name of East and West Florida."[42] And Article 8 provided, according to the English version, that

> all the grants of land made before the 24th of January 1818, by his Catholic majesty, or by his lawful authorities, in the said territories ceded by his majesty to the United States, shall be ratified and confirmed to the persons in possession of the lands, to the same extent that the same grants would be valid, if the territories had remained under the dominion of his Catholic majesty.[43]

II. THE COURT AND THE TREATY OF SAN ILDEFONSO—JUDICIAL DEFERENCE TO THE POLITICAL BRANCHES IN TREATY INTERPRETATION

As the case was presented to the Supreme Court by the very distinguished lawyers involved, including Daniel Webster arguing on behalf of the plaintiffs, the first issue was the correct construction of the Treaty of San Ildefonso between France and Spain: Had Spain ceded to France the territory between the Mississippi and the Perdido, or only the land west of the Mississippi? By far the greater part of the lengthy *Foster* opinion focused on whether the territory at issue was part of the territory that Spain had agreed to retrocede to France in 1800 and that the United States had accordingly purchased in 1803. This part of the opinion included some discussion of the respective roles of the courts and the political branches in treaty interpretation, and is sometimes cited today for the proposition that the courts must follow the executive branch's

38 *Foster*, 27 U.S. (2 Pet.) at 308.

39 *Id.* (citing 3 Stat. 371).

40 *Id.* at 310.

41 Treaty of Amity, Settlement, and Limits, Between the United States of America and his Catholic Majesty, U.S.-Spain, Feb. 22, 1819, 8 Stat. 252.

42 *Quoted in Foster*, 27 U.S. (2 Pet.) at 310 (citing the " 'treaty of amity, settlement and limits, between the United States of America and the king of Spain,' . . . signed at Washington, on the 22d day of February 1819").

43 *Quoted in id.*

interpretation of a U.S. treaty[44]—a proposition that is in some tension with Chief Justice Marshall's statement in *Marbury v. Madison*[45] that it is the province and duty of *the courts* to say what the law is. Upon closer inspection, *Foster* does not support judicial deference to the executive's interpretations of treaties to which the United States is a party.

Chief Justice Marshall began his analysis by reviewing the negotiating history of the Treaty of San Ildefonso of 1800 and examining the language of the pertinent provision and its subsequent application by the parties. The Court concluded that the relevant treaty provisions were ambiguous:

> We shall say only, that the language of the article may admit of either construction, and it is scarcely possible to consider the arguments on either side, without believing that they proceed from a conviction of their truth. The phrase on which the controversy mainly depends, that Spain retrocedes Louisiana with the same extent that it had when France possessed it, might so readily have been expressed in plain language, that it is difficult to resist the persuasion that the ambiguity was intentional. Had Louisiana been retroceded with the same extent that it had when France ceded it to Spain, or with the same extent that it had before the cession of any part of it to England, no controversy respecting its limits could have arisen. Had the parties concurred in their intention, a plain mode of expressing that intention would have presented itself to them. But Spain has always manifested infinite repugnance to the surrender of territory, and was probably unwilling to give back more than she had received. The introduction of ambiguous phrases into the treaty, which power might afterwards construe according to circumstances, was a measure which the strong and the politic might not be disinclined to employ.
>
> However this may be, it is, we think, incontestable, that the American construction of the article, if not entirely free from question, is supported by arguments of great strength which cannot be easily confuted.[46]

Only after having concluded that the treaty itself was ambiguous and that the U.S. interpretation was supported by strong arguments did the Court address the question of the respective roles of the judiciary and the political branches in treaty interpretation. It wrote:

> In a controversy between two nations concerning national boundary, it is scarcely possible that the courts of either should

---

44 *See supra* note 3.

45 5 U.S. (1 Cranch) 137 (1803).

46 *Foster*, 27 U.S. (2 Pet.) at 306–07. *See also id.* at 267 (concession by Foster's counsel that provision was "not . . . free from ambiguity").

> refuse to abide by the measures adopted by its own government. There being no common tribunal to decide between them, each determines for itself on its own rights, and if they cannot adjust their differences peaceably, the right remains with the strongest. The judiciary is not that department of the government, to which the assertion of its interests against foreign powers is confided; and its duty commonly is to decide upon individual rights, according to those principles which the political departments of the nation have established. If the course of the nation has been a plain one, its courts would hesitate to pronounce it erroneous.[47]

Although this language is sometimes cited for the proposition that the courts must defer to the President's interpretation of treaties, it is clear that the Court did not have deference to *the executive* in mind. As noted, the U.S. interpretation of the treaty that was accepted by the Court was manifested in a succession of *statutes*. The Court described each statute in some detail.[48] Thus, when the Court wrote that the courts' "duty commonly is to decide upon individual rights, according to those principles which the political departments of the nation has established," it was referring to principles established by Congress and the President acting together through legislation. The Court said so in the very next paragraph:

> We think then, however individual judges might construe the treaty of St Ildefonso, it is the province of the Court to conform its decisions to the will *of the legislature*, if that will has been clearly expressed.[49]

Indeed, given the clarity with which Congress had acted in connection with the very grants at issue in the case, what is most remarkable about the *Foster* opinion is the extent to which the Court hedged its deference. As noted, Congress had enacted the Mobile Act in 1804 on the basis of its view that the territory between the Mississippi and the Perdido had been ceded to the United States by France in 1803. Later the same year, Congress passed a law expressly nullifying grants of land by Spain in the ceded territory. Under the "last-in-time" rule, treaties and statutes are regarded as having the same stature, and accordingly the most recent prevails in the event of a conflict.[50] In *Foster*, however, the Court decided to defer to the legislative interpretation of the

---

47 *Id.* at 307.

48 *See id.* at 308–09.

49 *Id.* at 307 (emphasis added). It is also worth noting that the Court here was suggesting deference to Congress in interpreting a treaty between France and Spain—a treaty that was not "the supreme Law of the Land" that the President must faithfully execute. On the other hand, the pertinent language of this treaty was incorporated into the 1803 treaty between France and the United States ceding Louisiana, which was the "supreme Law of the Land." Treaty Between the United States of America and the French Republic, *supra* note 13, art. I.

50 *See* Whitney v. Robertson, 124 U.S. 190, 194 (1887) (establishing the last-in-time rule and setting forth its underlying rationale).

Treaty of Paris only after concluding that the treaty was ambiguous and that the U.S. interpretation was supported by strong arguments.[51] Additionally, in urging deference to the political branches, the Court emphasized that this was a dispute among nations concerning a national boundary.[52]

Foster thus reflects a very limited degree of judicial deference to *legislative* interpretations of treaties. It calls for deference to a reasonable interpretation by Congress of a treaty that addresses national boundaries. It cannot be taken as support for deference to the executive's treaty interpretations, or even deference to Congress's unreasonable interpretations or its interpretations of treaties on other subjects.[53]

III. THE COURT AND THE ADAMS-ONÍS TREATY

Of course, under the last-in-time rule, a subsequent treaty would prevail over an earlier conflicting statute. Accordingly, the Court in *Foster* went on to consider whether a later treaty—the Adams-Onís Treaty of 1819, which resolved the dispute between the United States and Spain over West Florida—superseded the statutes nullifying the grant to Joydra.[54] (Although the last-in time rule was not articulated until much later, it is noteworthy that the Court in *Foster* operated under the assumption that a later treaty would supersede an earlier statute in the event of aa conflict.) The Court had little trouble concluding that Article 2 of that treaty was consistent with the U.S. interpretation of the 1800 and 1803 treaties. According to that Article, his Catholic majesty ceded to the United States the territory east of the Mississippi "which belonged to him."[55] The Court surmised, reasonably, that this language was

---

[51] This part of *Foster* is thus of a piece with *Murray v. The Schooner Charming Betsy*, 6 U.S. (2 Cranch) 64, 118 (1804), which established, as a corollary to the last-in-time rule, that federal statutes "ought never to be construed to violate the law of nations if any other possible construction remains." For more on the *Charming Betsy* case, see Roger Alford's chapter in this volume. Roger P. Alford, Charming Betsy*: International Law as a Rule of Statutory Construction, in* INTERNATIONAL LAW STORIES (John E. Noyes, Laura A. Dickinson, Mark Weston Janis & Carlos M. Vázquez eds., 2d ed., 2025).

[52] *Foster*, 27 U.S. (2 Pet.) at 309 ("A question like this, *respecting the boundaries of nations*, is, as has been truly said, more a political than a legal question, and in its discussion, the courts of every country must respect the pronounced will of the legislature." (emphasis added)). *See also* Baker v. Carr, 369 U.S. 186, 212 (1962).

[53] The U.S. government cited the language from *Foster* quoted above, at text accompanying note 47, in the *Hamdan* case, for the proposition that treaty violations are a matter for international negotiations and reclamations, but not judicial redress. *See* Brief of Respondents at 30, Hamdan v. Rumsfeld, 548 U.S. 557 (2006) (No. 05–184). The Court's references in *Foster* to the resolution of inter-state boundary disputes by force rather than through the judiciary, however, were qualified by its recognition that the judiciary had a duty "to decide upon individual rights according to the principles which the political departments of the nation have established," 27 U.S. (2 Pet.) at 307, which of course include treaties and statutes. For more on *Hamdan*, see Oona Hathaway's chapter in this volume. Oona A. Hathaway, Hamdan v. Rumsfeld*: Domestic Enforcement of International Law, in* INTERNATIONAL LAW STORIES (John E. Noyes, Laura A. Dickinson, Mark Weston Janis & Carlos M. Vázquez eds., 2d ed., 2025).

[54] *See Foster*, 27 U.S. (2 Pet.) at 310.

[55] *Quoted in id.* at 276.

adopted to elide the dispute about which of those lands in fact had belonged to Spain. The language was chosen, the Court believed, to permit both sides to continue to insist on the rightness of their respective interpretations of the prior treaties.[56] The Court accordingly concluded that Article 8 of the treaty, which provided (in the English version) that "all the grants of land made before January 24 1818 . . . in the said territories ceded by his Catholic majesty . . . shall be ratified and confirmed," could be read by the United States to apply only to grants respecting land in the territory that the United States had not previously claimed.[57]

The Court had more difficulty with a declaration that Spain had attached to its ratification of the treaty. The declaration was intended to resolve a complication concerning three grants made by Spain after January 24, 1818, but bearing an earlier date.[58] The United States insisted on an express annulment of these grants, and Spain eventually agreed. Accordingly, Spain appended a declaration to its instruments of ratification for the purpose of "avoiding any doubt or ambiguity concerning the meaning of the eighth article of the treaty."[59] The declaration provided that "the said three grants have remained and do remain entirely annulled and invalid."[60] Because one of the grants was for land west of the Perdido River, in territory that the United States had claimed before 1819, the plaintiffs argued that the declaration supported an inference that other grants west of the Perdido fell within the United States' obligation under Article 8 to "ratify and confirm" Spanish grants.[61]

With respect to this argument, the Court was divided. Chief Justice Marshall and one other Justice were inclined to accept the plaintiffs' argument, but a majority of the Court was of the opinion that the declaration was not intended to approve grants that would otherwise have been invalid.[62] In the view of the Justices in the majority, the declaration removed any doubt about whether these three specific grants were covered by Article 8 without expressing any view on whether those grants (or other grants of land within the disputed territory) would have been covered by Article 8 in the absence of the declaration.[63]

---

56 *Id.* at 311. The Court's surmise appears to have been accurate. *See* BROOKS, *supra* note 30, at 163–64.

57 *See Foster*, 27 U.S. (2 Pet.) at 311.

58 These were three large grants deemed fraudulent by the United States, made by the King of Spain to the Duke of Alagón, the Count of Punon Rostro, and Don Pedro de Vargas. *Id.* at 312.

59 *Id.* (quoting a clause inserted by the king of Spain during his ratification).

60 *Id.*

61 *Id.* at 312–13.

62 *Id.* at 313.

63 *Id.* ("The form of the ratification ought not, in their opinion, to change the natural construction of the words of the eighth article, nor extend them to embrace grants not otherwise intended to be confirmed by it.").

Given the majority's view that the Article 8 obligation to "ratify and confirm" Spanish grants did not extend to grants of land west of the Perdido, the Court could have ended its analysis at this point. The discussion of the non-self-executing nature of Article 8 of the Adams-Onís Treaty could have been incorporated into a concurring opinion of Chief Justice Marshall and one other Justice, for whom alone that question was relevant.[64] Instead, the entire Court joined the portion of Marshall's opinion relating to self-execution, thus making this discussion either an alternative holding of *Foster* or obiter dictum. Though the specific conclusion that Article 8 of the Adams-Onís treaty was not self-executing proved to be short-lived, the Court's recognition of a distinction between self-executing and non-self-executing treaties has survived. The question that has confounded the courts, however, has been how to distinguish a self-executing treaty from a non-self-executing treaty.

IV. THE BIRTH OF THE DOCTRINE OF NON-SELF-EXECUTION

As Chief Justice Marshall read it, Article 8 of the Adams-Onís Treaty required the United States to "ratify and confirm" Spanish grants of land west of the Perdido, even though the United States had claimed that territory since 1803. Even so, Marshall did not think that Article 8 required a ruling in favor of the plaintiffs. The obligation imposed by that Article, he concluded, was addressed "to the political, not the judicial department,"[65] and thus had to be implemented by Congress before it could be applied by the courts. This discussion gave birth to the doctrine that some treaties are not self-executing and hence must be legislatively implemented before they can be enforced in court.[66]

The idea that certain treaties require legislative implementation before they may be applied by the courts is in some tension with the Supremacy Clause, whose text and history seem to establish that treaties in the United States have the force of law and are enforceable in the courts without implementing legislation. Before examining the Court's analysis of this issue, it is useful to sketch the story of the adoption of the Supremacy Clause, insofar as it relates to treaties.

The Supremacy Clause's declaration that treaties are the "supreme Law of the Land" was the Framers' solution to one of the most significant deficiencies of the government established by the Articles of

---

[64] *Cf.* David Sloss, *When Do Treaties Create Individually Enforceable Rights?*, 45 COLUM. J. TRANSNAT'L L. 20, 51 (2006) (arguing that self-execution discussion in *Foster* should be treated as concurring opinion).

[65] *Foster*, 27 U.S. (2 Pet.) at 314.

[66] Although I refer in the text to self-executing and non-self-executing treaties, it should be borne in mind that the same treaty may include self-executing and non-self-executing provisions. *See* Carlos Manuel Vázquez, *Treaty-Based Rights and Remedies of Individuals*, 92 COLUM. L. REV. 1082, 1128 n.179 (1992). This article also provides a more extended discussion, with supporting citations, of the history of the Supremacy Clause as it relates to treaties, which is sketched in the next several paragraphs. *See id.* at 1104–06.

Confederation.[67] The Articles gave Congress the power to conclude treaties, but did not address their status or create a mechanism to secure compliance. States failed to comply with treaty obligations, causing significant problems for the central government. Potential treaty partners lacked confidence in the United States' ability to secure compliance with treaties and were deterred from concluding potentially advantageous treaties with the United States. Because of treaty violations by the states, U.S. treaty partners refused to comply with their treaty obligations towards the United States, including obligations essential to the nation's security. For example, the Treaty of Peace with Great Britain required the British to abandon forts they held in western New York, which were of immense importance to the defense of the western frontier, but the British refused to do so, citing as justification the United States' failure to comply with its obligation under the same treaty to ensure the repayment of debts owed to British Loyalists.[68] The Founders feared that these and other treaty violations by the states would result in war.[69]

Because there were no national courts for the purpose, compliance with the treaty obligation to repay British debts depended on the courts of the states. Those courts, however, adhered to the British rule on treaty enforcement, which was (and remains) that treaties lack the status of domestic law and accordingly must always be implemented by the legislature before they may be applied in court.[70] Since Congress lacked the power to enact implementing legislation, and the state legislatures lacked the will to do so, treaty violations remained unremediable in court.

There was general agreement at the Constitutional Convention that the Constitution had to establish a mechanism for federal enforcement of treaties. Several options were considered. One rejected proposal would have been consistent with the British rule; it would have empowered Congress to nullify state laws that contravened treaties. Ultimately, the

---

67 *See, e.g.*, Ware v. Hylton, 3 U.S. (3 Dall.) 199, 277 (1796) (Iredell, J., on Circuit) ("The extreme inconveniences felt from such a system dictated the remedy which the constitution has now provided, 'that all treaties made or which shall be made under the authority of the United States, shall be the supreme law of the land; and that the judges in every State shall be bound thereby, any thing in the constitution or laws of any State to the contrary notwithstanding.' "), *rev'd on other grounds*, 3 U.S. (3 Dall.) 199 (1796). Justice Iredell read his opinion from the bench when the Court delivered its judgment reversing him. The Court disagreed with Iredell's too-narrow construction of the treaty, not his views regarding the effect of the Supremacy Clause.

68 *See* FREDERICK W. MARKS III, INDEPENDENCE ON TRIAL: FOREIGN AFFAIRS AND THE MAKING OF THE CONSTITUTION 5–11 (1973).

69 *See id.* at 12.

70 *See Ware*, 3 U.S. (3 Dall.) at 276 (Iredell, J., on Circuit) ("I believe no suit was ever maintained in any court in the United States, merely on the footing of the treaty when an act of the legislature stood in the way. It was to remove the obstacle arriving from such an opinion, that Congress recommended [to the states] the repeal of all acts inconsistent with the due execution of the treaty. And I must with due submission say, that in my opinion without such a repeal, no British creditor could have maintained a suit in virtue of the treaty, where any legislative impediment existed, until the present constitution of the United States was formed.").

Framers decided instead to declare that treaties would, once made, have the status of supreme federal law enforceable in the courts. The clear effect of the clause's declaration that treaties are the "supreme Law of the Land," and its instruction to the courts to apply them notwithstanding any conflicting state law, was to reverse the British rule that all treaties required implementation by the legislature before they could be enforced in the courts. The clear purpose behind the new rule was to avert treaty violations attributable to the United States, permitting the treaties' enforcement in the courts without the need for intervention by either the state or federal legislatures. This effect of the Supremacy Clause was recognized early on in Supreme Court decisions such as *Ware v. Hylton*[71] and in Justice Story's *Commentaries on the Constitution*.[72]

In its alternative holding (or obiter dicta) in *Foster*, the Court expressed the view that, notwithstanding the Supremacy Clause, some treaties do require implementing legislation before they may be enforced in the courts. The distinction between self-executing and non-self-executing treaties has confounded modern lower courts.[73] It even tripped up the father of the distinction, who abandoned the conclusion he had reached in *Foster* when Article 8 came before him again four years later in *Percheman*. That even the great Chief Justice found it necessary to reverse himself so quickly is not surprising. He embraced the distinction without benefit of adversarial briefing by counsel, who appear not to have raised the issue. As discussed below, Marshall eventually came to recognize the unusually complex nature of the question he had posed and answered all too casually in *Foster*.

Although much is obscure about the distinction Marshall had in mind in *Foster*, several points emerge with clarity from the opinion. First, Marshall leaves no doubt that the concept of a non-self-executing treaty is an exception to or limitation of the general principle established by the Supremacy Clause that treaties are judicially enforceable without implementing legislation. The Court began its analysis by describing the status of treaties in countries that do not have a constitutional rule like the one set forth in our Supremacy Clause:

> A treaty is in its nature a contract between two nations, not a legislative act. It does not generally effect, of itself, the object to be accomplished, especially so far as its operation is infra-territorial; but is carried into execution by the sovereign power of the respective parties to the instrument.[74]

---

71 3 U.S. (3 Dall.) 199 (1796).

72 1–3 JOSEPH STORY, COMMENTARIES ON THE CONSTITUTION OF THE UNITED STATES (Boston, Hilliard, Gray & Co. 1833).

73 *See, e.g.*, United States v. Postal, 589 F.2d 862, 876 (5th Cir. 1979), *cert. denied*, 444 U.S. 832 (1979) (pronouncing the distinction between self-executing and non-self-executing treaties the "most confounding" in U.S. treaty law).

74 Foster v. Neilson, 27 U.S. (2 Pet.) 253, 314 (1829).

That the Court understood this to be the rule in countries without a Supremacy Clause is made clear by the paragraph that immediately follows, which also makes clear that the United States follows a different rule—the rule embodied in the Supremacy Clause:

> In the United States a different principle is established. Our constitution declares a treaty to be the law of the land. It is, consequently, to be regarded in courts of justice as equivalent to an act of the legislature, whenever it operates of itself without the aid of any legislative provision.[75]

This last qualification is the source of the distinction between self-executing and non-self-executing treaties. It is clear from the context that the Court understood the latter as an exception to the general rule established by the Supremacy Clause.

Second, the *Foster* opinion leaves no doubt that the need for implementing legislation comes from the treaty itself. The distinction Marshall had in mind was between a treaty that purports to "act[ ] directly on the subject"[76] and a treaty in which "either of the parties engages to perform a particular act."[77] A treaty in the latter category "addresses itself to the political, not the judicial department; and the legislature must execute the contract, before it can become a rule for the Court."[78] Thus, *Foster* establishes that, unlike the British, we do not have a constitutional rule requiring implementing legislation for every treaty.[79] It recognizes that a need for implementing legislation may be created for particular treaties by the treaty itself. In other words, the treaty itself can alter the default rule established by the Supremacy Clause.

Third, *Foster* makes clear what it means to say that a treaty is self-executing. A self-executing treaty is "to be regarded in courts" as "equivalent to an act of the legislature." Thus, like a legislative act, a self-executing treaty supersedes inconsistent state law, as stated explicitly in the Supremacy Clause. Such a treaty also supersedes existing federal statutes. Thus, if Article 8 had been self-executing, it "would have repealed those acts of congress which were repugnant to it,"[80] including the 1804 statute nullifying Spanish grants. If such treaties are to be

---

[75] *Id.*

[76] *Id.*

[77] *Id.*

[78] *Id.*

[79] It has subsequently become clear that our Constitution does require legislative implementation of certain treaties because certain things can be done only by statute. For example, it is well established that a treaty cannot make conduct criminal. Thus, a treaty that requires the criminalization of conduct is non-self-executing by virtue of the Constitution. *See generally* Carlos Manuel Vázquez, *The Four Doctrines of Self-Executing Treaties*, 89 AM. J. INT'L L. 695, 718 (1995). In *Foster*, however, the need for legislation came from the treaty, not from the Constitution. The presumption of self-execution that I argue was recognized by *Percheman* is a presumption that implementing legislation is not required by the treaty itself.

[80] *Foster*, 27 U.S. (2 Pet.) at 314–15.

treated by courts as equivalent to federal statutes, then they are to be enforced in the courts in the same circumstances as federal statutes having like content. They may not be enforceable by particular parties in particular circumstances, but the reasons for finding them unenforceable must be the same as for federal statutes of like content.[81] Importantly, they are not to be held unenforceable because they are "contracts between nations" that under international law are enforceable only by nations and only through diplomacy or other state-to-state mechanisms. As the Court recognized in *Foster*, the Supremacy Clause establishes a "different principle" in the United States. The Founders made treaties enforceable in the courts in order to avert or remedy violations of treaties that, if left unremedied, would leave the United States vulnerable to such state-to-state enforcement mechanisms as war.

Far more obscure were Marshall's reasons for concluding that the treaty provision before him was non-self-executing. For Marshall, the classification turned on the treaty's language:

> The article under consideration does not declare that all the grants made by his catholic majesty before the 24th of January 1818, shall be valid to the same extent as if the ceded territories had remained under his dominion. It does not say that those grants are hereby confirmed. Had such been its language, it would have acted directly on the subject, and would have repealed those acts of congress which were repugnant to it . . . .[82]

Marshall contrasted such language with the actual language of the article—that the grants "shall be ratified and confirmed"—which "seems to be the language of contract."[83] Because Article 8 was so phrased, "the ratification and confirmation which are promised must be the act of the legislature."[84]

Marshall's contract analogy is of limited usefulness in distinguishing self-executing from non-self-executing treaties. Marshall appears to have had a particular type of contract in mind—an executory contract, as distinguished from an executed contract, which he presumably would have regarded as self-executing. Because contracts can be of either type, the contract analogy does not help us classify a treaty provision as self-executing or not. If Marshall was drawing on then-prevailing criteria for distinguishing one type of contract from the other, his unarticulated grounds for likening Article 8 to an executory contract are obscure to the modern reader.

---

81 For elaboration of this point, *see* Vázquez, *supra* note 7.

82 *Foster*, 27 U.S. (2 Pet.) at 314–15.

83 *Id.* at 315.

84 *Id.*

Nor is the analysis much advanced by Marshall's statement that, by Article 8, the United States "engage[d] to perform a particular act."[85] The Court here appears to hold that a treaty that requires an affirmative act on the part of the United States requires implementing legislation. But, if the "particular act" that Marshall had in mind was "ratification" of the grants, then it is unclear why such an act could not be performed by the judiciary in the context of particular cases. On the other hand, if the "particular act" to which Marshall referred was an act of legislation, then this language in the opinion is merely a restatement of the conclusion that Article 8 contemplated implementing legislation. It does not help us tell whether a treaty contemplates implementing legislation.

In the end, the modern reader of *Foster* is left to infer that the Court concluded that Article 8 contemplated implementing legislation because the treaty employed action verbs ("ratify" and "confirm") in the future imperative tense. By contrast, the Court appears to have been ready to regard treaty provisions as self-executing if phrased in continuous verbs (such as "be"), either in the future tense ("shall be [valid]") or in the present tense ("is [hereby confirmed]"). Whatever his reasoning, Marshall clearly reached his conclusion far too casually, as he himself would probably have been the first to admit in the light of his subsequent about-face in *Percheman*.[86] In the latter case, Marshall recognized that the language of Article 8 was in fact ambiguous and that the provision could have been read as "acting upon the subject." *Percheman* represents both a clarification and a tightening of the Supreme Court's test for determining when a treaty is "address[ed] . . . to the political . . . department."

V. *PERCHEMAN* AND THE PRESUMPTION OF SELF-EXECUTION

The Court had occasion to revisit its holding concerning the non-self-executing nature of Article 8 of the Adams-Onís Treaty in *United States v. Percheman*. The action had been brought in the superior court of the district of East Florida by Juan Percheman, who had been a captain in the Spanish army and who, in 1815, received from the Spanish governor a grant of two thousand acres of land in East Florida as a reward for services rendered in St. Augustine during the British invasion of 1812–1813.[87] Percheman brought suit to confirm his title pursuant to a waiver of sovereign immunity applicable to such suits. The district court ruled in his favor, and the United States sought Supreme Court review.[88]

---

85 *Id.* at 314.

86 United States v. Percheman, 32 U.S. (7 Pet.) 51 (1833).

87 *Id.* at 82–83.

88 Transcript of Record at 10, United States v. Percheman, 32 U.S. (7 Pet.) 51 (1833) (No. 35), *reprinted in* UNITED STATES SUPREME COURT RECORDS AND BRIEFS, 1832–1978 (opinion of the Superior Court, District East Florida).

Unlike the land claimed by Foster and Elam, the land claimed by Percheman lay in territory over which Spain had undisputed sovereignty at the time of the grant. Like Foster and Elam, Percheman relied on Article 8 of the Adams-Onís Treaty. This time, the Court held that Article 8 was self-executing.[89]

In supporting his claim under Article 8, Percheman brought to the Court's attention the version of Article 8 in the Spanish language, which was equally authoritative. As quoted by the Court in English, the Spanish version provided that the grants "shall remain ratified and confirmed to the persons in possession of them, etc."[90] This new evidence gave the Court some cover to reverse its holding in *Foster* that Article 8 contemplated implementing legislation:

> In the case of *Foster v. Neilson*, 2 Pet. 253, this court considered [the English version of Article 8] as importing contract. The Spanish part of the treaty was not then brought to our view, and we then supposed, that there was no variance between them. We did not suppose, that there was even a formal difference of expression in the same instrument, drawn up in the language of each party. Had this circumstance been known, we believe it would have produced the construction which we now give to the article.[91]

But the Court's about-face was not based exclusively on the Spanish text. First, the Court thought it proper to interpret Article 8 in the light of customary international law.[92] Under customary international law, as the Court understood it, a cession of territory from one nation to another cedes sovereignty over the land but not ownership of the land.[93] In other words, private property rights in the land would have remained unaffected by such cessions even in the absence of a treaty provision, such as Article 8, designed to secure such rights. "[I]f this security would have

---

89 *Percheman*, 32 U.S. (7 Pet.) at 89.

90 *Id.* at 88. The untranslated Spanish version conveys even more clearly the parties' intent to "act upon the subject":

> Todas las concesiones de terrenos hechas por Su Majestad Católica o por sus legítimas autoridades antes del 24 de Enero de 1818 en los expresados territorios que Su Majestad cede a los Estados Unidos *quedarán ratificadas y reconocidas* a las personas que estén en posesión de ellas del mismo modo que lo serian si Su Majestad hubiese continuado en el dominio de estos territories.

Treaty of Amity, Settlement, and Limits, Between the United States of America and His Catholic Majesty (Adams-Onís Treaty), U.S.-Spain, Feb. 22, 1819, Perfected International Treaties ("Treaty Series"), 1778–1945, RG 11, M1247, Roll 23 (National Archives Microfilm Publication) (emphasis added).

91 *Percheman*, 32 U.S. (7 Pet.) at 89.

92 *Id.* at 88 (stating that the Court's explication of customary international law "ought to be kept in view, when we construe the eighth article of the treaty, and the acts which have been passed by congress for the ascertainment and adjustment of titles acquired under the Spanish government").

93 *Id.* at 86–87 ("The modern usage of nations, which has become law, would be violated; that sense of justice and of right which is acknowledged and felt by the whole civilized world would be outraged, if private property should be generally confiscated, and private rights annulled . . . even in the case of conquest . . . .").

been complete without the article, the United States could have no motive for insisting on the interposition of government in order to give validity to titles which, according to the usages of the civilized world, were already valid."[94]

Second, the Court in addition recognized that, even without considering the Spanish text, the English text that it had so casually read as contemplating implementing legislation was actually ambiguous in this respect:

> Although the words "shall be ratified and confirmed," are properly the words of contract, stipulating for some future legislative act; they are not necessarily so. They may import that they "shall be ratified and confirmed" by force of the instrument itself.[95]

For this reason, "[n]o violence is done to the language of the treaty by a construction which conforms the English and Spanish to each other."[96] The Court's recognition that the words that it had confidently understood in *Foster* to call for implementing legislation were in fact ambiguous suggests that the Court now understood that greater caution was necessary in drawing conclusions about whether a treaty in fact contemplates legislation.

Perhaps most importantly, *Percheman* clarifies what exactly it takes to alter the constitutional default rule that treaties in the United States do not require implementing legislation. As noted above, in recognizing that the English text could be read as either contemplating implementing legislation or not, the Court described a treaty in the latter category (that is, a self-executing treaty) as one that accomplishes the desired end "by force of the instrument itself."[97] It described a treaty in the former category (i.e., a non-self-executing treaty) as one that "stipulate[es] for some future legislative act."[98] To stipulate is to specify or to state clearly or expressly. Thus, if a non-self-executing treaty is one that stipulates that its obligations are to be accomplished through subsequent legislation, then a clear statement to that effect would appear to be required. To the same effect, the Court elsewhere framed the question as whether the United States had "insist[ed] on the interposition of government"[99] to accomplish the object of the treaty. These formulations, considered alongside the Court's implicit recognition that greater caution was required in distinguishing self-executing from non-self-executing treaties, are best read as recognizing that the Supremacy Clause establishes a presumption that treaties do not contemplate implementing

94 *Id.* at 88.

95 *Id.* at 89.

96 *Id.*

97 *Id.*

98 *Id.*

99 *Id.* at 88; *see supra* text accompanying note 94.

legislation, a presumption that can be rebutted through treaty language "stipulating" or "insist[ing] on" the need for implementing legislation.

Asking whether the treaty contains an affirmative "stipulation" manifesting an "insist[ence]" that the object of the treaty be accomplished through "a future legislative act" was a significant advance over the I-know-it-when-see-it approach taken by the Court in *Foster*. As the Court appears to have realized the moment it received adversarial briefing on the point, answering the question posed by *Foster* without clear evidence of an intent to require legislation is a task fraught with difficulties. The question involves a highly complex tangle of international and domestic law. For some countries, the question whether judicial enforcement must be preceded by legislative implementation of the treaty is governed exclusively by domestic law. As we have seen, that was (and remains) the case for the United Kingdom, where treaties must be implemented by Parliament before they may be enforced in court, regardless of what the parties intended.[100] *Foster* recognized that, under our constitutional rule, implementing legislation is generally not needed unless the treaty itself requires it. Thus, the issue can turn on the parties' intent on the matter. However, although the parties to a treaty can in theory reach an agreement about whether the judiciary may enforce the treaty without prior involvement by the legislature, they will rarely concern themselves with such a question. States negotiating treaties are generally concerned with ends and not means;[101] they will usually be indifferent about whether judicial involvement can precede legislative involvement. Indeed, as noted, negotiators from some countries will be powerless to negotiate about that issue.

Two main conclusions follow. First, if the parties rarely address this question in the treaty, most cases will be decided by the default rule. *Foster* and *Percheman* correctly concluded that the Supremacy Clause establishes as our constitutional default rule that treaties generally do not require implementing legislation. The clause provides that the judges in every state shall be bound by treaties once "made"—that is, once they have been ratified by the President after receiving the consent of two-thirds of the Senate.[102] Had the Court adopted the contrary default rule, the judges in every state would be bound by very few treaties because the parties to a treaty rarely concern themselves with the manner in which treaty obligations will be enforced within the parties' domestic legal systems. Second, only a clear statement that legislation is required should suffice to overcome the default rule. Because the parties will rarely

---

100 *See supra* note 70 and accompanying text.

101 *Cf.* 1 OPPENHEIM'S INTERNATIONAL LAW § 21, at 82–83 (Robert Jennings & Arthur Watts eds., 1996) ("From the standpoint of international law states are generally free as to the manner in which, domestically, they put themselves in the position to meet their international obligations . . . . These are matters for each state to determine for itself according to its own constitutional practices.").

102 U.S. CONST. art. II, § 2 (The President "shall have power, by and with the advice and consent of the Senate, to make treaties, provided two thirds of the Senators present concur.").

be concerned about the need for prior legislative implementation, it is highly unlikely that they chose the treaty's language to convey their intent about that issue. As Chief Justice Marshall belatedly came to recognize, answering the question by reference to any but the clearest stipulation in the treaty is hazardous, especially when the parties speak different languages or have different constitutional rules concerning the need for legislative implementation of treaties.

That the Constitution establishes a presumption of self-execution is further supported by the complete absence of Supreme Court decisions until *Medellín* unambiguously denying relief on the ground that the treaty at issue was non-self-executing.[103] During that period, the Court came closest to denying relief on this basis in its decision in *Sosa v. Alvarez-Machain,*[104] in which it noted in dictum that the International Covenant on Civil and Political Rights[105] was not judicially enforceable because the United States had declared, upon ratifying it, that the treaty would be non-self-executing.[106] There has been much debate about whether the "non-self-executing" declarations that the United States has attached to its ratification of human rights treaties were intended to render the treaties to which they are attached judicially unenforceable,[107] and, if so, whether such declarations can validly accomplish that goal.[108] This is not the place to join that debate, but it is worth stressing that a conclusion that such declarations are valid would not conflict with a reading of *Foster* and *Percheman* as establishing a presumption of self-execution. Indeed, non-self-executing declarations might be regarded as modern-day "stipulations" of the type the Court in *Percheman* had in mind.[109]

"Non-self-execution" declarations may indeed be the most important legacy of the *Foster* decision. Even if understood to create a constitutional default rule of self-execution, *Foster* and *Percheman* allow the treaty-makers, with respect to particular treaties, to override the presumption

---

103 *See* Vázquez, *supra* note 79, at 716 & n.96.

104 Sosa v. Alvarez-Machain, 542 U.S. 692 (2004).

105 International Covenant on Civil and Political Rights, *opened for signature* Dec. 16, 1966, 999 U.N.T.S. 171 (ratified by the United States June 8, 1992).

106 *Sosa,* 542 U.S. at 734 (citing 138 CONG. REC. 8071 (1992)).

107 *See, e.g.,* David Sloss, *The Domestication of Human Rights: Non-Self-Executing Declarations and Human Rights Treaties,* 24 YALE J. INT'L L. 129, 220 (1999) (arguing that such declarations clarify that the relevant treaties do not create private rights of action, but do not preclude defensive enforcement of the treaties.).

108 *See, e.g.,* Curtis A. Bradley & Jack L. Goldsmith, *Treaties, Human Rights and Conditional Consent,* 149 U. PA. L. REV. 399, 401 (2000); Charles H. Dearborn, Note, *The Domestic Legal Effect of Declarations that Treaty Provisions are not Self-Executing,* 57 TEX. L. REV. 233, 243 (1979); Stefan A. Riesenfeld & Frederick M. Abbott, *The Scope of the U.S. Senate Control over the Conclusion and Operation of Treaties,* 67 CHI.-KENT L. REV. 571, 599 (1991); Jordan Paust, *Avoiding "Fraudulent" Executive Policy: Analysis of Non-Self-Execution of the Covenant on Civil and Political Rights,* 42 DEPAUL L. REV. 1253, 1260 (1993); John Quigley, *The International Covenant on Civil and Political Rights and the Supremacy Clause,* 42 DEPAUL L. REV. 1287, 1301 (1993).

109 For an extended discussion of the validity of "non-self-execution" declarations, *see* Vázquez, *supra* note 7, at 667–94.

that treaties in the United States do not require implementing legislation. The treaty-makers have taken up that implicit invitation in recent years by expressly addressing the domestic legal effect of the treaties they conclude. If these declarations are indeed valid, and the treaty-makers increasingly resort to them, then it may some day become the case that, notwithstanding the Supremacy Clause, most U.S. treaties do require implementing legislation. But, if so, that would be because the presumption of self-execution established by the Supremacy Clause and recognized in *Percheman* would have been overcome with respect to particular treaties. The *constitutional* rule in the United States is (and would remain) that treaties do not require implementing legislation unless they stipulate that they do.

VI. *MEDELLÍN*'S MUDDLE

After *Percheman*, the Supreme Court did not again unambiguously rely on the doctrine of "non-self-executing" treaties in denying a treaty-based claim for almost two centuries.[110] Although the 2008 decision in *Medellín v. Texas*[111] was unambiguous in relying on this doctrine, its basis for finding the relevant treaty to be non-self-executing was anything but. The majority opinion by Chief Justice Roberts put forward a multitude of reasons for reaching that conclusion, none persuasive on its own. The Court's reliance on multiple grounds for its conclusion makes it difficult to read *Medellín* as standing for any particular test for determining whether a treaty is self-executing.[112] Nevertheless, it is fair to say that Chief Justice Roberts overlooked the lessons his predecessor learned years earlier when the self-execution issue first came before the Court with full briefing.

José Ernesto Medellín, a Mexican national, was convicted in a Texas court of murder and sentenced to death, and he sought post-conviction relief in the Texas courts on the ground that his conviction was tainted by the failure of Texas officials to notify him upon arrest that he had a right to consult with Mexican consular officials, as required by the Vienna Convention on Consular Relations, a treaty to which both the United States and Mexico are parties.[113] The Texas courts denied relief on the

[110] A reporters' note in the *Fourth Restatement of Foreign Relations* Law states that the Court denied relief in *Cameron Septic Tank Co. v. Knoxville*, 227 U.S. 39 (1923), on the ground that the treaty was non-self-executing. *See* RESTATEMENT (FOURTH) OF FOREIGN RELATIONS LAW § 310 reporters' note 1 (2019) [hereinafter RESTATEMENT (FOURTH)]. *But see* Vázquez, *supra* note 7, at 601 n.8 (arguing that *Cameron Septic Tank* did not ultimately deny relief on this basis).

[111] Medellín v. Texas, 552 U.S. 491 (2008).

[112] *Cf.* RESTATEMENT (FOURTH), *supra* note 110, § 310 reporters' note 2 ("The unusual circumstances of *Medellín*—involving an effort to enforce in a domestic court a decision of the International Court of Justice to preempt State criminal law, counsel against generalizing too much from the Court's finding there of non-self-execution, and make it difficult to derive from that decision any clear test for determining when treaty provisions should or should not be regarded as self-executing.")

[113] Vienna Convention on Consular Relations art. 36, Apr. 24, 1963, 21 U.S.T. 77, 596 U.N.T.S. 261. *See Medellín*, 552 U.S. at 498.

ground that he had procedurally defaulted his Vienna Convention claim by failing to raise it at trial.[114] In response, Medellín relied on the decision of the International Court of Justice in *Case Concerning Avena and Other Mexican Nationals* (Mexico v. United States), holding that Medellín and fifty other named Mexican nationals incarcerated in the United States had a right to "review and reconsideration" of their state-court convictions and sentences notwithstanding any claimed procedural default.[115] His argument was supported by Article 94 of the United Nations Charter, another treaty to which Mexico and the United States are both parties, which provides that "each Member of the United Nations undertakes to comply with the decision of the International Court of Justice in any case to which it is a party."[116] But the Supreme Court denied relief, holding that the obligation imposed by Article 94 was non-self-executing, and that, accordingly, the ICJ's judgment in *Avena* was not enforceable in U.S. courts without prior legislative implementation.

In concluding that Article 94 was non-self-executing, the Court interpreted *Foster* as establishing a "distinction between treaties that automatically have effect as domestic law, and those that—while they constitute international law commitments—do not by themselves function as binding federal law."[117] The idea that some treaties do not constitute "binding federal law" flies in the face of the text of the Supremacy Clause, which establishes that "all" treaties of the United States are "the supreme Law of the Land."[118] Nothing in *Foster* supports the majority's understanding. The majority's suggestion here and elsewhere in the opinion that a non-self-executing treaty lacks the force of domestic law conflicts so clearly with the Constitution's text that the *Fourth Restatement of Foreign Relations Law* expressly rejects this view.[119] A non-self-executing treaty must instead be understood as the Court in *Foster* understood it—that is, as a treaty that is not judicially enforceable *even though* it has the status of supreme federal law.

Elsewhere, the Court in *Medellín* cited a lower-court opinion for the proposition that "while treaties 'may comprise international commitments . . . they are not domestic law unless Congress has either enacted implementing statutes or the treaty itself conveys an intention that it be "self-executing" and is ratified on these terms.' "[120] This formulation suggests that treaties are by default non-self-executing, and that affirmative evidence of an intent to make them self-executing is necessary to rebut that presumption. Of course, this is the opposite of the presumption *Percheman* appears to establish. The majority only cited

---

114 *See Medellín*, 552 U.S. at 498.

115 2004 I.C.J. 12 (Mar. 31). *See Medellín*, 552 U.S. at 497–98.

116 U.N. Charter art. 94.

117 *Medellín*, 552 U.S. at 504.

118 U.S. CONST. art. VI, cl. 2.

119 RESTATEMENT (FOURTH), *supra* note 110, § 310 reporters' note 12.

120 *Medellín*, 552 U.S. at 505 (quoting Igartua-De La Rosa v. United States, 417 F.3d 145, 150 (1st Cir. 2005) (en banc)).

Percheman once, however, and solely for the proposition that it overruled *Foster* "on other grounds."[121] By this, the Court appears to have meant that *Percheman* touched only *Foster*'s holding that the relevant provision of the Adams-Onís treaty was non-self-executing, not its more general discussion of how to distinguish self-executing from non-self-executing treaties. As indicated above, this is a far too narrow reading of the extent to which Marshall's opinion in *Percheman* altered the Court's approach to the more general question. As discussed above, *Percheman* is best understood as having limited the *Foster* alternative holding (or dictum) precisely on the question of how to distinguish self-executing from non-self-executing treaties.

The dissent by Justice Breyer perfectly and pithily captures the problem with the majority's suggestion that a treaty's self-executing status depends on the existence of evidence that the treaty was intended to be self-executing. Because, as discussed above, the parties to a treaty rarely if ever concern themselves with the question whether a treaty will be directly enforceable in the domestic courts or instead require implementing legislation, Justice Breyer rightly points out that searching for such evidence is tantamount to "hunting the snark."[122] As with the majority's suggestion that non-self-executing treaties lack the force of domestic law, the *Fourth Restatement* rejects a broad interpretation of *Medellín* as recognizing a presumption that treaties are not self-executing.[123]

The *Restatement* does read *Medellín* as inconsistent with the claim that there is a presumption that treaties are self-executing.[124] The Court's muddled opinion in *Medellín* is susceptible to numerous interpretations, however,[125] including readings consistent with *Percheman*'s presumption that treaties are presumptively self-executing.[126] The Court began its analysis of Article 94 by focusing on the article's text. It noted that, rather than saying that the parties to an ICJ judgment "shall" or "must" comply with the judgment, the treaty says that parties "undertake to comply" with such judgments, and it understood the wording of the provision as contemplating future action by the political branches to comply with ICJ judgments.[127] The distinction the majority drew between a treaty providing that the partiers shall or must comply and a treaty saying that the parties "undertake" to comply is puzzling to anyone with a background in international law, as it is well

---

121 *Medellín*, 552 U.S. at 505.

122 *Medellín*, 552 U.S. at 549 (Breyer, J., dissenting).

123 RESTATEMENT (FOURTH), *supra* note 110, § 310 reporters' note 3.

124 *Id.*

125 For a description of six possible interpretations, *see* Vázquez, *supra* note 7, at 651–67.

126 See in particular interpretations "d" and "f." *Id.* at 657–58 and 660–67.

127 *Medellín*, 552 U.S. at 508.

established that an "undertaking" is a hard, immediate obligation.[128] Colloquially, however, the word "undertake" can be understood as a synonym for "endeavor," which suggests a softer obligation.[129] That the Court understood article 94 to impose an obligation on parties to "do their best" to comply is also supported by the majority's statement elsewhere in the opinion that Article 94 preserved the "option of noncompliance."[130] If the Court's conclusion that Article 94 imposed non-self-executing obligations was based on its reading of the provision as merely imposing an obligation to use "best efforts" to comply, then the decision is consistent with a presumption that treaties imposing hard and determinate obligations are presumptively enforceable in court without prior legislative implementation.[131]

The part of the Chief Justice's opinion addressing the validity of presidential power to require compliance with non-self-executing treaties further supports this reading of *Medellín*. President George W. Bush had sent the Attorney General a memorandum indicating that the United States would comply with the *Avena* judgment by having state courts provide the required "review and reconsideration."[132] The Court held that the President lacks the power to instruct states to comply with non-self-executing treaties. In holding that the President lacks this authority, the Court applied the three-part classification of Justice Jackson's concurrence in *Youngstown Sheet and Tube v. Sawyer*.[133] The Court concluded that President Bush's memorandum fell in *Youngstown*'s third category, where presidential power is at its lowest ebb.[134] Presidential acts fall in *Youngstown*'s third category when the President acts in the face of an affirmative congressional (or in this case treaty-based) prohibition. The Court's view that the presidential memorandum fell in the third category was thus based on its view that the treaty affirmatively contemplated legislative implementation. The Roberts opinion's classification of the memorandum as falling in *Youngstown*'s third category thus appears to contemplate that a treaty is self-executing in the absence of affirmative evidence for concluding that it was intended to require legislative implementation. This reasoning is consistent with

---

[128] *See* Application of the Convention on the Prevention and Punishment of the Crime of Genocide (Bosn. & Herz. v. Serb. & Mont.), 2007 I.C.J. 43, ¶ 162 (Feb. 26) ("The ordinary meaning of the word 'undertake' is to give a formal promise, to bind or engage oneself, to give a pledge or promise, to agree, to accept an obligation. It is a word regularly used in treaties setting out the obligations of the Contracting Parties . . . . It is not merely hortatory or purposive. The undertaking is unqualified . . . ."); RESTATEMENT (THIRD) OF FOREIGN RELATIONS LAW § 301 reporters' note 2 (1987) (citing as "[a]n example of a nonbinding agreement" an instrument that "avoids words of legal undertaking").

[129] *See* Vázquez, *supra* note 7, at 662–64.

[130] *Medellín*, 552 U.S. at 511.

[131] *See generally* Vázquez, *supra* note 7, at 660–67.

[132] *Medellín*, 552 U.S. at 498.

[133] 343 U.S. 579, 635–38 (1952) (Jackson, J., concurring).

[134] *Medellín*, 552 U.S. at 527. *See generally* Vazquez, *supra* note 7, at 657–58; Carlos M. Vázquez, *Less Than Zero*, 102 AM. J. INT'L L. 563 (2008).

Percheman's presumption that a treaty is self-executing unless it "stipulates for an affirmative legislative act."

In the end, *Medellín* is best interpreted as not resting on *Foster*'s holding that certain treaties are non-self-executing because of what they say about whether domestic implementation is required, but as instead resting on the Court's view that Article 94 imposes at most an obligation to endeavor to comply with ICJ judgments, an obligation that is non-justiciable because it calls for an initial policy determination of a kind clearly for nonjudicial discretion.[135] So understood, *Medellin*'s holding is consistent with *Percheman*'s holding that treaties imposing obligations that do not call for the exercise of nonjudicial discretion are presumed to be judicially enforceable without the need for implementing legislation. There are, admittedly, other parts of the opinion that point the other way, but that can be said about any attempt to make sense of the muddled opinion in *Medellín*.

VII. CONCLUSION

Foster v. Neilson is best approached as a cautionary tale. The Court reached the "self-execution" issue unnecessarily, given the majority's conclusion that the treaty at issue did not apply to the grants in question. The "non-self-execution" argument does not appear to have been raised by the parties. The Court concluded that Article 8 of the Adams-Onís Treaty was non-self-executing based on its casual reading of the ambiguous text of the English version of the article, which did not correspond to the perfectly clear and equally authoritative Spanish version not before the Court. The holding that resulted from this mistranslation was quickly repudiated in *Percheman* once the Court received adversarial briefing of the issue, and the doctrine that emerged from *Foster* did not again supply the basis of a Supreme Court holding until *Medellín*. Even so, the doctrine has flourished in (and confounded) the lower courts. It has even been emulated in some foreign legal systems (which have similarly found it confounding).[136] Although it is too late in the day to reject the doctrine altogether, it is not too late to confine the doctrine to its proper scope by reaffirming the presumption of self-execution recognized in *Percheman*. *Medellín* does not stand in the way.

---

[135] For an extensive defense of this reading of *Medellín*, see Vázquez, *supra* note 7, at 660–65.

[136] *See* Duncan B. Hollis & Carlos M. Vázquez, *Treaty Self-Execution as "Foreign" Foreign Relations Law*, *in* CURTIS A. BRADLEY, THE OXFORD HANDBOOK OF COMPARATIVE FOREIGN RELATIONS LAW 467 (2019).

11

William S. Dodge

The Paquete Habana: Customary International Law as Part of Our Law

"International law is part of our law, and must be ascertained and administered by the courts of justice of appropriate jurisdiction as often as questions of right depending upon it are duly presented for their determination."[1] These lines from Justice Gray's majority opinion in *The Paquete Habana* have become the classic statement of the incorporation of customary international law in the U.S. legal system and of the courts' duty to enforce that law.[2] There was nothing new in this declaration itself, or in *The Paquete Habana*'s statements about consulting the works of scholars and the evolving nature of international law. Each of these principles dates back at least to the eighteenth century.

But in the meantime, the underlying conception of international law had changed. Once based on natural law, inspired by God and deduced by reason, international law now embraced positivism and was founded on state practice and consent.[3] *The Paquete Habana* reflects this transition, but it also stands for continuity—reiterating eighteenth-century principles in an age of legal positivism. It teaches that, despite significant changes in the international and domestic legal orders over more than two hundred years of U.S. history, courts should respect and accommodate the original understanding of customary international law

---

1 The Paquete Habana, 175 U.S. 677, 700 (1900).

2 *See* Sosa v. Alvarez-Machain, 542 U.S. 692, 730 (2004); First National City Bank v. Banco Para El Comercio Exterior de Cuba, 462 U.S. 611, 622 (1983); Banco Nacional de Cuba v. Sabbatino, 376 U.S. 398, 423 (1964); Filartiga v. Pena-Irala, 630 F.2d 876, 880, 886–87 (2d Cir. 1980); *see also* MARK WESTON JANIS, INTERNATIONAL LAW 113 (8th ed. 2021) (calling *The Paquete Habana*'s statement the "classic utterance by the Supreme Court" on the topic of incorporation); Michael J. Glennon, *Raising* The Paquete Habana*: Is Violation of Customary International Law by the Executive Unconstitutional?*, 80 NW. U. L. REV. 321, 322 (1985) (referring to *The Paquete Habana* as "the leading case concerning the incorporation of international law into United States domestic law").

3 *See* David J. Bederman, *Customary International Law in the Supreme Court, 1861–1900, in* INTERNATIONAL LAW IN THE U.S. SUPREME COURT: CONTINUITY AND CHANGE 89, 91–100 (David L. Sloss, Michael D. Ramsey & William S. Dodge eds., 2011); MARK WESTON JANIS, THE AMERICAN TRADITION OF INTERNATIONAL LAW: GREAT EXPECTATIONS 1789–1914, at 117–33 (2004); ARTHUR NUSSBAUM, A CONCISE HISTORY OF THE LAW OF NATIONS 222–25 (1947); Edwin D. Dickinson, *Changing Concepts and the Doctrine of Incorporation,* 26 AM. J. INT'L L. 239, 252–60 (1932).

as part of the domestic legal system. That teaching is as relevant in the twenty-first century as it was at the start of the twentieth.

The Paquete Habana is a formidable opinion, marshaling five centuries of state practice and the writings of scholars from ten countries to support its holding that coastal fishing vessels were exempt from capture under international law during the U.S. war with Spain.[4] Justice Gray tried to fortify his opinion further by showing that the President had committed the United States to observe the law of nations and that other U.S. officials recognized the exemption for coastal fishing vessels.[5] But like Thetis dipping her son Achilles in the River Styx, Gray's effort to strengthen his opinion left it with a vulnerable heel, for in emphasizing the President's agreement with the law of nations in this case, he raised the possibility that the President might disregard it in another. "[W]here there is no treaty, and no controlling executive or legislative act or judicial decision," Gray wrote, "resort must be had to the customs and usages of civilized nations."[6] As Professor Henkin noted, this "opaque, confused, and confusing dictum"[7] has "troubled our jurisprudence for a hundred years."[8]

I. HOW THE CASE GOT TO THE SUPREME COURT

The *Paquete Habana* sailed from Havana harbor on March 25, 1898, to begin a month-long fishing expedition at the western end of Cuba. She was a 43-foot sloop, with a crew of three, operating under a license issued by the Spanish Government.[9] The *Lola* left Havana on April 11 for a shorter trip to the Yucatan Peninsula. She was a 51-foot schooner with a crew of six and no fishing license.[10]

Cuba was then a colony of Spain. For three years, Spanish authorities had struggled to put down a Cuban insurgency,[11] most notoriously with a policy of "reconcentration" that forced people from the countryside into fortified areas where thousands died from unsanitary conditions.[12] Reports of atrocities in the American "yellow press," reaching a public already hostile to European involvement in the western hemisphere and generally sympathetic to U.S. expansion, produced strong anti-Spanish feelings.[13] Then, on February 15, 1898, an enormous explosion ripped through the battleship *Maine*, sending her to the bottom

4 *The Paquete Habana*, 175 U.S. at 686–700.

5 *Id.* at 700–08.

6 *Id.* at 700.

7 LOUIS HENKIN, FOREIGN AFFAIRS AND THE UNITED STATES CONSTITUTION 235 (2d ed. 1996).

8 *Id.* at 240.

9 *The Paquete Habana*, 175 U.S. at 678–79.

10 *Id.* at 679.

11 ADA FERRER, CUBA: AN AMERICAN HISTORY 144–53 (2021).

12 *See* DAVID F. TRASK, THE WAR WITH SPAIN IN 1898, at 1–11 (1981); LEWIS L. GOULD, THE SPANISH-AMERICAN WAR AND PRESIDENT MCKINLEY 22 (1982).

13 GOULD, *supra* note 12, at 23–25.

of Havana harbor, with a loss of 266 lives.[14] From then on, "Cuban issues consumed the body politic, displacing all other concerns."[15]

After negotiations failed to convince Spain to grant Cuba independence, President McKinley sent a message to Congress on April 11 asking for authority to intervene.[16] Congress responded on April 20, 1898, with a Joint Resolution declaring "[t]hat the people of the Island of Cuba are, and of right ought to be, free and independent"; demanding "that the Government of Spain at once relinquish its authority and government in the Island of Cuba and withdraw its land and naval forces from Cuba and Cuban waters"; and directing the President "to use the entire land and naval forces of the United States, and to call into the actual service of the United States the militia of the several States, to such an extent as may be necessary to carry these resolutions into effect."[17]

On April 21, the Secretary of the Navy, John Davis Long, instructed Admiral William T. Sampson to "immediately institute a blockade of the north coast of Cuba, extending from Cardenas on the east to Bahia Honda on the west,"[18] an area that encompassed the port of Havana.[19] President McKinley proclaimed the blockade the next day and stated that the United States would maintain it "in pursuance of the laws of the United States and the law of nations applicable to such cases."[20] Congress declared war against Spain on April 25.[21] The declaration was retroactive to April 21, thereby legitimizing the blockade already in effect.[22] President McKinley followed with another proclamation on April 26, reciting "that such war should be conducted upon principles in harmony with the present views of nations and sanctioned by their recent practice" and setting forth detailed rules for the conduct of the blockade and the capture of prizes.[23] The proclamation did not mention fishing vessels.

---

14 A U.S. investigation attributed the explosion to an external cause, while a Spanish investigation came to the opposite conclusion. TRASK, *supra* note 12, at 35. Later reviews of the evidence confirmed the Spanish view that the explosion was caused internally, probably by a fire in the ship's coal bunker that ignited its magazine. *Id.*; GOULD, *supra* note 12, at 35.

15 TRASK, *supra* note 12, at xiii, 29.

16 *Id.* at 52–53.

17 J. Res. 24, 55th Cong., 30 Stat. 738 (1898). The Joint Resolution further disclaimed "any disposition or intention to exercise sovereignty, jurisdiction, or control over said Island except for the pacification thereof, and assert[ed] its determination, when that is accomplished, to leave the government and control of the Island to its people." *Id.* at 739.

18 Annual Report of the Navy Department for the Year 1898: Appendix to the Report of the Chief of the Bureau of Navigation 175 (1898) [hereinafter Navy Report Appendix].

19 For fuller discussion of the planning and execution of the blockade, *see* Scott W. Stucky, The Paquete Habana*: A Case History in the Development of International Law*, 15 U. BALT. L. REV. 1, 8–13 (1985).

20 Proclamation No. 6, 30 Stat. 1769 (1898).

21 Act of April 25, 1898, ch. 189, 30 Stat. 364 (1898).

22 TRASK, *supra* note 12, at 57.

23 Proclamation No. 8, 30 Stat. 1770 (1898).

Unaware of these great events, the *Paquete Habana* started back to Havana with approximately 8800 pounds of live fish. She was captured on April 25 by the gunboat *Castine* about eleven miles from Havana. She offered no resistance and was taken to Key West, Florida, where she and her cargo were condemned as prize of war and sold for $490.[24] The *Lola* was seized two days later with a cargo of about 10,000 pounds of live fish, taken to Key West, condemned, and sold for $800.[25] These boats were just two of many vessels in the same circumstances.[26] On April 28, Admiral Sampson wrote to Secretary Long:

> I find that a large number of fishing schooners are attempting to get into Havana from their fishing grounds near the Florida reefs and coasts. They are generally manned by excellent seamen, belonging to the maritime inscription of Spain, who have already served in the Spanish navy, and who are liable to further service. As these trained men are naval reserves, have a semi-military character, and would be most valuable to the Spaniards as artillerymen, either afloat or ashore, I recommend that they should be detained [as] prisoners of war, and that I should be authorized to deliver them to the commanding officer of the army at Key West.[27]

Secretary Long replied on April 30: "Spanish fishing vessels attempting to violate blockade are subject, with crew, to capture, and any such vessel or crew considered likely to aid enemy may be detained."[28]

The right of belligerent nations to capture enemy ships as prizes of war is as old as naval warfare.[29] In the early days, captures were made by privateers—private ships granted a commission for this purpose—who were entitled to keep the proceeds from enemy ships lawfully captured as prize.[30] The 1856 Declaration of Paris outlawed privateering.[31] Although the United States did not sign this declaration, President McKinley's April 26th proclamation stated "that the policy of this Government will be not to resort to privateering, but to adhere to the rules of the

---

[24] The Paquete Habana, 175 U.S. 677, 679, 713 (1900); Brief for the United States at 3, The Paquete Habana, 175 U.S. 677 (1900) (Nos. 395, 396).

[25] *The Paquete Habana*, 175 U.S. at 679, 714; Brief for the United States, *supra* note 24, at 4.

[26] Claimants and the United States stipulated that the decisions in *The Paquete Habana* and *The Lola* would resolve a total of ten other cases involving fishing vessels. *See* Brief for Claimants at 1, 68–71, The Paquete Habana, 175 U.S. 677 (1900) (Nos. 395, 396).

[27] *The Paquete Habana*, 175 U.S. at 712–13 (quoting Navy Report Appendix, *supra* note 18, at 178).

[28] *Id.* at 713 (quoting Navy Report Appendix, *supra* note 18, at 178).

[29] 11 J.H.W. VERZIJL, W.P. HEERE & J.P.S. OFFERHAUS, INTERNATIONAL LAW IN HISTORICAL PERSPECTIVE: THE LAW OF MARITIME PRIZE 120 (1992); *see also* David J. Bederman, *The Feigned Demise of Prize*, 9 EMORY INT'L L. REV. 31 (1995).

[30] VERZIJL, *supra* note 29, at 152–68. It was to this end that the U.S. Constitution gave Congress the power to "grant Letters of Marque and Reprisal, and make Rules concerning Captures on Land and Water." U.S. CONST. art. I, § 8, cl. 11.

[31] VERZIJL, *supra* note 29, at 169–71.

Declaration of Paris."[32] Thus, it was U.S. naval vessels that captured enemy ships during the war with Spain. The captain and crews of these vessels were entitled to the proceeds of lawful captures, as well as bounties established by Congress, but they were also liable for damages in the event of a wrongful capture.[33]

The rights and wrongs of capture had developed over centuries in the decisions of prize courts. Although these were national courts, they aspired to apply a uniform law of nations. Lord Mansfield noted that "[e]very country sues in these Courts of the others, which are all governed by one and the same law, equally known to each other."[34] Justice Story declared that "the Court of prize is emphatically a Court of the law of nations; and it takes neither its character nor its rules from the mere municipal regulations of any country."[35]

In 1898, the federal district courts had original jurisdiction over prize cases, with appeals lying directly to the Supreme Court. The war with Spain produced a burst of such cases, and between November 1, 1899, and the middle of January 1900 the Supreme Court heard argument in nine prize cases.[36]

II. THE SUPREME COURT'S OPINION

Professor Fiss has noted the tendency of historians to identify a period in the Supreme Court's history with its Chief Justice and to rate such Courts. In his volume of the *Holmes Devise History of the Supreme Court*, Fiss observes that "the Court over which Melville Weston Fuller presided, from 1888 to 1910, ranks among the worst."[37] It "was composed of a group of seven or eight justices who largely shared the same basic premises and outlook."[38] They were "business-oriented and conservative."[39] But for all their homogeneity on other issues, the members of the Fuller Court differed sharply in prize cases.[40]

---

32 Proclamation No. 8, 30 Stat. 1770, 1771 (1898).

33 *See* Arnold W. Knauth, *Prize Law Reconsidered*, 46 COLUM. L. REV. 69, 70–74 (1946) (discussing prize money and bounties under U.S. law).

34 Lindo v. Rodney (1782) 99 Eng. Rep. 385, 388 (K.B.).

35 The Schooner Adeline, 13 U.S. (9 Cranch) 244, 284 (1815).

36 The Pedro, 175 U.S. 354 (1899); The Guido, 175 U.S. 382 (1899); The Buena Ventura, 175 U.S. 384 (1899); The Paquete Habana, 175 U.S. 677 (1900); The Newfoundland, 176 U.S. 97 (1900); The Adula, 176 U.S. 361 (1900); The Panama, 176 U.S. 535 (1900); The Benito Estenger, 176 U.S. 568 (1900); The Carlos F. Roses, 177 U.S. 655 (1900).

37 8 OWEN M. FISS, THE OLIVER WENDELL HOLMES DEVISE HISTORY OF THE SUPREME COURT OF THE UNITED STATES: TROUBLED BEGINNINGS OF THE MODERN STATE, 1888–1910, at 3 (1993).

38 *Id.* at 35.

39 *Id.* at 31.

40 *See* Henry M. Holt, *Recent Development and Tendency of the Law of Prize*, 12 YALE L.J. 306, 316–17 (1903) ("It is also interesting and noticeable that dissenting views have been expressed almost invariably, and about equally whether the judgment of the court was for condemnation or restitution."). Fiss does not discuss prize cases, limiting his

Before the Supreme Court, counsel for the fishermen made two principal arguments. First, he argued that by the President's proclamation of April 26, 1898, "the United States publicly declared that its policy was in full accord with the principles of modern international law."[41] Relying mostly on treatise writers, he asserted that "both by law and by uniform practice coast fishing boats are exempt from capture so long as they devote themselves exclusively to fishing."[42] Second, claimants' counsel argued that, because Congress's resolution of April 20, 1898, recognized the Cuban people as free and independent, the fishermen were entitled to the rights and privileges of neutrals or allies. "It cannot be conceived that those whom it was our policy and intention to protect and aid," he wrote, "should suffer either in their persons or their property by reason of our warfare against the very ones from whose domination we sought to deliver them."[43]

To the latter argument, the United States replied that a declaration by Congress that the Cuban people were free could not make them so and that under decisions dating from the Civil War persons living in a hostile state should be treated as enemies, regardless of their sympathies.[44] In response to the international law argument, the United States acknowledged the language in the President's proclamation,[45] but countered with three main points. First, while admitting that "[i]nternational law is largely to be collected from the practice of different nations and the authority of writers,"[46] the United States argued that many writers on international law—especially Continental writers, but even some English ones—went too far and did not express the law "as it is, but rather as they conceive it ought to be."[47] Second, the United States argued that American prize law had always followed English rather than Continental rules and that "the English rule is to consider the question as discretionary with the executive and as requiring an express ordinance of exemption."[48] In this case, "the discretion lodged in the Executive has been exercised . . . by the commanders of the capturing vessels, against the contention of the claimants."[49] Third, the United States argued that any exemption applied only to "small open boats" and not to sloops and

---

consideration of the Spanish-American war to the *Insular Cases*. *See* FISS, *supra* note 37, at 225–56.

41 Brief for Claimants, *supra* note 26, at 7.

42 *Id.* at 33.

43 *Id.* at 37. Counsel further argued that no presumption of hostile character should arise from the boats' having flown the Spanish flag, *id.* at 49–51, and that the vessels should at least have been given the opportunity to remove the Spanish flag before being condemned, *id.* at 52–55.

44 Brief for the United States, *supra* note 24, at 5–9.

45 *Id.* at 9.

46 *Id.* at 14.

47 *Id.* at 16.

48 *Id.* at 11.

49 *Id.*

schooners like the *Paquete Habana* and the *Lola*.[50] Each of the government's arguments addressed the content of international law. Nowhere did the United States assert that the President or his subordinates could violate that law.[51]

By a vote of six to three, the Court reversed the condemnations on the ground that coastal fishing vessels were exempt from capture under international law.[52] As senior Justice in the majority, Justice Horace Gray assigned the opinion to himself. Gray was known as the Court's "legal historian"[53] and was renowned for his "great erudition."[54] His methodological approach "emphasized the role of legal precedent: the tracing of decisions as far back as possible in order to establish their historic continuity," an approach that gave "many of Gray's decisions the status of monographs on the issues concerned."[55] *The Paquete Habana* fits that description.

First, Gray had to deal with the question whether the Supreme Court lacked jurisdiction, since the amount in dispute did not exceed $2000 and the district court had not certified the question as one of general importance.[56] He held that the Judiciary Act of 1891 establishing the Circuit Courts of Appeals had implicitly repealed previous pecuniary limits on the Supreme Court's jurisdiction, for the intent of Congress was "to make the nature of the case, and not the amount in dispute, the test of the appellate jurisdiction of this court."[57] Here, Gray had an insider's knowledge, for in 1890 he had authored a report to the Senate expressing the Justices' views on various judicial reform proposals.[58]

Gray then came to the principal question in the case, and he summarized his conclusion at the start: "By an ancient usage among civilized nations, beginning centuries ago, and gradually ripening into a

---

50 *Id.* at 9–10; *see also id.* at 23–25.

51 *See also* Jordan J. Paust, Paquete *and the President: Rediscovering the Brief for the United States*, 34 VA. J. INT'L L. 981 (1994). Indeed, the United States did not even assert that deference was owed to the executive's interpretation of international law. *See* Brief for the United States, *supra* note 24, at 14–25.

52 In a later decision, the Court rejected the argument that Cubans should not be treated as enemies for the purposes of prize law. *See* The Benito Estenger, 176 U.S. 568, 571 (1900) ("The general rule is that in war the citizens or subjects of the belligerents are enemies to each other without regard to individual sentiments or dispositions, and that political status determines the question of enemy ownership.").

53 Robert M. Spector, *Legal Historian on the United States Supreme Court: Justice Horace Gray, Jr., and the Historical Method*, 12 AM. J. LEGAL HIST. 181 (1968).

54 FISS, *supra* note 37, at 30.

55 Louis Filler, *Horace Gray*, *in* 2 THE JUSTICES OF THE UNITED STATES SUPREME COURT: THEIR LIVES AND MAJOR OPINIONS 666, 668 (Leon Friedman & Fred L. Israel eds., 1997).

56 The Court raised the issue during oral argument and asked the parties to file supplemental briefs on the question. *See* Supplemental Brief for Claimants-Appellants, The Paquete Habana, 175 U.S. 677 (1900) (Nos. 395, 396); Brief for the United States on the Question of Jurisdiction, The Paquete Habana, 175 U.S. 677 (Nos. 395, 396).

57 *The Paquete Habana*, 175 U.S. at 681.

58 WILLIARD L. KING, MELVILLE WESTON FULLER: CHIEF JUSTICE OF THE UNITED STATES 1888–1910, at 150–51 (1950).

rule of international law, coast fishing vessels, pursuing their vocation of catching and bringing in fresh fish, have been recognized as exempt, with their cargos and crews, from capture as prize of war."[59] True to his methodological preferences, Justice Gray resolved "to trace the history of the rule, from the earliest accessible sources."[60] The earliest sources he found were orders issued by King Henry IV of England in 1403 and 1406 implementing a treaty with the King of France.[61] A discussion of other treaties and the practices of other nations followed, down to the war between England and France following the French revolution.[62] Here Gray paused, for he was faced not only with a 1798 English order expressly directing the seizure of fishing boats but also with Sir William Scott's decision in *The Young Jacob and Johanna*, in which the great admiralty judge stated that the rule against capturing "small fishing vessels . . . was a rule of comity only, and not of legal decision."[63]

Gray's response was to observe that international law had evolved since 1798: "the period of a hundred years which has since elapsed is amply sufficient to have enabled what originally may have rested in custom or comity, courtesy or concession, to grow, by the general assent of civilized nations, into a settled rule of international law."[64] He followed with an account of nineteenth-century state practice through the Napoleonic wars, the Mexican-American War of 1848, the Crimean War of 1854, the Franco-Austrian War of 1859, the Franco-Prussian War of 1870, and the Sino-Japanese War of 1894.[65] French courts exempted coastal fishing vessels from capture throughout the Napoleonic Wars, and England soon changed its policy, issuing orders in council in 1806 and 1810 prohibiting the taking of vessels bringing in fresh fish.[66] During the U.S. war with Mexico in 1846, the commander blockading Mexico's east coast expressly exempted fishing vessels, and although the commander blockading the west coast ordered the capture of "all vessels under the Mexican flag," evidence showed that the exemption of coastal fishing vessels was observed in practice.[67] English practice during the Crimean

59 *The Paquete Habana*, 175 U.S. at 686.

60 *Id.*

61 *Id.* at 687.

62 *Id.* at 687–91.

63 (1798) 165 Eng. Rep. 81, 81 (Adm.). Scott, later Lord Stowell, was the leading admiralty judge of his day and his decisions had a great impact on American law and practice. *See* HENRY J. BOURGUIGNON, SIR WILLIAM SCOTT, LORD STOWELL: JUDGE OF THE HIGH COURT OF ADMIRALTY, 1798–1828, at 280–85 (1987).

64 *The Paquete Habana*, 175 U.S. at 694.

65 *Id.* at 694–700.

66 *Id.* at 694–95.

67 *Id.* at 696–98. Three days after oral argument, the United States filed an additional statement disclosing instructions during the war with Mexico that "Mexican boats engaged exclusively in fishing on any part of the coast will be allowed to pursue their labours unmolested." Statement on Behalf of the United States Relative to Exemption Allowed to Fishing Vessels in the Mexican War at 4, The Paquete Habana, 175 U.S. 677 (1900) (Nos. 395, 396); *see also* Supplemental Brief for Claimants-Appellants, *supra* note 56, at 7–9.

War of 1854 was more problematic, for it was conceded that England had destroyed many Russian fishing boats and storehouses, but Gray distinguished these as large commercial establishments supplying the military.[68] Thus Gray concluded that since 1806 "no instance has been found in which the exemption from capture of private coast fishing vessels honestly pursuing their peaceful industry has been denied by England or by any other nation."[69]

Then came the paragraph for which *The Paquete Habana* is famous:

> International law is part of our law, and must be ascertained and administered by the courts of justice of appropriate jurisdiction as often as questions of right depending upon it are duly presented for their determination. For this purpose, where there is no treaty and no controlling executive or legislative act or judicial decision, resort must be had to the customs and usages of civilized nations, and, as evidence of these, to the works of jurists and commentators who by years of labor, research, and experience have made themselves peculiarly well acquainted with the subjects of which they treat. Such works are resorted to by judicial tribunals, not for the speculations of their authors concerning what the law ought to be, but for trustworthy evidence of what the law really is.[70]

This passage introduced the scholarly works to which Gray turned next. Wheaton, Kent, Pistoye and Duverdy, De Cussy, Ortolan, Calvo, Heffter, Kaltenborn, Bluntschli, Perels, De Boeck, Hall, Lawrence, Ferguson, Attlmayr, Negrin, Testa, and Fiore were all marshaled[71] to support "the established rule of international law . . . that coast fishing vessels, with their implements and supplies, cargoes and crews, unarmed, and honestly pursuing their peaceful calling of catching and bringing in fresh fish, are exempt from capture as prize of war."[72] Gray was quick to point out the limitations of this rule. It did not apply to vessels "employed for a warlike purpose, or in such a way as to give aid or information to the enemy."[73] It did not apply "when military or naval operations create a necessity to which all private interests must give way."[74] And it did not apply to "vessels employed on the high seas" whose catch was "not

---

68 *The Paquete Habana*, 175 U.S. at 699–700.

69 *Id.* at 700.

70 *Id.*

71 *Id.* at 700–08.

72 *Id.* at 708. Some of the treatise writers suggested reasons for the rule, noting that coastal fishermen were poor, contributed little to national wealth, and provided no military benefit. *See id.* at 700–08. Perhaps Hall summarized the rationale best: "It is indisputable that coasting fishery is the sole means of livelihood of a very large number of families . . . and that the seizure of boats, while inflicting extreme hardship on their owners, is as a measure of general application wholly ineffective against the hostile state." WILLIAM EDWARD HALL, A TREATISE ON INTERNATIONAL LAW § 148, at 468 (4th ed. 1895).

73 *The Paquete Habana*, 175 U.S. at 708.

74 *Id.*

brought fresh to market."[75] But the *Paquete Habana* and the *Lola* came within the rule rather than the exceptions.[76]

Gray endeavored to show that the U.S. policy during the war with Spain had been to adopt rather than to violate this rule of international law. He quoted President McKinley's April 22 proclamation that the navy would maintain the blockade " 'in pursuance of the laws of the United States, and the law of nations applicable to such cases' "[77] and his April 26 proclamation reciting that the " 'war should be conducted upon principles in harmony with the present views of nations and sanctioned by their recent practice.' "[78] Gray read Admiral Sampson's April 28th message recommending the capture of fishing boats as "assum[ing] that he was not authorized, without express order, to arrest coast fishermen peaceably pursuing their calling"[79] and Secretary Long's reply as intending that coastal fishing vessels "should not be interfered with, so long as they neither attempted to violate the blockade, nor were considered likely to aid the enemy."[80] The last of these readings was fanciful. Cuban fishing boats could not avoid violating the blockade if they were to get back to port, and Secretary Long expressly directed that they were " 'subject . . . to capture,' "[81] thus ignoring the rule of international law that Gray so painstakingly established.

Chief Justice Fuller dissented, joined by Justices Harlan and McKenna. He maintained that there was no such rule of international law; that even if there were, the *Paquete Habana* and the *Lola* did not fall within it; and that in any event the President was not bound by it. Fuller quoted Sir William Scott's decision in *The Young Jacob and Johanna* to the effect that the rule was one " 'of comity only' "[82] and read the nineteenth-century practice as not universally acknowledging the exemption.[83] He dismissed the scholars that Gray cited as "lucumbrations [that] may be persuasive, but are not authoritative."[84] Even if such a rule existed, the Chief Justice doubted that these two ships fell within it. To him they seemed more like the high-seas vessels that Gray acknowledged to be excluded from the rule.[85]

---

75 *Id.*

76 *Id.* at 713–14.

77 *Id.* at 712 (quoting Proclamation No. 6, 30 Stat. 1769 (1898)).

78 *Id.* (quoting Proclamation No. 8, 30 Stat. 1770, 1770–71 (1898)).

79 *Id.* at 713.

80 *Id.*

81 *Id.* (quoting Navy Report Appendix, *supra* note 18, at 178).

82 *Id.* (Fuller, C.J., dissenting) (quoting The Young Jacob and Johanna (1798) 165 Eng. Rep. 81, 81 (Adm.)).

83 *Id.* at 719–20.

84 *Id.* at 720.

85 Fuller noted the boats' sizes, the substantial distances they had traveled from Havana, and their ownership by persons other than their captains and crews. *Id.* at 718. "They were engaged in what were substantially commercial ventures, and the mere fact that the fish were kept alive . . . did not render them any the less an article of trade than if they had been brought in cured." *Id.* at 718–19.

Fuller's most striking assertion, though, was that a court could not enforce international law against the executive. Quoting Chief Justice Marshall's opinion in *Brown v. United States*,[86] he argued that international law does not operate directly but only " 'through the sovereign power.' "[87]

> "This usage is a guide which the sovereign follows or abandons at his will. The rule, like other precepts of morality, of humanity and even of wisdom, is addressed to the judgment of the sovereign; and although it cannot be disregarded by him without obloquy, yet it may be disregarded."[88]

Fuller thus rejected the position that customary international law "*proprio vigore* limits the sovereign power in war."[89] He concluded "that exemption from the rigors of war is in the control of the Executive. He is bound by no immutable rule on the subject. It is for him to apply, or to modify, or to deny altogether such immunity as may have been usually extended."[90]

In the majority opinion, Gray admitted that there were words in *Brown v. United States*, "which, taken by themselves, might seem inconsistent with the position above maintained of the duty of a prize court to take judicial notice of a rule of international law, established by the general usage of civilized nations, as to the kind of property subject to capture."[91] As Gray pointed out, however, *Brown* held that the executive could not condemn enemy property without express authority from Congress.[92] In this case, Gray argued, there was no express authority from either Congress or the President.[93]

To summarize, *The Paquete Habana* made four important statements about international law: first, that it is "part of our law"; second, that to ascertain it courts may look to "the works of jurists and commentators"; third, that it evolves so that a practice once resting in comity might "ripen[ ] into a rule of international law"; and fourth, that

---

86 12 U.S. (8 Cranch) 110 (1814).

87 *The Paquete Habana*, 175 U.S. at 715 (Fuller, C.J., dissenting) (quoting *Brown*, 12 U.S. (8 Cranch) at 128).

88 *Id.*

89 *Id.* at 716.

90 *Id.* at 720. Fuller also read the executive's actions differently than Gray. The reference in the President's April 26th proclamation about " 'principles in harmony with the present views of nations and sanctioned by their recent practice' " was limited to the government's policy not to resort to privateering. *Id.* at 716 (quoting Proclamation No. 8, 30 Stat. 1770, 1770–71 (1898)). Fuller further noted that the captures of the *Paquete Habana* and the *Lola* had been ratified by the executive branch as consistent with its policy. *Id.* at 717.

91 *Id.* at 710 (majority opinion).

92 *Id.* at 711; *see Brown*, 12 U.S. (8 Cranch) at 129 ("It appears to the Court, that the power of confiscating enemy property is in the legislature, and that the legislature has not yet declared its will to confiscate property which was within our territory at the declaration of war.").

93 *The Paquete Habana*, 175 U.S. at 711.

resort to international law might not be necessary when there was a "controlling executive . . . act."[94] Of these four statements, only the last was new to American law. But each of them took on new significance because of the transition in international law from natural law to positivism.

From Natural Law to Positivism. During the nineteenth century, American law in general shifted from natural law to positivism.[95] In international law, a similar shift occurred, with courts and scholars increasingly looking to the practice of states rather than deductions from reason.[96] The law of nations had long been recognized to have both natural and positive elements. Grotius defined it as the body of law "concerned with the mutual relations among states or rulers of states, whether derived from nature, or established by divine ordinances, or having its origin in custom and tacit agreement."[97] Later writers tested the extremes, viewing the law of nations as purely a product of natural law (Pufendorf and Burlamaqui)[98] or as purely a product of positive law (Rachel and Moser).[99] But the authorities upon whom eighteenth-century Americans leaned most heavily emphasized the role of natural law. Vattel titled his work *The Law of Nations or the Principles of Natural Law Applied to the Conduct and to the Affairs of Nations and of Sovereigns* and wrote that "the *Law of Nations* is in its origin no other than the *Law of Nature applied to Nations*."[100] Blackstone stated that the law of nations "depends entirely upon the rules of natural law, or upon mutual compacts, treaties, leagues, and agreements."[101] Yet over the course of the nineteenth century, writers in America and elsewhere came to see international law as resting not upon the law of nature but upon the consent of states, as evidenced by their practices.[102]

To illustrate the difference in approach, one may contrast two opinions on the legality of the slave trade under international law. Sitting

---

94 *Id.* at 686, 700.

95 *See generally* Stephen M. Feldman, *From Premodern to Modern American Jurisprudence: The Onset of Positivism*, 50 VAND. L. REV. 1387 (1997). Natural law was "either revealed by God or discoverable through human reason," whereas positive law was made by human beings. *Id.* at 1396.

96 *See* William S. Dodge, The Charming Betsy *and* The Paquete Habana, *in* LANDMARK CASES IN PUBLIC INTERNATIONAL LAW 11, 19–24 (Eirik Bjorge & Cameron Miles eds., 2017) (discussing changes in the U.S. approach to international law during the nineteenth century).

97 HUGO GROTIUS, DE JURE BELLI AC PACIS 9 (1646) (Francis W. Kelsey trans. 1925); *see also* Dickinson, *supra* note 3, at 244 (noting that "the law of nations in the system of Grotius was a combination of elements derived from the divine law of revelation, the natural law of right reason, and positive law of custom and agreement").

98 *See* Dickinson, *supra* note 3, at 244–47.

99 *See id.* at 251–52.

100 E. DE VATTEL, THE LAW OF NATIONS § 6 (1758) (Charles G. Fenwick trans. 1916) (emphasis in original).

101 1 WILLIAM BLACKSTONE, COMMENTARIES ON THE LAWS OF ENGLAND *43 (1769); *see also* 4 *id.* at *66 ("The law of nations is a system of rules, deducible by natural reason, and established by universal consent among the civilized inhabitants of the world . . . .").

102 *See generally* sources cited *supra* note 3.

as a Circuit Justice in *United States v. The La Jeune Eugenie*, Justice Story approached the question from the perspective of natural law.[103] He wrote that "every doctrine, that may be fairly deduced by correct reasoning from the rights and duties of nations, and the nature of moral obligation, may theoretically be said to exist in the law of nations."[104] The African slave trade, Story reasoned, was "repugnant to the great principles of Christian duty, the dictates of natural religion, the obligations of good faith and morality, and the eternal maxims of social justice."[105] It was "sufficient to stamp any trade as interdicted by public law, when it can be justly affirmed, that it is repugnant to the general principles of justice and humanity."[106] When the same question reached the Supreme Court a few years later in *The Antelope*, Chief Justice Marshall reached the opposite conclusion using a positivist approach. That the slave trade was "contrary to the law of nature," Marshall wrote, "will scarcely be denied."[107] But for "a jurist," the test of international law was to be found "in those principles of action which are sanctioned by the usages, the national acts, and the general assent, of that portion of the world of which he considers himself a part, and to whose law the appeal is made."[108] The legality of the slave trade was supported by two centuries of practice.[109] While nations might renounce the trade for themselves, such renunciations could not bind others, "and this traffic remains lawful to those whose governments have not forbidden it."[110]

To be sure, international law's transition from natural law to positivism did not happen all at once, but "[t]he concepts of the positivist school gained steadily in influence throughout the 19th century."[111] By the end of the nineteenth century there had been a decided shift from the sort of reasoning Justice Story employed in *The La Jeune Eugenie* to the sort that Chief Justice Marshall used in *The Antelope*. *The Paquete Habana* was decided during what Professor Bederman has called "the period of 'high positivism' in international law."[112] As we shall see, Justice

---

[103] *See* 26 F. Cas 832, 846 (C.C.D. Mass. 1822) (No. 15,551). Story's opinion contains positivist elements as well, and he acknowledged that the law of nations could be "modified by practice." *Id.*

[104] *Id.*

[105] *Id.*

[106] *Id.*

[107] 23 U.S. 66, 120 (1825).

[108] *Id.* at 121.

[109] *Id.* at 121–22.

[110] *Id.* at 122.

[111] Dickinson, *supra* note 3, at 252.

[112] DAVID J. BEDERMAN, THE SPIRIT OF INTERNATIONAL LAW 11 (2002); *see also id.* at 7 ("Positivism reigned supreme in international relations from 1848 to 1919."); NUSSBAUM, *supra* note 3, at 222 ("In the science of international law, the nineteenth century marks the flourishing of positivism.").

The pendulum has since swung back towards greater acceptance of natural law. BEDERMAN, *supra*, at 9. Writing in 1955, Professor Lauterpacht observed:

> It is now generally admitted that, in the absence of rules of law based on the practice of States, International Law may be fittingly supplemented and

Gray's opinion reflects the shift to positivism in various ways but, at the same time, it establishes an important continuity between the eighteenth century and the twentieth.

International Law as Part of Our Law. When Justice Gray wrote that "[i]nternational law is part of our law, and must be ascertained and administered by the courts of justice of appropriate jurisdiction as often as questions of right depending upon it are duly presented for their determination,"[113] he was saying nothing new.[114] In English law, the incorporation of the law of nations is generally traced to Lord Mansfield's decision in *Triquet v. Bath*,[115] a case involving the immunity of a foreign minister's servant from arrest. Mansfield traced the principle further back to Lord Talbot's decision in *Barbuit's Case*,[116] another suit involving the immunities of public ministers. Mansfield had been counsel in *Barbuit's Case* and reported Lord Talbot as having declared "[t]hat the law of nations, in its full extent was part of the law of England."[117] A few years later, William Blackstone (who had in turn been counsel in *Triquet*) set down the principle in his *Commentaries on the Laws of England*: "the law of nations . . . is here adopted in it's [sic] full extent by the common law, and is held to be a part of the law of the land."[118]

> fertilised by recourse to rules of justice and to general principles of law, it being immaterial whether these rules are defined as a Law of Nature in the sense used by Grotius, or a modern Law of Nature with a variable content, or as flowing from the 'initial hypothesis' of International Law, or from the fundamental assumption of the social nature of States as members of the international community, or, in short, from reason.

H. LAUTERPACHT, INTERNATIONAL LAW: A TREATISE BY L. OPPENHEIM 107 (8th ed. 1955). Developments such as the Nuremberg Tribunal and the Universal Declaration of Human Rights are difficult to understand in terms of purely positive law. *See* BEDERMAN, *supra*, at 9; Quincy Wright, *Legal Positivism and the Nuremberg Judgment*, 42 AM. J. INT'L L. 405 (1948).

113 The Paquete Habana, 175 U.S. 677, 700 (1900).

114 Indeed, Gray himself said almost the same thing five years earlier in a case involving the enforcement of foreign judgments, *Hilton v. Guyot*, 159 U.S. 113, 163 (1895):

> International law, in its widest and most comprehensive sense—including not only questions of right between nations, governed by what has been appropriately called the law of nations; but also questions arising under what is usually called private international law, or the conflict of laws . . .—is part of our law, and must be ascertained and administered by the courts of justice as often as such questions are presented in litigation between man and man, duly submitted to their determination.

115 (1764) 97 Eng. Rep. 936 (K.B.); *see also* Heathfield v. Chilton (1767) 98 Eng. Rep. 50, 50 (K.B.) (Mansfield, L.J.) ("The privileges of public ministers and their retinue depend upon the law of nations; which is part of the common law of England.").

116 (1736) 25 Eng. Rep. 777 (Ch.).

117 Triquet v. Bath (1764) 97 Eng. Rep. 936, 938 (K.B.) (quoting Barbuit's Case (1736) 25 Eng. Rep. 777, 778, n.1 (Ch.)). A note to the report of *Barbuit's Case* states that "the Court seems to have determined that . . . the law of nations (which in its fullest extent was and formed part of the law of *England*) was the rule of decision in cases of this kind." *Id.* Mansfield, however, relied on his own note of the case. *See Triquet*, 97 Eng. Rep. at 938.

118 4 BLACKSTONE, *supra* note 101, at *67.

The colonists carried this principle with them to America, where it was applied in a variety of circumstances as general common law.[119] As in England, the law of nations governed the immunities of public ministers and their servants. In a 1792 opinion on this subject, Attorney General Edmund Randolph noted that "[t]he law of nations, although not specially adopted by the constitution or any municipal act, is essentially a part of the law of the land."[120]

The law of nations also formed part of the common law for criminal prosecutions.[121] In 1784, a French citizen was convicted by the Pennsylvania Supreme Court of assaulting the French Consul General and thereby violating "the law of Nations," which the court held, "in its full extent, is part of the law of this State."[122] In 1793, President Washington's Neutrality Proclamation promised prosecutions "against all persons who shall, within the cognizance of the courts of the United States, violate the laws of nations, with respect to the powers at war, or any of them."[123] And when charging the grand jury in one of these prosecutions, Justice James Iredell stated that "[t]he Common Law of England, from which our own is derived, fully recognizes the principles of the Law of Nations, and applies them in all cases falling under its jurisdiction, where the nature of the subject requires it."[124] The Judiciary Act of 1789 also opened the doors of the federal courts to tort suits alleging violations of the law of nations, providing that the district courts would have cognizance "of all causes where an alien sues for a tort only in violation of the law of nations or a treaty of the United States."[125]

---

[119] *See* Curtis A. Bradley & Jack L. Goldsmith, *Customary International Law as Federal Common Law: A Critique of the Modern Position*, 110 HARV. L. REV. 815, 820 (1997) ("Prior to *Erie*, [customary international law] was viewed as part of the general common law most famously identified with *Swift v. Tyson*."); Harold Hongju Koh, *Transnational Public Law Litigation*, 100 YALE L.J. 2347, 2354 (1991) ("[T]hroughout the early nineteenth century, American courts regularly construed and applied the unwritten law of nations as part of the 'general common law,' particularly to resolve commercial disputes, without regard to whether it should be characterized as federal or state.").

[120] 1 Op. Att'y Gen. 26, 27 (1792).

[121] *See* David L. Sloss, Michael D. Ramsey & William S. Dodge, *International Law in the U.S. Supreme Court to 1860*, *in* INTERNATIONAL LAW IN THE U.S. SUPREME COURT, *supra* note 3, at 7, 26–27.

[122] Respublica v. De Longchamps, 1 U.S. (1 Dall.) 111, 116 (Pa. 1784).

[123] Proclamation of Neutrality (Apr. 22, 1793), *in* 32 THE WRITINGS OF GEORGE WASHINGTON FROM THE ORIGINAL MANUSCRIPT SOURCES, 1745–1799, at 430–31 (John C. Fitzpatrick ed., 1939).

[124] Charge to the Grand Jury of Justice James Iredell for the District of South Carolina (May 12, 1794), *quoted in* Stewart Jay, *The Status of the Law of Nations in Early American Law*, 42 VAND. L. REV. 819, 825 (1989).

[125] An Act to establish the Judicial Courts of the United States, ch. 20, § 9, 1 Stat. 73, 77 (1789). *See* Sosa v. Alvarez-Machain, 542 U.S. 692, 712–24 (2004). *See generally* William S. Dodge, *The Historical Origins of the Alien Tort Statute: A Response to the "Originalists"*, 19 HASTINGS INT'L & COMP. L. REV. 221 (1996); Anne-Marie Burley [Slaughter], *The Alien Tort Statute and the Judiciary Act of 1789: A Badge of Honor*, 83 AM. J. INT'L L. 461 (1989); William R. Casto, *The Federal Courts' Protective Jurisdiction over Torts Committed in Violation of the Law of Nations*, 18 CONN. L. REV. 467 (1986).

Finally, the federal courts consistently applied the law of nations in cases arising under their admiralty and maritime jurisdiction.[126] Justice Story noted that piracy was "an offence against the law of nations (which is part of the common law)."[127] And Chief Justice Marshall declared in another prize case that "the court is bound by the law of nations which is a part of the law of the land."[128]

If Justice Gray's statement that "[i]nternational law is part of our law" was not new, it was nonetheless significant in affirming that this was *still* true. In the eighteenth century, both the law of nations and the common law were thought to rest upon principles of natural law, and it seemed perfectly natural for judges to articulate and apply the former in the same way that they articulated and applied the latter.[129] As Professor Dickinson observed, in the seventeenth and eighteenth centuries "[a]ll law, national no less than international, was being tested by the standards of what was assumed to be a rational, universal, and immutable system."[130] "In an age dominated by such ideas, nothing could have been more plausible than the conclusion that international law formed an integral part of the national law governing matters of international concern."[131] By the end of the nineteenth century, however, positivism had triumphed, and international law was to be found in state practice and consent.[132] This changed the sources to which Justice Gray would look, but it did not alter the basic principle that courts had an obligation to determine and apply international law.

The Works of Jurists and Commentators. To ascertain the rules of international law, Justice Gray wrote, "resort must be had to the customs and usages of civilized nations, and, as evidence of these, to the works of jurists and commentators who by years of labor, research, and experience have made themselves peculiarly well acquainted with the subjects of which they treat."[133] Again, there was nothing new in the sources Gray listed, but there was a difference in his treatment of scholars, which marked the transition from natural law to positivism.

English and American courts had long consulted treatises on international law as well as the practices of states. In *Triquet v. Bath*, Lord Mansfield attributed to Lord Talbot's decision in *Buvot v. Barbut*

---

126 *See* Sloss, Ramsey & Dodge, *supra* note 121, at 23–25.

127 United States v. Smith, 18 U.S. (5 Wheat.) 153, 161 (1820).

128 The Nereide, 13 U.S. (9 Cranch) 388, 423 (1815).

129 *See* J.L. BRIERLY, THE LAW OF NATIONS 87 (6th ed. 1963) ("It was natural therefore that judges should think of the two kinds of law [international law and common law] not as two unrelated systems, but as the application to different subject matters of different parts of one great system of law.").

130 Dickinson, *supra* note 3, at 253.

131 *Id.*

132 *See supra* notes 95–112 and accompanying text.

133 The Paquete Habana, 175 U.S. 677, 700 (1900); *see also* Hilton v. Guyot, 159 U.S. 113, 163 (1895) (stating that to ascertain the rules of international law "the courts must obtain such aid as they can from judicial decisions, from the works of jurists and commentators, and from the acts and usages of civilized nations").

the principle "[t]hat the law of nations was to be collected from the practice of different nations, and the authority of writers."[134] The Pennsylvania Supreme Court said precisely the same thing in 1784.[135] The law of nations concerning piracy, Justice Story wrote in 1820, "may be ascertained by consulting the works of jurists, writing professedly on public law; or by the general usage and practice of nations; or by judicial decisions recognising and enforcing that law."[136]

But the writers whom these English and American courts consulted often made little reference to state practice. This was for two reasons. First, their natural law premises led them to believe that the law of nations could be deduced from the dictates of reason.[137] Second, records of state practice were woefully inadequate. As Professor Dickinson has warned, "if it seems to us . . . that the classical publicists built too freely upon speculative premises, it must be remembered that frequently they had nothing else to build upon."[138] The nineteenth century witnessed not only the rise of positivism but also the systematic publication of diplomatic correspondence, treaties, and other evidence of state practice.[139] This brought about a "radical change . . . in the province of the text-writer, the change from the region of speculation to that of practice."[140] "The modern writer on International Law," one observer noted in 1915, "merely records the practice of States; and, if that practice is sufficiently certain and continuous, he deduces a rule therefrom."[141] *The Paquete Habana* reflected this transition to positivism when it cautioned that "[s]uch works are resorted to by judicial tribunals, not for

---

[134] (1764) 97 Eng. Rep. 936, 938 (K.B.). There is no mention of this principle, however, in the official report of the case. *See* Barbuit's Case (1736) 25 Eng. Rep. 777 (Ch.).

[135] Respublica v. De Longchamps, 1 U.S. (1 Dall.) 111, 116 (Pa. 1784) ("the law of Nations . . . is to be collected from the practice of different Nations, and the authority of writers").

[136] United States v. Smith, 18 U.S. (5 Wheat.) 153, 160–61 (1820); *see also* 1 JAMES KENT, COMMENTARIES ON AMERICAN LAW 19 (1826) ("England and the United States have been equally disposed to acknowledge the authority of the works of jurists, writing professedly on public law, and the binding force of the general usage and practice of nations, and the still greater respect due to judicial decisions recognizing and enforcing the law of nations."); HENRY WHEATON, ELEMENTS OF INTERNATIONAL LAW § 15, at 23 (Richard Henry Dana ed., 8th ed. 1866) ("Text-writers of authority, showing what is the approved usage of nations, or the general opinion respecting their mutual conduct, with the definitions and modifications introduced by general consent.").

[137] *See, e.g.*, United States v. The La Jeune Eugenie, 26 F. Cas. 846 (C.C.D. Mass. 1822) (No. 15,551) (Story, J.) ("every doctrine, that may be fairly deduced by correct reasoning from the rights and duties of nations, and the nature of moral obligation, may theoretically be said to exist in the law of nations"); 4 BLACKSTONE, *supra* note 101, at *66 (referring to the law of nations as "a system of rules, deducible by natural reason").

[138] Dickinson, *supra* note 3, at 242.

[139] *Id.* (noting that "[i]t was only in the 19th century that more or less systematic publication of such records was commenced in earnest").

[140] CYRIL M. PICCIOTTO, THE RELATION OF INTERNATIONAL LAW TO THE LAW OF ENGLAND AND OF THE UNITED STATES 121 (1915).

[141] *Id.*

the speculations of their authors concerning what the law ought to be, but for trustworthy evidence of what the law really is."[142]

That courts were capable of distinguishing genuine from spurious claims under international law was demonstrated in Justice Gray's other prize decision for the Court arising from the war with Spain. In *The Panama*, the Court rejected a claim that mail ships were exempt from capture under international law.[143] Gray noted the limits of international agreements on the subject,[144] adding that "the writers on international law concur in affirming that no provision for the immunity of mail ships from capture has as yet been adopted by such a general consent of civilized nations as to constitute a rule of international law."[145]

Ripening into a Rule of International Law. There was also nothing new in the idea that international law could evolve and that "what originally may have rested in custom or comity" could grow "into a settled rule of international law."[146] Early American jurists knew that ancient Greece and Rome had practices they found barbaric.[147] Early Supreme Court decisions are full of references to the "the modern law of nations,"[148] as are the papers of early American statesmen.[149] In *The La Jeune Eugenie*, Justice Story declared that "[i]t does not follow . . . that because a principle cannot be found settled by the consent or practice of nations at one time, it is to be concluded, that at no subsequent period the principle can be considered as incorporated into the public code of nations,"[150] and he noted that "[s]ome doctrines, which we, as well as

[142] The Paquete Habana, 175 U.S. 677, 700 (1900).

[143] 176 U.S. 535 (1900).

[144] *Id.* at 541–42.

[145] *Id.* at 542. In another case, the Court split 5–4 over whether international law required that, in the case of a blockade that had not been formally declared, a ship was entitled to approach the blockade to see if it was still in effect without being captured. The majority rejected the international law argument, stating that it could not accept the opinion of a treatise writer "as overruling in particular the prior decisions of this court," The Adula, 176 U.S. 361, 371 (1900), while the dissent (which Justice Gray joined) argued that the capture "was contrary to well-established principles of international law." *Id.* at 389 (Shiras, J., dissenting).

[146] *The Paquete Habana*, 175 U.S. at 694. "International comity" has been described as "deference to foreign states that is not required by international law." RESTATEMENT (FOURTH) OF FOREIGN RELATIONS LAW, pt. IV, ch. 1, intro. note (2018); *see also* William S. Dodge, *International Comity in American Law*, 115 COLUM. L. REV. 2071 (2015).

[147] *See* 1 KENT, *supra* note 136, at 4 ("The law of nations, as understood by the European world, and by us, is the offspring of modern times.").

[148] *See, e.g.*, Ware v. Hilton, 3 U.S. (3 Dall.) 199, 224, 229 (1796) (opinion of Chase, J.); *id.* at 269 (opinion of Iredell, J.); *id.* at 281 (opinion of Wilson, J.); Brown v. United States, 12 U.S. (8 Cranch) 110, 128 (1814); *id.* at 139, 145, 147 (Story, J., dissenting); The Commercen, 14 U.S. (1 Wheat.) 382, 387 (1816).

[149] *See, e.g.*, Proclamation of Neutrality (Apr. 22, 1793), *in* 32 THE WRITINGS OF GEORGE WASHINGTON FROM THE ORIGINAL MANUSCRIPT SOURCES, 1745–1799, at 430–31 (J.C. Fitzpatrick ed., 1939) (referring to "the modern usage of nations"); Letter from Thomas Jefferson to Thomas Pinckney (May 7, 1793), *in* 7 THE WORKS OF THOMAS JEFFERSON 312, 314 (P.L. Ford ed., 1904) (referring to "the principles of that law [of nations] as they have been liberalized in latter times by the refinement of manners & morals, and evidenced by the Declarations, Stipulations, and Practice of every civilized Nation.").

[150] 26 F. Cas. 832, 846 (C.C.D. Mass. 1822) (No. 15,551).

Great Britain, admit to belong to the law of nations, are of but recent origin and application."[151]

The transition from natural law to positivism facilitated the evolution of international law, for the practices of nations changed more readily than the laws of nature. Under a natural law theory, changes in international law had to be explained by changes in political philosophy[152] or religion.[153] Under a positivist theory, changes in international law flowed from changes in state practice indicating assent to a new rule. Thus, in *The Scotia* the Supreme Court found that changes in maritime rules made by Britain and the United States and accepted by other commercial states had ripened into rules of international law.[154] "Many of the usages which prevail, and which have the force of law," the Court said, "doubtless originated in the positive prescriptions of some single state, which were at first of limited effect, but which when generally accepted became of universal obligation."[155] The Court further noted "that unless general assent is efficacious to give sanction to international law, there never can be that growth and development of maritime rules which the constant changes in the instruments and necessities of navigation require."[156]

The Paquete Habana reflected positivist ideas of how customary international law evolves. Justice Gray found his rule in state practice, particularly over the prior century.[157] He looked to the writings of scholars only as "evidence of these [customs and usages]," and "not for the speculations of their authors concerning what the law ought to be."[158] And he concluded on the basis of this evidence that the rule against capturing

---

151 *Id.* Although Story approached the question of the slave trade from the perspective of natural law, he acknowledged that the law of nations could be "modified by practice," *id.*, and one sees in these quotations the positivist strand in Story's opinion. For further discussion of *The La Jeune Eugenie*, see *supra* notes 103–106 and accompanying text.

152 *See, e.g.*, Charge to the Grand Jury of Justice James Iredell for the District of South Carolina (May 12, 1794), *quoted in* Jay, *supra* note 124, at 824 (observing that the law of nations had been expounded "with a spirit of freedom and enlarged liberality of mind entirely suited to the high improvements the present age has made in all kinds of political reasoning").

153 For example, Chancellor Kent explained:

> The law of nations, so far as it is founded on the principles of natural law, is equally binding in every age, and upon all mankind. But the Christian nations of Europe, and their descendants on this side of the Atlantic, by the vast superiority of their attainments in arts, and science, and commerce, as well as in policy and government; and, above all, by the brighter light, the more certain truths, and the more definite sanction, which Christianity has communicated to the ethical jurisprudence of the ancients, have established a law of nations peculiar to themselves.

1 KENT, *supra* note 136, at 3.

154 81 U.S. (8 Wall.) 170, 188 (1871).

155 *Id.* at 187.

156 *Id.* at 188.

157 The Paquete Habana, 175 U.S. 677, 694–700 (1900).

158 *Id.* at 700.

coastal fishing vessels had grown, "by the general assent of civilized nations, into a settled rule of international law."[159]

Acknowledging Gray's positivist approach, one may still ask whether his evidence is convincing. Two prominent critics of customary international law have argued that it is not.[160] Professors Goldsmith and Posner write: "The bulk of the evidence suggests that nations refrain from seizing fishing vessels when there is no military or economic value in doing so. *The Paquete Habana*, an important casebook symbol of the power of [customary international law], is a hollow shell."[161]

Both Gray and his critics agree that it is the nineteenth-century evidence of state practice that matters.[162] Goldsmith and Posner argue that "the period from 1815 to 1900 was one of relative peace in Europe,"[163] that wars like the Franco-Prussian War should not count because they were not naval wars,[164] and that "during the one war in which the fishing vessel exemption rule was clearly tested—the Crimean War—the rule was violated."[165] This evaluation of the evidence, however, is highly selective. First, by beginning the nineteenth century in 1815, Goldsmith and Posner exclude evidence from the Napoleonic Wars on which Justice Gray relied.[166] Second, they pick on an example to which Gray devoted not even a sentence—the Franco-Prussian War[167]—while ignoring evidence from the more relevant Mexican-American War.[168] And third, they fail to note that Gray read British practice during the Crimean War as consistent with his rule because the property destroyed consisted of large commercial establishments supplying the Russian military.[169]

Goldsmith and Posner also criticize Gray's reliance on treatise writers as redundant if these writers were consulted only for their knowledge of the state practice the Court had already discussed.[170] But readers may draw different conclusions from the same facts, as illustrated by Goldsmith and Posner's differences with Gray over the proper interpretation of the evidence from the Crimean War. Although a court may not avoid the responsibility to evaluate the evidence of state

---

159 *Id.* at 694.

160 *See* Jack L. Goldsmith & Eric A. Posner, *Understanding the Resemblance Between Modern and Traditional Customary International Law*, 40 VA. J. INT'L L. 639 (2000) [hereinafter Goldsmith & Posner, *Resemblance*]. The argument is repeated in JACK L. GOLDSMITH & ERIC A. POSNER, THE LIMITS OF INTERNATIONAL LAW 66–78 (2005). For some critical responses to Goldsmith and Posner's more general thesis, see *Symposium: The Limits of International Law*, 34 GA. J. INT'L & COMP. L. 253 (2006).

161 Goldsmith & Posner, *Resemblance*, *supra* note 160, at 672.

162 *Id.* at 643, 647–51; *The Paquete Habana*, 175 U.S. at 694, 700.

163 Goldsmith & Posner, *Resemblance*, *supra* note 160, at 648.

164 *Id.* at 648–49.

165 *Id.* at 649.

166 *See The Paquete Habana*, 175 U.S. at 694–96.

167 *See id.* at 699.

168 *See id.* at 696–99.

169 *See id.* at 699–700.

170 *See* Goldsmith & Posner, *Resemblance*, *supra* note 160, at 650.

practice itself, surely its conclusions are strengthened by agreement with experts on international law. As Chancellor Kent observed, "[i]n cases where the principal jurists agree, the presumption will be very great in favour of the solidity of their maxims."[171]

Finally, Goldsmith and Posner argue that the practice of exempting coastal fishing vessels from capture is better explained by self-interest than legal obligation.[172] They argue that navies often had "more valuable opportunities to pursue—for example, defending the coastline or attacking the enemy's navy"[173]—and that therefore "a belligerent's refusal to seize enemy fishing vessels . . . is no more surprising than[ ] its refusal to sink its own ships."[174] In fact, though, both captors and their countries had substantial reasons to seize fishing vessels. The captains and crews of capturing ships were entitled to at least part of the proceeds of the captured ship and its cargo, and in the United States to bounties as well, which Congress did not abolish until just after the war with Spain.[175] From the countries' perspective, the crews of coastal fishing vessels might be used in the enemy's navy (which is why Admiral Sampson sought permission to seize them[176]) or at least feed the enemy's population. The exemption from capture that coast fishing vessels enjoyed throughout the years cannot be explained by self-interest alone but only by a sense of obligation founded, as Justice Gray wrote, "on considerations of humanity to a poor and industrious order of men, and of the mutual convenience of belligerent States."[177] In short, *The Paquete Habana* is no "hollow shell."[178] It is rather a textbook example of ascertaining customary international law from state practice.

Controlling Executive Act. If there was much that was not new in *The Paquete Habana*, there was one thing that was—Justice Gray's suggestion that customary international law might be superseded as a rule of decision by a "controlling executive . . . act."[179] For the purpose of ascertaining and administering international law, he wrote, "where there is no treaty and no controlling executive or legislative act or judicial decision, resort must be had to the customs and usages of civilized

---

171 *See* 1 KENT, *supra* note 136, at 18.

172 *See* Goldsmith & Posner, *Resemblance, supra* note 160, at 672.

173 *Id.* at 655.

174 *Id.* at 655–56.

175 *See* Act of Mar. 3, 1899, ch. 413, § 13, 30 Stat. 1004, 1007 (1899) ("And all provisions of law authorizing the distribution among captors of the whole or any portion of the proceeds of vessels, or any property hereafter captured, condemned as prize, or providing for the payment of bounty for the sinking or destruction of vessels of the enemy hereafter occurring in time of war, are hereby repealed."); *see also* Knauth, *supra* note 33, at 70–74 (discussing prize money and bounties under U.S. law).

176 The Paquete Habana, 175 U.S. 677, 712–13 (1900) (quoting Navy Report Appendix, *supra* note 18, at 178).

177 *Id.* at 708.

178 Goldsmith & Posner, *Resemblance, supra* note 160, at 672.

179 *The Paquete Habana*, 175 U.S. at 700.

nations."[180] Later in the opinion he stated that the exemption for coastal fishing vessels was a rule of international law that courts were bound "to give effect to, in the absence of any treaty or other public act of their own government in relation to the matter."[181] And later still he rejected the notion that a court could condemn coastal fishing vessels, "which are exempt by the general consent of civilized nations from capture, and which no act of Congress or order of the President has expressly authorized to be taken and confiscated."[182]

The idea that a treaty might supersede the law of nations predates *The Paquete Habana*. Vattel thought that treaties could depart from international law rules based on state practice but not from those based on natural law.[183] But he maintained that treaties contravening natural law rules could nevertheless be binding on the nations that signed them.[184] In 1871, the Supreme Court held that Congress could supersede treaties with Indian tribes,[185] and in 1884 it extended that holding to treaties with foreign nations.[186]

Early American courts also thought that statutes could supersede the law of nations in at least some cases.[187] In *Ware v. Hilton*,[188] the Supreme Court considered the validity of a Virginia statute confiscating debts owed to British creditors during the Revolutionary War. "It is admitted, that Virginia could not confiscate private debts without a violation of the modern law of nations," Justice Chase wrote, "yet if in fact, she has so done, the law is obligatory on all the citizens of Virginia, and on her Courts of Justice; and, in my opinion, on all the Courts of the

---

180 *Id.*

181 *Id.* at 708.

182 *Id.* at 711.

183 VATTEL, *supra* note 100, § 9. Vattel recognized four categories of the law of nations: (1) the necessary; (2) the voluntary; (3) the conventional; and (4) the customary. The conventional law of nations consisted of treaties. The other three categories were unwritten law. The necessary and the voluntary law of nations were based on natural law, whereas the customary law of nations was based on state practice. *See* William S. Dodge, *Customary International Law, Congress, and the Courts: Origins of the Later-in-Time Rule*, *in* MAKING TRANSNATIONAL LAW WORK IN THE GLOBAL ECONOMY: ESSAYS IN HONOUR OF DETLEV VAGTS 531, 534 (Pieter H.F. Bekker, Rudolf Dolzer & Michael Waibel eds., 2010).

184 VATTEL, *supra* note 100, § 9 ("We shall see, however, that [treaties and customs contrary to the necessary law of nations] are not always conformable to the *inner* law of conscience, and yet . . . such conventions and treaties are often valid by the *external* law.") (emphasis in original).

185 The Cherokee Tobacco, 78 U.S. (11 Wall.) 616, 621 (1870).

186 The Head Money Cases, 112 U.S. 580, 597, 599 (1884); *see also* Chinese Exclusion Case, 130 U.S. 581, 600 (1889); Whitney v. Robertson, 124 U.S. 190, 194 (1888). *See generally* Detlev F. Vagts, *The United States and Its Treaties: Observance and Breach*, 95 AM. J. INT'L L. 313, 313–18 (2001).

187 Of course, statutes might also supplement or clarify existing international law, and the Constitution of the United States expressly gave Congress with the power "[t]o define and punish . . . Offences against the Law of Nations." U.S. CONST. art I, § 8, cl. 10. On the history of the Offenses Clause, see Sarah H. Cleveland & William S. Dodge, *Defining and Punishing Offenses Under Treaties*, 124 YALE L.J. 2202, 2210–33 (2015).

188 3 U.S. (3 Dall.) 199 (1796).

United States."[189] The same idea is implicit in Chief Justice Marshall's statement in *Murray v. The Schooner Charming Betsy* that "an act of congress ought never to be construed to violate the law of nations if any other possible construction remains"[190] and explicit in his remark in *The Nereide* that "[t]ill such an act be passed, the Court is bound by the law of nations which is a part of the law of the land."[191] Some early decisions maintained that a statute could not supersede international law rules that were based on natural law.[192] But that exception was first ignored and then lost as U.S. understandings of international law transitioned to positivism.[193]

The Supreme Court had also previously held that a judicial decision interpreting the law of nations could be controlling even if the law of nations had changed. In *The Lottawanna*,[194] the Court was asked to overrule an earlier decision interpreting general maritime law because the practice of other nations had changed. "To ascertain . . . what the maritime law of this country is, it is not enough to read the French, German, Italian, and other foreign works on the subject, or the codes which they have framed," the Court wrote.[195] The Court's prior decisions were "conclusive on the subject; and we see no sufficient ground for disturbing them."[196] In another prize case argued around the same time as *The Paquete Habana*, the Court was again asked to overrule a prior decision interpreting international law; it again refused.[197]

By contrast, the possibility that an act of the executive alone could supersede customary international law seems to have been completely new. In the 1790s, it was accepted by writers on both sides of the debate over the Washington administration's neutrality prosecutions that the law of nations was among those laws that the President had a constitutional obligation to execute faithfully.[198] During the War of 1812,

189 *Id.* at 229 (Chase, J.).

190 6 U.S. (2 Cranch) 64, 118 (1804).

191 13 U.S. (9 Cranch) 388, 423 (1815).

192 *See, e.g.*, Miller v. The Ship Resolution, 2 U.S. 1, 4 (Fed. Ct. App. 1781) ("The municipal laws of a country cannot change the law of nations, so as to bind the subjects of another nation . . . .") (referring to the rights of neutral countries).

193 *See* Dodge, *supra* note 183, at 536–55.

194 88 U.S. 558 (1874).

195 *Id.* at 576.

196 *Id.* at 578.

197 *See* The Adula, 176 U.S. 361, 371 (1900) ("We cannot change our rulings to conform to the opinions of foreign writers as to what they suppose to be the existing law upon the subject."). The question continues to arise today; *see, e.g.*, United States v. Said, 798 F.3d 182, 189 (4th Cir. 2015) (interpreting federal piracy statute to conform to modern international law rather than 1820 Supreme Court decision).

198 U.S. CONST. art. II, § 3 (stating that the President "shall take Care that the Laws be faithfully executed"); *see* ALEXANDER HAMILTON, LETTERS OF PACIFICUS, No. 1 (1793), *reprinted in* 15 THE PAPERS OF ALEXANDER HAMILTON 33, 40 (Harold C. Syrett ed., 1969) ("The Executive is charged with the execution of all laws, the laws of Nations as well as the Municipal law, which recognises and adopts those laws."); *id.* at 43 ("the President is the constitutional Executor of the laws. Our Treaties and the laws of Nations form a part of the law of the land."); JAMES MADISON, LETTERS OF HELVIDIUS, No. 2 (1793), *reprinted in* 15

the Supreme Court held in *Brown v. United States* that the executive could not even exercise the United States' right under the law of nations to condemn enemy property without express authorization from Congress.[199] When Chief Justice Marshall wrote that the law of nations "is a guide which the sovereign follows or abandons at his will"[200]—the remark upon which Chief Justice Fuller relied so heavily in his *Paquete Habana* dissent—Marshall simply meant that confiscation was not automatic and that Congress could chose to exercise its right under the law of nations or not. In dissent, Justice Story argued that the executive could condemn enemy property without express authorization from Congress but was even more explicit that the President could not violate international law: "he cannot lawfully transcend the rules of warfare established among civilized nations[.] He cannot lawfully exercise powers or authorize proceedings which the civilized world repudiates and disclaims."[201]

Certainly, Justice Gray could have given a much stronger rebuttal to Chief Justice Fuller's reliance on *Brown*. Gray seems to have misread *Brown* as saying that the property at issue in that case could not be captured under the law of nations.[202] He therefore did not take Fuller to task for misquoting Marshall by implying discretion to violate customary international law from passages concerned solely with discretion to enforce rights under that law. Nor did he make the point that if it is for Congress rather than the President to make rules concerning the capture of enemy property consistent with the law of nations, then *a fortiori* it is for Congress to authorize any captures that would violate that law.

The nineteenth-century rise of positivism required more deference to legislative decisions to violate international law, as reflected in the later-in-time rule, but it did not require more deference to the executive acting alone. Although the Supreme Court held in *The Prize Cases* that President Lincoln's declaration of a blockade during the Civil War was

---

THE PAPERS OF JAMES MADISON 86 (Thomas A. Mason et al. eds., 1985) (referring to Hamilton's point about the law of nations as a "truth").

199 12 U.S. (8 Cranch) 110, 129 (1814) ("It appears to the Court, that the power of confiscating enemy property is in the legislature, and that the legislature has not yet declared its will to confiscate property which was within our territory at the declaration of war.").

200 *Id.* at 128. The word "his" is easily explained. Marshall was speaking of sovereigns in general, and apart from a few republics like the United States, most sovereigns were indeed individual men.

201 *Id.* at 153 (Story, J., dissenting). In *The Schooner Exchange v. McFadden*, decided two years earlier, Chief Justice Marshall found a usage of nations exempting foreign warships from the jurisdiction of national courts, but added that "[w]ithout doubt, the sovereign of the place is capable of destroying this implication." 11 U.S. (7 Cranch) 116, 146 (1812). As in *Brown*, Marshall would have understood "the sovereign" to be Congress and the President acting together rather than the President acting alone.

202 *See* The Paquete Habana, 175 U.S. 677, 711 (1900) (referring to *Brown*'s "decision that enemy property on land, which by the modern usage of nations is not subject to capture as prize of war, cannot be condemned by a prize court"). *Cf. Brown*, 12 U.S. (8 Cranch) at 122 ("That war gives to the sovereign full right to take the persons and confiscate the property of the enemy wherever found, is conceded.").

"conclusive evidence" of a state of war authorizing such a blockade,[203] the Court never suggested that the executive could violate customary international law, which it continued to ascertain and apply in case after case.[204] As Professor White has shown, the late-nineteenth-century orthodoxy assumed that authority over foreign affairs was fixed by the text of the Constitution.[205] At a time when even the notion that Congress could delegate some of its textual authority over international trade to the President was controversial,[206] arguing for extra-constitutional authority in the President to supersede international law would have been difficult. As we have seen, the briefs for the United States made no such argument, asserting only that international law did not require an exemption for fishing boats (or at least not these fishing boats).[207] Chief Justice Fuller's contention that the executive was not bound by international law in the conduct of war was based upon a plain misreading of *Brown*[208] and gathered just three votes. It was not until the early decades of the twentieth century that the Supreme Court would begin its expansive interpretation of executive power in foreign affairs, culminating in its *Curtiss-Wright* decision.[209] Against this background, it seems implausible that Justice Gray meant to suggest in *The Paquete Habana* that the President acting alone could violate international law.

What Gray appears to have been doing instead was emphasizing that, in this particular case, "no act of Congress or order of the President has expressly authorized [the vessels] to be taken and confiscated."[210] Indeed, he went on to say that "[t]he position taken by the United States during the recent war with Spain was quite in accord with the rule of international law, now generally recognized by civilized nations, in

---

[203] 67 U.S. (2 Black) 635, 670 (1862). The Court reasoned that the Civil War was a special case not requiring a congressional declaration of war, noting that "[a] civil war is never solemnly declared," *id.* at 666, and that the Constitution did not give Congress the power to declare war against a state. *Id.* at 668.

[204] *See, e.g.*, *id.* at 666 ("The right of prize and capture . . . is governed and adjudged under the law of nations."); The Springbok, 72 U.S. (5 Wall.) 1, 21 (1866) (noting that London and Nassau were "both neutral ports within the definitions of neutrality furnished by the international law"); The Peterhoff, 72 U.S. (5 Wall.) 28, 56 (1866) (applying rules of international law on free trade of neutrals with belligerents).

[205] *See* G. Edward White, *The Transformation of the Constitutional Regime of Foreign Relations*, 85 VA. L. REV. 1, 8 (1999).

[206] *See id.* at 15–18 (discussing Field v. Clark, 143 U.S. 649 (1892)).

[207] *See supra* notes 45–51 and accompanying text.

[208] *See supra* notes 86–90 and accompanying text.

[209] United States v. Curtiss-Wright Export Corp., 299 U.S. 304, 320 (1936) (describing the President "as the sole organ of the federal government in the field of international relations"). *See generally* White, *supra* note 205. More recently, the Supreme Court has declined to read *Curtiss-Wright* as accepting "unbounded" executive power over foreign affairs. Zivotofsky v. Kerry, 576 U.S. 1, 20 (2015); *see also id.* at 66 (Roberts, C.J., dissenting) ("[O]ur precedents have never accepted such a sweeping understanding of executive power.").

[210] The Paquete Habana, 175 U.S. 677, 711 (1900); *see also id.* at 700 ("where there is no treaty, and no controlling executive or legislative act or judicial decision"); *id.* at 708 ("in the absence of any treaty or other public act of their own government").

regard to coast fishing vessels."[211] But by emphasizing that no executive act superseded customary international law in this case, Gray opened the door to the argument that an executive act might do so in another. He thus gave *The Paquete Habana* its Achilles heel.

III. THE IMMEDIATE IMPACT OF *THE PAQUETE HABANA*

On remand, the cases of the *Paquete Habana*, the *Lola*, and ten other boats were referred to a commissioner for an assessment of damages. For the *Paquete Habana*, he awarded $4500 and the highest price for the fish in Havana during the blockade, plus interest at eight percent,[212] which the District Court ordered the United States to pay.[213] The United States appealed, arguing that the captors should have to pay and that the damages were excessive. Justice Gray had resigned in 1902, and the opinion was assigned to his successor Justice Holmes. Holmes held that a decree against the United States was proper because "it has so far adopted the acts of capture that it would be hard to say that under the circumstances of these cases it has not made those acts its own."[214] But he also found the damages excessive and unsupported by the evidence.[215] The case was remanded once again to the District Court, and there is no record of the ultimate amounts paid.[216]

Other nations quickly accepted the rule that coastal fishing vessels are exempt from capture under international law.[217] In 1907, the Second Hague Conference adopted the exemption in Article 3 of Hague Convention XI.[218] In 1914, without deciding whether this Convention applied, British courts abandoned their traditional position and concluded that the exemption had "become a sufficiently settled doctrine in the law of nations."[219] Of Justice Gray's opinion, the British court wrote: "It is full of research, learning, and historical interest. As such an elaborate and complete résumé is available in that judgment, it would be a work of supererogation . . . to attempt to perform a similar task."[220] However, the rule protecting coastal fishing vessels soon became

---

211 *Id.* at 712.

212 The Paquete Habana, 189 U.S. 453, 467 (1903).

213 *Id.* at 464.

214 *Id.*

215 *Id.* at 466–67.

216 *See* Stucky, *supra* note 19, at 35 n.210.

217 *See id.* at 36–44.

218 *See* Hague Convention XI: Convention Relative to Certain Restrictions with Regard to the Exercise of the Right to Capture in Naval Warfare, art. 3, Oct. 18, 1907, 36 Stat. 2936, 1 Bevans 711. ("Vessels used exclusively for fishing along the coast or small boats employed in local trade are exempt from capture, as well as their appliances, rigging, tackle, and cargo. They cease to be exempt as soon as they take any part whatever in hostilities.").

219 The Berlin (1914) 2 Lloyd's Prize Cases 43, 67.

220 *Id.* at 63–64.

irrelevant as mines and submarines made coastal blockades of enemy ports too dangerous.[221]

The more general significance of *The Paquete Habana* for international law in the United States was quickly realized. James Brown Scott, editor of the newly founded *American Journal of International Law*, called it a "remarkable opinion," which settled the propositions "that international law is law; that it is part of our municipal law; that our courts take judicial notice of it as such."[222] He also praised the opinion for sketching the sources of international law "with a masterly hand."[223] John Bassett Moore held the case up as the "clearest and most precise application" of the principle that international law evolves through "the general and gradual transformation of international opinion and practice."[224] These writers made no mention of *The Paquete Habana*'s dictum concerning "controlling executive . . . acts," which lay dormant for more than eighty years.

IV. THE IMPORTANCE OF *THE PAQUETE HABANA* TODAY

Those eighty years were not kind to the people of Cuba. A series of elected leaders soon gave way to the dictatorships of Gerardo Machado and Fulgencia Batista. In 1959, communist forces led by Fidel Castro forced Batista from power. By the end of 1962, more than 250,000 Cubans had fled the communist regime, many settling in Miami, Florida.[225]

In 1980, Castro declared the port of Mariel open, and more than 100,000 Cubans headed to the United States in what became known as the Mariel Boatlift.[226] Some Mariel Cubans with criminal records were held by the United States. Others, without criminal records, were initially paroled into the United States but then had their paroles revoked and were incarcerated. A district court found that the prolonged arbitrary detention of this second group violated international law but that the Attorney General's decision to hold them constituted a "controlling executive act."[227] In *Garcia-Mir v. Meese*, the Eleventh Circuit

---

[221] Stucky, *supra* note 19, at 41.

[222] James Brown Scott, *The Legal Nature of International Law*, 1 AM. J. INT'L L. 831, 859–60 (1907).

[223] *Id.* at 859.

[224] John Bassett Moore, *International Law: Its Present and Future*, 1 AM. J. INT'L L. 11, 11 (1907). The author of *A Digest of International Law* (8 vols. 1906), Moore had rejoined the State Department from Columbia Law School during the war with Spain, serving as First Assistant Secretary of State and then as secretary to the Paris Peace Commission. GOULD, *supra* note 12, at 60, 99.

[225] FERRER, *supra* note 11, at 401.

[226] *Id.* at 411–19.

[227] Fernandez-Roque v. Smith, 622 F. Supp. 887, 903 (N.D. Ga. 1985).

affirmed,[228] arousing a storm of controversy over whether the executive acting alone may supersede customary international law.[229]

Twenty years later, the Bush administration invoked Justice Gray's dictum to argue that detainees in the "war on terror" held at Guantánamo Bay, Cuba were not entitled to the protections of customary international law. A memorandum from the Department of Justice's Office of Legal Counsel stated that "under clear Supreme Court precedent, any presidential decision in the current conflict concerning the detention and trial of al Qaeda or Taliban militia prisoners would constitute a 'controlling' Executive act that would immediately and completely override any customary international law norms."[230]

Putting *The Paquete Habana*'s controversial dictum to one side, its other teachings remain important. In *Sosa v. Alvarez-Machain*,[231] the Supreme Court recognized an implied cause of action under the Alien Tort Statute (ATS)[232] for violations of modern human-rights norms.[233] The Court acknowledged that the law of nations violations that the First Congress had in mind in 1789 were limited to violations of safe-conducts, infringements of the rights of ambassadors, and piracy.[234] But, having earlier quoted *The Paquete Habana*'s line about usage "gradually ripening into a rule of international law,"[235] the Court refused to limit the ATS cause of action to those three offenses. Instead, the Court authorized claims "based on the present-day law of nations" so long as they "rest on a norm of international character accepted by the civilized world and defined with a specificity comparable to the features of the 18th-century paradigms we have recognized."[236]

The *Sosa* Court also looked to *The Paquete Habana* for guidance on how to determine modern customary international law, quoting in full its

---

[228] 788 F.2d 1446, 1453–55 (11th Cir.), *cert. denied*, 479 U.S. 889 (1986). In *Gisbert v. U.S. Attorney General*, 988 F.2d 1437, 1447–48 (5th Cir. 1993), the Fifth Circuit followed *Garcia-Mir*, but with the important difference that the Fifth Circuit found the indefinite detention authorized by statute. *See id.* at 1446.

[229] *See generally Agora: May the President Violate Customary Law?*, 80 AM. J. INT'L L. 913 (1986); *Agora: May the President Violate Customary Law? (Cont'd)*, 81 AM. J. INT'L L. 371 (1987).

[230] Memorandum for Alberto R. Gonzales, Counsel to the President, and William J. Haynes II, General Counsel of the Department of Defense, from Jay S. Bybee, Assistant Attorney General at 35 (Jan. 22, 2002), *available at* http://www.washingtonpost.com/wp-srv/nation/documents/012202bybee.pdf. In *In re Guantanamo Detainee Cases*, 355 F. Supp. 2d 443 (D.D.C. 2005), the district court found it unnecessary to reach the issue, having concluded that all the detainees had rights under the due process clause of the Fifth Amendment and that some might also have rights under the Geneva Conventions. *See id.* at 481.

[231] 542 U.S. 692 (2004).

[232] 28 U.S.C. § 1350 ("The district courts shall have original jurisdiction of any civil action by an alien for a tort only, committed in violation of the law of nations or a treaty of the United States.").

[233] *Sosa*, 542 U.S. at 725.

[234] *Id.* at 724.

[235] *Id.* at 715.

[236] *Id.* at 725.

passage about "the customs and usages of civilized nations" and "the works of jurists and commentators."[237] The Court considered the Universal Declaration of Human Rights, the International Covenant on Civil and Political Rights, the *Restatement (Third) of the Foreign Relations Law of the United States*, a scholarly survey of national constitutions, and a decision of the International Court of Justice before concluding that the plaintiff had not established a well-defined norm against detentions as brief as his.[238]

Most significantly, the *Sosa* Court relied on *The Paquete Habana* for the proposition that international law is part of our law.[239] Justice Scalia objected that when the ATS was passed in 1789 the law of nations was part of general common law[240] and that *Erie Railroad Co. v. Tompkins*[241] ended the federal courts' role in ascertaining and applying such law.[242] "[T]he creation of post-*Erie* federal common law," he wrote, "is so far removed from that general-common-law adjudication which applied the 'law of nations' that it would be anachronistic to find authorization to do the former in a statutory grant of jurisdiction that was thought to enable the latter."[243] But as in *The Paquete Habana*, the Court chose continuity over change. Quoting Justice Gray's opinion, along with earlier and later decisions, the majority noted that "[f]or two centuries we have affirmed that the domestic law of the United States recognized the law of nations."[244] When Congress passed the ATS, it expected federal courts to identify and enforce the law of nations, the Court continued, and "it would be unreasonable to assume that the First Congress would have expected federal courts to lose all capacity to recognize enforceable international norms simply because the common law might lose some metaphysical cachet on the road to modern realism."[245]

In the two decades since *Sosa* was decided, the Supreme Court has whittled down the ATS cause of action. The Court has applied the presumption against extraterritoriality to the cause of action,[246] held that foreign corporations may not be sued,[247] and insisted on substantial conduct in the United States when domestic corporations are the defendants.[248] But in none of these cases has the Court questioned the

---

237 *Id.* at 734 (quoting The Paquete Habana, 175 U.S. 677, 700 (1900)).

238 *Id.* at 734–38 & n.27.

239 *Id.* at 730 (quoting *The Paquete Habana*, 175 U.S. at 700).

240 *Id.* at 739 (Scalia, J., concurring).

241 304 U.S. 64 (1938).

242 *Sosa*, 542 U.S. at 746 (Scalia, J., concurring).

243 *Id.* at 745.

244 *Id.* at 729–30.

245 *Id.* at 730.

246 Kiobel v. Royal Dutch Petroleum Co., 569 U.S. 108 (2013).

247 Jesner v. Arab Bank, PLC, 584 U.S. 241 (2018).

248 Nestlé USA, Inc. v. Doe, 593 U.S. 628 (2021).

basic principles laid down in *The Paquete Habana*,[249] and lower courts continue to cite them in deciding human rights cases under the ATS.[250]

Since the founding of the United States, international law and our understanding of its place in the U.S. domestic legal system have both changed significantly. As one survey concluded, "there are few aspects of the Supreme Court's international law doctrine that remain the same as they were 200 years ago."[251] In *The Paquete Habana*, Justice Gray skillfully navigated the changing seas of nineteenth-century international law, holding to certain fixed stars by adapting old principles to international law's new positivism. Since then, international law has continued to change. Old topics such as prize law have sunk from view, while new ones such as human rights have arisen. Meanwhile, *Erie*'s reconceptualization of common law ripped up one of the maps that previously guided the incorporation of customary international law into the U.S. legal system. If, in the twenty-first century, the Supreme Court is to hold to those same fixed stars, skillful steering is still required.

---

249 The only mention of *The Paquete Habana* in these three opinions is found in Justice Gorsuch's *Jesner* concurrence, which acknowledges that international law is "part of our law" but suggests that this means it is part of general common law rather than federal common law. *Jesner*, 584 U.S. at 287 (Gorsuch, J., concurring in part) (quoting The Paquete Habana, 175 U.S. 677, 700 (1900)).

250 *See, e.g.*, Doe I v. Cisco Sys., Inc., 73 F.4th 700, 717 (9th Cir. 2023); Aziz v. Alcolac, Inc., 658 F.3d 388, 399 (4th Cir. 2011); Flomo v. Firestone Nat. Rubber Co., LLC, 643 F.3d 1013, 1015 (7th Cir. 2011); Abdullahi v. Pfizer, Inc., 562 F.3d 163, 174 (2d Cir. 2009); Aldana v. Del Monte Fresh Produce, N.A., Inc., 452 F.3d 1284, 1285 (11th Cir. 2006).

251 David L. Sloss, Michael D. Ramsey & William S. Dodge, *Conclusion: Continuity and Change over Two Centuries*, *in* INTERNATIONAL LAW IN THE U.S. SUPREME COURT, *supra* note 3, at 589.

12

Mark Weston Janis

Missouri v. Holland: Birds, Wars, and Rights

A 1920 judgment of Oliver Wendell Holmes, Jr., *Missouri v. Holland*,[1] one of the most important decisions related to international relations rendered by the U.S. Supreme Court, is wonderfully short. On its facts, the case is about migratory birds, but *Missouri v. Holland* is really much more than that. Justice Holmes's opinion goes to centuries-old questions about the respective international roles of the central government and the states, questions of federalism posed anew for every American generation. America's peculiar (dare we call it "exceptional"?) constitutional system builds in so many conflicts between the sovereign powers of Washington and those of the now-fifty state governments as to perennially raise the question: Is the United States fundamentally *united* or are we at root really merely a collection of *states*? This omnipresent federalist tension impacts on America's complicated constitutional endeavor to deal with the rest of the world, leads to difficulties with international law, and exasperates foreign governments.

As the archetypical case respecting America's federalist engagement with international law, *Missouri v. Holland* has been much and ably discussed. This short essay cannot replace or record the many accounts of Holmes's opinion. What it can do is, first, explain the immediate context of the case, showing how *Missouri v. Holland* arose at a time when the hunting of migratory birds was politically controversial. Second, it can explore the historical and legal setting of the case, putting it into more than a century of the American experience in grappling with national/state relations—relations that were at their worst in the Civil War, a conflict that did not spare Oliver Wendell Holmes, Jr. Third, it can tell some of the story of the case's evolution, relating how the subsequent decades saw *Missouri v. Holland* become a battlefield in other political struggles, notably about human rights.

I. BIRDS

To begin with the case's immediate context, by the 1880s, Americans, becoming ever more environmentally conscious, were increasingly

1 252 U.S. 416 (1920).

concerned about the slaughter of migratory birds, even, as with passenger pigeons, resulting in the total extinction of a species. The hunting problem was exacerbated both by technological developments in weaponry and by economic demand for slaughtered birds, not only for food but for fashion, especially for plumes on ladies' hats. Bird watchers, farmers who relied on birds to destroy pests, and sport hunters all joined forces in new conservationist organizations, notably the Audubon Society, founded in 1886, to battle against those they called "market hunters" and "game hogs," who were responsible for destroying migratory birds in large numbers.[2] The problem was aptly and proudly personified by a "game hog" in *Twenty Year Snipe Shooting, 1867–1887*: "The birds (snipes) were such migrants [in Louisiana] and only in the country for a short time, I had no mercy on them, and killed all I could."[3]

The first regulatory success of the conservationists was in sponsoring state legislation making trade in hunted birds difficult or illegal. Their triumph at the state level was sealed in 1896, in *Geer v. Connecticut*,[4] in which the U.S. Supreme Court upheld a Connecticut statute prohibiting the export of protected game birds out of state.[5] Ironically, *Geer* would soon become a stumbling block for the conservationists. Justice White's opinion holding that, under the U.S. Constitution, Connecticut had sovereign police power over migratory birds only temporarily in the state would come to threaten the constitutionality of any exclusive federal regulation of the same birds.

Realizing that, because migratory game birds were so transitory, patch-work state protection might not be enough, the conservationists decided to promote protective legislation on a national basis. This came first in 1900 with the Lacey Act,[6] which provided for the labeling of packages with birds or bird parts to indicate their contents and origin, and then in 1904 with the never-enacted Shiras bill, which aimed to provide for full federal regulation of the hunting of migratory birds. Finally, in 1913, the Weeks-McLean Act was passed, a statute that asserted a federal right to subject the killing of migratory birds to exclusive national control.[7] Thirty-two conservationist organizations supported Weeks-McLean in testimony before the Senate and House Agricultural Committees.[8]

---

2 KURKPATRICK DORSEY, THE DAWN OF CONSERVATION DIPLOMACY: U.S.-CANADIAN WILDLIFE PROTECTION TREATIES IN THE PROGRESSIVE ERA 167–91 (1998).

3 *Quoted in* JOHN C. PHILLIPS, MIGRATORY BIRD PROTECTION IN NORTH AMERICA 5–6 (1934).

4 161 U.S. 519 (1896).

5 DORSEY, *supra* note 2, at 177–78.

6 16 U.S.C. §§ 3371 *et seq.*

7 DORSEY, *supra* note 2, at 178–91. Weeks-McLean, known as the "migratory birds provision," was part of the March 4, 1913, Appropriations Act for the Department of Agriculture, Pub. L. No. 63–145, 37 Stat. 828, 847 (1913).

8 DORSEY, *supra* note 2, at 9.

Even among its advocates, there was doubt whether Weeks-McLean could be sustained as it stood. It appeared that the Act might be successfully challenged as an unconstitutional federal incursion upon state sovereignty. Elihu Root, Secretary of War for Presidents William McKinley and Theodore Roosevelt and later Secretary of State for Roosevelt, a prominent international lawyer and the founder and first President of the American Society of International Law, was then a U.S. Senator from New York. Root was, apparently, the first to suggest that Weeks-McLean could be constitutionally bolstered if it were supported by a U.S. treaty. In January 1913, Root proposed a Senate resolution, ultimately not adopted, that "the President be requested to propose to the Governments of other North American countries the negotiation of a convention for the mutual protection and preservation of migratory birds." Such a treaty might have comforted President William Howard Taft, who was otherwise inclined to veto Weeks-McLean. However, a treaty at this stage proved unnecessary because, confusingly, Taft, seemingly inadvertently, signed measures including Weeks-McLean on his last but rushed day in office, March 4, 1913; he later insisted he had not done so.[9]

Fortunately for the conservationists, the incoming President, Woodrow Wilson, was far keener to protect migratory birds than was Taft. Worried that Weeks-McLean might be declared unconstitutional in the courts, Wilson's administration, as early as April 1913, began exploring the possibility of negotiating international migratory bird agreements with Mexico and Canada. Meanwhile, states-rights opponents of Weeks-McLean began to launch legal challenges to the Act's constitutionality.[10]

No treaty yet in hand, conservationists were forced to defend Weeks-McLean as it stood. They immediately launched a publicity campaign to support the Act's constitutionality. In November 1913, the counsel to the American Game Protective Association, Walter S. Haskill, speaking to the American Ornithologists' Union, reported that he had "discussed the subject with several United States Supreme Court Judges, who said the courts would support it. I do not want to prophesy what will happen if we go to the Supreme Court. We do not wish litigation, but I think we shall be sustained if we are attacked."[11]

In March 1914, another conservationist, William Hornaday, blasted those challenging Weeks-McLean:

> The gamehogs of America now are forming permanent organizations, and establishing campaign funds and monthly publications, for the purpose of recovering and protecting their slaughtering privileges!

---

[9] *Id.* at 187–88; PHILLIPS, *supra* note 3, at 11–13.

[10] DORSEY, *supra* note 2, at 192–201.

[11] *Quoted in Defends Federal Bird Law*, N.Y. TIMES, Nov. 14, 1913, at 8.

> In the early days of the fight, the opposition was largely individual and therefore routed without great difficulty. But the time came when the lawless ones, the gamehogs and the commercial interests, began to band together, raise big sums of money and hire lawyers and lobbyists to defeat the protectionists, who were really getting big results in the saving of wild life. The market gunners, the game dealers, the hotel and restaurant men, the millinery importers and the makers of automatic and pump shotguns now know that to preserve their killing privileges, they must contribute money. To them it is business, and they subscribe as business men do subscribe when their projects are threatened.[12]

However, Weeks-McLean was soon struck down by lower courts as unconstitutional. In 1914, in *United States v. Shauver*,[13] an Arkansas defendant successfully objected to his indictment for hunting in violation of Weeks-McLean. U.S. District Judge Trieber held, *inter alia* relying on *Geer*, that "animals ferae naturae, denominated as game, are owned by the states, not as proprietors, but in their sovereign capacity as the representatives and for the benefit of all their people in common."[14] If it were useful for Congress to regulate migratory birds, the judge suggested, "[i]t is the people who alone can amend the Constitution," and it was "the duty of the court . . . to declare the act void."[15] Similarly, in 1915, in *United States v. McCullagh*, U.S. District Judge Pollock held for a defendant in Kansas: "the title and exclusive power of control over wild game coming within the borders of a state of this country resides in the state and not in the nation."[16]

Conservationists were persuaded that they did not want *Shauver* or *McCullagh* to reach the U.S. Supreme Court before a treaty could be agreed. Along with Elihu Root, they came to believe that an international agreement was the best way to ensure the constitutionality of federal regulation. Negotiations with Canada prospered and, on August 29, 1916, the Senate approved the nation's first migratory birds treaty, which President Wilson soon ratified.[17] The *New York Times* reported: "The chief purpose of both the treaty and the regulations is to save from extinction the migratory game birds, whose number has been reduced by more than one-half in the last forty years, and to protect those birds which help the farmer by eating the insects that prey upon his crops."[18] An

---

12 William T. Hornaday, *The Seamy Side of the Protection of Wild Game*, N.Y. TIMES, Mar. 8, 1914, at 51.

13 214 F. 154 (E.D. Ark. 1914).

14 *Id.* at 157.

15 *Id.* at 160.

16 221 F. 288, 294 (D. Kan. 1915).

17 Convention for the Protection of Migratory Birds, U.S.-U.K., *signed* Aug. 16, 1916, 39 Stat. 1702 (1916). *See* DORSEY, *supra* note 2, at 200–01; PHILLIPS, *supra* note 3, at 13–20.

18 *Saving the Birds*, N.Y. TIMES, Sept. 2, 1916, at 6.

Enabling Act to implement the treaty was passed by Congress and, on July 3, 1918, approved by President Wilson.[19] The new law limited the national hunting season to no more than three-and-a-half months and strove to equalize hunting opportunities among the several states.[20]

Now it was time to test the constitutionality of federal regulation of migratory birds *with* a treaty back-up. Enter *Missouri v. Holland.* On July 2, 1919, U.S. District Judge Van Valkenburgh decided the case at the trial court level.[21] George L. Samples and W.C. Lapp were accused by Holland, a federal game warden, of hunting and killing migratory birds in Missouri in violation of the new Treaty Enabling Act. Samples and Lapp were joined by the state of Missouri in challenging the charges on the ground that the Act was an unconstitutional federal infringement of the sovereign powers of the states. Judge Van Valkenburgh, following, *inter alia, Geer, Shauver,* and *McCullogh,* held that "in the absence of treaty there appears to have been no delegation of paramount authority to the federal government."[22] Hence, "this act, in the absence of [a] treaty, would be unconstitutional, as exceeding the legitimate powers of Congress."[23] Crucially, Judge Van Valkenburgh ruled that the existence of the U.S.-Canadian migratory birds treaty transformed the constitutional situation: "That the power to make treaties is a substantial power of highest degree, delegated by the states to the federal government by the terms of the Constitution, is beyond controversy."[24] As an exclusive federal power, the validity of the Act solely "depends upon whether this treaty was a valid exercise of federal authority as delegated by the Constitution."[25] A treaty, so long as it does not contradict the Constitution, is valid if it "is a compact made between two or more nations, entered into for the common advancement of their interests and the interests of civilization."[26] Since the United States and Canada both were to benefit by the protection of migratory birds, "the subject-matter comes properly within the treaty making power."[27] The demurrers to the indictments were overruled. The Treaty Enabling Act, in the opinion of Judge Van Valkenburgh, was constitutional.[28]

Nine months later, on April 19, 1920, Associate Justice Oliver Wendell Holmes, Jr., delivered the judgment of the Supreme Court in

---

19 Migratory Bird Treaty Act, Pub. L. No. 65–786, 49 Stat. 755 (1916) (codified as amended at 16 U.S.C. §§ 703–712). *See* PHILLIPS, *supra* note 3, at 20.

20 *Win Fight to Save Birds: House Passes Treaty Enabling Act for Protection of Migratory Game*, N.Y. TIMES, June 7, 1918, at 13.

21 258 F. 479 (W.D. Mo. 1919).

22 *Id.* at 481.

23 *Id.*

24 *Id.*

25 *Id.* at 482.

26 *Id.*

27 *Id.* at 484.

28 *Id.* at 485.

Missouri v. Holland.[29] Holmes's opinion is only five pages long. After about a page devoted to the background of the case, Holmes posed the key issue: "the question raised is the general one whether the treaty and statute are void as an interference with the rights reserved to the states."[30] Holmes began his answer by setting out the constitutional framework:

> To answer this question it is not enough to refer to the Tenth Amendment, reserving the powers not delegated to the United States, because by Article II, § 2, the power to make treaties is delegated expressly, and by Article VI treaties made under the authority of the United States, along with the Constitution and laws of the United States made in pursuance thereof, are declared the supreme law of the land. If the treaty is valid there can be no dispute about the validity of the statute under Article 1, § 8, as a necessary and proper means to execute the powers of the Government. The language of the Constitution as to the supremacy of treaties being general, the question before us is narrowed to an inquiry into the ground upon which the present supposed exception is placed.[31]

Then came the most controversial part of Holmes's opinion. Holmes distinguished *Shauver* and *McCullagh* because neither faced legislation grounded on the treaty power. This new foundation, of course, was just the remedy proposed by Elihu Root. Moreover, it was the important new piece of the puzzle identified by Judge Van Valkenburgh in the trial court. Here is Holmes's version of the distinction:

> It is said that a treaty cannot be valid if it infringes the Constitution, that there are limits, therefore, to the treaty-making power, and that one such limit is that what an act of Congress could not do unaided, in derogation of the powers reserved to the States, a treaty cannot do. An earlier act of Congress that attempted by itself and not in pursuance of a treaty to regulate the killing of migratory birds within the States had been held bad in the District Court. *United States* v. *Shauver*, 214 Fed. 154, *United States* v. *McCullagh*, 221 Fed. 288. Those decisions were supported by arguments that migratory birds were owned by the States in their sovereign capacity for the benefit of their people, and that under cases like *Geer* v. *Connecticut*, 161 U.S. 519, this control was one that Congress had no power to displace. The same argument is supposed to apply now with equal force.
>
> Whether the two cases cited were decided rightly or not they cannot be accepted as a test of the treaty power. Acts of

---

29 252 U.S. 416 (1920).

30 *Id.* at 432.

31 *Id.*

> Congress are the supreme law of the land only when made in pursuance of the Constitution, while treaties are declared to be so when made under the authority of the United States. It is open to question whether the authority of the United States means more than the formal acts prescribed to make the convention. We do not mean to imply that there are no qualifications to the treaty-making power; but they must be ascertained in a different way. It is obvious that there may be matters of the sharpest exigency for the national well being that an act of Congress could not deal with but that a treaty followed by such an act could, and it is not lightly to be assumed that, in matters requiring national action, "a power which must belong to and somewhere reside in every civilized government" is not to be found. *Andrews* v. *Andrews*, 188 U.S. 14, 33. What was said in that case with regard to the powers of the States applies with equal force to the powers of the nation in cases where the States individually are incompetent to act. We are not yet discussing the particular case before us but only are considering the validity of the test proposed. With regard to that we may add that when we are dealing with words that also are a constituent act, like the Constitution of the United States, we must realize that they have called into life a being the development of which could not have been foreseen completely by the most gifted of its begetters. It was enough for them to realize or to hope that they had created an organism; it has taken a century and has cost their successors much sweat and blood to prove that they created a nation. The case before us must be considered in the light of our whole experience and not merely in that of what was said a hundred years ago. The treaty in question does not contravene any prohibitory words to be found in the Constitution. The only question is whether it is forbidden by some invisible radiation from the general terms of the Tenth Amendment. We must consider what this country has become in deciding what that Amendment has reserved.[32]

Note that Holmes, unlike Root and Van Valkenburgh, drew upon the history of the American experience, distinguishing the time of the Constitution's founders from his own, e.g., "it has taken a century and has cost their successors much sweat and blood to prove that they had created a nation."[33] Finally, Holmes turned to the facts at hand, the case of the migratory birds:

> The State as we have intimated founds its claim of exclusive authority upon an assertion of title to migratory birds, an assertion that is embodied in statute. No doubt it is true that as between a State and its inhabitants the State may regulate

[32] *Id.* at 432–34.

[33] *Id.* at 433.

the killing and sale of such birds, but it does not follow that its authority is exclusive of paramount powers. To put the claim of the State upon title is to lean upon a slender reed. Wild birds are not in the possession of anyone; and possession is the beginning of ownership. The whole foundation of the State's rights is the presence within their jurisdiction of birds that yesterday had not arrived, tomorrow may be in another State and in a week a thousand miles away.

. . . No doubt the great body of private relations usually fall within the control of the State, but a treaty may override its power. We do not have to invoke the later developments of constitutional law for this proposition; it was recognized as early as *Hopkirk* v. *Bell*, 3 Cranch 454, with regard to statutes of limitation, and even earlier, as to confiscation, in *Ware* v. *Hylton*, 3 Dall. 199. . . .

Here a national interest of very nearly the first magnitude is involved. It can be protected only by national action in concert with that of another power. The subject matter is only transitorily within the State and has no permanent habitat therein. But for the treaty and the statute there soon might be no birds for any powers to deal with. We see nothing in the Constitution that compels the Government to sit by while a food supply is cut off and the protectors of our forests and our crops are destroyed. It is not sufficient to rely upon the States. The reliance is vain, and were it otherwise, the question is whether the United States is forbidden to act. We are of opinion that the treaty and statute must be upheld.[34]

II. WARS

To understand *Missouri v. Holland*, it is not enough to comprehend the political controversies of 1880–1920 surrounding migratory birds. Holmes's opinion was set in a much deeper and disturbing political context. Throughout American independence there has always been disagreement, sometimes violent, about the balance of sovereign powers between the states and the national government. This disagreement was one of the root causes of the most awful American conflagration, the Civil War 1860–1865. Importantly, Mr. Justice Holmes had himself witnessed and suffered in the War between the States, as a Union Army officer fighting for the nation and against those Americans in the Confederacy who defended the cause of states' rights.

The territory of the thirteen rebellious American states had originally been colonized by Britain, Holland, France, Sweden, and Spain, but by 1775 all were, from New Hampshire in the north to Georgia in the south, British colonies. Some, like British-founded Virginia and

[34] *Id.* at 434–35.

Massachusetts and Dutch-founded New Netherlands (become New York), were already more than 150 years old. Each had its own social, political, and legal traditions. They had differing established or predominant religions: Church of England, Congregational, Roman Catholic, Quaker. Their chief uniting aspect was common opposition to British control and taxation. When Massachusetts first rebelled in 1775 at Lexington and Concord, the thirteen states met in Philadelphia more or less as an international assembly. Perhaps it was the decision to appoint a Virginian, George Washington, to lead what was at first a largely New England army that was the fateful decision moving this international collection of American states toward a unified American nation. That the thirteen states made any such move was, as is widely known, probably as much a matter of self-preservation as an attempt at nation-building. Benjamin Franklin famously said: "We must all hang together, or assuredly we will all hang separately."[35]

As Franklin and the other Founding Fathers put their lives on the line for their new United States of America, so Holmes and millions of young Americans ninety years later fought to preserve the national Union. About 340,000 died for the Union; another 134,000 perished vainly striving to establish the states-rights Confederacy.[36] Oliver Wendell Holmes, Jr., the son of the famous Cambridge poet and physician, Oliver Wendell Holmes, was twenty years old, an 1861 graduate of Harvard College, when on July 23, 1861, he joined the 20th Massachusetts Volunteer Regiment. The 20th Massachusetts, with men drawn from all over the state, was led not only by self-acknowledged "blue bloods" like Holmes, but by immigrants, German and Polish officers among others. Though the officers, at least, were more committed to the cause of the Union than to the abolition of slavery, Holmes was counted among the minority for whom the anti-slavery cause was also important.[37]

Between 1861 and 1865, the 20th Massachusetts fought at Ball's Bluff, Fair Oaks, Antietam, Fredericksburg, Chancellorsville, Gettysburg, and the Wilderness. Officers of the 20th Massachusetts were all personally known to Holmes. Many were friends, some relations. Those who died in action included William Putnam, Ferdinand Dreher, Charles Lowell, William Bartlett, Nathan Hayward, Charles Cabot, Paul Revere, Henry Ropes, Sumner Paine, and, perhaps most painful of all to Holmes, a close personal friend, Henry Abbott. Holmes himself was

---

[35] Benjamin Franklin, At the signing of the Declaration of Independence (July 4, 1776), *reprinted in* JOHN BARTLETT, FAMILIAR QUOTATIONS 348 (Emily Morison Beck et al. eds., 15th ed. 1980).

[36] The Civil War saw more than 600,000 Americans killed in battle or in theater, a total greater than those who died in all the other U.S. wars combined, including the Revolution, Mexican-American, Spanish-American, World War I and II, Vietnam, Iraq, and Afghanistan.

[37] MARK DEWOLFE HOWE, JUSTICE OLIVER WENDELL HOLMES: VOLUME 1: THE SHAPING YEARS 1841–1870, at 80–86 (1957); SILAS BENT, JUSTICE OLIVER WENDELL HOLMES: A BIOGRAPHY 73–124 (1932).

wounded three times. He was twice near death, once when shot in the chest at Ball's Bluff in October 1861, and again when shot in the neck at Antietam in September 1862.[38] After Henry Abbott was killed in the 1864 Wilderness campaign, Holmes wrote, "nearly every Regimental off[icer] I know or cared for is dead or wounded."[39] Is it too difficult to understand why Holmes fifty-six years later in *Missouri v. Holland* wrote: "It was enough for [the Founding Fathers] to realize or to hope that they had created an organism; it has taken a century and has cost their successors much sweat and blood to prove that they had created a nation"? So many had died to preserve a living Constitution.

III. RIGHTS

The modern controversies about *Missouri v. Holland* have had more to do with human rights and particularly with that central embarrassment of American exceptionalism, race relations, than with either conservation, the case's immediate context, or with war and peace, the case's historic setting. It is doubtful that this consequence was foreseen by Justice Holmes, although, in a way, it was fitting. Holmes's own military service was played out in America's Civil War, which was, as much as anything, about the future of American slavery, testing whether national abolitionists or states-rights slave owners would predominate. Although the nationalist cause won the Civil War in 1865, the states-rights movement was far from obliterated. States-rights assertions that discriminatory regimes, most reprehensible in the Southern states, could and should resist national equal rights legislation, continued to color American political and legal history for another century. *Missouri v. Holland* was perceived as a threat to states-rights segregationist advocates and thus became a battleground of its own.

In formal legal doctrine, *Missouri v. Holland* quickly became what it has remained ever since: the principal judicial precedent supporting the supremacy of national treaties against state laws. Immediately in 1920, Chandler Anderson in the *American Journal of International Law* noted that *Missouri v. Holland* showed "that the treaty-making power is a *national* rather than a *federal* power, and that this distinction measures the whole difference between its jurisdiction and the jurisdiction of Congress in relation to the so-called reserved powers."[40] In 1924, the Supreme Court in *Asakura v. City of Seattle*, following *Missouri v. Holland*, relied on a bilateral treaty with Japan to invalidate a discriminatory municipal ordinance depriving a Japanese immigrant, ineligible because of his race to become a U.S. citizen, of his pawn broker license.[41] In 1937, in *United States v. Belmont*, the public policy of New

---

[38] HOWE, *supra* note 37, at 80–175; G. EDWARD WHITE, JUSTICE OLIVER WENDELL HOLMES: LAW AND THE INNER SELF 49–86 (1993).

[39] *Quoted in* WHITE, *supra* note 38, at 79.

[40] Chandler P. Andersen, *The Extension of Congressional Jurisdiction by the Treaty-Making Power*, 14 AM. J. INT'L L. 400, 400 (1920) (emphasis in original).

[41] 265 U.S. 332, 341 (1924).

York state was held irrelevant respecting a treaty accepting the nationalization of private property in Russia:

> In respect of all international negotiations and compacts, and in respect of our foreign relations generally, state lines disappear. As to such purposes the State of New York does not exist. Within the field of its powers, whatever the United States rightfully undertakes, it necessarily has warrant to consummate. And when judicial authority is invoked in aid of such consummation, state constitutions, state laws, and state policies are irrelevant to the inquiry and decision. It is inconceivable that any of them can be interposed as an obstacle to the effective operation of a federal constitutional power. Cf. *Missouri v. Holland*, 252 U.S. 416; *Asakura v. Seattle*, 265 U.S. 332, 341.[42]

Since it confirmed the national treaty power, *Missouri v. Holland* was soon perceived as a possible means for increasing the power of the national government vis-à-vis the states. Sometimes this possibility was viewed favorably. In 1924, a note in the *Michigan Law Review* argued that since labor regulation had become a regular topic of international agreements, *Missouri v. Holland* now permitted national regulation of labor conditions that would be otherwise unconstitutional under then-existing U.S. constitutional law.[43]

However, others soon saw the nationalistic possibilities of *Missouri v. Holland* less favorably. That a law professor at the University of Kentucky viewed *Missouri v. Holland* in just such a different light, was illuminated by his article's title: *Missouri v. Holland—A Judicial Mile-Post on the Road to Absolutism*.[44] In Professor Forrest Revere Black's opinion, Justice Holmes's judgment "will give aid and comfort to the advocates of unlimited power."[45] Black saw a vigorous use of the treaty power by judges as suspiciously un-American: "the judge who will be the most proficient and the most admired will be the one who is most steeped in the practices of other governments, the one who has mastered the international precedents, whether their source be in absolute monarchy, soviet or republic."[46]

In 1934, the international lawyer, Pitman Potter, launched an equally heated rebuttal:

> International law is superior in authority to national constitutional law, and the latter may not validly contravene the former; the treaty-making power is possessed by the national state by virtue of international, not national, law. . . .

---

[42] 301 U.S. 324, 331–32 (1937).

[43] Note and Comment, *Labor Legislation Under the Treaty Power*, 22 MICH. L. REV. 457, 457–63 (1924).

[44] Forrest Revere Black, *Missouri v. Holland—A Judicial Mile-Post on the Road to Absolutism*, 25 ILL. L. REV. 911 (1931).

[45] *Id.* at 916.

[46] *Id.* at 921.

> It is also hardly to be expected that such a conclusion will be acceptable to the fanatically nationalistic confraternity of the constitutional lawyers or to extreme nationalists generally, but it is submitted that it is both theoretically sound and socially valuable from either an international or a national point of view.[47]

The nationalist/states-rights debate about *Missouri v. Holland* became even more vehement after the Second World War when new international human rights treaties began to emerge. The states-rights fear was that either national legislation would implement the new human rights treaties or that the human rights treaties would be deemed to be self-executing by the federal courts. In either case, the separate-but-equal doctrine that many of the states had implemented to preserve discriminatory racial practices after the abolition of slavery and the slave codes could be imperiled.

An important opponent of *Missouri v. Holland* at the time was Frank Holman, President of the American Bar Association, who, in 1949, wrote scathingly of what he termed "so-called human rights," a term "of recent usage and as yet without any adequate or accepted definition."[48] Holman attacked the human rights proposals of the Economic and Social Council of the United Nations, which had promulgated in 1947 "a so-called Declaration of Human Rights and a so-called Covenant on Human Rights,"[49] led by its Commission on Human Rights, which had drafted these documents. The Commission was chaired by Eleanor Roosevelt, whom Holman characterized as "not a person trained in legal draftsmanship, but primarily a social reformer."[50] The result was, he felt, "nebulous and ambiguous and the latter portion of which [the Covenant] sets up a collective concept of government for all the peoples of the world including ourselves."[51] Rather than adopting the American theory that rights are "personal and inalienable," the "whole International Bill of Rights program is predicated on the un-American theory that basic rights can be created by legislative action and that, along with basic rights, the social and economic well-being of our citizens may be defined, fixed, and limited by international declaration."[52]

---

47 Pitman B. Potter, *Inhibitions Upon the Treaty-Making Power of the United States*, 28 AM. J. INT'L L. 456, 473–74 (1934).

48 Frank E. Holman, *International Proposals Affecting So-Called Human Rights*, 14 LAW & CONTEMP. PROBS. 479, 479 (1949).

49 *Id.* (citing Universal Declaration of Human Rights, G.A. Res. 217A (III), U.N. Doc. A/810, at 71 (Dec. 10, 1948)). The "so-called Covenant on Human Rights" finally emerged in 1966 in the form of two treaties, the International Covenant on Civil and Political Rights, Dec. 16, 1966, 999 U.N.T.S. 171, and the International Covenant on Economic, Social and Cultural Rights, Dec. 16, 1966, 993 U.N.T.S. 3. It took another decade for these treaties to enter into force.

50 Holman, *supra* note 48, at 479.

51 *Id.* at 480.

52 *Id.* at 481.

Besides viewing the U.N. Human Rights Declaration as "an attempt to fasten on the peoples of the world, including ourselves, a collectivist theory of government,"[53] Holman saw the Human Rights Declaration as threatening to upset American racial segregation. He attacked the Declaration's Article 16, which provided that "men and women, without any limitation due to race, nationality or religion, shall have the right to marry and to found a family," because it meant that "mixed marriages between the races are allowable without regard to state or national law or policy forbidding such marriages."[54]

Similarly, Holman complained that another part of the U.N.'s human rights program, the Genocide Convention,[55] could require that "public officials as well as private citizens are to be made amenable to international tribunals for a variety of ill-defined and ambiguous acts of 'genocide'—to the extent that the causing of 'mental harm' to a member of a group or complicity in so doing is an act of 'genocide.' "[56] He gave as examples segregating "colored recruits to the National Guard," and suppressing race riots of "Negroes" in Detroit, Italians in New Orleans, and Japanese on the West Coast.[57] Turning from the threat that African-Americans, Italians, and Japanese posed to domestic tranquility, to the role of treaties in U.S. law, Holman noted that the United States, almost alone, made treaties self-executing: "Hence, if a covenant like the Genocide Convention is ratified as a treaty, it will supersede every city ordinance, every county ordinance, every state law, and every state constitution."[58]

The most celebrated attack on the national treaty powers of *Missouri v. Holland* came in 1953, in the proposed Bricker Amendment. Senator John Bricker of Ohio complained that "[i]n the treaty-making power, as interpreted in *Missouri v. Holland*, a way has been found to amend the Constitution by resorting to Article VI, a preference to the more difficult method laid down in Article V."[59]

Senator Bricker's proposed amendment read:

> Sec. 1. A provision of a treaty which conflicts with this Constitution shall not be of any force or effect.
>
> Sec. 2. A treaty shall become effective as internal law in the United States only through legislation which would be valid in the absence of a treaty.

---

[53] *Id.* at 482.

[54] *Id.* at 482–83.

[55] Convention on the Prevention and Punishment of the Crime of Genocide, Jan. 12, 1951, 78 U.N.T.S. 277.

[56] Holman, *supra* note 48, at 486–87.

[57] *Id.* at 487.

[58] *Id.*

[59] John W. Bricker, *Making Treaties and Other International Agreements,* 289 ANNALS AM. ACAD. POL. & SOC. SCI. 134, 136 (1953).

> Sec. 3. Congress shall have power to regulate all executive and other agreements with any foreign power or international organization. All such agreements shall be subject to the limitations imposed on treaties by this article.[60]

Approving the views of Holman and the American Bar Association, Senator Bricker condemned the Genocide Convention. He argued that the ABA's "analysis of the Genocide Convention disclosed a grave threat to freedom of speech and press and the rights of persons accused of crimes."[61] Section 2 of the Bricker Amendment, of course, would have repudiated the rule in *Missouri v. Holland*.[62] Rejecting the position of Eisenhower's Secretary of State, John Foster Dulles, that reversing *Missouri v. Holland* would create a "no man's land in foreign affairs," Senator Bricker wrote that "the United States got along very well for many years without benefit of the *Missouri v. Holland* doctrine."[63] Section 2 of the Bricker Amendment was needed, he felt, because the "supremacy clause of Article VI as interpreted in *Missouri v. Holland* empowers Congress, acting pursuant to a treaty to strip the states of their reserved powers under the Constitution."[64]

Joining Holman and Senator Bricker was Donald Richberg, who lamented that "[u]nhappily, in the year 1920 the Supreme Court apparently sanctioned almost unlimited exercises of the treaty power, in the famous opinion of Mr. Justice Holmes in *Missouri v. Holland*."[65] Again, the perceived danger was the human rights treaties:

> The advocates of various forms of world government, including the adoption of such international laws as are constantly proposed through the United Nations (such as the Human Rights Covenant and the Genocide Convention) find great comfort and support in the use of the treaty power as expanded in recent years by executive action and supported by decisions and opinions of the Supreme Court . . . .[66]

Richberg attacked what he called "the sarcastic inquiry in Mr. Justice Holmes' opinion as to whether a treaty may be 'forbidden by some invisible radiation from the general terms of the Tenth Amendment.' "[67] With even more sarcasm, Richberg wrote,

> With due deference to the normal wisdom and sanity of Mr. Justice Holmes' opinions, it may be suggested that there is nothing "invisible" in that express provision in the Constitution

---

[60] *Id.* at 136–37.

[61] *Id.* at 138.

[62] *Id.* at 139.

[63] *Id.*

[64] *Id.* at 140.

[65] Donald R. Richberg, *The Bricker Amendment and the Treaty Power*, 39 VA. L. REV. 753, 756 (1953).

[66] *Id.* at 760.

[67] *Id.* at 760–61 (quoting *Missouri v. Holland*, 252 U.S. 416, 434 (1920)).

> to the effect that the United States Government has no powers except those delegated to it by the Constitution and that all other powers of government remain in the states except so far as they have been denied even to the states by the people.[68]

Richberg concluded: "should the constitutional Government of the United States be preserved, or should the people of the United States by inaction consent to the gradual destruction of our form of government and the gradual but sure substitution of international lawmaking to govern the people of the United States?"[69]

However, the Bricker Amendment had formidable Republican opposition. Alongside Secretary of State Dulles stood Arthur Dean, a leading New York lawyer, partner of Sullivan and Cromwell, Dulles's old law firm, and an influential Republican. Dean, staying entirely clear of the racial overtones of Holman, Bricker, and Richberg, relied on the established legal doctrine of constitutional supremacy over any treaty:

> Probably the greatest force behind the [Bricker and related] amendment proposals in the past year or two has been the mistaken but widespread belief that treaties "conflicting" with the Constitution have overridden it, that the Supreme Court has allowed or is in serious danger of allowing the Constitution to—in effect—be amended by treaty instead of by the regular amending process. And yet, the possibility of such amendment by treaty has certainly never been admitted by the Supreme Court.[70]

Dean argued that the "whole history of our form of government is such that it is inconceivable that the Supreme Court would ever permit constitutional amendment by treaty."[71] Turning to *Missouri v. Holland*, he maintained that the Migratory Bird Act "certainly did not override or conflict with the Tenth Amendment."[72] Dean concluded that the tempest surrounding the case was unwarranted:

> Much of the press comment on the Bricker Amendment seemed to regard *Missouri v. Holland* as some strange and foreign devil suddenly loosed upon a contented country by a pack of scheming individuals. Clearly, it was no such thing; it was in the same current as a century and more of precedent; it was indeed in accord with the considered judgment of the legislative, executive, and judicial branches of government.[73]

---

[68] *Id.* at 761.

[69] *Id.* at 764.

[70] Arthur H. Dean, *Amending the Treaty Power*, 6 STAN. L. REV. 589, 594 (1954).

[71] *Id.*

[72] *Id.* at 599.

[73] *Id.* at 600.

The Eisenhower administration confirmed Dean's defense of *Missouri v. Holland* in a 1955 U.S. State Department circular:

> Treaties should be designed to promote United States interests by securing action by foreign governments in a way deemed advantageous to the United States. Treaties are not to be used as a device for the purpose of effecting internal social changes or try to circumvent the constitutional procedures in relation to what are essentially matters of domestic concern.[74]

It was the view of Professor Louis Henkin that "persuading President Eisenhower and Secretary of State Dulles to oppose the [Bricker] Amendment" and ultimately defeat it did more to protect the principle of *Missouri v. Holland* than it did to promote the case of human rights: "[T]he human rights movement paid a high price for that victory. To help defeat the amendment, the Eisenhower administration promised that the United States would not accede to international human rights covenants or conventions."[75]

Finally, the momentum for the Bricker Amendment was derailed by two essentially internal developments. First, and probably most important, was the increasing assertion of national domestic power to combat segregation and racism. This movement appeared not only in the judgments of the U.S. Supreme Court, most notably *Brown v. Board of Education*,[76] but in actions by the executive, e.g., President Eisenhower's decision to send the 101st Airborne to Little Rock, Arkansas, to enforce school desegregation,[77] and by Congress, e.g., the 1964 Civil Rights Voting Act.[78] The national domestic judicial, executive, and legislative challenges to segregation shifted the states-rights battle from international to national affairs. Second in importance was the 1957 decision of the Supreme Court in *Reid v. Covert*.[79] This too took much of the steam out of the states-rights challenge to the Supreme Court.

Reid v. Covert concerned overseas military trials of two American women accused of murdering their servicemen husbands. In the case of Mrs. Covert, there was "an executive agreement . . . in effect between the United States and Great Britain which permitted United States' military courts to exercise exclusive jurisdiction over offenses committed in Great

---

[74] U.S. DEP'T OF STATE, CIRCULAR NO. 175 (1955), *reprinted in* 50 AM. J. INT'L L. 784 (1956).

[75] Louis Henkin, *Comment: U.S. Ratification of Human Rights Conventions: The Ghost of Senator Bricker*, 89 AM. J. INT'L L. 341, 348–49 (1995).

[76] 347 U.S. 483 (1954).

[77] ROBERT FREDRICK BURK, THE EISENHOWER ADMINISTRATION AND BLACK CIVIL RIGHTS 174–203 (1984).

[78] Pub. L. No. 88–352, 78 Stat. 241 (1964) (codified as amended at scattered sections of 42 U.S.C.).

[79] 354 U.S. 1 (1957).

Britain by American servicemen or their dependents."[80] In the opinion by Justice Black, joined by four others, the Supreme Court held:

> Even though a court-martial does not give an accused trial by jury and other Bill of Rights protections, the Government contends that Art. 2(11) of the [Uniform Code of Military Justice], insofar as it provides for the military trial of dependents accompanying the armed forces in Great Britain and Japan, can be sustained as legislation which is necessary and proper to carry out the United States' obligations under the international agreements made with those countries. The obvious and decisive answer to this, of course, is that no agreement with a foreign nation can confer power on the Congress, or on any other branch of Government, which is free from the restraints of the Constitution.[81]

Affirming "the supremacy of the constitution over a treaty,"[82] the Court distinguished *Missouri v. Holland*:

> There is nothing in *Missouri v. Holland*, 252 U.S. 416, which is contrary to the position taken here. There the Court carefully noted that the treaty involved was not inconsistent with any specific provision of the Constitution. The Court was concerned with the Tenth Amendment which reserves to the states or the people all power not delegated to the National Government. To the extent that the United States can validly make treaties, the people and the States have delegated their power to the National Government and the Tenth Amendment is no barrier.[83]

Reid v. Covert, alongside the success of the civil rights movement, seemed to put the nationalist/states-rights controversy over the Bricker Amendment and *Missouri v. Holland* to rest for almost four decades. But the re-emergence of a stronger states-rights jurisprudence from the U.S. Supreme Court in the 1990's, notably in *New York v. United States*,[84] *United States v. Lopez*,[85] and *Boerne v. Flores*,[86] led some to suggest that, given the importance of modern treaty law, it might again be time to consider overturning *Missouri v. Holland*. Looking especially at the modern importance of treaty law, Professor Curtis Bradley argued in 1998:

> *Holland* also was decided at a time when customary international law, rather than treaties, was the dominant form

---

80 *Id.* at 15.

81 *Id.* at 16.

82 *Id.* at 17.

83 *Id.* at 18.

84 505 U.S. 144 (1992).

85 514 U.S. 549 (1995).

86 521 U.S. 507 (1997).

> of international law. Since then, however, there has been a proliferation of treaties, as well as the rise of numerous multilateral treaty regimes, such that treaties "have become the principal vehicle for making law for the international system." This shift from custom to code has meant that international law is now more specific and regulates a substantially wider range of subjects. As Professor Mark Janis has observed, "[v]irtually every human activity is to some degree the object of some treaty." These changes have thus substantially heightened the significance of the treaty power in this country.[87]

For Bradley, as for the states-rights advocates before him, especially of concern was "the area of international human rights law, which purports to regulate the relationship between nations and their own citizens."[88] He gave as examples the possible nationalist imposition of international standards on the states pertaining to religious toleration,[89] the rights of the child,[90] women's rights,[91] affirmative action,[92] the Genocide Convention,[93] and the death penalty.[94] Supporting "overruling some of the reasoning in *Holland*,"[95] Bradley wrote, "we must make a choice. As we continue with what is in essence an 'international New Deal,' we must decide whether federalism is worth preserving. If it is, the nationalist view of the treaty power should be reconsidered."[96]

This modern states-rights attack on *Missouri v. Holland* generated a strong nationalist defense of the case. Notably, Professor David Golove answered Professor Bradley and defended the historical and doctrinal foundations of *Missouri v. Holland*.[97] Revealingly, Professor Golove answered Professor Bradley's states-rights/nationalist "choice" in an opposite way:

> *Missouri*'s importance extends beyond the constitutional law of foreign affairs. As Justice Holmes recognized, the treaty power raises questions going to the root of our identity as a nation. Its ultimate triumph did not come easily but flowed out of the national identity successfully forged on the field of battle. The founders may have believed that "if we are to be one nation

87 Curtis A. Bradley, *The Treaty Power and American Federalism*, 97 MICH. L. REV. 390, 459–60 (1998) (quoting MARK WESTON JANIS, AN INTRODUCTION TO INTERNATIONAL LAW 13 (2d ed. 1993)).

88 *Id.* at 396.

89 *Id.* at 401.

90 *Id.* at 402.

91 *Id.* at 402–03.

92 *Id.* at 403.

93 *Id.* at 403–04.

94 *Id.* at 404–06.

95 *Id.* at 460.

96 *Id.* at 461.

97 David M. Golove, *Treaty-Making and the Nation: The Historical Foundations of the Nationalist Conception of the Treaty Power*, 98 MICH. L. REV. 1075 (2000).

> in any respect, it clearly ought to be in respect to other nations." It took a Civil War to make it so. That national identity is a remarkable achievement and one which ought to be carefully nurtured. At its core is a sense of unity in our relations with other nations. Frittering away that national unity can be accomplished only at the cost of once again raising the question why we are a nation at all.[98]

Indeed, it is just this choice between the states-rights and nationalist persuasions that is built in by the U.S. Constitution and that accounts for the seemingly eternal American debate about the issues symbolized by *Missouri v. Holland*. Significantly, a recent important Supreme Court decision about the foreign affairs powers can be taken to opt for the nationalist position. In *Crosby v. National Foreign Trade Council*, the Supreme Court reviewed the decisions of the district court judge and a unanimous court of appeals, which had held invalid a Massachusetts statute attempting to punish companies that did business with the repressive government of Burma.[99] A unanimous Supreme Court affirmed, striking down the Massachusetts Burma Law. In Mr. Justice Souter's words:

> Because the state Act's provisions conflict with Congress's specific delegation to the President of flexible discretion, with limitation of sanctions to a limited scope of actions and acts, and with direction to develop a comprehensive, multilateral strategy under the federal Act, it is preempted, and its application is unconstitutional, under the Supremacy Clause.[100]

In 2014, in *Bond v. United States*,[101] the Supreme Court faced "the most direct challenge since *Holland* to the congressional powers to legislate pursuant to treaty."[102] The Supreme Court resisted calls that *Missouri* be limited or overturned,[103] holding instead that the Chemical Weapons Convention[104] did not apply to a petty domestic dispute.[105]

---

[98] *Id.* at 1314–15 (quoting THE FEDERALIST NO. 42, at 264 (James Madison) (Clinton Rossiter ed., 1961)).

[99] 530 U.S. 363 (2000).

[100] *Id.* at 388.

[101] 572 U.S. 844 (2014).

[102] Margaret E. McGuinness, *Treaties, Federalism, and the Contested Legacy of* Missouri v. Holland, *in* SUPREME LAW OF THE LAND?: DEBATING THE CONTEMPORARY EFFECTS OF TREATIES WITHIN THE UNITED STATES LEGAL SYSTEM 179, 214 (Gregory H. Fox, Paul R. Dubinsky & Brad R. Roth eds., 2017).

[103] *Id.* at 213–21.

[104] Convention on the Prohibition of the Development, Production, Stockpiling and Use of Chemical Weapons and on their Destruction, *opened for signature* Jan. 13, 1993, S. TREATY DOC. NO. 103–21 (1993), 1974 U.N.T.S. 317.

[105] *See* Adam Liptak, *Chemical Weapons Treaty Does Not Apply to Petty Crime, Justices Rule*, N.Y. TIMES, June 3, 2014, at A13.

IV. CONCLUSION

It is doubtful that *Crosby* or *Bond* or any subsequent judgment of the Supreme Court will ever absolutely resolve the built-in constitutional conflict between the protection of the rights of the American states and those of the U.S. nation vis-à-vis the treaty power. Albeit *Missouri v. Holland* was a victory for the power of the national government to make international law free of the sovereign assertions of the fifty states, U.S. practice shows again and again that the politics of states' rights remains a powerful political force. As with the Eisenhower administration at the time of the Bricker Amendment, modern American Presidents, as well as the Senate and House of Representatives, are and will sometimes be reluctant, for political if not legal reasons, to impose international rules in areas where the states traditionally exert sovereign powers. No doubt other countries will continue to be exasperated to learn that the U.S. national government will sometimes refuse to act internationally and instead defer to states' rights.

What *Missouri v. Holland* does, however, establish is that when the national political will is strong enough to employ the treaty power to implement international rules against the states, the Supreme Court and the Constitution will permit it, so long as the treaty does not violate an explicit term of the Constitution and is reasonably "international" in focus. This appears to be the lesson drawn not only from *Missouri v. Holland* in its immediate political context, migratory birds, but that drawn from the painful experiences of American political history, notably the Civil War, which has probably settled, once and for all, in Justice Holmes's words, that we Americans have spent "much sweat and blood to prove that [we have] created a nation."[106]

---

[106] 252 U.S. 416, 433 (1920).

13

Oona A. Hathaway

Hamdan v. Rumsfeld: Domestic Enforcement of International Law

International law has long been subjected to the charge that it isn't really law—at least not in the sense that we usually imagine law. There is no international police force standing ready to enforce the laws of the international community against states that violate them. There is no mandatory universal court system that can adjudicate violations and assess penalties. And, with a few exceptions, there is no mechanism for penalizing states found to have fallen short of the law's rules. This has led some to conclude that most of international law is little more than cheap talk—words not backed up deeds and, hence, without any real force.

And yet this view of international law misses much of what makes international law relevant and powerful: International law is not only enforced by states against one another, but it is also enforced by states *against themselves*. That is to say, it is enforced by domestic courts and political institutions that pressure their own government to live up to the promises it has made; it is enforced by individuals and interest groups that pressure the political branches of government to live up to international legal commitments they have made, whether they can be enforced in the courts or not; and it is enforced by individuals or groups that use a state's domestic court system to enforce international law through litigation. It is this missing part of the picture—the enforcement of international law at home—that this chapter brings to light.[1]

International law that fails to provide for international sanctions is not doomed to failure. It simply falls back on a second, and potentially far more powerful, line of defense against violations within states

---

[1] This chapter builds on earlier academic work that lays out the theoretical claims in more detail, including Oona A. Hathaway, *Why Do Countries Commit to Human Rights Treaties?*, 51 J. CONFLICT RESOL. 588 (2007) [hereinafter Hathaway, *Why Do Countries Commit?*]; Oona A. Hathaway & Ariel Lavinbuk, *Rationalism and Revisionism in International Law*, 119 HARV. L. REV. 1404 (2006); Oona A. Hathaway, *Between Power and Principle: An Integrated Theory of International Law*, 72 U. CHI. L. REV. 469 (2005); Oona A. Hathaway, *The Cost of Commitment*, 55 STAN. L. REV. 1821 (2003); Oona A. Hathaway, *Do Human Rights Treaties Make a Difference?*, 111 YALE L.J. 1989 (2002).

themselves: the dance of politics and the domestic rule of law. International law both depends on and empowers existing checks and balances within a state. It gives courts a basis for reining in damaging behavior by the political branches or gives political actors an external source of authority and legitimacy to point to in their efforts to challenge and contain abuses of power by government officials.

Still, relying on enforcement at home is not without drawbacks. Not all states will engage in domestic enforcement, nor will states that do engage in domestic enforcement do so all the time. In states where domestic political and legal institutions hold the government to its legal obligations, government actors have difficulty ignoring international law for long periods of time without being called to account. But in weak or autocratic states, governments can often make international legal commitments and then ignore them without fear of domestic repercussions. Similarly, in states with judiciaries that are corrupted by politics, violence, or money, judges are unable to make independent decisions, and the threat of litigation is likely to be largely ineffective. And even in states with independent judiciaries, the effectiveness of legal commitment varies depending on whether such commitments are binding as a matter of domestic law or not.[2]

This brings us to the case that is the subject of this chapter: *Hamdan v. Rumsfeld*.[3] Widely recognized as one of the most important international law cases in the United States in the last several decades, *Hamdan* powerfully illustrates both the promise and limits of domestic enforcement of international law. The circumstances that gave rise to the case demonstrate the hurdles that domestic enforcement of international law faces in even the most robust democracies. As we shall see, the *Hamdan* case and those that preceded it arose from systematic efforts by the George W. Bush administration to create an exclusive zone of authority over those captured in what the administration referred to as the "war on terror"—many of whom, it would later become clear, had been subject to detention at CIA "black sites" and torture, in clear violation of international law. By shielding its actions from oversight, the administration aimed to exercise unfettered discretion over what rights would be afforded to those it held and who would judge these detainees' guilt or innocence. The case thus stands as a stark reminder that the domestic enforcement of international law relies not only on the existence of robust rule-of-law institutions, but also on the ability of those institutions to reach the cases in which international legal rules are at stake.

---

2 Democratic states are much more likely to improve their human rights practices after ratifying a human rights treaty than are non-democratic states. *See* Hathaway, *Do Human Rights Treaties Make a Difference?*, *supra* note 1. Democratic states are less likely to ratify human rights treaties when their practices are out of compliance than are non-democratic states. *See* Hathaway, *The Cost of Commitment*, *supra* note 1; Hathaway, *Why Do Countries Commit?*, *supra* note 1.

3 Hamdan v. Rumsfeld, 548 U.S. 557 (2006).

And yet *Hamdan* also offers a more hopeful message: Domestic enforcement of international law can succeed even where there is stringent resistance by the most powerful of political actors. In the face of claims by the administration that it alone should judge the legality of its actions in the war on terror, the Court responded with a resounding "no." As Justice Breyer put it in his concurrence, "[t]he Court's conclusion ultimately rests upon a single ground: Congress has not issued the Executive a 'blank check.' "[4] Thus, even as it showcases the limits of international law, the case stands, too, for the hopeful message that domestic enforcement of international law can bring even the most powerful actors to account. Where there is no international enforcement of international law, where the nation at odds with the law is the most powerful in the world, and where the executive resists the constraints of international law—even then the law can hold sway. The story of *Hamdan* is the story of both the fragility and the power of domestic enforcement of international law, and in this story lie broader lessons for the promise and limits of international law as a whole.

This chapter begins with the circumstances behind the *Hamdan* case. It starts by examining how the terrorist attacks on the World Trade Center on September 11, 2001, led to reactions that threatened to undermine international law in the United States and the world. As the second section shows, these challenges did not go unanswered. They prompted responses in the media, in U.S. and world politics, and in the courts. As the third section explains, these responses culminated in the decision that is the central focus of this story—*Hamdan v. Rumsfeld*. But, as we shall see in the final section, the Supreme Court's decision in this case is not the end of the story. The battle over the fate of domestic enforcement of international law in the war on terror continued in the years that followed. What began as a hopeful assertion of the authority of law has, in the years since, led to a political stalemate that has resulted in lengthy and largely ineffective trials as well as the likely indefinite detention without trial of many of those who still remain in Guantánamo. This has left Camp X-Ray as both a symbol of America's aspiration to assert the authority of law and a painful reminder of its imperfection.

I. THE WAR AGAINST TERROR AND CAMP X-RAY

Just over a week after the devastating attacks on the World Trade Center, President George W. Bush stood before a joint session of Congress. "On September the 11th," he declared, "night fell on a different world, a world where freedom itself is under attack." He announced the commencement of a "war on terror"—a campaign "unlike any we have

[4] *Id.* at 636 (Breyer, J., concurring).

ever seen"—that would "not end until every terrorist group of global reach has been found, stopped and defeated."[5]

The first target of the new war was the Taliban government of Afghanistan—a government that had openly harbored terrorist Osama bin Laden and his al-Qaeda terrorist network, which was suspected of plotting the September 11 attacks. By the end of October, U.S. and British troops had entered Afghanistan in what U.S. forces dubbed "Operation Enduring Freedom," and coalition forces had captured hundreds of suspected Taliban soldiers and al-Qaeda members.[6] U.S. forces would capture and hold more than 83,000 prisoners in the war on terror by the end of 2005.[7]

It soon became apparent that the U.S. government had decided not to afford those it had captured the full range of protections defined by the international law of war. The Bush administration instead openly questioned the relevance of the four international agreements known collectively as the "Geneva Conventions"—agreements that together form the core of international humanitarian law.[8] These Conventions, the U.S. administration argued, did not apply to the detainees in the war on terror. They were created to protect nonparticipating civilians and soldiers engaged in classic state-to-state military conflict, not the "unlawful combatants" who had been captured in Afghanistan.[9] As then-White House counsel Alberto Gonzales put it in early 2002, "the war against terrorism is a new kind of war" and "this new paradigm renders obsolete Geneva's strict limitations on questioning of enemy prisoners and renders quaint some of its provisions."[10]

---

[5] President George W. Bush, Address to a Joint Session of Cong. and the Am. People (Sept. 20, 2001), https://georgewbush-whitehouse.archives.gov/news/releases/2001/09/2001 0920-8.html.

[6] Though the initial attacks were carried out exclusively by U.S. and British forces, a significant number of other countries soon offered support, including Canada, France, Italy, Spain, Portugal, Germany, Australia, Pakistan, and New Zealand.

[7] Katherine Shrader, *Detainees Top 83,000, U.S. Officials Say*, SEATTLE TIMES (Nov. 17, 2005), https://www.seattletimes.com/nation-world/detainees-top-83000-us-officials-say/.

[8] *See* Geneva Convention for the Amelioration of the Condition of the Wounded and Sick in Armed Forces in the Field, Aug. 12, 1949, 6 U.S.T. 3114, 75 U.N.T.S. 31; Geneva Convention for the Amelioration of the Condition of Wounded, Sick and Shipwrecked Members of Armed Forces at Sea, Aug. 12, 1949, 6 U.S.T. 3217, 75 U.N.T.S. 85; Geneva Convention Relative to the Treatment of Prisoners of War, Aug. 12, 1949, 6 U.S.T. 3116, 75 U.N.T.S. 135 [hereinafter Geneva Convention III]; Geneva Convention Relative to the Protection of Civilian Persons in Time of War, Aug. 12, 1949, 6 U.S.T. 3516, 75 U.N.T.S. 287.

[9] Secretary of Defense Donald Rumsfeld asserted that "technically unlawful combatants do not have any rights under the Geneva Conventions." *Defense Department Briefing*, C-SPAN (Jan. 11, 2002), https://www.c-span.org/video/?168158-1/defense-department-briefing. The term "unlawful combatant" does not appear in the Geneva Conventions.

[10] Memorandum from Alberto R. Gonzales, U.S. Att'y Gen., to President George W. Bush, Decision Re Application of the Geneva Convention on Prisoners of War to the Conflict with Al Qaeda and the Taliban 2 (Jan 25, 2002), https://nsarchive2.gwu.edu/torturing democracy/documents/20020125.pdf.

Only a month into the war in Afghanistan, President Bush issued a Military Order, entitled "Detention, Treatment, and Trial of Certain Non-Citizens in the War on Terrorism."[11] The Order authorized the creation of military commissions to try any non-U.S. citizen captured in the armed conflict if the President determined "there is reason to believe that such individual, at the relevant times . . . is or was a member of the organization known as al Qaida" or "has engaged in, aided or abetted, or conspired to commit acts of international terrorism, or acts in preparation therefor . . . ."[12] The Order further provided that individuals subject to the Order would have no remedy in U.S. courts, the courts of any foreign nation, or any international tribunal.[13] Thus began what would become a sustained effort not only to test and exceed the limits of international humanitarian law, but also to insulate the resulting actions from the scrutiny of the courts. This insulation of government action from enforcement of the law would, in turn, make possible an unchecked tide of violations.

Freed from the conventions of domestic law or direct oversight by domestic courts, the commissions promised to offer few procedural protections to the accused: "Given the danger to the safety of the United States and the nature of international terrorism," the President's Order stated, "it is not practicable to apply in military commissions under this order the principles of law and the rules of evidence generally recognized in the trial of criminal cases in the United States district courts."[14] The rules the administration outlined to guide the commissions provided that evidence need only have "probative value to a reasonable person,"[15] a standard that is generally regarded to permit the admission of hearsay and other types of usually inadmissible evidence, such as testimony obtained through coercion or even torture. Furthermore, the accused detainees would be afforded no right to know the evidence against them if doing so might compromise national security—a dramatic departure from the procedures of not only civilian courts, but courts-martial as well.[16]

---

[11] Detention, Treatment, and Trial of Certain Non-Citizens in the War Against Terrorism, 66 Fed. Reg. 57,833 § 2 (Nov. 13, 2001) [hereinafter November 13 Order].

[12] *Id.* § 7.

[13] *Id.*

[14] *Id.* § 1.

[15] The regulations were laid out in the Department of Defense Military Commission Order No. 1, which was issued pursuant to the President's November 13 Order, *supra* note 11. U.S. Dep't of Defense, Military Commission Order No. 1: Procedures for Trials by Military Commissions of Certain Non-United States Citizens in the War Against Terrorism (Mar. 21, 2002), https://www.mc.mil/Portals/0/MCO%20No.%201%20(Mar.%2021,%20 2002).pdf.

[16] The Order provided that evidence and proceedings would be subject to Executive Order 12,958, which provides rules for classifying, safeguarding, and declassifying national security information. November 13 Order, *supra* note 11, § 4. Many other procedural protections ordinarily afforded criminal defendants were not required to be observed by the commissions, including, for example, judicial review by an independent civilian court (as is available for courts-martial), a public hearing, and the right of the defendants to confront

Meanwhile, the U.S. government began to transport detainees from Afghanistan to Camp X-Ray, a military base located at Guantánamo Bay, Cuba, in January 2002.[17] Within a few weeks, hundreds of detainees had been relocated to the base. From the administration's point of view, the base had two significant advantages that made it, as then-Secretary of Defense Donald Rumsfeld later put it, "the least worst place we could have selected,"[18] It was physically isolated and hence offered excellent security, and it was not located on U.S. territory, sitting instead on land that is on long-term lease from the Cuban government. Consequently, the prisoners held there would not have the same legal protections they would have had were they held in the United States—including, it was hoped, the ability to challenge their detention in U.S. federal court. As a retired Air Force attorney put it, "[t]he government wants to keep them out of any place in the U.S. where they can claim protections."[19] The physical isolation also made it possible to hold the prisoners incommunicado, with little or no access to the press, non-military lawyers, or family members. The Guantánamo base would serve as a prison, interrogation center, and judicial facility rolled into one—run and overseen by the Department of Defense and the White House.

International law was an unsurprising casualty of this exclusive arrangement. In February 2002, over the opposition of Secretary of State Colin Powell, the administration declared in a memo with the subject line "Humane Treatment of al Qaeda and Taliban Detainees" that "none of the provisions of Geneva" apply to the conflict with the Taliban or al-Qaeda.[20] The memo stated that captured Taliban detainees were "unlawful combatants" who did not qualify as prisoners of war and al-Qaeda detainees "also do not qualify as prisoners of war."[21] In a series of memoranda throughout 2002, administration officials offered and defended the legality of torturing detainees.[22] These memos argued that as long as detainees were held outside the United States—and therefore outside the reach of domestic enforcement—the government could ignore domestic laws and outdated international legal rules and instead write its own rules to fit the challenges of the new war on terror.

It was not until 2014 that the full range of horrors that resulted would become public in sometimes graphic detail. That year, the Senate

---

the evidence against them. Moreover, the Order permitted indefinite detention without charge. November 13 Order, *supra* note 11.

17 Steve Vogel, *Afghan Prisoners Going to Gray Area*, WASH. POST (Jan. 8, 2002), https://www.washingtonpost.com/archive/politics/2002/01/09/afghan-prisoners-going-to-gray-area/0bc69bad-4cb5-469c-956a-2f22d84755a8/.

18 *Id.*

19 *Id.* (quoting former Air Force attorney Michael F. Noone).

20 Memorandum from President George W. Bush to the Vice President, et al., Re: Humane Treatment of al Qaeda and Taliban Detainees (Feb. 7, 2002), https://nsarchive2.gwu.edu/torturingdemocracy/documents/20020207-2.pdf.

21 *Id.*

22 A series of memos in which the administration devised arguments permitting torture can be found at http://www.nytimes.com/ref/international/24MEMO–GUIDE.html.

Select Committee on Intelligence released a lengthy report on the Central Intelligence Agency's post-9/11 detention and interrogation program, providing detailed evidence that the United States had detained and tortured terrorism suspects at secret black sites located around the world.[23] Many of these detainees were later transferred to Guantánamo Bay, where several are still detained more than two decades later. The torture to which they were subject had many longstanding consequences, including making it extremely difficult to try them.[24]

II. CHALLENGE IN COURT: THE DOMESTIC ENFORCEMENT OF INTERNATIONAL LAW BEGINS

Almost as soon as the U.S. government began holding detainees in Afghanistan, there emerged first a trickle and then a flow of allegations of detainee torture and abuse. As the war expanded into Iraq and detainees were moved to Guantánamo Bay, the allegations followed. Claimed abuses included inhumane interrogation procedures, sexual humiliation, extended solitary confinement,[25] and psychological abuse.[26] The International Committee of the Red Cross later submitted confidential reports to the U.S. government detailing evidence that the U.S. military's treatment of detainees at Guantánamo involved psychological and physical coercion that was "tantamount to torture," in clear violation of international law.[27]

Human rights groups both at home and abroad worked to bring these abuses to light and to encourage the U.S. public to press their government to afford detainees basic protections. With the country at war, memories of September 11 still fresh, and Republicans in charge of both houses of Congress, these efforts met with little success. The international press, rights organizations, and political leaders from around the world decried

---

[23] SENATE SELECT COMMITTEE ON INTELLIGENCE, COMMITTEE STUDY OF THE CENTRAL INTELLIGENCE AGENCY'S DETENTION AND INTERROGATION PROGRAM, S. REP. NO. 113–288 (2014).

[24] *See* Carol Rosenberg, *The Legacy of America's Post-9/11 Turn to Torture*, N.Y. TIMES (Sept. 12, 2021), https://www.nytimes.com/2021/09/12/us/politics/torture-post-9-11.html.

[25] *See* Tania Branigan & Vikram Dodd, *Fight Against Terror: Afghanistan to Guantanamo Bay—The Story of Three British Detainees*, GUARDIAN, Aug. 4, 2004, at 5; John Hendren, *The Conflict in Iraq: Army Limits Methods Used on Detainees*, L.A. TIMES, May 15, 2004, at A1; James Meek, *Welcome to Guantánamo: A Special Investigation into the Prison that Shames American Justice*, GUARDIAN, Dec. 3, 2003, at 1; Paul Waugh, *My Torture Hell in Camp Delta Cage*, EVENING STANDARD, Aug. 3, 2004, at A4 (detailing detainee abuse at Camp Delta in Guantánamo Bay).

[26] *Guantánamo: Shameful Regime of Detention Without Trial*, INDEPENDENT, Jan. 10, 2005, at 25. For further discussion, see Laura A. Dickinson, *Abu Ghraib: The Battle Over Institutional Culture and Respect for International Law within the U.S. Military*, *in* INTERNATIONAL LAW STORIES (John E. Noyes, Laura A. Dickinson, Mark Weston Janis & Carlos Vázquez eds., 2d ed., 2025), in this volume.

[27] Neil A. Lewis, *Red Cross Finds Detainee Abuse in Guantanamo*, N.Y. TIMES (Nov. 30, 2004), https://www.nytimes.com/2004/11/30/politics/red-cross-finds-detainee-abuse-in-guantanamo.html.

U.S. actions at Guantánamo and pressed for the release of those detained.[28] This pressure had minimal effect. Yet more formal international enforcement of the Geneva Conventions' requirements was impossible because the United States is a veto-wielding member of the United Nations Security Council and hence possesses the power to stop any enforcement action by the United Nations in its tracks.[29]

Groups and individuals thus began to challenge the administration in the courts. Within months of the U.S. invasion of Afghanistan, the administration's policy on detainees was under attack in U.S. domestic court in tens and eventually hundreds of cases. Through these cases, the courts began the *domestic enforcement* of international law in the war on terror.

Two cases that wound their way to the Supreme Court in 2004, *Rasul v. Bush*[30] and *Al Odah v. United States*,[31] presented what the Supreme Court called the "narrow but important question" of whether the United States could hear challenges to the legality of the detention of foreign nationals captured abroad and held at Guantánamo Bay.[32] Through their relatives and attorneys, they challenged the legality of their detention, arguing that they had not been combatants against the United States.[33] They asserted that they had not been formally charged with any illegal acts, had not been permitted to meet with their legal counsel, and had not received access to a court or tribunal; they sought access to counsel, freedom from interrogation, and release from custody.[34] At stake in these cases was whether the administration's efforts to insulate its actions from legal oversight would succeed. Would domestic courts be able to enforce the law against a recalcitrant administration, or would the administration's actions be immune from domestic enforcement?

---

[28] *See, e.g.*, Alison Healy, *Large Crowd Expected at Anti-war Rally in Dublin*, IRISH TIMES, Mar. 29, 2003, at 8; José María Irujo, *Unica: Pleas for Spaniard in Guantanamo to be Released Rejected by US Government*, EL PAIS, Mar. 31, 2003, at 1; François Sergent, *Kenneth Roth, président de Human Rights Watch, dénonce les abus de Bush: "Les Etats-Unis réécrivent les lois de la guerre,"* LIBERATION, Mar. 22, 2002, at 9; Andrew Gumbel, *Campaigners Begin Legal Battle to Shut Down Camp X-Ray*, INDEPENDENT, July 10, 2002, at 10.

[29] The situation remains under investigation by the International Criminal Court, which has jurisdiction because Afghanistan has long been a state party to the Rome Statute of the International Criminal Court. However, the prosecutor has deprioritized lines of inquiry into alleged crimes by U.S. forces. *See Situation in the Islamic Republic of Afghanistan*, INTERNATIONAL CRIMINAL COURT, https://www.icc-cpi.int/afghanistan (last visited Aug. 20, 2024).

[30] Rasul v. Bush, 542 U.S. 466 (2004).

[31] 542 U.S. 466 (2004).

[32] *Rasul*, 542 U.S. at 470.

[33] Al Odah v. United States, 321 F.3d 1134, 1138 (D.C. Cir. 2003).

[34] Rasul and the other British citizen on the petition were released from custody on March 10, 2004, more than three months before the case was decided. The case proceeded because other men on the petition were still being held. 542 U.S. at 470–71. *See* Carol Rosenberg, *They Won Guantanamo's Supreme Court Cases. Where Are They Now?*, N.Y. TIMES (Jan. 11, 2023), https://www.nytimes.com/2023/01/11/us/politics/guantanamo-bay-landmark-cases.html.

A third case involving detainee rights also made its way up through the courts, landing on the Supreme Court's docket during the same term as *Rasul* and *Al Odah*.[35] The case was filed on behalf of Yasser Esam Hamdi, who had been captured by a coalition of military groups opposed to the Taliban government known as the "Northern Alliance" in November 2001. Alleged to have fought on behalf of the Taliban, Hamdi was turned over to the U.S. military, which detained and interrogated him in Afghanistan before transferring him to Guantánamo Bay in January 2002. In April, upon learning that he was a U.S. citizen, the government again transferred him, this time to a military brig in Norfolk Naval Station in Norfolk, Virginia, and eventually to a brig in Charleston, South Carolina.[36] Labeled an "enemy combatant" who therefore was not entitled to the protections of either the criminal laws or the law of war, Hamdi was held without being charged, and was not permitted to meet with his family or attorneys.

In May 2002, Hamdi's attorneys filed a writ of habeas corpus in U.S. district court challenging Hamdi's detention and his label as an "enemy combatant." Twice the district court declared the evidence against him insufficient to justify his detention as an "enemy combatant," and twice the Fourth Circuit Court of Appeals reversed the decision in his favor, finally ruling that the district court did not have jurisdiction to question the executive's designation of Hamdi as an enemy combatant and that Hamdi was afforded no protection by the Geneva Conventions.[37] The Supreme Court granted certiorari to determine whether the executive could unilaterally declare Hamdi an "enemy combatant" and hold him indefinitely without the traditional procedural protections granted criminal defendants. Again, the threshold issue in the case was whether the domestic courts had the power to engage in oversight of the administration's actions in the war on terror. Could the administration unilaterally label a U.S. citizen an enemy combatant and thereby insulate his detention from domestic court oversight?

Even as the cases came before the Supreme Court, the war in Iraq began to take a turn for the worse. The *Rasul* and *Al Odah* cases were

---

[35] Hamdi v. Rumsfeld, 542 U.S. 507 (2004). The Supreme Court also heard another case, *Rumsfeld v. Padilla*, 542 U.S. 426 (2004), which involved a U.S. citizen who was captured in Chicago and suspected of involvement in a plot to set off a "dirty bomb" in the United States. President Bush declared Padilla an enemy combatant on June 9, 2002, and ordered him detained. He was subsequently transferred from civilian detention to the Charleston Naval Brig in South Carolina. His attorney filed suit as his "next friend" against Donald Rumsfeld, challenging his detention and designation as an enemy combatant. The district court and Second Circuit Court of Appeals both decided in his favor and ordered him transferred to civilian authorities. The Supreme Court granted certiorari. In a decision issued on the same day as *Hamdi* and *Rasul*, the Supreme Court declined to reach the merits of the case, deciding instead that the case had been filed in the wrong federal court and hence had to be dismissed.

[36] Though he was raised in Saudi Arabia, he was born in Louisiana during a brief stay there by his parents. Jan Crawford Greenburg, *Court Takes Terror Case: Justices Face Clash over "Combatants,"* CHI. TRIB., Jan. 10, 2004, at C1.

[37] Hamdi v. Rumsfeld, 316 F.3d 450, 468 (4th Cir. 2003).

consolidated and argued together before the Court on April 20, 2004, and *Hamdi* was argued just over a week later, on April 28. During oral argument, a Justice asked Deputy Solicitor General Paul Clement what constrained the administration's treatment of detainees if not the federal courts. Clement answered that "where there is a war . . . you have to trust the executive to make the kind of quintessential military judgments that are involved in things like that."[38]

That same night, CBS News showed photos on "60 Minutes II" of horrific abuse at the Abu Ghraib prison in Iraq. Some of the starkest images showed naked prisoners stacked in a human pyramid and a prisoner with a hood on his head and wires attached to his fingers.[39] Less than a month after oral argument, news outlets reported that the International Committee of the Red Cross had submitted a confidential report to the U.S. government concluding that in military sections of Abu Ghraib, "methods of physical and psychological coercion used by the interrogators appeared to be part of the standard operating procedures by military intelligence personnel to obtain confessions and extract information"—tactics that it found amounted to serious violations of the Geneva Conventions.[40] The evidence of widespread abuse of detainees was a stark counterargument to Clement's exhortation that the Court should "trust the executive."[41]

On a single day at the end of its term in June 2004, the Supreme Court issued its decisions in all three cases and with them a stinging rebuke to the Executive Branch. The Court reaffirmed the principle that the courts have the power to say when the President has gone too far, even when doing so involves placing limits on the President's ability to act in the war on terror.

In the *Rasul* and *Al Odah* cases, the Court held that the federal courts had jurisdiction over the habeas corpus petitions filed by detainees held at Guantánamo Bay.[42] In so holding, the Court rejected the administration's claim that it could unilaterally declare persons captured in the war on terror "enemy combatants" and hold them at Guantánamo indefinitely without any outside scrutiny. Though the cases were remanded back to the lower courts for substantive review, leaving the petitioning detainees' fates in some doubt, the decision was nonetheless hailed by human rights groups as a major victory. The decision represented the first time that the Supreme Court had permitted foreign

---

38 Transcript of Oral Argument at 23, Rumsfeld v. Padilla, 542 U.S. 426 (2004) (No. 03-1027).

39 *Photos Show U.S. Troops Apparently Abusing Iraqis*, L.A. TIMES, Apr. 29, 2004, at 8.

40 Alexander Higgins, Associated Press, *Red Cross Report Describes Abuse in Iraq*, WFMYNews2.com (May 10, 2004), https://www.wfmynews2.com/article/news/red-cross-report-describes-abuse-in-iraq/83-402372330.

41 Transcript of Oral Argument, *supra* note 38, at 23.

42 Rasul v. Bush, 542 U.S. 466, 483 (2004).

citizens not located in the United States to sue the U.S. government. The Court refused to allow Guantánamo Bay to be treated as a law-free zone.

Though no single opinion received a majority vote in *Hamdi*, the message of the Court was clear: Hamdi could not remain imprisoned at the unchecked discretion of the Executive Branch.[43] Five of the Justices agreed that Congress had given the President the power to detain U.S. citizens as "enemy combatants" when it passed the Authorization for the Use of Military Force in September 2001.[44] And yet the plurality (joined in this part by two additional justices, forming a majority) held that "history and common sense teach us that an unchecked system of detention carries the potential to become a means for oppression and abuse of others who do not present that sort of threat."[45] A majority of the Court agreed that, once detained, Hamdi had to be granted certain due process protections, including the right to challenge his status and detention, the right to access to counsel, and the right to have an impartial decision maker hear the proceedings on remand.[46] Despite the divided decision, commentators concluded that the Supreme Court had acted to sharply limit the unilateral powers claimed by the Bush administration.[47] And, indeed, several months later, Hamdi was released to Saudi Arabia after agreeing to relinquish his U.S. citizenship.[48]

Together, these decisions stood as a bold declaration by the Supreme Court that it would oversee the administration's actions in the war on terror and that the protections of domestic and international law could and would be enforced by U.S. domestic courts. The favorable decisions led to a flood of similar cases. Soon more than three hundred habeas petitions had been filed in federal court on behalf of detainees at Guantánamo.[49]

Meanwhile, the consequences of the "war on terror" continued to pour forth. Further evidence of abuses at Abu Ghraib emerged during the trials of the soldiers that participated in the abuse.[50] It soon became clear

---

43 All of the Justices except Justice Thomas agreed on this point. Hamdi v. Rumsfeld, 542 U.S. 507, 579 (2004) (Thomas, J., dissenting).

44 *See* Authorization for Use of Military Force, Pub. L. No. 107–40, 115 Stat. 224 (2001).

45 *Hamdi*, 542 U.S. at 530.

46 Notably, only four of the six Justices who agreed that due process protections were warranted also agreed that Congress had in fact granted the President the power to detain Hamdi. *See id.* at 541.

47 *See, e.g.*, Naftali Bendavid, *Justices Rule that Detainees Get Day in Court: Guantánamo Bay Inmates Granted Similar Rights*, CHI. TRIB., June 29, 2004, at C1.

48 *CNN Daybreak: Voting Problems* (CNN television broadcast Oct. 14, 2004); *NewsHour with Jim Lehrer: Hamdi to Be Released* (PBS television broadcast Sept. 23, 2004).

49 Corine Hegland, *The Guantánamo Bar*, NAT'L J., Mar. 18, 2006, at 50.

50 One of the more notorious cases involved Private Lynndie England, who pled guilty to seven violations of the Uniform Code of Military Justice, after pictures of her watching and participating in prisoner abuse came to light. *See* Kate Zernike, *Plea Deal Is Set for G.I. Pictured in Abuses in Iraq*, N.Y. TIMES (Apr. 30, 2005), https://www.nytimes.com/2005/04/30/us/plea-deal-is-set-for-gi-pictured-in-abuses-in-iraq.html.

that Abu Ghraib was "only the tip of the iceberg."[51] As Reed Brody, special counsel for Human Rights Watch, put it, "abuse of detainees has happened all over—from Afghanistan to Guantánamo Bay to a lot of third-country dungeons where the United States has sent prisoners."[52]

Amid the ongoing evidence of widespread abuses at U.S. detention facilities in Iraq and allegations of abuse at Guantánamo, Congress, which to this point had remained largely silent on the issue of detainee treatment, began to intervene. Republican Senator John McCain—himself a former prisoner of war who had been held and tortured in a Vietnam prison camp for five years—presented an amendment to the U.S. Senate Department of Defense Authorization bill. The "McCain Amendment" promised to prohibit inhumane treatment of prisoners held by the United States, regardless of where they are located, and confined interrogation techniques to those specified in the *Army Field Manual*. Introduced to the Senate on October 3, 2005, it quickly won widespread support, passing two days later with ninety votes in favor and only nine against.

The administration responded to the bill by pressuring its sponsors to exempt the CIA from the ban on the use of cruel, inhuman, and degrading treatment. In a private forty-five-minute meeting on October 20, Vice President Cheney and CIA Director Porter J. Goss pressured Senator McCain to support the exemption, arguing that the President needed "flexibility" to wage the global war on terrorism.[53] On November 2, news broke that made clear why the administration had been so intent on securing the exemption.[54] Reporter Dana Priest reported that the CIA had been operating a network of secret prisons since shortly after September 11 in eight countries, including Thailand, Afghanistan, and several countries in Eastern Europe, as well as at the Guantánamo Bay prison. More than one hundred suspected terrorists had been funneled through the detention facilities, referred to in internal classified memos as "black sites." CIA interrogators in the sites were authorized by the Agency to use "enhanced interrogation techniques," some of which—including "waterboarding" prisoners to create the sensation of drowning—are widely regarded as torture and cruel, inhuman, and degrading treatment.[55]

In December 2005, the House joined the Senate to overwhelmingly endorse Senator McCain's measure to bar cruel and inhumane treatment of prisoners in U.S. custody anywhere in the world in what was regarded

---

[51] HUMAN RIGHTS WATCH, US: ABU GHRAIB ONLY THE "TIP OF THE ICEBERG" (Apr. 27, 2005).

[52] *Id.*

[53] Eric Schmitt, *Exception Sought in Detainee Abuse Ban*, N.Y. TIMES (Oct. 25, 2005), https://www.nytimes.com/2005/10/25/us/exception-sought-in-detainee-abuse-ban.html.

[54] *See* Dana Priest, *CIA Holds Terror Suspects in Secret Prisons*, WASH. POST (Nov. 2, 2005), https://www.washingtonpost.com/archive/politics/2005/11/02/cia-holds-terror-suspects-in-secret-prisons/767f0160-cde4-41f2-a691-ba989990039c/.

[55] *Id.*

by the press at the time as an "unusual bipartisan rebuke to the Bush Administration."[56] The measure was signed into law by President Bush as the "Detainee Treatment Act" just before the close of 2005.[57]

Many in the human rights community, however, worried that what appeared on the surface to be a rebuke of the President might instead effectively sanction torture. The concerns were far from groundless. The new law limited interrogation methods to those listed in the *Army Field Manual on Intelligence Interrogation*.[58] The Department of Defense considered amending the *Manual* to allow harsh interrogation methods for enemy combatants—plans that were eventually abandoned under public scrutiny.[59] Even more concerning, the law had been amended to limit suspected foreign terrorists' access to U.S. courts.[60] In a move widely regarded as an effort to overturn the Supreme Court's earlier decision in *Rasul* by "stripping" significant jurisdiction over habeas corpus petitions from the federal courts, the amendment restricted review of military tribunal decisions to the U.S. Court of Appeals for the District of Columbia while at the same time significantly limiting the scope of review that court could provide. Equally concerning, the Act permitted the use of statements "obtained as a result of coercion" if their probative value was deemed sufficient while at the same time protecting U.S. government personnel from civil action or criminal prosecution for acts committed against detainees if they "did not know that the practices were unlawful."[61]

In a controversial signing statement that accompanied the Act, the President declared that the Executive Branch would construe the Act "in a manner consistent with the constitutional authority of the President to

[56] Eric Schmitt, *House Defies Bush and Backs McCain on Detainee Torture*, N.Y. TIMES, Dec. 15, 2005, at A14.

[57] Detainee Treatment Act of 2005, Pub. L. No. 109–148, §§ 1001–1006, 119 Stat. 2739 (codified at 42 U.S.C. § 2000dd–1).

[58] *Id.* § 1002(a).

[59] To evade the intended limits, the Department of Defense considered adding a classified annex to the *Field Manual* detailing permitted interrogation techniques or, alternatively, putting forth two sets of interrogation guidelines, one for those designated as prisoners of war and one for those designated as enemy combatants. However, the *Field Manual* that was approved included neither. *See* U.S. DEP'T OF THE ARMY, FIELD MANUAL NO. 2–22.3, HUMAN INTELLIGENCE COLLECTOR OPERATIONS (2006).

[60] Dan Eggen, *Senate Approves Plan to Limit Detainee Access to Courts*, WASH. POST (Nov. 11, 2005), https://www.washingtonpost.com/archive/politics/2005/11/11/senate-approves-plan-to-limit-detainee-access-to-courts/c54ea7de-5ffb-4962-a841-2aea9c550297/.

[61] Detainee Treatment Act § 1004(a). The Act goes on to explain that "[g]ood faith reliance on advice of counsel should be an important factor, among others, to consider in assessing whether a person of ordinary sense and understanding would have known the practices to be unlawful." *Id.* This likely referred to memos from the Office of Legal Counsel (OLC) finding most "extraordinary interrogation techniques" legal. Most of the relevant memos can be found at *Torturing Democracy: Documents by Chronology*, NAT'L SEC. ARCHIVE (last updated Aug. 2017), https://nsarchive2.gwu.edu/torturingdemocracy/documents.

supervise the unitary Executive Branch and as Commander in Chief."[62] Three key Republican senators, including John McCain, fired back with a joint statement rejecting Bush's claim that he could unilaterally waive the restrictions on cruel, inhuman, and degrading treatment against detainees. "The Congress declined when asked by administration officials to include a presidential waiver of the restrictions included in our legislation," they declared. "Our committee intends through strict oversight to monitor the administration's implementation of the new law."[63] A year later, however, no public hearings or Senate debate had been held on detainee treatment despite continuing reports of abuse.

Thus what began as an effort to assert limits on the President's treatment of detainees in the war on terror looked poised to end as a congressional stamp of approval on the President's plan to "hold people indefinitely without a hearing and beyond the reach of U.S. law and checks and balances."[64] The first test of this Act—and whether the administration's efforts to avoid domestic enforcement of international law by keeping the federal courts from overseeing its conduct in the war on terror—would come in the very case it was intended to force out of the courts: *Hamdan v. Rumsfeld*.

III. *HAMDAN V. RUMSFELD*

In many ways, it was mere happenstance that led Salim Ahmed Hamdan to the center of one of the most important international law cases in the United States of the last several decades. For the first quarter-century of his life, Hamdan led a largely uneventful existence. Born in a rural tribal village in South Yemen, he earned the rough equivalent of a fourth-grade education before his parents both died of illness and he left school. He went to live with relatives and was soon living on his own, working a variety of odd jobs.[65] There was no sign that Hamdan was particularly religious. Indeed, he seemed to have no plans beyond marrying and finding a decent job. He was twenty-six years old and working as a taxi driver in the Yemeni city of Sana in 1996 when a Saudi named Nasser al-Bahri recruited him to join a group of men leaving for Tajikistan, offering to pay for his travel as well as a salary.[66]

---

[62] Press Release, President George W. Bush, President's Statement on Signing of H.R. 2863 (Dec. 30, 2005), https://georgewbush-whitehouse.archives.gov/news/releases/2005/12/20051230-8.html.

[63] Charlie Savage, *3 GOP Senators Blast Bush Bid to Bypass Torture Ban*, BOSTON GLOBE, Jan. 5, 2006, at A3. *See, e.g.*, *Recent Developments*, 19 HARV. HUM. RTS. J. 257, 263 (2006).

[64] Eggen, *supra* note 60 (quoting a statement by the Center for Constitutional Rights).

[65] Jonathan Mahler, *The Bush Administration vs. Salim Hamdan*, N.Y. TIMES MAG. (Jan. 8, 2006), https://www.nytimes.com/2006/01/08/magazine/the-bush-administration-vs-salim-hamdan.html.

[66] *Id.*

Hamdan joined al-Bahri and thirty-five other Yemenis on a grueling six-month trip to Tajikistan to fight alongside the Islamist insurgency against the Russian-backed government. When they were turned back at the border, one of the group's members suggested that they go see a man named Osama bin Laden. Recently expelled from Sudan, bin Laden had relocated to Afghanistan, where he had begun working to rebuild al-Qaeda. He was seeking recruits to join him in his efforts to drive the United States from the region. After listening to bin Laden's teachings for three days, al-Bahri and many of his companions agreed to join al-Qaeda. Al-Bahri soon helped arrange for Hamdan to work as a driver on a farm owned by bin Laden for a salary of $200 per month. About seven months later, Hamdan began working as one of bin Laden's personal drivers.[67]

Over the course of five years, Hamdan is alleged to have performed many different jobs for bin Laden—most often serving as his personal bodyguard and driver.[68] It is unknown how much responsibility Hamdan was given or how much he was involved in planning al-Qaeda's terrorist activities.[69] Although he undoubtedly had access to information regarding the group's activities and plans, his lawyers contend that he primarily served as an employee.[70]

In 1999, Hamdan married a Yemeni woman and brought her to Afghanistan. When the United States invaded Afghanistan in October 2001, she fled with their child across the Pakistani border, eventually making her way back to Yemen. Hamdan was attempting to join her when he was captured by warlords near the Pakistani border and turned over to the U.S. military for a $5000 reward.[71] After spending six months in prison in Bagram and Kandahar, he was transported along with nearly five hundred other detainees to Guantánamo Bay.

On July 3, 2003, the President determined that Hamdan and five of his fellow detainees at Guantánamo were eligible for trial by military commission.[72] Hamdan was assigned military counsel in December 2003—forty-four-year-old Lieutenant Commander Charles Swift of the U.S. Navy. Swift later recounted arriving at his assignment on the first day as defense counsel for the military commissions to find that "[n]o one

---

67 *Id.*; Carol Rosenberg, *Detainee Stunned By Court Victory*, SEATTLE TIMES, July 1, 2006, at A14; Petition for Writ of Certiorari app. H, Hamdan v. Rumsfeld, 548 U.S. 557 (2006) (No. 05–184) (affidavit of Salim Hamdan).

68 Linda Greenhouse, *Justices, 5–3, Broadly Reject Bush Plan to Try Detainees,* N.Y. TIMES, June 30, 2006, at A6.

69 *See Lawyer Says Prisoner "Humble," Not "Jubilant,"* CHI. TRIB. (June 30, 2006), https://www.chicagotribune.com/2006/06/30/lawyer-says-prisoner-humble-not-jubilant/ ("Hamdan contends he worked as a driver for bin Laden in Afghanistan only to make a living for his family.").

70 Mahler, *supra* note 65.

71 *Id.*

72 Hamdan v. Rumsfeld, 415 F.3d 33, 35 (D.C. Cir. 2005) ("On July 3, 2003, the President determined 'that there is reason to believe that [Hamdan] was a member of Al Qaeda or was otherwise involved in terrorism directed against the United States.' ").

involved in the Commission process appeared eager to begin the process."[73] The Chief Prosecutor made clear that Hamdan's access to legal counsel was contingent on his guilty plea.[74] "I had the unenviable task of going down to this guy from Yemen in the uniform of people who had been treating him badly and saying, 'If you don't make a deal you may never see me again,' " Swift recalled.[75] After he met Hamdan on January 30, 2004, however, it was clear to him that Hamdan wanted to fight the charges against him.

At this point, Swift had been working for months with Neal Katyal, a professor at Georgetown University Law Center who had recently clerked for Supreme Court Justice Stephen Breyer and was widely regarded a leading constitutional law expert. A known hawk on national security issues who served for a time as national security advisor to the Deputy Attorney General,[76] Katyal surprised some when he volunteered to work with defense lawyers to challenge the military commissions. But he was appalled by what he saw as a "blatantly unconstitutional" plan for trying the suspected terrorists.[77] Hamdan's case, he and Swift decided, was the test case they had been waiting for.

Katyal drafted an agreement allowing Swift to serve as Hamdan's "next friend" in a lawsuit against his employer. It was a bold move for Swift, who had made his career in the military.[78] Swift later explained that he decided to mount a challenge to the administration's policies because he was "fearful of the dangerous precedent that could be set by denying international standards of justice to those swept up in the war on terrorism."[79] With the help of lawyers they enlisted from the Seattle-based law firm Perkins Coie and law students from Yale and Georgetown, Swift and Katyal then filed a demand for charges and a speedy trial pursuant to Article 10 of the Universal Code of Military Justice (UCMJ).[80] After the legal advisor to the Appointing Authority ruled that the UCMJ did not apply to Hamdan, they filed a habeas petition on Hamdan's behalf

---

73 *Detainees: Hearing Before the S. Comm. on the Judiciary*, 109th Cong. 305 (2005) (statement of Charles Swift, defense counsel, Office of Department of Defense Military Commissions).

74 *Id.* at 307.

75 *Lawyer Says Prisoner "Humble," Not "Jubilant," supra* note 69 (quoting Swift).

76 *See Neal K. Katyal*, GEORGETOWN LAW, https://www.law.georgetown.edu/faculty/neal-k-katyal/ (last updated July 15, 2024); Elizabeth Amon, *Defending Detainees*, LAW.COM (Sept. 15, 2004, 12:00 AM), https://www.law.com/almID/900005540391/.

77 *Quoted in* Dan Froomkin, *A Challenge to Presidential Power*, YALE ALUMNI MAG. (Sept.–Oct. 2006), http://archives.yalealumnimagazine.com/issues/2006_09/where.html.

78 Indeed, Swift was later forced to retire under the military's up-or-out system when he was passed over for a promotion—a decision he learned of just two weeks after winning the *Hamdan* case in the Supreme Court and which many viewed as retaliation for his decision to challenge the government's detainee policies. *The Cost of Doing Your Duty*, N.Y. TIMES (Oct. 11, 2006), https://www.nytimes.com/2006/10/11/opinion/the-cost-of-doing-your-duty.html.

79 Carol Williams, *Lonely Victory for U.S. Navy Lawyer*, L.A. TIMES (June 30, 2006), https://www.latimes.com/archives/la-xpm-2006-jun-30-na-lawyer30-story.html.

80 Uniform Code of Military Justice, 10 U.S.C. §§ 801–946 (2000).

in the Western District of Washington in April 2004.[81] The case, *Hamdan v. Rumsfeld*, was born.[82]

Though the President had determined that Hamdan was eligible for trial by military commission in July 2003, it was not until just over a year later—and only after Hamdan's lawyers had filed the habeas petition in U.S. district court—that he was formally charged. Hamdan was accused of conspiracy to commit the offenses of "attacking civilians; attacking civilian objects; murder by an unprivileged belligerent; destruction of property by an unprivileged belligerent; and terrorism."[83] Concurrently, as a result of the Supreme Court's decision in *Hamdi v. Rumsfeld*,[84] a Combatant Status Review Tribunal reviewed Hamdan's detention and on July 7, 2004, declared that Hamdan had been correctly classified as an enemy combatant and was therefore subject to detention. Hence, "proceedings before the military commission commenced."[85]

Asked later why Hamdan's case was the one that made it to the center of debate, Katyal said it was a matter of substance, timing, and the strength of the case.[86] Most important, Katyal and Swift were looking for a case involving a link to al-Qaeda or some other non-state actor rather than a more conventional conflict (such as the war with Afghanistan). Hamdan was also among the first detainees declared triable by the military commission. Moreover, the case against him seemed extraordinarily thin. Katyal and Swift chose this case from among the others "because this was a guy they couldn't allege had done anything personally wrong. He drove a bad guy, but that didn't make him much of a criminal."[87] It was far from clear, however, that the courts would agree—or that Hamdan could even reach a court that would hear his claims.

District Court. Hamdan's lawyers filed his petition for habeas corpus in U.S. district court, where they made six central claims: First, Hamdan was denied his right to a speedy trial under the UCMJ when being held for years without charge. Second, the nature and length of his detention violated the Third Geneva Convention and Common Article 3 of the Geneva Conventions. Third, the establishment of the military commission by the President violated the separation of powers. Fourth,

---

[81] Pursuant to the Ninth Circuit's ruling in *Gherebi v. Bush*, 374 F.3d 727 (9th Cir. 2004), the case was moved to the D.C. District Court and docketed on September 2, 2004. Hamdan v. Rumsfeld, 344 F. Supp. 2d 152, 156 (D.D.C. 2004).

[82] "Hamdan's counsel, Charles Swift, initially filed the petition in this case in his own name as Hamdan's next friend. The government challenged Swift's standing to do so. At a conference on September 14, 2004, the petition was amended, by consent and *nunc pro tunc*, to be in Hamdan's name only." 344 F. Supp. 2d at 156 n.3.

[83] Hamdan v. Rumsfeld, 344 F. Supp. 2d 152, 156 (2004) (quoting Dep't of Def., *Military Commission List of Charges for Salim Ahmed Hamdan*).

[84] Hamdi v. Rumsfeld, 542 U.S. 507 (2004).

[85] Hamdan v. Rumsfeld, 548 U.S. 557, 571 (2006).

[86] Interview by Oona Hathaway with Neal Katyal, Professor, Geo. Univ. L. Ctr. (Oct. 30, 2006).

[87] *Id.*

the military commission had exceeded its authority to try violations of the law of war because the crime of conspiracy is not a war crime. Fifth, the establishment of the military commission violated the Equal Protection Clause of the Fifth Amendment and 42 U.S.C. § 1981. Sixth and finally, the President's November 13 Order did not, on its face, apply to Hamdan.

On November 8, 2004, Judge James Robertson granted Hamdan's petition in part.[88] He ruled that the President had the power to create military commissions only under the law of war as authorized by Congress[89] and that, furthermore, the government had not properly determined whether Hamdan was a prisoner of war under the Third Geneva Convention. That Convention guarantees that prisoners of war are "sentenced only if the sentence has been pronounced by the same courts according to the same procedure as in the case of members of the armed forces of the Detaining Power."[90] Judge Robertson found that "[t]he Military Commission is not such a court. Its procedures are not such procedures."[91] Under Article 5 of the Third Geneva Convention, until such a determination was made, Hamdan was therefore entitled to all the protections of POW status, including trial by court-martial.[92]

Moreover, Robertson found that even if Hamdan were not a prisoner of war, the military commission still had to comply with the UCMJ, which stated:

> procedures . . . in courts-martial, military commissions and other courts of inquiry, may be prescribed by the President by regulations which shall, so far as he considers practicable, apply the principles of law and the rules of evidence generally recognized in the trial of criminal cases in the United States district courts, but which may not be *contrary to or inconsistent with* this chapter.[93]

Hamdan's exclusion from his own trial, Robertson found, was "directly contrary to the UCMJ's right to be present"[94] and furthermore conflicted with the U.S. conception of fundamental fairness. The military commissions thus did not comply with the procedures set forth by

---

88 Hamdan v. Rumsfeld, 344 F. Supp. 2d 152, 152 (D.D.C. 2004).

89 The UCMJ stated, "[t]he provisions of this chapter conferring jurisdiction upon courts-martial do not deprive military commissions, provost courts, or other military tribunals of concurrent jurisdiction with respect to offenders or offenses that by statute or by the law of war may be tried by military commissions, provost courts, or other military tribunals." 10 U.S.C. § 821.

90 Geneva Convention III, *supra* note 8, 6 U.S.T. at 3394, 75 U.N.T.S. at 212.

91 344 F. Supp. 2d at 160.

92 Geneva Convention III, *supra* note 8, 6 U.S.T. at 3324, 75 U.N.T.S. at 34.

93 10 U.S.C. § 836 (emphasis added).

94 344 F. Supp. 2d at 172.

Congress, and, therefore, the President's authority was "at its lowest ebb."[95]

Furthermore, Robertson ruled not only that the Geneva Conventions applied to the conflict with al-Qaeda, rejecting the government's arguments to the contrary,[96] but also that most of the provisions were self-executing—that is, were judicially enforceable.[97] Specifically, Robertson found that the prohibition against "the passing of sentences and the carrying out of executions without previous judgment pronounced by a regularly constituted court affording all the judicial guarantees as indispensable by civilized peoples"[98] provided a modicum of protection for Hamdan even if he was not eligible for prisoner-of-war status.

It was a striking victory that called into question the entire apparatus the administration had built to hold and try suspected terrorists at Guantánamo outside the reach of U.S. courts. The Bush administration, calling the Robertson ruling an "unprecedented intrusion" into presidential powers, responded by seeking full review in the D.C. Circuit Court within ten days.[99]

Circuit Court. On July 15, 2005, the Court of Appeals for the District of Columbia reversed the decision of the district court.[100] Judge Randolph, joined by then-Judge Roberts (who would soon be promoted to the U.S. Supreme Court), wrote the opinion of the court; Judge Williams filed a concurring opinion. The court agreed with the district court that it could—and should—exercise jurisdiction over Hamdan's habeas corpus petition. Yet the circuit court disagreed with the lower court on the merits of Hamdan's claims. It found that Congress had authorized the military commissions in the Authorization for the Use of Military Force (AUMF)[101] and in the UCMJ.[102] The court further held that the military commissions were not "contrary to or inconsistent with" the UCMJ, reasoning that

> the UCMJ takes care to distinguish between "courts-martial" and "military commissions" .... The terms are not used interchangeably, and the majority of the UCMJ's procedural requirements refer only to courts-martial. The district court's approach would obliterate this distinction. A far more sensible reading is that in establishing military commissions, the

---

[95] *See id.* at 160 (quoting Youngstown Sheet & Tube Co. v. Sawyer, 343 U.S. 579, 637 (1952)).

[96] The government argued that Common Article 3 should be applied only to domestic conflicts or conflicts "not of an international character." Brief for Respondents at 48, Hamdan v. Rumsfeld, 548 U.S. 557 (2006) (No. 05–184). It argued that the conflict with al-Qaeda was clearly international in scope and therefore Common Article 3 did not apply. *Id.*

[97] 344 F. Supp. 2d at 164–65.

[98] Geneva Convention III, *supra* note 8, 6 U.S.T. at 3320, 75 U.N.T.S. at 34.

[99] Tony Mauro, *Inadmissible: Fast Track,* LEGAL TIMES, Nov. 29, 2004, at 4.

[100] Hamdan v. Rumsfeld, 415 F.3d 33, 33 (D.C. Cir. 2005).

[101] *Id.* at 37–38; *see* Authorization for Use of Military Force, Pub. L. No. 107–40, 115 Stat. 224 (2001).

[102] 415 F.3d at 38, 42–43; *see* 10 U.S.C. §§ 821, 836(a).

> President may not adopt procedures that are "contrary to or inconsistent with" the UCMJ's provisions governing military commissions.[103]

The court interpreted an earlier case, *Johnson v. Eisentrager*,[104] to have established that the Geneva Conventions could not be judicially enforced. Furthermore, the court determined that the Conventions did not apply to Hamdan because the conflict with al-Qaeda was not covered by the Conventions.[105] Last, the court held, even if the Conventions did apply to him, Hamdan could get no relief, because comity required that the judicial branch "defer to ongoing military proceedings."[106] The court dismissed the remaining claims without discussion.

Supreme Court. On August 8, 2005, Hamdan's lawyers filed a petition for writ of certiorari in the U.S. Supreme Court. The Supreme Court granted certiorari on November 7, 2005, to determine whether the military commission established by the President to try petitioner and others similarly situated for alleged war crimes in the war on terror was duly authorized under the 2001 AUMF, the UCMJ, or the inherent powers of the President and whether Hamdan and others held at Guantánamo could challenge the legality of their detention by the Executive Branch through a writ of habeas corpus in the federal courts.

By a vote of five Justices to three, the Court ruled in Hamdan's favor.[107] The decision, announced on June 29, 2006, included a dizzying array of concurrences and dissenting opinions that stretched across 185 pages of the U.S. Reports. Justice Stevens wrote for the majority of the Court on most of the issues (but for a plurality on some). He began with the threshold question of whether the Court could even hear the case. Seeking to take advantage of the jurisdiction-stripping provisions that had been added to the Detainee Treatment Act days after the Court granted the writ of certiorari in the *Hamdan* case, the government had argued, first in a motion to dismiss the writ of certiorari and then in its merits brief, that the case ought to be dismissed. The Detainee Treatment Act, the government argued, had the effect of repealing federal jurisdiction over detainee habeas actions—including those, like *Hamdan*,

---

103 415 F.3d at 41–42.

104 Johnson v. Eisentrager, 339 U.S. 763 (1950). *Johnson v. Eisentrager* concerned German nationals convicted by military commission in China. The Court stated in dicta that the 1929 Geneva Conventions were non-self-executing. The court of appeals in *Hamdan* argued by analogy that the 1949 Geneva Conventions were likewise judicially unenforceable. 415 F.3d at 40.

105 415 F.3d at 41.

106 *Id.* at 42.

107 Hamdan v. Rumsfeld, 548 U.S. 557 (2006). Justice Stevens delivered the judgment and opinion of the Court, in which Justices Ginsburg, Souter, and Breyer joined, and in which Justice Kennedy joined in part. Justices Kennedy and Breyer both filed separate concurring opinions. Justices Scalia, Thomas, and Alito all filed and joined each other's dissenting opinions. Chief Justice Roberts took no part in the consideration or decision of the case because of his role in deciding the case at the circuit court level. For details on Roberts's involvement in the case, see Jim VandeHei, *Judge Heard Terrorism Case as He Interviewed for Seat*, WASH. POST, Aug. 17, 2005, at A4.

that were presently pending before the courts.[108] Stevens, writing for the Court, concluded that the Act's jurisdiction-stripping provisions did not apply to cases that were, like Hamdan's, pending on the date of enactment.[109] The Court likewise rejected the government's argument that principles of comity should lead it to abstain from the case, citing the public importance of the questions raised and the duty that rests on the courts " 'to preserve unimpaired the constitutional safeguards of civil liberty.' "[110] The Court thus once again decisively rejected the administration's—and Congress's—efforts to exclude it from overseeing the Executive Branch's conduct toward detainees held in the war on terror.[111] The Court would oversee the administration's conduct and subject its actions to scrutiny in light of domestic and international legal limits.

On the merits, the Court concluded that Congress in Article 21 of the UCMJ had explicitly authorized the use of military commissions created by the executive, *provided that* the commissions comply with the law of war.[112] In Hamdan's case, the commission was operating in violation of that limited mandate. First, a plurality of the Court held that the commission exceeded its powers by trying Hamdan for a crime that fell outside the law of war. "Conspiracy," the only charge levied against him, was not a violation of the law of war, the plurality held, because it was neither proscribed by statute nor by domestic or international sources of the common law of war.[113]

Second, the Court held that the procedures that the government had decreed for the commissions were woefully inadequate. They are inconsistent "not only with the American common law of war, but also with the rest of the UCMJ, insofar as applicable, and with the 'rules and precepts of the law of nations.' "[114] The UCMJ imposes a variety of

---

[108] It was likely not coincidental that the President's signing statement specifically stated that he understood the Act's jurisdiction-stripping provisions to apply to pending cases, as well as those not yet filed.

[109] 548 U.S. at 572–83.

[110] *Id.* at 588 (quoting *Ex parte* Quirin, 317 U.S. 1, 19 (1942)).

[111] This is true at least with regard to those who filed their cases before the DTA became law.

[112] 548 U.S. at 593. The Court also held that nothing in either the 2001 AUMF or the 2005 DTA expanded this authorization. 548 U.S. at 593–94; *see* Authorization for Use of Military Force, Pub. L. No. 107–40, 115 Stat. 224 (2001); Detainee Treatment Act of 2005, Pub. L. No. 109–148, §§ 1001–1006, 119 Stat. 2739 (codified at 42 U.S.C. § 2000dd–1).

[113] 548 U.S. at 601–13. Justices Stevens, Souter, Ginsburg, and Breyer formed the plurality on this point. Justice Kennedy joined these four Justices to form a majority on the rest of the case, but he did not join Parts V and VI–D–iv, concluding that there was no need to decide whether Common Article 3 of the Conventions requires that the accused have the right to be present at all stages of a criminal trial or to address the validity of the conspiracy charge against Hamdan. *Id.* at 653–55 (Kennedy, J., concurring in part).

[114] *Id.* at 613 (quoting *Ex parte* Quirin, 317 U.S. 1, 28 (1942)). Two restrictions are placed on the President's power to promulgate rules of procedure—no rule can be "contrary to or inconsistent with" the UCMJ, and the rules must be "uniform insofar as practicable." In other words, courts-martial and military commissions are subject to the same procedures

procedural protections, including a requirement that the rules applied to military commissions must be the same as those applied to courts-martial "insofar as practicable."[115] And yet the procedures outlined for the commissions deviated from the procedures for courts-martial in ways that were not adequately justified. For example, the commissions would "permit the admission of *any* evidence that, in the opinion of the presiding officer, 'would have probative value to a reasonable person.' "[116] Under this test, the Court explained, testimonial hearsay and evidence obtained through coercion would be fully admissible. A vote of two-thirds of the commission members was sufficient for a guilty verdict, and appeals are taken to a three-member review panel composed of military officers and designated by the Secretary of Defense. Hence the review was in the sole purview of the Executive Branch. Moreover, a conviction could be based on evidence that the defendant had not seen or heard, and a defendant could be excluded from his own trial for reasons other than his own behavior.[117]

Finally, the Court directly addressed international law, specifically the applicability of the Geneva Conventions. It found that the military commission convened to try Hamdan was established in violation of Common Article 3 of the Geneva Conventions.[118] It rejected the D.C. Circuit's holding that the Geneva Conventions did not "confer on Hamdan a right to enforce its provisions in Court."[119] Regardless of whether the Conventions were an independent source of law "binding on the Government's actions and furnishing petitioner with any enforceable right," compliance with the law of war "is the condition upon which the authority set forth in Article 21 [of the UCMJ] is granted."[120] In short, whether or not the Conventions create an enforceable right on their own, they apply via their incorporation into the statute.

The Court next rejected the government's argument that Common Article 3 did not apply to Hamdan because it did not apply to the conflict with al-Qaeda. The Court explained that "[t]he term 'conflict not of an international character' is used here in contradistinction to a conflict

---

unless impracticable. The Court held that the government had shown no reason why such uniformity was impracticable in this case. *Id.* at 621–24.

115 10 U.S.C. § 836.

116 548 U.S. at 614 (quoting Commission Order No. 1, § 6(D)(1)) (emphasis in original).

117 Justice Kennedy declined to decide whether Common Article 3 necessarily requires that "the accused has the right to be present at all stages of a criminal trial." *Id.* at 653–54 (Kennedy, J., concurring in part). Hence the decision is a plurality on this last point.

118 Some of the language in Justice Stevens's opinion can be read to suggest that other portions of the Geneva Conventions are independently enforceable. Justice Kennedy specifically reserved on this issue: "There should be reluctance, furthermore, to reach unnecessarily the question whether, as the plurality seems to conclude, . . . Article 75 of Protocol I to the Geneva Conventions is binding law notwithstanding the earlier decision by our Government not to accede to the Protocol." *Id.* at 654.

119 Hamdan v. Rumsfeld, 415 F.3d 33, 40 (D.C. Cir. 2005). *See supra* text accompanying note 104.

120 548 U.S. at 627–28.

between nations"[121] and was intended to provide "some minimal protection, falling short of full protection under the Conventions, to individuals associated with neither a signatory nor even a nonsignatory 'Power' who are involved in a conflict 'in the territory of' a signatory."[122]

Having decided that Common Article 3 was both enforceable and applied to Hamdan, the Court held that the military commissions failed to provide Hamdan the protections required by the Conventions. The Conventions, the Court explained, require that Hamdan be tried by a " 'regularly constituted court affording all the judicial guarantees which are recognized as indispensable by civilized peoples' "[123]—a requirement that was not satisfied by the military tribunals. At a minimum, "a military commission 'can be "regularly constituted" by the standards of our military justice system only if some practical need explains deviations from court-martial practice' "—a need that had not been demonstrated.[124] The Court thus concluded:

> Common Article 3 obviously tolerates a great degree of flexibility in trying individuals captured during armed conflict; its requirements are general ones, crafted to accommodate a wide variety of legal systems. But *requirements* they are nonetheless. The commission that the President has convened to try Hamdan does not meet those requirements.[125]

And so the Court once again pushed back against efforts by the administration to shield its actions from outside scrutiny. Once again the Court refused Executive Branch claims of unilateral authority to act in the war on terror without significant oversight of its actions by the courts. And once again the Court found that when it pulled back the curtain, the actions that were revealed fell far short of the standards established by both domestic and international law. In revealing these weaknesses in the system, however, the Court also revealed its core strength. For all the abuses and violations of the law, as terrible as they were and are, the case itself—and the decision of the Court in favor of a suspected enemy of the state and against the country's own representatives—signaled the country's deep and abiding commitment to the very principles that had been broken.

---

121 548 U.S. at 630 (quoting Geneva Convention III, *supra* note 8, 6 U.S.T. at 3318–20, 75 U.N.T.S. at 32–34).

122 *Id.* (quoting Geneva Convention III, *supra* note 8, 6 U.S.T. at 3318–20, 75 U.N.T.S. at 32–34).

123 *Id.* (quoting Geneva Convention III, *supra* note 8, 6 U.S.T. at 3318–20, 75 U.N.T.S. at 32–34).

124 *Id.* at 632–33 (quoting Kennedy, J., concurring in part).

125 *Id.* at 635 (emphasis in original).

IV. THE AFTERMATH

Widely viewed as a sharp rebuke to the Bush administration,[126] the Court's decision was met with jubilation in the human rights community. *Time* called the opinion "185 pages [that] can be summarized in two words: Start over."[127] The *New York Times* reported that "the decision was such a sweeping and categorical defeat for the administration that it left human rights lawyers who have pressed this and other cases on behalf of Guantánamo detainees almost speechless with surprise and delight."[128] The *Chicago Tribune*, likewise, called it an elimination of "a central pillar of the president's anti-terrorism strategy" and "signaled a limit to judicial deference to the executive branch on a key question of war powers."[129] The *Washington Post* proclaimed that the decision was "clearly a setback for the White House."[130] In a subsequent analysis piece, the *Post* gave even more gravitas to the decision, finding that it struck down not only a specific presidential policy but also the "governing philosophy of a leader who at repeated turns has operated on the principle that it is better to act than to ask permission."[131] Walter Dellinger declared, "Hamdan is simply the most important decision on presidential power and the rule of law ever."[132] Even presidential power enthusiast John Yoo recognized the importance of the Court's assertion of power: it "could affect detention conditions, interrogation methods, the use of force," he said. "It could affect every aspect of the war on terror."[133]

The Bush administration was quick to respond. At a press conference in Chicago, President Bush stated unequivocally, "I am willing to abide by the ruling of the Supreme Court" and expressed his intent to work with Congress in drafting new legislation to address the Court's concerns. At the same time, Bush also tried to limit the decision to military commissions, asserting that "[t]hey were silent on . . . whether or not we should have used Guantánamo. In other words, they accepted the use of

---

[126] *See, e.g.*, David Sanger, *Court's Ruling Is Likely To Force Negotiations Over Presidential Power*, N.Y. TIMES (June 30, 2006), https://www.nytimes.com/2006/06/30/washington/courts-ruling-is-likely-to-force-negotiations-over-presidential.html.

[127] Nathan Thornburgh, *Gitmo. How to Fix It*, TIME MAG., July 10, 2006, at 22.

[128] Greenhouse, *supra* note 68.

[129] Andrew Zajac, *Tribunals Ruled Illegal; Court: Guantanamo Trials Violate U.S., Global Laws*, CHI. TRIB., June 30, 2006, at C1.

[130] Charles Lane, *High Court Rejects Detainee Tribunals; 5 to 3 Ruling Curbs President's Claim of Wartime Power*, WASH. POST, June 30, 2006, at A1.

[131] Peter Baker & Michael Abramowitz, *A Governing Philosophy Rebuffed*, WASH. POST, June 30, 2006, at A1. *See also* Sidney Blumenthal, *The Imperial Presidency Crushed*, SALON (July 6, 2006), http://salon.com/opinion/blumenthal/2006/07/06/hamdan/index_np.html (arguing that the decision "has thrown Bush's war paradigm into profound crisis").

[132] Walter Dellinger, *The Most Important Decision on Presidential Power. Ever.*, SLATE MAG. (June 29, 2006), http://www.slate.com/id/2144476/entry/2144825.

[133] Adam Liptak, *The Court Enters the War, Loudly*, N.Y. TIMES (July 2, 2006), https://www.nytimes.com/2006/07/02/weekinreview/the-court-enters-the-war-loudly.html.

Guantánamo, the decision I made."[134] He further declared, "I'm not going to jeopardize the safety of the American people. People have got to understand that."[135]

A briefing with unnamed "Senior Administration Officials" reiterated the President's interpretation, asserting that "[n]othing in the holding affects the authority of the president in wartime to detain enemy combatants through the duration of hostilities. . . . [N]othing in the holding affects the status of Guantanamo Bay or the continued detention of enemy combatants there one way or the other."[136] At the same time, officials confirmed the administration's willingness to follow the decision and expressed its intent to work with Congress.[137]

Others in the administration were less accommodating. Attorney General Alberto Gonzales complained, "[w]hat this decision has done is, it's hampered our ability to move forward with a tool which we had hoped would be available to the president of the United States in dealing with terrorists."[138] Capitol Hill Republicans were even more combative. House Majority Leader John Boehner accused Democrats who supported the *Hamdan* decision as advocating for "special privileges for terrorists" and further commented that "Al Qaeda . . . is surely pleased at the show of support from Capitol Hill Democrats."[139]

Despite these words of defiance, the administration and its allies on Capitol Hill seemed for a time to be ready to make some important changes in their handling of detainees. The 2014 Senate Select Committee on Intelligence Report found that, "[i]n late 2005 and 2006, the Detainee Treatment Act and then the U.S. Supreme Court decision in *Hamdan v. Rumsfeld* caused the CIA to again temporarily suspend the use of its enhanced interrogation techniques."[140] On September 6, 2006, the Department of Defense issued a revised *Army Field Manual* along with an accompanying Department of Defense Directive 2310.[141]

---

[134] President George W. Bush, Press Conference by the President, Museum of Science and Industry, Chicago, Illinois (July 7, 2006), https://georgewbush-whitehouse.archives.gov/news/releases/2006/07/20060707-1.html.

[135] Josh Gerstein, *Court Sidelines Bush's War Crimes Strategy*, N.Y. SUN, June 30, 2006, at A1.

[136] *Transcript of Teleconference with Senior Officials Regarding Supreme Court's Ruling in the Hamdan Case*, U.S. NEWS WIRE, June 30, 2006, LEXIS (database updated July 2006).

[137] *Id.*

[138] Blumenthal, *supra* note 131.

[139] Press Release, Rep. John Boehner, Capitol Hill Democrats Advocate Special Privileges for Terrorists (June 30, 2006), *quoted in McCain, Feinstein Debate Terrorist Trials*, ABC NEWS (July 2, 2006, 10:59 AM), https://abcnews.go.com/ThisWeek/story?id=2145372&page=1.

[140] SENATE SELECT COMMITTEE ON INTELLIGENCE, COMMITTEE STUDY OF THE CENTRAL INTELLIGENCE AGENCY'S DETENTION AND INTERROGATION PROGRAM, S. REP. NO. 113–288, at xxv (2014).

[141] HEADQUARTERS, DEP'T OF THE ARMY, FM 2–22.3 (FM 34–52) HUMAN INTELLIGENCE COLLECTOR OPERATIONS (Sept. 2006), https://www.marines.mil/Portals/1/Publications/FM%202-22.3%20%20Human%20Intelligence%20Collector%20Operations_1.pdf (known as Army Field Manual); U.S. DEP'T OF DEF., DOD DIRECTIVE 2310.01E (2006),

Together, they prohibited the use of unlawful and abusive techniques, and committed to compliance with Common Article 3 of the Geneva Conventions.

Yet this hopeful move was quickly overshadowed by sweeping new legislation passed in the waning days of the 109th Congress. Shortly before members of Congress left Washington to campaign for reelection in their home states, Congress passed the Military Commissions Act of 2006.[142]

The Act's stated purpose was to "facilitate bringing to justice terrorists and other unlawful enemy combatants through full and fair trials by military commissions, and for other purposes."[143] In many ways, however, the Act was a repudiation of the *Hamdan* decision. Where the Court found the rules of international law placed limits on the commissions, the Act declared the Conventions judicially unenforceable[144]—even going so far as to forbid courts from relying on "foreign or international source of law" in any cases involving military commissions.[145] Where the Court had insisted on independently considering whether the administration's actions were consistent with international law, the Act criminalized grave breaches but gave the President the exclusive authority to interpret the meaning and the application of the Geneva Conventions for violations that are not grave breaches.[146] Where the Court resisted efforts to strip the federal courts of jurisdiction over the habeas petitions of detainees, the Act stripped the statutory right of habeas corpus from non-citizen enemy combatants,[147] while giving the President the sole authority to determine enemy combatant status. Where the Court had insisted on more significant procedural protections for detainees, the Act eliminated them—including the right to a speedy trial and most protections against hearsay. It also permitted the use of statements obtained through the use of cruel, inhuman, or degrading treatment if obtained prior to the enactment of the Detainee Treatment Act of 2005. Where the Court had held the commissions' authority limited to trying violations of the law of war, the Act expanded that authority to include a variety of crimes—including conspiracy.[148]

---

https://www.esd.whs.mil/Portals/54/Documents/DD/issuances/dodd/231001e.pdf?ver=6y1Oz3QqY1slOmu_p9g9Fw%3d%3d.

142 Military Commissions Act of 2006, Pub. L. No. 109–366, 120 Stat. 2600.

143 *Id.*

144 There are questions as to whether this limitation is constitutional. *See* Carlos Manuel Vázquez, *The Military Commissions Act, the Geneva Conventions, and the Courts: A Critical Guide*, 101 AM. J. INT'L L. 73, 88–92 (2007).

145 Military Commissions Act § 6(a)(2).

146 *Id.* § 6(a)(3).

147 The Supreme Court later determined this was unconstitutional in *Boumediene v. Bush*, 553 U.S. 723 (2008).

148 Military Commissions Act § 3. The decision to include conspiracy later became a subject of significant litigation over the question whether it was, in fact, a war crime cognizable by a military commission. *See, e.g.*, Benjamin R. Farley, *The D.C. Circuit,*

Almost immediately after President Bush signed the Act into law, the government moved to dismiss the pending habeas corpus petitions of the roughly 430 detainees remaining at Guantánamo. In early November 2006, the *New York Times* reported, "[t]he Bush administration's successful effort to have Congress eliminate the right of Guantánamo prisoners to challenge their detentions before federal judges is now moving toward what may be an epic battle in the courts."[149]

In 2007, Hamdan, having been detained at this point for five years at Guantánamo, was charged under the new Act with conspiracy and providing material support for terrorism. He was put on trial before the new military commissions. The military judges in the case, however, dismissed the case, ruling that the military had not followed procedures to declare him and a fellow detainee "unlawful enemy combatants," and thus the commissions lacked jurisdiction over the case.[150] This decision required all of the remaining detainees' cases to be reviewed to determine whether they were "unlawful enemy combatants" subject to the jurisdiction of the commissions.

Later that year, Hamdan's designation was reviewed, and he was determined to be an unlawful enemy combatant and thus subject to the jurisdiction of the commission. In 2008, he was tried before the commission. A jury acquitted him of conspiracy but convicted him of material support for terrorism, and he was sentenced to sixty-six months imprisonment. With credit for time served, this left him with only five additional months on his sentence. Although the government asserted that it could continue to detain him until the end of hostilities, it transferred him to Yemen in late 2008, where he was released. Even after release, Hamdan continued to challenge his conviction in court. In 2012, the DC Circuit Court of Appeals decided that "material support for terrorism was not an international law war crime at the time Hamdan engaged in the relevant conduct" and thus it vacated his conviction for material support for terrorism.[151]

While campaigning for president, Barack Obama promised he would close the Guantánamo Bay detention center. But progress toward that goal was slow, and in 2015, Congress placed a restriction in the National Defense Authorization Act prohibiting the use of federal money to bring detainees to the United States for any purpose, including prosecution or

---

Conspiracy, and the Guantanamo Military Commissions: Third Time's the Charm?, JUST SEC. (Sept. 4, 2020), https://www.justsecurity.org/72280/the-d-c-circuit-conspiracy-and-the-guantanamo-military-commissions-third-times-the-charm/.

149 Neil A. Lewis, *Appeals Court Weighs Prisoners' Right to Fight Detention*, N.Y. TIMES, Nov. 7, 2006, at A15.

150 William Glaberson, *Military Judges Dismiss Charges for 2 Detainees*, N.Y. TIMES, June 5, 2007, at A1.

151 Hamdan v. United States, 696 F.3d 1238 (D.C. Cir. 2012). In the interim, Congress worked with newly elected President Barack Obama to enact some modest reforms to the military commissions. Military Commissions Act of 2009, Pub. L. 111–84, § 1801, 123 Stat. 2190, 2574. These reforms brought the commissions closer to ordinary courts-martial but kept what many regard as a delegitimized tribunal in place.

continued detention.[152] It also required the Secretary of Defense to personally certify to a variety of conditions before releasing detainees abroad.[153] In part as a result, fifteen detainees remain at Guantánamo at the start of 2025, close to two decades after Hamdan's victory in the Supreme Court. Seven of them have been charged with war crimes in the military commission system, two have been convicted, three are held in "indefinite law-of-war detention," and three have been recommended for transfer to another country.[154]

V. CONCLUSION

The story of the post-September 11 era is by now a familiar one. In the name of the "flexibility" allegedly essential to protecting national security, the U.S. administration repeatedly sought to evade domestic and international legal restrictions on its treatment of detainees in the war on terror by avoiding review by domestic federal courts. It succeeded for a time in creating islands of exclusive authority—in Afghanistan, in Iraq, at Guantánamo, and at CIA "black sites." With no international or domestic enforcement mechanism behind it, and facing the executive leadership of the most powerful nation in the world, international law appeared consigned to irrelevance. Meanwhile, the troops, CIA officials, and contractors on the ground—given misleading legal guidance and placed under pressure to produce results—abused detainees, inflicting cruel, inhuman and degrading treatment and torture.

Yet international law was not entirely powerless. For into the breach created by the administration's insistence on its own exclusive authority came the domestic courts—sporadically and with imperfect long-term effect, but with a clear determination to assert the authority of the rule of law. This is ultimately what makes *Hamdan v. Rumsfeld* important. It stands for the principle that the courts—and not the President—have the authority to say what the law is and that the courts have the power to insist that the most basic principles of domestic and international law must be observed.

Enforcement of international law in domestic courts is essential to the effectiveness of that law. When the courts fail, the law fails too. Domestic enforcement means that international law can have sweeping effects even in a world in which such law is only rarely enforced through international tribunals. This domestic enforcement of international law—the enforcement of the law by domestic institutions including against their own government—represents a critical tool for enforcing international law around the globe.

---

[152] National Defense Authorization Act of 2016, § 1031, Pub. L. 114–92, 129 Stat. 735 (2015).

[153] *Id.* § 1034.

[154] *The Guantánamo Docket*, N.Y. TIMES, https://www.nytimes.com/interactive/2021/us/guantanamo-bay-detainees.html (last updated Jan. 11, 2025).

IV. INTERNATIONAL LAW AND INTERSTATE CONFLICTS

14

John E. Noyes

The *Caroline*: International Law and Resort to Force

During the night of December 29, 1837, approximately forty-five volunteers under the command of British naval officer Andrew Drew left Chippewa, in the British province of Upper Canada, and rowed five boats across the Niagara River. They sought the U.S. merchant vessel *Caroline*, docked at Schlosser, New York. This ship was supplying U.S. supporters of an uprising against British rule in Upper Canada who had occupied a British island from which they were shelling Chippewa. Drew and his men stormed the vessel; both crew members and attackers were injured, and at least one man died. Drew's men towed the *Caroline* out into the Niagara River, set her on fire, and left her to drift toward Niagara Falls. The ship sank, with parts of the wreckage plummeting over the Falls.

The *Caroline* incident led to a famous international law formulation concerning limits on resort to force. U.S. Secretary of State Daniel Webster wrote, in a diplomatic note to British Ambassador Henry Fox, that a state using force extraterritorially to defend itself must "show a necessity of self-defence, instant, overwhelming, leaving no choice of means, and no moment for deliberation." Under Webster's *Caroline* test, "even supposing the necessity of the moment authorized" forces to enter foreign territory, those forces must have done "nothing unreasonable or excessive; since the act, justified by the necessity of self-defence, must be limited by that necessity, and kept clearly within it."[1] The British government agreed with this test, although the two countries disagreed about how it applied to the facts.

The *Caroline* self-defense test is still invoked today, more than 175 years after it was first articulated. Over the years, publicists, tribunals, and government officials have interpreted the test in different ways, illustrating the challenges of taking a legal formulation from one historical context and applying it in another. This chapter explores why Webster developed his test, how it has been invoked, and why it has retained currency.

1 Letter from Daniel Webster to Henry Stephen Fox (Apr. 24, 1841) [hereinafter Webster's *Caroline* Letter], *in* 29 BRITISH AND FOREIGN STATE PAPERS 1129, 1138 (1857), *reprinted in* THE PAPERS OF DANIEL WEBSTER: DIPLOMATIC PAPERS, VOL. 1, 1841–1843, at 58, 67 (Kenneth E. Shewmaker ed., 1983) [hereinafter DIPLOMATIC PAPERS].

The U.S.-Canadian Frontier in 1837

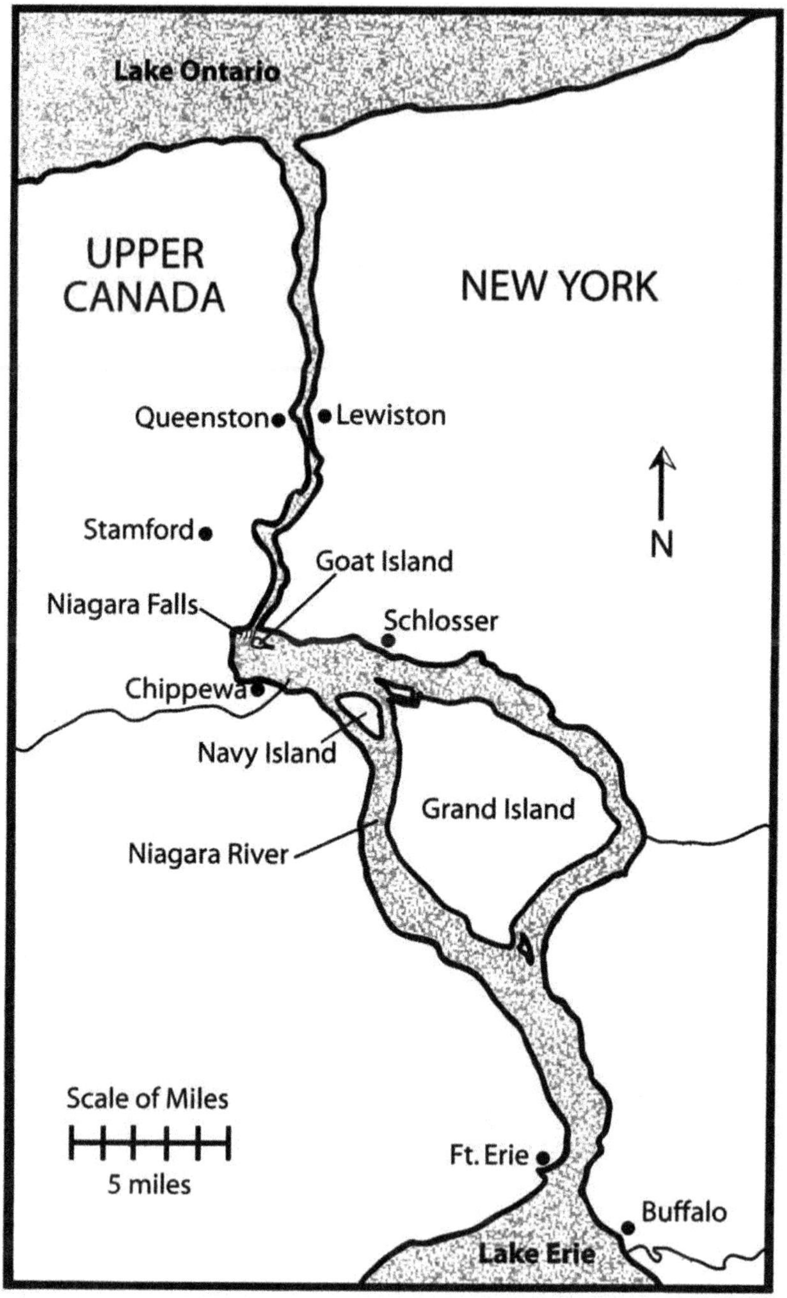

Although the *Caroline* story is most often linked to the law of self-defense, it offers other lessons as well. First, it shows how international law may affect the resolution of sensitive international political disputes. The *Caroline* dispute did not lead to a case before an international judicial or arbitral body, but U.S. and British diplomats relied on international law in negotiating a settlement. Second, the trial of the Canadian Alexander McLeod for murder and arson in connection with the destruction of the *Caroline* illustrates that U.S. courts have long applied international law to individuals. Third, the *Caroline* story highlights the challenges federalism may pose to the effective use of international law by the United States.

I. BACKGROUND[2]

U.S.-British relations were strained during the 1830s. There was lingering bitterness over the War of 1812, when the British had burned government buildings in Washington, D.C. British interference with U.S. shipping complicated relations, and boundary disputes remained unsettled.

Tensions ran high along the U.S. border with the British colony of Upper Canada because of an insurrection against British rule there.[3] Several hundred Canadian rebels, believing themselves not fairly represented by the British government, attacked York (now part of Toronto) in early December 1837. The attack failed, and the rebels' leader William Mackenzie, a political reformer and newspaper publisher, fled to upstate New York, there seeking support for the insurrection.

The Upper Canadian rebellion attracted U.S. sympathizers who drew parallels to the overthrow of British colonial rule in the Revolutionary War. Many also thought that a change of government to the north would open up economic opportunities for U.S. citizens; some even hoped that Upper Canada would become part of the United States. Several thousand New York "Patriots" joined "Hunters' Lodges," fomenting anti-British sentiment and helping the insurgents in Upper Canada.[4] Although U.S. law provided penalties for its citizens who aided endeavors directed against the territory of any foreign country with

---

2 For a thoroughly researched and insightful account of the *Caroline* incident, see CRAIG FORCESE, DESTROYING THE CAROLINE: THE FRONTIER RAID THAT RESHAPED THE RIGHT TO WAR (2018). *See also* HOWARD JONES, TO THE WEBSTER-ASHBURTON TREATY: A STUDY IN ANGLO-AMERICAN RELATIONS, 1783–1843 (1977); KENNETH R. STEVENS, BORDER DIPLOMACY: THE *CAROLINE* AND MCLEOD AFFAIRS IN ANGLO-AMERICAN-CANADIAN RELATIONS, 1837–1842 (1989); R.Y. Jennings, *The* Caroline *and McLeod Cases*, 32 AM. J. INT'L L. 82 (1938).

3 In 1841, Upper Canada (today's Ontario) and Lower Canada (Quebec) would merge to form the Province of Canada. The self-governing Dominion of Canada, comprised of the Province of Canada, New Brunswick, and Nova Scotia, was created in 1867. British North America Act, 1867, 30–31 Vict., ch. 3 (U.K.).

4 Estimates of the number of Patriots along the entire U.S.-Canadian border ranged from 15,000 to 200,000. THE PAPERS OF DANIEL WEBSTER: CORRESPONDENCE, VOL. 5, 1840–1843, at 174 n.4 (Harold D. Moser ed., 1982) [hereinafter CORRESPONDENCE]. One contemporary observer thought the Hunters' Lodges would contribute 10,000 volunteers in case of a war. Letter from Jacob Merritt Howard to Daniel Webster (Apr. 6, 1841), *in* DIPLOMATIC PAPERS, *supra* note 1, at 53, 54–55.

which the United States was at peace, the Canadian frontier was long and difficult to police.[5]

The British attack on the *Caroline* followed a build-up of U.S. citizens and equipment on Navy Island, a British island in the Niagara River three miles upstream from Niagara Falls. The Navy Island force began to gather in mid-December 1837. Several hundred men and a few women soon occupied the island, bombarding houses in Chippewa, Upper Canada, and Canadian boats. The British feared that Navy Island could become a staging ground for attacks into Upper Canada.

The insurgents took steps to strengthen their position, hiring the *Caroline*, a 45-ton, 71-foot merchant steamer, to transport supplies, munitions, and recruits from New York to the island. The vessel made several trips beginning on December 28th, mooring for the night of December 29th at Schlosser, New York, the site of an inn and a wharf on the U.S. shore across from Navy Island.

Colonel Allan McNab, who commanded British forces in the area, met with Captain Andrew Drew to discuss the Navy Island buildup. A direct attack across the strong Niagara River current against the fortified island was not feasible, so McNab ordered Drew to "cut out" the supply vessel. Drew understood his orders to authorize action against the *Caroline* "wherever found."[6] On the night of December 29th Drew and his men rowed across the Niagara River to attack the vessel at Schlosser, where they seized and destroyed her. Conflicting accounts circulated about the number of people killed and wounded during the attack, although the only person consistently identified as having been killed was Amos Durfee of Buffalo, New York.

The attack prompted a furor in upstate New York. Headlines in the *Buffalo Star* suggest the mood: "BRITISH OUTRAGE!! The American soil invaded and unarmed and unresisting Americans Butchered in Cold Blood!!"[7] Cries mounted for U.S. retaliation and even for a declaration of war against the United Kingdom. In Washington, D.C., a more moderate stance prevailed. President Martin Van Buren thought a war would be disastrous and reacted by sending General Winfield Scott to upstate New York, directing him to encourage respect for U.S. nonintervention laws. The United States soon strengthened those laws, authorizing the seizure

[5] Act of Apr. 20, 1818, ch. 88, § 6, 3 Stat. 447, 449. U.S. federal officials issued arrest warrants for individuals who aided rebels and sent customs collectors to stop shipments of arms and supplies to the insurgency, but the public, along with some local government officials, supported the Patriots. The U.S. district attorney in northern New York feared efforts "to prevent the due administration of justice." Letter from N.S. Benton to Secretary of State John Forsyth (Dec. 26, 1837), *in* H.R. EXEC. DOC. NO. 25–74, at 43, 44 (1838).

[6] [ANDREW] DREW, A NARRATIVE OF THE CAPTURE AND DESTRUCTION OF THE STEAMER 'CAROLINE' 6 (1864); Letter from Col. A.N. McNab to Lt.-Col. Strachan (Dec. 30, 1837), *in* British Foreign Office Records 881/9. *See* FORCESE, *supra* note 2, at 37–38.

[7] *Quoted in* E.A. Cruikshank, *The Invasion of Navy Island in 1837–8*, 32 ONTARIO HIST. SOC'Y PAPERS & REC. 7, 47 (1937). For a review of the news coverage, see FORCESE, *supra* note 2, at 61–64.

of munitions and vessels to be used against any country with which the U.S. government was not at war.[8]

Scott had to rely largely on persuasion rather than force in carrying out his mission, for the United States did not keep a large army during peacetime, and the militia Scott raised was weak.[9] He thwarted one insurgent plan to replace the *Caroline* with another ship simply by outbidding Patriots for her. Scott encouraged the Patriots to abandon Navy Island, which they did in mid-January 1838 in the face of heavy British bombardment and cold weather. Many Americans remained outraged by the *Caroline* incident, however, and Patriots unsuccessfully launched several new attacks into Upper Canada.[10]

British officials, predictably, viewed the *Caroline* affair in a different light. They saw the destruction of the vessel as necessary and expressed frustration at the U.S. government's inability or unwillingness to control attacks on Canada by U.S. citizens. Upper Canada's legislature approved court martial trials and the death penalty for foreigners engaged in anti-British acts,[11] and British authorities threatened severe consequences for the United States should it fail to control Patriots' attacks. In the words of Lieutenant Governor Francis Head, "we would not stand with 'folded arms' to allow ourselves to be surrounded and hustled out of Upper Canada by a mob."[12] The British government, concerned about the continuing activities of the Patriots, increased the British fleet on the Great Lakes[13] and stood ready to pursue Patriots into the United States in response to attacks in British territory.[14]

Those trying to determine the responsibility of the *Caroline*'s attackers relied heavily on international law. Lawyers, judges, legislators, and commentators saw the incident as linked inextricably to international law questions concerning neutrality, the legality of resort to force, and the immunity of soldiers engaged in armed conflicts. Soon

---

8 Act of Mar. 10, 1838, ch. 31, 5 Stat. 212. *See* Edward Dumbauld, *Neutrality Laws of the United States*, 7 AM. J. INT'L L. 258 (1937).

9 Almost all regular U.S. soldiers were then stationed in Florida and on the western frontier.

10 *See* FORCESE, *supra* note 2, at 50–54.

11 Ch. III, An Act to protect the Inhabitants of this Province against Lawless Aggressions form Subjects of Foreign Countries, at Peace with Her Majesty, Jan. 12, 1838, *in* STATUTES OF HER MAJESTY'S PROVINCE OF UPPER CANADA, PASSED IN THE THIRD SESSION OF THE THIRTEENTH PROVINCIAL PARLIAMENT 7 (1838), https://www.canadiana.ca/view/oocihm.9_10042_46/2 (last visited Jan. 15, 2025).

12 Explanatory Memorandum Addressed by Sir Francis Head to Lord Glenelg (May 21, 1838), *in* 9 IRISH UNIVERSITY PRESS SERIES OF BRITISH PARLIAMENTARY PAPERS 1837–38, at 516, 521 (1969).

13 The naval buildup was controversial, because in the Rush-Bagot Agreement, Exchange of Notes Concerning the Naval Forces to Be Maintained on the Great Lakes, U.S.-U.K., Apr. 28–29, 1817, 8 Stat. 231, the United States and the United Kingdom had agreed to reduce armed vessels on the Great Lakes. *See* STEVENS, *supra* note 2, at 51–52, 132–34.

14 Letter from Viscount Palmerston to Henry S. Fox (Dec. 15, 1838), *in* British Foreign Office Records 5/321, 115/68.

after the destruction of the *Caroline*, U.S. and British diplomats invoked international law in their negotiations.

II. THE *CAROLINE* DISPUTE AND THE *McLEOD* CASE

International Law and Diplomacy, 1838. On January 5, 1838, U.S. Secretary of State John Forsyth complained to Henry Fox, the British ambassador in Washington, about the "extraordinary outrage committed from Her Britannic Majesty's province of Upper Canada, on the persons and property of citizens of The United States, within the jurisdiction of the State of New York."[15] Fox both condemned the invasion of the British territory of Navy Island by armed U.S. citizens and justified the destruction of the *Caroline* on the grounds of "the necessity of self-defence and self-preservation."[16]

The U.S. government formally demanded reparations in a letter from Andrew Stevenson, the U.S. minister in London, to Viscount Palmerston, the British Foreign Secretary, on May 22, 1838. Stevenson relied on principles of international law to argue the illegality of British interference with U.S. "right and sovereignty." Although the United Kingdom could treat U.S. citizens as enemies if they were captured fighting the British government in British territory, the attack on the *Caroline* in the United States contravened the "sacred" principle of immunity of neutral territory. Even if those on board the *Caroline* had violated "the neutrality of the United States and the rights of war" by aiding Canadian insurgents, the violators "were alone amenable to the laws of the United States." Stevenson recognized a narrow exception to the inviolability of neutral territory for "state necessity," but "all publicists" on the law of nations agreed "that the necessity which can justify the invasion of neutral territory must be imminent and extreme, and involving impending destruction." To suppose that the destruction of the *Caroline* "was dictated by the extreme necessity of self-preservation," Stevenson maintained, "would be preposterous."[17] Later U.S. protests would echo Stevenson's emphasis on the need to respect neutral territory.

---

15 Letter from Mr. Forsyth to Mr. Fox (Jan. 5, 1838), *in* 26 BRITISH AND FOREIGN STATE PAPERS 1837–1838, at 1376, 1376–77 (1855).

16 Letter from Mr. Fox to Mr. Forsyth (Jan. 4, 1838), *in* People v. McLeod, 25 Wend. 483, 487 n.* (N.Y. Sup. Ct. 1841); Letter from Mr. Fox to Mr. Forsyth (Feb. 6, 1838), *in McLeod*, 25 Wend. at 490, 491 n.*. Fox also condemned the *Caroline*'s "piratical character," a claim the British government dropped after the Law Officers of the Crown, who provided legal advice to British government departments, opined that pirates were "Common Sea Rovers who acknowledge no Sovereign and no Law, and support themselves by pillage and depredations at sea." Letter from J. Dodson to Viscount Palmerston (May 18, 1841), *in* 2 INTERNATIONAL LAW OPINIONS 229 ([Arnold D.] McNair ed., 1956); *see* Letter from Viscount Palmerston to Andrew Stevenson (Aug. 27, 1841), *in* DIPLOMATIC PAPERS, *supra* note 1, at 124, 127–28.

17 Letter from Mr. Stevenson to Viscount Palmerston (May 22, 1838), *in* H.R. EXEC. DOC. NO. 25–183, at 2 (1838).

Destruction of the American Steamboat *Caroline*

On June 6, 1838, Palmerston promised to give Stevenson's demand for redress due consideration.[18] Palmerston, occupied by events in Europe, believed that the United States did not want to risk war and that tensions would dissipate.[19] He was not eager to address the *Caroline* matter apart from other issues complicating U.S.-British relations and did not respond substantively until August 1841. His response, when it came, was prompted by the New York arrest and trial of Alexander McLeod, whose story is inextricably linked to that of the *Caroline*.

The Arrest of Alexander McLeod and the* Caroline *Test. The *Caroline* dispute simmered during 1838–1840, but events in late 1840 brought the matter again to the forefront. On November 12, 1840, authorities in Lewiston, New York arrested Alexander McLeod, a deputy sheriff from Upper Canada who had worked to undermine the efforts of the Patriots, on charges related to the destruction of the *Caroline*.[20] According to his February 1841 grand jury indictment, McLeod, "not having the fear of God before his eyes, but being moved and seduced by the instigation of the devil," had murdered Amos Durfee, destroyed

---

[18] Letter from Viscount Palmerston to Mr. Stevenson (June 6, 1838), *in* H.R. EXEC. DOC. NO. 25–183, at 9, 10 (1838).

[19] *See* FORCESE, *supra* note 2, at 77–80.

[20] For accounts of McLeod's arrest, detention, and indictment, see STEVENS, *supra* note 2, at 71–83; Alastair Watt, *The Case of Alexander McLeod*, 12 CAN. HIST. REV. 145, 153–55, 159–67 (1931).

personal property (the *Caroline*) with deadly weapons, and committed several other related crimes.[21] At his arraignment, McLeod pled not guilty, and he was imprisoned pending trial.

December 1840 diplomatic exchanges between British Ambassador Fox and U.S. Secretary of State Forsyth[22] foreshadowed positions that would become entrenched after the new administration of President William Henry Harrison took office in March 1841. Harrison named Daniel Webster Secretary of State, and Webster continued in that position after Harrison died a month after his inauguration and John Tyler became President. Webster, a former U.S. Congressman and Senator and one of the most highly respected lawyers and politicians in the United States, formulated the famous *Caroline* test in reply to a March 12, 1841, letter from Fox.[23]

In his letter, Fox wanted to set aside the question whether the attack on the *Caroline* was, on the one hand, a justifiable use of force or, on the other, an unjustifiable invasion of U.S. territory. Either way, wrote Fox, McLeod should be released: it was "contrary to the universal practice of Civilized Nations to fix individual responsibility upon persons who with the sanction or by the orders of the Constituted Authorities of a State engage in Military or Naval Enterprizes in their Country's cause." He also criticized the view that the U.S. federal government, with which any foreign government must deal on matters of international law and diplomacy, should leave the matter to be handled by the state of New York.

Webster, in his reply of April 24, 1841, agreed with Fox about the lack of personal responsibility for individuals involved in "an act of public force."[24] But despite this international law principle, Webster continued, the federal government could not order McLeod's release, for "in the United States, as in England, persons confined under judicial process, can be released from that confinement only by judicial process." McLeod's rights, Webster assured Fox, "are no less safe" in New York state court than in federal court, since "the law of Nations . . . in civilized States, is to be respected in all courts."

Webster then, in the same letter, renewed U.S. protests concerning the destruction of the *Caroline*. He maintained that the British attack on

---

21 The indictment is reproduced in 2 GOULD'S STENOGRAPHIC REPORTER 17–19 (1841) [hereinafter GOULD].

22 Letter from Mr. Fox to Mr. Forsyth (Dec. 13, 1840), *in* People v. McLeod, 25 Wend. 500, 501 n.* (N.Y. Sup. Ct. 1841); Letter from Mr. Forsyth to Mr. Fox, (Dec. 26, [1840]), *in McLeod*, 25 Wend. at 501, 503.

23 Letter from Henry Stephen Fox to Daniel Webster (Mar. 12, 1841), *in* DIPLOMATIC PAPERS, *supra* note 1, at 41. Webster admired British culture, favored peaceful means of resolving U.S.-British disputes, and sought to increase British investment in the United States. *See* MAURICE G. BAXTER, ONE AND INSEPARABLE: DANIEL WEBSTER AND THE UNION 320 (1978); FORCESE, *supra* note 2, at 91–92.

24 The quotations in this and the next three paragraphs are from Webster's *Caroline* Letter, *supra* note 1, unless otherwise noted.

the *Caroline*—a hostile act "within the territory of a Power at peace"—violated international law. There followed a long disquisition on principles of nonintervention and neutrality. The United States had long relied on its status as a neutral to object to French and British interference with U.S. shipping and to avoid being drawn into European conflicts. Webster did not, however, argue that neutral territory was absolutely inviolable; the United States itself, during the second decade of the nineteenth century, had used force in Florida—then neutral Spanish territory—in order to repel or prevent cross-border attacks by Seminoles and their allies into the United States. In 1818, President James Monroe, in his annual address to Congress, had stressed the "sacred" right of self-defense, asserting that with "Spanish authority almost extinct" in Florida, U.S. forces could "pursu[e] these savages" in Spanish territory.[25] The British government had invoked these U.S. incursions in defending its destruction of the *Caroline*.[26]

Webster defended U.S. actions in upstate New York. He acknowledged the rule that a neutral country's citizens could not intervene in conflicts inside another country. Such conduct would allow "individuals to make war on their own authority" and could compromise their own government's international relations. The United States had not "permitted" its citizens to participate in military expeditions against the British government of Upper Canada, although "irregularities, violences and conflicts," unintended by both sides, might well occur along the long U.S.-Canadian border. "All that can be expected, from either government" in such cases, Webster wrote, "is good faith, a sincere desire to preserve peace and do justice, the use of all proper means of prevention, and, that if offences cannot, nevertheless, be always prevented, the offenders shall still be justly punished." If some individuals had escaped punishment in the United States, "this is no more than happens in regard to other laws."

It was against this background that Webster penned his famous passage:

> Under these circumstances, . . . it will be for Her Majesty's Government to show, upon what state of facts, and rules of national law, the destruction of the "Caroline" is to be defended. It will be for that Government to show a necessity of self-defence, instant, overwhelming, leaving no choice of means, and no moment for deliberation. It will be for it to show, also, that the local authorities of Canada,—even supposing the necessity of the moment authorized them to enter the territories of the United States at all,—did nothing unreasonable or excessive;

[25] James Monroe, Second Annual Message (Nov. 16, 1818), *in* 2 JAMES D. RICHARDSON, A COMPILATION OF THE MESSAGES AND PAPERS OF THE PRESIDENTS, 1789–1897, at 39, 40–41 (1897).

[26] *See, e.g.*, Letter from Daniel Webster to [Edward] Everett (Oct. 16, 1839), *in* 18 THE WRITINGS AND SPEECHES OF DANIEL WEBSTER 71 (Fletcher Webster ed., 1903). *See also* FORCESE, *supra* note 2, at 155–62.

> since the act justified by the necessity of self-defence, must be limited by that necessity, and kept clearly within it. It must be shown that admonition or remonstrances to the persons on board the "Caroline" was impracticable, or would have been unavailing; it must be shown that daylight could not be waited for; that there could be no attempt at discrimination, between the innocent and the guilty; that it would not have been enough to seize and detain the vessel; but that there was a necessity, present and inevitable, for attacking her, in the darkness of the night, while moored to the shore, and while unarmed men were asleep on board, killing some and wound[ing] others, and then drawing her into the current, above the cataract, setting her on fire, and, careless to know whether there might not be in her the innocent with the guilty, or the living with the dead, committing her to a fate which fills the imagination with horror. A necessity for all this, the Government of the United States cannot believe to have existed.

The British government eventually responded to Webster's letter, but its response awaited the outcome of New York's case against McLeod.

The attention accorded McLeod's arrest and detention was by no means limited to diplomatic exchanges. The U.S. Congress and the British Parliament debated the matter.[27] British newspapers and officials uniformly condemned McLeod's arrest and detention as an affront to British honor. U.S. Ambassador Stevenson reported from London "[t]hat the Press and the people, are under deep excitement" and that "the strongest feelings of indignation are entertained and expressed towards the U. States, growing out of the affair of the Caroline, & especially the detention of McLeod."[28] U.S. and, especially, British officials thought war likely should McLeod be convicted and executed, and both countries began military preparations.[29]

On the eve of McLeod's trial, the views of the U.S. and British governments were clear. Both agreed that if McLeod was following military orders, he should be immune from prosecution in the United States. But the British complained that the U.S. system of federalism—the "peculiar laws and institutions" of the United States—could allow a New York court to rule against the position of the federal government "in bar of national responsibility."[30] Despite Daniel Webster's confident

---

[27] *Hansard's Parliamentary Debates* and the *Congressional Globe* chronicle numerous debates during 1841 and 1842.

[28] Letter from Andrew Stevenson to Daniel Webster (Mar. 18, 1841), *in* DIPLOMATIC PAPERS, *supra* note 1, at 49.

[29] *See* FORCESE, *supra* note 2, at 85–89, 94–100, 106. France and Russia were also concerned about the implications of a U.S.-U.K. war. *See* Lewis Cass, U.S. Minister to France, to Secretary of State Daniel Webster (Mar. 15, 1841), *in* DIPLOMATIC PAPERS, *supra* note 1, at 44; Despatch from Count Nesselrode to Alexander de Bodisco (Mar. 18/30, 1841), *in* DIPLOMATIC PAPERS, *supra* note 1, at 51; STEVENS, *supra* note 2, at 99, 189 n.36.

[30] Letter from Henry Stephen Fox to Lord Aberdeen (Oct. 12, 1841), *quoted in* FORCESE, *supra* note 2, at 92.

assertion in his April 1841 letter to British Ambassador Fox that the law of nations would be fairly applied in New York courts, he too worried that its misapplication could lead to war or otherwise damage U.S.-U.K. relations.

As for the merits of using force to destroy the *Caroline*, the two countries disagreed, each emphasizing facts or accusations that put the other side in a poor light. The British stressed that the *Caroline* had been ferrying supplies and reinforcements to U.S. nationals who were occupying Britain's Navy Island and bombarding the Canadian mainland. Ambassador Fox believed that the nominally neutral United States had supported public unrest in New York against British rule in Upper Canada; British officials saw the raid as a necessary act of self-defense "against a people whom their own Government either could not or would not control."[31] The United States, however, saw its territory—the neutral territory of a sovereign nation—as virtually inviolable, and the British attack on U.S. soil a breach of international law.

McLeod's Trial. Secretary of State Daniel Webster took a personal interest in the case against Alexander McLeod. In March 1841, Webster implored New York Governor William H. Seward to intervene in McLeod's case and thus "relieve this Government from embarrassments and the Country from some dangers of collision with a foreign power."[32] Seward, sensitive to the political climate in New York, refused to pardon McLeod or otherwise interfere in the trial.[33] When McLeod, arguing that his imprisonment was unlawful, sought a writ of habeas corpus from the New York Supreme Court, Webster took a room at the Astor Hotel in New York City where the court sat, in order to keep up to date with the case and to cooperate with the defense team.[34]

Justice Esek Cowen, who wrote the unanimous July 1841 opinion denying McLeod's habeas petition, discussed international law extensively. He found that because the British claimed to be at peace with the United States, no "public war" existed that might deprive the court of jurisdiction; that even if a Canadian civil war existed, McLeod could be punished for his acts in New York, because a state of civil war could not extend into the territory of the neutral United States; that even during a

---

[31] Letter from Francis Bond Head to Henry Stephen Fox (Jan. 8, 1838), *quoted in* FORCESE, *supra* note 2, at 74.

[32] Letter from Daniel Webster to William H. Seward (Mar. 17, 1841), *in* DIPLOMATIC PAPERS, *supra* note 1, at 49.

[33] *See* Letter from William H. Seward to Daniel Webster (Mar. 22, 1841), *in* DIPLOMATIC PAPERS, *supra* note 1, at 53; STEVENS, *supra* note 2, at 94–95. An executive initiative alone could not have halted the prosecution of a New York criminal case; dismissal of an indictment was a matter of judicial discretion. *See* People v. McLeod, 25 Wend. 483, 573 (N.Y. Sup. Ct. 1841); 2 REVISED STATUTES OF THE STATE OF NEW YORK § 54, at 609 (1836).

[34] *See* Letter from Daniel Webster to Daniel Fletcher Webster (May 10, 1841), *in* DIPLOMATIC PAPERS, *supra* note 1, at 72; Letter from Daniel Webster to Joshua Spencer (Sept. 21, 1841), *in* DIPLOMATIC PAPERS, *supra* note 1, at 146. For New York's habeas statute, see 2 REVISED STATUTES OF THE STATE OF NEW YORK § 50, at 471 (1836), *quoted in* *McLeod*, 25 Wend. at 547.

war, furthermore, a soldier could be punished for a "deed of infamy," as was sufficiently alleged in McLeod's indictment; and that self-defense, a doctrine Cowen found would have been available only had the *Caroline* itself been directly assaulting the Canadian shore, did not justify the British attack.[35]

The court's ruling provoked strong reactions. British Ambassador Fox thought the denial of McLeod's habeas petition showed the federal government's weakness, and he stressed that U.S. actions would determine whether the United States would avoid the "heavy calamity of War."[36] Viscount Palmerston, the British Foreign Secretary, complained about McLeod's detention to U.S. Ambassador Stevenson.[37] Cowen's opinion also energized the Patriots, who thought a war would ultimately lead to the overthrow of British control in its Canadian colony. New York's Governor Seward and federal officials increased security measures along the border.[38]

Secretary of State Daniel Webster called Justice Cowen's opinion "hollow, false, & almost dishonest, from beginning to end."[39] New York Superior Court Judge Daniel Tallmadge published a critique of the opinion, finding it "unsound in all its parts"; he stressed that under international law, a "lawful war" need not be formally declared, and that those participating in the attack under government commission could not be individually responsible for the attack on the *Caroline*.[40] State supreme court justices, leading attorneys and politicians, Harvard Law Professor Simon Greenleaf, and the noted legal publicist James Kent effusively praised Tallmadge's work and agreed with his view that the New York habeas statute and international law provided ample authority to release someone in McLeod's position.[41]

---

35 *McLeod*, 25 Wend. at 587. According to Justice Cowen, the requirement of such a prior assault was "no narrow technical rule peculiar to the common law; but the law of nature and of nations, the same everywhere . . . . It is easily applied both as between individuals in civil society and nations at peace." *Id.* at 588 (citing WILLIAM BLACKSTONE, 3 COMMENTARIES *4). Cowen did not cite or discuss the "instant, overwhelming" self-defense test that Webster had asserted less than two months earlier.

36 Letter from H.S. Fox to Daniel Webster (Sept. 5, 1841), *in* DIPLOMATIC PAPERS, *supra* note 1, at 114, 115.

37 Letter from Viscount Palmerston to Andrew Stevenson (Aug. 27, 1841), *in* DIPLOMATIC PAPERS, *supra* note 1, at 124; Letter from Viscount Palmerston to Andrew Stevenson (Sept. 2, 1841), *in* DIPLOMATIC PAPERS, *supra* note 1, at 138.

38 *See* STEVENS, *supra* note 2, at 123–25.

39 Letter from Daniel Webster to Joseph Story (July 16, [1841]), *in* DIPLOMATIC PAPERS, *supra* note 1, at 99.

40 DANIEL TALLMADGE, REVIEW OF THE OPINION OF JUDGE COWEN, OF THE SUPREME COURT OF THE STATE OF NEW YORK, IN THE CASE OF ALEXANDER MCLEOD 43 (rev. ed. 1841), *reprinted in* 26 Wend. 663, 699 (1841). In contrast, an unlawful war was one conducted for "havoc and pillage," and those participating in an unlawful war could be prosecuted by a country harmed by their actions. TALLMADGE, *supra*, at 18, 26 Wend. at 673.

41 *See* 26 Wend. at 699–706; Letter from Chancellor Kent to Daniel Webster (Dec. 21, 1842), *in* DIPLOMATIC PAPERS, *supra* note 1, at 708. For defenses of Cowen's opinion, see Comment, *The Supreme Court of New York, and Mr. Webster, on the McLeod Question*, 10

Against the backdrop of the tense political situation, McLeod's attorneys, President Tyler, and other U.S. officials debated their next steps. One possibility was to appeal Justice Cowen's habeas ruling to the New York Supreme Court of Errors and thence perhaps to the U.S. Supreme Court. Alexander McLeod, however, had been in jail for eight months and wanted a quick trial. Webster hoped the trial would vindicate the view of the U.S. and British governments, and of Judge Tallmadge, that McLeod was immune from prosecution.[42]

McLeod's trial began on Monday morning, October 4, 1841, in the Circuit Court in Utica, New York, with Judge Philo Gridley presiding.[43] The trial, which lasted eight days, was a spectacle. Officials made extensive security arrangements, crowds gathered, and the press reported details of the trial. Willis Hall, the New York Attorney General, opened the prosecution's case by reminding the jury that the New York Supreme Court had decided, in its habeas opinion, that Durfee's alleged murder "was not to be governed by the laws of war, but of peace. . . . Blood has been shed upon our soil."[44]

Joshua Spencer, McLeod's highly respected attorney, presented two defenses. First, he asserted that official British orders authorized using military force to destroy the *Caroline*, which he deemed a "necessary act" to protect British subjects, property, and territory. Under the law of nations, any "individual who formed part of that public force of Great Britain stands excused . . . from all the consequences of his action under those orders."[45] Second, he denied that McLeod was even present during the attack.

Spencer linked his international law argument to U.S. foreign policy prerogatives. He tried to introduce diplomatic correspondence concerning the *Caroline* to show that the federal government had "taken cognizance" of the "entire transaction."[46] Judge Gridley rejected this assertion and refused to admit the diplomatic correspondence into evidence. The defense also tried to invoke the *Caroline* self-defense test that Daniel

---

U.S. MAG. & DEMOCRATIC REV. 487 (1842); Note, *Rufus Choate: XIII*, 19 ALB. L.J. 506, 507–08 (1878).

42 *See* Letter from Daniel Webster to Joshua Spencer (July 15, 1841), *in* DIPLOMATIC PAPERS, *supra* note 1, at 98; Letter from Daniel Webster to Joshua Spencer (Aug. 6, 1841), *in* DIPLOMATIC PAPERS, *supra* note 1, at 100; BAXTER, *supra* note 23, at 326–27.

43 In 1841, New York's court system included Circuit Courts and the Supreme Court, both trial courts of general jurisdiction; Courts of Chancery, which heard matters of equity; and the Supreme Court of Errors, which was composed of state senators and Supreme Court justices and which exercised appellate jurisdiction. The New York Constitution of 1846 abolished the Courts of Chancery, the Circuit Courts, and the Supreme Court of Errors; reorganized the Supreme Court; and created a new Court of Appeals, which became the highest appellate court in the state. *See* 2 CHARLES Z. LINCOLN, THE CONSTITUTIONAL HISTORY OF NEW YORK 140–64 (1906).

44 GOULD, *supra* note 21, at 41. Volume 2 of *Gould's Stenographic Reporter* contains a thorough account of the trial and reprints many relevant documents. A condensed trial report appears in 7 AMERICAN STATE TRIALS 61–323 (John D. Lawson ed., 1916).

45 GOULD, *supra* note 21, at 86.

46 *Id.* at 103.

Webster had devised six months earlier—the "instant, overwhelming, leaving no choice of means" formulation—noting that the New York Supreme Court had not heard arguments about it during the habeas proceedings. According to the defense, this language suggested "a class of cases in which even neutral territory may be entered for a hostile purpose." Gridley refused to apply Webster's test, cryptically proclaiming the doctrine "unsound."[47] Overall, the trial involved "the absence of any thing like war,"[48] and the New York court would try McLeod under the state's criminal laws.

McLeod thus had to rely on its second line of argument—that he was not present when the *Caroline* was attacked on December 29, 1837. McLeod testified he had spent that night at a friend's house in Stamford, Canada, and other witnesses corroborated his testimony. Spencer also introduced sworn depositions from at least one member of each of the boats under Captain Drew's command, each such statement indicating that McLeod was not part of the attacking party. All these detailed depositions were read in full in court over a two-day period, a process the jury—nine farmers, one physician, and two merchants—found mind-numbing.[49] The defense's case was nonetheless persuasive. At the end of the trial, the jury deliberated less than half an hour before returning a verdict of "Not Guilty."

III. THE DIPLOMATIC DENOUEMENT AND McLEOD'S FATE

McLeod's acquittal lessened but did not altogether remove U.S.-British tensions related to the *Caroline* incident. Anti-British insurgents from New York blew up a lock in Canada and attacked British vessels.[50] The British government continued to seek assurances that anyone who took part in the *Caroline* attack would not be held personally responsible. Secretary of State Webster and President Tyler worried that another British subject might be arrested in connection with the death of Amos Durfee and the destruction of the *Caroline*, tried in state court, and convicted. Indeed, New York authorities arrested several other British citizens for Durfee's murder and for arson, lending credence to Webster's and Tyler's concern.[51] When John Horgan, a Canadian journalist, was taken into custody in New York early in 1842 and then released for insufficient evidence, Joshua Spencer, McLeod's attorney, thought Horgan's discharge "a wonder" and concluded that "we shall have no

---

47 *Id.* at 106.

48 *Id.* at 105.

49 *See id.* at 145.

50 FORCESE, *supra* note 2, at 113.

51 *See* STEVENS, *supra* note 2, at 161–62; Watt, *supra* note 20, at 162–63.

repose on the frontier" unless "the whole ground of the Caroline affair . . . be embraced in a treaty of settlement."[52]

Despite the debates about whether the *Caroline*'s attackers were entitled to immunity from criminal prosecution, U.S. jurists, publicists, and government officials agreed that the British destruction of the vessel was illegal at international law. In December 1841, President Tyler reminded Congress that the British government had neither "atone[d]" for its "violation of territorial sovereignty" nor "renounce[d] as a rule of future action the precedent which has been set in the affair at Schlosser."[53]

Efforts to settle the *Caroline* dispute would not have moved forward as expeditiously as they did without McLeod's acquittal and a change of government in the United Kingdom. Lord Aberdeen, who became Foreign Secretary in September 1841 when Robert Peel's Tory government took office, sought to ease tensions with the United States. He would not act while McLeod's case was pending,[54] but soon after McLeod's release in October 1841, Aberdeen appointed Lord Ashburton (Alexander Baring) to negotiate outstanding disputes with the United States. Ashburton, a banker and a skilled diplomat who had married the daughter of a U.S. Senator and had cultivated American friends, knew Secretary of State Daniel Webster and understood U.S. perspectives.

The most important bilateral controversy was the unsettled boundary between much of the northeastern United States and Canada, but Ashburton and Webster also discussed the boundaries of the northwestern United States, joint cruising to suppress the slave trade, extradition, the British policy of stopping U.S. vessels on the high seas, and the *Caroline* incident.[55] The 1842 Webster-Ashburton Treaty set out the boundary between the northeastern United States and Canada, and the negotiations helped resolve some of the other controversies between the two countries.[56]

The *Caroline* affair was not settled by treaty, however, but by diplomatic exchanges. On July 27th, 1842, Secretary of State Webster wrote Ashburton, enclosing portions of his April 24, 1841, letter setting out the *Caroline* test: the use of force in neutral foreign territory was legal when there existed "a necessity of self-defence, instant, overwhelming, leaving no choice of means, and no moment for deliberation," and when the force used was not "unreasonable or excessive," limited by the

[52] Letter from Joshua A. Spencer to Daniel Webster (Apr. 8, 1842), *in* DIPLOMATIC PAPERS, *supra* note 1, at 532.

[53] John Tyler, First Annual Message (Dec. 7, 1841), *in* 4 JAMES D. RICHARDSON, A COMPILATION OF THE MESSAGES AND PAPERS OF THE PRESIDENTS, 1789–1897, at 74, 76–77 (1897).

[54] *See* Letter from Christopher Hughes to Daniel Webster (Sept. 18, 1841), *in* CORRESPONDENCE, *supra* note 4, at 153, 154.

[55] *See* BAXTER, *supra* note 23, at 336–59; JONES, *supra* note 2.

[56] Treaty of Aug. 9, 1842, U.S.-U.K., 8 Stat. 572.

necessity of self-defense.[57] Ashburton's reply of July 28th agreed with the *Caroline* test, reinforcing its status:

> [W]e are perfectly agreed as to the general principles of international law applicable to this unfortunate case. Respect for the inviolable character of the territory of independent nations is the most essential foundation of civilization. . . . Her Majesty's Government set the highest possible value on this principle, and are sensible of their duty to support it by their conduct and example for the maintenance of peace and order in the world. . . .
>
> . . . But however strong this duty may be it is admitted by all writers, by all jurists, by the occasional practice of nations, not excepting your own, that a strong overpowering necessity may arise when this great principle may and must be suspended. It must be so for the shortest possible period during the continuance of an admitted overruling necessity, and strictly confined within the narrowest limits imposed by that necessity. "Self" defence is the first law of our nature, and it must be recognised by every code which professes to regulate the conditions and relations of man. Upon this modification, if I may so call it, of the great general principle, we seem also to be agreed, and on this part of the subject I have done little more than repeat the sentiments, though in less forcible language, admitted and maintained by you in the letter to which you refer me.[58]

Ashburton then argued that, on the facts, the attack on the *Caroline* involved just such a "strong overpowering necessity" and satisfied Webster's test. Ashburton noted that the British had first protested the build-up of arms on Navy Island—British territory—but to no effect. If, Ashburton asked rhetorically, "cannon are moving and setting up in a battery which can reach you and are actually destroying life and property by their fire, If you have remonstrated . . . and see no prospect of relief, when begins your right to defend yourself, should you have no other means of doing so, than by seizing your assailant on the verge of a neutral territory?" The *Caroline* was the means "by which numbers and arms were hourly increasing." The military commander in Canada lacked "the remotest reason . . . to expect to be relieved from this state of suffering by the protective intervention of any American authority." In sum, "the facts which you say would alone justify the act, viz., 'a necessity of self defence, instant, overwhelming, leaving no choice of means and no moment for

---

[57] Letter from Daniel Webster to Lord Ashburton (July 27, 1842), *in* DIPLOMATIC PAPERS, *supra* note 1, at 650.

[58] Letter from Lord Ashburton to Daniel Webster (July 28, 1842), *in* DIPLOMATIC PAPERS, *supra* note 1, at 651, 651–52. The quotations in the next two paragraphs are also from this letter.

deliberation,' were . . . applicable to this case in as high a degree as they ever were to any case of a similar description in the history of nations."

Ashburton coupled this justification for the attack with a carefully worded "apology":

> I am instructed to assure you . . . that far from thinking that an event of this kind should be lightly risked, [Her Majesty's Government] would unfeignedly deprecate its recurrence. Looking back to what passed at this distance of time, what is perhaps most to be regretted, is, that some explanation and apology for this occurrence was not immediately made; this, with a frank explanation of the necessity of the case, might and probably would have prevented much of the exasperation and of the subsequent complaints and recriminations to which it gave rise. . . .
>
> . . . I have to repeat the assurance of regret [Her Majesty's Government] feel that the event of which I am treating should have disturbed the harmony they so anxiously wish to maintain with the American people and Government.

President Tyler deemed Ashburton's letter sufficient to settle the *Caroline* dispute, and the United States dropped its 1838 claim for compensation.[59] Webster wrote to Ashburton again on August 6, 1842:

> The President sees with pleasure that your Lordship fully admits those great principles of public law, applicable to cases of this kind, which this Government has expressed; and that on your part, as on ours, respect for the inviolable character of the territory of independent States is deemed the most essential foundation of civilization. . . . Undoubtedly it is just, that while it is admitted that exceptions growing out of the great law of self-defence do exist, those exceptions should be confined to cases in which "the necessity of self-defence is instant, overwhelming, and leaving no choice of means, and no moment for deliberation."[60]

The two countries still disagreed about whether the facts justified Britain's use of force. Webster noted, however, that since "it is now admitted that an explanation and apology for this violation was due at the time," President Tyler had decided to "make this subject . . . the topic of no further discussion between the two Governments."[61]

As for Alexander McLeod, whose arrest and trial had so heightened the political tensions surrounding the *Caroline* incident, his acquittal of course meant his freedom. He quickly returned to Canada, fearing

---

59 *See* ROBERT V. REMINI, DANIEL WEBSTER 559–60 (1997).

60 Letter from Daniel Webster to Lord Ashburton (Aug. 6, 1842), *in* DIPLOMATIC PAPERS, *supra* note 1, at 669.

61 *Id.*

retaliation from members of Hunters' Lodges. There he became a storekeeper, married, and raised a family.[62] McLeod sought compensation for his eleven months in U.S. prison through a binational claims commission established by an 1853 U.S.-British treaty.[63] The claims commissioners ruled, by a vote of two to one, that they could not evaluate the merits of McLeod's claim against the United States. The 1853 treaty only authorized decisions concerning "unsettled" claims, and the majority concluded that the 1842 Webster-Ashburton diplomatic correspondence had settled matters related to the *Caroline*.[64] McLeod also petitioned British colonial authorities for relief, and the British government ultimately, in 1855, awarded him an annual pension of £200 (approximately $31,000 today) for deprivations suffered while imprisoned in New York.

The *Caroline* incident and McLeod's arrest and trial also led the United States to reallocate jurisdiction in habeas cases. In August 1842, Congress enacted a statute providing that federal courts could hear habeas petitions from foreigners who were in state custody in the United States for acts done pursuant to orders "of any foreign State or Sovereignty, the validity and effect whereof depend upon the law of nations."[65] The statute was designed to avoid someone in McLeod's position from being detained with no federal habeas avenue of relief.

IV. THE LASTING SIGNIFICANCE OF THE *CAROLINE* INCIDENT

International Law, Diplomacy, Individuals, and Federalism. Although the *Caroline* is best known for its self-defense test, three other aspects of the incident deserve brief mention. First, the story of the *Caroline* demonstrates that international law may affect the outcome of even tense international controversies. International law formed the language of diplomatic discourse used to conceptualize, negotiate, and, in this case, help resolve a sensitive international dispute.

Second, the incident shows that international law may directly concern the rights of individuals. When Alexander McLeod was arrested, British diplomats invoked "the universal practice of Civilized Nations" not to hold individuals responsible for participating in their country's military enterprises, a legal proposition with which Secretary of State

---

[62] *See* JONES, *supra* note 2, at 65–67; STEVENS, *supra* note 2, at 170. For the fates of other key figures in the *Caroline* affair, see FORCESE, *supra* note 2, at 251–60.

[63] Convention between the United States of America and Her Britannic Majesty, Feb. 8, 1853, 10 Stat. 988.

[64] 3 JOHN BASSETT MOORE, HISTORY AND DIGEST OF THE INTERNATIONAL ARBITRATIONS TO WHICH THE UNITED STATES HAS BEEN A PARTY 2419–28 (1898); *see* Jennings, *supra* note 2, at 96–99.

[65] Act of Aug. 29, 1842, 5 Stat. 539 (now codified, as amended, at 28 U.S.C. § 2241(c)(4)). *See* David J. Bederman, *The Cautionary Tale of Alexander McLeod: Superior Orders and the American Writ of Habeas Corpus*, 41 EMORY L.J. 515 (1992).

Webster agreed.[66] The law of nations was also used in municipal court proceedings involving individual rights. Daniel Webster wrote that "the law of nations . . . is to be respected in all courts,"[67] McLeod's attorneys invoked the law of nations, and the N.Y. Attorney General acknowledged its applicability.[68] The N.Y. Supreme Court in McLeod's habeas case recognized that during his trial, a judge should direct a jury "to obey the law of nations."[69] Politicians, law professors, and other judges acknowledged that the *McLeod* case involved international law, although they sometimes disputed its rules. *McLeod* and the *Caroline* diplomatic correspondence demonstrate that—well before the post-World War II development of international human rights law—international law applied to individuals.[70]

Third, the *McLeod* case illustrates the challenges for international law and international relations occasioned by the U.S. system of federalism. When New York's judges denied McLeod the international legal immunity to which the federal government believed him entitled, U.S.-U.K. political tensions escalated. Such federalism concerns have recurred throughout U.S. history. As Professor Mark Janis has written, "[t]his omnipresent federalist tension impacts on America's complicated constitutional endeavor to deal with the rest of the world, leads to difficulties with international law, and exasperates foreign governments."[71]

Self-Defense and the* Caroline *Test. The *Caroline* test, requiring an "instant, overwhelming" necessity for self-defense and confining the force used to that which is not "unreasonable or excessive" and is "limited by that necessity," has remained important over the years. Today, "[i]n a massive body of literature," the *Caroline* "has become the litmus test in international law for self-defence and a constant feature in international law deliberations."[72] States and international tribunals, as well as publicists, have invoked Webster's formulation in a variety of instances from the nineteenth to the twenty-first centuries.[73]

Why has the *Caroline* test, formulated during a fact-specific bilateral controversy in 1841, endured in international law? To answer that

---

66 Letter from Henry Stephen Fox to Daniel Webster (Mar. 12, 1841), *in* DIPLOMATIC PAPERS, *supra* note 1, at 41, 43; Webster's *Caroline* Letter, *supra* note 1.

67 Webster's *Caroline* Letter, *supra* note 1.

68 People v. McLeod, 25 Wend. 483, 532 (N.Y. Sup. Ct. 1841).

69 *Id.* at 603.

70 *See also* MARK WESTON JANIS, THE AMERICAN TRADITION OF INTERNATIONAL LAW: GREAT EXPECTATIONS 1789–1914, at 1–24 (2004).

71 *Quoting* Mark Janis's chapter in this volume. Mark Weston Janis, Missouri v. Holland*: Birds, Wars, and Rights, in* INTERNATIONAL LAW STORIES (John E. Noyes, Laura A. Dickinson, Mark Weston Janis & Carlos M. Vázquez eds., 2d ed., 2025).

72 FORCESE, *supra* note 2, at 206.

73 *See id.* at 192–96, 207–08, 218–19, 225–27; Edward Collins, Jr. & Martin A. Rogoff, *The* Caroline *Incident of 1837, the McLeod Affair of 1840–1841, and the Development of International Law*, 20 AM. REV. CANADIAN STUD. 81, 88–90 (1990); PAPERS RELATING TO THE FOREIGN RELATIONS OF THE UNITED STATES 977–78 (1917).

question, we look at five different periods: (1) the time of the *Caroline* incident; (2) the late nineteenth century, when, according to some scholars, a state's unilateral discretion to resort to war was not limited by international law; (3) the aftermath of World War I, when multilateral treaty-based constraints on recourse to force took root; (4) the post-World War II era in which the United Nations Charter and its limitations on use of force became fundamental touchstones; and (5) the twenty-first century, when force has been used in self-defense against non-state terrorists.

Self-Defense in 1841. When Daniel Webster developed the *Caroline* test in 1841, jurists and diplomats relied heavily on natural law. Natural law, based on principles of justice and right reason, had long been propounded by philosophers and theologians. States, deemed moral entities, were governed by natural law, which approved "just wars." A just war must be based on legitimate authority, avoided unless necessary, engaged in for a just cause, and undertaken with right intention—although the difficulty of proving proper intention was, by the early nineteenth century, leading jurists to deemphasize that factor.[74] States and jurists also invoked the "law of nations," which increasingly emphasized human agency and consistent patterns of state practice.

Within the just war tradition as understood at this time, wars could be "perfect" or "imperfect." A perfect war required a formal declaration; in the *Caroline* incident, neither Britain nor the United States had declared war. Yet undeclared, imperfect wars could also be just. One type of imperfect war involved a defensive use of force, fought on the grounds of self-preservation.[75] Self-preservation was a murky and malleable concept. In general, a state could rely on self-preservation not only to counter direct threats to its very existence, but also to prevent hypothetical threats to its important interests. For example, when in 1807 the United Kingdom invaded Copenhagen and seized Danish warships, the British government invoked self-preservation: Britain was at war with Napoleon's France and feared that France might capture the Danish fleet and use the warships against Britain. But Denmark was neutral, and French capture or use of the Danish fleet was not certain.[76] Although the term "self-preservation" was used in some of the *Caroline* diplomatic correspondence,[77] Webster, in crafting his *Caroline* test, resisted relying on a broad self-preservation framework, which Britain might invoke to justify a war against the United States.

---

[74] *See* FORCESE, *supra* note 2, at 133. For a brief history of various meanings of just war, see YORAM DINSTEIN, WAR, AGGRESSION AND SELF-DEFENCE ¶¶ 181–193 (6th ed. 2017).

[75] The possibility that Britain was engaged in a civil war, another type of imperfect war, was also considered in connection with McLeod's claim of immunity. *See supra* text accompanying note 35.

[76] *See* FORCESE, *supra* note 2, at 141–45.

[77] *See, e.g.*, *supra* text accompanying note 17.

Instead, Webster's famous test focused on a "form of self-defense" involving "non-consensual cross-border counter-force against hostile organized armed groups within a foreign State."[78] Self-defense was not a new concept in international relations in 1841, but it was often conflated with self-preservation.[79] Webster's signal achievement was to synthesize self-defense antecedents into a succinct, restrictive legal formulation. With respect to the *Caroline* attack, Britain had to meet a stringent test, demonstrating the "necessity of self-defence" (a formulation that excluded retaliation or revenge), immediacy of need ("instant, overwhelming, leaving no choice of means, and no moment for deliberation"), and proportionality ("nothing unreasonable or excessive"). All of Webster's discussions of necessity were linked to self-defense. His formulation did not depend on a state's policy choice to undertake a defensive war of self-preservation in the face of some prospective and attenuated danger, but on objective notions of necessity and proportionality, narrowly defined.

For Webster, Britain's destruction of the *Caroline* in neutral U.S. territory demanded a strong response, especially given the popular outrage about it. Yet Webster believed that war with Britain would economically devastate the United States, and he pursued a peaceful solution to the *Caroline* incident. His nuanced self-defense formulation—recall that the United States had used force in neutral Spanish Florida just a few years before the *Caroline* incident, and Webster's test accordingly did not proclaim the absolute inviolability of neutral territory[80]—contributed to a diplomatic resolution of the tense dispute. But the *Caroline* test has endured far beyond this incident, and in enduring has changed to apply in broader settings and to reflect different historical conceptions of international law.

Self-Defense in the Late Nineteenth Century. A different international law paradigm governing resort to force, one linked to conceptions of state-centric positivism, gained support by the late nineteenth century. Customary international law, influenced by state practice and the consensus of publicists, increasingly supplemented or replaced natural law conceptions.[81] Some prominent scholars saw the just war doctrine as vague, subject to manipulation by self-interested states,

---

78 DINSTEIN, *supra* note 74, ¶ 768.

79 *See* STANIMIR A. ALEXANDROV, SELF-DEFENSE AGAINST THE USE OF FORCE IN INTERNATIONAL LAW 23 (1996).

80 *See supra* text accompanying notes 25–26. President John Tyler asserted a more absolute approach toward the inviolability of U.S. territory in reporting to Congress about the *Caroline*'s destruction: "The territory of the United States must be regarded as sacredly secure against all such invasions until they shall voluntarily acknowledge their inability to acquit themselves of their duties to others." Tyler, *supra* note 53, at 76. That is, before Britain could use force in U.S. territory, the neutral United States itself needed to explicitly announce that it could not control anti-British insurgent activity within U.S. borders.

81 For discussion of the rise of state-centric positivism in the late nineteenth century, see the story of *The Paquete Habana* in this volume. William S. Dodge, The Paquete Habana*: Customary International Law as Part of Our Law*, *in* INTERNATIONAL LAW STORIES (John E. Noyes, Laura A. Dickinson, Mark Weston Janis & Carlos M. Vázquez eds., 2d ed., 2025).

and insufficiently related to their actual practice. In their view, international law must "accept war, independent of the justice of its origin, as a relation which the parties to it may set up as they choose";[82] "[w]ar became the supreme right of sovereign states and the very hallmark of their sovereignty."[83] Yet those positions were not routinely espoused during this period, according to Professor Agatha Verdebout. Her in-depth analysis of state practice and academic commentary has demonstrated that, even in the late nineteenth century, international law was not entirely indifferent to recourse to war, and natural law limits on the use of force carried weight.[84] Although states had much discretion in deciding whether to go to war, their discretion was not legally unbounded. In addition, other constraints on resort to war—among them national constitutional restrictions and public opposition to wars' expense, commercial disruption, and trauma—remained very real. Peace societies, churches, and leading public figures in Britain and the United States promoted international arbitration to resolve disputes by peaceful means.[85]

States and commentators also endorsed legal limits on recourse to force short of war, and self-defense retained doctrinal significance. Both the *Caroline* test's strict limits on recourse to force in self-defense and the use of diplomacy to resolve the *Caroline* incident fit with late nineteenth-century Anglo-American ideas about progress toward minimizing uses of force and developing peaceful mechanisms of dispute settlement. Publicists in this period cited Webster's test, though they gave it different emphases: U.S. treatise writers were more likely to cite it in discussing neutral rights than were British writers, some of whom still conflated self-defense with self-preservation.[86]

Self-Defense After World War I. A third paradigm took hold after World War I. The use of force came to be regarded as a matter of "international community" concern. The Great War demonstrated that bilateral accords and reliance on principles of justice and natural law had not prevented horrendous violence and devastation. The world turned to multilateral treaties and international institutions to limit recourse to force. The 1919 League of Nations Covenant required that interstate

---

[82] W.E. HALL, A TREATISE ON INTERNATIONAL LAW § 16, at 64–65 (4th ed. 1895).

[83] H. Lauterpacht, *The Grotian Tradition in International Law*, 23 BRIT. Y.B. INT'L L. 1, 39 (1946). Another scholar, also looking back after two world wars and aware of post-war efforts to prohibit recourse to force, wrote that the late nineteenth century rejected "any legal distinction between just and unjust use of force" as "necessarily unreal so long as there was no international authority to apply it." C.H.M. Waldock, *The Regulation of the Use of Force by Individual States in International Law*, 81 RECUEIL DES COURS 451, 456–57 (1952).

[84] *See* AGATHA VERDEBOUT, REWRITING HISTORIES OF THE USE OF FORCE: THE NARRATIVES OF "INDIFFERENCE" (2021); Mary Ellen O'Connell, *Symposium on Rewriting Histories of the Use of Force: The Natural Law Past and Future of the Prohibition on the Use of Force*, OPINIO JURIS (Feb. 2, 2023), https://opiniojuris.org/2023/02/17/symposium-on-rewriting-histories-of-the-use-of-force-the-natural-law-past-and-future-of-the-prohibition-on-the-use-of-force/.

[85] *See* JANIS, *supra* note 70, at 95–116.

[86] *See* FORCESE, *supra* note 2, at 170–77.

disputes "likely to lead to a rupture" were to be referred to arbitration, the new Permanent Court of International Justice, or enquiry by the League Council; no country could go to war for three months after the ensuing arbitral award, judicial decision, or Council report. Should a state contravene these "cooling off" requirements, the Council could issue recommendations, and should a state launch a war in violation of the League Covenant, other countries undertook to impose financial and economic sanctions on the aggressor.[87] In addition, the aspirational 1928 Kellogg-Briand Pact banned recourse to "war as an instrument of national policy."[88]

In this environment, self-defense, still regarded as an inherent right of states though increasingly referred to as a rule of customary international law, became the "single, indisputable way to circumvent League rules."[89] Although the Kellogg-Briand Pact did not explicitly mention a right of self-defense—doing so could make it "far too easy for the unscrupulous to mold events to accord with an agreed definition"[90]—its negotiators emphasized that nothing in the Pact affected that right.[91] Commentators concerned with limiting uses of force under the rubric of self-defense turned to the *Caroline* test as the applicable legal definition. Robert Jennings, writing at the centennial of the *Caroline* incident, referred to Webster's formulation as the "*locus classicus*" of self-defense.[92] Publicists increasingly applied the test to situations far different from its original context; the *Caroline* test became "shorn of its facts."[93]

That said, states rejected overbroad applications of Webster's test. When in 1931 Japan bombarded and overran a Chinese barracks in Manchuria, seized a nearby Chinese city, and then captured and occupied a wide area of China, Japan cited the *Caroline* test, claiming the right to forcefully defend itself in Chinese territory in response to an imminent danger. Japan said it was responding to an explosion on a Japanese-controlled railroad in Manchuria and risked being overrun by China's numerically superior forces. Unlike the situation in the *Caroline*, however, the invading state (here Japan) was not invoking self-defense to respond to attacks or threats against its own territory. The Japanese government also did not mention the part of Webster's formula providing that self-defense could not involve any "unreasonable or excessive" use of force and had to be proportional to the necessity that justified self-

---

[87] League of Nations Covenant arts. 12–13, 15–16.

[88] Treaty Providing for the Renunciation of War as an Instrument of National Policy art. 1, Aug. 27, 1928, 46 Stat. 2343, 94 L.N.T.S. 57.

[89] FORCESE, *supra* note 2, at 183.

[90] U.S. Secretary of State Frank B. Kellogg, *quoted in id.* at 186.

[91] In one influential diplomatic note the U.S. government asserted that nothing in the Pact "restricts or impairs in any way the right of self-defense. That right is inherent in every sovereign state and is implicit in every treaty." Identic Notes of the Government of the United States, June 23, 1928, 22 AM. J. INT'L L. SUPP. 109, 109 (1928).

[92] Jennings, *supra* note 2, at 92.

[93] *See* FORCESE, *supra* note 2, at 190.

defense. A League of Nations commission and other states rejected Japan's use of force for its territorial aggrandizement.[94]

The post-World War II Nuremberg Tribunal applied pre-1940 law to find Nazi Germany's 1940 invasion and occupation of Norway illegal, quoting the *Caroline* test to conclude that the invasion was not defensive but instead an illegal "aggressive war." According to the Tribunal, "preventive action in foreign territories is justified only in the case of 'an instant and overwhelming necessity for self-defence, leaving no choice of means and no moment of deliberation,' " and no Allied landing was imminent.[95]

Self-Defense and the United Nations Charter. A fourth use of force paradigm, still important today, is grounded in the international peace and security provisions of the United Nations Charter, adopted at the end of World War II. The Charter's provisions concerning the use of force differ significantly from those in pre-World War II international law. A major innovation was the collective security system established in Chapter VII of the Charter, under which the U.N. Security Council could authorize the use of force to preserve international peace and security.[96] In addition, Article 2(3) of the Charter requires that "all Members shall settle their international disputes by peaceful means"; it does not, as did the League Covenant, leave open the possibility that a state might legally use force after a cooling off period. And instead of just outlawing recourse to war as an instrument of national policy as did the Kellogg-Briand Pact, Article 2(4) broadly prohibits the use of unconsented-to "force": "All Members shall refrain in their international relations from the threat or use of force against the territorial integrity or political independence of any state, or in any manner inconsistent with the Purposes of the United Nations."[97] Today the use of force proscribed by Article 2(4) is widely regarded as a peremptory (*jus cogens*) norm.[98]

Finally, the U.N. Charter, unlike the League of Nations Covenant and the Kellogg-Briand Pact, explicitly refers to the "inherent right of . . . self-defense." Article 51, adopted to ensure that Latin American collective self-defense arrangements could coexist with the Charter's new global collective security system, recognizes both individual and collective self-defense:

> Nothing in the present Charter shall impair the inherent right of individual or collective self-defense if an armed attack

[94] *See id.* at 192–96.

[95] Nurnberg Trial, 6 F.R.D. 69, 99–101 (1946).

[96] *See* U.N. Charter arts. 39–51.

[97] Although Article 2(4) does not prohibit the use or threat of economic or psychological pressure, it otherwise is typically interpreted broadly. *See* DINSTEIN, *supra* note 74, ¶¶ 243–267.

[98] *See* Case Concerning Military and Paramilitary Activities in and against Nicaragua (Nicar. v. U.S.), 1986 I.C.J. 14, ¶ 90 (June 27); DINSTEIN, *supra* note 74, ¶¶ 297–309.

> occurs against a Member of the United Nations until the Security Council has taken the measures necessary to maintain international peace and security. Measures taken by members in the exercise of this right of self-defense shall be immediately reported to the Security Council and shall not in any way affect the authority and responsibility of the Security Council under the present Charter to take at any time such action as it deems necessary in order to maintain or restore international peace and security.

Article 51 has become centrally important in assessing the legality of extraterritorial uses of force, for the Security Council is often prevented from acting; any of its permanent members—China, France, Russia, the United Kingdom, and the United States—may veto proposed Council measures.

Even states with Council vetoes attempt to justify their uses of force by invoking self-defense. When Russia invaded Ukraine in 2022, Russia unconvincingly argued that it acted in self-defense against threats posed by the United States and NATO countries. Russia's argument was roundly denounced. It faced no armed attack, actual or imminent, and the Ukrainian regions of Donbas and Luhansk, which Russia asserted it was defending, were not recognized as states entitled to a right of collective self-defense.[99]

In order to define and limit the inherent right of self-defense referred to in Article 51, jurists after World War II seized on the *Caroline* test. They conceptualized its core elements as part of customary international law and extended its application to fact situations far different from that of the original incident. For example, some have claimed that Webster's formulation could justify states using force not just to defend against armed attacks in their territory but also to protect their nationals abroad.[100] And as discussed next, others have argued that the *Caroline* self-defense criteria justify responses to potential rather than ongoing attacks—despite the fact that the original incident involved Britain's response to an ongoing bombardment and despite the literal "if an armed attack occurs" limitation of Article 51.

Self-Defense in Response to Nuclear and Terrorist Threats. Does the U.N. Charter provide appropriate protections for states seeking to defend themselves against modern threats of nuclear or terrorist attacks? After the Charter's adoption, commentators, aware that the U.N. Security Council, hamstrung by Cold War politics, was unable to take effective action, asked whether Article 51 could accommodate anticipatory

---

[99] *See, e.g.*, James A. Green et al., *Russia's Attack on Ukraine and the* Jus ad Bellum, 9 J. USE FORCE & INT'L L. 4 (2022).

[100] The issue arose in debates over Israel's 1976 use of force in Entebbe, Uganda. Israel invoked the *Caroline* test to justify its efforts to save its nationals there. U.N. SCOR, 31st Sess., 1939th mtg., U.N. Doc. S/PV.1939, ¶ 115 (July 9, 1976). Other states disagreed, arguing that Israel was not responding to an attack.

responses to such threats. Some argued for a non-restrictive interpretation of Article 51, invoking the *Caroline* test as embodying the inherent right of self-defense referred to in Article 51. The Article 51 phrase "if an armed attack occurs," in this view, precludes propaganda attacks or minor border incidents from giving rise to the right to use of force in self-defense, but should not be read to impair that essential, inherent right.[101] Such non-restrictivists argued that Webster's formulation allowed the use of force in self-defense if the need for it was imminent.[102]

In contrast, restrictivists noted that the *Caroline* incident on its facts involved Britain's response to an actual attack on British soil. They feared that a doctrine of anticipatory self-defense would expand the situations in which states unilaterally could use force extraterritoriality, and thus undercut necessary preconditions to both international peace and the development of human rights. The restrictivists believed that the Article 51 phrase "if an armed attack occurs" means what it says: the door should not be opened to the use of defensive force on the amorphous grounds that an attack was imminent. Nevertheless, if a state "embarked upon an apparently irreversible course of action," that could satisfy Article 51's armed attack requirement and justify using force in self-defense.[103] With respect to nuclear threats, a state need not wait until warheads are launched before responding defensively. Both sides in the debate about the permissibility of anticipatory self-defense accepted the Charter paradigm and argued about the *Caroline* test within this paradigm.

How close in time must an attack be in order to be "imminent"? The *Caroline* test emphasized a temporal element—an "instant, overwhelming" need for an extraterritorial use of force of force that left "no moment for deliberation." Although many international lawyers came to believe that the *Caroline* test and the U.N. Charter permitted anticipatory self-defense as a legal response to imminent attacks,[104] the use of force to respond to prospective, attenuated threats was a different matter. When in 1991 Israeli forces destroyed the core of Iraq's Osiraq

---

[101] As a textual matter, non-restrictivists justified anticipatory self-defense by construing "if an armed attack occurs" not to mean "only if," or at least not to mean "after an armed attack has occurred." They also noted the context of Article 51's adoption, stressing that it was meant to ensure that the right to band together in collective self-defense arrangements would continue until the Security Council exercised its authority. *See, e.g.*, ALEXANDROV, *supra* note 79, at 99–100; FORCESE, *supra* note 2, at 213–14; LELAND M. GOODRICH & EDVARD HAMBRO, CHARTER OF THE UNITED NATIONS: COMMENTARY AND DOCUMENTS 297–99 (2d ed. 1949).

[102] Oscar Schachter, *The Right of States to Use Armed Force*, 82 MICH. L. REV. 1620, 1635 (1984).

[103] DINSTEIN, *supra* note 74, ¶ 609. "The casting of the die, rather than the actual opening of fire, is what starts the armed attack." *Id.*

[104] *See* THOMAS M. FRANCK, RECOURSE TO FORCE: STATE ACTION AGAINST THREATS AND ARMED ATTACKS 50, 67, 97–108 (2002); A MORE SECURE WORLD: OUR SHARED RESPONSIBILITY: REPORT OF THE SECRETARY-GENERAL'S HIGH-LEVEL PANEL ON THREATS, CHALLENGES AND CHANGE ¶ 188, U.N. Doc. A/59/565 (2004).

nuclear reactor, not yet completely built, Israel argued that its attack was a necessary act of anticipatory self-defense because Iraq would have used the reactor to build an atomic weapon to attack Israel. Other states criticized the legality of Israel's response because, even if the reactor might pose a threat, there was nothing imminent about it. The *Caroline* test figured in debates at the U.N. Security Council, which unanimously condemned Israel's attack as a violation of the U.N. Charter.[105]

The legality of defensive use of force to prevent prospective, rather than imminent, attacks has been revisited following the 2001 terrorist attacks in U.S. territory (9/11). Unilateral use of force in self-defense, some argue—echoing Britain's view of the United States at the time of the *Caroline* incident—is justified in the territory of states "unable or unwilling" to control such threatening actors. The Bush administration's 2002 *National Security Strategy* set out the U.S. doctrine of "preemptive self-defense," which would allow the use of force against prospective threats in addition to temporally imminent attacks. According to the *National Security Strategy*, "[w]e must adapt the concept of imminent threat to the capabilities and objectives of today's adversaries. . . . The greater the threat, the greater is the risk of inaction."[106] In this view, imminence is not just a question of timing:

> Whether an armed attack may be regarded as "imminent" will fall to be assessed by reference to all relevant circumstances, including (a) the nature and immediacy of the threat, (b) the probability of an attack, (c) whether the anticipated attack is part of a concerted pattern of continuing armed activity, (d) the likely scale of the attack and the injury, loss, or damage likely to result therefrom in the absence of mitigating action, and (e) the likelihood that there will be other opportunities to undertake effective action in self-defense that may be expected to cause less serious collateral injury, loss, or damage.[107]

Supporters of preemptive self-defense have invoked Webster's *Caroline* formulation, arguing that Webster's "instant, overwhelming" language was a context-specific application of the more fundamental concept of necessity.[108]

But using force to counter a possible future attack—one that is neither under way nor imminent—may lead to abuses. As Professor Michael Reisman has written, if preemptive force were to become

[105] S.C. Res. 487, U.N. Doc S/RES/487 (June 19, 1981). *See* U.N. SCOR 36th Sess., 2282d mtg., U.N. Doc. S/PV.2282, ¶ 14 (June 15, 1981) (comments of Uganda's delegate); *id.* 2283d mtg., U.N. Doc. S/PV.2283, ¶ 148 (June 15, 1981) (comments of Sierra Leone's delegate).

[106] NATIONAL SECURITY STRATEGY OF THE UNITED STATES OF AMERICA 15 (Sept. 2002).

[107] Daniel Bethlehem, *Self-Defense Against an Actual or Imminent Attack by Nonstate Actors*, 106 AM. J. INT'L L. 770, 775–76 (2012).

[108] *See* Memorandum from U.S. Dep't of State Legal Adviser William H. Taft, IV, to Members of the ASIL-CFR Roundtable, Nov. 18, 2002, https://www.cfr.org/backgrounders.

"generally available in international law, it could, even more than [anticipatory self-defense responding to imminent threats], lead to more international violence by lowering the threshold for unilaterally determined contingencies that warrant acts of self-defense."[109] Preemptive self-defense risks undermining the traditional self-defense limits of necessity and proportionality. It may be impossible to know whether less intrusive measures could prevent a non-imminent attack. It may also be impossible to determine what "defensive" measures are proportional if an attack is not imminent enough to allow sizing up its potential effects.[110]

The fact that forceful responses to terrorist threats may target non-state actors rather than states poses its own complications. When Article 51 was drafted, the primary concern was using force in self-defense to respond to armed attacks attributable to other states.[111] However, the *Caroline* incident involved extraterritorial self-defense in response to attacks by non-state actors: British forces attacked, in U.S. territory, a vessel used by private U.S. citizens who were shelling British Canada. And after 9/11, the United Nations and most states have accepted that a non-state actor itself may launch an armed attack, leading to a forceful defensive response under Article 51.[112] When self-defense is asserted against prospective attacks by terrorists, however, it may be unclear whether the state from which they operate is in fact "unable or unwilling" to control them—one asserted precondition for a defensive response in that state's territory. In addition, modern uses of force in self-defense against non-state actors is often not as straightforward as Britain's in-and-out destruction of the *Caroline* almost two centuries ago. Extraterritorial counter-terrorist uses of force could be protracted, and bombing suspected terrorists could damage their host state's infrastructure or kill many ordinary civilians. In those situations, the host state might mount its own defensive responses and thus escalate a conflict.[113]

Today the limits of necessity and proportionality that Webster stressed in the *Caroline* test remain fundamental parts of the law of self-defense.[114] Necessity sets a self-defense threshold: the lack of any

---

109 W. Michael Reisman, *Remarks*, 2003 AM. SOC'Y INT'L L. PROC. 142, 143.

110 *See* MARY ELLEN O'CONNELL, THE MYTH OF PREEMPTIVE SELF-DEFENSE 19–20 (Am. Soc'y Int'l L. Task Force on Terrorism, 2002); *The Chatham House Principles of International Law on the Use of Force in Self-Defence*, 55 INT'L & COMP. L.Q. 963, 969–71 (2006).

111 *See* Kimberly J. Trapp, *Can Non-state Actors Mount an Armed Attack?*, *in* THE OXFORD HANDBOOK OF THE USE OF FORCE IN INTERNATIONAL LAW 679 (Marc Weller ed., 2015) [hereinafter OXFORD HANDBOOK].

112 *See* FORCESE, *supra* note 2, at 231, 336 n.5; *Chatham House Principles*, *supra* note 110, at 968.

113 *See* FORCESE, *supra* note 2, at 241–42; Craig Martin, *Challenging and Refining the "Unwilling or Unable" Doctrine*, 52 VAND. J. TRANSNAT'L L. 387 (2021).

114 "The *Caroline* is an invaluable tool in aiding any understanding of the contemporary criteria" of necessity and proportionality, "due to its similarities to, and influence upon them." James A. Green, *Docking the* Caroline*: Understanding the Relevance*

practical alternative to the use of force. Punitive reprisals and force directed solely at targets of opportunity do not meet this necessity requirement. Necessity also links to the proportionality limit, which in Webster's formulation provided that the response to an attack must involve "nothing unreasonable or excessive" and must be confined within the necessity giving rise to the defensive measures. Many today agree that proportionality means that the use of force in self-defense may only involve military actions needed to stop and repel the danger.[115] Although the significance of the temporal, "instant, overwhelming" portion of the *Caroline* test is debated today, the international law necessity and proportionality limits on self-defense endure.

V. CONCLUSION

Why should the *Caroline* test, articulated in 1841, have survived into the twenty-first century? Commentators have done much to promote it, and the test has the attraction of succinctly summarizing factors, notably necessity and proportionality, that have long seemed sensible and just. The *Caroline* test also owes much of its venerability to its pliability. States and publicists have applied it in fact situations far different from those of the *Caroline* incident and have adapted it to fit changing conceptions of international law. The test's concepts of immediacy, necessity, and proportionality are not rigid and may be applied in new settings and legal contexts. This pliability has been useful: a test that did not evolve beyond its original bilateral setting to accommodate essential defensive uses of force in a range of contexts would likely have become obsolete.

---

of the Formula in Contemporary Customary International Law Concerning Self-Defense, 14 CARDOZO J. INT'L & COMP. L. 429, 476 (2006). Parties to cases before the International Court of Justice have invoked Webster's *Caroline* test as reflecting the international law on self-defense, *see* FORCESE, *supra* note 2, at 206–07, 336 n.26, and the Court itself, albeit without citing the *Caroline*, has recognized proportionality and necessity as essential components of the "inherent right of self-defense." *E.g.*, Case Concerning Military and Paramilitary Activities in and against Nicaragua (Nicar. v. U.S.), 1986 I.C.J. 14, ¶ 194 (June 27). *See generally* JUDITH GARDAM, NECESSITY, PROPORTIONALITY AND THE USE OF FORCE BY STATES (2004).

Although the *Caroline* test has traditionally been linked to the law of self-defense, the International Law Commission has cited it as an example of the general concept of necessity, one of the circumstances precluding wrongfulness in the law of state responsibility. *See* JAMES CRAWFORD, THE INTERNATIONAL LAW COMMISSION'S ARTICLES ON STATE RESPONSIBILITY 179–80 (2002). The ILC's retrospective cutting of "the historical umbilical cord of the *Caroline* incident to self-defence" has been criticized as "artificial and erroneous." DINSTEIN, *supra* note 74, at ¶ 767. *See also* Olivier Corten, *Necessity*, *in* OXFORD HANDBOOK, *supra* note 109, at 861, 863–67.

115 *See* FORCESE, *supra* note 2, at 25–36, 347 n.20; *see also* DINSTEIN, *supra* note 74, ¶¶ 743–745. Determining what measures are proportional requires a difficult assessment and balancing of several (perhaps non-static) factors, including the scope and duration of a (perhaps only threatened) attack and of a defensive response, the reactions of third states, and the identity of the actors and factions involved (and links between them). Proportionality is also a central concept in international humanitarian law—the *jus in bello*—which concerns conduct during armed conflicts, *e.g.*, targeting civilians or using proscribed weaponry.

Analyses of self-defense under Article 51 of the U.N. Charter have at times relied on the *Caroline* test, drawing on it to flesh out the meaning of the "inherent right" of self-defense to which that Article refers. The Charter's general prohibition on recourse to force remains a cornerstone of the international legal order. At present, because the Security Council has often not been able to prevent armed conflicts or to authorize forceful responses to illegal uses of force, self-defense plays an outsize role in justifying recourse to force.[116]

What difference, if any, has the *Caroline* test made in constraining recourse to force? International law and legal process may at times contribute to resolving even highly politicized international disputes. In the *Caroline* incident itself, although the British government never conceded that it acted illegally and the U.S. government never conceded that the British attack was justified, bilateral agreement on the *Caroline* test helped both countries put the dispute behind them. The Nuremberg Tribunal found that the *Caroline* test provided no justification for Nazi Germany's invasion of Norway in the early years of World War II, punishing those responsible.[117] More generally, transboundary attacks not justifiable as self-defense have led to the imposition of sanctions against attackers and the non-recognition of territorial gains.[118]

Although international law rules of course have not eliminated illegal uses of force, the law governing recourse to force has nevertheless shaped attitudes, arguments, and actions. The *Caroline* self-defense test has helped frame debates over the legality of uses of force. The test's necessity and proportionality conditions also serve an aspirational function. These values reflect hope that international law may limit some of the suffering and devastation associated with states' recourse to force.

---

116 *But cf.* W. Michael Reisman, *Criteria for the Lawful Use of Force in International Law*, 10 YALE J. INT'L L. 279 (1985) (arguing that international law should not preclude states from unilaterally resorting to force to promote a range of values, including safeguarding populations threatened by atrocities or ensuring the right of peoples to determine their political futures).

117 *See supra* text accompanying note 95.

118 For example, Russia's 2014 invasion and occupation of Crimea and, especially, Russia's 2022 invasion of other parts of Ukraine triggered harsh sanctions and other anti-Russian measures. *See, e.g.*, OONA A. HATHAWAY & SCOTT J. SHAPIRO, THE INTERNATIONALISTS: HOW A RADICAL PLAN TO OUTLAW WAR REMADE THE WORLD 390–94 (2017); U.S. Dep't of State, *How the United States Is Holding Russia and Belarus to Account*, https://2021-2025.state.gov/holding-russia-and-belarus-to-account/ (last visited Mar. 20, 2025); European Commission, *Sanctions adopted following Russia's military aggression against Ukraine*, https://finance.ec.europa.eu/eu-and-world/sanctions-restrictive-measures/sanctions-adopted-following-russias-military-aggression-against-ukraine_en (last visited Jan. 15, 2025). Russia cannot credibly justify its invasions as self-defense. *See* Green et al., *supra* note 99, and *supra* text accompanying note 99.

15

Eric Talbot Jensen

A Century After the *S.S. Lotus* Case: A Modern Understanding

In 2027, the international community will mark the 100th anniversary of the Permanent Court of International Justice's (PCIJ) *Case of the S.S. "Lotus"* (France v. Turkey).[1] As the predecessor to the International Court of Justice (ICJ),[2] the principal judicial organ of the United Nations, the PCIJ played a key role in international law development during the first half of the twentieth century. *Lotus* is one of the PCIJ's most famous early cases, making a review of the case as it approaches its century mark an important legal study.

I. SIGNIFICANCE OF THE *LOTUS* CASE

The *Lotus* case has been labelled a "momentous judgment."[3] The case revolved around a collision between a French and a Turkish vessel on the high seas in 1926 and raised significant questions regarding the extent of a state's jurisdiction, particularly with respect to ships on the high seas. In response to the collision, Turkey arrested Lieutenant Demons, the French officer on watch during the collision, and prosecuted him under Turkish law. France, as the flag state of the *S.S. Lotus*, argued before the PCIJ that Turkey had violated international law by prosecuting Lt. Demons. Conversely, Turkey claimed jurisdiction over Demons, asserting its right to prosecute him based on the argument that the effects of the collision were felt in Turkey.

On its facts, this case was about the application of jurisdiction, and particularly territorial jurisdiction, to a collision between the two ships on the high seas. More importantly, it has come to stand for a foundational perspective on international law—that international law is a fundamentally permissive regime, such that unless a state is specifically prohibited from taking an action, it is free to do so.

Illustrating this point, and as will be discussed below, two of the most famous quotes from the case are:

---

1 S.S. "Lotus" (Fr. v. Turk.) (*Lotus*), 1927 P.C.I.J. (ser. A) No. 10 (Sept. 7).

2 U.N. Charter art. 92, para. 1.

3 George Wendell Berge, *The Case of the S.S. "Lotus,"* 26 MICH. L. REV. 361, 361 (1928).

1) "Restrictions upon the independence of States cannot . . . be presumed";[4] and

2) States have a "wide measure of discretion which is only limited in certain cases by prohibitive rules."[5]

These two statements epitomize the permissive regime for states—unless there is a specific treaty provision, a prohibition based in customary international law, or some general principle of international law, states may act based on their interests.

Despite espousing such well-recognized principles of international law, the Court was split evenly on the decision and required the deciding vote of the President of the Court to resolve the issue. This chapter will look in detail at the *Lotus* case, examining first its historical underpinnings and then the actual decision. The chapter will then canvas alternative views, including both the dissent and subsequent practice that has narrowed the application of the *Lotus* decision through the evolution of international custom and treaty law. Finally, the article will speculate on how the *Lotus* case may continue to be used in the future.

II. CONTINUING IMPORTANCE OF THE *LOTUS* CASE

Before turning to the facts and decision in *Lotus*, it is instructive to look at contemporary statements that point to its continuing importance. Such statements are many, and only a few can be listed here, but these give a sense of the on-going significance of the principles laid out in the case.

With respect to the principle of jurisdiction, Stéphane Beaulac encapsulated her view by writing, "[i]n examining jurisdiction in international law from a historical perspective, most people—be they in academia, government, or elsewhere—would agree that the concept, even in modern times, needs to be considered in light of the judgment of the Permanent Court of International Justice (PCIJ) in the 1927 case of *SS Lotus* between France and Turkey."[6] Danielle Ireland-Piper expressed a similar view, calling *Lotus* a "turning point in jurisdictional jurisprudence."[7] Armin van Bogdandy and Markus Rau wrote that the *Lotus* case is "still one of the most often cited international law cases."[8] Curries and Kindred recognized it as the "starting point" for modern

---

4 *Lotus*, 1927 P.C.I.J. (ser. A) No. 10, at 18.

5 *Id.* at 19.

6 Stéphane Beaulac, *The Lotus Case in Context—Sovereignty, Westphalia, Vattel and Positivism*, *in* THE OXFORD HANDBOOK OF JURISDICTION IN INTERNATIONAL LAW 41, 41 (Stephen Allen et al. eds., 2018).

7 Danielle Ireland-Piper, *Prosecutions of Extraterritorial Criminal Conduct and the Abuse of Rights Doctrine*, 9 UTRECHT L. REV 68, 68–69 (2013).

8 Armin van Bogdandy & Markus Rau, *The Lotus*, *in* 6 THE MAX PLANCK ENCYCLOPEDIA OF PUBLIC INTERNATIONAL LAW 946, 948 (Rüdiger Wolfrum ed., 2d ed. 2012).

expanded assertions of jurisdiction.[9] Ganesh described the case as perhaps the "only full exposition of the concept of jurisdiction by an international court," though also noting some of its more modern detractors.[10]

Asaf Lubin, in an article discussing enforcement jurisdiction in cases of cyber criminality, asked: "Can a collision between two steamers on the high seas in 1926 really teach us something of value about internet governance in 2021?"[11] He argued that some modification on the edges may be necessary, but he did not undermine the fundamental principles of *Lotus*.

Speaking more broadly about the "*Lotus* principle," An Hertogen described current views of the decision in her article, "*Letting* Lotus *Bloom*":

> Those representing states continue to invoke the *Lotus* principle in international disputes. This is not surprising since the voluntarism proclaimed in the principle puts a state in the driver's seat when it comes to the development of restrictions. . . . In contrast, lawyers who take a more constitutional or cosmopolitan approach to international law have labelled the principle's approach of looking for an express prohibition as being outdated or even retrograde.[12]

These are a mere sampling of the acknowledgements of the importance and impact of the *Lotus* case. It is timely, then, as the case nears its 100-year anniversary, to review it in some detail and consider the international law principles it espoused. Clearly, many view the case as still legally important. It will be the task of this chapter to look again at *Lotus* and assess what it still stands for after the passage of so much time, and where it might continue to have an impact in the future.

---

[9] Robert J. Curries & Hugh M. Kindred, *Flux and Fragmentation in the International Law of State Jurisdiction: The Synecdochal Example of Canada's Domestic Court Conflicts over Accountability for International Human Rights Violations*, *in* THE PRACTICE OF INTERNATIONAL AND NATIONAL COURTS AND THE (DE-)FRAGMENTATION OF INTERNATIONAL LAW 217, 220 (Ole Kristian Fauchald & André Nollkaemper eds., 2012).

[10] Aravind Ganesh, *The European Union's Human Rights Obligations Towards Distant Strangers*, 37 MICH. J. INT'L L. 475, 492 (2016).

[11] Asaf Lubin, *The Prohibition on Extraterritorial Enforcement Jurisdiction in the Datasphere*, *in* HANDBOOK ON EXTRATERRITORIALITY IN INTERNATIONAL LAW 1, 2 (Austen L. Parrish & Cedric Ryngaert eds., 2022).

[12] An Hertogen, *Letting* Lotus *Bloom*, 26 EUR. J. INT'L L. 901, 902–03 (2016). Hertogen went on to argue:

> The article therefore rejects calls for discarding the *Lotus* judgment as an outdated and wrongly decided precedent. In other words, it is the prevailing reading of the *Lotus* judgment expressed in the *Lotus* principle, rather than the judgment itself, that needs to be discarded as inaccurate. Instead, an alternative reading that centres on the judgment's reference to the "co-existence of independent communities" is proposed.

Id. at 904.

III. FACTS

Perhaps one advantage of the *Lotus* case over other PCIJ cases is that the facts were uncontested. As will be discussed below, the parties agreed on the facts, leaving no fact-finding role for the Court. Rather, the Court was able to focus solely on the legal questions posed. Though the facts were not in dispute, their review and the historical setting in which they sit are key to understanding the legal ruling.

Historical Context. Understanding the importance of the *Lotus* decision requires placing it in historical context, beginning with the 1648 Peace of Westphalia. As described by Stéphane Beaulac, the Peace of Westphalia and its embrace of sovereignty as "the foundational basis of international jurisdiction"[13] was a key building block in establishing the bases for state interaction. As Dionisio Anzilotti rightly stated, Westphalia is "the starting point of the historical development of the present international law."[14]

As a result of the Peace of Westphalia and the gradual integration of state sovereignty as a fundamental aspect of international relations, the doctrine of state jurisdiction also became a key aspect of international law. Though the doctrines of jurisdiction were not fully developed in 1648, the specific question of territorial jurisdiction and how states exercised exclusive rights to jurisdiction or shared those rights became the major question of the *Lotus* case.

Without the context of the Peace of Westphalia and the subsequent entrenchment of the ideas and powers attached to state sovereignty, the discussion in the *Lotus* case would have been very different. It is only the underlying acceptance of the foundational underpinnings of sovereignty that made the territorial claims of jurisdiction the prominent legal concept at issue in the case.

In addition, the states of Turkey and France also shared a recent history of interaction. Turkey was only four years into independence after the dissolution of the Ottoman Empire in the wake of World War I. Continued French presence in the Levant added additional opportunities for interaction, and often conflict, including competing claims by both states to areas in Syria. The newly independent state of Turkey was anxious to be recognized as an independent and equal sovereign by its European neighbors.[15] The negotiations surrounding the 1923 Treaty of Lausanne discussed below are indicative of this desire by Turkey.

---

13 Beaulac, *supra* note 6, at 43.

14 DIONISIO ANZILOTTI, COURS DE DROIT INTERNATIONAL, I: INTRODUCTION: THÉORIES, GÉNÉRALES (Receuil Sirey, 1929), *quoted in* Beaulac, *supra* note 6, at 43.

15 Douglas Guilfoyle, SS Lotus (France v Turkey) *(1927)*, *in* LANDMARK CASES IN PUBLIC INTERNATIONAL LAW 89, 91–92 (Eirik Bjorge & Cameron Miles eds., 2017).

Facts of the Case. The *Lotus* case arose from a collision between two vessels, the French-flagged steamship *Lotus* and the Turkish-flagged ship *Boz-Kourt*. The facts, as submitted to the Court, were uncontested.[16]

> On August 2nd, 1926, just before midnight, a collision occurred between the French mail steamer Lotus, proceeding to Constantinople, and the Turkish collier Boz-Kourt, between five and six nautical miles to the north of Cape Sigri (Mitylene). The Boz-Kourt, which was cut in two, sank, and eight Turkish nationals who were on board perished. After having done everything possible to succour the shipwrecked persons, of whom ten were able to be saved, the Lotus continued on its course to Constantinople, where it arrived on August 3rd.[17]

With respect to the personnel involved, the parties agreed that Lt. Demons was a French citizen and was directing the movement of the *S.S. Lotus*. Hassan Bey, whom the sailors on the *Lotus* retrieved from the wreckage, was captaining the *Boz-Kourt*.[18] The accident happened on the high seas,[19] an area outside the territorial jurisdiction of any state.[20] This fact is significant with respect to the legal arguments that eventually served as the basis for the contention between France and Turkey.

Once Lt. Demons arrived in Constantinople with the survivors of the *Boz-Kourt*, he filed a report with the French Consulate-General and the harbor master, after which the local police were alerted to the collision.[21] The Turkish authorities soon arrested the captains of both ships "pending trial,"[22] interrogated them, and charged both with involuntary manslaughter under Article 6 of the Turkish Criminal Code.[23]

French authorities in Turkey immediately objected to the assertion of jurisdiction by Turkey over Lt. Demons, demanding that he be turned over to the French for judicial resolution of the case.[24] Nevertheless, Demons was tried in Turkish courts, convicted, and sentenced to eighty days imprisonment and a fine of 6,000 Turkish pounds.[25]

Concurrently, France was making continuous protestations to the Turkish government. As a result of those diplomatic interventions, the Turkish government notified the French government that "it would have no objection to the reference of the conflict of jurisdiction to the court at the Hague." An agreement was signed on October 12 under Article 40 of

---

16 S.S. "Lotus" (Fr. v. Turk.), 1927 P.C.I.J. (ser. A) No. 10, at 10 (Sept. 7); Guilfoyle, *supra* note 15, at 94–95.

17 *Lotus*, 1927 P.C.I.J. (ser. A) No. 10, at 10. *See also* Beaulac, *supra* note 6, at 49.

18 *Lotus*, 1927 P.C.I.J. (ser. A) No. 10, at 10.

19 Beaulac, *supra* note 6, at 49.

20 *Lotus*, 1927 P.C.I.J. (ser. A) No. 10, at 12.

21 *Id.* at 10.

22 *Id.*

23 Beaulac, *supra* note 6, at 49.

24 *Id.*; *Lotus*, 1927 P.C.I.J. (ser. A) No. 10, at 11.

25 Beaulac, *supra* note 6 at 49.

the Statute of the Permanent Court, and the events in the case transitioned from Turkey to the PCIJ.[26]

IV. JUDICIAL PROCEEDINGS AT THE PCIJ

When the case arrived at the Permanent Court of International Justice, the primary question before the Court was whether Turkey violated international law by asserting jurisdiction over Lt. Demons in a case that occurred on the high seas.[27] According to the special agreement by which France and Turkey authorized the Court to hear the case, the Court was charged with determining:

> Has Turkey, contrary to Article 15 of the Convention of Lausanne of July 24th, 1923, respecting conditions of residence and business and jurisdiction, acted in conflict with the principles of international law—and if so, what principles—by instituting, following the collision which occurred on August 2nd, 1926, on the high seas between the French steamer *Lotus* and the Turkish steamer *Boz-Kourt* and upon the arrival of the French steamer at Constantinople—as well as against the captain of the Turkish steamship—joint criminal proceedings in pursuance of Turkish law against M. Demons, officer of the watch on board the *Lotus* at the time of the collision, in consequence of the loss of the *Boz-Kourt* having involved the death of eight Turkish sailors and passengers?[28]

As introduced above, an important underlying legal consideration was the Convention Respecting Conditions of Residence and Business and Jurisdiction, signed by both parties at Lausanne on July 24, 1923. This Convention was signed in conjunction with the Peace Treaty ending hostilities between the Allied Powers and Turkey. At issue was Article 15 of the Convention, which states: "Subject to the provisions of Article 16, all questions of jurisdiction shall, as between Turkey and the other contracting Powers, be decided in accordance with the principles of international law."[29] During the negotiations of the Convention, there

---

26 *Id.*

27 *Id.*

28 *Lotus*, 1927 P.C.I.J. (ser. A) No. 10, at 5.

29 *Quoted in id.* at 16; *see* Treaty of Lausanne, July 24, 1923, 28 L.N.T.S. 11. Article 16 of the Convention states:

> In matters of personal status, i.e., all questions relating to marriage, conjugal rights, divorce, judicial separation, dower, paternity affiliation, adoption, capacity, majority, guardianship, trusteeship and interdiction; in matters relating to succession to personality, whether by will or on intestacy, and the distribution and winding up of estates; and family law in general, it is agreed between Turkey and the other contracting Powers that, as regards non-Moslem nationals of such Powers in Turkey, the national tribunals or other competent national authorities established in the country of which the party whose personal status is in question will alone have jurisdiction. The present stipulation does not affect the special attributions of consuls in matters of status in accordance with international law or special agreements which may be concluded, nor the right of Turkish courts to request and receive evidence

was some dispute over the meaning of the words "principles of international law" in Article 15. Turkey had asserted at the negotiations that such principles allowed the assertion of jurisdiction "to crimes committed in the territory of a third state." France, Italy, and the United Kingdom all disagreed with this proposal, which was eventually not included in the text of the Convention.[30]

Arguments of the Parties. The proceedings were somewhat abbreviated based on the desires of the parties.[31] Across the proceedings, France argued six main points: 1) The rejection of Turkey's arguments during the negotiations at Lausanne should apply to the Court's interpretation of the Convention; 2) A state may not exercise extraterritorial jurisdiction without an express provision that allows it; 3) With reference to prior cases, in collisions on the high seas, the flag state was the only state with jurisdictional competence; 4) The Court should not apply an "effects-based" territorial jurisdiction to this case; 5) Turkey had to establish some positive law granting it the right to exercise jurisdiction in this case because none could be presumed; and 6) The Turkish domestic law that allowed jurisdiction was contrary to international law.[32]

Turkey also made six main arguments: 1) Article 15 of the Lausanne Convention only mandated that Turkey not act in any manner contrary to international law; 2) Turkish domestic law reflected Italian domestic law and was not contrary to international law; 3) Turkey was able to assert territorial effects jurisdiction based on the fact that the *Boz-Kourt* was a Turkish flagged vessel; 4) Because this was a connected offense, involving both Turkish and French citizens, Turkey was permitted to assert jurisdiction; 5) In the absence of a provision of international law "debarring" Turkey from asserting jurisdiction, Turkey was free to do so; and 6) France had no right to claim indemnities.[33]

These arguments, and counter-arguments, made clear that Turkey and France had very different views of the content of international law at the time, particularly with respect to the nature of international law and the application of territorial jurisdiction. The Court, under the direction

---

> respecting matters acknowledged above as being within the competence of the national tribunals or authorities of the parties concerned.
>
> By way of exception to the first paragraph of this article, the Turkish courts will also have jurisdiction in the matters referred to therein, if all the parties to the case submit in writing to the jurisdiction of the said courts. In such case the Turkish courts will apply the national law of the parties.

Article 16 did not preclude Turkey's exercise of jurisdiction over Lt. Demons because, although he was a non-Moslem French citizen, the subject matter of *Lotus* did not involve family law or another matter that Article 16 reserved to the exclusive jurisdiction of other countries.

30 *Lotus*, 1927 P.C.I.J. (ser. A) No. 10, at 16–17.

31 *Id.* at 5.

32 *Id.* at 6–8; Guilfoyle, *supra* note 15, at 95–96.

33 *Lotus*, 1927 P.C.I.J. (ser. A) No. 10, at 8–9; Guilfoyle, *supra* note 15, at 96.

of President Max Huber who would eventually cast the deciding vote, set about to resolve these issues.[34]

V. DECISION AND LEGAL REASONING

The central legal question before the PCIJ was whether the exercise of jurisdiction was a permissive international law regime, allowing a state to assert jurisdiction unless prohibited from doing so, or a regime where specific authority was required for each assertion of jurisdiction. In the Court's own words, "The French Government contends that the Turkish Courts, in order to have jurisdiction, should be able to point to some title to jurisdiction recognized by international law in favour of Turkey. On the other hand, the Turkish Government takes the view that Article 15 allows Turkey jurisdiction whenever such jurisdiction does not come into conflict with a principle of international law."[35]

Ultimately, the ICJ sided with Turkey and upheld its right to exercise jurisdiction over the collision. The Court acknowledged that under customary international law, states could exercise their jurisdiction to regulate activities that had a substantial connection to their territory. The collision between the *S.S. Lotus* and the *Boz-Kourt* was deemed to have had a direct and immediate connection to Turkish territory, as it resulted in the loss of lives and property associated with a Turkish-flagged vessel on the high seas. How the Court got there deserves attention.

Turkey's Extraterritorial Argument Under Its Domestic Law. One of Turkey's arguments was that its domestic law provided a method of exercising extraterritorial jurisdiction that would extend to the facts of the *Lotus* case. Turkey argued that Article 6 of the Turkish criminal code established an extraterritorial application of jurisdiction based on the theory of what we would now describe as either protective[36] or passive personality jurisdiction.[37] Article 6 allowed Turkish courts to assert jurisdiction over "Any foreigner who . . . commits an offence abroad to the prejudice of Turkey or of a Turkish subject, for which offence Turkish law prescribes a penalty."[38]

The Court dismissed this provision of Turkish law as unimportant to the case because "the question submitted to the Court is not whether that article is compatible with the principles of international law; it is more general. The Court is asked to state whether or not the principles of international law prevent Turkey from instituting criminal proceedings against Lieutenant Demons under Turkish law."[39] The assertion of

34 OLE SPIERMANN, INTERNATIONAL LEGAL ARGUMENT IN THE PERMANENT COURT OF INTERNATIONAL JUSTICE: THE RISE OF THE INTERNATIONAL JUDICIARY 247–48 (2005).

35 *Lotus*, 1927 P.C.I.J. (ser. A) No. 10, at 18.

36 RESTATEMENT (FOURTH) OF FOREIGN RELATIONS LAW § 412 (2018).

37 *Id.* § 411.

38 *Lotus*, 1927 P.C.I.J. (ser. A) No. 10, at 14.

39 *Id.* at 15.

extraterritorial jurisdiction based on one of these theories was strongly advocated at the time of the case,[40] but the Court did not rely on either theory. As Hertogen astutely pointed out, "[t]he assimilation of a ship to the territory of its flag state framed the question as one of objective territorial jurisdiction where actions in one state are inseparable from its effects in the territory of another state, rather than one involving the passive personality principle or the protective principle."[41]

Under current understandings of international law, there are generally three categories of jurisdiction: 1) prescriptive, or "the authority of a state to make law applicable to persons, property, or conduct"; 2) enforcement, or "the authority of a state to exercise its power to compel compliance with law"; and 3) adjudicative, or "the authority of a state to apply law to persons or things, in particular through the processes of its courts or administrative tribunals."[42] Within prescriptive jurisdiction, there are generally six methods of applying jurisdiction: 1) territorial; 2) territorial effects; 3) nationality; 4) passive personality; 5) protective; and 6) universal.[43]

Territorial jurisdiction allows a state to exercise authority "with respect to persons, property, and conduct within its territory."[44] Territorial effects jurisdiction allows prescribing conduct that "has a substantial effect within its territory." Nationality jurisdiction is based on the "conduct, interests, status and relations of its nationals and residents outside its territory." Passive personality jurisdiction relates to conduct outside its territory that harms its nationals. Protective jurisdiction covers conduct "directed against the security" of a state, or "against a limited class of other fundamental . . . interests." Universal jurisdiction allows any state to prescribe laws concerning a certain small class of crimes, including piracy, slavery, and genocide.[45]

While all these current understandings of jurisdiction were not settled at the time of the *Lotus* case, the connection between territory and sovereignty was well established. Only one year after Max Huber provided the tie-breaking vote at the PCIJ in the *Lotus* case, he conducted his famous arbitration in the "Island of Palmas" where he stated that "[s]overeignty in the relations between States signifies independence. Independence in regard to a portion of the globe is the right to exercise therein, to the exclusion of any other State, the function of a State."[46] As noted above, the parties in *Lotus* held divergent views about territorial jurisdiction. The PCIJ understood its task to resolve this key issue. In

[40] Berge, *supra* note 3, at 380–81. The author argued "this claim [of Article 6] is not essential to sustain Turkey's jurisdiction in the Lotus case, where the effects of the offence were felt on a Turkish vessel under Turkish jurisdiction."

[41] Hertogen, *supra* note 12, at 905.

[42] RESTATEMENT (FOURTH), *supra* note 36, § 401.

[43] *See id.* § 402.

[44] *Id.* § 402(1)(a).

[45] *Id.* § 402(1).

[46] Island of Palmas Case (Neth. v. U.S.), 2 R.I.A.A. 829, 838 (Perm. Ct. Arb. 1928).

doing so the Court stated, "it is the very fact of the institution of proceedings [against Lt. Demons] which is held by France to be contrary to those principles. Thus the French Government at once protested against his arrest, quite independently of the question as to what clause of her legislation was relied upon by Turkey to justify it."[47]

The Permissive Nature of International Law. After emphasizing that the dispute at the PCIJ involved international rather than domestic law, the Court turned its attention to the nature of the international legal system. In doing so, the Court built its basis for eventually opining on the permissive nature of the legal regime. To begin, the Court confirmed the voluntarist nature of international law, citing both the need for individual states to accept conventions and the foundational nature of state practice in the establishment of custom.[48] As the Court stated, "[i]nternational law governs relations between independent States. The rules of law binding upon States therefore emanate from their own free will as expressed in conventions or by usages generally accepted as expressing principles of law and established in order to regulate the relations between these co-existing independent communities or with a view to the achievement of common aims."[49]

The PCIJ's reference to "usages generally accepted as expressing principles of law" is one of the first pronouncements of the connection between state practice and *opinio juris* that is so well ensconced in international law today.[50] This connection of state practice to legal obligation appears in the Statute of the International Court of Justice, as it had in the PCIJ Statute before it,[51] but, as Guilfoyle pointed out, was not a staple of international jurisprudence when the *Lotus* case was decided.

It is this voluntarist reliance on free will and its importance in the formulation of international law that led the Court to state the oft-quoted dictum from the case: "Restrictions upon the independence of States cannot therefore be presumed."[52] States were, however, legally bound by restrictions they accepted in treaties or in rules of customary international law. As an example, the Court noted the restriction on the exercise of enforcement jurisdiction on the territory of another state.[53]

---

47 S.S. "Lotus" (Fr. v. Turk.), 1927 P.C.I.J. (ser. A) No. 10, at 15 (Sept. 7); *see also* Berge, *supra* note 3, at 379.

48 Beaulac, *supra* note 6, at 49–52, 53–54.

49 *Lotus*, 1927 P.C.I.J. (ser. A) No. 10, at 18.

50 Guilfoyle, *supra* note 15, at 103.

51 *See* Statute of the International Court of Justice art. 38(1)(b), June 26, 1945, 59 Stat. 1055, 1060; Statute of the Permanent Court of International Justice art. 38(2), Dec. 16, 1920, 6 L.N.T.S. 390.

52 *Lotus*, 1927 P.C.I.J. (ser. A) No. 10, at 18; *see also* Berge, *supra* note 3, at 377, who contemporaneously argued that "[t]he chief source of international law is general consent, express or implied. In the absence of law on the subject, freedom of national action is presumed."

53 Sean D. Yates, *Will the Canadian Courts Make Meng Wanzhou's Case Their Own* Lotus*?*, 4 SCHOLARS INT'L J. L., CRIME & JUST. 136, 137 (2021).

The Court endorsed the view that each state possessed exclusive territorial enforcement jurisdiction,[54] both in terms of having the exclusive right to exercise enforcement jurisdiction in its own territory and being precluded from exercising the same in the territory of another state. The Court then stated that "[i]t does not, however, follow that international law prohibits a State from exercising jurisdiction in its own territory, in respect of any case which relates to acts which have taken place abroad, and in which it cannot rely on some permissive rule of international law."[55] Rather, "[f]ar from laying down a general prohibition to the effect that States may not extend the application of their laws and the jurisdiction of their courts to persons, property, and acts outside their territory, it leaves them in this respect a wide measure of discretion which is only limited in certain cases by prohibitive rules."[56]

In support of this interpretation of international law, the Court noted the "efforts [that] have been made for many years past, both in Europe and America, to prepare conventions the effect of which would be precisely to limit the discretion at present left to States in this respect by international law."[57] This line of reasoning led the *Lotus* Court to conclude that "the contention of the French Government to the effect that Turkey must in each case be able to cite a rule of international law authorizing her to exercise jurisdiction, is opposed to the generally accepted international law to which Article 15 of the Convention of Lausanne refers."[58]

Here then, is the basis for the *Lotus* Court's most far-reaching impact on international law. The Court's progression from the voluntarist nature of international law to the assumption that in such a regime, restrictions may not be presumed, and then to the acceptance of the existence of certain codified or accepted restrictions that do serve to limit states' potential actions, all work together to establish a strong foundation for the *Lotus* Court's assertion that international law is a permissive regime and that in the absence of a specific prohibition, states are free to act.

A casual reader may be tempted to attribute this statement on the permissive nature of international law to the formulation of the question in the special agreement between France and Turkey that brought the case to trial. In fact, the Court started with that approach itself. Commenting on the importance of the formulation of the special agreement, the Court stated: "According to the special agreement, therefore, it is not a question of stating principles which would permit Turkey to take criminal proceedings, but of formulating the principles, if any, which might have been violated by such proceedings."[59] But the

---

54 *Lotus*, 1927 P.C.I.J. (ser. A) No. 10, at 18–19.

55 *Id.* at 19.

56 *Id.*

57 *Id.*

58 *Id.*

59 *Id.* at 18.

Court immediately followed that statement by noting, "[t]his way of stating the question is also dictated by the very nature and existing conditions of international law."[60] In other words, regardless of the particular wording of the special agreement, the nature of international law also dictated that the Court take this same approach.[61]

Some writers have argued that the Court's approach was indeed necessitated by the nature of international law. Berge exemplified this view when he wrote in 1931,

> the burden of proof was on France to show that Turkey had violated the principles of international law, and that, in the absence of such a showing, jurisdiction was proper; that restrictions upon the right of a state to exercise its jurisdiction are not to be presumed in the absence of a clear showing that they exist; that there is no rule of international law that would forbid Turkey to base jurisdiction upon the fact that the offense took effect on a Turkish vessel and, consequently, on a place assimilated for jurisdictional purposes to Turkish territory; and that this was properly a case for concurrent jurisdiction.[62]

Several modern scholars have, however, argued that the Court's decision is less about ensconcing the permissive nature of international law than it is about portraying the regime as cooperative and designed to "limit[ ] the possibility of conflict between the different states involved."[63] Others have argued that the Court's approach of adopting the permissive rule was simply the easiest approach to take and that "in this particular case it did not matter the approach one took to the question because the positive law already supplied an answer."[64] What commentators do seem to agree on is that this case represents a high point of state-centric positivism.[65]

Nevertheless, for many the *Lotus* case continues to stand for the permissive regime the PCIJ espoused and provides the basis for many legal arguments that remain mostly uncontested today.

Applying the Permissive Regime. Once the Court had embraced and defined the permissive nature of international law, it then turned to applying that principle to the facts of the case, and sought to ascertain if any codified or accepted rule of international law supported the assertions of France that:

---

[60] *Id.*

[61] Berge, *supra* note 3, at 369.

[62] Wendell Berge, *Criminal Jurisdiction and the Territorial Principle*, 30 MICH. L. REV. 238, 246 (1931) [hereinafter Berge 1931].

[63] Hertogen, *supra* note 12, at 910. Hertogen argued that "the real difference between the majority and the dissents is thus not one of prohibition or permission but, rather, the respective judges' understanding of the limits on the exercise of prescriptive or adjudicative jurisdiction that followed from the concept of territorial sovereignty."

[64] Guilfoyle, *supra* note 15, at 102.

[65] Beaulac, *supra* note 6, at 47–49; SPIERMANN, *supra* note 34, at 249, 261–62.

The Peace Palace, The Hague
Home of the Permanent Court of International Justice
and the International Court of Justice

> (1) International law does not allow a State to take proceedings with regard to offences committed by foreigners abroad, simply by reason of the nationality of the victim; and such is the situation in the present case because the offence must be regarded as having been committed on board the French vessel.
>
> (2) International law recognizes the exclusive jurisdiction of the State whose flag is flown as regards everything which occurs on board a ship on the high seas.
>
> (3) Lastly, this principle is especially applicable in a collision case.[66]

The Court dispensed with France's first assertion by stating that "No argument has come to the knowledge of the Court from which it could be deduced that States recognize themselves to be under an obligation towards each other only to have regard to the place where the author of the offence happens to be at the time of the offence."[67] As a result, the Court concluded, "once it is admitted that the effects of the offence were

[66] S.S. "Lotus" (Fr. v. Turk.), 1927 P.C.I.J. (ser. A) No. 10, at 22 (Sept. 7).

[67] *Id.* at 23.

produced on the Turkish vessel, it becomes impossible to hold that there is a rule of international law which prohibits Turkey from prosecuting Lieutenant Demons because of the fact that the author of the offence was on board the French ship."[68]

With respect to the second French contention, the Court recognized the exclusive jurisdiction of the flag state. "It is certainly true that—apart from certain special cases which are defined by international law—vessels on the high seas are subject to no authority except that of the State whose flag they fly."[69] However, the Court continued that "it by no means follows that a State can never in its own territory exercise jurisdiction over acts which have occurred on board a foreign ship on the high seas."[70] Rather, the Court argued that the application of territorial jurisdiction to the flagged ship leads to the opposite conclusion.

> It follows that what occurs on board a vessel on the high seas must be regarded as if it occurred on the territory of the State whose flag the ship flies. If, therefore, a guilty act committed on the high seas produces its effects on a vessel flying another flag or in foreign territory, the same principles must be applied as if the territories of two different States were concerned, and the conclusion must therefore be drawn that there is no rule of international law prohibiting the State to which the ship on which the effects of the offence have taken place belongs, from regarding the offence as having been committed in its territory and prosecuting, accordingly, the delinquent.[71]

The Court thus embraced the effects doctrine of territorial sovereignty and found no other prohibitive rule that would prevent its application to the specific facts of the case. As Beaulac noted with respect to the Court's acknowledgement of the basis for France's argument, "the general ban in international law, alluded to by the PCIJ . . . is on extraterritorial enforcement jurisdiction, not extraterritorial prescriptive jurisdiction or extraterritorial adjudicative jurisdiction. As far as prescriptive jurisdiction is concerned, so long as no enforcement is involved, sovereign states may have legislation that reaches outside its territory."[72]

France argued that flag ship jurisdiction is exclusive, relying on the teachings of publicists among other international sources. In response, the Court found "the existence of such a rule has not been conclusively proved."[73] When the *S.S. Lotus* and the *Boz-Kourt* collided, law of the sea norms were not as well-established as they are today. The *Lotus* case reflected the state practice and international law principles of its time. As will be shown below, the international community reacted to the *Lotus*

---

68 *Id.*

69 *Id.* at 25.

70 *Id.*

71 *Id.*

72 Beaulac, *supra* note 6, at 51–52.

73 *Lotus*, 1927 P.C.I.J. (ser. A) No. 10, at 26.

decision by adopting the 1952 Brussels Convention for the Unification of Certain Rules Relating to Penal Jurisdiction[74] and other treaties that would have led to finding Turkey's exercise of jurisdiction over Lt. Demons invalid.[75] However, based on the lack of codified law at that time that restricted Turkey's assertion of jurisdiction, the Court determined France's assertion had no accepted legal basis.

With regard to France's third assertion—that a principle of exclusive flag state jurisdiction applied in collision cases—the Court briefly looked at inconsistent domestic cases on the issue. It found that "as municipal jurisprudence is thus divided, it is hardly possible to see in it an indication of the existence of the restrictive rule of international law which alone could serve as a basis for the contention of the French Government."[76]

In deciding the *Lotus* case as it did, the PCIJ established the principle that states are free to exercise jurisdiction unless otherwise prohibited from doing so, while still responding to the sovereignty-driven exclusivity of enforcement jurisdiction. With respect to the high seas, in the absence of a specific treaty provision to the contrary, a state may, where the effects of the action are felt by that state, exercise concurrent jurisdiction with the flag state. In doing so, the Court solidified the principle of objective territoriality, which means that a state may assert jurisdiction over acts that have an effect on its territory, including flagged vessels.[77] Thus, in the Court's own words, "[i]t is only natural that each [country] should be able to exercise jurisdiction and to do so in respect of the incident as a whole. It is therefore a case of concurrent jurisdiction."[78]

Having decided that jurisdiction was concurrent and not exclusive, the Court ruled that "Turkey, by instituting, in virtue of the discretion which international law leaves to every sovereign State, the criminal proceedings in question, has not, in the absence of such principles, acted in a manner contrary to the principles of international law within the meaning of the special agreement."[79]

Such is the decision of the *S.S. Lotus* case. The determination that jurisdiction was concurrent allowed Turkey to continue to assert jurisdiction over the collision, including over the French officer, Lt.

---

[74] International Convention for the Unification of Certain Rules Relating to Penal Jurisdiction in Matters of Collision or Other Incidents of Navigation, May 10, 1952, 439 U.N.T.S. 233 [hereinafter Collision Convention].

[75] Yates also argued that "custom and practice have developed in the way States approach issues of jurisdiction that clearly run contrary to the *Lotus* position." Yates, *supra* note 53, at 137.

[76] *Lotus*, 1927 P.C.I.J. (ser. A) No. 10, at 29.

[77] Suzanne Kingston, *Territoriality in EU (Tax) Law: A Sacred Principle, or Dépassé?*, *in* INTERNATIONAL TAX LAW AND NEW CHALLENGES FROM CONSTITUTIONAL AND LEGAL PLURALISM 23 (Joachim Englisch ed., 2016).

[78] *Lotus*, 1927 P.C.I.J. (ser. A) No. 10, at 30–31.

[79] *Id.* at 31.

Demons. Perhaps more importantly, the case announced the *Lotus* principle that continues to influence international law today.

VI. SUBSEQUENT ICJ PRACTICE

One measure of how influential a judicial decision is over time is whether subsequent courts follow or quote that decision. The ICJ has quoted *Lotus* in three subsequent cases. Two of those references—the *North Sea Continental Shelf* cases[80] and the *Nicaragua* case[81]—do not deal with the jurisdiction issue discussed here. The third reference—the *Nuclear Weapons Advisory Opinion*[82]—"refers to the *Lotus* principle of sovereignty (and jurisdiction) and how it relates to the nature of international normativity."[83] In that opinion, the Court quoted some of the key points in the *Lotus* case, such as that "restrictions upon the independence of states cannot . . . be presumed" and that states have a "wide measure of discretion which is only limited in certain cases by prohibitive rules."[84] Perhaps as important, Beaulac, after discussing the impact of *Lotus* on both the *Corfu Channel*[85] and *Kosovo*[86] cases, asserted that the ICJ seemed to be "using a logic emphasizing international law as a system permitting everything that is not prohibited."[87]

On the other hand, Hugh Handyside argued that the Court's opinion in the *Nuclear Weapons* case is not as clear as some commentators might contend. Handyside stated that the Court "did not look favorably on the *Lotus* principle as a presumption, a residual principle, or a combination of the two."[88] Perhaps reinforcing Handyside's view, in a separate opinion to the *Arrest Warrants* case,[89] Judges Higgins, Kooijmans, and Buergenthal argued that the *Lotus* decision "represents the high water mark of laissez-faire in international relations,"[90] and dissenting Judge

---

80 North Sea Continental Shelf Cases (Ger./Den.; Ger./Neth.), 1969 I.C.J. 3, ¶ 78 (Feb. 20).

81 Military and Paramilitary Activities in and against Nicaragua (Nicar. v. U.S.), 1986 I.C.J. 14, ¶ 29 (June 27).

82 Legality of the Threat or Use of Nuclear Weapons, Advisory Opinion, 1996 I.C.J. 226, ¶ 21 (July 8).

83 Beaulac, *supra* note 6, at 55.

84 *Legality of the Threat or Use of Nuclear Weapons*, 1996 I.C.J. 226, ¶ 21, at 238.

85 Corfu Channel (U.K. v. Alb.), 1949 I.C.J. 4 (Apr. 9).

86 Accordance with International Law of the Unilateral Declaration of Independence in Respect of Kosovo, Advisory Opinion, 2010 I.C.J. 403 (July 22); Roman Kwiecień, *On Some Contemporary Challenges to Statehood in the International Legal Order: International Law Between Lotus and Global Administrative Law*, 51 ARCHIV DES VÖLKERRECHTS 279, 283 (2013).

87 Beaulac, *supra* note 6, at 56.

88 Hugh Handyside, *The* Lotus *Principle in ICJ Jurisprudence: Was the Ship Ever Afloat?*, 29 MICH. J. INT'L L. 71, 89 (2007).

89 Arrest Warrant of 11 April 2000 (Dem. Rep. Congo v. Belg.), 2002 I.C.J. 3 (Feb. 14).

90 *Id.* at 78.

Van den Wyngaert argued that "a more restrictive approach should be adopted today."[91]

Further clarity on the Court's current disposition toward the *Lotus* case will likely come with time. However, even at its inception, the case certainly garnered alternate views as to its holding, particularly with respect to the permissive nature of international law.

VII. ALTERNATE VIEWS

Both when *Lotus* was decided and later, there have been alternate views about the permissive nature of international law. As mentioned above, the PCIJ judges split six to six, requiring the President of the Court to cast the deciding vote. Many academics also immediately rejected the decision. And eventually, the community of states also rejected portions of the decision.

Dissenting Opinions. Though six judges disagreed with the majority opinion, they did not disagree for the same reasons, causing each to submit his own dissenting opinion.

Judge Loder. As stated in Judge Loder's dissenting opinion, "the [majority's] contention [is] that under international law, everything which is not prohibited is permitted. In other words, . . . under international law, every door is open unless it is closed by treaty or by established custom. . . . It seems to me that the contention is at variance with the spirit of international law."[92]

Though seemingly disagreeing with the permissive regime of international law, Judge Loder focused on the assertion of jurisdiction, alleging that Turkey should not have been allowed to assert jurisdiction over another state's national. He critiqued what today is called the passive personality basis of jurisdiction. "The criminal law of a State may extend to crimes and offences committed abroad by its nationals, since such nationals are subject to the law of their own country; but it cannot extend to offences committed by a foreigner in foreign territory, without infringing the sovereign rights of the foreign State concerned, since in that State the State enacting the law has no jurisdiction."[93]

Judge Loder also, while accepting the effects basis for jurisdiction in some cases, rejected its application here. Arguing that "the case which the Court has to consider bears no resemblance to [accepted situations where effects jurisdiction applies,] [t]he officer of the *Lotus*, who had never set foot on board the *Boz-Kourt*, had no intention of injuring

---

[91] *Id.* at 169.

[92] S.S. "Lotus" (Fr. v. Turk.), 1927 P.C.I.J. (ser. A) No. 10, at 34 (Sept. 7). "Judge Loder did not accept the Court's view of international law that every door is open to the jurisdiction of a nation 'unless it is closed by treaty or by established custom.' " Berge, *supra* note 3, at 371.

[93] *Lotus*, 1927 P.C.I.J. (ser. A) No. 10, at 35.

anyone, and no such intention is imputed to him."[94] The persuasiveness of Loder's dissent has caused even modern scholars to comment that he "cemented his place in judicial history with his dissenting opinion in the *S.S. Lotus* case."[95]

Judge Weiss. As noted by Berge, "Judge Weiss found in Turkey's assertion of jurisdiction a violation of two principles of international law: (I) the principle of the sovereignty of states in criminal matters, and (2) the principle of the freedom of the high seas, including the application of the law of the flag, which is its corollary."[96] As Judge Weiss noted, "[t]he Turkish Government, in proceeding against the French Lieutenant Demons upon the basis of acts which had taken place outside Turkish territory on a vessel flying the French flag has disregarded those two fundamental principles of international law; it has consequently acted in contravention of Article 15 of the Lausanne Convention."[97]

Judge Lord Finlay. Lord Finlay did not agree with the majority's assertion of the permissive nature of international law. Again, Berge supplied a sound summary of Lord Finlay's objection to the majority's decision: "Lord Finlay questioned that France, in order to succeed, had to point to some definite rule of international law forbidding what Turkey did. He thought it was enough if the fair application of principles usually accepted by nations negatived such jurisdiction."[98] Hence, Finlay concluded,

> Of course, every country has the right to protect the persons and the property of its citizens. If a wrong is done, the State may demand redress and enforce it, but the assertion that any State can by any law of its own assume criminal jurisdiction in respect of alleged crimes committed abroad or on the high seas is a new one. The government of the country of the injured person may call upon the government of the country where the injury was committed to have the offenders punished in due course by law, but it cannot make laws for their punishment in its own courts, except in pursuance of a convention with the other Power affected.[99]

Judge Nyholm. Judge Nyholm took the opposite view of the majority, regarding the territorial principle as the preeminent basis for jurisdiction. He would have required an international agreement creating an exception to territorial jurisdiction to allow Turkey to exercise jurisdiction as it did. He wrote,

---

94 *Id.* at 37.

95 Henri de Waele, *A New League of Extraordinary Gentlemen? The Professionalization of International Law Scholarship in the Netherlands, 1919–1940*, 31 EUR. J. INT'L L. 1005, 1020 (2020).

96 Berge, *supra* note 3, at 372.

97 *Lotus*, 1927 P.C.I.J. (ser. A) No. 10, at 40, 49.

98 Berge, *supra* note 3, at 372.

99 *Lotus*, 1927 P.C.I.J. (ser. A) No. 10, at 50, 58.

> [T]he exception to the territorial principle which must be established to provide a legal sanction for the exercise of jurisdiction by Turkey, and which forms the subject of the present dispute, does not exist. It is impossible to hold with the judgment that, over and above positive international law, there is a kind of international law which amounts to this: that the absence of a rule prohibiting an action suffices to render that action permissible, for not only is it in most cases inadmissible thus to deduce permission from the absence of a prohibition, but furthermore in the present case one is confronted with the territorial principle, which is definitely established, whilst the possible exceptions to it—and in particular the exception which would be required to give Turkey criminal jurisdiction in this case—are not.[100]

As Berge summarized Nyholm, "[i]nstead of reasoning that failing a rule of positive international law, the relations of states are governed by absolute freedom, we should say that failing a clear cut exception, the general rule of international law, which is the territorial rule, should apply."[101]

Judge Moore. Judge Moore, the U.S. judge on the PCIJ, also dissented from the Court's decision and submitted a separate opinion. He nevertheless agreed with much of the Court's reasoning, and was siding with the majority until the very end of the deliberations.[102] As he stated in introducing his dissenting opinion:

> [M]y dissent was based solely on the connection of the pending case with Article 6 of the Turkish Penal Code .... In the judgment of the Court that there is no rule of international law by virtue of which the penal cognizance of a collision at sea, resulting in loss of life, belongs exclusively to the country of the ship by or by means of which the wrong was done, I concur, thus making for the judgment on that question, as submitted by the *compromis*, a definitely ascertained majority of seven to five. But, as I have reached my conclusions, both on the general question and on the point on which I dissent, by a somewhat independent course of reasoning, I deem it to be my duty to deliver a separate opinion.[103]

On Judge Moore's point of dissent, Berge summarized his position thus: "Judge Moore believed that since Turkey had defended Article 6 of its Penal Code, consideration of it could not be overlooked. On this he differed with the Court which had not found it necessary to consider Article 6. Judge Moore was unable to justify Article 6 under international

---

100 *Id.* at 59, 63.

101 Berge, *supra* note 3, at 373.

102 SPIERMANN, *supra* note 34, at 258.

103 *Lotus*, 1927 P.C.I.J. (ser. A) No. 10, at 65.

law."[104] It is interesting to speculate on whether Judge Moore would have dissented had the vote not been six to six since he did not disagree with the fundamental argument about the permissive regime of international law.

Judge Altamira. Judge Altamira dissented based on his conviction that territorial jurisdiction did not allow the exception that Turkey was seeking. As Judge Altamira argued, "[t]herefore, exceptions to these principles, in so far as they allow a foreign jurisdiction to be exercised over the citizens of a given State, have only been recognized in extreme cases where it has been absolutely necessary or inevitable."[105] He then went on to argue that this situation was not such a case.

Judge Altamira also objected to Turkey's reliance on Article 6. As Berge summarized his views:

> It is general agreement that makes rules of international law. Municipal legislation is not capable of changing it . . . . There is no agreement . . . as to the type of legislation adopted by Turkey in Article 6 . . . . The will of one state or of a few states cannot in and of itself create an exception to the territorial principle, if general consent to such an exception is lacking.[106]

Themes. Though none of the dissenting judges opted to join any other opinion, Hertogen argued that there is at least some thematic joinder between them. She maintained that Judges Weiss and Finlay argued that the question came down to finding in international law an authorization for Turkey's exercise of criminal jurisdiction. She pointed out that "Judges Loder, Nyholm, and Altamira did not address the prohibition or permission question explicitly, but criticized the majority's opinion for being too deferential to states."[107]

Allowing for the various reasons for dissent, and considering Judge Moore's position, it seems clear that at least several of the dissenters did not openly object to the majority's endorsement of the permissive nature of the international law regime, and that on at least that point, the decision was stronger than its final six to six vote indicated.

Academics. In addition to the dissents, other prominent voices writing soon after the *Lotus* decision disagreed with the majority. Among them was the renowned jurist Hersh Lauterpacht. As Kwiecień mentioned,

> Hersch Lauterpacht was an especially virulent critic of the doctrine. He primarily questioned the legal significance of the presumptive freedom of the action of States, which was emphasized by the PCIJ. Lauterpacht regarded the doctrine as

---

104 Berge, *supra* note 3, at 373.

105 *Lotus*, 1927 P.C.I.J. (ser. A) No. 10, at 95.

106 Berge, *supra* note 3, at 374.

107 Hertogen, *supra* note 12, at 906.

> a "double-edged sword" in judicial proceedings, as each and every party might refer to it in order to support their claim. He perceived it to be of little practical importance, as it reduced the essence of a dispute to a question of the burden of proof. However, the most significant reason for Lauterpacht's rejection of the presumptive freedom of the action of States stems from his view that the doctrine undermines the basis of the validity of the international legal order.[108]

Lauterpacht's contemporaneous view reflected the profound impact of the *Lotus* case and its implications for the understanding and interpretation of international law, and the divided nature of the case's reception.

Modern scholars have taken various views, as discussed in Part II above. It seems that Spiermann's account[109] of the PCIJ judges' acknowledgement of the importance and controversial nature of the decision has proven true, even after almost 100 years of international law codification and development, some of which will be discussed next.

Subsequent International Law. While much of the previous discussion has focused on subsequent academic discourse and later ICJ decisions, states have also taken actions that have demonstrated their embrace, or not, of the *Lotus* maritime jurisdiction principle and the idea of international law as a fundamentally permissive regime. Since states continue to play a key role in the formulation and application of international law, at least some discussion here is useful.

Maritime Jurisdiction. The impact of the *Lotus* case "sent shockwaves through the maritime community and prompted international regulation on the issue of criminal jurisdiction over high seas collisions."[110] Discussions among states subsequent to the *Lotus* decision congealed in opposition to the decision. This was reflected in several subsequent international treaties, including the 1952 Brussels Convention for the Unification of Certain Rules Relating to Penal Jurisdiction[111] and the 1982 United Nations Convention on the Law of the Sea (LOS Convention),[112] providing that a state in Turkey's position in the *Lotus* case could not exercise criminal jurisdiction with respect to a maritime collision case on the high seas.[113] Article 97 of the LOS

---

108 Kwiecień, *supra* note 86, at 283–84; *see* HERSCH LAUTERPACHT, PRIVATE LAW SOURCES AND ANALOGIES OF INTERNATIONAL LAW (1927).

109 SPIERMANN, *supra* note 34, at 247–48.

110 Hertogen, *supra* note 12, at 905.

111 Collision Convention, *supra* note 74, art. 1.

112 U.N. Convention on the Law of the Sea, *opened for signature* Dec. 10, 1982, 1833 U.N.T.S. 397.

113 Yoshifumi Tanaka has disputed the notion that a ship is a floating bit of state territory:

> The legal basis of the principle of the exclusive jurisdiction of the flag State was sometimes explained by the theory of the territoriality of the ship. According to this theory, a ship is considered as a "floating island" or a "detached part of the territory of the State to which it belongs" [here citing *Lotus*]. Nonetheless, the theory of the territoriality of the ship is contrary to the fact that, in certain

Convention is titled "Penal jurisdiction in matters of collision or any other incident of navigation," and states:

> In the event of a collision or any other incident of navigation concerning a ship on the high seas, involving the penal or disciplinary responsibility of the master or of any other person in the service of the ship, no penal or disciplinary proceedings may be instituted against such person except before the judicial or administrative authorities either of the flag State or of the State of which such person is a national.[114]

Though the LOS Convention specifically changed the discrete rule of maritime jurisdiction supported in the *Lotus* case, it did not detract from the *Lotus* principle announcing the permissive nature of international law. In fact, the response by states of explicitly codifying the opposing view is at least some evidence that states felt a specific restriction was necessary to prevent continued reliance on the fundamentally permissive regime of international law.

Jurisdiction. In addition to the specific question of maritime jurisdiction, the *Lotus* case also laid out some basic principles on jurisdiction more generally, as discussed above. As Raustiala has stated with respect to the connection between territory and jurisdiction, "Westphalian sovereignty thus creates a system in which legal jurisdiction is congruent with sovereign territorial borders."[115]

Writing only four years after the *Lotus* decision, Wendell Berge used the decision to support his argument that a restriction of the application of jurisdiction to the land territory of a state is no longer possible or preferred in modern society. He argued that "the trend is unmistakably away from absolutely logical territorial restrictions on criminal jurisdiction" and that policy "dictates that the territorial principle should be liberalized whenever real situations in a world of rapid change demand such liberalization."[116]

Berge proved prophetic concerning the developing nature of the doctrine of jurisdiction. Indeed, two key points about jurisdiction have become much clearer after the *Lotus* case: 1) the general acceptance of

---

> circumstances, merchant vessels are subject to the right of visit by foreign warships, and vessels within internal waters and the territorial seas are in principle under the territorial sovereignty of the coastal State. Hence the theory of the territoriality of the ship is obsolete and indefensible for practical reasons. The principle of the exclusive jurisdiction of the flag State should be considered as a corollary of the freedom of the high seas and the requirement of the submission of the high seas to law . . . . Considering that the high seas are not subject to any national jurisdiction and that there is no centralised authority governing the high seas, legal order on the high seas can be ensured primarily by the flag State.

YOSHIFUMI TANAKA, THE INTERNATIONAL LAW OF THE SEA 206 (4th ed. 2023).

[114] U.N. Convention on the Law of the Sea, *supra* note 112, art. 97(1); *see* Hertogen, *supra* note 12, at 906.

[115] Kal Raustiala, *The Geography of Justice*, 73 FORDHAM L. REV. 2501, 2509 (2005).

[116] Berge 1931, *supra* note 62, at 269.

concurrent jurisdiction and 2) the lack of hierarchy among various types of prescriptive jurisdiction. The PCIJ's embrace of concurrent jurisdiction, and its implication of non-hierarchical application of prescriptive jurisdiction has prevailed in today's international law. As stated in the *Restatement (Fourth) of the Foreign Relations Law of the United States*,

> Instances of concurrent prescriptive jurisdiction are common, and international law recognizes no hierarchy of bases of jurisdiction. According to Crawford:
>
> > [While the] sufficiency of grounds for jurisdiction is normally considered relative to the rights of other states . . . [t]here is no assumption (even in criminal cases) that individuals or corporations will be regulated only once, and situations of multiple jurisdictional competence occur frequently. In such situations there is no "natural regulator" and the consequences of multiple laws applying to the same transaction are managed rather than avoided—double taxation being a case in point.[117]

Applying today's understanding of concurrent territorial and territorial effects jurisdiction, the judges in the PCIJ would certainly have needed less argument to justify their decision.

International Law as Fundamentally Permissive. The discussions among academics, the further references of the ICJ to the *Lotus* principle, and the effects of codification on the specific jurisdictional question at issue in *Lotus* have been documented above. The approach of states on the more general issue of permissiveness in international law deserves further discussion. While it might seem obvious that states would benefit from embracing the approach adopted in the *Lotus* case, few official pronouncements provide clarity on this issue.

In the United States, for example, only a few recent official statements directly pronounce on the continuing applicability of the *Lotus* principle. One recent statement is shared below, along with a practical example that illustrates the United States applying the *Lotus* principle in cyber operations.

The International Law Commission (ILC) has recently engaged in a project on identifying customary international law. As part of the process, the ILC sought input from states. In a 2018 response, the United States Department of State said the following concerning *opinio juris*:

> The United States believes that it is important that the Draft Conclusion and commentary adhere to common, widely used language on this issue, both to avoid suggesting any conflict

[117] RESTATEMENT (FOURTH), *supra* note 36, § 407, reporters' note 3 (quoting JAMES CRAWFORD, BROWNLIE'S PRINCIPLES OF PUBLIC INTERNATIONAL LAW 457 (8th ed. 2012)); *see also* S.S. "Lotus" (Fr. v. Turk.), 1927 P.C.I.J. (ser. A) No. 10, at 34 (Sept. 7).

> with existing State practice and in order to avoid being misunderstood to affect the longstanding principle that States are free to act in the absence of a legal restriction. See The Case of the S.S. "Lotus," P.C.I.J., Series A, No. 10 (1927) p. 18. States are not required to establish *opinio juris* or that a general and consistent practice of States supports an action as lawful before they can lawfully engage in a practice that is not otherwise legally restricted.[118]

This U.S. endorsement of international law as fundamentally permissive, with specific reference to the *Lotus* case, is a strong statement about the longevity of the *Lotus* principle.

In 1999, cyber capabilities were barely known to the world at large. However, some governments, including the United States, had already started to think about how international law might be applied to cyber operations. In a 1999 assessment written for the Department of Defense Office of General Counsel, the author argued that "[a]n unauthorized electronic intrusion into another nation's computer systems may very well end up being regarded as a violation of the victim's sovereignty. It may even be regarded as equivalent to a physical trespass into a nation's territory, but such issues have yet to be addressed in the international community."[119] The author then concluded, "[u]nless the nations decide to negotiate a treaty addressing computer network attacks, which seems unlikely any time in the near future, international law in this area will develop through the actions of nations and through the positions the nations adopt publicly as events unfold."[120]

The reader may regard this statement as more about *non liquet*—a situation where there is no applicable law or the law is unclear—than the permissive nature of international law.[121] However, subsequent activity by the United States indicates that it views the international system as allowing actions unless specifically prohibited. For example, the United States has been very forthright in stating its strategy of defend forward and its doctrine of persistent engagement.[122] Under this strategy, U.S.

---

[118] Int'l Law Comm'n, Identification of Customary International Law Comments and Observations Received from Governments, U.N. Doc. A/CN.4/716, at 37 (2018).

[119] OFF. OF GEN. COUNS., U.S. DEP'T OF DEF., AN ASSESSMENT OF INTERNATIONAL LEGAL ISSUES IN INFORMATION OPERATIONS 18 (2d ed. 1999).

[120] *Id.* at 23.

[121] For brief discussions of the application of the *Lotus* case to the principle of *non liquet*, see Guilfoyle, *supra* note 15, at 91; Handyside, *supra* note 88, at 78–80.

[122] According to the U.S. Cyberspace Solarium Commission,

> Defend forward is a proactive, rather than reactive, approach to adversary cyber threats. Specifically, it addresses the fact that the United States has not created credible and sufficient costs against malicious adversary behavior below the level of armed attack—even as the United States has prevented cyberattacks of significant consequences. Therefore, defend forward posits that the United States must shift from responding to malicious behavior after it has already occurred to proactively observing, pursuing, and countering adversary operations and imposing costs to change adversary behavior. By shaping the strategic environment and creating meaningful costs for malicious behavior,

government agencies conduct cyber operations on the infrastructure of other nations, in order to secure U.S. interests. These actions are often done with the permission of the other countries, but often not. Because there is an on-going debate among states on the proper application of sovereignty to transnational cyber operations,[123] this action by the United States signals that it feels free to conduct cyber operations within the sovereign territory of other states because no specific rule prohibits it. In line with the continuing vitality of the principle reflected in the Department of State communication quoted above, this is at least one clear example of the application of that approach to international law in practice.

VIII. CONCLUSION

The *S.S. Lotus* case represents a pivotal moment in international law, asserting a specific understanding of international law. Not only did the case reinforce the Westphalian system of state sovereignty and equality, but it also established the principle that international law is a fundamentally permissive regime and that states are free to take actions, absent an explicit prohibition. Despite the fact that the specific principle supporting the assertion of jurisdiction by Turkey has been subsequently rejected by the international community, the wide discretion granted to states generally remains as a fundamental structural aspect of the international legal regime.

Nonetheless, many voices, including noted scholars and perhaps even the ICJ itself, have questioned the continuing validity of the *Lotus* principle. As the *Lotus* case approaches its century mark, the rapidly changing modern world may lead to the eventual desuetude of the principle. Alternatively, the *Lotus* principle may reemerge and regain general acceptance. In another hundred years, we may still be discussing *Lotus* as a seminal International Law Story.

> defend forward aims to disrupt and defeat ongoing malicious adversary cyber campaigns, deter future campaigns, and reinforce favorable international norms of behavior. This posture implies persistent engagement with adversaries as part of an overall integrated effort to apply every authority, access, and capability possible (e.g., laws, financial regulation, diplomacy, education) to the defense of cyberspace in a manner consistent with international law.

U.S. CYBERSPACE SOLARIUM COMM'N, FINAL REPORT 24 (2020), https://www.solarium.gov/.

123 *See* Jeremy Wright, U.K. Att'y Gen., Att'y Gen.'s Off., Speech by Attorney General Wright on Cyber and International Law in the 21st Century (May 23, 2018), https://www.gov.uk/government/speeches/cyber-and-international-law-in-the-21st-century; GOV'T OF THE NETH., LETTER TO THE PARLIAMENT ON THE INTERNATIONAL LEGAL ORDER IN CYBERSPACE app. (2019) (Appendix: International Law in Cyberspace), https://www.government.nl/documents/parliamentary-documents/2019/09/26/letter-to-the-parliament-on-the-international-legal-order-in-cyberspace.

16

David J. Bederman*

The *Reparation for Injuries* Case: The Law of Nations Is Transformed into International Law

The *Reparation for Injuries* advisory opinion, handed down by the International Court of Justice (ICJ) in 1949, continues to exert a strong influence over the course of international law, even to this day. It also remains a bit of an enigma. Starting with the curiously cumbersome title of the case, and then its strange narrative structure, the ICJ's opinion seems to be an abstract disquisition, without any reference to fact or reality. The truth, however, is that the opinion represents the culmination of the early, momentous years of the United Nations as an organization. The events leading to the rendering of the advisory opinion are weirdly resonant with those of our own time. And, most important of all, the enduring truths and impact of the Court's rulings remain significant for anyone's understanding of how international law has evolved as a struggling, and imperfect, system to manage conflict and competition between states and non-state actors.

On the surface, the *Reparation for Injuries Sustained in the Service of the United Nations* opinion, which was the second advisory opinion rendered by the ICJ, addressed the question whether the United Nations had legal personality, including the ability to bring suit against a government or state. The case arose out of circumstances that also were a direct challenge to the new organization. In the wake of World War II, violence broke out in Palestine. As the British Mandate of Palestine ended, the nascent Jewish state and its unwelcoming Arab neighbors engaged in deadly conflicts that threatened once again to set the world to war. The United Nations was introduced to its first challenge, to bring peace to the Middle East. According to commentators of the day, the United Nations' ability to meet this challenge would determine the future of the world organization.

* This chapter, by the late David Bederman, is reprinted from the first edition of this book. David J. Bederman, *The* Reparation for Injuries *Case: The Law of Nations Is Transformed into International Law*, *in* INTERNATIONAL LAW STORIES 307 (John E. Noyes, Laura A. Dickinson & Mark Weston Janis eds., 2007).

The work of the United Nations to bring peace in Palestine was halted abruptly on September 17, 1948, when the Count Folke Bernadotte, nephew of the King of Sweden and Chairman of the Swedish Red Cross, the United Nations Mediator to Palestine, was assassinated in Jerusalem. The assassins were Jewish fighters belonging to an underground terrorist organization called the Fatherland Front, a secret faction of one of the most extreme Zionist terrorist organizations in Israel—the Stern Gang. The event created an international outcry—Arab, Israeli, and world leaders were outraged by the act, and the United Nations was called on to respond.

The response of the World Court will be addressed later in the essay. First the events that led to the case—the situation in Palestine and the assassination of Count Bernadotte—will be unfolded.

I. THE BACKGROUND AND CONTEXT OF THE *REPARATION FOR INJURIES* OPINION

The Events Leading to the Assassination. A war in the British Mandate of Palestine had been brewing for several decades. In 1917, in the Balfour Declaration, Britain had welcomed the creation of a Jewish homeland in Palestine, which had just been liberated from Ottoman Turkish control in the last stages of the First World War. As part of the creation of the League of Nations, the first truly international organization devoted to global peace and security, a system of "mandates" was established by which one or more Great Powers would administer a colonial area for a future transition to self-government and independence. The League gave Great Britain control over the Palestinian Mandate. From that time forward, Jewish immigration to the Holy Land increased, and Palestine's small Jewish community began to grow dramatically. The events of the Holocaust in Europe brought the situation to a head. Jewish immigration swelled as Jews fled the Nazi concentration camps of Europe and the Middle East for the land of Palestine.[1] The British had decided to end the Mandate, but no solution had been reached as to what would then happen to Palestine. The feared outcome was a Jewish state that would be immediately attacked by the states of the Arab League. The British Mandate ended, and on May 13, 1948, the British High Commissioner left Palestine without a successor regime. The independent state of Israel was proclaimed, receiving de facto recognition immediately from the United States. An armed attack by the states of the Arab League was expected any day.[2]

Immediately it was felt that the war in Palestine could once again set the world to war. Peaceful relations between the United States and the U.S.S.R. began to deteriorate. The United States feared that

---

1 TED SCHWARZ, WALKING WITH THE DAMNED: THE SHOCKING MURDER OF THE MAN WHO FREED 30,000 PRISONERS FROM THE NAZIS 77–80, 90–94 (1992).

2 AMITZUR ILAN, BERNADOTTE IN PALESTINE, 1948: A STUDY IN CONTEMPORARY HUMANITARIAN KNIGHT-ERRANTRY 57–58 (1989).

Palestine would be a new ground for this emerging conflict between the communist and capitalist worlds.[3] The newly formed United Nations sought to intervene in Palestine. The task was seen as the first challenge to the Organization, and some predicted that if it were to fail, so would the United Nations.[4]

The United Nations first addressed the question of Palestine in 1947. The General Assembly issued the partition resolution on November 29, 1947, which proposed the division of the British Mandate into two states, one Jewish and one Arab. The Galilee, the fertile region in the north, would be divided, as would the Negev desert in the south. The City of Jerusalem and the surrounding area would be a *corpus separatum*, a separate body to be governed by the United Nations. When the state of Israel was proclaimed and the attack by Arab states imminent, it was clear that the United Nations would not be able to enforce the partition resolution on the parties in the region, and that a different approach must be adopted.[5]

An office of the United Nations Mediator to Palestine was created on May 14th, with a three-part mandate, involving care of the population of Palestine, protection of the holy places, and ending the conflict. The mediator would first attempt to establish a cease-fire between the warring parties and then mediate a permanent solution to the crisis in Palestine. On May 20, 1948, the U.N. Security Council, after a mere seven minutes of deliberation, decided to ask Count Folke Bernadotte of Sweden to be the United Nations' Mediator for Palestine.[6]

The Count Folke Bernadotte was born in 1895 to Prince Oscar Carl August, younger brother of King Gustav of Sweden. The Count's father renounced his title and the right to succeed to the throne of Sweden in order to marry a commoner. The marriage was for love, and was a happy marriage.[7] The Count Bernadotte likewise married outside the European nobility when he married Estelle Manville, the New York heiress, daughter of the former head of the Johns-Manville Corporation.[8] Before his marriage, the Count attended military school and was an officer in the Swedish Dragoon Guards. After leaving the military, the Count became involved in humanitarian efforts. Count Folke Bernadotte's first entrance into history was during World War II, when he flew between Berlin and Stockholm, conducting negotiations for the release of Scandinavian internees in German concentration camps. He succeeded in negotiating for the release of 20,000 Jewish and Christian internees in

---

3 *Id.* at 55.

4 Anne O'Hare McCormick, *The Mediator in Palestine Wields His Authority*, N.Y. TIMES, June 14, 1949, at 22.

5 ILAN, *supra* note 2, at 55; G.A. Res 181(II), U.N. Doc. A/519 (Nov. 29, 1947).

6 ILAN, *supra* note 2, at 55–58; Walter Sullivan, *Count Bernadotte of Sweden To Be Mediator in Palestine*, N.Y. TIMES, May 21, 1948, at 1.

7 Sullivan, *supra* note 6, at 3; Raymond Daniel, *A Resolute Man In Search of Peace*, N.Y. TIMES, June 27, 1948, at 11.

8 Sullivan, *supra* note 6, at 3.

exchange for a much smaller number of German prisoners of war held in Swedish POW camps.

When Count Bernadotte was offered the position of United Nations Mediator to Palestine, Estelle and he lived in Stockholm with their two children, Ockie, 16, and Bertil, 12. The Count accepted the position immediately, while acknowledging that he had no background knowledge of the situation in Palestine.[9] At the beginning of the mission, the Count stated that there was "only a one percent chance" that he could succeed, but that it was still worth the effort to take the one percent chance to prevent another war that could again spread across the world.[10]

The mediator's task was to first establish a cease-fire, so that he could then begin negotiations between the parties that could lead to a peaceful solution to the conflict. The three duties of the mediator were to bring the parties to a peaceful resolution of the conflict, to arrange for services to ensure the safety and well-being of the population, and to protect the holy places.[11] After a short trip to Paris to confer with officials and other members of his mediation team at the United Nations, including the American member of the team, Dr. Ralph Bunche, the mediator began a circuit of Middle East cities, to meet with the leaders of the warring parties.[12]

Count Bernadotte stopped in Cairo on May 28th on his way to Tel Aviv, where he arrived on May 31st. After meeting with Israel's Prime Minister David Ben-Gurion and the Foreign Minister, Moshe Shertok, the Count left for other Middle Eastern cities. A threatening Security Council resolution on May 29th ordered the parties to submit to a four-week truce beginning on June 1st, a deadline that passed without consequence. After two weeks of shuttling around the Middle Eastern capitols, Bernadotte succeeded in achieving agreement on a four-week truce, to begin on June 11, 1948.[13]

With the cease-fire in place, the mediator directed his attention toward creating a permanent resolution to the conflict. The Count settled in Rhodes, and on the Greek island he met with "technical experts" from both sides to discuss possible solutions to the conflict. On June 28th, the mediator sent a proposal for a final settlement to the Provisional Government of Israel and to the Arab leaders. The proposal was sent in a report to the United Nations on July 4th and released publicly to newspapers.[14]

---

[9] *Evans Leaving for Palestine*, N.Y. TIMES, May 22, 1948, at 2 [hereinafter *Leaving*]; Sam Pope Brewer, *Mediator Speeds Move*, N.Y. TIMES, June 22, 1948, at 19.

[10] McCormick, *supra* note 4, at 22.

[11] Sullivan, *supra* note 6, at 3.

[12] *Leaving, supra* note 9, at 2.

[13] ILAN, *supra* note 2, at 73; *Bernadotte in Tel Aviv*, N.Y. TIMES, June 1, 1948, at 10.

[14] Brewer, *supra* note 9, at 19; *Text of Bernadotte's Proposals for a Palestine Settlement*, N.Y. TIMES, July 5, 1948, at 2.

The mediator's proposal departed from the division of land laid out in the November partition resolution, instead aligning more with the placement of troops in Palestine during the cease-fire. Under the Bernadotte proposal, the whole of the northern area would be given to Israel and the whole of the southern Negev given to an Arab state. The most controversial changes in the proposal were first the Count's suggestion that Jerusalem be not an internationalized city, but given to the Arab state, and second that the Arab Palestine be annexed to Trans-Jordan.[15]

The Israeli state rejected the proposal, refusing to consider giving up its claim to Jerusalem, as did the Arab states, which were not yet willing to even implicitly recognize a state of Israel. The end of the four-week truce approached, and attempts to extend the truce failed. While the Count gained Israeli agreement near the final days, the Arab states were not willing to extend the truce, citing Israeli violations of its terms.[16]

Fighting resumed by July 9th, and the Count returned to New York to present reports to the U.N. Security Council. The mediator admitted that the cease-fire had ended. In New York, Count Bernadotte succeeded in obtaining a more strongly worded Security Council resolution on July 15th. The resolution called for the parties to submit to a truce by a date set by the mediator and threatened that failure to comply would be considered a "break of the peace," which would entitle the Security Council to impose economic sanctions and even armed intervention. Count Bernadotte announced from New York that the cease-fire must begin at 3:00 p.m. on July 18th. On the 16th, Israel agreed to the truce, and on the 17th the Arab League also accepted, having faced depressing defeats since the resumption of fighting.[17]

The second truce was marked with massive violations and poor supervision on the part of the U.N. staff. Additional attempts at negotiation failed to produce results, and the mediator left the region for several weeks. During that time, the Count Bernadotte began to prepare a second proposal for a final solution to the conflict. The proposal was to be presented at the United Nations in New York on September 19th. The mediator hoped that a new proposal could be accepted and adopted by the United Nations to replace the long-outdated but never revised partition resolution. On September 17th, Count Folke Bernadotte returned to the Holy Land to conduct several more meetings before presenting his proposals in New York.[18]

---

15 Thomas J. Hamilton, *Mediator Offers Holy City to Arabs in His Peace Plan*, N.Y. TIMES, July 5, 1948, at 1.

16 *Messages to U.N. From Bernadotte and Shertok*, N.Y. TIMES, July 9, 1948, at 2; ILAN, *supra* note 2, at 125.

17 ILAN, *supra* note 2, at 145–49.

18 *Id.* at 145–87; Aege Lundstrom, *Epilogue: the 17th of September*, *in* FOLKE BERNADOTTE, TO JERUSALEM 245, 245 (Joan Bulman trans., 1951).

The Assassination of Count Bernadotte. Only in the past couple decades has the full story of the assassination plot become known. At the time of the killing, very little was publicly known. The Count Bernadotte had earned the enmity of the extremist factions within Israel. At the time of the emergence of the state, multiple militias were acting autonomously outside the control of the nascent government. One of these organizations was the Stern Gang, named for its founder, Abraham Stern, and founded for the purpose of driving out the British and founding a Jewish state on the entirety of the biblical land of Israel. After Stern's death at the hands of the British, the leadership of the organization was taken up by three individuals: Nathan Yelin-Mor (also known as Friedman-Yellin), Dr. Israel Eldad, and Yitzhak Shamir.[19]

The Stern Gang loathed any outside interference and hated the United Nations with the same fervor as the British. Count Bernadotte had gained specific hatred for, among other things, proposing that Jerusalem be given to the Arab state with only partial autonomy for the Jewish community in the city. The Gang published threats against the U.N. Mediator. Posters attributed to the Stern Gang appeared in Jerusalem and Tel Aviv immediately before the assassination telling the U.N. Mediator to get out of Israel.[20]

On September 17th, Count Folke Bernadotte flew into the airport in Kalandia, between Jerusalem and Ramallah. As the plane drew near the airport, statements were heard over the radio that any plane attempting to land would be shot at. The Count joked with the pilot, and the plane landed without incident. These warnings were, in fact, meant to prevent the Count from conducting his meetings in Ramallah with Arab fighters in that city, not to forewarn of an assassination plot. The Count traveled in an armored car during the first half of the day. After attending meetings in Ramallah, Count Bernadotte and his entourage traveled to Jerusalem. On the road, his car was hit by sniper fire, but no one was injured. In Jerusalem, the Count stopped at the YMCA building, which was home to the U.S. delegation. The mediator continued on through the Israeli-held parts of Jerusalem.[21]

The Count's entourage consisted of three vehicles. Two carried Red Cross flags, and the mediator's car carried the flag of the United Nations. Count Bernadotte had refused to keep his movements in the Holy Land secret throughout his time as mediator, and it was unmistakable who was in this group of vehicles. As his car wound through the Jewish suburb of Lev Merhavia, it encountered an Israeli roadblock. As it approached, the barrier was raised and lowered several times, in the end lowering to block passage. When the cars approached, the soldier stated that he did not know how to treat the entourage, and then let the cars pass. Unknown at

---

19 ILAN, *supra* note 2, at 193–97, 203.

20 *Id.* at 202; Julian Louis Meltzer, *His Car Ambushed*, N.Y. TIMES, Sept. 18, 1948, at 1.

21 SCHWARZ, *supra* note 1, at 301.

the time was that the movement of the barrier was a signal to the assassins.[22]

The cars continued on, and again were blocked by an army-like jeep in the center of the road. There were four men in Israeli army uniforms. One man remained in the jeep, two approached the vehicles and halted near the first. The fourth man approached the window of the mediator's vehicle. The Count and the rest of the entourage were reaching for their identity papers, assuming this was another checkpoint. The fourth man pointed a gun through the window of the car and shot the Count Bernadotte and the French Colonel Serdot at close range. The driver of the mediator's car got out and began to struggle with the gunman, who retreated to the jeep with the other men and sped away. The Colonel was clearly dead at the scene, but the Count was rushed to Hadassah Hospital. He was declared dead on arrival.[23]

In the weeks before the assassination, the three leaders of the Stern Gang had decided in secret meetings that the Count must be assassinated, but knew that they must keep some distance from the act. They formed a small unit of four men, named the Fatherland Front, to carry out the assassination. The unit likely included Yehoshua Cohen and Meshulam Markover, who came forward in 1988 after Cohen's death to admit his own and Cohen's part in the assassination.[24]

The Stern Gang had the mediator under surveillance and knew exactly the routes by which the Count planned to travel on September 17, 1948. The plan was to stop the entourage pretending to be a regular army checkpoint. The first to identify Bernadotte was to shoot. In fact, that person was Yehoshua Cohen. As investigators later noted, the assassins were well-prepared, knowing the exact route the mediator was to take through Jerusalem, the car in which the mediator was to ride, and, as it appeared, the mediator's exact position in that car.[25]

The Martyr of Peace. Telegrams were sent to the United Nations informing the world of the death of Count Folke Bernadotte, and a report by Dr. Ralph Bunche was cabled to New York, detailing what was known of the attack by unknown assailants. Dr. Bunche was appointed the new head of the United Nations Mission in Palestine.[26] International outrage was immediate and fervent. Anger at Israel for failing to protect the Count was nearly universal. Arab leaders praised the Count and decried the Israeli assassination, stating that the Jewish nation could not be trusted. Israeli leaders denounced the act and praised the mediator,

---

22 *Id.* at 303; ILAN, *supra* note 2, at 213, 219.

23 SCHWARZ, *supra* note 1, at 303–04; *Bernadotte's Aide Describes Killing*, N.Y. TIMES, Sept. 19, 1948, at 52.

24 SCHWARZ, *supra* note 1, at 299; John Kifner, *Two Recount 1948 Killing in Israel*, N.Y. TIMES, Sept. 12, 1988, at A3.

25 ILAN, *supra* note 2, at 219–20; *Yehoshua Cohen Dies; Linked to 1948 Killing*, N.Y. TIMES, Aug. 12, 1986, at D24.

26 *Text of Report to U.N.*, N.Y. TIMES, Sept. 18, 1948, at 3.

promising to make every effort to bring his killers to justice.[27] The Israeli Foreign Minister sent the following telegram to the King of Sweden, the Countess Bernadotte, and U.N. Secretary-General Trygve Lie:

> Deeply shocked by outrageous murder of Count Bernadotte by criminal outlaws who are execrated by the entire people of Israel and the Jewish community of Jerusalem. On behalf of the Government of Israel I beg to express our feelings of grief and profound sympathy. The Government of Israel is adopting the sternest measures to bring the criminals to justice.[28]

Israel's hopes that U.N. membership would be granted to the new state soon were put on hold. It was clear that the future of the new state would now only partly depend on its success against the Arab armies.[29] The assassination of the United Nations Mediator was as great a threat to Israel's survival as the legions of Arab armies. As one editorial stated, "No Arab armies could have done so much harm in so short a time."[30]

The future of the United Nations was also at stake in these events. The organization was called on to respond to this terrible attack, which not only was directed against an agent of the United Nations and a member of the royal family of Sweden, but at the institution of the United Nations as a whole and its role as peacemaker in the world.[31] The success or failure of the Bernadotte mission had already been considered determinative of the success of the world organization. Now the United Nations faced a new challenge. Count Bernadotte was one of eight members of the Mission to Palestine who lost his life during the course of the mission. For the United Nations to maintain credibility, it must find some way to respond to the attacks on its personnel and its status in the world. If Count Bernadotte had been merely a representative of the Kingdom of Sweden, the procedures by which states interact to obtain indemnity and apology were known. However, an attack on the representative of the United Nations was an attack on all states.[32]

As world leaders praised Count Bernadotte, called on the United Nations to respond, and denounced Israel for allowing the assassination to take place, there were also calls for peace in the Middle East to be established "as 'a living monument' to Count Bernadotte."[33] The Syrian president called the mediator "an apostle of peace, and a servant of

---

[27] *World Expresses Sorrow at Death*, N.Y. TIMES, Sept. 19, 1948, at 55 [hereinafter *World Expresses Sorrow*]; *Arabs Say Death is a Loss to Peace*, N.Y. TIMES, Sept. 18, 1948, at 2.

[28] *Quoted in Shot at Point-Blank Range*, N.Y. TIMES, Sept. 18, 1948, at 3.

[29] Thomas J. Hamilton, *U.N. Move is Swift*, N.Y. TIMES, Sept. 18, 1948, at 1–2.

[30] *The U.N. Must Act*, N.Y. TIMES, Sept. 19, 1948, at E8 [hereinafter *Must Act*].

[31] *The U.N.'s First Martyr*, N.Y. TIMES, Sept. 18, 1948, at 16 [hereinafter *U.N. Martyr*].

[32] *Must Act*, *supra* note 30, at E8.

[33] *Id.*

humanity."[34] Newspapers named the Count the "U.N.'s first martyr."[35] Criticisms of the mediator's work stated that he had not enough knowledge of the situation in the Middle East, and that his first proposals had done more to hinder the establishment of a permanent agreement than help. The mediator's last report was finished immediately before his death and was submitted to the United Nations posthumously. The two guides for the continuation of the mediation process in the Middle East were General Assembly Resolution 181 and the final report, known as the Bernadotte Plan.[36]

While a permanent solution to the conflict was not found, the efforts of Dr. Ralph Bunche achieved an armistice between Israel and the Arab states—Egypt, Jordan, Syria, and Lebanon—in the early months of 1949. For his efforts at ending the Middle East conflict, he received the Nobel Peace Prize in 1949. Dr. Bunche credited the United Nations, the late Count Folke Bernadotte, and the U.N. staff in Palestine for the prize.[37] After the armistice was achieved, Dr. Bunche traveled to Stockholm to lay flowers on the grave of Count Bernadotte. He told the press that the armistice achieved at Rhodes was "nothing but the results of Count Bernadotte's work."[38] Before the assassination, many assumed that the prize would be given to Count Folke Bernadotte if he were to achieve lasting peace in the Middle East. Sweden saw the prize as a tribute to the late Count.[39]

Responses to the Assassination. The first reports from the U.N. envoys in Jerusalem strongly condemned Israel for failing to provide adequate protection for the United Nations Mediator. The assassination had taken place in a part of Jerusalem completely under the control of the Israeli Provisional Government.[40] Immediately after the Prime Minister of Israel, David Ben-Gurion, learned of the assassination, the city of Jerusalem was closed and about 200 members of the Stern Gang were arrested.[41] All of the actual assassins managed to escape arrest.

The newspapers at the time reported only the massive round-up of the Stern Gang. Historians later revealed that the arrested individuals were moved to a prison in Jaffa where they were treated like heroes, and experienced total freedom in the prison, able to mingle and to come and go as they pleased. When Prime Minister Ben-Gurion learned of this situation, he had the inmates transferred to a prison with less

---

[34] *Quoted in World Expresses Sorrow*, *supra* note 27, at 55.

[35] *U.N. Martyr*, *supra* note 31, at 16.

[36] Thomas J. Hamilton, *Jessup Gives Aims*, N.Y. TIMES, Nov. 24, 1948, at 1, 4.

[37] *Bunche of U.N. Is Selected for 1950 Nobel Peace Prize*, N.Y. TIMES, Sept. 23, 1950, at 1; *Bunche Surprised By News of Prize*, N.Y. TIMES, Sept. 23, 1950, at 4.

[38] *Bernadotte is Honored*, N.Y. TIMES, Apr. 12, 1949, at 14.

[39] Hamilton, *supra* note 29, at 2; *Sweden Hails Dr. Bunche*, N.Y. TIMES, Sept. 24, 1950, at 4.

[40] *Text of Report to U.N.*, *supra* note 26, at 3.

[41] Julian Louis Meltzer, *Jerusalem Sealed*, N.Y. TIMES, Sept. 19, 1948, at 1.

sympathetic guards.[42] Several members and leaders of the Stern Gang faced charges, but no one was directly charged with the assassination. The Stern Gang was allowed to participate in the upcoming elections as a political group, "The Fighters," and six of the twelve individuals on the ballot were imprisoned and facing prosecution. Israeli law provided that, if they were elected, the charges would be dropped and the candidates would be released. The plan succeeded, and among those elected and released was Friedman-Yellin, one of the three leaders of the organization. All members of the Stern Gang were released five months after the assassination under a general amnesty.[43]

Israel submitted to the United Nations a report on the death of the mediator stating that there was a lack of evidence, and that all efforts had failed to produce any evidence that might help determine the identity of the killers. The "Fatherland Front" accepted responsibility for the act and even apologized for the death of the French colonel, whom they had thought was the British chief-of-staff, General Lundstrom. Not for several decades did a member of the Stern Gang accept responsibility for the assassination.[44] When Friedman-Yellin was on trial, he obstinately refused to admit that the organization had any role in planning the assassination, and persisted in his claim that the Fatherland Front was a splinter group acting independently.[45]

II. THE INTERNATIONAL COURT OF JUSTICE'S ADVISORY OPINION

A Question for the World Court. The question of whether the United Nations would seek indemnities for personnel killed in Israel during the peacekeeping mission had been raised even before Count Folke Bernadotte's death, ironically enough by the mediator himself. Several members of the peacekeeping mission had been killed on either side at the time of his death, and he had suggested in one of his last reports that the United Nations reserve the right to seek indemnities. Several months after the mediator's death, the General Assembly of the United Nations submitted a question for consideration to the International Court of Justice. It was the second request for an advisory opinion given to the international adjudicatory body.

As propounded by the U.N. General Assembly, the questions to be decided by the ICJ were:

> I. In the event of an agent of the United Nations in the performance of his duties suffering injury in circumstances

[42] SCHWARZ, *supra* note 1, at 305–06.

[43] *Police Chief Absolves Sternist*, N.Y. TIMES, Jan. 5, 1949, at 14; Gene Currivan, *Sternists Active in Election Drive*, N.Y. TIMES, Jan. 15, 1949, at 6; *Nathan Yallin-Mor, 66, A Leader of Stern Gang*, N.Y. TIMES, Feb. 19, 1980, at B4.

[44] ILAN, *supra* note 2, at 233–38; Lundstrom, *supra* note 18, at 262; *Stern Group Chief, Aide are Arrested*, N.Y. TIMES, Oct. 1, 1948, at 4.

[45] *Sternist Reiterates Denial*, N.Y. TIMES, Dec. 22, 1948, at 18.

> involving the responsibility of a State, has the United Nations, as an organization, the capacity to bring an international claim against the responsible *de jure* or *de facto* government with a view to obtaining the reparation due in respect of the damage caused (*a*) to the United Nations, (*b*) to the victim or to the persons entitled through him?
>
> II. In the event of an affirmative reply to point I (*b*), how is action by the United Nations to be reconciled with such rights as may be possessed by the State of which the victim is a national?[46]

At the invitation of the Court, a number of governments submitted observations on issues raised by the questions propounded by the United Nations General Assembly. The governments of India, China, France, the United States, and the United Kingdom provided written statements, the tenor of which was largely supportive of the U.N.'s right to bring a claim under the circumstances presented by the Bernadotte assassination.[47] The ICJ heard arguments on March 7–9, 1949. The United Nations Organization itself (through its legal advisers) and the governments of Belgium, France, and Great Britain made oral submissions.[48]

The Court's Opinion. The Court issued its opinion on April 11, 1949, which, in short, stated that the United Nations had the legal ability to seek indemnities from any state or government. After some preliminaries,[49] the Court considered whether the United Nations had the "capacity" to bring an international claim for the injuries sustained by one of its employees or agents. Quite curiously, the advisory opinion in no way describes the situation or events leading up to the General Assembly's request.[50] Neither Israel nor Sweden (the countries most intimately involved in the dispute) are ever identified. Count Bernadotte is nowhere mentioned by name. The opinion appears to be an arid exercise is legal casuistry, divorced from any facts or context, and empty of any meaning. Indeed, the very title given to the opinion—"*Reparation for Injuries Suffered in the Service of the United Nations*"—appears to have been deliberately formulated by the Court to understate and minimize the underlying facts.[51] To call the assassination of a high-

---

[46] G.A. Res. 195 (III) (Dec. 3, 1948); *see also* Reparation for Injuries Suffered in the Service of the United Nations, Order, 1948 I.C.J. 121 (Dec. 11).

[47] *See* Reparation for Injuries Suffered in the Service of the United Nations, Memorials, Pleadings and Documents, 1949 I.C.J. pt. I, § C, at 12–42.

[48] *See id.* pt. II, at 50–130.

[49] Reparation for Injuries Suffered in the Service of the United Nations, Advisory Opinion, 1949 I.C.J. 174, 174–78 (Apr. 11).

[50] The International Court of Justice (like its predecessor from 1921–1939, the Permanent Court of International Justice) modeled its working habits on French and German appeals tribunals, and not on the common-law mode of judicial law-making (with its emphasis on the distinctive factual and procedural posture of cases for decision) used in such countries as the United States and Great Britain.

[51] It has been common practice for the Court to select the most innocuous names for both its advisory opinions and its judgments in contentious cases. *See, e.g.*, Aerial Incident

ranking United Nations mediator a kind of "injury" would seem to be understatement at best, or political correctness at its worst.

But if one reads between the lines of the decision, despite the apparent absence of any factual context, one will readily discern that the Court appreciated the momentousness of its decision. Looking first to the Charter of the United Nations, and not finding a specific provision dealing with the capacity of the Organization to bring such claims, the Court nevertheless inferred that the Charter intended that the United Nations have an enduring character, and a legal personality, that qualified it to bring claims in cases where the interests of the Organization have been affected by the conduct of states in relation to the Organization's employees or agents.[52] Perhaps most astonishingly of all, the Court held that the United Nations could press its claims even against those countries that were not members of the Organization at the time of the relevant incident (as Israel had not yet been admitted to U.N. membership), because the Organization was endowed with a special character that gave it such standing.[53]

Moreover, the Court ruled,[54] the U.N.'s interests in bringing a claim for the violation of its own interests did not preclude it from also claiming on behalf of its agent, even though that person had his own country of nationality or citizenship (Sweden in Count Bernadotte's case). Recognizing that this, too, was a novel question, the Court broke from the then-prevailing law of diplomatic protection and held that the United Nations could make a claim on behalf of Count Bernadotte's estate and family. Indeed, the Court observed, in order for the Organization to be effective it would need to have the power to vindicate the rights of its employees, even in cases where they were injured by the conduct of their own country of nationality.[55] The Court recognized that there could be situations where the U.N.'s right of "functional protection" could conflict with another state's prerogative of "diplomatic protection" for its dead or injured citizen, but that these situations would be worked out in practice, and, in any event, would never lead to situations of double recovery for the victim or his family.[56]

The fifteen members of the Court ruled unanimously that the United Nations could bring a claim against a state (and even against a non-member) for damages that the Organization, itself, had sustained.[57] The

---

of October 7th, 1952 (U.S. v. U.S.S.R.), 1956 I.C.J. 9 (Mar. 14) (the first of a long line of cases involving shoot-downs of civil or military aircraft over another state's airspace); Case Concerning Military and Paramilitary Activities in and against Nicaragua (Nicar. v. U.S.), 1984 I.C.J. 169 (Provisional Measures) (May 10) (the first of a series of decisions concerning the U.S. secret war against the Sandinista regime in Nicaragua).

[52] *Reparation for Injuries*, 1949 I.C.J. at 178–81.

[53] *See id.* at 185.

[54] *See id.* at 181–84.

[55] *See id.* at 183–84, 186.

[56] *See id.* at 185–86.

[57] *See id.* at 187.

members of the Court divided (11–4), however, as to whether the Organization could bring a claim on behalf of the injured "victim or to persons entitled through him,"[58] with the majority voting that it could. Lastly, the vote was 10–5 in favor of the principle that:

> When the United Nations as an Organization is bringing a claim for reparation of damage caused to its agent, it can only do so by basing its claim upon a breach of obligations due to itself; respect for this rule will usually prevent a conflict between the action of the United Nations and such rights as the agent's national State may possess, and thus bring about a reconciliation between their claims; moreover, this reconciliation must depend upon considerations applicable to each particular case, and upon agreements to be made between the Organization and individual States, either generally or in each case.[59]

Judges Alvarez and Azevedo filed individual concurring opinions in the case,[60] while Judge Hackworth (from the United States),[61] Judge Badawi Pasha,[62] and Judge Krylov (from the Soviet Union) issued dissenting opinions.[63] Ironically enough, a decision of the Court that has come to have iconic significance for the development of international law was issued over the dissents of judges representing the then-superpowers.

Shortly after the advisory opinion was rendered, the General Assembly issued a resolution giving the Secretary-General full authority to pursue indemnities in the case of Count Folke Bernadotte and the ten other U.N. personnel who had lost their lives in the conflict in Palestine. The Secretary-General submitted one letter to Israel. And thus matters stood until the next year, when Sweden took up the cause of its fallen nobleman.

Sweden Steps in. Sweden was not satisfied with Israel's cursory investigation into the killing of the mediator, and the United Nations had failed to produce any results since the decision regarding reparations claims by the International Court of Justice.[64] Early in 1950, Sweden conducted its own investigation into the assassination and into Israel's efforts to track down the killers. The Swedish investigators released a report in March of 1950 that was highly critical of the Israeli efforts to track down those who murdered the Swedish Count. The report was delivered first to Israel and later to the United Nations Security Council,

---

58 *Id.*

59 *Id.* at 188.

60 *See id.* at 190–96.

61 *See id.* at 196–204.

62 *See id.* at 205–16.

63 *See id.* at 217–19.

64 *Sweden Explains Stand*, N.Y. TIMES, May 14, 1949, at 7.

though Sweden did not request that the body address the report in session.[65]

The report alleged that the Israeli investigation was conducted in such a manner that the investigators felt obliged to doubt whether there was any real will to find the perpetrators. The Israeli authorities did not begin to investigate the crime scene until twenty-four hours after the assassination, by which time most of the evidence had been moved or carried off. The jeep used in the shootings was never located. Witnesses had only been lightly questioned, and what was discovered had not been followed up on. Although 200 members of the Stern Gang had been arrested, none had been brought before the witnesses to the murder for identification. The Swedish report was harsh, in essence charging Israel with covering up the murder and conducting a sham investigation that had no intention of finding the perpetrators of the crime.[66]

Israel began a reinvestigation into the assassinations, and on June 19, 1950, conceded almost all the allegations in the Swedish report. However, Israel maintained that the lack of care in the investigation was due to the inefficiency of the newly formed government and to the lack of coordination between the police and military investigations. During the series of diplomatic exchanges that precipitated the statement, Israel had offered a large indemnity to Count Bernadotte's family and a small sum to the United Nations. The Countess asked that the money be all given to the United Nations, and in the final statement and apology by Israel, Israel agreed to pay indemnity to the United Nations in the sum of $54,628, an amount over twice the yearly salary of the United Nations Mediator to Palestine.[67]

The Kingdom of Sweden afterwards formally recognized the new state of Israel, and the United Nations received its check on June 29, 1950.[68] The Countess Bernadotte's benevolence in requesting that the money be given to the United Nations was founded in part on her own ideals as well as respect for her husband's. After the Count's death, Countess Bernadotte became active in U.N. work on prisoner of war issues.[69] When the check was received by the United Nations, Secretary-General Trygve Lie accepted the payment and Israel's apology as "substantial compliance" with the demands that the United Nations had

---

65 *Sweden Hits Israel in Count's Death*, N.Y. TIMES, Mar. 10, 1950, at 17; *Bernadotte Report Goes to U.N. Council*, N.Y. TIMES, Mar. 31, 1950, at 4.

66 *Sweden Hits Israel in Count's Death*, *supra* note 65, at 17.

67 *Israel Apologizes in Death of Count*, N.Y. TIMES, June 20, 1950, at 14; *Israel to Apologize in Bernadotte Death*, N.Y. TIMES, May 26, 1950, at 7; *Israel May Pay Indemnity in Slaying of Bernadotte*, N.Y. TIMES, May 25, 1950, at 13; *Report on Bernadotte Killing*, N.Y. TIMES, May 18, 1950, at 7.

68 *$54,628 Indemnity to U.N.*, N.Y. TIMES, June 30, 1950; at 9; *Swedish Note Closes Bernadotte Incident*, N.Y. TIMES, July 6, 1950, at 15.

69 Mac R. Johnson, *Countess Bernadotte Works on U.N. Prisoner of War Problems*, WASH. POST, Aug. 12, 1951, at S4.

made on its own behalf, expressing satisfaction that Israel did not consider the hunt for the mediator's killers to be over.[70]

III. THE ENDURING SIGNIFICANCE OF THE *REPARATION* OPINION

Initially, the World Court's opinion in the *Reparation for Injuries* case was regarded merely as a relatively minor footnote to the emerging body of law concerning the United Nations as an international institution.[71] It was only over the course of the following decades that the opinion came to be regarded as significant for a number of areas of public international law. Indeed, the opinion impacted five separate and distinct doctrinal realms of international law. In ascending order of generality, the *Reparation* opinion has: (1) recast our understanding of the role of non-state actors and the international law of terrorism; (2) established the basic contours of the constitutional law of international organizations, and particularly the United Nations; (3) refashioned the role and function of international institutions in the global legal order; (4) inaugurated a new set of "super-treaty" systems—or "objective regimes"—that can bind even non-parties; and (5) fundamentally transformed the way we think about the actors in the global legal system, and thus ended the era of the "law of nations" and ushered in our contemporary vision of international law.

Each of these developments will be reviewed, in turn, in order to fully appreciate the extraordinary impact the *Reparation for Injuries* opinion has had in creating our modern international legal system. Indeed, it might be fair to say that the *Reparation* opinion, as modest as it may seem at first reading, is one of the distinguishing features of the general architecture of the international legal system.

Terrorism and Non-State Actors. In dwelling on the broader, and more theoretical, aspects of the *Reparation* opinion, it is very easy to forget that the case concerns terrorism, and the responsibility of governments to prevent acts of terrorism by non-state actors or groups, and, if those acts nonetheless occur, to take all necessary steps to apprehend and punish the perpetrators. Count Bernadotte's assassination by the Stern Gang was a spectacular act of terrorism, designed as a direct provocation by extremists to derail an international peace process that was showing modest success in bringing more cooperative Jewish and Arab elements in Palestine to the negotiating table. The Bernadotte assassination set a pattern for acts of terrorism directed against peace processes and moderate elements within societies

---

70 *$54,628 Indemnity to U.N.*, *supra* note 68, at 9.

71 *See, e.g.*, Yuen-li Liang, *Reparation for Injuries Suffered in the Service of the United Nations*, 43 AM. J. INT'L L. 460 (1949); Manley O. Hudson, *The Twenty-Eighth Year of the World Court*, 44 AM. J. INT'L L. 1, 12–18 (1950).

in conflict. As we are all too-depressingly aware, this pattern has been replicated in sectarian violence all around the world.

While the *Reparation* opinion does not mention the underlying facts that gave rise to the United Nations' potential claim against Israel, they were notorious to everyone at that time. As already discussed, the United Nations expected Israel to compensate the Organization and the Bernadotte family, insofar as the provisional government of Israel had failed to protect him, even after threats against Bernadotte had been publicly made. As the Court hinted in its opinion, Israel was not even a recognized state at the time of the events. That is why the Court refers, in the language of the General Assembly resolution requesting the advisory opinion, elliptically to Israel as either a "*de jure*" or "*de facto*" government.[72] It was enough for the International Court of Justice that Israel qualified as a state of some sort: "the Court is authorized to assume that the damage suffered involves the responsibility of a State, and it is not called upon to express an opinion upon the various ways in which that responsibility might be engaged."[73]

One outgrowth of the *Reparation for Injuries* opinion was the development of treaty-based international law to prevent and punish those acts of violence directed at what are known as "internationally protected persons." The 1973 Convention on the Prevention and Punishment of Crimes Against Internationally Protected Persons was a land-mark convention,[74] designed to address the circumstances giving rise to the Bernadotte assassination and the subsequent *Reparation* opinion. In addition to covering heads of state, and those individually accorded diplomatic status, the Convention also covers a wider category of "internationally protected persons," which was defined to include:

> any representative or official of a State or any official or other agent of an international organization of an intergovernmental character who, at the time when and in the place where a crime against him, his official premises, his private accommodation or his means of transport is committed, is entitled pursuant to international law to special protection from any attack on his person, freedom or dignity, as well as members of his family forming part of his household.[75]

The Convention requires states parties to exercise criminal jurisdiction over offenders (whether based on territorial or nationality jurisdiction), to either extradite or prosecute such offenders, and to take all measures to punish them.[76]

---

[72] *See* 1949 I.C.J. at 175–76, 180.

[73] *Id.* at 184.

[74] Convention on the Prevention and Punishment of Crimes Against Internationally Protected Persons, Including Diplomatic Agents, Dec. 14, 1973, 28 U.S.T. 1975, 1035 U.N.T.S. 167.

[75] *Id.* art. 1(b).

[76] *Id.* arts. 3–4, 6–7.

All of this begs, of course, a larger question very much on our minds today: whether non-state actors, without any links to any established government or state regime, can also be responsible under international law for acts of terrorism. While the ICJ's advisory opinion is silent on this specific matter, the rest of the Court's holdings (as will be discussed below) clearly indicate that it was in the contemplation of the judges in 1949 that non-state actors could be responsible for international crimes, and that such conduct would be attributable to the country that either gave them safe-haven or protection, or (in a more traditional sense) failed to take measures to ensure the security of international officials like Bernadotte.

In many respects, then, the international community's response to the terrorist attacks of September 11, 2001—especially the elimination of regimes (such as the Taliban in Afghanistan) that provided a safe-haven for Al Qaeda operatives—was premised on the World Court's response to the Bernadotte assassination. While the dividing line between state and non-state actors was sharper in 1949 than it is today, the Court's ruling (in this and many other respects, which will be considered below) foreshadowed significant changes in international law.

The Constitutional Law of the United Nations. The Court's advisory opinion in the *Reparation for Injuries* case has come to also be regarded as positively seminal for the development of the constitutional law of the United Nations. It may seem odd to refer to the "constitutional law" of an international institution, which, as the Court noted, is not to be treated as a state.[77] But, like many countries that have a fundamental law known as a "constitution," the United Nations Organization has a constituent document: the United Nations Charter, adopted by the victorious powers after the Second World War.[78] A close reading of the *Reparation for Injuries* opinion reveals some very significant truths about the nature of constitutional interpretation, especially for an instrument (e.g., the U.N. Charter) that can be viewed both as a treaty or contract between member states, and also as a constitutional text.

The U.N. Charter contained no provision specifically addressing the question of whether the Organization could address an international claim to a state, either on its own behalf or that of an injured agent.[79] There was thus no textual basis for the Court to rule one way or the other on this issue. And although there was some discussion at the San Francisco Conference on International Organization, which drafted the Charter, as to the general legal personality of the United Nations, there was nothing debated about the particular right to bring an international

---

77 *See* 1949 I.C.J. at 179 ("[T]he Organization is an international person. That is not the same thing as saying that it is a State, which it certainly is not . . . .").

78 Charter of the United Nations, June 26, 1945, 59 Stat. 1031.

79 *See* 1949 I.C.J. at 178 ("To answer this question, which is not settled by the actual terms of the Charter, we must consider what characteristics it was intended thereby to give to the Organization.").

claim. So, there was no argument to be made to the Court that the intent of the drafters of the Charter was to either grant, or deny, such a power to the Organization. If the U.N. Charter was merely regarded as a treaty text—a literal contract between nations—the lack of either any text or intent to give the United Nations the right to address an international claim would probably have been fatal to the Organization's chances of success, at least in regard to bringing a claim on behalf of the Bernadotte family.

But the U.N. Charter is not "merely" a contract between sovereign nations. It is also a constituent document for an organic being: a new international institution. How, then, does one interpret a text like the Charter, when there is no textual hook for a power, nor any evidence that the creators of the Organization desired such a power to be exercised? In a vitally important move, the Court made these observations:

> The Court is here faced with a new situation. The questions to which it gives rise can only be solved by realizing that the situation is dominated by the provisions of the Charter considered in the light of the principles of international law. . . .
>
> The Charter does not expressly confer upon the Organization the capacity to include, in its claim for reparation, damage caused to the victim or to persons entitled through him. The Court must therefore begin by enquiring whether the provisions of the Charter concerning the functions of the Organization, and the part played by its agents in the performance of those functions, imply for the Organization power to afford its agents the limited protection that would consist in the bringing of a claim on their behalf for reparation for damage suffered in such circumstances. Under international law, the Organization must be deemed to have those powers which, though not expressly provided in the Charter, are conferred upon it by necessary implication as being essential to the performance of its duties.
>
> Having regard to its purposes and functions already referred to, the Organization may find it necessary, and has in fact found it necessary, to entrust its agents with important missions to be performed in disturbed parts of the world. Many missions, from their very nature, involve the agents in unusual dangers to which ordinary persons are not exposed. For the same reason, the injuries suffered by its agents in these circumstances will sometimes have occurred in such a manner that their national State would not be justified in bringing a claim for reparation on the ground of diplomatic protection, or, at any rate, would not feel disposed to do so. Both to ensure the efficient and independent performance of these missions and to afford effective support to its agents, the Organization must provide them with adequate protection.

> In order that the agent may perform his duties satisfactorily, he must feel that this protection is assured to him by the Organization, and that he may count on it. To ensure the independence of the agent, and, consequently, the independent action of the Organization itself, it is essential that in performing his duties he need not have to rely on any other protection than that of the Organization (save of course for the more direct and immediate protection due from the State in whose territory he may be). In particular, he should not have to rely on the protection of his own State. If he had to rely on that State, his independence might well be compromised, contrary to the principle applied by Article 100 of the Charter. And lastly, it is essential that—whether the agent belongs to a powerful or to a weak State; to one more affected or less affected by the complications of international life; to one in sympathy or not in sympathy with the mission of the agent—he should know that in the performance of his duties he is under the protection of the Organization. This assurance is even more necessary when the agent is stateless.
>
> Upon examination of the character of the functions entrusted to the Organization and of the nature of the missions of its agents, it becomes clear that the capacity of the Organization to exercise a measure of functional protection of its agents arises by necessary intendment out of the Charter.[80]

This passage is worth setting out at length, because it reflects the emergence of a new approach[81] of constitutional interpretation for provisions of treaties establishing international institutions: the goal of effectuating the wider purposes of the organization. This has come to be called a purposivist, or teleological, approach to Charter interpretation. The World Court thus ruled that, even in the absence of dispositive text or clear intent, it could find that the Organization had inherent powers, even those beyond the original contemplation of the creators of the institution, so long as those powers were required for the "effective discharge" of the Organization's functions and purposes.[82] These inherent powers, the Court hinted, need not even be derived, as implied powers, from other provisions in the Charter or even the general structure of the instrument.

Needless to say, this purposivist approach worked a potential revolution in the constitutional law of the United Nations. The

---

80 *Id.* at 182–84.

81 One cannot say, though, that this approach was utterly unprecedented. The Court did cite an earlier decision of the Permanent Court of International Justice for this proposition. *See id.* at 182–83 (citing Competence of the International Labor Organization, 1926 P.C.I.J. ser. B, No. 13, at 18 (July 23) (interpreting the ILO Convention, consistent with its "aim and scope")). *But see id.* at 214 (Badawi Pasha, J., dissenting) (questioning relevance of the 1923 PCIJ decision).

82 *Id.* at 179, 180.

Organization would be free to grow and develop over time, to acquire new power and authority, without necessary reference to the original restrictions imagined by the founding countries. This approach gave incredible power to the organs of the United Nations, but most of all to the Court itself, which (presumably) might have the last word about the limits of the U.N.'s power. The Court has not been shy to exercise this authority as being the ultimate arbiter of the Charter's meaning.

In his dissent,[83] Judge Hackworth expressed concern that the *Reparation* opinion set a dangerous precedent by permitting an international organization to assert powers that were neither textually granted by its members in its charter or constituent instrument, nor fairly implied from other provisions. Hackworth was dubious that an international institution should be granted "inherent" powers and was worried that an organization would quickly acquire a life of its own:

> There can be no gainsaying the fact that the Organization is one of delegated and enumerated powers. It is to be presumed that such powers as the Member States desired to confer upon it are stated either in the Charter or in complementary agreements concluded by them. Powers not expressed cannot freely be implied. Implied powers flow from a grant of expressed powers, and are limited to those that are "necessary" to the exercise of powers expressly granted. No necessity for the exercise of the power here in question has been shown to exist. There is no impelling reason, if any at all, why the Organization should become the sponsor of claims on behalf of its employees, even though limited to those arising while the employee is in line of duty. These employees are still nationals of their respective countries, and the customary methods of handling such claims are still available in full vigour.[84]

Drawing on the idiom of American constitutionalism, and the actual language of such landmark cases as *McCulloch v. Maryland*,[85] Hackworth feared giving international institutions potentially unlimited powers. An institution, he worried, driven by a majority of its members, could subvert its original purposes.

Not surprisingly, one of the major themes of the "constitutional law" of the United Nations and other organizations has been the issue of adjudicating charges that the organization has exceeded its intended role and has engaged in *ultra vires* acts. In a later case, the *Certain Expenses of the United Nations* opinion,[86] the problem was framed starkly. In the 1960s, both France and the Soviet Union had objected to the deployment of U.N. peacekeeping forces in Africa and the Middle East. Both had

83 *Id.* at 196 (Hackworth, J., dissenting).

84 *Id.* at 198.

85 17 U.S. (4 Wheat.) 316, 353, 356, 405–07, 412, 416 (1819) (Marshall, C.J.).

86 1962 I.C.J. 151 (July 20).

refused to pay their share of the costs of these forces and were thus in arrears on their dues to the Organization. The question for the Court was whether the cost of these forces, deployed by the U.N. General Assembly (and not by the Security Council, as argued by the French and Soviets) was a proper "expense" of the United Nations within the meaning of the Charter.

The World Court decided that the costs of peacekeeping ordered by the General Assembly were a legitimate "expense" of the United Nations and thus France and the Soviet Union were obliged to pay their fair share. The Court rejected the "separation of powers" argument made by the two countries and ruled that peacekeeping was within the scope of the powers of the General Assembly, and was not exclusively within the authority of the Security Council. More importantly, the Court ruled, if organizational "dissenters" were unhappy with a decision made by the institution, their only recourse was to argue that the *ultra vires* act was contrary to the entire object and purpose of the organization, not that a certain decision should have been made by another organ within the institution. Thus, the ability of a minority to object to the conduct of an international institution was severely circumscribed. The World Court has thus, in a sequence of decisions, expanded the legal personality of international institutions to permit them to take on a "life of their own," even in defiance of the will of a substantial number of their members.

The Nature and Legal Personality of International Organizations. It followed from the *Reparation* opinion that international organizations, while not having the full bundle of rights and duties that states have under international law, certainly have many of the twigs. As the Court observed:

> Accordingly, the Court has come to the conclusion that the Organization is an international person. That is not the same thing as saying that it is a State, which it certainly is not, or that its legal personality and rights and duties are the same as those of a State. Still less is it the same thing as saying that it is "a super-State," whatever that expression may mean. It does not even imply that all its rights and duties must be upon the international plane, any more than all the rights and duties of a State must be upon that plane. What it does mean is that it is a subject of international law and capable of possessing international rights and duties, and that it has capacity to maintain its rights by bringing international claims.[87]

Following from the *Reparation for Injuries* opinion, international institutions can conclude binding treaties not only with each other, but with states. Indeed, the Court specifically mentioned, in the 1949 opinion,

---

87 1949 I.C.J. at 179.

the U.N.'s conclusion of a convention on its privileges and immunities.[88] These instruments between one or more international institutions, or between an international organization and one or more states, are governed by customary international law and a special, International Law Commission-drafted convention for that purpose.[89] International organizations often have standing before international tribunals, not only to raise claims for reparations when they have suffered some kind of loss, but also (more generally) to protect their interests. Institutions also have organic jurisdiction over internal matters (like employee discipline) with which states may not interfere.

That does, however, leave a number of unresolved issues regarding the prerogatives of international organizations. Some of these concern the privileges and immunities of institutions, and the ability of those organizations to avoid scrutiny, under domestic law mechanisms. Perhaps more significant are the problems associated with what business lawyers would call "piercing the corporate veil." If, by acquiring international legal personality, an institution is establishing itself as a separate subject of international law, that can cause legal mischief and produce unfair results.

That was illustrated by the story of an international organization called the International Tin Council (ITC). The ITC implemented what was known as a "commodity stabilization agreement." The Council included members from both tin-producing and tin-consuming countries. The ITC worked to keep tin prices within an established and acceptable range. It did this by buying and selling vast stocks of tin. When prices were too low, the ITC would buy supplies to add to its buffer stock, driving prices up. When prices were too high, the Council would sell from its buffers, thus sending prices down. This is classic price-fixing and, if engaged in by any party other than an international organization, would clearly violate the antitrust laws of most nations around the world.

But in the late 1970s and early 1980s, the ITC's house of cards collapsed, as tin prices dropped and dropped, despite its intervention in purchasing all available supplies. The ITC quite literally ran out of funds and could not meet its obligations when it came time to pay for the tin it had purchased. The ITC thus became the first international institution to figuratively declare bankruptcy, leaving many creditors (including major banks in Australia and Britain) holding millions of dollars of bad promissory notes. Not surprisingly, the banks sued the ITC for contract breaches, and (realizing that the Council was an empty pocket) also

---

[88] *Id.* at 179 (citing Convention on the Privileges and Immunities of the United Nations § 35, Feb. 13, 1946, 21 U.S.T. 1418, 1 U.N.T.S. 15 (ratified by the United States on Apr. 29, 1970)).

[89] *See* Vienna Convention on the Law of Treaties Concluded Between States and International Organizations or Between International Organizations, Mar. 21, 1986, U.N. Doc. A/CONF.129/15, 25 I.L.M. 543, 547 (1986).

impleaded the member states of the Council, arguing that they should be responsible for their agent's misdeeds.

The ITC's legal status and, more importantly, the ability of the banks to pierce the Council's corporate veil, were litigated in British courts applying both international and domestic law. In decisions issued in 1988 and 1989, Britain's highest court, the House of Lords, ruled that the ITC's member states were not responsible for the organization's bad debts.[90] The ITC had sufficiently separate legal personality, under both the English law of corporations and international institutional law, to prevent such a piercing. Interestingly, this holding was followed by U.S. courts, even though the United States was not a member of the Council (unlike Britain, which was) and thus was not obliged to respect its immunities or legal personality. The *Reparation* opinion has thus, in some sense, contributed to an injustice: if international institutions are to be treated as their own legal persons, then that means that the member states can insulate themselves from liability, even where they are really directing the organization's day-to-day activities.

The responsibility of international organizations has also been tested in a caustic, new environment: failed peacekeeping or peace-building missions. Especially during the 1990s, the United Nations came under public scrutiny for the misdeeds of its peacekeepers, especially in the former Yugoslavia, including charges of dereliction of duty, willful neglect of vulnerable populations, and even sexual assault against (and forced prostitution of) female victims whom the peacekeepers were charged with protecting. The United Nations' own International Law Commission has been debating rules of responsibility for international institutions in these (and similar) circumstances, but (to date) without any treaty instrument being produced.

So, while it is significant that the *Reparation for Injuries* opinion firmly and conclusively determined that international organizations are subjects of international law—and are endowed with rights and duties on the international plane (although not to the same degree as states)—one can question whether, in all circumstances, this is an unalloyed good. International institutions are certainly entitled to a degree of international legal personality, and in that sense the World Court's 1949 opinion was not wholly unprecedented,[91] but the enduring question for the international community is what the separate and distinctive legal personality of these institutions practically means in many controversial situations.

"Objective Regimes"—Treaties Binding on Non-Parties. If the International Court of Justice in the *Reparation for Injuries* opinion had simply been content in making its core ruling—that international

---

[90] *See* J.H. Rayner Ltd. v. Dep't of Trade & Indus., [1989] 3 W.L.R. 969, [1990] 2 App. Cas. 418, 500, 81 I.L.R. 670 (H.L.) (U.K.).

[91] *See* David J. Bederman, *The Souls of International Organizations: Legal Personality and the Lighthouse at Cape Spartel*, 36 VA. J. INT'L L. 275 (1996).

institutions are endowed with legal personality sufficient for the United Nations to have the capacity to bring a claim not only for the violation of its own interests, but also of its employees and agents—it would still be regarded as a landmark decision. But it went on to make two other holdings, both of which would revolutionize the theory and structure of public international law.

The first was, strictly speaking, necessary to its decision. As already observed, at the time that Count Bernadotte was assassinated, Israel was not formally recognized as a state by the international community, and thus not a member of the United Nations Organization itself. That raised the intriguing question of whether the international legal personality of the United Nations was even binding on Israel, such that Israel even had to respond to an international claim addressed to it. The World Court summarily raised, and dismissed, this argument in these terms:

> Accordingly the question is whether the Organization has capacity to bring a claim against the defendant State to recover reparation in respect of that damage or whether, on the contrary, the defendant State, not being a member, is justified in raising the objection that the Organization lacks the capacity to bring an international claim. On this point, the Court's opinion is that fifty States, representing the vast majority of the members of the international community, had the power, in conformity with international law, to bring into being an entity possessing objective international personality, and not merely personality recognized by them alone, together with capacity to bring international claims.[92]

Essentially, the Court ruled that the U.N. Charter was a "super-treaty," binding equally on parties and non-parties, as an "objective regime." This principle was in contradistinction to the typical, black-letter rule of treaty law that an international agreement could only impose obligations on a party that had signified its intent to be bound by it.[93] This is sometimes referred to as the principle of "*ius tertii*."

What exactly the Court imagined as being "objective regimes," aside from the U.N. Charter, is a bit of a mystery. The judges on the Court might have believed that the U.N. Charter was unique in this respect. Indeed, according to Article 2, paragraph 6 of the Charter, non-members of the Organization were placed under a distinctive set of obligations.[94] Judge Krylov of the Soviet Union, in his dissent, mentioned this provision, but correctly observed that that "this paragraph has very little connexion with the right of the United Nations to bring an international

---

[92] 1949 I.C.J. at 185.

[93] *See* Vienna Convention on the Law of Treaties art. 34, May 23, 1969, 1155 U.N.T.S. 331.

[94] U.N. Charter art. 2, para. 6 (providing that non-member states must act in accordance with the principles of the Charter for the maintenance of international peace and security).

claim with a view to obtaining reparation for damage."[95] Judge Krylov thus concluded: "It is true that the non-member States cannot fail to recognize the existence of the United Nations as an objective fact. But, in order that they may be bound by a legal obligation to the Organization, it is necessary that the latter should conclude a special agreement with these States."[96]

Since the time of the *Reparation for Injuries* opinion, international law experts and publicists have nominated other treaty regimes as objective regimes.[97] Most often mentioned[98] is the Antarctic Treaty System, established by the Antarctic Treaty of 1959.[99] But, occasionally, some forms of human rights and collective security regimes are also characterized in this way.[100]

Perhaps such vagueness might be expected, since the whole notion of "objective regimes" runs counter to a bedrock, classical principle of the discipline: international law is binding on states only to the extent they wish to be bound. The issue today is whether law for the international community is exclusively the product of consent by the participants in the system (however manifested) or also includes enduring truths that somehow reflect the values of that community? In just a short paragraph, the International Court of Justice opened the possibility that international law could be a normative force to condition state behavior, quite apart from the principle of consent.

Transforming the "Law of Nations" into "International Law." The announcement of "objective regimes" was an extraordinary move in the *Reparation for Injuries* opinion. It nonetheless pales in comparison with a threshold observation made by the Court:

> The subjects of law in any legal system are not necessarily identical in their nature or in the extent of their rights, and their nature depends upon the needs of the community. Throughout its history, the development of international law has been influenced by the requirements of international life, and the progressive increase in the collective activities of States

---

95 1949 I.C.J. at 218 (Krylov, J., dissenting).

96 *Id.* at 218–19 (Krylov, J., dissenting).

97 *See, e.g.*, Summary Records of the 877th Meeting, [1966] Y.B. Int'l L. Comm'n 227, 231, U.N. Doc. A/CN.4/SER.A/1966.

98 *See* Bruno Simma, *The Antarctic Treaty as a Treaty Providing for an 'Objective Regime,'* 19 CORNELL INT'L L.J. 189 (1986). *See also* Dennis W. Arrow, *Seabeds, Sovereignty and Objective Regimes*, 7 FORDHAM INT'L L.J. 169, 209 (1984) (discussing *erga omnes* and "objective regimes").

99 Antarctic Treaty, Dec. 1, 1959, 12 U.S.T. 794, 402 U.N.T.S. 71.

100 *See* Report of the International Law Commission on the Work of Its 35th Session, [1983] 2 Y.B. Int'l L. Comm'n pt. 2, at 1, 41, U.N. Doc. A/38/10; Surya P. Subedi, *The Doctrine of Objective Regimes in International Law and the Competence of the United Nations to Impose Territorial or Peace Settlements on States*, 37 GER. Y.B. INT'L L. 162 (1994).

> has already given rise to instances of action upon the international plane by certain entities which are not States.[101]

With this simple statement, the World Court proclaimed the end of the classical system of the "law of nations," and ushered in the contemporary concept of "international law."

The law of nations was the outgrowth of the Westphalian state system concluded at the end of the Thirty Years' War (1618–1648), one of the most bloody and cataclysmic conflicts in European history. As originally conceived by the European states of the seventeenth and eighteenth centuries—and by such international law publicists at Vitoria, Suarez, Gentili, Grotius, Pufendorf, and Bynkershoek—the original law of nations was an amalgam of natural law principles (binding on individuals and rulers equally) and of state practice (reflected in custom and treaties).

But beginning in the late eighteenth century (and especially in the writings of Vattel), a strong positivist element to the law of nations emerged. Natural law principles mattered less, and, instead, state practice and state consent to the rules of the international community mattered more. Under this vision of the law of nations, there was only one set of actors, one type of player, in international relations. That was the nation-state. Nothing and no one else had any standing to assert international law rights and duties. To put it another way, during this "post-classical" period of high positivism, the law of nations recognized only states as having international legal personality.

The post-classical vision of the "law of nations" was utterly and completely state-centered. Since only states had rights and duties under international law, other sorts of individuals and entities had no international standing whatsoever. Individuals were regarded as mere "objects" of international law, quite literally acted upon by "real" international legal "subjects." The post-classical understanding of the law of nations was that individuals had no standing to bring claims against states, except through mechanisms of diplomatic protection, where one country espoused or addressed the claim of one of its own nationals against another, perpetrator country. Indeed, except in rare circumstances (where individuals had placed themselves outside the realm of diplomatic protection, such as taking up piracy and becoming the enemy of all mankind (*hostes humanis generis*)), individuals had neither rights nor duties under international law. As the ultimate application of these principles, the law of nations was completely disinterested in the manner in which a state treated its own citizens.

The Second World War and its aftermath revolutionized international law, and this sea-change was reflected in the World Court's well-chosen sentences about the nature of the international community and the subjects of international law. The same set of principles that

[101] 1949 I.C.J. at 178.

made it possible for the Court to embrace the notion of "collective activities of States" by endowing such new international institutions as the United Nations with international legal personality, also grounded the notion that international law ought to accept that individuals have international rights and duties not utterly tied to state prerogative. The public and wide-spread revulsion of the international community at the human rights abuses of the Nazi German and Imperial Japanese forces during the Second World War created the conditions for a new recognition of human rights norms. And so, when the International Court of Justice declared an end to states' monopoly on the identity and instruments of the law in the international community, it was heralding the end of one epoch and signaling the transition to a new era of a democratic, accessible, relevant, and transparent regime for international law.

In declaring the demise of the old "law of nations," the Court was also recognizing that the international legal system was growing and maturing. In a sense, international law was starting to appear and act like many domestic legal systems, and that is why the Court observed that "the subjects of law in any legal system are not necessarily identical in their nature or in the extent of their rights, and their nature depends upon the needs of the community."[102] Contemporary international law can accommodate the idea that there can be a diversity of international legal subjects—nation-states, international institutions, transnational corporations, individuals, non-governmental organizations, and other forms of non-state actors. They serve different functions and have divergent sets of rights and duties under international law. As the Court observed for international organizations (such as the United Nations), they do not have the same rights and duties as states, nor would we expect them to do so. In the same way, individual actors in international relations have a different set of rights and responsibilities.

What the International Court of Justice made clear in the *Reparation for Injuries* opinion was that the functional nature of international legal actors, and indeed the entire success of international law as a legal system, are gauged by the "needs of the [international] community."[103] What matters for the international legal system is what works. The World Court's advisory opinion thus reflects a pragmatic and open approach to the future development of international law, uninfluenced by the old formalisms and shibboleths of the law of nations. The real legal legacy of the World Court's 1949 *Reparation for Injuries* opinion was to usher in a new sense of doctrinal confidence, of hopeful optimism, and sustained intent for a new world legal order.

It is an international legal regime that—nearly sixty years later, and despite its many faults and dysfunctions—we still live in, and that still accounts for whatever peace, prosperity, and human dignity we enjoy on this planet. To read the *Reparation for Injuries* opinion in this light, after

---

102 *Id.*

103 *Id.*

all of these years, is to understand the very beginnings of our contemporary international legal world.

IV. THE REST OF THE STORY

To end this narrative on that valedictory note would do a disservice to the individual whose tragic, violent, and unnecessary death impelled the events leading to the issuance of the International Court of Justice's advisory opinion in the *Reparation for Injuries* case. The human drama of that story, having been eliminated from the Court's own text, deserves to be retold and remembered. So, one might legitimately ask, what became of Count Folke Bernadotte's family and his assassins?

In the late 1970s and early 1980s, as the leaders of the erstwhile Stern Gang approached the ends of their lives, the truth of the Bernadotte assassination became known as former members and others told their stories to reporters. Former Prime Minister David Ben Gurion spoke to his biographer about the assassination, and gave the list of names of individuals who had been suspected to have committed the act. Not enough evidence was present to convict or even bring charges against anyone. One of the names on the list was Yehoshua Cohen, who was by this time a close friend and neighbor of Ben Gurion. When asked, the former Prime Minister told his biographer that Cohen had admitted to him that he had taken part in the killing of Count Bernadotte. Yehoshua Cohen refused to add anything to the statements of Ben Gurion and died a few years later.[104]

Other leaders in the Stern Gang also revealed their role in the planning of the assassination, and the fact that they had decided to have the killing attributed to the "Fatherland Front" in order to ease pressure on the Stern Gang. Two of the individuals who were directly involved in the killing came forward in the early 1980s. Yehoshua Seitler claimed to have planned and orchestrated the assassination. Meshulam Markover declared that he was one of the four individuals who carried out the plans, and affirmed that Yehoshua Cohen not only was one of the four, but had been the individual to shoot the mediator while the other three provided cover. Their motivation for coming forward was once again to frustrate the United Nations from imposing what they saw as an unacceptable solution to the conflict in the Holy Land.[105] So, as before, those wishing to disrupt peace movements and initiatives sought to use violence to intimidate or kill.

And there is also the irony that a thin line separates terrorists and statesmen, insurrectionists and diplomats. One individual implicated in the killings was Yitzhak Shamir, one of the three leaders of the Stern Gang, who later went on to become Prime Minister of Israel during 1983–1984. During his time in office, as reports continued to be revealed

---

[104] *Yehoshua Cohen Dies; Linked to 1948 Killing*, *supra* note 25, at D24.

[105] Kifner, *supra* note 24, at A3.

regarding his role in the planning of the assassination, he refused to comment. His press office stated merely that the Prime Minister had no role in the planning or execution of the assassination.[106]

On a more hopeful note, Countess Estelle Bernadotte, Folke's widow, an American by birth, resettled years later in the United States and became a significant patroness of efforts to promote international humanitarian law.[107] While the Count's family may have hoped for an enduring and lasting peace in the Middle East as the main legacy of his life, that, alas, has not come to pass in the years and decades since his assassination. Instead, Count Bernadotte's most poignant bequest for later generations may be an international court opinion that neither bears his name, nor even tells his story, but nonetheless stands for important and enduring truths about the rule of law in international relations.

---

[106] *Id.*; Thomas L. Friedman, *Israel's Other Half: Yitzhak Shamir*, N.Y. TIMES, Oct. 21, 1986, at A8.

[107] *See* Johnson, *supra* note 69, at S4.

17

Mary Ellen O'Connell

The *Nicaragua* Case: Preserving World Peace and the World Court

The *Nicaragua* case (*Military and Paramilitary Activities in and against Nicaragua*) was filed in 1984. Forty years later it stands out as the International Court of Justice's (ICJ) most important decision to date. It concerns the world's hard-earned rules restricting the use of force in international relations. Just as importantly, it concerns the use of force by a superpower against a small, impoverished state. The Court's main decision in the case confirmed and reinforced international law's general prohibition on the use of force. The Court also handed a victory to the small state, Nicaragua, against the superpower, the United States of America. As a result, the decision helped modify the Court's image as an elitist, pro-North institution. It set the context for another Global South challenge to a militarily superior state, the Republic of South Africa's case against the State of Israel filed at the very end of 2023.[1]

The positive results of the *Nicaragua* case came at a price for the Court, however. U.S. officials were not pleased. They argued that the Court, like other organs and agencies of the United Nations, had, by the time of the case, become biased against the United States. Their primary evidence of this bias was the fact the Court had taken jurisdiction in the case. The Court did, indeed, have a technical basis on which it could have reasonably avoided taking jurisdiction in major parts of the case, but contrary to the U.S. public position, the judges could not reasonably have rejected the entire case. Fifteen of sixteen judges voted to find jurisdiction on some basis. Only the U.S. judge found no basis for jurisdiction. Nevertheless, U.S. officials characterized the vote on jurisdiction as highly unfair. They refused to participate further in the case, at least officially, and condemned the use of the Court as a political tool by Nicaragua.[2] Paradoxically, not long after the decision, the United States

---

1 *See* Application of Convention on the Prevention and Punishment of the Crime of Genocide in the Gaza Strip (S. Afr. v. Isr.), Application, 2023 I.C.J. (Dec. 29), https://www.icj-cij.org/case/192/institution-proceedings.

2 *US Withdrawal Another Blow to "World Court,"* FIN. TIMES, Oct. 15, 1985, at 10. The United States did not, however, terminate the many compromissory clauses it has in numerous bilateral and multilateral treaties agreeing to ICJ jurisdiction. In 1987, it invoked one of these treaties to take Italy to the Court to settle a claim by U.S. nationals of

began acknowledging *Nicaragua* as the authoritative decision on use of force. This has been acceptance in word, not deed. U.S. conduct has continued to dishonor the United Nations Charter principles on the use of force as interpreted by the International Court in 1986.[3] Nicaragua's own story has been one of long years of oppression and human rights violations by the very individuals who sought vindication of sovereign rights and peace under international law at the ICJ.[4]

The United States had tried to prevent the case from becoming the accepted verdict on U.S. use of force by refusing to participate. It could then assert the Court had not heard its side of the evidence. The case reached its influential status despite the U.S. absence. Indeed, the U.S. decision was taken as an elitist dismissal of Nicaragua, the ICJ, and international law. In addition, the Court had plenty of evidence of the U.S. position. Few gave credence to the view the Court could not fully adjudicate the claims, and the United States soon dropped the argument.

The ICJ has no provision for default judgments. It must undertake a thorough review of both sides of a dispute. Nicaragua made voluminous submissions, presenting witnesses—including high government officials—and participating in weeks of oral argument. For its part, the United States sent the Court's registrar a document called *Revolution Beyond Our Borders*, outlining alleged wrongdoing by Nicaragua.[5] To assure itself per Article 53 of its Statute that its judgment was "well-founded in fact and law," the Court reviewed *Revolution Beyond Our Borders*, as well as statements of U.S. officials. The judges also had the benefit of U.S. Judge Stephen Schwebel's perspective. In addition, it had volumes of pleadings by the United States in the earlier phases of the case.[6] The Court was able to produce a 150-page decision on the merits with separate and dissenting opinions totaling over 400 pages, including almost 300 pages of opinion and factual annexes by Judge Schwebel. The decision on the merits is remembered forty years later as a clear win for Nicaragua and defeat for the United States. Lingering criticism is of the wish for more analysis by the Court to help in applying the law on the use of force to ongoing situations.

Against the odds, then, the *Nicaragua* case became a major milestone in international law's development as a legal system. Forty

---

unlawful expropriation. Elettronica Sicula S.p.A. (ELSI) (U.S. v. It.), 1989 I.C.J. 15 (June 14). The case was heard by a chamber of the Court composed of five judges selected by the parties.

3 For two comprehensive assessments of international law on the use of force confirming these observations on the influence of the case, see CHRISTINE GRAY, INTERNATIONAL LAW AND THE USE OF FORCE (4th ed. 2018), and SELF DEFENCE AGAINST NON-STATE ACTORS (Mary Ellen O'Connell, Christian J. Tams & Dire Tladi eds., 2019).

4 *See* Amnesty International, *Nicaragua, A Continuum of Repression and Systematic Human Rights Violations under the Ortega-Murillo Government* (Apr. 18, 2023), https://www.amnesty.org/en/latest/news/2023/04/nicaragua-systematic-human-rights-violations-ortega-murillo/.

5 *See infra* text accompanying note 65.

6 *See infra* text accompanying notes 32–66.

years after the adoption of the United Nations Charter, the case served to reinforce and reinvigorate the rules restricting armed force. It did so in a setting that also strengthened international law in its rightful place above power and above politics in the world community. Forty years after the decision, it is the *locus classicus* on use of force but too often, like the Charter itself, is honored in the breach. Yet, the decision sparked a boom in business at the Court. Despite U.S. charges of bias and unfairness, the *Nicaragua* case won new respect for the Court, especially in the Global South.

Many stories can be told related to the *Nicaragua* case—stories about the judges, the lawyers, the history, the aftermath, and the legal issues dealt with over hundreds of pages.[7] This story focuses on those aspects of the case that most likely account for its prominence today: the fact that the Court applied the law regulating the use of force by states and did so on behalf of a small state against a far more powerful one. The ICJ itself also benefited from its bold decision. It went from an institution where little happened to one where the judges complain about their heavy case load. The *Nicaragua* case reaffirmed that the primary goal of international law is the preservation of peace and that the way to achieve that goal is through substantive norms against armed conflict and institutions for the peaceful resolution of disputes, especially courts. South Africa's 2023 case against Israel renewed awareness of all of these reaffirmations of *Nicaragua*.

I. INTERNATIONAL LAW, ARMED CONFLICT, AND BACKGROUND TO THE *NICARAGUA* CASE

The purpose of international law, like all law, is to allow human beings to live peacefully in community. Modern international law originated in 1648 with the Peace of Westphalia, treaties ending Europe's bloody Thirty Years' War.[8] The treaties laid down certain principles designed to prevent new conflicts and instituted means to enforce compliance, including collective action against wrongdoers. With the rise of the concept of absolute state sovereignty, however, the theoretical underpinning of international law's control of war declined. Promoters of sovereignty, like Vattel, elevated the state and the will of the state, in effect, to be above the law. It became increasingly difficult throughout the nineteenth century to argue that a prince could not go to war whenever he wished. What was international law, however, if it could not regulate the ultimate violence of international society? In fact, international lawyers never conceded that the prohibition of force is not a fundamental principle of international law. Yet as Agatha Verdebout shows, in the

---

[7] For more, see TERRY D. GILL, LITIGATION STRATEGY AT THE INTERNATIONAL COURT: A CASE STUDY OF THE NICARAGUA V. UNITED STATES DISPUTE (1989).

[8] For a longer treatment of humanity's attempt to control the use of force through law, see MARY ELLEN O'CONNELL, INTERNATIONAL LAW AND THE USE OF FORCE (3d ed. 2022).

cognitive dissonance of World War I and the continued suppression of natural law in favor of positive law, international lawyers sought to codify the prohibition in increasingly strict positive law instruments culminating in the U.N. Charter.[9]

By 1945, national leaders, led by the United States, were ready to agree to a general treaty-based prohibition on the use of force by states in Article 2(4) of the United Nations Charter and to grant to the U.N. Security Council the authority to enforce the prohibition. The United States remained a champion of the Charter and its limits on resort to armed force until the 1960s. Then, influenced by the teaching of Hans Morgenthau, political scientists began to warn of a too-strict adherence to international law in the ultimate questions confronting U.S. leaders. "Legalism-moralism" was presented as a danger to be avoided. Still, the power of international law was also understood by U.S. leaders and was not simply tossed aside. Starting with the Cuban missile crisis and continuing until today, the United States has justified its many uses of force in terms of the U.N. Charter—though too often in ways that test credulity. By the time Nicaragua took the United States to the ICJ for violating the Charter, Thomas Franck had already published his article, *Who Killed Article 2(4)?*[10] Franck argued that given the high level of violence in the world the Charter prohibition on force had not proven viable. Louis Henkin, in his firm and eloquent response to Franck, pointed to the normative commitment of the world community to law against war.[11] No responsible leader had called for a world without law superior to state will. The ICJ incorporated a view very much like Henkin's in its decision in the *Nicaragua* case.

The case began with an application by Nicaragua, citing numerous uses of force by the United States and its proxies against Nicaragua's Sandinista government. The decision to bring a case had not been taken lightly. The United States had been intervening militarily in Nicaragua since the 1850s:

> Throughout its history, Nicaragua has been dominated by the United States, from the brief conquest of the country by William Walker in the 1850s, through the repeated intervention of the U.S. Marines in the first three decades of the twentieth century, to the installation of the first General Somoza in 1933 . . . and the forty-five years of U.S. military and economic support for the Somoza family dictatorship.[12]

---

9 AGATHA VERDEBOUT, REWRITING HISTORIES OF THE USE OF FORCE: THE NARRATIVE OF "INDIFFERENCE" (2021).

10 Thomas M. Franck, *Who Killed Article 2(4)? or: Changing Norms Governing the Use of Force by States*, 64 AM. J. INT'L L. 809 (1970).

11 Louis Henkin, *The Reports of the Death of Article 2(4) Are Greatly Exaggerated*, 65 AM. J. INT'L L. 544, 545 (1971).

12 Paul S. Reichler, *Holding America to Its Own Best Standards: Abe Chayes and Nicaragua in the World Court,* 42 HARV. INT'L L.J. 15, 42 (2001).

The United States had exercised significant influence over the Nicaraguan government, acting both overtly and covertly to promote its own agenda in Central America. As President Truman said of General Somoza, "He's a bastard but he's our bastard."[13] Somoza, too, acknowledged the close relationship: "Over a period of years, we sent over fourteen thousand men through various military training programs in the United States. . . . Due to our close association with the U.S., Nicaragua was often referred to as 'the little U.S.A.' of Central America."[14] Then, however, during the presidency of Jimmy Carter, the United States underwent a profound shift in foreign policy. The United States began to promote international human rights, and President Carter withdrew support from Somoza in light of the serious human rights abuses committed by his regime.

Soon after, in July 1979, Somoza was successfully overthrown. The new revolutionary government of the "Sandinistas" embarked on a plan to improve literacy rates, health care, and social security. The United States began providing "what was to be a $130 million aid program for Nicaragua," and "[b]y January 1981 the US had provided more aid than any other government."[15] However, in May 1980 Congress added a condition that the President certify that Nicaragua was not supporting terrorism or violence in other countries.[16] Despite reports of Nicaraguan assistance to anti-government forces in El Salvador in September 1980, President Carter, in an attempt to maintain friendly relations with Nicaragua, certified to Congress that there was no conclusive evidence of Sandinista support for El Salvadoran guerrilla rebels.

By January 1981, Carter was gone, and Ronald Reagan was in charge. Reagan shifted U.S. foreign policy away from human rights promotion to a determined anti-communist campaign. The Sandinistas were Marxists. On April 1, 1981, the United States cut off aid to Nicaragua, even though Nicaraguan arms shipments to guerrillas in El Salvador had been curtailed. While the United States was shifting its relations with Nicaragua, the Sandinistas made little effort to establish good relations with the new U.S. administration in Washington. The Sandinista anthem continued to include the line, "We shall fight against the Yankee, the enemy of humanity."[17]

---

13 *Quoted in* Hunter R. Clark & Amanda Velazquez, *Foreign Direct Investment in Latin America: Nicaragua—A Case Study*, 16 AM. U. INT'L L. REV. 743, 783 (2001).

14 JACK COZ, NICARAGUA BETRAYED 262 (1980) (quoting Anastasio Somoza) (quoted in HOLLY SKLAR, WASHINGTON'S WAR ON NICARAGUA 7 (1988)).

15 Central Intelligence Agency, *Nicaragua Under the Sandinistas: A Bill of Particulars*, at 1, https://www.cia.gov/readingroom/docs/CIA-RDP85M00363R000801790005-6.pdf.

16 Special Central American Assistance Act of 1979, Pub. L. No. 96–257, § 536(g), 21 U.S.C. § 2151 (1980).

17 The anthem with this anti-U.S. lyric was apparently dropped in the 1990s. *See* Alvaro Cruz, *Sandinistas change anti-US anthem*, UNITED PRESS INT'L (Sept. 7, 1996), https://www.upi.com/Archives/1996/09/07/Sandinistas-change-anti-US-anthem/2253842068800/.

Central America

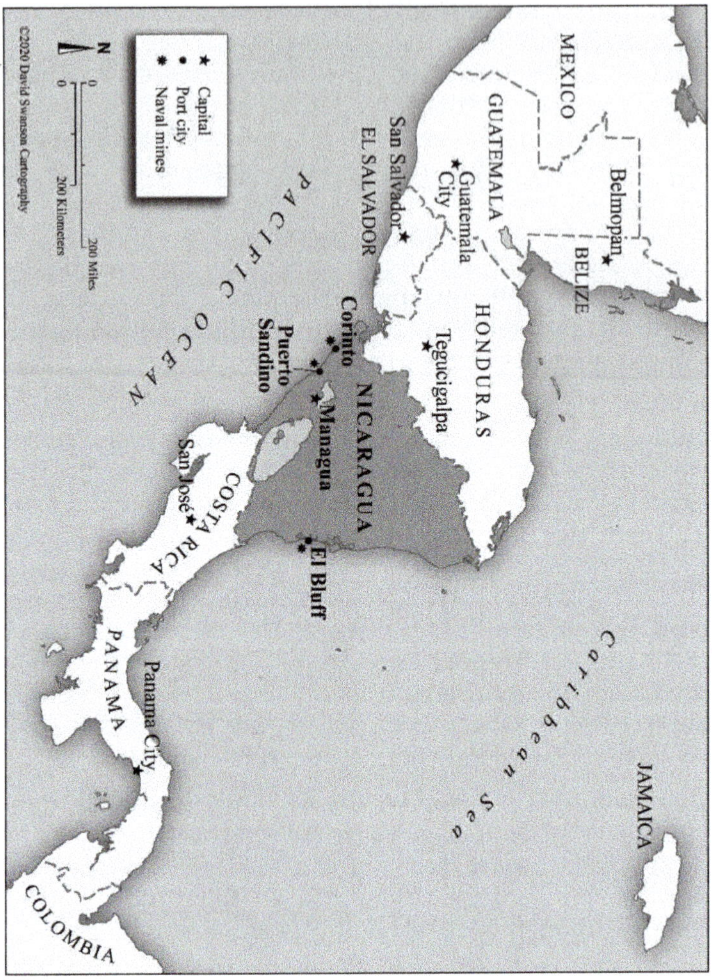

By late 1981, many of the fears of Sandinista officials were realized. The United States had embarked on a full-fledged policy of hostility toward Nicaragua with the creation of the anti-Sandinista Contra forces. Initially, the Contras were composed of and directed by former members of Somoza's National Guard. They were fully funded by the United States, operating from bases primarily in Honduras. By 1982, the Contras received sophisticated training and weapons from the U.S. government, and their forces grew to over 10,000. The Sandinistas responded to this increase in what they portrayed as a mercenary force by pursuing a two-track policy. First, the Sandinistas built Nicaragua's army to become the second largest in Latin America, after Cuba's. Both Cuba and the Soviet Union were its major suppliers. Second, the Sandinistas pursued diplomatic options, especially through a multilateral grouping known as the Contadoras, and also bilaterally with the United States.[18]

The Reagan administration was, however, determined to eliminate the Sandinistas and prevent new Marxist regimes in the Americas. Its preferred means for pursuing this goal were through support for anti-Marxist groups attempting to overthrow Marxist regimes or by keeping anti-Marxist governments in power. These policies were key aspects of what came to be known as the "Reagan Doctrine."[19] The administration did not favor negotiation.[20]

Although Congress was concerned about overthrowing governments and limited the funds available to the President for this purpose, the U.S. Central Intelligence Agency (CIA) easily circumvented funding restrictions on its Central American activities. In 1983, the CIA organized a new Contra force in Costa Rica, subjecting the Sandinistas to Contra pressure from both the north (Honduras) and the south (Costa Rica). The CIA published a field manual entitled *Psychological Operations in Guerrilla Warfare*, known as the "*CIA Murder Manual*." This manual instructed the Contras on tactics, including kidnapping "all officials or agents of the Sandinista government" and shaming and humiliating "the 'personal symbols' of the government of repression in the presence of the people."[21] Nicaragua described other U.S. anti-Sandinista activities in its application to the ICJ: "[The U.S.] military and paramilitary activities have resulted in death or bodily harm to more than 3,000 Nicaraguan citizens, and destruction of property valued at more than $200,000,000 including bridges, port facilities, airports, power stations, oil pipelines and storage facilities, agricultural cooperatives, schools, hospitals, day-care centers and homes."[22]

While the United States was engaging in attacks on Nicaragua in an attempt to weaken, and eventually overthrow, the Sandinista regime,

---

[18] The Contadoras group was formed by Colombia, Mexico, Panama, and Venezuela specifically to address conflict in Nicaragua, El Salvador, and Guatemala. THE CONTADORA, DOCUMENT OF OBJECTIVES (Panama City, Sept. 9, 1983).

[19] The "Reagan Doctrine" refers to the Reagan administration's (1981–1988) support for anti-communist insurgent movements worldwide. *See* LOUIS HENKIN ET AL., RIGHT V. MIGHT, INTERNATIONAL LAW AND THE USE OF FORCE (2d ed. 1991).

[20] As Paul Reichler, one of Nicaragua's legal counsel, explained, the Reagan administration

> torpedoed Contadora by ignoring it, and by pressuring Honduras and El Salvador, whose shaky, military-backed regimes were heavily dependent on U.S. support, to resist reaching any agreements that would let Nicaragua off the hook. . . . No one in the U.S. government would meet with Foreign Minister d'Escoto when he came to Washington to present . . . [peace] treaties . . . in its zeal to isolate and destroy the Nicaraguan revolution.

Reichler, *supra* note 12, at 21.

[21] Central Intelligence Agency, *Psychological Operations in Guerilla Warfare*, at 28, *available at* https://www.cia.gov/readingroom/docs/DOC_0000526690.pdf (last visited May 23, 2024).

[22] Military and Paramilitary Activities in and against Nicaragua (Nicar. v. U.S.), Application Instituting Proceedings, 1984 I.C.J. 2, 20 (Apr. 9). In Annex A to the Application, Nicaragua detailed in chronological order the attacks against Nicaragua.

Nicaragua's neighbors, El Salvador, Guatemala, Honduras, and Costa Rica, were charging Nicaragua with supporting forces opposed to their governments. Honduran Ambassador Roberto Martinez, speaking at the Organization of American States (OAS), accused the Sandinistas of destabilizing Central America:

> [T]he totalitarian Nicaraguan regime is the main factor in the emergence of the regional crisis, because it has unleashed actions aimed at destabilizing governments in other Central American countries. These actions include, among others, direct support for terrorist and subversive groups. . . . The incidents show the aggravation of the Central American situation as the direct and immediate result of the warmongering and threatening attitude of the Sandinist regime.[23]

In this charged atmosphere, Nicaragua contemplated bringing a case against the United States at the ICJ. Going to the Court, according to Paul Reichler, one of Nicaragua's American lawyers, would change the debate: "The question would no longer be a simplistic one . . . whether the Sandinistas were Communists whose very existence threatened U.S. interests. . . . [M]embers of Congress would have to ask themselves whether U.S. national interests were truly served when America wantonly disregarded, and thereby undermined, the most fundamental principles of international law."[24] Moreover, by asking this question and attempting to hold up a mirror showing Congress the reality of the situation in Nicaragua, the Nicaraguan officials hoped to reveal "an international outlaw guilty of the same offenses—trampling on the political independence and territorial sovereignty of a small and defenseless nation—that Americans associated with the adversary they disdainfully called the 'evil empire' [i.e., the Soviet Union]."[25] Because the World Court was highly regarded in the United States, a judgment in Nicaragua's favor could turn the tide of opinion in Congress and slow, if not completely stop, the funding of the Contra forces.

In January of 1984, after extensive research and consideration, the government of Nicaragua formally decided to institute a case against the United States at the ICJ. Nicaragua had already recruited Reichler and had consulted with friendly governments to weigh the consequences of taking on the world's most powerful state. Abe Chayes was recruited next. Chayes was a law professor at Harvard Law School at the time, but he had been the Legal Adviser to the State Department during the Kennedy administration. The team also included Ian Brownlie, professor at the University of Oxford, and Alain Pellet, professor at the University of Paris (Nord), both leading experts on the law prohibiting the use of force.

---

[23] Tegucigalpa Domestic Service in Spanish, July 14, 1983, *in* FBIS—Daily Report Latin America, July 20, 1983.

[24] Reichler, *supra* note 12, at 22–23.

[25] *Id.* at 23.

The team decided that they would file the application on April 9, 1984. Shortly before, an investigative reporter for the *Wall Street Journal* broke the story of the mining of Nicaraguan harbors by the CIA.[26] Various newspapers and members of Congress called the mining an act of war, bringing attention to the legality of U.S. actions in Nicaragua. On April 6, U.S. officials learned of Nicaragua's intention to file a case in the ICJ and reacted by announcing that they would modify America's 1946 acceptance of the ICJ's optional compulsory jurisdiction by excluding Central American disputes.[27] They filed a declaration with the Secretary-

---

[26] David Rogers, *U.S. Role in Mining Nicaraguan Harbors Reportedly Is Larger than First Thought*, WALL ST. J., Apr. 6, 1984, at 6.

[27] The ICJ Statute provides in Article 36 for compulsory jurisdiction where parties declare they accept it:

> 1. The jurisdiction of the Court comprises all cases which the parties refer to it and all matters specially provided for in the Charter of the United Nations or in treaties and conventions in force.
>
> 2. The states parties to the present Statute may at any time declare that they recognize as compulsory *ipso facto* and without special agreement, in relation to any other state accepting the same obligation, the jurisdiction of the Court in all legal disputes concerning:
>
> a. the interpretation of a treaty;
>
> b. any question of international law;
>
> c. the existence of any fact which, if established, would constitute a breach of an international obligation;
>
> d. the nature or extent of the reparation to be made for the breach of an international obligation.
>
> 3. The declarations referred to above may be made unconditionally or on condition of reciprocity on the part of several or certain states, or for a certain time.
>
> 4. Such declarations shall be deposited with the Secretary-General of the United Nations, who shall transmit copies thereof to the parties to the Statute and to the Registrar of the Court.
>
> 5. Declarations made under Article 36 of the Statute of the Permanent Court of International Justice and which are still in force shall be deemed, as between the parties to the present Statute, to be acceptances of the compulsory jurisdiction of the International Court of Justice for the period which they still have to run and in accordance with their terms.
>
> 6. In the event of a dispute as to whether the Court has jurisdiction, the matter shall be settled by the decision of the Court.

The U.S. declaration accepting the Court's compulsory jurisdiction read in part:

> I, Harry S. Truman . . . declare on behalf of the United States of America . . . that the United States of America recognizes as compulsory *ipso facto* and without special agreement, in relation to any other state accepting the same obligation, the jurisdiction of the International Court of Justice in all legal disputes hereafter arising concerning
>
> a. the interpretation of a treaty;
>
> b. any question of international law;
>
> c. the existence of any fact which, if established, would constitute a breach of an international obligation;
>
> d. the nature or extent of the reparation to be made for the breach of an international obligation; . . .
>
> *Provided further*, that this declaration shall remain in force for a period of five years and thereafter until the expiration of six months after notice may be given to terminate this declaration.

Declaration on the Part of the United States of America, Aug. 14, 1946, 61 Stat. 1218.

General of the United Nations stating, with reference to the 1946 declaration, that "the aforesaid declaration shall not apply to disputes with any Central American State or arising out of or related to events in Central America, any of which disputes shall be settled in such manners as the parties to them may agree."[28] The declaration only underscored for some that the Reagan administration was carrying out actions in Central America that it was not publicly willing to defend.

II. THE CASE

Despite the U.S. attempt with its last-minute declaration to avoid the Court, the *Nicaragua* case remained on the ICJ's docket for seven years. The Court issued four major decisions, totaling almost 800 pages, on provisional measures, El Salvador's request to intervene, jurisdiction and admissibility, and, finally, the merits. The case was only removed from the docket in 1991 at Nicaragua's request.

Provisional Measures. Nicaragua filed its application with the Court on April 9, 1984, as planned, ignoring the U.S. declaration. The application set out Nicaragua's basic claims, as well as a request for an order of provisional measures of protection pending the resolution of the case. Nicaragua wanted the Court to order the United States to cease all military activities against Nicaragua and all interference in its internal affairs.

The ICJ orders provisional measures in cases of urgency where evidence indicates a *prima facie* basis for jurisdiction. Nicaragua referred in its application to its acceptance of the optional jurisdiction of the Court under Article 36(2) of the ICJ Statute, as well as to the U.S. acceptance of this basis of jurisdiction.[29] In a letter dated April 24, 1984, Nicaragua also referred to other treaties that provided for jurisdiction, although it did not cite any treaties specifically.[30]

The United States informed the Court on April 13 that, in light of its announced modification of April 6, the Court had no jurisdiction in the case. The United States communicated again on April 23, mentioning for the first time that Nicaragua had never perfected its 1929 acceptance of the Permanent Court of International Justice's optional jurisdiction and that this failure meant Nicaragua had never validly accepted the ICJ's optional jurisdiction either.

The ICJ held hearings on the request for provisional measures on April 25 and 27. U.S. representatives attended these hearings but refused to argue in detail on the question of provisional measures because it insisted there was no jurisdiction. The Court found evidence of

[28] Letter from U.S. Secretary of State to Javier Perez de Cuellar, U.N. Secretary-General, Apr. 6, 1984, 23 I.L.M. 670 (1984).

[29] *See supra* note 27.

[30] *See* Military and Paramilitary Activities in and against Nicaragua (Nicar. v. U.S.), 1984 I.C.J. 169, 169–75 (May 10).

Nicaragua's acceptance of the compulsory jurisdiction of the Permanent Court of International Justice, the predecessor of the ICJ—evidence the United States subsequently contested. The Court concluded that, in light of Article 36(5) of the ICJ Statute, Nicaragua's evidence supported a finding of *prima facie* jurisdiction. The Court would revisit this issue at the jurisdiction and admissibility stage of the case.[31]

While the United States focused primarily on jurisdiction, it also argued that it was Nicaragua, not the United States, that was using unlawful force in Central America. The U.S. used a line of reasoning reminiscent of Iran's argument in the *Hostages* case[32] that the ICJ should not take jurisdiction because the fact situation was too complex for a court and that a multilateral negotiating process (the Contadora process) was underway and could be disrupted if the ICJ took the case. Nicaragua responded that the Court was a uniquely competent and appropriate place for resolution of the legal issues Nicaragua had presented. It could, as it had in *Hostages*, respond to a crisis at the same time as negotiations and other procedures were ongoing.

The ICJ agreed with Nicaragua and ordered provisional measures pending the outcome of the case. It voted unanimously to dismiss the U.S. request for a blanket rejection of the case. It also voted unanimously that the United States stop blockading Nicaraguan ports and laying mines and that that the parties should not aggravate the situation or in any way prejudice the outcome of the case. However, the vote was fourteen to one that the United States not threaten, use force against, or intervene in Nicaragua's internal affairs. The American judge, Stephen Schwebel, wrote a lengthy dissent that this part of the order should have been aimed at Nicaragua, too, even though the United States had not claimed that Nicaragua was using force against it or intervening in its affairs. Schwebel criticized the order for failing to treat the parties equally. The U.S. government took up the theme of unequal treatment thereafter, arguing that the Court was unfair to the United States and biased in favor of Nicaragua.

On close examination, the charge of bias is not borne out. Respecting the provisional measures order, for example, equal treatment as the United States characterized it would have required an order to Nicaragua to stop attacking the United States, despite the fact the U.S. made no claim that Nicaragua had attacked it or even intended to attack it. Judge Schwebel made the novel argument that the Court should have made the order on behalf of states not before it, El Salvador, Costa Rica, and Honduras. He suggested the United States was acting for these states and the order could be made to Nicaragua on an *erga omnes* theory or by

---

31 *See infra* text accompanying notes 43–51.

32 Case Concerning United States Diplomatic and Consular Staff in Tehran (U.S. v. Iran), 1980 I.C.J. 34 (May 24).

the Court's own power to fashion a remedy.[33] The British judge, Robert Jennings, and the German judge, Hermann Mosler, also thought this part of the order should have required Nicaragua to refrain from intervening and using force against any state. They emphasized the need for all parties to resolve disputes peacefully.[34]

This aspect of Schwebel's opinion, however, was not as influential as the fact that he, Jennings, and Mosler had joined in the votes against the United States on such concrete orders as ceasing the mining of Nicaragua's harbors and ending attacks on port facilities. These votes were a sensation. Judges of the ICJ are supposed to be impartial, but the sad history has been and continues to be that judges most often vote for their states of nationality or for the states that put them on the Court as judges *ad hoc* when no national is already a member of the Court. Judge Schwebel voted against the United States on a concrete point of military strategy. His vote sent a strong message. It was around the time of the provisional measures order that the United States ended the secret mining of Nicaraguan harbors.[35] The U.S. Congress voted to cut funding to the Executive Branch for future mining. Two years later, the ICJ noted that the United States had complied with its order to cease mining and other interference with Nicaragua's ports[36]—a rare occasion, hardly remarked upon decades later, of compliance with ICJ provisional measures.

El Salvador's Attempt to Intervene. Following the decision on provisional measures, El Salvador attempted to intervene under Article 63 of the ICJ Statute. Article 63 permits intervention of right for any state concerned about the interpretation of a treaty to which the intervening state is a party. Nicaragua had cited the U.N. Charter, the Charter of the Organization of American States, and other treaties in which El Salvador proclaimed an interest. All of the judges except Judge Schwebel voted that El Salvador's attempt to intervene was premature.[37] The majority said that to allow a state to intervene before the Court had decided whether it even had jurisdiction made little sense. El Salvador could have a hearing on intervention after the decision on jurisdiction. Oddly, five (Western) judges voting against intervention nevertheless voted to hold a hearing. They wrote it would be "in accordance with judicial

33 *Military and Paramilitary Activities*, 1984 I.C.J. at 190 (Dissenting Opinion of Judge Schwebel).

34 *Id.* at 189 (Separate Opinion of Judges Mosler and Jennings).

35 N.Y. TIMES, May 11, 1984, at A8 (statement of Mr. Hughes, U.S. Dep't of State). *See also* Mary Ellen O'Connell, *Prospects for Enforcing Monetary Judgments of the International Court of Justice: A Study of Nicaragua's Judgment Against the United States*, 30 VA. J. INT'L L. 891, 892 n.8 (1990)).

36 Military and Paramilitary Activities in and against Nicaragua (Nicar. v. U.S.), 1986 I.C.J. 14, 143–44 (June 27).

37 Military and Paramilitary Activities in and against Nicaragua (Nicar. v. U.S.), Declaration of Intervention, Order, 1984 I.C.J. 215 (Oct. 4).

propriety."[38] The United States cited the failure to hold a hearing as another example of bias. Three months later, when the Court found it had jurisdiction, El Salvador did not renew its attempt to intervene.

Jurisdiction and Admissibility. On November 26, 1984, the Court issued its decision on both jurisdiction and admissibility. It found it had jurisdiction on two bases. First, both the United States and Nicaragua had validly accepted its optional compulsory jurisdiction. In addition, the parties had a bilateral Treaty of Friendship, Commerce and Navigation (FCN) that committed them to go to the ICJ to resolve disputes under that treaty.[39] Some of the criticism of the Court's decision on its optional jurisdiction overlooks this second basis for jurisdiction in the case. The Court also found the case admissible, ironically, for many of the same reasons it had found the U.S. case against Iran admissible just five years previously in the *Hostages* case, brought by the United States against Iran.[40]

The optional compulsory jurisdiction issue took up the greater part of the decision on jurisdiction and admissibility, and probably remains the most criticized aspect of the decisions in the case. The Court's optional jurisdiction was originally devised for the 1920 Statute of the Permanent Court of International Justice (PCIJ), the predecessor of the ICJ, as an interim step toward general compulsory jurisdiction.[41] Once the PCIJ was established, promoting the "World Court" and compulsory jurisdiction became a major cause for international law scholars and the world's peace movements alike.[42]

The ICJ had already reviewed Nicaragua's Article 36(2) declaration accepting the PCIJ's compulsory jurisdiction in the provisional measures phase. It took up the declaration again during its full consideration of jurisdiction.[43] It seems that in 1929 Nicaragua signed a declaration accepting the optional compulsory jurisdiction of the PCIJ, the same provision found in the ICJ's Statute. That meant Nicaragua had accepted the PCIJ's jurisdiction on the basis of reciprocity with every other state that had declared its acceptance. Declarations of acceptance of

[38] *Id.* at 219 (Separate Opinion of Judges Ruda, Mosler, Ago, Jennings, and de Lacharrière).

[39] Treaty of Friendship, Commerce and Navigation, U.S.-Nicar., Jan. 21, 1956, 9 U.S.T. 449 [hereinafter FCN Treaty].

[40] Case Concerning United States Diplomatic and Consular Staff in Tehran (U.S. v. Iran), 1980 I.C.J. 34 (May 24).

[41] Lorna Lloyd, *"A Springboard for the Future": A Historical Examination of Britain's Role in Shaping the Optional Clause of the Permanent Court of International Justice*, 79 AM. J. INT'L L. 28, 40–41 (1985).

[42] *See, e.g.*, Bernard H. Oxman, *Complementary Agreements and Compulsory Jurisdiction*, 95 AM. J. INT'L L. 227 (2001). Elihu Root, a U.S. Senator, Secretary of State, Secretary of War, and founder of the American Society of International Law, had been the U.S. member of the drafting committee. He spent much of his career promoting international courts.

[43] Military and Paramilitary Activities in and against Nicaragua (Nicar. v. U.S.), 1984 I.C.J. 392, 399 (Nov. 26).

compulsory jurisdiction required no ratification, but the PCIJ Statute did require ratification before a state could become a party to it. In 1938 Nicaragua sent a telegram announcing that the relevant branches of its government had finally approved Nicaraguan ratification of the PCIJ Statute and that the instrument of ratification was to follow. Apparently, the document never arrived at the office of the treaty depositary in Geneva.[44]

Nicaraguan officials argued that their predecessors had ratified the Statute of the PCIJ and had sent the instrument of ratification to Geneva. Nicaragua suggested that given the fact World War II was in full progress when the document was sent by ship to Europe, its ratification document might have been sunk along with the ship carrying it.[45]

After World War II, the ICJ was created to succeed the PCIJ and to become the chief legal organ of the new United Nations. The Statute of the ICJ was virtually the same as that of the PCIJ, but it did provide for the transition to the new court, including in Article 36(5), which states:

> Declarations made under Article 36 of the Statute of the Permanent Court of International Justice and which are still in force shall be deemed, as between the parties to the present Statute, to be acceptances of the compulsory jurisdiction of the International Court of Justice for the period which they still have to run and in accordance with their terms.

The French version is slightly different. It says that declarations that have not yet expired can be deemed acceptances of the ICJ's compulsory jurisdiction ("*pour un duré qui n'est pas encore expiré*").[46] The Court decided that while Nicaragua's declaration had never come into force, it had also never "expired." As soon as Nicaragua became a party to the U.N. Charter and the ICJ Statute, its Article 36(2) declaration became binding.

In addition to this structural argument, the Court also pointed to the treatment of the declaration after 1946. Nicaragua was listed as a party to the PCIJ in the *Yearbooks* of the ICJ and other publications. The United States was never a party to the PCIJ, but became a party to the ICJ and accepted the Court's compulsory jurisdiction in 1946.[47] Beginning with the 1955–1956 *Yearbook*, editors began adding a footnote mentioning that Nicaragua's instrument of ratification had never been received. Still, in Nicaragua's previous case at the ICJ, the 1960 *King of*

[44] *Id.*

[45] *Id.* at 399–400.

[46] Compare *LaGrand*, in which the Court again looked to the French version of the Statute for language supporting its decision that the Court's provisional measures are binding. LaGrand Case (F.R.G. v. U.S.), 2001 I.C.J. 466, 504–05 (June 27).

[47] Declaration on the Part of the United States of America, Aug. 14, 1946, 61 Stat. 1218; *see supra* note 27.

Spain case,[48] Honduras had referred to Nicaragua's 1929 acceptance.[49] The ICJ reviewed the U.S. evidence that Nicaragua did not consider itself bound by its declaration, although the Court found these indications vague compared with the evidence supporting the contrary view. By the time the case was filed in 1984, the Court determined that Nicaragua had acquiesced in public recognition that it had accepted the Court's compulsory jurisdiction.[50] This perhaps generous view of the matter was, as the Court pointed out, consistent with the purpose of Article 36(5), which was to maintain progress toward the great goal of compulsory jurisdiction. The vote was eleven to five in favor of jurisdiction under the optional clause.[51]

There was another indication of public recognition respecting Nicaragua's declaration—one the Court does not mention. Recall that on April 6, 1984, just three days before Nicaragua filed the case, the United States had attempted to modify its own optional clause declaration by excluding Central American cases. The U.S. attempt at modification indicated that it believed Nicaragua had a valid declaration. The U.S. attempt also indicates that there was no unfair surprise when the Court found Nicaragua's declaration valid.

Almost twenty years previously, the ICJ had dismissed a case by Liberia and Ethiopia against South Africa on a narrow reading of standing,[52] a reading that reversed a position it had taken earlier in the same case.[53] That decision had seemed to many to be a case of pure preference for a white, prosperous state against black, impoverished ones. In the *Nicaragua* case, the ICJ read a jurisdiction provision broadly, giving some the impression of favoring a small, impoverished state. Perhaps it was significant that the President of the Court at the time of the jurisdiction decision in the *Nicaragua* case was T.O. Elias, an African.

The Court had a number of other issues to deal with in the decision on jurisdiction and admissibility in addition to the important question of the optional clause. The U.S. attempt to exclude Central American cases from the scope of its optional clause declaration three days before Nicaragua filed its cases was easily dismissed by the Court. The 1946 U.S. declaration accepting the Court's optional jurisdiction included a six-month notice provision for termination.[54] The ICJ did not allow the United States to ignore the notice provision in making a "modification" to

48 Arbitral Award Made by the King of Spain on 23 December 1906 (Hond. v. Nicar.), 1960 I.C.J. 192 (Nov. 18).

49 *Military and Paramilitary Activities*, 1984 I.C.J. at 399–400.

50 *Id.* at 411.

51 *See also* Military and Paramilitary Activities in and against Nicaragua (Nicar. v. U.S.), 1986 I.C.J. 14, 158, 161–65 (June 27) (Separate Opinion of Judge Lachs).

52 South West Africa Cases, Second Phase (Eth. v. S. Afr.; Liber. v. S. Afr.), 1966 I.C.J. 6 (July 18).

53 South West Africa Cases, Preliminary Objections (Eth. v. S. Afr.; Liber. v. S. Afr.), 1962 I.C.J. 319 (Dec. 21).

54 *See supra* note 27.

its acceptance.[55] Indeed, allowing modifications or terminations without some reasonable period of notice would, of course, make nonsense of the system of compulsory jurisdiction, allowing states to modify declarations to restrict their acceptance as soon as they learned of an impending application.

The Court did give effect to a reservation in the U.S. acceptance of compulsory jurisdiction. The reservation, named for Senator Vandenberg, excluded from the scope of acceptance any case involving a treaty that did not include other affected states. The Court found this reservation applied but put off until the merits stage its precise impact.[56]

The Court also turned briefly to the bilateral Treaty of Friendship, Commerce and Navigation,[57] finding that the treaty's conditions for triggering the Court's jurisdiction had all been met. Only Judges Schwebel and Ruda voted against finding jurisdiction under the treaty. Judge Ruda had voted in favor of the compulsory jurisdiction ground, however, so only Judge Schwebel found no ground for jurisdiction at all.

The last part of the opinion concerns the five arguments made by the United States against admissibility. None of these were particularly persuasive: the absence of indispensable parties; preference for a regional peace process; separation of powers between the Security Council and the Court; non-justiciability; and failure to exhaust established procedures of peaceful settlement.[58] Several of these arguments were dismissed by the Court relying on the *Hostages*[59] and *Corfu Channel*[60] cases, two cases involving on-going crises being pursued in multiple fora, including the Security Council. The United States itself had argued in the *Hostages* case that the Court had jurisdiction over questions of international law at the same time the Security Council was dealing with political aspects of a matter.[61] The Court found no basis in international law for the assertions that regional peace processes had priority in peaceful settlement or that such processes had to be exhausted before going to the premier body for peaceful settlement, the ICJ. The judges voted unanimously to reject the five U.S. arguments.

Despite the fact that fifteen judges—all but the U.S. judge—found jurisdiction in the case and that all sixteen found the case admissible, the United States took the very public position that the Court was wrong. According to the Reagan administration, the "objectives of the court were being subverted by the efforts of Nicaragua and its Cuban and Soviet

---

55 *Military and Paramilitary Activities*, 1984 I.C.J. at 419–21.

56 *Id.* at 421–23.

57 FCN Treaty, *supra* note 39.

58 *Military and Paramilitary Activities*, 1984 I.C.J. at 429–41.

59 Case Concerning United States Diplomatic and Consular Staff in Tehran (U.S. v. Iran), 1980 I.C.J. 34 (May 24).

60 Corfu Channel (U.K. v. Alb.), 1949 I.C.J. 4 (Apr. 9).

61 *Diplomatic and Consular Staff*, 1980 I.C.J. at 20–24.

sponsors to use the court as a political weapon."[62] Consequently, the United States notified the Court in January 1985 that it would no longer participate in the case. When oral arguments went forward in September, the United States informed the Court that it also would be terminating its acceptance of the Court's compulsory jurisdiction. Editorial page opinion in the United States ranged from utter dismay at the abandonment of an American ideal of peaceful settlement of disputes through courts to congratulations to the Reagan administration for its realism.[63]

Merits. The Court's judgment on the merits deals with such important matters as the nature of customary international law, the parameters of collective self-defense, the principles of necessity and proportionality, and state responsibility for the actions of non-state actors. The Court's various decisions on these questions turned significantly on its findings of fact. So the first issue the Court addressed was the sufficiency of the evidence. Judge Schwebel in his dissenting opinion on the merits accused the Court of believing "false testimony" by Nicaraguan government representatives.[64] The Court acknowledged that the United States had not been there to counter this testimony, but the U.S. publication, *Revolution Beyond Our Borders*, supplemented the U.S. submissions in the provisional measures, intervention, and jurisdiction phases. The Court also had Judge Schwebel's perspective. He appended an almost 300-page dissenting opinion, which the other judges also had available during deliberations.[65] Schwebel's strongly worded dissent attracted no other judge, but it probably does account for lingering doubts about the Court's findings. Given all of the material before it, however, and Schwebel's arguments, the Court made a sound assessment of the facts. If there were points on which the United States thought the Court erred, it must be accepted, as the Court pointed out, that the U.S. forfeited "the opportunity to counter the factual allegations of its opponent."[66]

After reviewing the sufficiency of the evidence, the Court turned next to the U.S. multilateral treaty reservation. The Court had already found the reservation valid during the jurisdiction phase. In the merits phase, the Court ruled that because El Salvador, Costa Rica, and Honduras could be affected by the Court's interpretation of treaties in the case, the

---

62 *US Withdrawal Another Blow to "World Court," supra* note 2; *see also* Norman Kemptster, *Court: U.S. Restricts Participation; U.S. Rejects "Compulsory" World Court Jurisdiction*, L.A. TIMES, Oct. 8, 1985, at 1.

63 *See, e.g., An Appalling Choice*, MIAMI HERALD, Oct. 9, 1985 ("The dreams of American idealists of both parties who sought a more-just world order were shattered."); *Parrying the World Court*, CHI. TRIBUNE, Oct. 9, 1985, at 14 ("The Reagan administration made the right decision by limiting its cooperation with the international court.").

64 Military and Paramilitary Activities in and against Nicaragua (Nicar. v. U.S.), 1986 I.C.J. 14, 259 (June 27) (Dissenting Opinion of Judge Schwebel).

65 E-mail from Judge Stephen Schwebel to Prof. Mary Ellen O'Connell (Jan. 31, 2007) (on file with the author).

66 *Military and Paramilitary Activities*, 1986 I.C.J. at 25.

Court would exclude consideration of the treaties cited by Nicaragua and instead base its decision on customary and general international law. Judge Jennings, the British judge, dissented on this point, arguing that no evidence of custom could be found clearly distinct from the important treaties in question. Judge Elias noted in his separate opinion, by contrast, that once the three potentially affected states refused to exercise their right to intervene, the matter should have ended there.[67] Treaties should have come into the case. Other judges joined him in voting against giving any effect to the multilateral treaty reservation. In their view, it was not only not relevant, it was an impermissible reservation.[68]

The majority, however, voted to go ahead without applying any multilateral treaty. They pointed out that, first, there *is* discernable evidence of rules on use of force that is quite separate from treaty rules. These rules would obviously apply in the case. Second, the Court found sufficient evidence that many treaty rules existed in identical form in customary international law. As for the first category, the general prohibition on the use of force found in U.N. Charter Article 2(4), both parties acknowledged it had become a rule of *jus cogens*.[69] As such it was non-derogable and more fundamental than a treaty rule. The Court reached this conclusion relying, in part, on the U.S.'s own pleadings in the case. The Court also found that such important rules as the principles of necessity and proportionality did not depend on treaties.[70]

The Court also found some rules identical in treaty and custom. In these cases, the Court could cite the treaty rule as it was co-extensive with the customary law rule. The *North Sea Continental Shelf Cases* had discussed the process whereby a rule that began as a treaty rule could develop into a rule of customary international law.[71]

The Court also dealt with the vexing problem of state practice contrary to the rules on the use of force. Some critics argue there are no rules of custom on resort to force because of the large amount of contrary practice.[72] Since the adoption of the U.N. Charter there have been plenty of cases of states using force unlawfully, begging the question of how a rule could be a rule of custom if it was so widely violated. Where is the "general practice" that Article 38 of the ICJ's own Statute requires for a customary norm? The Court responded in a highly significant observation on the nature of customary international law:

> It is not to be expected that in the practice of States the application of the rules in question should have been perfect, in

---

67 *Id.* at 178 (Separate Opinion of Judge Elias).

68 *See id.* at 174, 178, 192, 201 (Separate Opinions of Judges Ruda, Elias, Sette-Camara, and Ni).

69 *Id.* at 100–01.

70 *Id.* at 98.

71 *Id.* (citing North Sea Continental Shelf Cases (F.R.G./Den.; F.R.G./Neth.), 1969 I.C.J. 3 (Feb. 20)).

72 *See, e.g.*, MICHAEL GLENNON, LIMITS OF LAW, PREROGATIVES OF POWER 84 (2001).

> the sense that States should have refrained, with complete consistency, from the use of force or from intervention in each other's internal affairs. The Court does not consider that, for a rule to be established as customary, the corresponding practice must be in absolutely rigorous conformity with the rule. In order to deduce the existence of customary rules, the Court deems it sufficient that the conduct of States should, in general, be consistent with such rules, and that instances of State conduct inconsistent with a given rule should generally have been treated as breaches of that rule, not as indications of the recognition of a new rule. If a State acts in a way *prima facie* incompatible with a recognized rule, but defends its conduct by appealing to exceptions or justifications contained within the rule itself, then whether or not the State's conduct is in fact justifiable on that basis, the significance of that attitude is to confirm rather than to weaken the rule.[73]

Looking to evidence of state practice and *opinio juris*, including U.N. General Assembly resolutions, arguments of the parties in their pleadings, and treaties, the Court could identify a number of rules of customary international law relevant to the case. It found, for example, that the right to resort to collective self-defense is triggered by an armed attack in customary international law and the Charter.[74]

The Court found evidence that between July 1979 and early 1981 arms had been supplied to rebels fighting the government of El Salvador from or through Nicaragua. The Court held that even if it assumed the Nicaraguan government had participated in supplying these weapons, this behavior did not amount to an armed attack.[75] The Court determined that an armed attack on El Salvador was the "*sine qua non*" that must exist to justify, as self-defense, armed attacks on Nicaragua of the kind the United States had carried out, including mining harbors and attacking port facilities, oil installations, and a naval base.[76] (The U.S. funding of the Contras also did not amount to an armed attack on Nicaragua.[77]) The Court found no evidence that the three states in

---

[73] *Military and Paramilitary Activities*, 1986 I.C.J. at 98.

[74] *Id.* at 102–04. The ICJ's focus on customary international law raises the issue why the Court did not focus on *jus cogens* when it needed to consider a different source of law other than treaties. *Jus cogens* norms, also known as peremptory norms, are not derived from treaties. Very few norms are in the category—the prohibitions of force, torture, slavery, genocide, apartheid, and a few others. These norms were once explained using natural law theory since they do not rely on the positive law methods of treaty or customary international law. By the time of *Nicaragua*, however, natural law was being suppressed. The ICJ has never discussed natural law or *jus cogens* in any detail beyond acknowledging the existence of peremptory norms. It appeared to treat *jus cogens* like customary international law, missing an opportunity to educate. *See* MARY ELLEN O'CONNELL, THE ART OF LAW IN THE INTERNATIONAL COMMUNITY ch. 2 (2019).

[75] *Military and Paramilitary Activities*, 1986 I.C.J. at 119.

[76] *Id.* at 118, 122–23. The Court said its decision did not concern anticipatory armed attacks, as the case concerned actions that had already occurred. *Id.* at 120.

[77] *Id.* at 118–19.

question had acted consistently with being under armed attack. Nor had the United States made a report to the Security Council explaining that its use of force against Nicaragua was in response to Nicaraguan attacks on its neighbors.[78]

The Court also emphasized that any armed attack giving rise to a right of self-defense or collective self-defense must be a significant attack.

> The Court sees no reason to deny that, in customary law, the prohibition of armed attacks may apply to the sending by a State of armed bands to the territory of another State, if such an operation, because of its scale and effects, would have been classified as an armed attack rather than as a mere frontier incident had it been carried out by regular armed forces.[79]

Attacks or provision of support to armed groups below the requisite threshold may violate the principle of non-intervention but not Article 2(4). Even where a significant armed attack does occur, the right of a state acting in individual or collective self-defense must conform its response to the restraining principles of necessity and proportionality:

> On the question of necessity, the Court observes that the United States measures taken in December 1981 . . . cannot be said to correspond to a "necessity." . . . First, these measures were only taken, and began to produce their effects, several months after the major offensive of the armed opposition against the Government of El Salvador had been completely repulsed (January 1981), and the actions of the opposition considerably reduced in consequence. Thus, it was possible to eliminate the main danger to the Salvadorian Government without the United States embarking on activities in and against Nicaragua. . . . Whether or not the assistance to the contras might meet the criterion of proportionality, the Court cannot regard . . . the mining of the Nicaraguan ports and the attacks on ports, oil installations, etc., as satisfying that criterion. . . . [T]he Court must also observe that the reaction of the United States in the context of what it regarded as self-defense was continued long after the period in which any presumed armed attack by Nicaragua could reasonably be contemplated.[80]

The Court is here referring to necessity and proportionality as an aspect of the *jus ad bellum*. It separately discussed the need for any state using force to respect the restraints found in the *jus in bello* (international humanitarian law).

---

[78] *Id.* at 120–23. Article 51 of the U.N. Charter requires that a report be made: "Measures taken by Members in the exercise of this right of self-defence shall be immediately reported to the Security Council."

[79] *Id.* at 103–04. "[I]t will be necessary to distinguish the most grave forms of the use of force (those constituting an armed attack) from other less grave forms." *Id.* at 101.

[80] *Id.* at 122–23.

In those cases where violence or intervention in a state is not sufficiently grave or where an armed response cannot be justified on the basis of necessity and proportionality, the victim state may turn to countermeasures. Countermeasures are actions short of armed force that may violate international law but are justifiable because they respond to a prior violation. Economic sanctions are the most common form of countermeasure. The Court explained that only the injured state may use countermeasures. International law does not permit "collective countermeasures."[81]

Without a basis in the right of collective self-defense, it was the United States, not Nicaragua, that had breached the Article 2(4) prohibition on the use of force through mining ships and air attacks.[82] U.S. financial, logistical, and training support to the Contras was not an armed attack on Nicaragua. This support did, however, violate the principle of nonintervention.[83] Provision of humanitarian assistance—food, medicine, and clothing—does not violate the principle of nonintervention.[84] Similarly, breach of economic treaties does not violate the principle of nonintervention.[85] Nevertheless, the Court found that such activity did breach the FCN Treaty, a separate wrong from intervention.[86]

The Court found in the U.S.'s favor on one important claim. The United States did not share responsibility for human rights violations committed by the Contras. The evidence of U.S. complicity in human rights violations was serious. The Court had before it the manual created by the CIA that advocated assassination, along with other criminal conduct. The Court chose, however, a high threshold for attribution to a state of the acts of non-state actors, namely that the state must "control" the non-state actor.[87] The United States did not control the Contras under the Court's test.

Seven judges appended separate opinions, and three added dissenting opinions. Four of the separate opinions expressed the view that the U.S. multilateral treaty reservation should not have been applied. By contrast, Judges Oda and Jennings wrote in their dissenting opinions that the Court had not given sufficient effect to the multilateral treaty reservation. Judge Schwebel's dissent was the most noteworthy, not least because of its length. It was the longest dissenting opinion in the Court's history. Previously, the longest dissent was by also by an American judge, Philip Jessup. That was a very different opinion. Judge

---

[81] *Id.* at 110–11, 127.

[82] *Id.* at 124–25.

[83] *Id.*

[84] *Id.* at 125.

[85] *Id.* at 126.

[86] *Id.* at 140–41.

[87] *Id.* at 64–65.

Jessup had found fault with the Court's decision *not* to hear the cases brought by Ethiopia and Liberia against South Africa.[88]

Schwebel went into great detail to undermine the credibility of the Nicaraguan officials who testified in the case. Three officials had stated that Nicaragua had had no involvement in providing arms or training to the national liberation front (the FMLN) fighting in El Salvador. Nicaragua's chief witness, a former CIA agent, testified that the Nicaraguan government had been involved in arms shipments in 1980 through January 1981. Although this testimony clashed with that of Nicaraguan officials, it did not really undermine the Court's conclusion on the point. The Court had accepted for the purpose of its ruling that Nicaragua had been involved in low-level weapons shipments until early 1981.[89]

Of the Court's important contributions to the jurisprudence on the use of force its emphasis on significance and scale of an attack may be the most important. The Charter is clear regarding the need for an armed attack to trigger the right of self-defense. It is less clear regarding the nature of the armed attack. The majority in *Nicaragua* decided, consistently with the principles and purposes of the U.N. Charter and the historic development of this area of international law, that only a significant armed attack will give rise to a right to use force in turn on the territory of the attacking state. This decision together with the application of the general principles of attribution, necessity, and

---

[88] *South West Africa Cases*, 1966 I.C.J. at 325 (Dissenting Opinion of Judge Jessup).

[89] On weapons shipments, the ICJ held:

> As regards El Salvador, the Court . . . is satisfied that between July 1979 and the early months of 1981, an intermittent flow of arms was routed via the territory of Nicaragua to the armed opposition in that country. The Court was not however satisfied that assistance has reached the Salvadorian armed opposition, on a scale of any significance, since the early months of 1981, or that the Government of Nicaragua was responsible for any flow of arms at either period. Even assuming that the supply of arms to the opposition in El Salvador could be treated as imputable to the Government of Nicaragua, to justify invocation of the right of collective self-defence in customary international law, it would have to be equated with an armed attack by Nicaragua on El Salvador. As stated above, the Court is unable to consider that, in customary international law, the provision of arms to the opposition in another State constitutes an armed attack on that State. Even at a time when the arms flow was at its peak, and again assuming the participation of the Nicaraguan Government, that would not constitute such armed attack.

Military and Paramilitary Activities, 1986 I.C.J. at 119.

The C.I.A. agent who testified for Nicaragua was Dr. David C. MacMichael. His obituary said that following his testimony he became "a pariah among former colleagues in the intelligence community." He was quoted for the view, however, that the ostracism had been worth it because his testimony " 'was my one ethical plus in a lifetime of unethical behavior.' " Clay Risen, *David C. MacMichael, 95, Is Dead: Ex-C.I.A. Analyst Blew the Whistle*, N.Y. TIMES, June 2, 2022, at A21.

proportionality all underscore that the international legal right to use force is highly limited.[90]

III. THE IMPACT OF THE *NICARAGUA* CASE

Four decades after the *Nicaragua* decision, the case's abiding impact has been on the international law governing the use of force and on the stature of the International Court of Justice. The Court's stature undoubtedly rose after the case and keeps rising. The judgment has at least preserved the prohibition on the use of force, despite unremitting attempts, by the United States in particular, to weaken it. The U.S.'s reputation for law compliance was harmed by the decision and even more, in the years that followed, by its actions violating the prohibition and its attempts to reinterpret the law to fit U.S. practice. In a dark irony, Nicaragua's reputation for law compliance is lower today than the U.S.'s.

Respecting the law on the use of force, it is increasingly significant that the ICJ referred to the prohibition on force as a *jus cogens* norm. In his separate opinion in the highly consequential *Advisory Opinion on the Legal Consequences of the Construction of a Wall in the Occupied Palestinian Territory*, Judge Elaraby emphasized that "[t]he prohibition of the use of force . . . is universally recognized as a *jus cogens* principle, a peremptory norm from which no derogation is permitted."[91] In the *Advisory Opinion on the Legality of the Threat or Use of Nuclear Weapons*, the Court found that self-defense is subject "to the conditions of necessity and proportionality."[92] The need to comply with these principles is well established in international law. It is not enough to point to an attack of some sort at some point in the past.

The Court repeated these points in the *Oil Platforms* case between Iran and the United States.[93] It emphasized that self-defense is only triggered by forms of force that amount to significant armed attacks.[94] It also pointed out that the nature of the target must be part of the consideration of whether a counter-attack is both necessary and proportionate under international law.[95]

Subsequent cases have taken up *Nicaragua*'s discussion of attribution. Judge Higgins explained in *The Wall* case, referencing *Nicaragua*, that "military action by irregulars could constitute an armed attack if these were sent by or on behalf of the State and if the activity

---

90 For contemporary scholarly reactions (mixed) to the *Nicaragua* case, see *Appraisals of the ICJ's Decision: Nicaragua v. United States (Merits)*, 81 AM. J. INT'L L. 77 (1987).

91 Legal Consequences of the Construction of a Wall in the Occupied Palestinian Territory, Advisory Opinion, 2004 I.C.J. 136, 246, ¶ 3.1 (July 9) (Separate Opinion of Judge Elaraby).

92 Legality of the Threat or Use of Nuclear Weapons, Advisory Opinion, 1996 I.C.J. 226, ¶ 41 (July 8) (citing *Military and Paramilitary Activities*, 1986 I.C.J. at 94).

93 Oil Platforms (Iran v. U.S.), 2003 I.C.J. 161, ¶ 51 (Nov. 6).

94 *Id.* (citing *Military and Paramilitary Activities*, 1986 I.C.J. at 101).

95 *Oil Platforms*, 2003 I.C.J. ¶ 76.

'because of its scale and effects, would have been classified as an armed attack . . . had it been carried out by regular armed forces.' "[96]

In *Case Concerning Armed Activities on the Territory of the Congo (Congo v. Uganda)*,[97] the Court cited the *Nicaragua* case no fewer than eighteen times. It emphasized the magnitude and duration of Uganda's use of force against Congo, amounting to a "grave violation of the prohibition on the use of force expressed in Article 2, paragraph 4, of the Charter."[98]

In *Bosnia and Herzegovina v. Serbia*,[99] it invoked *Nicaragua*'s test for attribution to the state of the acts of non-state actors. This is a test of control, not the lesser test of coordination and material support found in a judgment of the International Criminal Tribunal for the former Yugoslavia.[100]

In addition to its impact on jurisprudence, the *Nicaragua* case also significantly impacted Nicaraguan and U.S. politics. Nicaraguan officials initially hailed the decision as a victory. Yet, it may well have launched the chain of events that led to the Sandinistas being ousted from power when they agreed after the case to permit elections. Nicaraguan President Daniel Ortega Saaverda said the ruling would give Nicaragua "more strength to resist, combat and defeat the aggressive, terrorist policy of the U.S. leaders."[101] Nicaraguan foreign minister Miguel d'Escoto praised the decision as a victory for not only Nicaragua but also for Latin America, the Third World, and all people who desire peace. Much of the international community shared his impression that the ICJ "clearly and definitely defended Nicaragua's rights to life, peace, self-determination, independence."[102] D'Escoto also acknowledged, however, that the victory at the ICJ was unlikely to mean the end of U.S. military activities against Nicaragua.

> We must remain alert, because although this has been a victory for peace, peace has not yet been achieved in Nicaragua because

---

[96] *Legal Consequences of the Construction of a Wall*, 2004 I.C.J. at 207, ¶ 33 (Separate Opinion of Judge Higgins) (quoting *Military and Paramilitary Activities*, 1986 I.C.J. at 103).

[97] Armed Activities in the Territory of the Congo (Congo v. Uganda), 2005 I.C.J. 168 (Dec. 19).

[98] *Id.* ¶ 165.

[99] *Id.* ¶ 160; Application of the Convention on the Prevention and Punishment of the Crime of Genocide (Bosn. & Herz. v. Serb. and Mont.), 2007 I.C.J. 47, ¶¶ 391–393 (Feb. 26).

[100] Prosecutor v. Tadić, Case No. IT–94–1–A, Judgment, ¶ 137 (Appeals Chamber, July 15, 1999).

[101] *Quoted in* Tracy Wilkinson, *President Ortega leads march, calls Contra aid a declaration of war*, UNITED PRESS INT'L (June 28, 1986), https://www.upi.com/Archives/1986/06/28/President-Ortega-leads-march-calls-Contra-aid-a-declaration-of-war/8179520315200/.

[102] *Interview with Foreign Minister Miguel d'Escoto Brockman by unidentified reporters at the International Court of Justice at The Hague*, Managua International Service in Spanish, June 27, 1986, *in* FBIS Daily Report—Latin America (FBIS–LAM–86–125), June 30, 1986.

> the United States continues with its warmongering stand. The United States continues on insisting on ousting our government and destroying our revolution, precisely because this revolution demands the right to independence.[103]

Indeed, the Reagan administration did not register any interest in complying with the judgment or entering into negotiations with Nicaragua on the question of damages. When the judgment on the merits was announced, State Department spokesman Charles Redman again questioned the competence of the ICJ to judge the case: the "opinion demonstrates what we have stated all along: the court is simply not equipped to deal with a case of this nature involving complex facts and intelligence information."[104]

The Court handed down its decision at the same time Congress and a special prosecutor were investigating the administration's funding of the Contras. By 1981 members of Congress had voiced doubts about the administration's policy of overthrowing the Sandinistas. Various appropriations bills through 1986 included restrictions on how the administration could spend funds to aid the Contras.[105] Congress imposed these limits in full awareness of the ICJ's decision in the *Nicaragua* case. The administration responded by seeking ways to fund the Contras, evading congressional restrictions. Several foreign governments were contacted to provide funds, and an elaborate scheme involving arms purchases by Iran was hatched. Because of Iran's involvement, the administration's attempts were later labeled the "Iran-Contra Affair" or "Iran-Contra Scandal." By the late 1980s the Reagan administration had become infamous for supporting the Contras in violation of U.S. domestic and international law.

In addition to Congress, members of the Contadora group[106] condemned continuing U.S. aid to the Contras. They feared it would increase tension in the region and undermine the Contadora peace process.[107] Mexican Foreign Secretary Bernardo Sepulveda Amor stated on behalf of the Contadora group that the U.S. decision to continue aid to the Contras was "a historic mistake that may damage inter-American relations" and the peace process.[108]

---

103 *Id.*

104 *Quoted in* Loren Jenkins, *World Court Says U.S. Violates International Law by Aiding Contras*, WASH. POST, June 27, 1986, at A1. *See also* Patrick M. Norton, *The* Nicaragua *Case: Political Questions Before the International Court of Justice*, 27 VA. J. INT'L L. 459 (1987); Dana Walker, *Experts: U.S., world court lose in Nicaragua Case*, UNITED PRESS INT'L (June 28, 1986), https://www.upi.com/Archives/1986/06/28/Experts-US-world-court-lose-in-Nicaragua-case/7775520315200/.

105 For details on the various spending bills, see Andrew W. Hayes, *The Boland Amendments and Foreign Affairs Deference*, 88 COLUM. L. REV. 1534, 1566–69 (1988).

106 *See supra* note 18.

107 *Wagner on U.S.-Contadora Relations, Debt Crisis*, Lima Caretas, June 30, 1986, *in* FBIS Daily Report—Latin America (FBIS–LAM–86–137), July 17, 1986.

108 *Quoted in* Roberto Gonzalez Perez, *Contadora Group Condemns U.S. Contra Aid Approval*, Mexico City XHDF Television Network, June 27, 1986, *in* FBIS Daily Report—

Under this pressure from inside and outside, the United States shifted course. Rather than funding militias, it began funding the political opposition in Nicaragua. The Sandinistas had associated themselves with law, courts, and peaceful process of change through the *Nicaragua* case. Now the United States demanded that the Sandinistas hold elections. They agreed, feeling confident in their popularity with the Nicaraguan people. They turned out not to be as popular as they thought.

One last filing was made in the *Nicaragua* case. In March 1988, the Sandinista government asked the ICJ to order the United States to pay $12 billion in damages. The Court made no ruling before February 25, 1990, when the Sandinistas were voted out of office. The new government, which had received generous—probably decisive—financial support during the campaign from the United States, did not, however, immediately withdraw the pending request at the Court. So, in late 1990, the United States informed Nicaragua's new leader, Violeta Chamarro, that a $300 million aid package would be held until the case was withdrawn.[109] In September 1991, Nicaragua formally requested that the Court remove the case from its list.[110]

This final event in the case, together with its impact on the U.S. political scene and the shift in U.S. policy, made a strong favorable impression on much of the world. For the International Court of Justice, the decision was a boon. Cases have poured into the Court, including important cases on the use of force. The prospects for peaceful settlement of disputes through the World Court appear as strong as ever. The Court helped preserve the Charter rules generally prohibiting the use of force among states, and the Court helped repair its own reputation as a body charged with applying the law evenhandedly to the powerful and weak alike. This new perception of the Court may also have helped support the perception of international law as real law, law superior to the decisions of national leaders, even the leaders of superpowers.

While the Court's decisions in the *Nicaragua* case did not result in an immediate end of the Reagan administration's policy of force in Central America or even a direct payment of damages, the case was still seen as a victory for small states and improved the standing of the Court in their eyes. One rough statistic indicates the impact: in the twenty years following the 1966 *South West Africa Cases*,[111] only about half a dozen cases were instituted by non-Western states. In the twenty years after

---

Latin America (FBIS–LAM–86–125), June 30, 1986. *See also Foreign Minister Deplores Nicaraguan Actions*, A.F.P. (Paris), July 9, 1986, *in* FBIS Daily Report—Latin America (FBIS–LAM–86–133), July 11, 1986.

[109] Scott Wallace, *Evading Justice*, NATION, Oct. 29, 1990, at 476.

[110] Military and Paramilitary Activities in and against Nicaragua (Nicar. v. U.S.), Order, 1991 I.C.J. 47 (Sept. 26).

[111] South West Africa Cases, Second Phase (Eth. v. S. Afr.; Liber. v. S. Afr.), 1966 I.C. J. 6 (July 18).

the 1986 *Nicaragua* case some fifty such cases had been submitted, and by 2024 the number had reached ninety-five.[112]

> By adjudicating in favor of a poor, Third World country like Nicaragua the I.C.J. has opened up an option to other Third World States whose citizens may feel that in this era of sovereign equality, some sovereigns are more equal than others. Aware of its rights as an international person, Nicaragua presented a well-argued case in a peaceful forum often regarded as an instrument of the First World.[113]

Opening this option to other Global South countries, the ICJ reinforced the basic principles of international law and reinvigorated a forum in which disputes can be resolved peacefully without fear of domination due to a disparity in size or military power.

The United States remains involved in cases at the ICJ.[114] The cases include contentious disputes brought under treaty provisions the United States agreed to in the 1950s and 1960s as well as advisory proceedings. These cases do not reflect any new embrace of the Court. Indeed, the Bush administration terminated a commitment to ICJ dispute settlement in a protocol to the Vienna Convention on Consular Relations in 2005.[115] The United States has not refused to participate in any case against it since the *Nicaragua* case. It rarely, however, complies with provisional measures orders or final judgments against it.

Daniel Ortega retook power in Nicaragua in 2006 and proceeded to hold on through repression and violence. The importance of law, the non-use of force, and the superiority of peaceful settlement of disputes through courts remains a lesson to be learned by the parties to the *Nicaragua* case and so many others.[116] This conclusion gained new support when South Africa instituted a case against Israel on behalf of the people of Gaza. U.S. officials called the case "meritless." Nicaragua sought to intervene on the side of South Africa[117] and to improve its own human rights reputation by bringing a related case against Germany for

---

[112] *See* Contentious Cases, https://www.icj-cij.org/contentious-cases (last visited July 24, 2024).

[113] Anna Leah T. Castañeda, *From Prerogative to Prohibition: Article 2(4) as Customary International Law in Nicaragua v. U.S.*, 38 ATENEO L.J. 1, 69 (1993).

[114] *See* Pending Cases, https://www.icj-cij.org/pending-cases (last visited July 24, 2024).

[115] Concerning the March 2005 U.S. withdrawal from the Optional Protocol to the Vienna Convention on Consular Relations concerning the Compulsory Settlement of Disputes, Apr. 24, 1963, 21 U.S.T. 326, 596 U.N.T.S. 488, see *Contemporary Practice of the United States Relating to International Law*, 99 AM. J. INT'L L. 489, 490 (2005).

[116] For a discussion of the Iraq invasion of 2003, the U.N. Charter, and the *Nicaragua* case, as well as some of the negative consequences for the United States of having failed to comply with international law respecting Iraq, see Mary Ellen O'Connell, *Occupation Failures and the Legality of Armed Conflict: The Case of Iraqi Cultural Prosperity,* 9 ART ANTIQUITY & L. 323 (2004).

[117] *Nicaragua Seeks to Join South Africa in World Court Genocide Case Against Israel,* REUTERS (Feb. 8, 2024), https://www.reuters.com/world/nicaragua-seeks-join-south-africa-world-court-genocide-case-against-israel-2024-02-08/.

its support of Israel.[118] Notably, Paul Reichler, who represented Nicaragua for many years in the ICJ, did not do so in the two Gaza-related cases. He moved on to advocate for the Palestinian Authority.[119] Those cases, like so many others at the ICJ, continue to draw on *Nicaragua*, the ICJ's most important judgment.

[118] Alleged Breaches of Certain International Obligations in respect of the Occupied Palestinian Territory (Nicar. v. Ger.), Application Instituting Proceedings (Mar. 1, 2024), https://www.icj-cij.org/sites/default/files/case-related/193/193-20240301-app-01-00-en.pdf.

[119] Legal Consequences arising from the Policies and Practices of Israel in the Occupied Palestinian Territory, including East Jerusalem, Verbatim Record, ¶ 3.1 (Feb. 19, 2024, 10 a.m.), https://www.icj-cij.org/sites/default/files/case-related/186/186-20240219-ora-01-00-bi.pdf.

Contributors

Roger P. Alford is a Professor of Law at Notre Dame Law School and former Deputy Assistant Attorney General in the Antitrust Division for the Department of Justice (2017–2019). He has written extensively on a variety of international law topics, including several articles related to the *Charming Betsy*. He is a graduate of Baylor University (B.A. 1985), Southern Baptist Theological Seminary (M.Div. 1988), New York University (J.D. 1991), and the University of Edinburgh (LL.M. 1992). He clerked for the Honorable James Buckley of the United States Court of Appeals for the District of Columbia and for two international tribunals, the Iran-United States Claims Tribunal in The Hague, Netherlands (1992–1994), and the Tribunal for Dormant Swiss Bank Accounts in Zurich, Switzerland (1999–2000). Prior to teaching he was an attorney with Hogan & Hartson (now Hogan Lovells) in Washington, D.C. He teaches International Law, Transnational Civil Litigation, International Commercial Arbitration, Global Antitrust, International Trade, and Constitutional Law.

David J. Bederman was the K.H. Gyr Professor of Private International Law at Emory University Law School in Atlanta, Georgia, until his death in 2011. His areas of expertise also included constitutional law, admiralty and maritime law, and legal history. Aside from his undergraduate studies at Princeton, he received a J.D. from the University of Virginia and both an M.Sc. and Ph.D. from the University of London, as well as the Diploma of the Hague Academy of International Law. Prior to his academic career, he practiced law in Washington, D.C., with the firm of Covington & Burling and worked as a legal advisor at the Iran/United States Claims Tribunal at The Hague. He wrote a number of books and dozens of articles and essays. His major publications include *International Law in Antiquity* (Cambridge University Press 2001), *The Spirit of International Law* (University of Georgia Press 2002), *International Law Frameworks* (Foundation Press, 3d ed. 2010), *The Classical Foundations of the American Constitution: Prevailing Wisdom* (Cambridge University Press 2008), and *Custom as a Source of Law* (Cambridge University Press 2010).

Laura A. Dickinson is the Lyle T. Alverson Professor of Law at The George Washington University Law School. Her work focuses on international human rights law, international humanitarian law, national security law, and foreign affairs privatization. She has authored numerous articles and book chapters, including scholarship that has appeared in the *American Journal of International Law*, the *Yale Journal of International Law*, the *Harvard National Security Journal*, the *NYU Journal of International Law and Politics*, the *William & Mary Law*

Review, the *Emory Law Journal*, and the *Southern California Law Review*. Her recent book, *Big Data and Armed Conflict*, co-edited with Ed Berg and published by Oxford University Press, grapples with international legal challenges presented by the growing use of big data in military operations. Her article entitled "National Security Policymaking in the Shadow of International Law," published in the *Utah Law Review*, won the 2021 Mike Lewis Prize for National Security Law Scholarship, awarded by the Strauss Center for International Security and Law at the University of Texas. And Professor Dickinson's prizewinning book, *Outsourcing War and Peace*, published by Yale University Press, examines the increasing outsourcing of military and security functions and considers the impact of this trend on core public values. Professor Dickinson served as Special Counsel to the General Counsel of the Department of Defense from 2016–2017 and was awarded the Secretary of Defense Medal for Exceptional Public Service for her work there. She has also served as a senior policy adviser to Harold Hongju Koh, Assistant Secretary of State for Democracy, Human Rights, and Labor at the U.S. Department of State, and is a former law clerk to U.S. Supreme Court Justices Harry A. Blackmun and Stephen G. Breyer.

William S. Dodge is the Lobingier Professor of Comparative Law and Jurisprudence at The George Washington University Law School. He is a reporter for the *Restatement (Fourth) of the Foreign Relations Law of the United States*. From 2011 to 2012, he served as Counselor on International Law to the Legal Adviser at the U.S. Department of State. Professor Dodge is a co-author of *Transnational Business Problems* (7th ed. 2024) and *Transnational Litigation in a Nutshell* (2d ed. 2021) and is the co-editor of *International Law in the U.S. Supreme Court: Continuity and Change* (2011). He has published more than 90 articles, essays, and chapters in law reviews and books. Professor Dodge received his B.A. and J.D. from Yale University and served as a law clerk to Judge William Norris of the United States Court of Appeals for the Ninth Circuit and U.S. Supreme Court Justice Harry Blackmun.

Jean Galbraith is a Professor at the University of Pennsylvania Carey Law School, where she focuses on U.S. foreign relations law and public international law. Her scholarship addresses the allocation of legal authority among U.S. governmental actors and, at the international level, between domestic actors and international regimes. Professor Galbraith received her B.A. *summa cum laude* from Harvard University and her J.D. from the University of California, Berkeley, School of Law. After graduating law school, she served as a law clerk at the D.C. Circuit (for Judge David Tatel) and at the Supreme Court of the United States (for Justice John Paul Stevens). She also spent a year as an Associate Legal Officer at the International Criminal Tribunal for the former Yugoslavia (for Judge Theodor Meron). She is a member of the American Law Institute and on the Board of Editors of the *American Journal of International Law*. At Penn Carey Law, she has three times received the

Harvey Levin Memorial Award for Teaching Excellence, which is awarded each year to one professor by vote of the graduating J.D. class.

James T. Gathii has been, since 2012, the Wing-Tat Lee Chair in International Law and Professor of Law at Loyola University Chicago School of Law. He is a graduate of the University of Nairobi, Kenya, and Harvard Law School. He sits on the board of editors of the *Journal of African Law* and the *Journal of International Trade Law and Policy*, among others, and serves as Co-Editor-in-Chief of the *African Journal of International Economic Law*. He is a founding member of the Third World Approaches to International Lw (TWAIL) network and a founding editor of Afronomicslaw.org, the blog on international economic law issues relating to Africa and the Global South. His books include *African Regional Trade Agreements as Legal Regimes* (Cambridge University Press 2011), *The Performance of Africa's International Courts: Using Litigation for Political, Legal, and Social Change* (Oxford University Press 2021), and *Transforming Climate Finance in an Era of Sovereign Debt Distress* (Sheria Publishing House 2023). He has authored over 100 articles and book chapters.

Claudio Grossman is a Professor of Law, Dean Emeritus, and the R. Geraldson Scholar for International and Humanitarian Law, at American University Washington College of Law. He served as Dean from 1994–2015. Professor Grossman is a member of the U.N. International Law Commission (2017–2027); a member of the Institut de Droit International since 2019; and President of the Inter-American Institute of Human Rights (2017–2027). From 2003–2016, he served as member and chairperson of the U.N. Committee against Torture (CAT), and in 2013, he chaired the U.N. Human Rights Treaty Bodies. He also served as a member of the Inter-American Commission on Human Rights (1994–2001), as well as its President. Professor Grossman participated in landmark human rights decisions within both the universal and Inter-American legal systems, including CAT's adoption of General Comment No. 3 on Reparations, and decisions of those organs concerning non-discrimination, freedom of expression, rape as torture, extraordinary renditions, disappearances, indigenous populations, amnesties, and reparations. Juan Mendez, José Miguel Vivanco, and Grossman served as lawyers for the Velásquez Rodríguez family in their case before the Inter-American system. Grossman was Agent for Chile in *Obligation to Negotiate Access to the Pacific Ocean (Bolivia v. Chile)* and Advocate in *Maritime Dispute (Perú v. Chile)* before the International Court of Justice. Grossman is the author of numerous publications concerning international law, human rights, and international education.

Nienke Grossman is a Professor of Law and Co-Director of the Center for International and Comparative Law at the University of Baltimore School of Law. Her scholarship is found in top international law publications, including the *American Journal of International Law* and the *Max Planck Encyclopedias of International Procedural Law* and *of Public International Law*, and she is co-editor of the forthcoming *Oxford Handbook of Women and International Law*. Professor Grossman was nominated by the United States and elected to the Inter-American Juridical Committee of the Organization of American States in 2024. In 2023, she was Special Advisor to the U.N. Special Rapporteur on the situation of human rights in the Democratic People's Republic of Korea. She has provided legal advice to Latin American States in cases before the International Court of Justice, and, in 2017, she served on an Independent Panel of Experts to evaluate candidates to the Inter-American Commission on Human Rights. She served on the American Society of International Law's Executive Council and as co-chair of its Women in International Law and International Courts and Tribunals Interest Groups. Professor Grossman is a graduate of Harvard College, Harvard Law School, and Georgetown University Law Center.

Oona A. Hathaway is the Gerard C. and Bernice Latrobe Smith Professor of International Law at Yale Law School, Professor of Political Science at the Yale University Department of Political Science, a faculty member at the Jackson School of Global Affairs, and Director of the Yale Law School Center for Global Legal Challenges. She is also a non-resident scholar at the Carnegie Endowment for Peace. She has been a member of the Advisory Committee on International Law for the Legal Adviser at the United States Department of State since 2005 and a member of the Council on Foreign Relations since 2011. In 2014–2015, she took leave to serve as Special Counsel to the General Counsel at the U.S. Department of Defense, where she was awarded the Office of the Secretary of Defense Award for Excellence. Earlier in her career, she served as a law clerk to Justice Sandra Day O'Connor of the U.S. Supreme Court and Judge Patricia Wald of the D.C. Circuit Court of Appeals. She has published more than forty law review articles and *The Internationalists: How a Radical Plan to Outlaw War Remade the World* (Simon & Schuster 2017) (with Scott Shapiro). She is also Executive Editor of and regular author at *Just Security*, and she writes often for popular publications such as *The Washington Post*, *New York Times*, and *Foreign Affairs*.

Natasha Holcroft-Emmess is a lecturer and tutor in law at Jesus College, University of Oxford, and a D.Phil. candidate in the Faculty of Law at the University of Oxford. She is a qualified (but non-practicing) barrister and solicitor who undertook her vocational training in London, at Matrix Chambers and Slaughter and May. She was admitted to the roll of solicitors in 2016 and called to the Bar of England and Wales in 2018. She has also worked as a lecturer and tutor in law at Keble College, Oxford, and served as Research Director at the Oxford Human Rights Hub. Her D.Phil. research concerns human rights in conflicts and crises, with a particular focus on derogation clauses in international human rights treaties.

Mark Weston Janis is the William F Starr Professor at the University of Connecticut School of Law and formerly Reader in Law and

Fellow of Exeter College, Oxford University. He graduated from Princeton, Oxford, where he was a Rhodes Scholar, and Harvard. He served as a U.S. Naval officer and practiced financial law with Sullivan & Cromwell in New York and Paris. He is a fellow commoner at The Queen's College, Oxford, and has taught as a visiting professor at Cornell, UCLA, Paris I & XIII, Aix-en-Provence, Heidelberg, Munster, Tilburg, Riga, and the San Diego summer faculty in Oxford and Paris. Professor Janis teaches International Law, European Human Rights Law, and Conflicts. He has written three widely read books: *An Introduction to International Law* (Aspen, 8th ed. 2021), *International Law Cases and Commentary* (West, 6th ed. 2020) (with John Noyes and Leila Sadat), and *European Human Rights Law* (Oxford University Press, 3d ed. 2008) (with Richard Kay and Anthony Bradley). He has also authored or edited other books, including *Religion and International Law* (Martinus Nijhoff 1991) and *America and the Law of Nations 1776–1939* (Oxford University Press 2010), and more than eighty articles.

Eric Talbot Jensen is the Robert W. Barker Professor of Law at Brigham Young University Law School. He also currently serves as the President of the American Branch of the International Society for Military Law and the Law of War, as a faculty member of the Global Cyber Institute, and as a Senior Fellow at the Lieber Institute for Law and Land Warfare. He has previously served on the Executive Council of the American Society of International Law and as the Special Counsel to the U.S. Department of Defense General Counsel. Prior to joining the BYU law faculty in 2011, Professor Jensen spent two years teaching at Fordham Law School in New York City and twenty years in the U.S. Army as both a Cavalry Officer and as a Judge Advocate. During his time as a Judge Advocate, Professor Jensen served in various positions including as the Chief of the Army's International Law Branch; Deputy Legal Advisor for Task Force Baghdad; Professor of International and Operational Law at The Judge Advocate General's Legal Center and School; legal advisor to the U.S. contingent of U.N. Forces deployed to Skopje, Macedonia as part of UNPREDEP; and legal advisor in Bosnia in support of Operation Joint Endeavor/Guard.

Harold Hongju Koh is Sterling Professor of International Law at Yale Law School, where he has taught since 1985 and was Dean from 2004–2009. He has served four U.S. administrations as Senior Advisor (2021) and Legal Adviser (2009–2013) at the Office of the Legal Adviser, U.S. Department of State; Assistant Secretary of State for Democracy, Human Rights and Labor (1998–2001); and Attorney-Adviser, Office of Legal Counsel, U.S. Department of Justice (1983–1985), and he clerked for Justice Harry A. Blackmun of the U.S. Supreme Court (1980–1981) and Judge Malcolm Richard Wilkey of the D.C. Circuit (1980–1981). Both inside and outside the government, Professor Koh has participated in nearly every Alien Tort case that has reached the U.S. Supreme Court since 1984, including as Counsel for Amici Curiae International Jurists in *Sosa v. Alvarez-Machain*. The author and co-author of nine books and more than 250 articles, he has appeared before many international tribunals and received eighteen honorary degrees, along with more than thirty human rights awards, including awards from the American Bar Association, the Burton Awards, and Columbia and Duke Law Schools for his lifetime achievements in international law.

Yasmin Liberman is an LL.M. graduate of New York University School of Law and a First Class Politics, Philosophy, and Law Graduate of King's College London. She has worked as a legal advisor to the Permanent Mission of Antigua and Barbuda to the United Nations and is a Junior Fellow at the Centre for International Governance and Dispute Resolution in London. She has co-authored and edited several publications on international law, including a Commentary on Article 54 of the Articles on State Responsibility, in *Articles on State Responsibility: A Commentary* (Pierre Bodeau-Livinec & Patricia Galvão-Teles eds.; D.-S. Robin assoc. ed., Oxford University Press, 2025 or 2026) (with Kate Parlett), and a special issue of the *King's Law Journal* on "The Legal Accountability of Transnational Institutions: Past, Present and Future" (Rishi Gulati & Philippa Webb eds., Vol. 34(3), 2023).

Theodor Meron, born in Poland in 1930, has been a Judge and, between March 2012 and January 2019, the President of the International Residual Mechanism for Criminal Tribunals. Judge Meron was also the President of the Appeals Chambers of the International Criminal Tribunal for the former Yugoslavia (ICTY) and the International Criminal Tribunal for Rwanda. He served a total of four terms as President of the ICTY and three terms as President of the Mechanism, a unique record in the international judiciary. A leading scholar of international humanitarian law, human rights, and international criminal law, Judge Meron is the author of more than a hundred articles and twelve books—mostly on international law and two on chivalry in Shakespeare—one of which, *Human Rights Law Making in the United Nations* (Oxford University, Clarendon Press 1986), received the Certificate of Merit from the American Society of International Law. Some of his books and articles helped build the legal foundations for international criminal tribunals. His most recent book is *Standing up for Justice* (Oxford University Press 2021). He has taught at New York University Law School, Harvard, Geneva, and Oxford. He is a member of the Institute of International Law and of the Council on Foreign Relations, a Fellow of the American Academy of Arts and Sciences, and the recipient of numerous awards, honors, and medals, such as the Hudson Medal (American Society of International Law) and the Haskins Prize (American Council of Learned Societies), Officer of the French Legion of Honor, Grand Officer of the French National Order of Merit, Officer of the Order of Merit of Poland, and Companion of the Most Distinguished Order of St. Michael and St. George of the United Kingdom. A past honorary President of the American Society of International Law, past Editor-in-Chief of the *American Journal of International Law*, and Visiting Fellow of All Souls College, Oxford, he is the Charles L. Denison Professor of Law Emeritus at New York University Law School and, since 2014, a Visiting Professor of Law at Oxford University. He is a Visiting Fellow at Mansfield College, Academic Associate of Oxford Bonavero Human Rights Institute, and Honorary Fellow at Trinity College. As a child and teenager, he survived the Holocaust in ghettos and a labor camp and later was smuggled out of Communist Poland and studied law in the Universities of Jerusalem, Harvard, and Cambridge. He has had distinguished and varied careers as a diplomat at the rank of Ambassador, Legal Adviser to the Foreign Ministry of Israel, Counselor on International Law to the U.S. State Department, and President of U.N. War Crimes Tribunals; as a leading professor of law; and now as an Oxford academic. He has written landmark decisions on genocide and war crimes and, as a legal adviser in Israel, he authored a famous opinion in 1967 declaring the illegality of settlements on the West Bank. He is considered one of the world's authorities on international justice and is now a special adviser on International Humanitarian Law to the Prosecutor of the International Criminal Court.

John E. Noyes is the Roger J. Traynor Professor of Law Emeritus at California Western School of Law. A graduate of Amherst College and the University of Virginia School of Law, he regularly taught International Law, Law of the Sea, and Conflict of Laws. During his career, he was a visiting faculty member at Connecticut, Roger Williams, Suffolk, Wake Forest, Victoria University (Wellington, New Zealand), and the University of San Diego Oxford and Paris programs. Professor Noyes's work with various international law organizations included service as President of the American Branch of the International Law Association, and he received the Branch's Charles Siegal Distinguished Service Award. He has written numerous book chapters, law review articles, and essays, focusing especially on the international law of the sea and international dispute resolution. Among his several books are *International Law Cases and Commentary* (West, 6th ed. 2020) (with Mark Janis and Leila Sadat) and *Cases and Materials on the Law of the Sea* (Brill, 2d ed. 2014) (with Erik Franckx, Kristen Juras, and Louis Sohn).

Mary Ellen O'Connell, J.D., Ph.D., is the Robert and Marion Short Professor of Law at the University of Notre Dame School of Law and Professor of International Peace Studies at Notre Dame's Kroc Institute. She focuses on general international law, international law on the use of force, international dispute resolution, and international legal theory. She is the author or editor of numerous books and articles, including "Banning Autonomous Weapons: A Legal and Ethical Mandate," 37(3) *Ethics & International Affairs* 287 (2023), and *The Art of Law in the International Community* (Cambridge University Press 2019). From 2010–2012, she was a vice president of the American Society of International Law, and from 2005–2010, she chaired the International Law Association Committee on the Use of Force. From 1993–1998,

Professor O'Connell was a professional military educator for the U.S. Department of Defense at the George C. Marshall European Center for Security Studies in Garmisch-Partenkirchen, Germany.

Yuval Shany is the Hersch Lauterpacht Chair in International Law and former Dean of the Law Faculty of the Hebrew University of Jerusalem. Professor Shany was a member of the U.N. Human Rights Committee from 2013 to 2020 (and served between 2018–2019 as Chair of the Committee). He currently teaches at the Center for Transnational Legal Studies at King's College in London and the Graduate Institute of International and Development Studies in Geneva, and he serves as a Senior Fellow at the Israel Democracy Institute. He holds degrees in law from the Hebrew University of Jerusalem (LL.B. 1995, *cum laude*), New York University (LL.M. 1997), and the University of London (Ph.D. 2001).

Carlos M. Vázquez is the Scott K. Ginsburg Professor of Law at the Georgetown University Law Center. He teaches and writes in the areas of International Law, Conflict of Laws, and Constitutional Law. His articles have appeared in the *Harvard Law Review*, *Yale Law Journal*, *Columbia Law Review*, and *American Journal of International Law*, among other journals. His article "The Four Doctrines of Self–Executing Treaties" won the Francis Deák Prize from the American Society of International Law. Professor Vázquez has been a member of the Inter–American Juridical Committee and the U.N. Committee for the Elimination of Racial Discrimination, and he has been a member of the Editorial Board of the *American Journal of International Law*. He is an advisor to the *Fourth Restatement of Foreign Relations Law* and serves on the U.S. State Department's Advisory Committee on International Law.

Philippa Webb is Professor of Public International Law, University of Oxford and the Blavatnik School of Government. She is also a barrister specializing in international law at Twenty Essex. She is a specialist in public international law and appears in domestic and international courts, including the International Court of Justice, the International Tribunal for the Law of the Sea, the European Court of Human Rights, and the U.K. Supreme Court. She is appointed to the United Kingdom Attorney General's Public International Law Panel of Counsel and is a founding board member of the Clooney Foundation for Justice. Professor Webb has held positions in the Presidency of the International Court of Justice, the Office of the Prosecutor at the International Criminal Court, and United Nations Headquarters. She was shortlisted for 2022 "Barrister of the Year" by *The Lawyer* magazine. Her publications include chapters on insulting speech and false speech in *Freedom of Speech in International Law* (Oxford University Press, Amal Clooney & David Neuberger eds., 2024); *The Right to a Fair Trial in International Law* (Oxford University Press 2021) (with Amal Clooney); and *Oppenheim's International Law: United Nations* (Oxford University Press, 2017) (with Rosalyn Higgins, Dapo Akande, Sandesh Sivakumaran, and James

Sloan). The latter two books have been awarded the American Society of International Law's Certificate of Merit. Her treatise, *The Law of State Immunity* (Oxford University Press, 3d ed. 2015) (with Hazel Fox), has been cited by leading courts around the world.

Acknowledgments

The editors thank each of the authors for their work in preparing such compelling law stories. Special thanks too to Georgetown University Law Center's Librarian Thanh Nguyen and the several Georgetown student research assistants—Brendan Glenn, Doug Hicks, Hyungi Lee, Li-Wen Ong, Olivia Pavao, and Jillian Rayes—who helped with citations. And special thanks as well to librarians Mary Kate Hunter and Traci Emerson Spackey at The George Washington University Law School (GW Law), along with GW Law School Research Fellow Tristan Barron, who also helped with citations.

Professor Roger P. Alford offers his gratitude and special thanks to Michael Klein (Notre Dame Law School J.D. 2023), McKenzie Bush (Notre Dame Law School J.D. 2024), and Max Himmelwright (Notre Dame Law School J.D. expected 2025) for their excellent research and editing assistance.

Professor David J. Bederman acknowledges the superb research assistance of Nicole Herther–Spiro, Emory Law class of 2007.

Professor Laura A. Dickinson acknowledges the excellent research assistance provided by Lee Sims and Simon Canick of the University of Connecticut School of Law Library.

Professor William S. Dodge thanks the late David Bederman, Curt Bradley, Sarah Cleveland, Reuel Schiller, Tony Sebok, and the participants in the 2005 Conference on International Law in U.S. Courts at Vanderbilt University School of Law for their thoughts and comments.

Professor James T. Gathii thanks Laura Dickinson and John Noyes for very helpful comments on earlier drafts. Thanks too to Bianca Stockmeier and Rama Izar for their research assistance.

Professor Claudio Grossman thanks Alice Rierner (WCL, J.D. '07) and Agustina del Campo (WCL, LL.M. '05; Impact Litigation Coordinator '05–'07) for their assistance on the first version of this chapter, and Marta Trevino Leyva (WCL, LL.M. '23) for checking additional references. He extends his gratitude to Washington College of Law for its constant support for research and service.

Professor Nienke Grossman thanks the editors for the invitation to contribute to this volume and for their comments, and Anthony Blanchfield-Felice (Baltimore, J.D. '23), Courtney Morgan (Baltimore, J.D. '23), and A. Rand (Baltimore, J.D. '24), for their excellent research assistance. She is grateful to her co-author, Claudio Grossman, for his encouragement and support, and for inspiring so many to use international law in the pursuit of justice.

Professor Oona A. Hathaway thanks Neal Katyal, Commander Charles Swift, Marty Lederman, and Sandy Levinson for offering their insights in the *Hamdan* case, and for their feedback on the earlier edition of this chapter. She also thanks Katherine Wiltenberg Todrys, Nicole Hallett, and Sumon Dantiki for their research assistance on the original version of this chapter, and Michael Sullivan for his excellent research assistance on the revised version.

Natasha Holcroft-Emmess thanks the editors for their guidance on drafts, and Professor Miles Jackson for his thoughtful comments, both on drafts and in discussions about *Hassan* and related cases.

Professor Mark Weston Janis acknowledges with thanks the excellent research work of Eric Hisey, Connecticut J.D. '07, and Thomas Plotkin, Connecticut J.D. '08, and the outstanding manuscript typing of Joan Wood.

Professor Harold Hongju Koh's essay grows out of his Foreword to William J. Aceves, *The Anatomy of Torture: A Documentary History of Filártiga v. Peña-Irala* (2007), a volume that unearthed much of the documentary evidence and information cited in the chapter. Professor Koh expresses his gratitude to Professor Drew S. Days III, John E. Huerta, and Bruce R. Kraus for their *Filártiga* memories, and to Yale law students Kate Desormeau and Danielle Morris for their outstanding research assistance.

Professor John E. Noyes thanks William Aceves, Michal Belknap, James Cooper, Dino Kritsiotis, Sarah Seene, and Mary Ellen O'Connell for their helpful comments on early drafts, and Amy Cordova, Steven Nikolov, Amy Moberly, and Linda Weathers for their research assistance on the version of this chapter that appeared in the first edition of this book. Bobbi Weaver provided essential research assistance for the revised version.

Professor Mary Ellen O'Connell thanks Kathryn Fuehrmeyer (J.D. Notre Dame '08) and Lenore VanderZee (J.D.; LL.M. Notre Dame '07) for their help with research.

Professor Yuval Shany thanks then-Professor and current International Court of Justice Judge Sarah Cleveland for her comments on an earlier draft of this chapter.

Professor Carlos M. Vázquez thanks Kevin Arlyck and Curtis Bradley for helpful comments, and Max Lang and Eric Rahn for excellent research assistance. Special thanks go to Thanh Nguyen and his team at the Edward Bennett Williams Library at Georgetown—Brendan Glenn, Doug Hicks, Hyungi Lee, Li-Wen Ong, Olivia Pavao, and Jillian Rayes—for their invaluable help with cite-checking.